MW01294293

Major League Baseball in the 1970s

Major League Baseball in the 1970s

A Modern Game Emerges

JOSEPH G. PRESTON

McFarland & Company, Inc., Publishers
Jefferson, North Carolina, and London

LIBRARY OF CONGRESS CATALOGUING-IN-PUBLICATION DATA

Preston, Joseph G., 1959–
    Major league baseball in the 1970s : a modern game emerges /
Joseph G. Preston
        p.   cm.
    Includes bibliographical references and index.

    ISBN 0-7864-1592-4 (softcover : 50# alkaline paper)

    1. Baseball — United States — History — 20th century.   2. Major
League Baseball (Organization) — History — 20th century.   I. Title.
GV863.A1P74   2004
796.357'64 — dc22   2003026007

British Library cataloguing data are available

©2004 Joseph G. Preston. All rights reserved

*No part of this book may be reproduced or transmitted in any form
or by any means, electronic or mechanical, including photocopying
or recording, or by any information storage and retrieval system,
without permission in writing from the publisher.*

On the cover: *inset* Dave McNally; *pitching* Andy Messersmith (courtesy
National Baseball Hall of Fame Library, Cooperstown, New York)

Manufactured in the United States of America

McFarland & Company, Inc., Publishers
    Box 611, Jefferson, North Carolina 28640
        www.mcfarlandpub.com

To June, Tina, and Gina

Contents

Preface

One of man's most persistent psychological traits as a species is his tendency to see himself as a participant in (or at least an eyewitness to) the most critical moments in human history. In 1976, for example, the Louis Harris polling organization asked 1,512 adults to rank the seven most recent presidents (Franklin Roosevelt through Gerald Ford) in terms of overall performance as well as six specific categories regarding personal integrity, competence in handling foreign affairs, and the like. Not surprisingly, Roosevelt and John F. Kennedy finished one-two in the poll, but what was more interesting was that support for the two presidents was emphatically split by the age of the respondent. People under 30 (those born after 1946) overwhelmingly chose JFK as best in all of the categories surveyed, while those over 50 (born before 1926) went for FDR by a similar margin.*

It was thus with some trepidation that I undertook this study of baseball in the decade that begot such disparate icons as disco music, Archie Bunker, and taped presidential conversations filled with deleted expletives. Yet in reviewing the era of my maturation I am constantly amazed by how many vexations, Hot Stove League debates, and pleasures of today's game have their roots in issues that first came onto the radar screen during the seventies. Wonder whether your team's favorite star is going to defect now that his contract has expired? Well, before 1975 nobody worried about that, because players were bound (or at least thought they were bound) to their teams in perpetuity. Thrilled by your city's new stadium? Chances are that they moved out of one that was either built or extensively remodeled during that era. Most of the liveliest current Hall of Fame debates (Bert Blyleven, Goose Gossage, Bruce Sutter, Jim Rice) center on men whose stars shone brightest during the decade, while much of today's on-field strategy is orchestrated by men who cut their teeth on '70s era baseball.

In a sense, producing a work regarding the 1970s game should be an easy

---

*David Wallechinsky, Irving Wallace and Amy Wallace, The People's Almanac Presents the Book of Lists, William Morrow and Company, Inc., New York, 1977, pp. 31–32.

task. Once Jim Bouton's *Ball Four* proved that there was a broad market for books about baseball and its characters a veritable avalanche of tomes was unleashed on the public. Players, managers, umpires, front office guys ... seemingly anybody who'd ever taken a whiff of locker room air was suddenly jumping on the literary bandwagon.

Contrary to popular belief, a remarkable number of the works produced during this period were quite good, though often for reasons unanticipated by their authors—it is often the unguarded or subconscious admission that is the most illuminating, and many of these books have such slips of the psychological guard in spades. Having said that, the kiss and tell aspects of Bouton's book seem to have resonated most with those that followed in his footsteps, and thus the serious student is confronted with a morass of beaver shots and cakes being sat upon en route to an understanding of the era and its leading lights. Moreover, many of these tomes were published rather quickly — that, in a sense, was part of their charm — and thus lack the reflection and insight that more polished works might provide.

In marked contrast to the contemporary timeframe, remarkably little has been written about the 1970s in recent years, with even fewer books addressing the interrelationship between the on- and off-field issues that characterized the decade. Randy Rieland's *The New Professionals: Baseball in the 1970s* (Redefinition, Inc. 1989) as well as Phil Pepe's *Talkin' Baseball: An Oral History of Baseball in the 1970s* (Ballantine Books, 1998) do a good job of covering many of the decade's highlights (Pepe's through conversations with such luminaries as Bowie Kuhn, Tommy Lasorda, and Al Hrabosky). But Pepe's book is anecdotal by design and as such does not aspire to provide a balanced appraisal of the issues touched upon, while the relative brevity of Rieland's work precludes extensive review of such topics as the origins of the DH rule, the 1979 umpire's strike, and Bill Veeck's latter day Chicago carnival/shipwreck.

My hope is that the reader will come away from this book with an understanding of how the game's stewardship, playing interests (which should not, at times, be confused with the players themselves), and on-field dynamics conspired to produce this most disparate of decades. An era in which the generations-old bond between player and owner—forced as it might have been — was irreparably broken. One in which short hair, black shoes, and low-cut stirrups shared the field with handlebar mustaches and a mule named "Charlie O." One in which black players began reminding the rest of us that it had been 25 years since Jackie Robinson broke baseball's color barrier ... and that too little had changed in the interim. One in which long-held assumptions regarding how the game was played were cast aside, replaced by even older ones, or parked on the bench while a bunch of aging sluggers DH'ed for them.

This book and I owe a special debt of gratitude to two individuals. It has been said that behind every great man there is a great woman: well, my case goes to show that even sub-average slobs like me can get lucky now and again. Without the support, confidence, and forbearance of my wife June (as well as helper Chihuahuas Tina and Gina) this work would never have gotten off the ground ... and the funny thing is that she gets better every day. Long-suffering Dodger fan (sounds funny, doesn't it, but oh so painfully true...) Stuart Richey gave graciously of his time in reviewing each chapter as it came off my computer. While I doubt Stuart initially understood how open-ended this commitment was, his insightful comments and suggestions have much to do with whatever qualities of humor and intellect the finished work possesses.

I hope you find half as much enjoyment in reading the book as I did in writing it.

Joseph Preston
January 2004

Introduction:
December 2, 1969

Under the reasonably sunny skies of Bal Harbour, Florida, the hierarchy of baseball's 24 major league teams gathered at the Americana Hotel to celebrate that annual bacchanal of power politics, deal-making, and hardware convention-style socialization: the winter meetings. As always, there was a just-full-enough plate of issues large and small to warrant gathering.

One was the executive summary of a $100,000 study completed by the University of Pennsylvania's Wharton School of Finance and Commerce on reorganizing baseball's management and league structure, which was presented and perfunctorily discussed. Though visionary in certain areas,[1] the report's emphasis on consolidating power in Commissioner Bowie Kuhn's office ultimately doomed its chances with a collective mindset that, 35 years after Kenesaw Mountain Landis's death, was still fearful of anointing another one of *those*.

Another issue placed a symbolic exclamation point on the senior circuit's opposition to key elements of the Wharton report: Chub Feeney was named to succeed the 72-year-old Warren Giles as National League president. It was a "déjà vu all over again" choice in many ways. Both Feeney and Giles were former general managers (Feeney with the Giants, Giles with the Reds). Both had been serious candidates for the commissioner's post before accepting the league presidency.[2] Most importantly, both were traditionalists and National League *uber alles* types at heart, a factor that would take on increased significance as the battle over the designated hitter heated up.

Finally, the normal bumper crop of we've-got-to-plug-that-hole/I-don't-care-just-get-him-*out*-of-here/we've-got-to-do-*something* trades had to be made:

- Desperate for an alternative at third base to the too young Wayne Garrett and the too old Ed Charles, the world champion Mets gambled on Joe Foy's uncertain glove. The cost: Amos Otis, a tantalizing and infuriating 22-year-old prospect who had fifteen seasons and four All-Star appearances in front of him. As for Foy, an offensive dropoff and 18 errors in 97 games sealed his fate in New York, prompting a similar acquisition (Jim Fregosi) the next winter at what would prove to be an even more horrendous cost (Nolan Ryan).

- Joe Pepitone's irreverent Mod Mod World act finally reached the end of its New York run, as the perennially disappointing first baseman was dispatched to Houston for 1965 Rookie of the Year and man without a position Curt Blefary.

- The Washington Senators swapped Dave Baldwin, a once-promising 31-year-old long reliever with 40 big league innings in front of him, for George Brunet, a well-traveled 34-year-old lefty who was only 144 frames away from embarking on a legendary Mexican League career that would end with his death on the team bus at age 56.[3]

It was a comfortable, familiar way to end a year that had been anything but comforting and familiar. Four expansion teams, a compromise commissioner, a preseason mini-strike, the historic cleaving of each league into subsidiary divisions, a contracted strike zone and less elevated pitcher's mound, a manager who cold-cocked his number two starter ... well, suffice it to say that 1969 had been a season with a little something for everyone. Yet for all of that, a record 27.2 million fans had been treated to a veritable offensive explosion (runs scored per game were up 15.2 percent over the depressed 1968 levels), a couple of thrilling pennant races courtesy of the new divisional setup, and a legitimate miracle team that (praise the Lord!) was based in the media capital of the world.

Given the inherent disaster potential, everyone was mildly astonished that 1969 turned out as well as it did. Unfortunately, the afterglow of this memorable season was chilled by the absence of one key group from the Bal Harbour proceedings— the players.

Reportedly miffed at being treated like a fifth wheel during the last two winterfests,[4] Marvin Miller had asked the 24 representatives of his Major League Baseball Players Association (MLBPA) to boycott the Bal Harbour meetings and gather instead in San Juan, Puerto Rico, some ten days hence. It was an irritating move by a man who often appeared to revel in his role as baseball's resident pain in the posterior, but seemingly of little significance. By all appearances the players' union was still far from cohesive; such stars as Chicago Cubs third baseman Ron Santo and 1967 Triple Crown winner Carl Yastrzemski had been vocal opponents of the preseason strike.[5] Kuhn would be a featured speaker at the gathering[6] and besides, exactly how earth-shattering could a meeting that the sporting press wasn't bothering to cover possibly be?[7]

Unfortunately, that particular blind spot would end up being an embarrassing gaffe for both the owners and press alike. Once Bowie's prying eyes and ears were safely shuttled out of the room, the players would take up a matter that would be a precursor of turbulent times to come. Curt Flood, one-time star center fielder for the St. Louis Cardinals, was seeking union support for a lawsuit that would eliminate the so-called reserve clause from baseball's standard contract. If successful, the manner in which the game had operated for the better part of a century would become obsolete overnight ... yet it would be nearly two weeks after the meeting's conclusion before the decision to back Flood became public.

Such was a perfect metaphor for how baseball as a whole was operating at that time.

Underneath the business-as-usual air of Bal Harbour lay deeper, more perilous issues that the assembled owners and their entourages were struggling to get their arms around. The attendance gain, for example, was the baseball equivalent of stating that the average temperature worldwide right now is 72 degrees. Four-fifths (80.1 percent) of the increase was accounted for by the four expansion teams, while an additional 38.4 percent went into the coffers of the ten pre-existing National League teams.[8] That's 118.5 percent of the gain accounted for so far for those who aren't scoring at home, which means that the American League ... well, let's just say that 1968 looked like a heck of a year in retrospect.

Not that looking up at the National League wasn't something of a habit for the AL. The junior circuit was steadily becoming so in more than just name. Per game attendance for the league's eight and then ten teams had trailed that of the NL for fourteen consecutive seasons. Even more embarrassingly, the NL outdrew the AL in all four cities in which the two leagues went head-to-head — in three of them by more than a two-to-one margin.[9] Initially, there had been a number of reasons advanced for the disparity — the National League's more intense pursuit of black athletes in the 1950s, the homesteading of the fast-growing California and Texas markets before the AL was able to act, the stifling dominance of the New York Yankees up to 1964 — but increasingly the difference was coming down to money, cash, green, scratch, bread, and bucks, in that order.

This disparity in resources would manifest itself in many ways. Within two seasons just one National League team would be playing in a stadium built before 1960, whereas only three AL clubs would be in premises built after that year. The NL's ownership group included scions of some of the nation's most prosperous companies (Anheuser-Busch, Seagram's, Wrigley, Perini) as well as several highly successful and visionary baseball entrepreneurs, while the American League had one solid businessman (Kansas City's Ewing Kauffman), a major company (CBS) that had presided over the decline and fall of the league's champagne franchise, and a hodgepodge of sportsmen and marginally financed operators. The senior circuit had returned to New York in

1962 with the backing of Whitney money; the AL's attempt to colonize the Pacific Northwest was on the verge of bankruptcy after one season.[10]

Ultimately, resources or the lack thereof will make themselves apparent on the field, and the American League was beginning to lag in the talent race — perhaps not so much among the best players, but certainly with the next group down. Baseball's centennial year was an average one in terms of new talent debuting: one Hall of Famer (Carlton Fisk), a guy who might make it yet (Steve Garvey), and a quartet who came reasonably close (Vida Blue, Darrell Evans, George Foster, and Thurman Munson). So far, so good, but the next nine after that are Bill Buckner, Jerry Reuss, Toby Harrah, Bill Russell, Gene Tenace, Gene Garber, Dave Cash, Ted Sizemore, and Bill (Spaceman) Lee, which makes the final score National League 9, American League 6 in the contest for the top 15 players.[11] Now, a three-player difference in terms of quality talent produced may seem like a small thing and it is — but maintain such an annual advantage over a decade or more and the variance becomes significant, as the NL's recent dominance in All-Star Game competition (seven straight) demonstrated.

Yet despite the offensive boost, even the mighty National League's per-game attendance levels were virtually identical to those seen two decades earlier.[12] Keep in mind that the postwar era had witnessed an unprecedented explosion in consumerism, one that had engulfed and enriched most facets of society. Professional basketball had become mainstream entertainment; pro football had grown from what pro basketball currently was to a legitimate contender for the title of America's National Pastime. Baseball had basically tread water.

The possible explanations for baseball's malaise seemed to involve virtually every characteristic of the game. The increasing uppercut mentality of hitters coupled with a generation of flamethrowing pitchers taking full advantage of the 1963–1968 playing conditions had caused strikeouts to soar beyond imagination — by 1969 a full 11 percent of all outs recorded consisted of some muscular guy going up to the plate, watching three go by, and returning to the bench.[13] The deluge of whiffs, walks (which had returned to historically high levels with the 1969 rule changes) and relief pitchers were creating tons of dead spots in what already seemed to the uninitiated like a less-than-action-packed game.

Then there were the organizational issues. Unlike its competitors for the entertainment dollar, baseball did very little to promote itself as a sport. Until 1969 the game had refrained from developing a centralized marketing function out of the fear that placing control of anything in the hands of the commissioner would be the first step down the road to another Landis-like 800-pound gorilla.[14] This was a critical omission in a game where the average team had perhaps three or four people involved in publicity and promotions at the staff level, plus a speaker's bureau if the club drew from a wide area. Furthermore, most of these people were normally in a club's second or even third line of command, a clear demonstration of where their function ranked in the hierarchy of things.[15]

Then again, the idea of commercializing the game beyond whatever happened their way via print and broadcast media was a concept that baseball had repeatedly shunned since the days of Bill Veeck and Larry MacPhail. It just wasn't the way things were done, in part because it cost money that these rich-but-not-that-rich people didn't have to gamble, but also because such practices weren't in keeping with the "civic duty" status that pervaded ownership circles at the time.

It may seem quaint to those accustomed to superstations and megabuck cable TV deals, but team ownership by the late 1960s had taken its place alongside opera companies and museums as a socially responsible endeavor for pillars of the local community. Well, perhaps "pillars" is a bit too strong — Astros Chieftain Judge Roy Hofheinz, for example, was an ex-mayor of Houston who once had his recalcitrant city council arrested en masse[16] — but by and large these people were upstanding citizens who liked the game, rather than sports entrepreneurs. Even the dying breed of owner-operators were becoming more owner than operator, increasingly leaving day-to-day details to longtime cronies and family members.

This is what made Mr. Charles Oscar Finley of the Oakland A's such a trial for baseball's lords (though in all fairness, Finley's status as baseball's resident juvenile delinquent didn't help matters). Charlie O, a salesman by trade, was a lot of things that "sportsmen" and upstanding citizens either aren't or don't want to position themselves as being: aggressive, risk-oriented, willing to push the limits to get that sale, self-confident to the extreme. As a result, Finley was perceived as a half-mad perpetual motion machine with an endless supply of ideas designed to shatter tradition, and little else. Yellow baseballs, cutting a walk to three balls and a whiff to two strikes to speed up the game,[17] dressing his team in colored uniforms rather than the traditional white or gray — Finley had oodles of schemes which, along with a penchant for showering his opposition with four-letter epithets at full volume,[18] made him something of a pariah among the power elite.

Of course, by attacking the game's foundations Finley was indirectly challenging those who were seated at the table with him. Only one of the "original eight" National League teams had changed hands since Gussie Busch's purchase of the St. Louis Cardinals in 1953 and half of all pre-1961 franchises were owned by individuals, families, or descendants whose baseball roots extended back at least to World War II.[19] It was only natural that such people should be resistant to changes in a game that had served them so well and by their lights continued to do so.

Assuming, of course, that the new generation of militant, "do your own thing" players could be brought back under control.

Baseball's pantheon of heroes had undergone a violent upheaval over the past few seasons, with virtually every marquee player of five years previous either gone or in serious decline. Sandy Koufax and Don Drysdale had been forced into early retirement via injury, Mickey Mantle's body had finally given out under the weight of accumulated abuse (not all of which was sustained on the playing field), and Willie Mays had gotten old overnight. While that left a number of fine players from the era behind, they just weren't oooh and aaah-type guys. Henry Aaron was a wonderful athlete, still in his prime at 36 and destined for historic numbers, but there was more than a grain of truth in Leo Durocher's comment that the most colorful thing about Henry was his home run trot.[20] Bob Gibson and Frank Robinson were terrific players and articulate men off the field, but each was getting a little long in the tooth for cult status and as for their on-field demeanors—well, Albert Belle was an absolute sweetheart compared to those two. Roberto Clemente was perceived by many to be a habitual whiner, Al Kaline had hit the downhill slopes of a steady but unspectacular career, and Ernie Banks' knees had gotten to the point at which even Mantle would have rejected them.

Thus, the field was wide open for younger players to step into the limelight—and that was exactly what worried baseball's moguls. Yes, there were some fine young men like Tom Seaver and Johnny Bench who looked ready to assume the point position, but behind them was a crop of troubled souls, outspoken nonconformists, and angry men that seemingly represented a microcosm of American youth at its nadir. Whispers were already rampant about two-time Cy Young Award winner Denny McLain's gambling addiction and consequent association with a cornucopia of mobsters, chiselers, and lowlifes that make Pete Rose's accomplices fifteen years later look like upstanding citizens.[21] Joe Pepitone and Ken (The Hawk) Harrelson were apparently too busy living the New Morality to fully develop their baseball skills—heck, at least Mantle had cooperated in keeping his alcohol abuse an in-house (though poorly kept) secret.

Then there were guys like Reggie Jackson, Richie (not yet Dick despite his best efforts) Allen, and Alex Johnson. Exceptionally talented men who were treated with the utmost respect by baseball standards and destined to become moderately wealthy, they criticized management and teammates alike with wild abandon, thumbed their noses at any rules that got in the way of their off-field lifestyle, refused to play the press game if they didn't want to, and acted like they had the power in the relationship.

Trouble was, they could possibly be right about that last one, and the owners had (or felt they had) Marvin Miller to blame for this new consciousness.

Since that lamentable day in 1965 when Miller had succeeded Robert Cannon (a part-time panjandrum who had demanded that the MLBPA offices be located in Chicago or Milwaukee so as to be convenient to his residence[22]) as head of the players' association—a one-time in-house organ that had formed in the aftermath of the Mexican League fiasco—it became a real union with the willingness to flex its muscle whenever necessary. At first Miller's demands were minor — an increase in pension funding and the minimum wage plus recognition of a player's right to employ an agent to bargain for him (that one had at least seemed minor at the time)[23] — but the trend was obvious. Furthermore, there was an increasing stridency in the statements of such respected player/union leaders as Tom Haller, Joe Torre, and future senator Jim Bunning that could not be ignored.

Thus, baseball's movers and shakers were poised on the precipice of a crazy, mixed-up, perilous world that December day. The worst nightmares of those assembled would be realized in the coming decade — escalating salaries (and, many would contend, player egos), an acrimonious strike that altered baseball's image forever, Sesame Street-style team mascots, and the breaking of the time-honored tradition that all players, including the pitcher, must play on offense as well as defense. Many would fail to adapt: more than half of 1969's winter meeting attendees would be dead or inactive ten years hence,[24] their places taken by what would have seemed to them to be a veritable rogues' gallery of hardheaded businessmen and hustlers. Yet by the end of the 1970s baseball would be enjoying unprecedented prosperity — a 60 percent increase in attendance, a four-year, $250 million television deal and untold millions more on the horizon for those lucky enough to have superstation deals. A lot of that largesse would be flowing in different directions, but everybody's piece of pie — no matter how many additional slices had been cut out of it — had distinctly increased in size.

How all this prosperity came about in the face of so many forces that seemed hell-bent on destroying the game to prove a point remains a mystery. Yet there is no doubt that the game itself — the one between the lines — had a major role in baseball's salvation. For multiple and sometimes contradictory reasons, the 1970s game evolved into a war of competing theories and ideologies. Innovations (some visionary, others ill-conceived) impacted virtually every facet of the game and made the era a second-guesser's dream. Whether baseball in the 1970s was a better game than in the eras that preceded and followed it is debatable; that it was entertaining and refreshing after a decade of Dead Ball Era tactics is undeniable.

This is how it all came about.

1

Curt Flood, the Man
Who Fought the Law

One of *Homo sapiens's* more charming traits as a species is our predilection for the lost cause, the martyr, the man who came close but couldn't quite get over the top. Bill Bevens, for example, is every bit as well remembered for what he didn't do as Don Larsen is for what he did. Mark McGwire may have set the single season home run record, but it was Sammy Sosa playing Avis to McGwire's Hertz who walked away with the MVP Award that year.

Which brings us to Curt Flood — the guy who fought The Law only to have The Law win.

As the 1969 season came to a close, Flood was the 31-year-old center fielder on a St. Louis Cardinals team that, while only a year separated from the World Series, was rapidly succumbing to the ravages of time. Flood was the Gold Glove center fielder of the post–Willie-Mays-at-his-peak period despite a weak throwing arm (the result of a 1965 injury aggravated a couple of years later[1]) and a consistent high average hitter with speed and doubles power, though not as many walks as one would like. In short, he was akin to what Benito Santiago would be to National League catchers some 20 years later: a fine player who may have seemed better than he was because there didn't happen to be a lot of quality competition around to argue the point.

Correctly evaluating the situation, the Cardinals decided to put together a CARE package of aging but still valuable players and drop it on the doorstep of the Philadelphia Phillies, a team that had one troubled superstar and a ton of aging but no longer valuable players. Thus, Flood, Tim McCarver (a high mileage 29-year-old catcher who was about to be shoved aside by Ted Simmons anyway), Joe Hoerner (a 33-year-old left-handed platoon closer), and Byron Browne were sent away for the troubled superstar (Dick Allen), Cookie Rojas, and Jerry Johnson. It was a prototypical deal for a fading team; such moves rarely work because another cog (in this case everybody on the St. Louis staff not named Bob Gibson) inevitably breaks down, but at least at the end of the season the general manager (GM) has evidence that he did everything he could.

Unfortunately, nobody in the Cardinals' front office bothered to let Flood know that he had been dealt.

According to the outfielder, this oversight was the event that precipitated his three-year odyssey through the American judicial system. "If I had been a foot-shuffling porter," Flood wrote in his autobiographical book *The Way It Is*, "they might have at least given me a pocket watch."[2] Furthermore, after twelve years of loyal service he didn't feel that being traded away like "a consignment of goods" was fitting treatment for an adult human being with rights and dignity.[3]

At least that's the way Flood frames it in his book, which was published at a point in time when it was beginning to look like he would come out on the wrong end of the stick. While such motives should by no means be discounted entirely — Flood was after all a sensitive, artistically inclined man — they were in all likelihood accompanied by some practical considerations:

1. Flood would be 32 by the time spring training camp opened and, like most athletes of similar age, was staring Father Time in the face.
2. The Phillies stunk and were likely to continue doing so for the foreseeable future.
3. Given 1 and 2 above, there was roughly a 100 percent chance that he was going to be swapped again as soon as the dust settled.
4. Wherever Flood went, it would be darned tough for him to manage his struggling St. Louis–based photographic business.

In short, it probably wasn't so much that Flood didn't want to be traded to Philadelphia, or that he didn't want to be traded without dignity — he just didn't want to be traded, period. That's not a novel concept in society. Similar agonies confront the typical upwardly mobile professional when considering a cross-country transfer — but it is one of those things a person accepts when he embarks upon a baseball career. For all the money that it generates, baseball is a relatively small business even today: the sum total of players, clubhouse boys, front office executives, and groundskeepers presently working for big league teams would be barely adequate to staff a decent sized Las Vegas hotel-casino. Thus when a player is dealt he has to go; his current employer can't add roster spots and there aren't any competing businesses across the street to offer one's services to.

So far so good, but when baseball's lords codified this common sense approach, they did what one normally does when drafting something that others have to live up to: they made it as advantageous for themselves as possible. Thus was born the so-called reserve clause in the game's standard contract — The Law, if you will, that Flood was destined to challenge.

It may be hard for modern fans to believe, but once upon a time players (or at least their baseball-related skills) really were owned by their teams. On the face of it, such servitude is a clear violation of the Thirteenth Amendment and Flood's attorneys argued his case largely on that basis.[4] However, let's consider the situation carefully before rushing to judgment. A team signs a young man with promising but imperfect skills to a contract and pays him a wage while he learns his trade in the minor leagues. Up to the moment that the young man makes his debut in the majors, he has been nothing but a drain upon the club's treasury — and for every phenom that makes it, five others will fall by the wayside as total losses. Why, baseball argued, should an organization not be able to maintain control over the fruits of its labor, especially when it has committed so much in the way of resources (financial and otherwise) up front? Furthermore, shouldn't a club have the ability to pass such control on to another team when it no longer needs the player in question in exchange for someone else that perhaps can fill a hole?

That, in essence, was the reserve clause. The idea was that a club that originally signed a player had the ability to either retain or assign him elsewhere as long as they desired to do so — which of course would be as long as he had any value. The player was free to bargain with the team as to the amount he would be paid for a given season, but with only one potential buyer for his services the bidding was unlikely to get too far out of hand.

In most businesses, such practices are defined as "restraint of trade" (lawyer talk for "illegal") under the provisions of the Sherman Antitrust Act of 1890. Baseball, though, according to a 1922 opinion by Supreme Court Justice Oliver Wendell Holmes, was not subject to the Act's Provisions.[5] Thus according to the Supreme Court of the United States, a team could indeed trade the rights to a baseball player as if he were "a consignment of goods," and furthermore, such Court heavyweights as Earl Warren, William O. Douglas, Hugo Black, and Felix Frankfurter had subsequently upheld Holmes' position.[6]

This was what Flood was up against as he first contacted a local attorney, who apparently advised that a suit against baseball would have a good chance of success. Recognizing, however, that such an action was probably going to go well beyond the capabilities of a typical trial lawyer, the duo went to Major League Baseball Players Association executive director Marvin Miller for help. According to Miller, the outfielder was given the appropriate cautions (i.e. ain't no way you're ever going to make a living in baseball again and get used to having a lawyer permanently attached to your wallet) and sent away to think this whole thing over.[7] Still, Flood wanted to go ahead and, after meeting with the player representatives at the MLBPA's San Juan meeting (the same one that Bowie Kuhn addressed in an attempt to position himself as the players' commissioner), received the union's financial backing for his legal fees as well as a heavyweight lawyer — former Supreme

With samples of his artwork and photographs from his glory days behind him, a pensive Curt Flood discusses his challenge to baseball's hallowed reserve clause. (*The Sporting News*)

Court Justice Arthur Goldberg.[8]

This is the sequence of events as reported by the key participants. However, while everything said in the paragraph above is almost certainly true in a literal sense, this is one of those occasions where how everything was said is probably just as important as what was said. Yes, Flood got worked up over this all by himself, but somebody had to refine that anger into the Messiah-like posture that he struck in the following months. Yes, the man was clearly naïve about what was to come, but his initial moves were both reasoned and conservative — in fact, Philadelphia GM John Quinn thought that a deal was in the bag after a meeting with the outfielder.[9] Finally, any constitutional lawyer worth his salt would have told Flood after a couple of hours of research that he had an arguable case, there was no way that the case was going to stop short of the Supreme Court (the appointment of Goldberg being proof positive of that), and there wasn't a hope in hell that an increasingly conservative-leaning Court was going to overrule a twice affirmed Oliver Wendell Holmes opinion.

Somebody had to talk Flood into this, and the most likely culprit is Marvin Miller. Miller's warning about the risks was as much fiduciary responsibility (as Flood's bargaining agent Miller would have been liable for a lawsuit if he hadn't provided such counsel) as sage advice. As a labor leader out of the Walter Reuther mold (motto: every great cause inevitably produces a martyr or two along the way), Miller's decision to back Flood was probably akin to the purchase of a lottery ticket. The cost was relatively low given the potential reward and if lightning did strike ... well, the MLBPA would have accomplished an end run around the owners' key salary control defense.

Once *Flood vs. Kuhn* was officially filed in New York's District Court, there was a veritable tidal wave of verbal support for Flood among major league players and longtime observers of the game, as well as the expected doomsday warnings from the game's Old Guard.[10] However, there was a strong undercurrent to much of the support that apparently was lost on Flood and his legal team: that revision, rather than outright elimination, of the reserve clause was a more realistic (and perhaps even desirable) goal.[11]

While baseball players as a group may not be 100 percent savvy in the ways of the world, they are far from total innocents. The owners' basic logic regarding the need to get a return for the years they put into the development of a player struck most as being eminently reasonable. Besides, by and large the owners and their front office personnel were nice guys (many ex-players) who treated their brethren well while extending an opportunity to do something that millions of young Americans would have given their eye-teeth for. By way of contrast, Flood's "I am a man" tone seemed somewhat abstract and strident. Flood wanted emancipation; his colleagues seemed perfectly happy with servitude so long as their cut of the pie increased.

Thus, when Flood's case was tried in front of Judge Irving Ben Cooper, a number of one-time figures in the game (Jackie Robinson, Hank Greenberg, Bill Veeck) took the stand on his behalf[12] — but not a single current player testified or even showed up as an expression of support. Flood was quite bitter about that in retrospect — the lack of moral support that is, not the lack of testimony — and considered his peers' timidity in the face of an unlikely blackball by owners to be rather unseemly given the risks he was taking.[13]

Overall, outside of a memorable appearance by Joe Garigiola as a defense (owners') witness,[14] the proceedings were about as exciting as such trials normally are. However, one witness did cause a minor stir with his comments — one that would reverberate as time passed. Marion Laboratories founder and Kansas City owner Ewing Kauffman admitted under cross-examination that the outfielder would probably have received between $100,000 and $125,000 as a Royal and that some sort of escalating pay scale (with free agency for the player if the club was unwilling to meet the scale) "wouldn't hurt a bit."[15]

Kauffman's comments were far from earth-shattering for a businessman accustomed to paying competitive rates for employees in a free marketplace. Major League Baseball, however, had been anything but a free marketplace for years and Kauffman's statements simply dramatized this dysfunctional aspect. In a differently constructed case, such an admission could have been fatally damaging to baseball's posture; however, the Flood legal team's emphasis on defeating the reserve clause *in toto* rather than simply negotiating for market based wages robbed the statement of much of its evidential power.

This was a key error that the later Messersmith and McNally actions would go to great lengths to avoid.

Kauffman's comments notwithstanding, Judge Cooper's August 12 decision was pretty much a total wipeout for Flood. The jurist began his opinion by admitting that he was "impressed with Flood's argument" (translation: It isn't your lawyers' fault that you lost) and suggested that "arbitration or modification" of the reserve clause might be possible to produce a result that would satisfy everybody (translation: Baseball is welcome to do it if they so desire but don't hold your breath). However, the meat of Cooper's thesis stated that baseball's antitrust exemption and the reserve clause spawned by it were based upon a Supreme Court decision: thus, only the Supreme Court could invalidate it.[16] Furthermore, he said, "Clearly the preponderance of creditable proof does not favor elimination of the reserve clause. With the sole exception of plaintiff [Flood] himself, it shows that even plaintiff's witnesses do not contend that it is wholly undesirable; in fact, they regard substantial portions meritorious...."[17]

The first point was no surprise (no one expected a district court judge to slam dunk Oliver Wendell Holmes), but the second one was a real stinger. Flood had gone for the home run — total elimination of the reserve clause — because that best served his goal of not being "a piece of property to be bought and sold irrespective of my wishes,"[18] and because that's the type of argument necessary to challenge a Supreme Court ruling. One can't just say, "I'll abide by your rules if Paragraph A and Footnote B are changed"; they must declare, "I don't care what happens to your silly little game — the rule is unconstitutional and it has to go."

Unfortunately for Flood, nobody else was willing to throw baseball into chaos: not the other players, not the people he called as witnesses ... and most ominously, not the judge either. Perhaps a different attorney would have found a way around the issue to make Flood's complaint more palatable, but between being Jack Kennedy's first Secretary of Labor, sitting on the Supreme Court, and serving as Ambassador to the United Nations, Arthur Goldberg hadn't actually tried a case in over ten years.[19] Add to that the fact that Goldberg was simultaneously running for Governor of New York....

By this time, Flood was worse than broke. His photographic business was in a shambles, the IRS was after him for delinquent taxes, he owed his ex-wife back alimony[20] — in short, he needed serious money and knew only one way to get it.

Thus Curt Flood opened the 1971 season as the starting center fielder for the Washington Senators.

To most businesses, throwing a financial lifeline to a guy that's dragging them through the courts (Flood's complaint was against Kuhn and the 24 team owners) is *prima facie* absurd. However, baseball's lords have long realized that theirs is a game contested by less than totally mature young men, some of whom will inevitably punch an umpire's light out (Johnny Allen) or jump their contract to play in an outlaw league (Sal Maglie) or dangle their manager out of a moving train (Babe Ruth). Thus, a unique (if sometimes patronizing) tolerance of those who transgress the rules has developed in baseball's executive suites. Besides, Denny McLain's acquisition had already established owner Bob Short's franchise as a halfway house for fallen angels, so in a sense Flood's signing to a one-year, $110,000 contract (with the specific provision that his suit against baseball would not be hindered as a result[21]) was a natural.

At least, until Flood discovered that the only thing worse than being a 32-year-old star playing for a down and out team was being a 33-year-old star whose talents had been allowed to rot for a year playing for a down and out team.

After 13 games it became clear to Flood that the AWOL season had robbed him of critical bat and foot speed. Recognizing that he was facing an uphill battle at his age to knock off the rust and return to anything approaching peak performance, the outfielder left the team for Spain, where he explored, painted a little, and awaited the Supreme Court's decision.[22] That part of the story is eminently fair and honorable; what is somewhat less worthy is the fact that Flood took off with $55,000 of Short's money in exchange for 35 less-than-stellar at-bats.[23]

It was a sad yet oddly appropriate ending, because Flood's case was just about as comatose as his baseball career. In the midst of a Supreme Court term that revolved around the famous *Roe vs. Wade* abortion case, the death penalty, and numerous obscenity cases, *Flood vs. Kuhn* was seen as a peewee.[24] The oral arguments presented by both sides were uninspired, the opinion assigned to one of the court's poorest legal craftsmen because it was considered to be a slam dunk, and the final text included an ode to 87 old-time players that two of the four concurring justices refused to join.[25] Future reviewers would make a lot out of the 5-to-3 vote and the opinion's reference to the "legal anomaly" that baseball represented, but that's really just 20-20 hindsight based on what is known today.

At the time, the flat fact of the matter was that Flood had lost, period, and the reserve clause wasn't going anywhere, period. Sure, some people like Kuhn and *The Sporting News* suggested that negotiation on the clause was now possible,[26] but the courts clearly weren't going to compel the owners to change it, it wasn't in their best (if perhaps myopic) interests to change it, so they saw little reason to change it.

As a result, Flood's legacy is not nearly as solid as many latter day observers make it out to be. While Curt's plight may engage our emotions because he struck a heroic pose, lost everything, and died relatively young and forgotten, his direct impact on subsequent events was essentially zip. Nearly thirty years after the fact, both the reserve clause (albeit in revised form) and baseball's antitrust exemption remain intact, and the two guys who did finally force the revisions went out of their way to distance themselves both tactically and publicly from Flood's arguments.

The one person who probably came out to the good in all of this was Marvin Miller. The Flood case served to confirm two things that Miller had probably suspected all along: first, that a direct assault on baseball's legal foundation was futile, and second, that his coalition was neither strong nor visionary enough yet to stick together on non–bread-and-butter issues. Thus, the MLBPA chief's tactics over the next few years focused upon maneuvering the owners out of their legal bunker by forcing a series of small concessions that undermined the reserve clause in fact. It was a serpentine way of doing business, and the public's image of Miller and the players' union was tarnished as a result. But, like Scott Boras today, Marvin was relatively oblivious to the opinions of those who were not his clients, and the players quickly realized that what the public thought of them as a group was somehow divorced from its opinion of them as individuals. In short, Dear Old Bob, our power-hitting left fielder, could still be Dear Old Bob even if he was a member of the hated players' union.

As for Flood, he ultimately returned to the United States, taking an apartment in Oakland underneath his mother's.[27] He painted, did some broadcasting work for the A's, ran the city's Little League program and, in a ironic twist of fate, served as commissioner of the ill-fated Seniors' League.[28] In many ways he was an imperfect martyr, but hey — if Bill Bevens hadn't walked ten men in the 8⅔ innings prior to Cookie Lavagetto, that fateful fastball that ended the game (and, ironically, Bevens's career) might have not caught quite as much of the plate.

Perhaps that's the best simile for Curt Flood's experience. Had he been of a slightly different makeup the whole thing would never have happened and baseball would probably still be where it is today. However, we'd be short one heck of a story — and one hopes that Flood ultimately found consolation in witnessing the unfolding of a future that, by and large, was the one he had striven for.

2

From the Literary
Corner, *Ball Four*

As anyone who has taken college level courses can attest, there are important books and there are great books. *Mein Kampf*, for example, is an important book — anybody who read it should have had no doubts as to what Adolf Hitler was going to do if he ever got his hands on the wheel of state. Having said that, art it ain't: any reader initially unaware that *Mein Kampf* was written by someone with an eighth grade education doesn't need to be told after perusing the book's opening chapter. *The Grapes of Wrath*, however, is a great work, at once a historically significant testament to the feeling of hopelessness that pervaded daily life at the bottom of the Depression as well as a good (though unremittingly depressing) read.

Somewhere between the two lies *Ball Four*, Jim Bouton's inside look at baseball from the worm's eye viewpoint.

For those who know nothing of the man or the book, Jim Bouton was a once fine pitcher (he won 39 games in two seasons for the Yankees at the tail end of the Mantle-Maris glory days) who had lost his stuff but not his intellect or sense of humor. Turning to the capricious knuckleball in an attempt to keep his career going, Bouton was one of the select few to benefit from MLB's periodic gift to AAAA (too good for the minors but not quite good enough for the Show) players — expansion. In training camp with the 1969 Seattle Pilots, he found himself surrounded by men in similar fixes — ex-Reds ace Jim O'Toole, former Orioles phenom Steve Barber, 1962-1963 NL batting champ Tommy Davis, and numerous other once-prized players now down on their luck. Sensing the human-interest elements inherent in this baseball ghetto, Bouton began recording his observations of the people around him as well as what they said and did ... and baseball would never be the same for his so doing.

Those that doubt the impact of *Ball Four* upon the game's psyche and image are advised to consider the hoopla that surrounded its publication.

Commissioner Bowie Kuhn attempted to discipline Bouton over his violation of "baseball's unwritten code about the confidentiality of the clubhouse."[1] Every owner and half of the players denounced it,[2] while talk shows clamored for the knuckleballer as a guest. For a number of years thereafter every baseball tome was compared to it. Yet for all of that, *Ball Four* is a gentle, almost quaint tale about overgrown man-children struggling to make a living in a profession from which they could be eliminated at any moment.

From a historical perspective, *Ball Four* represented the first unvarnished look inside the locker room of a typical ball club — not one full of stars headed towards glory, but one stocked with average or less-than-average players on a long trip to nowhere. For the 1969 Seattle Pilots, the sheer joy of playing baseball at the major league level is what it's all about. Roughly half the team probably would have observed the season from the vantage point of an AAA bench under normal circumstances and only a select few (Mike Marshall, Marty Pattin, Tommy Davis, and Tommy Harper) had much in the way of careers in front of them. Thus the more earthy aspects of baseball life — greenies, beaver shooting, pranks — take center stage for a Pilots team that both individually and as a whole knows that the nothing-special present is as good as it will ever get.

Taken at that level, *Ball Four* is a reasonably interesting if moderately embarrassing exposé of an American institution, nothing that 100 other books that preceded it weren't. Yet somehow this humble study of a group of overgrown frat rats struck a chord with the American public, and in so doing changed the course of baseball writing forever.

Before *Ball Four*, writers were often co-conspirators in management's attempt to paint an All-American face on their all-too American boys. It is hard for modern day observers to imagine the lengths sportswriters took to hide Mickey Mantle's drunkenness from the public — but hide it they did, because in so doing their lines of communication to baseball's best team and player remained open. Once *Ball Four* was published there was no mystique left to protect, but to baseball's utter amazement the fans proved accepting of heroes that drank too much, looked up the skirts of unsuspecting women and hated the people they worked for — perhaps because they themselves enjoyed the same pursuits. Thus in the veritable twinkling of an eye the era of hero-worshipping journalism came to a close, leaving its practitioners no alternative but to ask the tough question, expose the blemish, and print the unguarded comment before someone else with a deadline to meet did.

A dramatization of how quickly and thoroughly the times changed can be seen in two *Sporting News* cover articles on Chicago Cubs third baseman Ron Santo. The first article, written by Edgar Munzel for the September 6, 1969, issue of the Bible of Baseball, focuses upon manager Leo Durocher's assessment of Santo's offensive and defensive prowess while depicting the Cub captain as "the perfect projection of the Durocher personality."[3] The second, penned by Jerome Holtzman nearly four years later, does not mention a single attribute of Santo's that would show up in a box score, focusing instead on Ron's psychological development. He is now "a very emotional fellow" who "can't hide his feelings"; a man whose one-time "boyish enthusiasm, an enthusiasm which didn't always help him" has been replaced by a "quiet maturity."[4]

Such increased scrutiny, as one might imagine, was less than welcomed by the players. Keep in mind that baseball's locker room cast was and still is primarily composed of twenty something guys wise in the ways of the world as only those who haven't been kicked in the teeth by Life can be. Everybody thinks they are smarter, wittier, and more sage than they actually are at that age, and without the "sanctity of the locker room" to protect them, their offhand comments were increasingly held up to public scrutiny — and, not surprisingly, ridicule. With bigger paychecks to protect, player comments became progressively more guarded, migrating towards the "baseball has been berry berry good to me" level of sophistication. Some, such as Steve Carlton and George Hendrick, took the "once burned, twice shy" maxim to its extreme, refusing to speak to the press at all.

The problem with such freeze-out tactics, though, is that the space reporters have to fill in their newspapers doesn't go away if a player clams up. Thus, writers became hungrier for anything that could masquerade as news, and as such were more willing to publish the unsubstantiated rumor or the unguarded remark.

Simultaneously, *Ball Four* opened up a whole new venue for baseball books. As the gross-out aspects of Bouton's book seemed to be the ones that lingered longest in the public mind, any athlete with a tape recorder and the willingness to rat out his teammates became a candidate for the bestseller list. Stories about men sitting on birthday cakes,[5] locker room fights, ballplayers' sex lives, and drug abuse became the grist of a torrent of books that would be published over the next decade, most of which have sunk back into the muck from whence they came. Yet the image that came forth from these books— that of the ballplayer as *Animal House* resident in good standing — survives for better or worse to this day.

Thus, *Ball Four's* place in history is assured, but as art ... well, it's a decent read.

The best way to think of *Ball Four* is as *The Jazz Singer* of baseball writing. For those who aren't Hollywood-centric, *The Jazz Singer* was the first feature-length talking picture (even though only about half of the film has a sound track attached to it) and is considered to be a cinematic landmark by film historians. Given all of that, one can be excused for wondering why nobody on God's green earth has seen this flick in the last 30 years, and the reasons for that are:

• The story line was passé even by 1927 standards (which didn't stop Neil Diamond from remaking it some 60 years later).

- The crude sound capabilities extant at the time forced The Jazz Singer to take on the aura of a filmed stage play.
- The supporting cast largely consisted of people that no one living ever heard of — and the reason for that becomes obvious after one viewing.

OK, so it isn't great art. But *The Jazz Singer* is historically significant, the plot is pleasant if a bit melodramatic, and those who have never seen Al Jolson before will understand why their great grandpa's generation considered him to be Frank Sinatra, The Beatles, and Michael Jackson all rolled into one. In short, it's an enjoyable movie that's worth a look if you're in the right frame of mind ... just don't expect too much from it.

Ball Four is in the same predicament. Thirty years after the fact, the kiss-and-tell aspects that made it such a sensation when originally published are old hat to anyone who didn't depart for Mars the day Janis Joplin OD'ed. Most of the insights about individual players are either (a) cardboard or (b) about people we don't remember, and they are compiled by a guy who comes across as strangely condescending towards the game he is struggling so mightily to maintain a bit part in. Simply put, Bouton is obviously a deep thinker about many things, but baseball isn't one of them — which goes a long way towards explaining his problems with virtually every authority figure (from the executive suite down to the locker room attendant) he comes in contact with.

Such faults keep *Ball Four* from being the grand opus that certain baseball geeks insist it is, but as straightforward entertainment, a milestone in writing about the game, and an engaging character study ... well, one can and will do a lot worse.

3

The Coming of the Sterile Ashtrays

Change was the watchword for early 1970s culture — in fact, it was one of the few things that the younger generation and their elders could agree upon. Admittedly, their goals were different: those who'd shed their blood on the sands of Iwo Jima generally wanted new, technologically superior copies of what they already had, while the younger generation simply wanted the icons of their elders (the ones who got us into this mess) done away with. Either way, stuff that had seemed pretty nifty keeno up to now was suddenly something to be parodied if the observer was kind, openly derided if he wasn't. Ernest Hemingway, bourbon, Cadillacs, country clubs, Schlitz beer — all of these one-time symbols of sophistication and the good life suddenly became objects of ridicule and were either relegated to the fringes of popular society or purged from it altogether.

Under such circumstances, it was no surprise that baseball, the traditional working man's sport, was directly in the crosshairs of a million Ray Kinsellas as well as their Field of Dream-ish fathers.

In a veritable instant, the game's greatest strength — its sense of continuity over the decades— became a weakness. It wasn't just that baseball's current stars under the offense-throttling rules of the mid- to late-1960s seemed like dwarves in comparison to the Ruths, Wagners, and Cobbs of yore, they were also literally playing in the late Hall of Famers' shadows. As late as 1968 half of all American League games were being played in venues that both predated the New Deal and looked it.[1] Between the natural effects of aging, decades of studied neglect, and multiple reconfigurations of variable architectural merit, the game's past was threatening to entomb its future. The 1969 rule changes would take time to restore the luster to baseball's offensive heroes, but fortunately a decade of jousting with city officials bore fruit at a time when the game most needed it....

... And thus the era of the multi-purpose stadium was upon us.

Of course, convert-o-parks were not a totally new phenomenon (St. Louis' Busch Stadium was the first of the breed in 1966), but the 1970-1971 period undoubtedly represented the trend's high watermark. A trio of strictly off-the-rack ballyards superseded three unique parks that Christy Mathewson would have had no problem getting around in:

- Assuming that one wasn't a slugger, Forbes Field — with its ivy covered walls, Schenley Park backdrop and the University of Pittsburgh's Cathedral of Learning looming over the left-field bleachers — was one of the National League's gems.[2] It gave way to Three Rivers Stadium, whose picturesque location overlooking the confluence of the Allegheny and Monongahela Rivers was invisible from within.
- Cincinnati's oft-reconfigured Crosley Field — host to the first night game in baseball history as well as a quirky left field terrace[3] — yielded to the relatively massive (it held nearly 22,000 more paying customers) and less flood-prone Riverfront Stadium.
- A piece of architectural history, Philadelphia's Shibe Park (nee Connie Mack Stadium) was the first baseball palace that couldn't be demolished with either a lighted match or a termite.[4] That wasn't enough to save it, though, as after a protracted gestation period (the Phillies originally thought they'd have a new park in time for the 1964 season[5]) Veterans Stadium rose in South Philly to replace it.

Yet a mere thirty years later, all three of these minor marvels have become concrete and synthetic turf dinosaurs, destined for (or in the case of Three Rivers, already consigned to) history's scrap heap alongside the more fabled brethren that they replaced. These parks are collectively (along with Busch, Atlanta's late Fulton County Stadium and several others) referred to as the "sterile ashtrays,"[6] symbols of raging monoculture that receive unrelenting criticism by fans and amateur architectural critics alike. For one thing, the new parks' multi-functional purpose by necessity pushed spectators away from the field of play, thus destroying the traditional closeness of the fans to the players. Additionally, their engulfing acres of highly profitable parking effectively divorced each stadium from its surrounding community, while their cookie-cutter dimensions and resolute symmetry seemed a poor substitute for the eccentric screens, jutting walls, and monuments in fair territory that they replaced.

Latter day observers frequently (and loudly) wonder what the designers of these oversized salad bowls must have been thinking. Did they have no sense of the history that was being obliterated with every swing of the wrecking ball? Would current designers feel compelled to construct so many odes to the past (remember the Mets' design of a couple of years back that essentially re-created Ebbets Field with a retractable roof overhead?) if a few more of the Real McCoys had been left standing?

History is often a heck of a lot more enjoyable when contemplated from a safe distance. Yes, the old parks were historically significant, and yes, two of these facilities were among the most aesthetically pleasing and thoughtfully constructed of their time (sorry, Reds fans: Crosley Field was more Erector Set project than architectural masterpiece). However, if one went back to the time and place and honestly considered the situation as those on the spot saw it, taking a sledgehammer to those stadiums was (sad to say) by this point in time more mercy killing than desecration.

Let's start off by taking a look at the parks themselves— not as seen today through Camden Yards-colored glasses, but as they actually existed at the turn of the decade.

First off, while Forbes, Shibe, and Crosley may well have been the bee's knees in 1920, so was the Stutz Bearcat — and nobody in his right mind would have driven one of those down the interstate fifty years later. As great as they were in their day, by 1970 each of these ballyards were:

(a) In need of major capital upgrades to remain competitive. In the days before cable TV deals and megabuck logoed merchandise lines, game day sales of tickets, concessions, and parking were critical to a club's financial success. Yet the three doomed parks trailed the pack in terms of capacity (Forbes being the largest of the trio at 35,000[7]) and none had much in the way of associated parking facilities— Phillies fans, for example, were leaving their cars in a coal yard.[8]

Furthermore, all three stadiums had lived through that character-building experience known as the Great Depression. In those days, the good-drawing clubs were averaging 7,000 fans a game. As for the others ... well, a 1933 Pirates team that finished a competitive second with five Hall of Famers in the everyday lineup drew a grand total of 288,747 fans.[9] It was a time when Shibe Park and Philadelphia A's owner Connie Mack first sold off one of the greatest talent pools ever assembled to pay the monthly bills, then built a 38-foot-high extension to the right field wall to discourage homeowners across the street from selling their rooftops as cheap seating.[10]

Ballpark upkeep, as one might imagine, was well down the list of Depression-era priorities, and the problem was exacerbated by the three teams' relatively poor showings in the early postwar years. (Cincinnati was spared this indignity to some extent when radio magnate Powell Crosley purchased the club in 1935. This brings up an interesting footnote: one of the key reasons why Wrigley Field and Fenway Park survive today is because each was owned during the lean years by a multi-millionaire/sportsman who was capable of maintaining the facilities despite the absence of adequate revenues.)

To dramatize the scope of the deferred maintenance problem, consider that Barney Dreyfess spent $2 million to build his Forbes Field showplace

The upper right-hand corner of the massive left-field grandstand is invisible in this picture of Forbes Field — which is perfectly fair, given that the people sitting in that area couldn't see home plate either. (*National Baseball Hall of Fame Library, Cooperstown, NY*)

in 1909.[11] Thirty-seven years later, Dreyfuss's son-in-law, Bill Benswanger, offered to sell the entire Pirates franchise — park, players, minor leagues, the works—to Bill Veeck for $1.6 million[12] at a time when brand new 35,000-seat venues (Milwaukee's County Stadium) were costing about $5 million to build.[13] Think about that one for a moment.

(b) Located in less-than desirable parts of town. The latter day idea of a stadium fitting into the surrounding neighborhood would have been hilarious to the majority of baseball's pioneers. Most of the old ballparks were built either on marginal sites or in relatively undeveloped locales: Ebbets Field, for example, rose on the site of a dump in a "stylish" area known as Pigtown.[14] Though the availability of public transit was an important consideration, none of these people spent so much as three seconds thinking about urban growth patterns or the demographics of the surrounding neighborhood. They simply put the parks up where the land could be assembled at reasonable cost and hoped for the best.

When the middle class flight to Green Acres began in earnest in the 1950s, these ballyards were doubly cursed: first by the loss of their traditional customer base, and secondly by the fact that they weren't in the most fashionable neighborhoods to begin with. As a result, the areas around the stadiums began to take on an ambiance that was less than comforting to the average suburbanite. A trip to the park became less a leisure activity than an involuntary immersion in the issues that threatened to tear the nation apart: poverty, joblessness, and race with a capital R. Perhaps the concerns of upwardly mobile fans were a touch overblown, but in recalling Connie Mack Stadium's final days, Phillies manager Frank Lucchesi characterized the surrounding neighborhood as so tough that "we had to give away two policeman with every admission."[15]

(c) Not all that much fun to watch a game at. A supposedly laudable feature of The Ballpark at Arlington is the columns holding up the right field bleacher roof. It's a nice old-timey touch in the view of many observers, trading a few obstructed-view seats for a look that was sure to be a hit with nostalgia-oriented fans.

Right — just so long as they aren't the ones sitting in the obstructed seats.

Before the advent of cantilevered construction techniques in the 1940s, pillars were required to hold up the second deck ... but that didn't keep teams from placing seats directly behind them. Piecemeal expansions often had unexpected consequences akin to the slight setback of Forbes Field's huge left-field bleacher that obscured home plate for those sitting in its upper right hand corner.[16] Playing field revisions could further compromise the experience (think Crosley Field was an intimate park by virtue of its small capacity? Think again: by the 1950s home plate was 78 feet from the grandstands, a direct result of the Reds' attempts to increase scoring in what traditionally had been a pitcher's park.[17]) The first deck of the Polo Grounds' left-field grandstands were an intimacy-robbing 16.8 feet above the field of play[18] and the center-field bleacher section so distant from home plate that only three balls were ever hit into it.[19]

In short, by the 1960s those wonderful old ballyards, as steeped (some might say pickled) in tradition as they might have been, were aging relics of a bygone day tucked away in areas that the average fan needed a better reason than the Houston Colt 45s to venture into. Something clearly needed to be done, and the worst part of it was that the average pre-cable TV, pre-luxury box team wasn't producing anything like the kind of cash flow necessary to foot the $50 million bill for new facilities.

Enter, unwillingly, the cities....

It's hard to recreate the sense of gloom — no, impending disaster — that prevailed in America's metropolises at the time. In just over a generation the entire middle class of many cities had simply vanished from the scene, and those who took their place were often disadvantaged, dissatisfied, and dis-

Even the addition of billboards and world championship pennants in the upper deck didn't liven up Three Rivers Stadium much in this view, photographed late in the park's life. However, Three Rivers did play host to two World Series in its 31-year tenure, as well as Ted Turner's "manager for a day" stunt ... and there wasn't an obstructed seat in the house. (*The Sporting News*)

mayed. Massive civic infrastructures were suddenly being supported by people to whom McDonald's was a good paying employer, and they did so about as well as anyone could reasonably have expected them to. The crumbling streets, schools with no books, and police and fire services that were reduced to damage control levels were just the tip of the iceberg; even with such draconian cuts, cities like New York, Philadelphia, and Cleveland (among others) were still going broke.

In the midst of all this tumult, baseball came calling with its hand out ... and the thinly veiled threat that the suburbs, an obscure industrial town, or some fast-growing Sunbelt locale was acceptable if the city fathers were unable to spring for new digs. The Los Angeles Angels chose to hang their shingle 35 miles from the city center in an area still dotted with orange groves, while Calvin Griffith had forsaken the nation's capital for a 50,000-person bedroom community somewhere in the wilds of Minnesota. Thus, when Phillies owner Bob Carpenter hinted in the midst of his ten-year battle for new facilities (which included two cliffhanger referendums) that New Jersey would be a perfectly adequate home for a Philadelphia team if needs be,[20] people listened — and believed.

Thus, the cities found themselves between the proverbial rock and hard place, needing champagne facilities on a beer bankroll. That Cincinnati, Philadelphia, and Pittsburgh would have solved their problem in much the same way — by building functional, no-frills structures that got the job done while making as few compromises as were absolutely necessary — is anything but surprising.

And on the whole they did quite well, thank you. Everybody who bought a ticket could now see the game — some of the seats may have been high enough that passing airplanes occasionally obscured the line of sight, but at least everybody could now tell if the ball was going towards second or short. Seats and aisles were wide enough that people could coexist without initiating consensual sexual activity. Concessionaires could serve organically inert (if not particularly nutritious) food to 40,000 hungry fans without threatening to burn the ballpark down due to substandard wiring.

Perhaps the parks were a little stark, but they were clean, modern, and the pride of their respective communities — and as such was featured prominently in the teams' contemporary yearbooks and advertising. Yes, the Gobi Desert of parking lots that surrounded each stadium did set the complexes apart from their communities, but convenient parking generated revenue that paid down bonds — and besides, the local neighborhood was (mum's the word) nothing to write home about anyway.

And, along with their partner-in-crime artificial turf, the multi-purpose stadiums drove a revolution in how the game was played.

Chemistry's contribution to modern baseball play has gotten a justifiably bad name in recent years for the number of contusions, achy knees, and Turf Toes that it has inflicted, but the covering required a more diverse skill set to play upon effectively. The resilient surface demanded quick reactions on ground balls and drives hit into the gaps while the relatively reliable hops made the diving stop an exciting addition to baseball's defensive scheme. Simultaneously, the increased velocity of the typical grounder forced infielders back to the edge of the outfield "grass" to maintain an adequate defensive arc, testing the limits of many an arm.

As the multi-purpose stadiums' influence spread, even teams with grass-covered home parks adapted to the new realities. By 1977 more than half of all National League games were played on the plastic stuff; even the Los Angeles Dodgers could expect the defensive limitations of their converted center fielder/double play combo of Dave Lopes and Bill Russell to be exposed some 40 times a season.[21]

With speed, quick reflexes, and a cannon arm taking their place alongside brute power and hand-eye coordination as prime attributes for the turf player, the search for the elusive "five tool" athlete became the Holy Grail of scouts everywhere. The Ted Kluszewskis, Frank Howards, and Harmon Killebrews that had been the prize catches of the previous generation gave way to the Cesar Cedenos, Ken Griffey Srs., and Amos Otises. Even the new breed of "pure power" hitters like Dave Parker, Mike Schmidt, and Dave Kingman (at least when he first came up) had wheels and defensive capabilities. Sure, an occasional Greg Luzinski might break through to play with his back turned to a Garry Maddox, but one pretty much had to be a 30-100-.300 guy to make a living that way.

In short, the new parks offered a quicker, more aggressive style of play in an environment that a normally conscientious dad could take his son to without concern — and the fans absolutely loved it.

The Philadelphia Phillies in 1969 were a foundering fifth place team that drew an anemic 519,000 fans (less than 7,000 more than the fledgling San Diego Padres, who didn't have all that tradition to fall back on) to witness their next-to-last season in Connie Mack Stadium.[22] By 1971 (their first season at the Vet) the Phils had progressed from foundering to nearly hopeless— perhaps seven guys on the roster actually had careers in front of them — yet attendance had nearly tripled.[23] The Cincinnati Reds drew just under a million fans (seventh best in the NL) in 1969 with an up-and-coming third place team in a terrific baseball town. Two years later they were a confused, sub-.500 disappointment ... that drew over a half million more fans.[24] Pittsburgh's situation is less clear cut — their move from contender to champion coincided with the park switch — but consider this: a Pirates team that won 88 games in 1969 drew over 100,000 fewer fans than a 90-win San Francisco Giants team. Two years later, the two faced off in the National League Championship Series— yet the Bucs, never seriously threatened after mid-August, outdrew a Giants team that won the divisional title on the season's final day by nearly 400,000 admissions.[25]

OK, so nowadays we think of these forums as defilers of baseball's holy landscape, cookie-cutter enclaves that superseded parks with genuine if quirky personality — but what is personality anyway? Is it something acquired by having funny concave walls as they did at Ebbets Field, or is it a product of watching Carl Furillo turning caroms off that wall into putouts at second base?

Each of the "sterile ashtrays" housed a world championship team. Each was home to multiple Hall of Famers during their biggest seasons. Each witnessed its share of dramatic and bizarre moments: Pete Rose knocking Ray Fosse and his career for a loop while scoring the 1970 All-Star Game's deciding run; Greg Luzinski hitting a titanic home run off the Vets' schmaltzy Liberty Bell[26]; Ted Turner pulling his ludicrous "manager for a day" stunt against the Bucs. Perhaps none of the sterile ashtrays will ever be featured in *Architectural Digest*, but none of them set fans back $75 a head for a "priceless" (as that famous credit card company is quick to remind us) moment with their kids, either.

The old baseball parks were wonderful in their time, but that time had passed by the 1970s— just as the multi-purpose stadiums that succeeded them are now headed into the twilight. That such parks-on-a-budget were capable of providing as many thrills as they did was one of the era's minor miracles ... as well as a driving force in the reshaping of the game and its relationship with its public.

4

The Man Who Gave His Body to Baseball

Every discipline is blessed with souls willing to sacrifice their physical well-being for the sake of their art. Football is an obvious one — heck, it's practically impossible to play in the NFL for more than a year or two without spending one's golden years hobbling around on an artificial joint. Muhammad Ali's boxing-induced Parkinson's Disease and Evel Knievel's multitude of broken bones are symbols of the price that certain men and women willingly pay for the glory that comes with the professional sporting life.

Such sacrifices, though usually accidental when they do occur (witness Tony Conigliaro), are relatively rare in baseball. Yet every so often even this theoretically non-contact sport will lure a hardy individual who will stop at nothing to improve his competitive position. In 1971 the ultimate expression of this spirit was embodied by a man who would later say, "Some men give their bodies to science. I gave mine to baseball."[1]

That man was a scrappy second baseman named Ronald Kenneth Hunt.

A natural third baseman who was moved to second early on because his original organization (the Milwaukee Braves) was desperate, Hunt was the primeval Todd Walker — a guy whose attitude and numbers seemed more attractive from a distance than they did on closer inspection. By no means a small man (6', 186), he'd shown decent power as a rookie playing in the Polo Grounds but was fated to spend his next seven years toiling in the National League's three most extreme pitcher's parks (Shea Stadium, followed by a year in Los Angeles and three in the Giants' wind-swept castle by the bay). As a result of this immersion into the world of the offensively deprived, Hunt began to emphasize bat control by progressively choking up on the stick. Ultimately, he would hold his bat as far up from the knob as any player of his day save Matty Alou and Felix Milan, prompting Phillies broadcaster Richie Ashburn to observe that Hunt should be forced to declare which end of the bat he intended to hit the ball with.[2]

33

(The concept of choking up on the bat, which had seen a big time revival in the 1960s when hits of any type were rare and precious things, declined steadily during the next decade to the point of near extinction by the mid-Reagan years. While the livelier offensive conditions had much to do with convincing even the weakest batters to maximize their leverage, it should be noted that many fine power hitters— Frank Robinson among them[3]— historically opted for an increased measure of bat control.)

As his hands migrated up the bat handle, Hunt of necessity began crowding the plate in order to reach the outside corner, ultimately ending up right on top of it à la Craig Biggio. Between that placement and a natural hitch that thrust his upper body over the dish while striding,[4] the man was both an easy target for anything tight and unable to do much to get out of the way.

And thus a legend was born...

Hunt's episodes in pain management became his signature talent. He was hit three times during a batting practice stint one spring — by the pitching machine.[5] Such punishment was anything but unusual for Hunt: while with the Giants he tied a major league record by being plunked three times in a single game.[6] People wondered aloud if the man did it on purpose. Montreal coach Jerry

Ron Hunt demonstrates the extreme choke grip that prompted Phillies broadcaster Richie Ashburn to quip that Hunt should have to declare which end of the bat he wanted to hit the ball with. Positioning himself almost on top of the plate à la Craig Biggio as a result, Hunt established the modern single season HBP mark — and became "the man who gave his body to baseball." (*The Sporting News*)

Zimmerman once said, "I swear he likes it. He just turns slightly and lets the balls bounce off."[7] From his own perspective, Hunt would always emphasize how much it hurt to be hit, while simultaneously pointing out that "my ability isn't that great. When you lack something, you make up for it in other ways. I won't give ground and if it helps me get on base more often, that's great."[8]

As modest and self-effacing as that comment sounds, Hunt's assessment of his skills and what it took for him to stay in the majors was right on the mark. A tendency towards excess weight[9] plus the cumulative effect of his various dings would progressively slow him both in the field and on the basepaths as the season progressed.[10] His exaggerated choke hold on the bat coupled with a short, choppy swing gave Hunt as little power as any major leaguer of his time — his last 1,270 at-bats in the Show would not yield a single homer or triple. Though his batting philosophy allowed him to make contact virtually at will (after yielding three hits to Hunt one night, Don Sutton lamented, "I'll bet if I threw the rosin bag he'd punch it into center field"[11]), the price of such bat control was less-than-impressive walk totals.

In short, being hit by the ball was a central if debilitating skill — the 50 point gain in on-base percentage that Hunt's special talent yielded in a typical year was the difference between a starting job and utility player hell.

The 1971 season represented the ultimate expression of the now Montreal Expos second baseman's masochistic art. Ding by painful ding, Hunt became the Roger Maris of hit batsmen that summer, supposedly breaking (oh, the irony) Hughie Jennings' 1896 single season record with an amazing 50 hit-by-pitches (HBPs), nearly twice as many as he would post in any other season.[12] His painful trek towards the record became a minor cause célèbre in the baseball world, in part because the Expos weren't doing anything else worthy of note and also because of the controversy surrounding Hunt's coopting of a portion of the strike zone for himself. After administering the record-setting plunk, Cub pitcher Milt Pappas indignantly stated, "He not only didn't try to get out of the way, but he actually leaned into … a breaking pitch. That's a joke."[13]

Maybe so, Milt, but it was an amazingly effective joke just the same — Hunt's incremental not-so-free passes combined with 58 walks and 145 conventional hits to produce a .402 on-base percentage (fourth in the league that year) and 89 runs scored (eighth).[14]

Alas, as is the case with so many artists, Hunt sacrificed much for his craft. Unlike Biggio he wore no body armor and thus was constantly fighting injuries—1971 would be the only season of Hunt's career in which he would play as many as 150 games. Though not disabled, he was anything but unaffected by the myriad dings: an early-season HBP caused Hunt's left hand to fly off the bat during his follow through.[15] By 1973 the sundry contusions and strains had reduced his defensive range to the point of inducing critical comments from closer Mike Marshall.[16] Perhaps Marshall was just on a roll that day (his ripping of Hunt came amidst a series of incidents and less-than-diplomatic statements that greased the skids for Iron Mike's departure that winter), but by 1974 Hunt was moved to third base where he simply didn't provide enough O to compete with the Mike Schmidts and Darrell Evanses of the world. Thus, at 33, he was history — but in departing the game Hunt left behind a Ruth-like record in his particular discipline.

A bit presumptuous perhaps? The career HBP leader of the modern era prior to Hunt's ascension was Minnie Minoso with 192[17]: Hunt bettered his mark by 23 percent despite playing 500 fewer games than Minoso did, and lacking the "advantage" of being a really good black player at a time when knocking down black guys was a revered pitching strategy.

Though Don Baylor would ultimately pass Hunt on the career bruise list (and in the process play Henry Aaron to his Ruth by needing 809 additional games to record 24 more HBPs), nobody has made a serious run at his single season mark since. Baylor's high water mark was 35 dings in 1986 while Biggio, armor and all, has never exceeded 34 in a campaign. Craig, by the way, is on the threshold of unseating Hunt from the number two spot but will do so as a matter of longevity than talent (as the 2004 season begins, Biggio has been hit two *fewer* times in 770 *more* games played).

Hunt's departure was one unmarked by great sorrow (like many artists he was a kind of grumpy guy who was never terribly popular with his teammates), but with the end of the 1974 season a truly unique character passed from baseball's scene. Scrappy and determined, Ron Hunt was a man who utilized every drop of talent that the Lord put into his body — and once that was all expended, he discovered a novel, if painful, way to keep on going.

5

The Angry Men

There is a fine line between anger (defined as a strong feeling of displeasure or hostility) and rage (the violent, explosive cousin of the above). Anger can be mixed with reason to fuel revolutions: rage repels reason and leads to riots and mob rule. Maintaining a fine sense of moral angst without crossing the border to the senseless destruction of rage has been one of man's greatest psychological challenges through the ages. Some of history's most compelling and fascinating stories revolve around those who seem to be permanently camped in the no-man's land between these two emotions: the alternately brutal and homespun Nikita Khrushchev was the breed's all-too-chilling Cold War model.

This gray Twilight Zone was the stomping grounds for a group of black baseball players who reached their athletic zenith in the early 1970s. Unwilling to sit at the back of a bus filled with people (players) that were second class citizens to begin with, this new generation of African-American stars were outspoken about their fate in the newly vigorous manner of the society around them. They were dissatisfied, they were demanding, they were as mad as hell and not going to take it anymore.

It was a madness that would sadly consume much of what they brought to baseball while breaking the spirits of those who harbored it.

Unlike the previous generation of black ballplayers, the men that came of age in the 1960s were primarily not Southerners, and thus baseball would provide a rude and somewhat belated introduction to the realities of life in a racist America. Dick Allen, for example, was from a small town in western Pennsylvania while Reggie Jackson from a suburb of Philadelphia. Though such men routinely experienced the covert racism that was part and parcel of the so-called Negro Experience in those days, along with the occasional overt act, none grew up having their blackness rubbed in their faces at every opportunity. Furthermore, many in the Jackie Robinson generation had been shielded as much as possible from the Southern minor league experience, leaving whole teams if not leagues as pioneer territory for racial integration until well into the 1960s.

Dick Allen, as late as 1963, was the first black to play professional base-ball in the state of Arkansas,[1] doing so in a town (Little Rock) where the National Guard had been called out just six years earlier to implement the integration of its schools. Not surprisingly, Allen's experience as the first African-American athlete in a place where race was a battleground was bit-ter at best. Catcalls of "nigger" were commonplace,[2] and he was lucky if slurs were the only things thrown his way from the stands. Segregated housing was a way of life that nobody in the Arkansas organization was interested in doing much about.[3] Taking to the streets at night was so dangerous (Allen's car was shot at twice[4]) that the future Phillie rarely ventured out of his room except to go to the ballpark.

Simultaneously, the national mood was evolving to the point where asserting one's rights was not only encouraged but seen as a duty. By the late 1960s, submitting to racism was almost as bad as having it inflicted upon one's self — a young black man of stature was expected to speak out and stand up for his principles ... at least in society as a whole.

Baseball, however, was not and is not a democratic society: it's a busi-ness much like General Motors in which people who do not conform to the organization's standards of conduct can be punished for their transgressions. There are, of course, limits to what either organization can do—both GM and baseball have those pesky unions to deal with — but every shop foreman worth his salt knows that there are a dozen ways to make a guy who gets out of line pay for so doing. He can be assigned unpleasant work, transferred to some odious locale, or minutely scrutinized so that the inevitable screw-up is not overlooked. Whether one approves of his activities or not, such is the treatment that John Rocker has been subjected to in recent years, and such (along with a graveling dose of patronization) was what these angry young black men received from their patrons.

This clash between sociology and Corporate America (sports division) would claim more than one career before running its course.

Consider Alex Johnson, an immensely strong right-handed hitter who played for eight different teams in his 13-year career. A thumper early on (he led the Pioneer League in homers in 1962[5]), Johnson, by the time he reached the majors, had converted himself into a line drive hitting machine of such ferocity that batting practice pitchers would routinely throw to him from behind a screen.[6] One of Johnson's training tricks was to start out hitting against a pitching machine at the regulation distance, than move Iron Mike progressively closer to him until it was within 45 feet of home plate — and he'd still hit rope after rope.[7] The result of this intensive effort was .300 aver-ages in each of his first three seasons as a regular, capped by the first (and to date only) batting championship won by a Los Angeles/California/Anaheim Angel.

Contemporary opinions notwithstanding, however, Johnson was a per-fect example of why a great swing does not necessarily make a great player.

The level cut robbed him of over-the-fence power — despite Alex's powerful physique his career high in homers was 17. He didn't take walks, was a poor percentage base runner and an atrocious fielder with remarkably limited range for a man with a fine throwing arm and above-average speed. In his later years he'd disdain the act of fielding entirely: when Rangers third base coach Jackie Moore would approach Alex with the news that he would be playing left field that day, Johnson would habitually frown before Moore could get a word out of his mouth.[8]

He haughtily rejected instruction of any kind. When Phillies coach Peanuts Lowrey tried to refine his ball-hawking, Johnson initially took offense, then dropped the first fly hit to him in a theatric attempt to emulate the technique ... which was also the last one he ever tried to field in that manner.[9] The Cardinals tried to alter his batting stance and swing — Johnson would brag in later years that "I made them trade me in St. Louis by my actions" for deigning to do such a thing.[10] In short, he was the kind of guy who had to hit .300 to play — and anybody who looked at him realized that such should not be the case.

Perhaps that sense of talent squandered was what made Alex's life so difficult to bear.

Characterizing Johnson as moody is about the same as describing Andruw Jones as a good fielder: sure it's true, but a certain something gets lost in the translation. In listening to Alex Johnson one got the impression that the man truly loved baseball — he just hated everything that went along with playing it, like teammates, managers, fans, and sportswriters. Johnson wanted to be left alone at all times, dressing in a corner of the locker room to be out of the line of fire for clubhouse pranks and close to the door for easy escape from reporters.[11] He wouldn't accept the traditional handshake from a teammate after hitting a home run: when Chico Ruiz once jokingly grabbed his hand after a dinger, Alex jumped off the bench and kicked Ruiz in the shin.[12] When Cardinals manager Red Schoendienst was asked why he'd insisted that such a great hitter be traded, he retorted, "Do something for me. Introduce yourself to Johnson and then come back and ask that question again."

The writer did so and immediately understood.[13]

None of this is to suggest that the man didn't have a way with words. To him, everybody in baseball was "dickhead."[14] Earl Lawson once observed that "what you have to remember is that when Alex says 'Mother,' he's just used half of his vocabulary."[15] When dealt to the Angels in November 1969, Johnson immediately scored points with the Anaheim faithful by stating, "I'd rather play in hell than for the Angels."[16] He was candid about his unwillingness to run out every ground ball, saying that "I think it's to my benefit to conserve myself a little bit.... You just have to pace yourself."[17] After having pulled a baserunning rock while with the Cincinnati Reds, manager Dave Bristol asked Johnson what he'd been thinking of. "Explaining to you what I

Perhaps as he was meant to be, Alex Johnson is alone with his thoughts behind the Anaheim Stadium batting cage prior to a 1970 game. (*The Sporting News*)

don't know is like trying to get back from where I ain't been" was Alex's reply.[18]

Now there's one that's hard to argue with....

Not surprisingly, reporters became Johnson's favorite whipping boys. To Alex's way of thinking, the fact that they reported what he said was the cause of all his problems— thus he would habitually launch into obscenity-laden tirades at full volume that would make it impossible for reporters to interview him or anyone within shouting distance.[19] After Bob Miller of the Los Angeles *Herald-Examiner* had given him an error on a play then hid his bat a few days later as a practical joke (Johnson carried his bats everywhere with him[20]), Alex dumped coffee grounds in Miller's typewriter.[21] The situation got so bad during Johnson's Anaheim days that the Angels press corps filed a formal complaint with the American League about Alex's abuse.[22]

In typical fashion, Johnson released a telegram stating that "in the future I will not talk with you in any manner, offensive or otherwise."[23]

Not that the writers didn't give it back to Alex in spades. A June 9, 1970, Baltimore *Evening Sun* cartoon depicted Johnson as a spike-toothed ape twirling a telephone pole over his head.[24] A Detroit *Free Press* columnist wrote, "Just to have to refer to Alex as an Angel all the time is repugnant," while suggesting that a sign should be posted outside the Halo clubhouse: "Beware of the Leftfielder: He Bites."[25] A Chicago sportswriter suggested that American League president Joe Cronin should suspend Johnson for his penchant of physically intimidating umpires.[26]

The 1971 season represented the apex of Alex's problems, partly because the Angels bombed despite three acquisitions (Tony Conigliaro, Ken Berry, and Jim Maloney) that were supposed to move them back into contention and partly because ... well, Johnson was his normal self. Alex combined his traditional disdain for spring training (during an exhibition game he positioned himself under the shade of a light standard[27]) with his penchant for running out routine ground balls at half speed to create friction with the Angels brass early on. The solution that manager Lefty Phillips and general manager Dick Walsh devised could best be called tough love: Johnson was benched on four occasions for lack of hustle and fined an amazing 29 times for a cornucopia of infractions ranging from not taking outfield practice to half-heartedly chasing balls during games.[28] The situation finally came to a head on June 26, when Johnson was suspended "for failure, as a member of this club, to give your best efforts towards the winning of American League baseball games played by the California Angels."[29]

Phillips and Walsh weren't hallucinating: Johnson's lack of effort was clear to his teammates as well, and they were both vocal and demonstrative in their distaste for Alex. The happy-go-lucky Ruiz, who was the godfather of Johnson's adopted daughter, pulled a gun on the batting champ in the clubhouse one day — an unnamed pitcher later commented that "if Chico did anything wrong, it was that he didn't pull the trigger."[30] After the Halos won two out of three games during one of Johnson's suspensions, a player commented, "As far as we are concerned, Alex can go home right now.... He does not care if we win or lose."[31] Clyde Wright wasn't alone when he said that "it takes a lot of pressure off when he's not out there"[32]; the pitching staff in total had called an impromptu meeting earlier in the season to air their complaints about Johnson's defensive efforts. On May 23, Phillips told the other 24 members of the team that Johnson would never play for him again.

His oath was met with sustained applause.[33]

Having read the previous, one might get the idea that Johnson's real first name was Damian. Yet off the field more than one person attested to the man's affability if not outright kindness. Johnson was a sucker for little tikes: Dick Allen remembered Alex giving piggyback rides to his kids,[34] while Texas Ranger catcher Rich Billings once observed that "if the world were filled with nothing but children, Alex Johnson would be the happiest one alive."[35] Once, when a Philadelphia clubhouse man called into Connie Mack Stadium saying that his car had broken down on the expressway, Johnson left to help fix the vehicle — in uniform.[36] When Alex discovered that the Angels' Kangaroo Court fines went to Minnie Rojas, the one-time Halo closer who was paralyzed in an automobile crash, he offered up a $500 check, saying, "Take my fines out of this and keep the change."[37]

Furthermore, when discussing his problems, Johnson would movingly reveal emotional scars of a type that caused teammate Tony Conigliaro to comment that "he's so hurt inside it's terrifying."[38] When preparing for the grievance hearing over Johnson's suspension, MLBPA chief Marvin Miller met with the outfielder to get his side of the story ... and ended up on the receiving end of a ten-hour monologue that frequently bordered on incoherence. Alex had diligently recorded scores of complaints and slights on whatever scraps of paper had been handy at the moment — ticket folders, the backs of used envelopes, matchbook covers, etc. Some were serious, some were trivial (assuming that one considered segregated pools and the like to be trivial), some predated his experience with baseball ... but all had exacted an obvious toll on this most sensitive of men.[39]

At the core of the amassed complaints were racism and the man's near-total inability to deal with it on any level.

Though he was born in Helena, Arkansas, Johnson's family had moved to Detroit early on, and while his existence was anything but cushy, his father's position at an auto plant made things easier than they were for many others. Yet Alex, unlike his brother Ron who would go onto a storied football career with the New York Giants, possessed a natural reserve that bordered on introversion: his father observed that "even as a boy around me at home, he [Alex] never said anything unless I spoke to him first."[40] In its classic sink or swim manner, baseball had tossed this youth into the deep end of the racism pool by dispatching him first to Miami and then to Little Rock for his minor league tutelage. Toss the *Animal House*-like sensitivities of the baseball locker room into the mix and what emerged was an incredibly bitter man with few natural outlets for his temper, one who could refuse to explain a less-than-obvious act by rationalizing that "it just wouldn't have done any good."

Thus, dickhead. Thus the intolerance for any prank, no matter how innocuous. Thus the anger at any slight, real or imagined. "Hell yes I'm bitter," Johnson said in one of his rare interviews with the local press. "I've been bitter since I learned I was black. The society into which I was born and in which I grew up and in which I play ball today is anti-black. My attitude is nothing more than a reaction to their attitude. But they don't keep their hatreds to themselves. They go out of their way to set up barriers, to make dirty little slights so that you're aware of their messed up feelings."[41]

Johnson's problems with the world were obvious and deep-seated (his victory over the Angels established mental illness as an injury[42]) but there were others whose problems, while less incapacitating, were every bit as damaging to the sport and themselves.

A prime example of this phenomenon was a 5' 11" all-sports athlete from Wampum, Pennsylvania, named Dick Allen.

Unlike Johnson, who was one of those guys who supposedly could have been a great player if whatever, Dick Allen really did put the rubber to the road. An incredibly muscular man (one reporter likened his upper body to a Rodin sculpture), Allen utilized the heaviest bat of his day[43] to hit the kind of homers that people remember 30-plus years later. Yet despite the inevitable strikeouts that came along with the clouts, Allen possessed excellent bat control, leading to oodles of walks and high batting averages at a time when remembering every .300 hitter in a given season wasn't much of a challenge.

Dick was a seven-time All-Star, an automatic selection when healthy and not in trouble. His 1964 rookie season (29 homers, 91 RBIs, .316 average) was given the circumstances as good as any ever recorded, while eight years later he was a no-brainer MVP choice in his first season as an American Leaguer.[44] While his .292 career average and 351 homers seem undistinguished in the current context, consider that as of 2002 the most similar player to Gary Sheffield at a like age was Dick Allen[45] — except that in Allen's day batting and slugging averages were 15 and 30 points lower respectively. Take Gary Sheffield, add 15 points in average and 30 points in slugging and the result is Jason Giambi with speed.

That's the kind of player Allen was.

Having said all of that, Sheffield is in many ways an eerily ironic pairing for this most troubled of men. Like Sheffield, Allen was one of those people who could say something off the wall and then be startled when others took it the wrong way. Like Sheffield, he got into numerous arguments with teammates, management, and fans, polarizing practically every team he was associated with. Like Sheffield, Allen had a casual attitude to rules as they applied to him.

And like Sheffield, he felt that racism was at the root of all of his problems.

In all fairness, Allen had more than a little basis for feeling persecuted. As the Arkansas Travelers' first black player, he received the kind of greeting one would expect such a pioneer to get, with people picketing his arrival at the Little Rock airport then showing up at his first game with signs such as "Don't Negro-ize Baseball" and "Nigger Go Home."[46] Threatening telephone calls with racial overtones followed his 1965 altercation with veteran outfielder Frank Thomas, while someone drove up on Allen's front lawn and spun his wheels on the grass during the same period.[47] When Allen cut the ulnar nerve and two tendons in his right hand while pushing a car, he was variously reported as having been injured in a barroom fight, by a jealous lover, or while exiting the bedroom of a teammate's wife.[48] Several years after Allen left the Phils, Chicago *Daily News* sportswriter Dave Nightingale began putting together a story on Dick's human side. "Don't trust a word the SOB says," one Philadelphia writer advised. "He's an inveterate liar."[49]

So much for the press' vaunted objectivity....

Yet for all of that, Allen was more than adept at creating his own trouble. Once he'd tired of Philadelphia Dick "began to set my own rules" that included stopping off at a series of bars on his way to the ballpark, missing batting practice, and showing up late for a game as a result of watching one of his horses run at Monmouth Park.[50] He drew words in the dirt with his spikes, continuing to do so after Commissioner Bowie Kuhn ordered him not to.[51] Once the Phillies traded him to the St. Louis Cardinals, Allen was the model of decorum until he tore a hamstring in mid-August and left town rather than be administered to by the Cardinals' team doctors.[52] During his second tour of duty with the Phillies in 1976, Allen became upset when he heard that Tony Taylor, a 40-year-old coach who'd batted 23 times all sea-

Sporting the physique that inspired one writer to liken him to a Rodin sculpture, Dick Allen was arguably the most gifted — and troubled — athelete of his era. A runaway choice for the 1972 MVP award, Allen would "retire" two years later while leading the AL in homers and was finished at 35, prompting him to ask, rhetorically, some years later: "I wonder how good I could have been?" (*National Baseball Hall of Fame Library, Cooperestown, NY*)

son, was going to be left off the postseason roster. By way of protest, Allen remained in the dugout while the rest of the team celebrated clinching the pennant in the first game of a double-header in Montreal, then moved to the clubhouse with the black players and Mike Schmidt for a private celebration during the second game.[53]

Not surprisingly, the Phillies went three and out in the playoffs to the Big Red Machine.

Regardless of the source, the result of it all was a persecution complex of massive proportions. Allen would comment for years about the horrors of 1963 Little Rock, yet the fans at the end of the season selected him as the Travelers' Most Popular Player.[54] After the incident at Monmouth, Allen was suspended for 26 days; when he returned he cleaned out his locker and dressed in an equipment room for the remainder of the season.[55] After feuding with the newly acquired Ron Santo in 1974 over the leadership of the

Dick Allen wearing his signature batting helmet. A response to debris thrown by Philadelphia fans (he would be dubbed "Crash," for crash helmet, by his Phillies teammates), Dick would wear the helmet both at the plate and in the field for the remainder of his career. (*National Baseball Hall of Fame Library, Cooperstown, NY*)

White Sox, Allen gathered his teammates together and tearfully told them he was retiring[56]—on September 13, with the White Sox two games under .500 but not completely out of the race.

Yet unlike Johnson, Allen had his immense productivity to fall back on, and thus was allowed to more or less do and say what he wished. The fines and suspensions that Philadelphia managers Gene Mauch and Bob Skinner levied on Dick were routinely overruled by owner Bob Carpenter, who invested untold hours in talking the young slugger out of retirement. Chuck Tanner made Allen's Chicago sojourn as convenient as it could possibly be — Dick didn't have to do interviews, take batting practice, or show up more than a half hour before game time.[57] Jack McKeon, Allen's manager during his final days in Oakland, didn't use Dick as a designated hitter because ... well, Dick neither wanted to perform the function or (depending on whom one believed) had to, given his agreement with owner Charlie Finley.[58]

Three of the four managers mentioned above were fired in part because of their inability to control Allen, and Tanner outlasted Dick in Chicago by a single season.

Managers and rules exist for a reason — namely, that the young men who comprise baseball's talent pool lack the worldliness and wisdom to act in their own best interests (not to mention those of the team) at all times. It's a problem that spans ethnic boundaries but one that Dick Allen, in his outrage against society in general, was unable to perceive. The years of lax training habits and nighttime benders quickly reduced Allen once he passed his 33rd birthday: in his three remaining seasons Dick would hit a combined .246 with 32 homers and 208 strikeouts in 885 at-bats. At age 30 Allen's career totals were similar to those of Duke Snider and Willie Stargell, meaning that Dick was headed for the Hall of Fame assuming he didn't come down with Eric Davis Disease. By the time Finley tired of him (after finding Allen in the clubhouse showering during the sixth inning of a game, Charlie said, "I wanted to show the world I could be the first to work with Dick Allen. I found out that I was like all the other suckers"[59]) his career stats were equivalent to those in the Willie Horton and Norm Cash strata of baseball society, i.e. nobody who's going to be invited to upstate New York anytime soon.

In a reflective moment some years later, Dick Allen would speculate on what his career might have been if only — though if only what is never defined. "I wonder how good I could have been," Allen began in a quiet voice. "It could have been a joy, a celebration. Instead, I played angry. In baseball, if a couple of things go wrong for you and those things get misperceived or distorted, you get a label. After a while that label becomes you and you become the label, whether that's really you or not. I was labeled an outlaw, and after a while that's what I became."[60]

That echo of "what if" is especially intriguing when considered in light of the accomplishments of one Reginald Martinez Jackson. Like Johnson and Allen, Reggie had a rough upbringing — in fact, on the day he left for Arizona State his father was in jail for running an illegal still.[61] Like Alex and Dick, Reggie's mouth caused him more than a little heartache, and like his predecessors, Jackson grew wary of the media as a result (though his natural yearning for the spotlight drew him back to the press corps in the manner of a moth returning to a flame). Like Johnson, few of his teammates liked him (Allen, despite his problems with management and selected individuals, was generally well-regarded by those he played with). And, like Allen and Johnson he was normally at war with authority, be it on field management or in the executive suite.

Yet for all of that Reggie managed to build a career that would ultimately result in Cooperstown glory. Though Jackson, like Allen, would age precipitously, posting only one really good season after his 33rd birthday, Reggie managed via hard work (try 1,200 sit-ups every morning[62]) to turn 40 in a big league uniform. The egocentric attitude that instigated Billy Martin's nationally televised screaming fit and a 1972 bout with Mike Epstein over complimentary tickets[63] mellowed to the point of self-parody in his declining years. He became more outspoken about the plight of black players in baseball, adopting a Willie Stargell-like elder statesman pose as time progressed (though Reggie's affinity for money and the spotlight would cause some to question his sincerity).

What was the difference between Jackson and his forebears? Well, as in so many things the answer is most likely complex — yet in any analysis, timing and the perspective that comes with it have to be key factors.

Reggie came along an important few years after Allen and Johnson, when most of the trails for black athletes had at least been tentatively blazed and national attitudes about prejudice were being codified into law. Not that his trek to the majors was pleasant by any means: Jackson spent plenty of hours in colored hotels and heard scores of "niggers" during his 1967 baseball apprenticeship in Birmingham.[64] As opposed to Allen's Arkansas experiences, though, the future Mr. October faced less in-your-face racism and did so with more supportive teammates and management — when some local bigwigs invited the team sans Jackson to a party, skipper John McNamara made it clear no Baron would show under such circumstances.[65] For his part, Reggie possessed the rare maturity to understand the limitations of a South in the throws of cataclysmic change. When legendary Alabama football coach Paul "Bear" Bryant, upon meeting the ex-Arizona State fullback, said matter of factly, "Now this is the kind of nigger boy I need to start my football program," Jackson took it as "the best he could do, his way of paying me a compliment."[66]

The mind boggles at how Alex Johnson might have handled such a situation....

Jackson came into prominence at a time when the player-owner relationship was evolving into one where the concept of bucking the power elite was no longer reserved for rebels without causes. In a perverse way the motley cast of characters he dealt with (Finley, Vida Blue, Dick Williams, Earl Weaver, Martin, Steinbrenner, Thurman Munson ... one would be hard pressed to name anybody who cavorted with a more impressive rogue's gallery) made his own excesses seem mild by way of comparison. He was also luckier in terms of the teams he played with, largely avoiding the second division outfits Johnson and Allen were habitually saddled with, mostly because tail-enders are the prime candidates for gambling on a troubled athlete.

Yet at the same time, Reggie knew when to pull away from the brink.

After a 1969 season in which he had made a serious run at 50 homers, Reggie decided that his services were worth $75,000 for the coming year.[67] It wasn't an unreasonable figure all things considered, but it ran directly into two painful facts of life: the reserve clause as interpreted at the time severely limited a player's bargaining power, and Charlie Finley was the kind of man who would take full advantage of such a situation.

After holding out until ten days before the start of the season (and thumbing his nose at Finley by playing in an Arizona State alumni game while doing so[68]) Jackson finally faced facts and signed for $45,000 plus a season's rent on a luxury apartment.[69] That should have settled matters, but ... well, each man was what he was and thus the 1970 season turned into a battle royal. After Reggie was a no-show for a midseason barbecue at Charlie's LaPorte, Indiana, estate, Finley announced that he was sending the slugger to the minors.[70] When Jackson refused to go (and Bowie Kuhn backed him up[71]) Charlie ordered him benched against lefties.[72] Things got so bad that after hitting a grand slam in a September home game, Reggie looked up at the owner's box, gave Finley the finger and according to sportswriter Jim Scott, "shouted up at Charles to perform an anatomically impossible act upon himself."[73]

Jackson's life was quickly spinning out of control. He demanded to be traded, darkly implying at one point that he had some sort of evidence that would keep him from having to play with the A's ever again.[74] He was roasted in the press, his wife left him, he posted the worst season of his prime years, and once succumbed to what he later termed "the strange sensation that I'd never be able to hit again."[75] Given the personalities involved, one could almost write the scenario....

... and yet it didn't happen. Reggie spent the winter in Puerto Rico playing for and living with Frank Robinson, a man to whom pouting and self-pity were anathema: Jackson would later say that his experience with Robinson made him "a better professional, a better man."[76] He signed early in 1971, accepting a pay cut in stride.[77] He even showed a surprising touch of humility: "I guess last season was a growing up period for me. My body wasn't right at the start of the season and my mind wasn't right later. But that's all behind me now. I'm no longer sore at Mr. Finley and he's no longer sore at me. I only want to play ball, play in every game."[78]

The 1971-model Jackson firmly reestablished his Cooperstown trajectory by clubbing 32 homers (one short of the league lead) while finishing in the top 10 in runs scored, hits, doubles, slugging percentage, and stolen bases.

Dick Allen would blow hot and cold about Reggie in his later years, characterizing him as the Don King of baseball. "Where were all of his strong opinions about blacks in baseball when he was in his prime?" Allen wondered aloud. "Then it was Reggie, Reggie, Reggie. Now that the curtain has come down on the Reggie Jackson career, he's suddenly a man with a lot to say. My question with Reggie has always been the same: Does he love baseball enough to be good for the game?"[79]

It's a valid query in certain ways, but one that begs a follow-up question: were Dick Allen and Alex Johnson ever good for the game? Each undoubtedly loved baseball and found in the competition a sense of solace that they were denied elsewhere. Yet neither proved capable of recognizing that their pact with the game extended beyond the field of play, that baseball's injustices were no worse or more malicious than those of society in general, or that working within the system might yield more results that wantonly tearing it asunder. Thus, by attempting to publicly exorcise their inner demons, both destroyed much if not all of what they accomplished — and regardless of any compassion posterity might have for their plight, Allen and Johnson will be forever viewed in that light.

In short, neither could get over being Angry Men long enough to be good for the game.

6

The End of the Age of Innocence

Most revolutions are born out of misconceptions that, while based upon perfectly rational analysis at the time, seem ludicrous in hindsight. Take the British: after a century of protecting their American territories from the French and various Indian tribes, they felt that the colonists should start shouldering some of the financial burden for their defense and thus initiated a series of taxes to recoup these costs. A perfectly reasonable proposition on the face of it — or at least it seems reasonable until one considers that Britain had never taxed the colonies before, yet intended to start now whether the Americans agreed or not. But what the heck: what were they going to do about it ... rebel?

Well, yes ... that was exactly what they were going to do.

Two centuries later, major league baseball was fated to restage this "give me liberty or give me death" battle with the game's ownership interests representing the fat cat British while Marvin Miller's nascent Major League Baseball Players Association took on the role of the scrappy Continentals. Like the American Revolution, the issue that triggered the players' insurrection was one that should have been easily resolvable. Like the Revolution, a series of perhaps inadvertent provocations and ill-timed statements rapidly escalated the conflict beyond anything that anyone was prepared for. Like the Revolution, a group of insurrectionists whose previous alliance had been loose became one in the face of the perceived oppressor. Like the Revolution, the fat cats' ultimate decision that asserting their authority wasn't worth the time and effort had more to do with the underdog's victory than any tactical moves or personal heroics.

And like the Revolution, the fat cats had no concept of the Rosemary's Baby they were unleashing upon the world via their acquiescence.

Between the collapse of the Fraternity of Professional Base Ball Players of America in the aftermath of the Federal League's 1915 demise[1] and the late

1960s, ownership's negotiations with its players on salary and benefit matters could be summed up succinctly—the owners told the players what they would get, and the players accepted it. Within limits management had kept pace with the Industrial Revolution by providing such things as pensions (the initial funding of which was one of the key factors driving the All-Star Game's creation[2]) and health care. However, since ownership was unilaterally setting the rules and dollar amounts vested in such benefits, the overall package was less lucrative than it might have been in another business. For example, the minimum wage for a major league player was set at $5,000 in 1947 ... and would rise by a mere $1,000 over the next 20 years.[3]

The players had made one attempt to band together immediately after World War II when an ex–National Labor Relations Board lawyer named Robert Murphy formed something he called the American Baseball Guild. The guild's goals were of a kind that would be near and dear to any labor leader's heart—improved benefits, locker rooms that were something less than an OSHA nightmare, that sort of thing. While Murphy did record some successes (the minimum wage was his crusade, along with a spring training allowance that came to be known as "Murphy money") the union's name proved to be more impressive than its actual strength. Internal subterfuge thwarted a proposed 1946 strike against the Pittsburgh Pirates as effectively as management's willingness to field a replacement team featuring the 72-year-old Honus Wagner, and once the players' divisions were exposed, the guild was quickly and completely excised from the baseball scene.[4] Though future Grapefruit Leaguers would come to accept his toils as their due, a generation later virtually no one knew how the term "Murphy money" had initially been derived.[5]

Coming on the heels of the Mexican League near-disaster (an attempt by the wealthy Pasquel brothers to form a third major league[6]) the Murphy episode convinced the owners that some sort of player voice within baseball was both inevitable and potentially useful as an early warning system for future insurrections. With the players cowed from those two experiences and their aftermath (his Mexican League escapade and subsequent suspension may have cost Sal Maglie a shot at Cooperstown), the spontaneous development of an acceptable guild replacement was unlikely from that quarter. Thus, the owners resorted to that most Machiavellian (and probably illegal) of industrial creations: an in-house union that would become known as the Major League Baseball Players Association.[7]

Though such an organization's ability to seriously push player rights was highly suspect, the rank and file was largely unconcerned about their union's incestuous relationship with management. While latter day observers might be shocked at such naiveté, keep in mind that the era's typical player was young, transitory within the game (their major league careers on average would last less than five seasons), relatively uneducated (it would be the mid-1970s before ex-collegians became a significant factor), and hailed primarily from Sunbelt areas in which unions were seedy entities learned about in movies like *On The Waterfront*.

What union sentiment there was came from the more experienced players (who of course had a larger stake in the game) and focused on pensions (again naturally, since these guys were spending a greater percentage of their working life within baseball). Even then, the common heritage that these veterans had with their less fortunate brethren made them virulently anti-strike by nature and inclination: as one-time NL player rep Bob Friend said, "It would destroy baseball if the fans were exposed to the spectacle of someone like Stan Musial picketing a ballpark."[8]

This was the situation and mindset that confronted Marvin Miller upon assuming the association's helm on July 1, 1966.

A Brooklyn-born son of a clothing salesman, Miller had more or less meandered his way through various governmental and union posts before taking a job as an economist for the United Steelworkers of America. Sixteen years with the steelworkers forged Miller's reputation as a strong negotiator with a knack for developing innovative solutions to surmount contract obstacles. However, changes in the union's leadership had him looking for alternate employment when the players' association in the person of future Hall of Famer Robin Roberts came calling.[9]

These are the salient facts to remember about Miller: that he was a union man through and through, and that he was an expert negotiator. Contemporary fan and sportswriter opinions about the MLBPA chief tend to be colored by a basic misconception of his role in baseball society — namely, that he had some sort of duty to the game as a whole. Such an idea, as we have grown to understand in our sadder but wiser latter day view, is silly to the point of Harlequin romanticism. Miller was merely the players' bargaining agent — in essence, the primordial Scott Boras. His blatantly adversarial relationship with the game's power brokers may have stunned sports fans but was nothing that Alcoa's executives wouldn't have been familiar with, the only difference being that eight-year-old kids don't dream of working the third shift on a continuous casting machine. While much was made of his Brooklyn upbringing and ability to recite the 1934 Dodgers' starting lineup,[10] Miller neither cared about baseball per se nor his maneuvers' impact on anyone save his association's members— and why should he, given that he didn't work for the fans or the game itself?

By 1972 Miller had won some significant gains for his union, including a minimum wage hike to $13,500, increased spring training and in-season meal money, and improved pension and health care benefits.[11] Still, stars as Carl Yastrzemski and Ron Santo had publicly broken ranks with the union chief during the 1969 pension negotiations while no active player had offered much support beyond lip service for Curt Flood. Thus, as the players' pension and health care plan came up for renegotiation, Miller was at once confident of his ability to squeeze further concessions out of a foe that he had

Marvin Miller works at his desk in this 1969 photograph. Despite having headed the Major League Baseball Players Association for three years, Miller's office (at least in this view) looks as if he'd moved in yesterday — no smiling photographs on the walls, no autographed baseballs on the desk, no nothing. This apparent lack of sentimentality would bode ill for baseball's barons in the years to come. (*The Sporting News*)

previously bested, yet queasy in regards to his membership's willingness to support a strike if such was warranted.

Two issues were at stake that spring. Given the rampant inflation of the day, the real value of the owners' annual contributions to the pension plan had eroded significantly over the previous agreement's three-year life span. To make up for this decline in purchasing power the players initially sought a 22 percent increase in owner contribution to the plan, a figure that had been scaled back to 17 percent by early March.[12] Also, baseball's insurer had notified both sides that the cost to maintain the players' current level of coverage would increase by an estimated $372,000 annually,[13] a figure that the players wanted the owners to fund in total.

It was the second point that would trigger the firestorm. In his initial offer to the players, baseball's chief negotiator, John Gaherin, actually agreed on the owners' behalf to fund any increase in the players' insurance costs.

That should have closed the matter, but Gaherin made the mistake of incorporating the $372,000 figure into the total dollar value of his offer to the players. After doing some comparison shopping, however, the owners discovered that they could secure identical coverage from another company for only $250,000 more than their current outlay and save on their costs for inactive players to boot. Accordingly, Gaherin, in a subsequent offer, adjusted the annual dollar value of his proposal downward by $122,000, arguing that the players were going to get the same coverage as before, and that the savings from utilizing a less expensive insurer should accrue to the owners.[14]

Well, yeah ... but what the players saw (or more properly, what Miller chose to have them see) was that the total pot of money the owners were offering had inexplicably declined. Never mind that the smaller number of dollars would accomplish the same goal — the key point was that the owners were suddenly proposing to spend less on Miller's minions than before, and any negotiator who'd let something like that go unchallenged was hardly worth his pay.

In response, the MLBPA chief decided to up the ante during his March 9 visit to the Chicago White Sox camp in Sarasota. In seven prior team meetings Miller had never hinted that negotiations were in jeopardy, but he abruptly changed his tune in this get-together and asked the White Sox players to give their player representatives the power to vote on a strike should the need arise.[15] Note that Miller at this point was *not* asking the players to walk out — what he wanted was authorization to have the players' association executive board (which consisted of the 48 player representatives and alternates) make the decision if negotiations did not progress satisfactorily.

The reason for this intermediate move became obvious as the votes were taken: the MLBPA's ability to stand united during a work action of even modest duration was far from assured. Keep in mind that up to this time no group of players had ever successfully struck any professional sport, and furthermore, these guys were not particularly union-savvy to begin with. Their association was a financial and public relations pygmy in relation to that of the owners, a significant disadvantage in a war that would inevitably be waged at least in part through the media. Finally, some calls for moderation were emanating from the player ranks, with Boston Red Sox star left-fielder Carl Yastrzemski's voice being among the most prominent. In a *Chicago Sun-Times* interview Yastrzemski observed, "You'd think we've been working in a factory these past five or six years. There isn't too much to fight about. As I understand it, all the club owners have to do is increase their contributions by $50,000 a ball club and that shouldn't be a hardship."[16]

While Yaz's comments to some extent ran counter to Miller's push for radical action, they also illustrated the chasm that separated the players' view of this melodrama from that of the owners. On one level Yastrzemski was correct: the proposed increases represented chump change in comparison to the $72 million NBC would pay for Game of the Week, All-Star Game, and postseason broadcast rights over the succeeding four year period.[17] Yet $72 million in revenue is not the same as $72 million in money that can be shared with players or used to buy yachts, especially in a quasi-business that represented no more than an expensive dalliance to people like Cincinnati *Inquirer* publisher and Reds managing partner Francis Dale ... or Montreal's Bronfman family, owners of the Expos and liquor giant Seagram's ... or "Mr. San Diego" C. Arnholt Smith, who controlled a conglomerate that included U.S. National Bank along with the Padres. To this strata of society, baseball was a business in the way consulting represents "work" for retired executives, i.e. an opportunity to wreak havoc via suggestions that no one in his right mind would propose if his career was on the line while claiming a bunch of nifty-keeno tax deductions. As for the money, well ... if a buck or two gets made in the process, so much the better.

The MLBPA's ongoing demands, however, posed a direct threat to this laissez-faire approach in which needy ex-players (the 75-year-old Charlie Grimm, for example, was still on the Cubs' payroll in 1973[18]), cronies, and ne'er-do-well relatives were routinely awarded top management positions. Miller's concept of the union-owner relationship (i.e. how they pay for what we get at the bargaining table is their problem) may have been apropos in a climate where profitability was the overriding goal, but baseball hadn't been into profit maximization since the days of bottle bats. Furthermore, the union chief's in-your-face bargaining tactics and barely concealed scorn for what he considered to be a cabal of robber barons and Neanderthals consistently rubbed these prideful — and very successful in the areas that mattered to them — men the wrong way. Thus, it should come as no surprise that after a March 22 ownership meeting in St. Petersburg a red-faced and angry Gussie Busch emerged declaring, "We voted unanimously to take a stand. We're not going to give them another god damn cent. If they want to strike, let 'em."[19]

Not surprising, perhaps, but ill considered just the same ... yet does anyone really believe that the world's largest brewing company's architect would have risked his bread and butter business on a moment of pique?

While Busch's statement served to galvanize the players' resolve, even Miller later admitted surprise at the level of solidarity this once-splintered group displayed at a March 31 meeting of the players' executive board in Dallas. Fully prepared to recommend that the issues be tabled until the Basic Agreement expired in 1973, the union chief was shocked to discover militancy in his ranks for a strike. After a four-hour discussion in which Miller outlined in graphic detail the potential consequences of such a decision, the player reps and alternates overrode his warnings by enthusiastically voting 47-0 to initiate the first strike in professional sports history.[20]

At least that's how Miller remembered it in his book *A Whole Different Ball Game*, and while his recollections could be accurate, one might also consider the contemporary comments of Dodger first baseman and player rep Wes Parker: "The meeting in Dallas was just a formality. Technically, it's true that Marvin advised us against striking — but only technically. Did you ever try to make love to a girl and have her say 'no' in such a way that you knew she meant 'yes'? That's the way it was with Marvin. He was saying 'no' but parenthetically he was saying 'yes.'[21]

While others such as Gary Peters and Rick Reichardt would refute Parker's allegations, and Parker himself would change his mind after the strike had ended,[22] one wonders if there wasn't more than a little bit of truth in his gut response to Miller's performance. Let's consider the known facts to that point in time:

- Miller had just come away with a 663 — 10 thumbs up for a strike vote from his meetings with the 24 clubs.[23] The idea that someone armed with such a mandate would be caught completely unaware by a display of militancy from his executive board is, to put it mildly, *prima facie* absurd. Furthermore, the union chief would only have been human if he'd at least subconsciously played upon the implications of Busch's statements in his initial presentation to the board.
- Any expression of enthusiasm from the player reps and alternates was doubly significant given the bull's eye that was painted on their backs, even in normal times. Over the previous year, 16 of the 24 player representatives had either been cut by their teams or traded away.[24]
- Having come this far, Miller had to recognize that backing away from the brink would have threatened the MLBPA's legitimacy with both the owners and its members. As Peters would sagely yet succinctly comment, "We just had to strike to maintain our association."[25]

To put it as gently as possible, the Marvin Miller that emerges from *A Whole Different Ball Game* is a man inherently suspicious of everybody's morals and intellectual capacity — those on his side of the table included.[26] That's a pretty typical mini-profile for a leader of men, by the way; it takes a healthy (some would say unhealthy) dose of self-confidence and, yes, arrogance to reach the top in any profession. It is the way of such men to "simplify" matters in their discussions with others (much in the way Miller "simplified" the insurance issue that instigated this donnybrook), perhaps subconsciously eliminating extraneous or contradictory data to make it easier for the rank and file to know which way to turn.

The result was Curt Flood redux. A group of player representatives accept significant risk to their personal livelihoods and withering criticism from the press so that Alex Johnson can earn an incremental $1,650 a year in benefits[27] for not running out grounders — and they choose to do so without dissension.

One wonders how much "advice" the representatives would have remembered Miller giving if they'd lost....

Management's initial public response to this display of player resolve was modest surprise followed quickly by renewed expressions of resolution. The owners' Player Relations Committee (PRC) clearly signaled its desire to play hardball: after a month of so-called negotiation, Gaherin's early March offer remained virtually unchanged.[28] When Miller proposed to end the walkout if the matter were submitted to binding arbitration, the PRC summarily rejected the offer,[29] in part because they saw no need to compromise and in part because doing so would represent an indirect assault on baseball's antitrust exemption. A suggestion to utilize a purported pension fund surplus to finance player demands was deemed imprudent by an actuarial firm other than the one baseball had done business with for 17 years[30] (one wonders, as Miller did publicly, why the owners decided to switch firms at so auspicious a moment).

The PRC's intransigence was for the most part buttressed by public opinion. While such stalwarts as *Sporting News* editor C.C. Johnson Spink led the charge,[31] fan comments such as the following one published in the April 2 Chicago *Tribune* were commonplace. In it, one Joe Ingram of St. Louis wrote simply that "I don't think that the players have a legitimate complaint. They certainly make more money than we do."[32]

Even ex-major leaguers such as Johnny Vander Meer and Rip Sewell (the mole that had leaked the American Baseball Guild's plan to strike the Pittsburgh Pirates in 1946) jumped on the establishment bandwagon. Sewell observed, "First the players wanted a hamburger and the owners gave them a hamburger. Then they wanted filet mignon and they gave them filet mignon. Then they wanted the whole darned cow and they gave them the cow. Now they want a pasture for the cow. You just can't satisfy them."[33]

Underneath the owners' monolithic front, though, lurked a tug of war over whether this battle to the death represented the best course of action. The PRC board was primarily composed of owner-as-laissez-faire-businessman types such as Gussie Busch's second in command Dick Meyer, Boston's Dick O'Connell (representing Tom Yawkey, the original dilettante owner) and New York Mets/Whitney money overseer M. Donald Grant. That such folks would be predisposed towards conceding little to the hired help is unsurprising, but over time such owners as Charlie Finley, Texas' Bob Short, Chicago's John Allyn, and Milwaukee's Bud Selig (i.e. the people with short bankrolls) began voicing their dissatisfaction with the stance of a committee that didn't represent their views. Finley, an insurance agent who well understood actuarial tables and the like, stated that he didn't see why some of the pension fund's excess assets couldn't be used — others, including Yankees' partner Mike Burke, echoed his sentiments.[34]

Faced with increasing dissent from within as well as governmental intervention (President Nixon asked both sides to sit down with J. Curtis Counts, director of the Federal Mediation and Conciliation Service[35]), the PRC began to move towards the players' position. By April 10 a reasonable compromise on the basic contractual issues had been reached with one important caveat: the players would forfeit their salaries for the days that they had been on strike but would still have to play the entire 162-game schedule.

The full season requirement was indicative of a second split within the ownership ranks. The financially stronger National League was loath to eliminate any profit-generating games from their schedule and thus proposed using doubleheaders and open dates to make up for the canceled contests. Their position was that a player's contract ran for a specific number of calendar days—if the league could squeeze more games into the days contracted for, so much the better. The struggling junior circuit, however, preferred pocketing the salary savings to rescheduling a bunch of early season games that they weren't going to make any money on anyway (the league in fact had been pushing a truncated 156-game regular season for years).[36]

In manufacturing terms the demand represented a work speedup (producing more units [games] in a shorter period of time without additional compensation), and in the union-conscious 1970s such a position represented a public relations disaster. Miller immediately seized upon this opportunity, commenting that "now the owners want to spank the players like little boys" and insisted with more than a little logic on his side that a group of workers producing 100 percent of the agreed-upon product should receive 100 percent of the agreed-upon pay.[37]

Between the AL's opposition and the proposal's rather petulant look, the chances for a cut-rate 162-game season quickly fizzled, and after several days of tiring negotiation over crossed t's and dotted i's, a one year agreement was finally reached. In exchange for the players forgoing nine days of pay, the owners would:

1. Increase their contribution to the pension fund by $500,000 (a 14 percent gain, give or take),
2. Shift the health care coverage to the new provider while retaining the savings (the instigating factor in this brouhaha, the health care issue had basically been agreed to weeks before), and
3. Stage an unbalanced schedule in which the Boston Red Sox would fall ½ game short of the Detroit Tigers in the AL East pennant race due in large part to the one additional contest that the Tigers were allowed to play.[38]

From a strict monetary point of view, the strike represented a costly fiasco for all involved. The average club forfeited something in the neighborhood of $175,000 to $200,000 as a direct result of the lost games,[39] and the lingering ill will in fan circles drove a 6.3 percent decline in National League per-game attendance figures for the truncated season that followed.[40] From the players' point of view, the modest gains achieved in the new contract were of roughly the same value as the salaries they had forgone to achieve them.[41] Furthermore, the deal's one-year duration meant that another spring without paychecks was a real — and immediate — possibility.

Yet from a historical perspective the 1972 strike signaled a seismic shift in the balance of power between players and owners. The Major League Baseball Players Association had managed to coalesce in the face of hardball owner tactics with a level of resolve that few believed possible, while management's previously monolithic front had in crisis quickly splintered into a series of warring factions. Marvin Miller's adept handling of the strike from an organizational, psychological and negotiation perspective won him the almost slavish support of his membership in the trials that were to follow.[42] The unity and consistency of approach that this relationship engendered would stand in bold contrast to the increasingly uncoordinated attempts by ownership to retain the shreds of what had been baseball's ode to the Antebellum South.

A less fortunate parallel theme to this new relationship was an industrial-management-style cynicism that came to dominate each sides' perspectives of the other. Player-management disagreements increasingly devolved into grievances or the threat thereof. When Astros pitcher George Culver begged off warming up one night due to a sore arm, manager Harry Walker questioned how such an injury could have occurred "from throwing that junk you use" ... so Culver naturally filed an unfair labor practice suit against Walker shortly thereafter.[43] Charges of racism and bad attitude flew back and forth between Reds outfielder Bobby Tolan and Cincinnati management in 1973: when Tolan was suspended (nominally for refusing to shave his beard) Bobby filed a grievance, got the suspension overturned ... and was traded at season's end.[44] Even managers got into the swing of this new, litigious era — the Employment Standards Division of the Department of Labor threatened an age discrimination suit against Royals owner Ewing Kauffman after Kauffman admitted that his 1972 firing of skipper Bob Lemon was in part because Lemon was too old.[45]

Much to everyone's surprise, however, the fans proved capable (after a short interlude) of divorcing these legal shenanigans from their affections for the game itself. One year after the pension fund and health care dust had settled, major league attendance topped 30 million for the first time with 17 of the 24 teams tallying in excess of one million admissions[46] (just four years earlier only half of the teams had surmounted the million mark[47]). This indirect acceptance of non-Marquis of Queensbury tactics at the bargaining table removed the last vestiges of civility from the proceedings, as Miller tacitly (and ironically) noted in his post-signing statement to the press: "Ironically, this should bring the players and owners closer together. You don't have a good relationship when there is a superior and an inferior working under peaceful conditions. But if they are working as equals the relationship is better, even if it's stormy."[48]

To anyone reading that statement without preconceptions, the future course of player-owner relations was clear. However, like the British in 1773, management would have difficulty recognizing the significance of baseball's 1972 version of the Boston Tea Party — thus placing themselves on a course towards a future in which many of them would become anachronisms.

7

The Pride of
Westchester High

Expectations can be deadly things. Take Ted Kennedy, the last surviving brother of that storied and star-crossed family. Once Jack and Bobby were dead the American liberal movement needed Teddy: never mind that he was a 36-year-old one-term senator in 1968 and possessed half the experience and savvy of his martyred brothers. Given time to mature and gain insight away from the spotlight, the younger Kennedy might well have met the expectations of those who yearned for a return to Camelot; instead, a series of personal and political missteps marginalized both him and the movement whose colors he bore.

The baseball world seems to be particularly prone to this type of Great White (or Black) Hope complex. Seemingly every year some hotshot teenager with a short resume but quick swing or hellacious fastball comes out of nowhere to be anointed as a downtrodden franchise's salvation. Occasionally a Dwight Gooden or Robin Yount will break through to keep the Pavlov's Dog of hope within us salivating, but for every Gooden there are ten Lance Dicksons who forfeit potentially fine careers on the altar of expediency.

Every era has its examples of the breed, but perhaps the quintessential penthouse to outhouse story is that of one David Clyde, a lanky lefty who for an instant was the nation's most famous Class of '73 grad.

Born in Kansas City, Clyde became a legend at Houston's Westchester High School. That may not seem like any great shakes to people in many parts of the country, but one must understand that high school athletics in Texas are a religion akin to presidential elections in the William Jennings Bryan era. A reasonably tall kid equipped with a good fastball, drop-off-the-edge-of-the-table curve, and the savvy to keep from falling in love with one or the other, Clyde was not only unbeatable but practically unhittable as well. He threw nine no-hitters while in high school, five of them in his senior year and two during the 1973 state championships in Austin.[1]

Given Clyde's 17-0 senior record, stuff, and left-handedness, it should come as no surprise that he was the number one choice in the 1973 amateur draft.[2] Unfortunately for him, that pick was owned by the home state Texas Rangers, and that is where the phenom's downfall began.

The Rangers in those days were owned by Bob Short, an ex-Minnesota politician, Democratic National Committee chairman, and owner of the then-Minneapolis Lakers.[3] Short's status as top dog on the draft heap was richly deserved: Jeff Burroughs and Toby Harrah were his only offensive players of long term value, while Jim Bibby would be the sole staff member of any stature to remain in the majors two years hence. As bad as that was, the Ranger talent void was exceeded only by the emptiness of its owner's pockets. Three years of operating in the nation's capital had reduced Short to strong-arming the league for permission to move to Texas[4]; once there, he was rewarded for bringing "major league" baseball to the Dallas area with fewer admissions than a 57-105 Senators' team had achieved the previous year.

It must have seemed like manna from heaven when Clyde, a sure-fire attraction as well as a kid who obviously had the tools to be a quality starter, dropped into his lap. Under the circumstances it would have been ridiculous to expect much restraint from Short, and thus a mere two weeks after his graduation the pride of Westchester High was on the Rangers hill for his first pro start against the Minnesota Twins.

And he won ... and more importantly did so before the first sellout crowd in Ranger history.[5] Allowing only one hit in five innings of work while striking out eight, Clyde received kudos from none other than legendary pitching coach Johnny Sain, who observed that "he wasn't just out there throwing, he was pitching."[6] Others were not as kind (though giving him credit for poise, Rod Carew considered Clyde's fast ball to be "nothing special"[7]), but the bottom line was:

1. The rookie was 1-0,
2. He hadn't been obviously overmatched by the pros, and most importantly,
3. He was a money machine, generating $150,000 in incremental ticket sales for his initial pair of home starts.[8]

Thus, Texas and to some extent the nation fell under the grip of what became known as Clydemania.

Clyde's second start against the lowly Milwaukee Brewers was nationally televised and, as if on cue, he won again. His next road appearance against the Red Sox drew the second largest crowd of the season to Fenway Park.[9] Over 113,000 people made their way to Arlington Stadium to witness Clyde's first four outings—this for a team that drew a mere 590,000 patrons all season long.[10]

There were flies in Clyde's ointment from the start, though, and as the

Fresh from back-to-back no-hitters in the 1973 Texas high school championship series at Austin, David Clyde's first two starts at Arlington Stadium generated an estimated $150,000 in incremental ticket sales for the financially teetering Rangers. Despite such promising origins, Clyde's big league career would produce just 18 wins along with a 4.63 ERA. (*The Sporting News*)

season progressed they became increasingly apparent. He suffered from Ismael Valdes Disease, periodically having his outings truncated by blisters on his pitching hand.[11] David began overthrowing his curve, losing command of the pitch and much of the speed differential between it and his heater.[12] Without an effective bender, hitters began to sit on Clyde's fastball, resulting in 106 hits allowed in 93 1/3 innings. Or perhaps the high-hit totals were a sign of fatigue: the phenom lasted a total of 38 innings in his last nine starts while posting a 7.34 ERA.[13]

Recognizing that they had a young man on their hands who needed to learn how to pitch, the Rangers coaches began descending on Clyde the next spring, ultimately rebuilding his motion and repertoire several times. They junked his curve in favor of a slower model — lacking confidence in the new pitch, Clyde rarely threw it after early May.[14] They worked with him to improve his control — in 1974 the former number one pick gave up 129 hits (including 14 homers) in 117 innings. He was sent to the minors and equipped with a slider — Clyde promptly hurt his golden arm.[15] A year of rest and further modifications resulted in a Steve Dalkowski-like 1977 season in which he struck out 148 men in 128 innings but walked 119 en route to a 5-7 record with a 5.84 ERA at AAA Tucson.[16]

At age 22, recently divorced, and totally screwed up mechanically (his future pitching coach Harvey Haddix would call the youngster "one of the worst throwers I've ever seen"[17]), David Clyde found himself reduced to trade throw-in status. Landing with the Cleveland Indians (a.k.a. second chance nirvana), Clyde revived somewhat in 1978 after Haddix came up with the novel idea of having him to go back to what he'd been doing in high school.[18] Unfortunately, David's once golden wing was too far gone by that time; a second bout of arm trouble spelled curtains for his career at the tender age of 24.

It is said that the road to hell is paved with good intentions, and from all indications such could not have been truer in Clyde's case. Everybody that worked with the kid waxed enthusiastic in regards to his work ethic and attitude. David was as mentally and emotionally mature as anyone constantly compared with Bob Feller can be: finding himself on the bubble during his first spring training camp, he said that "if they say I must go back to the minors, then fine. I'll go and work just as hard to get back here."[19] While Clyde generally played for awful teams at the big league level, the people who supervised his development included such respected coaching minds as Haddix, Whitey Herzog, Billy Martin, Jeff Torborg, Dave Duncan, and Art Fowler.

Yet for all the intellect and goodwill that was backing him up, the flat fact of the matter was that most of those who crossed David Clyde's path were at the time in precarious straits. Bob Short was within a year of selling the franchise at zero profit to Brad Corbett.[20] Whitey Herzog, Clyde's first manager, would not be around for the end of the phenom's rookie season. Herzog's replacement, Martin, was the personification of insecurity and paranoia.

Torborg's managerial tenure in Cleveland would outlast Clyde's by less than two months.

In short, these people didn't have time for Clyde to develop naturally. They needed results *now*, and thus were prone to tinkering with his approach — junk a pitch, change his stride, learn a change-up, whatever. A more seasoned professional might have resisted many of these efforts, but Clyde was a good kid who did what he was told and even worse recognized how much of everybody's future was riding on him. According to Martin, the youngster's drive to perform was so great that he could barely hit the backstop in his early 1974 spring training efforts.[21]

Thus the result of all that coaching, maturity, and raw material was an 18-33 career record with a 4.63 ERA.

How good could he have been if all the cooks could have been kept from spoiling the soup? It's easy to write Clyde off as another in the line of over-hyped youngsters that includes the Clint brothers (Hurdle and Hartung), and the Rangers phenom's 5.03 1973 ERA (the league figure was 3.73) does little to dispel such notions. Still, through his 20th birthday David Clyde's 7-17 career record and 4.66 ERA in 210 innings were remarkably similar to the numbers posted by Curt Simmons, the longtime Phillies and Cardinals starter of the 1950s and 1960s.[22] Though Simmons pitched under somewhat tougher circumstances than Clyde did, the similarities between the two are more than skin deep: both were lefties of virtually the same height and weight; both were hard throwers lacking an effective change of pace; both had less than classic pitching motions that invited tinkering by their coaches[23]; and both suffered arm injuries early on.[24]

Whether Clyde would have matched Simmons' 193 victories under better circumstances is anybody's guess. Perhaps the arm problems that terminated his career so quickly were inevitable. Or, had his arm held out, he may have faced the temptations other driven players of his generation succumbed to, such as recreational drug use. Perhaps a big contract or two would have eroded his competitive edge.

Perhaps ... but one still has to wonder what his upside would have, save Short's desperation for revenue. Or if the Rangers had focused on what he could do rather than trying for the quick fix. Or if he'd served a bullpen apprenticeship before being thrown into the rotation.

Yes, expectations can be such deadly things.

8

Charlie Finley's
Big Happy Family

Remember when chemistry was a critical element in assembling a contender? The baseball equivalent of alchemy, chemistry's key tenet was that a team at war with itself could not win. Under this theory, swapping a talented troublemaker for someone of lesser ability who meshed with the organization could, under the right circumstances, magically transform a contender into a champion. Chemistry was the reason Dick Allen drove in 89 or more runs with four different teams in four years. It made Steve Carlton as valuable as Rick Wise, uprooted Ted Simmons from his St. Louis home after six All-Star appearances in nine years, and transformed Jeffrey Leonard into a San Francisco icon despite never hitting more than 21 homers in a season.

As with scriptures that seemingly justify both eternal brotherhood and car bombings, chemistry was a wonderfully versatile theory. If a team like the 1969 Mets that featured maybe three guys modern fans have heard of defeats a Cub team stocked with three Hall of Famers and a fourth guy (Ron Santo) who should be as well, the result was attributed to chemistry. Either

1. The victors came together as the result of
   • a Chuck Tanner-type manager "letting 'em play"
   • a Dick Williams-type manager instilling discipline
   • some slugger with a lot of heart and guts coming on board

Or,

2. The losing team fell apart when
   • the Chuck Tanner-type manager lost control of the clubhouse
   • the Dick Williams-type manager's disciplinary tactics led to a player revolt
   • the new slugger turned out to be a clubhouse lawyer.

This easy-to-stand-on-its-head rationale is what made the concept of chemistry so alluring to baseball's executive suites. Intangible qualities that benefited a team one season could easily be transformed into the logic for next year's trade or firing. Fans and sportswriters might temporarily howl over the departure of some longtime favorite, but "he just didn't fit in with our philosophy" was an unassailable defense. Quantifiable things like homers and ERAs are dangerous rationales, because anybody with a third grade education will know by the end of the season if their general manager was screwer or screwee, but chemistry was like ketchup: an all-purpose flavor enhancer capable of making practically anything palatable.

Like the emperor's new clothes, the myth of chemistry represented a Titanic destined to crash into an iceberg of reality, and that reality materialized in the fog-shrouded gloom of San Francisco Bay's eastern shoreline.

In the early 1970s an unlikely colossus arose in Oakland, one that by conventional standards lacked any trace of decorum, tact, or humility. The Mustache Gang A's represented a microcosm of the Establishment — New Generation battle for supremacy raging throughout society in those days. In one corner stood owner Charles O. Finley, an alternately paternalistic and slave-driving idea man — cross Simon Legree with Professor Clyde Crashcup and one gets the general idea. Opposing Finley was a psychologist's delight of overblown egos, fragile psyches, and Mike Tyson wannabes who often were as intent on battling one another as they were the front office or opposing teams. Between the two stood a series of six men representing a full spectrum of managerial styles, all of whom posted winning records but left embittered to a greater or lesser degree. Every season was a symphony of clubhouse fist fights, bickering, front office parsimony bordering on the ludicrous and roster moves oftentimes made out of pique.

In terms of chemistry, the Mustache Crew was up there with oil and vinegar — it took a whole lot of shaking to keep them together — and yet they won.

Perhaps the most unlikely facet of this soap opera was the once-genteel organization that brought it forth. A Tiffany franchise for much of the first third of the century, the Athletics fell on hard times as the Depression and Connie Mack's advancing age consigned them more often than not to the American League's lower depths. New ownership and a migration to Kansas City had little effect; the new chieftain (Arnold Johnson) was a baseball neophyte who quickly fell under the spell of Yankee general manager George Weiss.[1] The result was a series of trades in which the A's provided New York with whatever good player they had at the moment in exchange for some prospect or spare part that Casey Stengel couldn't work into his complex platoon arrangements. The trades looked worse than they were — such fine players as Norm Siebern and Jerry Lumpe came aboard in the various deals — but the net effect was to make Kansas City at the time of Johnson's 1960 demise look more a Yankee rest home than a serious competitor.

Enter one Charles Oscar Finley.

A few people in this world are typecast for the roles they play on life's stage. John Wayne, for example, was meant to make westerns— despite fine performances in other genres, it's always a bit disconcerting to see him in anything other than a ten-gallon hat. A geek like Bill Gates has no business running anything other than a computer company. Queen Elizabeth II, Charles Manson, Bill Clinton — none of these people could be mistaken for anything other than what they are.

As for Charlie Finley, well … if anyone more suited to be a salesman has ever walked the earth, we'd all be hip deep in aluminum siding.

A steel mill laborer whose life of physical toil was ended by tuberculosis, Finley concocted the idea of selling group insurance to doctors while he was spending 27 months in an Indiana sanatorium. Within two years he'd sold a comprehensive health plan to the American College of Surgeons, and by the late 1950s Charlie's Chicago-based insurance brokerage business was a cash machine running on autopilot.[2] A one-time semi-pro first baseman, Finley's attentions naturally began to swerve towards the game of his youth. He made an unsuccessful run at the Detroit Tigers after Walter Briggs' death and was for a time a minor partner in Bill Veeck's 1959 purchase of the White Sox. In the duplicitous manner for which he would become famous, Finley attempted to break up Veeck's group from within so as to buy the Sox himself. When unmasked he hardly paused to catch his breath before offering $250,000 for Bill's $100 option to purchase the team.[3] After being kicked out of the Chicago consortium, Finley finally managed to purchase the A's from Johnson's estate and almost immediately began to make things happen.

Of course, "making things happen" is not necessarily the same as making progress....

He struggled mightily at first, initially hoarding his makeshift farm system's progeny, then trading them for overaged "name" players like Rocky Colovito and Jim Gentile when the youth movement didn't blossom quickly enough for his taste.[4] Yet for all of his early travails, the man possessed the U.S. Grant quality of drawing some invaluable lesson from every misstep, a trait that helped Finley seize his big chance when it came ambling by in 1965.

Recognizing the undesirability of perpetual tenth place teams, Major League Baseball initiated the amateur draft, a round-robin in which each organization would for the first time have equal access to the country's top high school and college players. For years the talent game had been pretty straightforward, with the rich teams' extensive scouting networks signing every good looking kid in sight while the also-rans made do with whoever fell through the cracks. Now the player acquisition biz was no longer first come, first served: a centralized scouting bureau provided evaluations for all teams, each round was conducted in the reverse order of the teams' prior year finish, and peer pressure held signing bonuses in check.

Finley immediately grasped the significance of this new innovation. As a perennial cellar dweller, he would have first crack at the best amateurs for several years, talent that could be acquired without sacrificing his top pitcher in exchange. If the A's chose well, the up-front cost of these bodies would be trivial in comparison to the 10-plus years of productivity that they could produce. Thus Finley dove headlong into the amateur pool, netting such prime beef as Rick Monday, Reggie Jackson, Sal Bando, and Gene Tenace in the first two drafts.[5]

As can be seen from the list above Charlie's top picks were primarily college men, an against-the-grain strategy in the days when baseball's development efforts were still tailored to the transformation of Dizzy Dean-like hayseeds into polished players. Lacking a strong farm system or the patience to build one, Finley recognized the cost-effectiveness and refined skills (due to improved coaching) of college players early on. Much of what Charlie accomplished and the speed with which it occurred (the A's improved from 59 to 82 wins in three years) was due to his grasp of this simple concept.

Once a player was selected, Finley made an intensive effort to establish rapport with the athlete and his family. He came across as fatherly and committed to winning, developing bonds that would be leveraged on more than one occasion to keep contract costs under control.[6] That Charlie's attentiveness was laced with a dose of calculation is likely, yet even steadfast detractors would marvel at his occasional bouts of generosity. Catfish Hunter and Vida Blue, for example, each received Cadillacs (Catfish's royal blue with a white vinyl top, Vida's baby blue) for winning 20 in 1971.[7]

Of course, none of this largesse was allowed to go uncommented upon in the national press either....

P.T. Barnum once told an assemblage of reporters, "I don't care what you say about me as long as you keep talking about me," and in that spirit the owner of the A's rarely missed any opportunity—crass or otherwise—to embed his and his team's persona in the public conscience. The man was a veritable idea geyser: some good (he was an early proponent of night World Series games[8]), some vulgar (the team's mule mascot Charlie O[9]), and some out in la-la land (Finley carried four catchers for a time in 1969 with the intent of pinch hitting whenever the luckless backstops were scheduled to bat[10]). He gave his young charges borderline bizarre nicknames, transforming Jim Hunter into Catfish, Johnny Odom into Blue Moon and attempting to turn Vida Blue into True Blue ("If Mr. Finley thinks it's such a great name, why doesn't he call himself True O. Finley?" Vida replied[11]). A stream of former stars such as Deron Johnson, Felipe Alou, and Billy Williams passed through Oakland because they had name value and were at the "I'll take anything to keep my career going for one more year" stage. The mustaches were his idea as well; the result of a 1972 Father's Day promotion that offered $300 to any player who would cultivate a hairy upper lip.[12]

Yet for all that, the bottom line was the bottom line with Finley—neither sentimentality nor ethics would deter him from prompt action against

The 1973 Mustache Gang. With decent but nothing special offensive stats, just three good starters and a bench overflowing with has-beens, they nonetheless dominated the American League — even when they weren't fighting amongst one another. (*National Baseball Hall of Fame Library, Cooperstown, NY*)

those not meeting his standards. When Mike Andrews committed two costly errors in Game 2 of the 1973 World Series, Charlie coerced him into signing a statement asking to be removed from the postseason roster due to a sore shoulder.[13] The manager's office had a revolving door attached to it — those subscribing to the auteur theory of management are invited to consider the spectrum of personalities (everything from the dour Hank Bauer to Everybody's Buddy Chuck Tanner) that led the A's in those years. When Reggie Jackson's 47-homer 1969 season was followed by a truncated, turbulent 1970 campaign in which he hit 23 dingers, Finley cut him by $5,000 to $40,000. By way of comparison, Jim Bouton of Ball Four fame had earned $27,000 a year earlier as an Astro set-up man.[14]

Ah, the penny pinching stories ... a generation of columnists should bow five times towards Finley's grave in honor of all the slow news days spiced up by Charlie's sometimes outrageous attempts to save a buck. To get a color TV for the clubhouse, the A's players were reduced to pooling their $25 gift certificates for appearing on the postgame show.[15] Fan mail was responded to with player-purchased stamps, if at all (Sal Bando would toss his in the trash when the pile got too high[16]) — heck, the club wouldn't even take their replies to the post office for them.[17] The grounds crew was reduced to such a skeleton level that Joe Rudi once turned an ankle stepping into a hole on the way to first base.[18] The Oakland pressroom was the only one in the league sans free beer.[19]

Well, that only goes to show that even the darkest cloud has its silver lining.

This penny wise but pound foolish attitude extended to the business side of Oakland operations as well, severely limiting Finley's ability to capitalize on the team's on-field success. In a blue collar city the A's imposed the majors' priciest ticket structure,[20] and as a result the 1972 and 1974 World Champions were handily outdrawn by a 1959 Kansas City team that finished 20 games under .500.[21] Difficulties in negotiating television rights relegated A's broadcasts to a UHF station early in their Oakland tenure and left the team without a TV contract of any type for the opening of the 1974 season.[22] Charlie's demanding personality drove continuous employee turnover — during the 1973 season the team's ticket manager, PR man, traveling secretary, and controller either left the organization or were fired (an unnamed employee quipped, "We're setting up a resignations desk. We used to take the roll daily, but now we do it at noon, too."[23]).

Down in the clubhouse, Finley's cheapness and cavalier attitude became a perverse rallying point. This was perhaps fortunate given the team's penchant for spending as much time on intramural battles as they did duking it out with the opposition — Fingers once likened being an A to "having a ringside seat for the Muhammad Ali — Joe Frazier fights."[24] Vida Blue scuffled with Blue Moon Odom after Odom got the nod to start Game 5 of the 1972 playoffs.[25] Odom returned the favor a couple of years later by brawling with Fingers prior to the first game of the 1974 World Series; Rollie came away from that one sporting a cut on his left cheek courtesy of Odom's diamond wedding ring.[26] Temperamental center fielder Bill North (he once attacked Royal reliever Doug Bird in retaliation for a beaning three years earlier when both were Midwest Leaguers[27]) scuffled with Jackson over a girl during the tight 1974 pennant race. Peacekeeper Ray Fosse ended up the big loser in that one, suffering a separated cervical disc that took a big chunk out of his season.[28]

An aggressive and aggrieved local press fueled the image of locker room turbulence. Finley's relations with the Fourth Estate had been strained since his Midwest days— Charlie once designated "Poison Pen Day" in honor of a Kansas City *Star* editor who'd suggested that then-manager Joe Gordon's lineups were being approved by the owner.[29] The team's PR effort was notoriously poor, as witnessed by a release announcing Don Mincher's retirement which misstated such basic data as the first baseman's career homer total and number of All-Star appearances.[30] Add to that witches' brew players such as Blue, who ducked autograph hounds by carrying a load of empty cardboard boxes out of the clubhouse with him[31] and ... well, those who don't help others are unlikely to be helped themselves.

The situation came to a head when Oakland *Tribune* sportswriter Ron Bergman was banned from team flights for writing uncomplimentary comments about the team's announcing staff[32]: thereafter, practically every club-

Reggie Jackson, 1975 — wearing vintage 1972 pants and a jersey from 1974. (*The Sporting News*)

house tiff made its way into the headlines. Joe Rudi's tirade when lifted for a pinch runner in Oakland's 1974 opener,[33] manager Alvin Dark's consultations with Finley over his lineup (shades of 1961),[34] Bando's heat-of-battle comments about Dark's managerial capabilities[35]—articles from those days are oftentimes more laundry lists of spicy gossip than cohesive stories.

Thus, on a chemistry scale, the A's were the rough equivalent of those trans-uranium elements at the end of the Periodic Table that require atom-smashers to produce and have a half-life measured in nanoseconds ... but oh, how they could play on the field.

A hundred years from now armchair baseball analysts are likely to regard the Mustache Gang as one of those teams that one had to be there to understand. Yes, the team sports three Hall of Famers, but only one (Reggie) is the kind of player whose stats scream "Cooperstown." As for the other two:

• Rollie Fingers' ERAs are good but not great, given the era and stadium he pitched in. Though durable and consistent, there's little in Fingers' record that vaults him over the Bruce Sutters, Dan Quisenberrys, and Lee Smiths that would follow — and there isn't room in the Hall of Fame for all of them. Take Mike Henneman's career, add a couple of seasons to the front and back of it and the result is Rollie's spitting image ... and Henneman didn't receive a single vote for immortality.

• Though a fine pitcher for five or six years, Catfish Hunter was worked into the ground by age 31 and thus posted career numbers similar to plenty of non-Cooperstownians. Luis Tiant recorded virtually identical totals with worse teams in tougher ballparks, yet Tiant fell just short of immortality. Teammate Vida Blue was a good match as well, but he's not in and not likely to be as long as anybody remembers him as a person. Tommy John and Jim Kaat had significantly superior careers and both are still awaiting enshrinement. Hunter is in the Tony Perez class of inductees: a nice guy who had some big seasons at the right time.

The same holds true for the rest of the roster. Vida Blue could have been as good as his press clippings had one thing or another not perpetually distracted him. Gene Tenace took the concept of plate discipline too far, working walks in situations when it probably would have been better from the team's perspective to try and drive a pitch. Bert Campaneris epitomized the class of leadoff hitters ignorant to the concept that first base can't be stolen. Joe Rudi was an overrated "underrated" player in the curious way that decent people who come up big with the flashbulbs popping have, though as Rudi himself once said, "I get more ink about not getting any ink than about what I do."[36]

A cursory review of the 1973 team backs up this impression of mediocrity. Offensively, the A's were in the middle of the AL pack in batting average, on-base percentage, and slugging, while ranking seventh in doubles and next to last in three baggers — an extraordinary performance given the team's good overall speed.[37] The starting rotation had exactly three good pitchers, its control was suspect, and the bench was overflowing with has-beens like Dal Maxvill and Jesus Alou.

Yet for all of that, the A's led the league in runs scored and were third in (fewest) runs allowed that season. The offensive figure is by far the more impressive — the Oakland Coliseum was a noted death trap for fly balls, given the chronically heavy and chilly air caused by the stadium's proximity to the bay (A's players dubbed it "the Mausoleum"[38]), acres of foul territory to chase down popups, and symmetrical fences that invariably channeled balls hit off them towards center field.

On the pitching side, Oakland was second in ERA primarily due to a marked stinginess in allowing hits, and a long, strong bullpen....

... and a team that scores the most runs while allowing the third fewest is likely to win a bunch of games.

How did that all happen with such a "good as the 2001 Toronto Blue Jays but no better" roster? In a sense it was chemistry, just chemistry of a different type:

1. *Virtually every key member of the 1972-1974 A's was in his prime during their World Championship run.* Outside of the DHs (who tended to be any old slugger who was available and cheap) and Blue (age 23), every Oakland regular was between 25 and 32: in short, entering into or in the midst of what are typically a player's prime seasons. Having a team's talent clock synchronized is a tremendous competitive advantage — field a roster at its athletic peak and it simply doesn't have to have as much natural ability as one filled with 23-year-old phenoms and 35-plus veterans.

   A good counterpoint to the A's is their 1973 American League Championship Series challengers, the Baltimore Orioles. Though possessing only two Hall of Famers (well, three if Earl Weaver is included with Jim Palmer and Brooks Robinson) Baltimore's talent is clearly deeper on a historical basis. Ex- or future MVPs Robinson, Boog Powell, and Don Baylor were on that team along with four Cy Young Awards split between Jim Palmer and Mike Cuellar. The 1971 National League (Earl Williams) and 1973 AL (Al Bumbry) Rookies of the Year were there, along with five current or future Gold Glove winners (Palmer, Robinson, Bobby Grich, Mark Belanger, and Paul Blair). Even the guys that didn't have bulging trophy cases were plenty good: Tommy Davis won a couple of NL batting crowns while Dave McNally was a four-time, 20-game winner.

   Given those credentials it's easy to conclude that Baltimore was the superior team ... and they clearly were if considered on the basis of their career totals. Grich, Baylor, and Doug DeCinces, though, were mere images of what they were going to be, while Powell, Brooks, Davis, McNally and Cuellar were on the downhill slopes. Sure, as a group they represented superior talents, but to hold down a regular position before or after one's peak seasons, one must by definition be a superior player. The typical guy who's three years in front of the beginning of his peak seasons (22) is still in the minors, while the average 35-year-old is back home wondering what happened to his fastball.

   By constructing a lineup of prime age players the odds were with Finley: the team was likely to peak simultaneously, perform at a consistently high level, and not fall prey to the nagging injuries that degrade even the finest veterans. And if Charlie was anything, he was a man who helped himself to the percentages whenever possible.

2. *There were no holes in the front line talent.* A surprisingly large number of good or even dominant teams have potentially crippling gaps in their talent bases. Take the 2001 Arizona Diamondbacks—while they won it all and deserved to as much as anyone did in that rugby scrum of a season, the Snakes were basically carried by three players having career years. Look beyond those guys, though, and one sees three rotation holes, no true closer, half a platoon at catcher, and a double play combination that was just this side of worthless.

It's tough to win under such circumstances—those subscribing to the Star Trek theory of parallel universes must suspect that there were many in which Arizona finished under .500 that year.

The A's, though, weren't like that. Yes, they had some players of dubious offensive merit like Ray Fosse and Dick Green in the lineup, but both provided solid to spectacular defense and weren't absolute zeros at the plate. Perhaps Campaneris wasn't the prototypical leadoff hitter people of the day thought he was, but 145 games per season of solid, dependable play on both sides of the ball is enormously valuable. While the rotation was weak at the back end due to Blue Moon Odom's premature demise, the A's had a Big Three capable of starting 110 games a season to minimize the problem, and a bullpen hip deep in durable, quality arms.

Outside of his infatuation with pinch runners, Finley didn't go for the type of player that in the modern idiom possesses "tools" but no skills that help a team win baseball games. His predilection for men that were good five years ago and cheap now resulted in notoriously weak benches throughout the team's salad days, but every key player on the roster contributed something concrete to the team's effort.

There is an old saying that a person should carefully consider the way he treats those met on the way up because they will be the same ones encountered on the way down, and Finley's inability to absorb that simple homily assured the Oakland's post-1974 demise. The Mike Andrews fiasco represented a turning point in Charlie's relationship with his locker room: seen as something of an eccentric uncle previously, the utility infielder's humiliation cast the calculating side of Finley's personality in high relief at an inopportune time.[39] Whatever credit Charlie had built up with the men he'd romanced as youngsters was gone in the blink of an eye, and once the Messersmith-McNally decision was handed down they could hardly wait to get away from him.

Simultaneously, Finley's ongoing war with Bowie Kuhn and his fellow owners first cost him the services of Catfish Hunter, then blocked him from raising capital via the sale of soon-to-be defectors. By 1978 the A's were draw-ing 6,500 fans per game to see a 69-93 team that won an offensive Triple Crown (last in batting average, on-base percentage, and slugging percent-age)[40] with a roster featuring eleven players making the major league mini-mum salary.[41] Unable to sustain further losses and in declining health, Charlie was essentially forced out of his beloved franchise, yet in so doing he left behind the key components of what would be a divisional champion just three years hence. Tony Armas was a 1978 Athletic, along with Dwayne Mur-phy, Wayne Gross, Rick Langford, Steve McCatty, Matt Keough, and Mike Norris, while a kid named Rickey Henderson was primed to join them in 1979.

In short, had Finley been able to hold out a few years longer, he'd have been back on top again … but to do so he wouldn't have been Charlie Fin-ley.

Despite the internal strife, bad manners, and ultimately ignominious downfall the early '70s A's ushered in a new era in team development. The false gods of team chemistry were increasingly cast aside in favor of a real-ization that maximizing runs scored while minimizing runs allowed repre-sented the best roster mix of all. Though perhaps less romantic and endearing than the black magic methodologies that preceded it, Finley's pragmatic approach was a fitting prologue to a game that was increasingly dominated by dollar signs and "business is business" decisions. That the man who ush-ered in this new reality was ultimately crushed by it was a delicious irony, yet the magnitude of Charles O. Finley's accomplishment cannot be ignored.

9

On the Origins
of the DH Rule

Cataclysmic change is most often born out of desperation rather than inspiration. The All-Star game, for example, did not arise out of some altruistic desire to entertain baseball fans. It came about because baseball's lords needed to fund a pension plan for ex-players, and because the 3,000-fan-per-game gates that were common during the Depression made it tough to pay the salaries of current players, much less retirees. To cite an example of how tough times were, a section of the left-field grandstand in Boston's Fenway Park burned down in 1926. The scorched columns were still there — and factored in play at times— when Tom Yawkey bought the Red Sox in 1933.[1]

The mound and strike zone changes prior to the 1969 season were primarily an attempt to snap the game out of a mid-1960s attendance funk: if the paying customer wanted more runs, then the paying customer would get more runs and to hell with tradition. Similarly, Branch Rickey was as much economist as social reformer in his signing of Jackie Robinson. Papa Branch knew that (1) good players meant good attendance, (2) good attendance meant money, and (3) that he (Rickey) had a profit-based incentive contract.[2] Thus, lofty ideals often take a back seat to greed in the development of new ideas— but as *Wall Street's* anti-hero Gordon Gekko observed: "The point ... is that greed, for lack of a better word, is good. Greed is right. Greed works. Greed clarifies, cuts through, and captures the essence of the evolutionary spirit."[3]

Now that's a line from a movie about a bad guy at his seductive worst, but Gekko's words wouldn't have captured so many people's imagination if they didn't have more than a grain of truth to them — or applicability in daily life.

All of which brings us to that most controversial of 1970s innovations, the designated hitter (DH) rule.

Conventional wisdom would have fans believe that the American League's goal in inaugurating the DH was to leaven what was becoming a dangerously stagnant game. With hit and walk totals plummeting to levels unseen since the Dead Ball Era while strikeouts and pitching changes soared beyond imagination, junior circuit baseball seemed to be evolving into a contest centered around keeping people from doing things. For the same reason that war pictures are inherently more popular than flicks about guys walking uneventful watches on the 38th Parallel, this proliferation of pitchers' duels was seen as hazardous to the game and owners' wallets, not necessarily in that order.

The funny thing was that nobody had a particularly good explanation for why all of this nothing seemed to be occurring in only one league. Still, the parallel nature of the AL's decline in batting (the league's average sunk to .239 in 1972) and attendance (off 14 percent from 1971)[4] suggested that some sort of offensive remedy was in order, and thus attention was focused upon the weakest link in the run-production chain, the pitcher. The number nine spot in the order and a trip to the concession stands had long been synonymous, but the long-term erosion in hurler hitting skills (the average American League pitcher hit .145 in 1972, with nearly 30 percent of their at-bats resulting in strikeouts[5]) had reduced the pitcher's turn at bat to yet another speed bump in a game that was already studded with them. By substituting someone capable of sustaining the game's offensive rhythm, tedious and otherwise illogical pitching changes could simultaneously be reduced in favor of that all-time crowd pleaser, runs.

Thus the American League, in contrast to the curmudgeonly senior circuit (which in fairness saw little need to tinker with a formula that was driving record business for them), boldly decided to go where no league had gone before — and thus produced baseball's answer to the field goal kicker.

Or at least, that's how the story goes....

The reality of the matter, though, centered less around abstract concepts like game tempo and had more to do with the size of AL bank accounts, which were nearing the level at which average Americans visit their friendly neighborhood payday check cashing outfit. By 1972, the American League's attendance figures lagged those of the senior circuit by 26 percent,[6] a disturbing deficit given the fact that the league had much the better of it from a competitive standpoint. An exciting Oakland A's team was both world champions and a veritable publicity magnet — not all of it good, but as P.T. Barnum once observed, "There is no such thing as bad publicity." The Eastern divisional race had been a four-way nail-biter ultimately decided by a single game that the Boston Red Sox lost to the strike. Conversely, both NL races were won handily by the usual suspects in cakewalks that generated little suspense after mid-August.

Yet even under such circumstances the AL had failed to make significant headway against the senior circuit juggernaut. Now, as in so many things, there were two sets of reasons for this differential — the obvious ones that everybody was talking about and the subtler strata that really made the difference. The obvious ones were as follows:

1. The AL game generated less offense — both in quantity and diversity — than did its National League counterpart. A typical visitor to a 1972 AL ballpark witnessed seven runs scored as opposed to just under eight at an NL park.[7] Stated in that manner the disparity seems almost trivial, but add it all up and the result is a differential of 12.7 percent in the total number of runs scored between the two leagues, a number which is big enough to catch anyone's attention.

   It was an across-the-board disparity too. The National League hit 15.6 percent more homers than the AL did, and if the 1961 Roger Maris/Mickey Mantle tag team event (reprised with a multi-ethnic cast in 1998) taught the junior circuit anything, it's that casual fans just love them taters. For the aficionado, the NL racked up 5.8 percent more doubles and a whopping 36 percent more triples, arguably the offensive highlight of any game. National League base stealers were both more prolific (11.8 percent more thefts) and successful (62.7 percent vs. 61.3 percent) in their attempts.[8]

2. The National League was perceived as producing superior talent — so much so that the AL seemed compelled to draw its premier players from the NL's leftovers. Statisticians may pooh-pooh the value of a single annual game in terms of evaluating the quality differential between two participants, but to the casual 1972 fan the NL's All-Star Game dominance was unignorably large. The National League had won nine of the previous ten midseason classics while out-homering the AL 16-9[9] — and since wins and big bombs are easy-to-comprehend events, a notion of NL invincibility above and beyond any real talent differential had taken root in the public conscience. Sure, six of those victories were by one run and four of them in extra innings,[10] but such subtleties are easily lost on what we now call "the Enquiring mind."

   As for the inter-league imports, the same held true — the differential wasn't that great, but the symbolic impact of those who did cross made the situation seem more profound than it was. The winners of the AL's two top awards in 1972, Dick Allen and Gaylord Perry, were more or less NL castoffs, the former a knight errant with emphasis on the errant part, the latter a good ol' boy with a jaundiced view of baseball ethics and legality. By way of comparison, Mike McCormick in 1967 was the only ex-American Leaguer to ever win a major senior circuit award — and the only reason he'd been tainted with the AL virus was because the Giants had thought that Jack Fisher was a better choice for the 1963 pennant chase.[11] Nolan Ryan, who was on the verge of setting the single season strikeout record, was a Mets' system product. Mike Cuellar, the 1969 AL Cy Young Award co-winner who won 18 games in 1972 with a 2.57 ERA, had become a junior circuit monster following three OK-but-nothing-special seasons in Houston. Dodgers reject Frank Howard had been the AL's leading home run hitter over the previous eight seasons. Tommie Harper, Leo Cardenas, Woodie Fryman, Pat Dobson, Alex Johnson,

Johnny Briggs, Wayne Granger, Amos Otis, Cookie Rojas, Vada Pinson — all were 1972 AL mainstays, and all had made the jump (taken the plunge?) after their National League careers had flamed out for one reason or another. Of course Vic Davallilo, Claude Osteen (though he started out with the Reds), Milt Pappas, Mike Marshall, and Al Downing were ex-American Leaguers who were having productive seasons in the 1972 National League, but when you're on a roll....

3. The NL had nicer parks to play in. As mentioned earlier, every National League team save the Chicago Cubs by 1972 was playing in stadiums built since 1960 — and Wrigley Field was half national treasure, half money pit for a benevolent centimillionaire. As for the AL, Comiskey Park had seen better days and Cleveland's "Mistake by the Lake" Municipal Stadium didn't even have all that many good days to look back on. Yankee Stadium and Metropolitan Stadium in Minnesota were decaying badly.[12] Milwaukee's County and Baltimore's Memorial stadiums were 1950s era Erector Set parks that had been built on the cheap and looked it.

Even the league's newer ballyards were less than auspicious. Arlington Stadium in Texas represented the Erector Set concept updated to the 1970s, while the Oakland Coliseum was both bland and blustery and Anaheim Stadium was on the verge of a hideous metamorphosis to accommodate football's Los Angeles Rams. Only Boston's Fenway Park, Kansas City's new Royals Stadium and arguably Tiger Stadium in Detroit (though the place looked like a oversized cannery from the outside) were anything that could be pointed to with pride.[13]

Now all of these are solid-sounding reasons with more than a little truth attached to them for the AL's relative malaise, but each argument's holes become obvious upon further inspection. Take the perceived quality differential — though frustrated fans of the time might have said so with conviction, the current Hall of Fame tally certainly doesn't suggest that the early '70s AL was viewed as a decidedly inferior venue. As of 2001, 15 of these supposedly inferior beings (Rod Carew, Luis Aparicio, Robin Yount, Nolan Ryan, Orlando Cepeda, Jim Palmer, Rollie Fingers, Carleton Fisk, Brooks Robinson, Gaylord Perry, Harmon Killebrew, Catfish Hunter, Reggie Jackson, Carl Yastrzemski, and Al Kaline) have been deemed worthy of enshrinement. Now that isn't quite as many as the 18 NL'ers of the same era who have gone in, but it's far from a mismatch and several of the NL guys like Willie Mays and Hoyt Wilhelm were prior generation holdovers on their last legs. Same with the hitting argument: if the league's offensive numbers are lower but the overall quality of the players is similar, couldn't it be because the pitching is better?

And as for the old parks? Since when has architectural merit had anything to do with the "beauty" of a given venue? The Polo Grounds may well have been the steel and masonry equivalent of a camel, but that detracts not one iota from the ballet-like brilliance of Willie Mays' catch in Game 1 of the 1954 World Series. Furthermore, given the modern day rush that municipalities are in to erect ersatz 1925-era edifices, one wonders how big a handicap the authentic retro look really was.

So, none of the above explanations are all that satisfying. OK, now let's look past the obvious:

1. The AL game was dampened by the fact that most of its teams played in pitcher's parks. One distinguishing characteristic of early 1900s ballyards was their relative size. With real estate prices low (at least in the less-than-prime areas where these parks were constructed) and home runs a relative rarity, concerns over playing field dimensions ran a poor third to stadium capacity and the limitations of the physical lot. As a result, Comiskey Park had a huge playing field — roughly 10 percent larger than the typical sterile ashtray stadium[14] — as did Tiger Stadium (though the distances along the lines were cozy) and the Bronx Bombers' home. Fenway Park is popularly considered to be tiny due to its small seating capacity as well as the Green Monster, but at 54,120 square feet Fenway's area of play to the right of second base is one of the largest of any current big league ballpark.[15]

    Exacerbating the matter was the fact that many of the other stadiums were either designed or placed in physical locations that made them good pitcher's forums. Cleveland's Municipal and Milwaukee's County Stadium along with the Oakland Coliseum lay alongside large, normally cold bodies of water which deadened fly balls hit at night. Memorial Stadium in Baltimore had a symmetrically-shaped fence that was high along the lines and tended to channel balls hit off it towards the middle of the field.[16] Even Arlington Stadium, with its heat, small amount of foul territory down the lines and wind that was perpetually blowing out, was by and large a pitcher's park due in part to the large number of night games necessitated by the midsummer Texas weather.[17]

2. The junior circuit had the worst of the location battle vis-à-vis its older competitor. Each league had eight metropolitan areas to itself. In the American League they were Milwaukee, Detroit, Dallas-Ft. Worth, Kansas City, Boston, Baltimore, Cleveland and Minneapolis-St. Paul. The National League's were Cincinnati, Montreal, St. Louis, San Diego, Atlanta, Houston, Pittsburgh, and Philadelphia.

    Of the eight solo AL cities, six were growing at rates significantly below the national average[18] and one of the other two (Dallas-Ft. Worth) hosted the league's weakest franchise. Only three of the eight AL-only towns housed teams with strong fan bases (Boston, Detroit and arguably Kansas City) while most of the remaining quintet were among the league's poorest draws. Conversely, half of the NL metropolises were growing rapidly[19] while the remainder, with the possible exception of Philadelphia, were traditionally vibrant baseball markets— and the Phillies would draw over two million fans annually as the team's fortunes improved in the mid-1970s.

In the four shared markets, the American League franchise was generally in the weaker geographic location. Whether the Yankees' South Bronx home across the East River from Manhattan was inferior to the Mets' venue near LaGuardia Airport is debatable, but in Chicago the Cubs were ensconced in a gentrifying North Side residential area while Comiskey Park backed up to a Mack Truck assembly plant.[20] The Angels had a fine stadium — but it was 35 miles away from the Dodgers' mountaintop location overlooking downtown Los Angeles. As for the Bay Area teams, well ... the NL got San Francisco and the AL got Oakland.

3. Junior circuit ownership was weaker both financially and operationally. On the face of it, the AL owners looked every bit as well-heeled and substantial as their NL brethren. They included:

- a brewery owner (Baltimore's Jerry Hoffberger)
- a major television network (CBS owned the Yankees in those days)
- a film star (Gene Autry)
- a very well connected politico (Texas' Bob Short)
- several operators that had been around forever (Calvin Griffith, Tom Yawkey, and Spike Briggs' descendants in Detroit), as well as
- a bunch of other guys who were wealthier than anybody has a right to be.

People in underdeveloped countries don't realize that they are poor until they see a rich person; in the same way, AL owners look remarkably solid and stolid until compared to the big boys in the opposite league. Hoffberger was no Gussie Busch. The Tiffany Network's stewardship of the AL's Tiffany franchise had been somewhere between bungling and hilarious. Short, Griffith, Chicago's John Allyn, and Cleveland's ownership group headed by Nick Mileti were perilously short bankrolled.[21]

In short, the AL was playing Avis to the senior circuit's Hertz — and as long as they offered the same product in the same venues with the same financial resources at their command, that situation was unlikely to change.

Place this question in front of 15 marketing gurus and after 14 of them are trampled in the rush to get your signature on a $500 per hour consulting agreement, the 15th will advise finding a way — any way — to differentiate the AL product from the NL's offering. It doesn't matter whether the differentiation improves the game, or makes it superior to the senior circuit's offering, or even makes sense, just as long as it's different.

That's the DH in a nutshell. When one considers the AL's problems (both real and perceived) it becomes obvious that the rule doesn't really address any of them. Yes, a designated hitter does eliminate an automatic out from the lineup, but as Dick Young pointed out in typical Dick Young fashion, "The

DH rule is doing nothing for the other eight men in the lineup. Most of them still can't hit the ball."[22] An additional hitter may reduce between-inning pitching changes, but those moves weren't the ones that took an eternity: it was the mid-inning switches that were the real time wasters, and those jumped with the added run-scoring potential. As for the "taking on the NL's factory seconds" stigma, the DH's inauguration opened up second careers for a ton of aging, decrepit NL alumni. For example, the top hitting DH of 1973 was Tommy Davis, a 34-year-old ex-National Leaguer whose knees were shot. The number three guy was Orlando Cepeda, a 35-year-old ex-National Leaguer whose knees were shot. Between Davis and Cepeda was Tony Oliva, proof positive that the AL could home-grow its own knee problems. Rico Carty (who habitually carried his wallet with him while on the field[23]), Frank Robinson, Deron Johnson, Jim Ray Hart, Downtown Ollie Brown — heck, if Dick (Dr. Strangeglove) Stuart had stuck around for a few more years, he'd have had it made.

Furthermore, it wasn't as if the DH hadn't been tried before. Designated hitters had been used a couple of times during spring training by major league clubs, and in 1969 were the subject of a year-long experiment by the AAA International League. Upon inception of the rule, the circuit was subjected to the same kind of outcry (mostly from managers and club officials) that the American League would hear four years later — ruins the traditions of the game, removes strategy, promotes half-good players, etc. There were even rumors that managers would ignore the rule entirely in an attempt to continue molding "complete players." They didn't, of course — no one was willing to yield such an obvious tactical advantage — but it should be kept in mind that these arguments weren't trivial or academic ones either; the league served as the final proving grounds for the top prospects of eight organizations.

In many ways the International League was prescient in its use of the designated hitter. In the modern manner the typical IL manager tended to utilize the DH as a quasi-day-off for his best players. While there was a bias towards utilizing defensively challenged mid-career guys in the role,[24] it would be a mistake to characterize these men as minor league losers: though their names might not ring many bells with modern fans, the majority would take at least one major league bow. The best of the bunch was probably Bob Robertson, a first baseman with soft hands and three minor league home run crowns who posted a couple of quality seasons with the Pirates before succumbing to knee problems and a complainer reputation.[25]

The experiment turned out to be one of those "the operation was a success but the patient died" type of things. Technically, the DH did everything the IL could have hoped for: runs scored per game increased by 12.6 percent over the 1969 level, while shutouts declined by more than a third. However, the response to all that extra offense was something akin to a passive boycott — despite a tight pennant race in which the top four teams ended up within 4½ games of one another, league-wide attendance figures fell by 18.7 percent. Perhaps the 1969 IL was less than star-studded (Dave Cash, Ralph Garr, and Jon Matlack are about it in terms of quality careers). Still, the 1970 crop wasn't all that much better and they sans the DH were enough to return attendance to within 13,000 bodies of the 1968 level.[26]

So what we have is a major rule change that didn't address the American League's core problems, didn't work when tried before, and would be opposed by 61 percent of fans responding to a *Sporting News* poll conducted after its first season of use.[27]

And yet it succeeded ... after a fashion.

Once the DH was approved by a just-good-enough 8-4 margin,[28] the new rule became a publicity man's dream: it drove everything else (including a moderately nasty fight with the players over extension of the Basic Agreement) from baseball's front page. Fans, sportswriters, managers, pitchers, retired players, dead Hall of Famers— people seemed to literally crawl out of the woodwork to offer sound-bite-style appraisals of the impending Armageddon. Mickey Lolich loved the idea in the way that a pitcher sporting a .110 career average and an expanding waistline might.[29] Earl Weaver hated it in the manner that a control freak that was already on top might.[30] Carl Yastrzemski thought that pitchers would become beanball freaks absent the threat of retribution at the plate.[31] Yankee outfielder Johnny Callison wondered aloud what 1940s great Johnny Mize was doing these days.[32] Rookie manager Whitey Herzog opined in the bedside manner for which he would become famous that his Rangers possessed the perfect DH in Rico Carty: when apprised of this comment, Carty was quick to assert, "I'm no invalid. I want to play both ways."[33]

At a nominal level, the impact that all of this controversy and chin wagging had on the AL's financial fortunes was both obvious and monumental:

- The league's batting average rose by 20 points in one year while runs scored rose by just under 25 percent on a per-game basis and shutouts declined by a similar amount.[34]
- Furthermore, the DH did not drain strategy from the AL game as some had feared. Yes, a layer of obvious ploys like pinch hitting for a Jack Aker (career average .076) or having him lay down a sacrifice bunt were purged, but these were by and large push button choices that are within the capability of a moderately intelligent six-year-old. The meat and potatoes decisions that separated an Earl Weaver from a Gene Mauch were basically unchanged by the rule — in fact, such differentials became more obvious without the automatic stuff obscuring the issue.
- Best of all, despite a couple of ho-hum pennant races and Henry Aaron's run at the magic 714 in the opposing league, AL turnstile counts rose by 12.2 percent to a new yearly record in 1973.[35]

For a league that had one foot on the financial ledge, anything that drew two million incremental fans was manna from heaven, and thus this once-experimental rule was destined to become a permanent dichotomy within baseball's family.

The long-term impact of the DH on the AL's fortunes, however, turned out to be much more problematic. If the rule's first-year impact had really been as pervasive as the attendance numbers suggest, logic would dictate that a couple of other things would have occurred as well. First, the American League would have continued to close the attendance gap with the senior circuit in future years. And, the stick-in-the-mud NL would ultimately have been forced to adopt the rule themselves.

Neither of these things happened. Junior circuit turnstile counts were basically flat over the following two seasons, growing again only as new ownership with new money (and new free agency rules to exploit) began to make its presence felt within the game.[36] The NL remains DH-less to this day and has never seriously considered implementing the rule, which to many serves as proof positive of the dinosaur-like tendencies prevalent in baseball's executive suites. Buying off on that scenario, though, leaves the provocative question of when a man like staunch DH opponent Walter O'Malley, whose concern for tradition at the expense of lucre is heralded by several generations of Brooklynites, became adverse to money.

Still, the inauguration of the designated hitter undoubtedly gave the American League a long-term leg up as witnessed by the fact that AL attendance did not decline after the rule's novelty factor wore off. All that off-season talk about the cessation of life as we know it on junior circuit diamonds achieved what any huckster from Professor Harold Hill of *Music Man* fame on would have predicted: it got people through the doors. Once there, these new fans found, perhaps to their surprise, that the American League game was not contested by guys with pillbox hats and bottle bats, but by a breed that played an exciting brand of baseball that might (heaven forbid) be every bit as good as the NL's.

As we will later see, the DH boom was too little and too late to save the incumbent AL owners, but at least it did allow a number of them to beat an honorable retreat from the game while kindling the league's renaissance. The rule remains to this day a political volleyball, a perfectly logical outcome given the balance of desperation vis-à-vis inspiration that prompted its birth.

As for whether or not greed really was good in this case....

10

Bobby Bonds and the Ghost of Baseball Future

Every so often someone comes along whose life serves as a glimpse through the looking glass darkly at what is to come for the rest of us. Steve Jobs's roller coaster ride from techno-geek building computers in his garage to head of Apple Computer (with a period of exile thrown in for dramatic effect) represented a microcosm of the surf that thousands of dot-commers are treading today. Malcolm X's trek from apolitical criminal to black revolutionary to man who envisioned the possibility of coexistence with Whitey would be followed by many in the generations after him. Lenny Bruce, John Belushi, Newt Gingrich — each served as tea leaves which, when read (usually in retrospect), portrayed so much of the triumph and tragedy that the future would hold. None of these men were universally loved, to say the least, because each displayed the all-too-human warts that we hope posterity will ignore.

In National Pastime terms, the Ghost of Baseball Future was embodied in one Bobby Lee Bonds, a man whose career personified the collision of inflated expectations with an increasingly money-driven game. In a very real sense Bonds was the prototype for the modern five-tool player — not that others before him hadn't possessed a full range of skills, but Bobby was the first to be commonly referred to in that manner, and utilized so that every capability became a critical part of his game.

It seems as if anybody who can hit a cutoff man on the fly and pop ten taters at Coors Field qualifies for five-tool playerhood nowadays, but Bobby was the real deal, showcasing each talent at one point or another during his big league career. He was fast, stealing as many as 48 bases in a season with an excellent success rate. He was born knowing how to work pitchers for ball four, taking 81 walks in his first full year and accepting 70 or more in eight of the ten seasons in which he played regularly. A powerful upper body and quick swing resulted in six 30-plus homer seasons.[1] He had the speed to play center field and the arm to play right (an area in which he exceeded his son Barry).

Yet despite all of those qualities, Barry's dad was fated to spend much of his career as a vagabond, playing for eight teams in as many years. It wasn't as if he were a truly bad egg — Bonds was in the main a very matter-of-fact fellow who would candidly discuss his failings — but it was just that ... well, no matter what he did, it wasn't quite good enough.

In a sense, Bonds's first mistake was to come up through the same organization that had spawned Willie Mays and then end up playing alongside the great man himself. Given Bobby's myriad talents, it was natural for Giants fans to think of him as the next Mays, which would have been fine except that Bonds's minor league high in homers was 26 and he hit .262 and .261 in his last two pre-Show seasons.[2] Anyway, once Bonds made the majors, his speed and strike zone judgment along with the presence of Mays, Willie McCovey, and eventually Dave Kingman pushed him into the leadoff role, and in 1970 he turned in one of the best seasons ever for a tablesetter. Playing 157 games, Bonds scored 134 runs, due in part to the big bats behind him, but also compiled a .302 average in a miserable hitter's park, along with 77 walks, 48 steals, and 72 extra base hits.

Think Willie Mays as a leadoff hitter and you get the general idea. Bonds reached base a good though nothing spectacular 280 times that year, but 120 of those occasions ended up with Bobby in scoring position under his own power.[3] A player who pops a single and stays close to the bag will generally require two hits to be plated: one that singles and steals second, or doubles in the first place takes only one ... and then there's Bonds's 26 dingers to consider as well.

The custom in Roman days was for conquering generals to have the slaves and booty their campaigns garnered paraded in front of them upon return to the capital — but at the same time someone was stationed behind the great man to whisper the warning that fame and glory were fleeting. We call it a reality check these days, and it's a tradition honored all too infrequently in sports ... and given his true skill level plus the situation that he would soon find himself in, few would have benefited from one more than Bobby Bonds.

First of all, Bonds really wasn't a .300 hitter: a chronic weakness for curveballs out of the strike zone (despite the best efforts of Preston Wilson and others, Bobby still holds the single season whiff record) would bar him from ever hitting as high as .290 again. Though he would wax philosophic over his futility — once quipping that "if I'm going to make [an] out I might as well strike out. It saves all that running to first base,"[4] the recurrent breezes became a cause célèbre with fans as well as many of his managers. More than one early '70s baseball man suggested that the then 24-year-old Bobby was capable of hitting .350 if he could somehow cut his strikeouts in half,[5] a sentiment that Angels skipper Dave Garcia echoed seven years later.

Garcia would, however, also add, "But if he did maybe he wouldn't be the same Bonds when it came to homers and runs batted in. On second thought, I think he'd better stay the way he is."[6]

Secondly, Bobby was a goals-oriented guy, which is a good thing except that:

1. He'd tend to set them on the high side,
2. He would, at least initially, share them with reporters,[7] thus incurring the public's wrath when things didn't go according to plan, and
3. It really bothered him when he fell short.

Finally, Bonds's Giants were fated to endure one of those periods where the holes would spring up faster than they could be patched. Mays's slow fade had been written on the wind by the time Bobby joined the club in 1968, but Willie McCovey's chronic knee problems along with the injury-induced decline of Jim Ray Hart blew holes in the power core that resisted solution. It was an odd situation: the San Francisco farm system during this era produced a bumper crop of long-term major leaguers like Bonds, Kingman, Gary Matthews, Ken Henderson, Chris Speier, and Garry Maddox, yet none outside of Bobby was quite capable of filling the key offensive roles that came available. Kingman's and Henderson's productivity came and went, Matthews was a fine overall offensive player who was stretched power-wise to hold down a middle of the order spot, while Speier and Maddox were really bottom of the order types.

As a result of this tumult, then-manager Charlie Fox regularly shuttled Bonds between the leadoff and power positions in his lineup, a course of action that forced Bobby to constantly change his hitting approach and would ultimately sour his relationship with the Giants' skipper.[8] One can sympathize with Fox's dilemma: after the 1970 trade of Ron Hunt, the Giants didn't have anybody else who could set the table on a consistent basis, but when McCovey's body gave way and Kingman wasn't hitting his weight, the lineup was critically short of power. The San Francisco rotation was unraveling via the sudden aging of Juan Marichal and the infinitely regrettable Gaylord Perry for Sam McDowell trade. A surprise 1971 divisional championship inflated expectations beyond reason.

Despite this less-than-ideal cauldron for developing one's skills, by mid-decade more than a few people in baseball viewed Bobby as being among the game's elite. A 1972 poll of managers, coaches, and players conducted by *Baseball Digest* picked Bonds over Roberto Clemente, Rusty Staub, and Frank Robinson as the NL's best right fielder.[9] Sparky Anderson termed him "baseball's most outstanding player" and considered it an outrage when Pete Rose, Billy Williams, and Cesar Cedeno were voted ahead of him for the 1973 All-Star team.[10] Columnist Ross Atkin of *The Christian Science Monitor* termed Bobby to be "the closest thing to a Superman there is in the game of baseball today."[11]

Still, an undercurrent of dissatisfaction always seemed to present itself whenever the achievements of this man with the big red S were discussed. Even the laudatory articles alluded to how much better he'd be once an injury cleared up or his K totals declined or whatever. Heck, Bobby himself once said, "Someday I'm going to put it all together, and when I do get it together the nation will be shocked."[12] For all the pats on the back, Bonds would only make three All-Star appearances and receive serious consideration in MVP Award balloting twice.[13] Rumors of drunkenness and drug use would swirl around him,[14] along with a bad attitude rep that wasn't helped by such offhand comments as "I don't see why you have to run down to first base every time to make an out."[15]

In short, Bonds's relationship with the Giants was one of those love-hate types that last until the player suffers through his next sub-par season. Thus, it should come as no surprise that after a poor, by his standards, 1974 campaign (he finished eighth in runs scored after being in the top two for the previous five years) Bonds was dealt to the New York Yankees for Bobby Murcer. Surprising, no, but historic (it was the first trade of $100,000-a-year players, a distinction that seems quaint today but got big play at the time[16]) and deliciously ironic just the same: the man who couldn't fill Willie Mays's shoes swapped for the man who couldn't fill Mickey Mantle's.

And thus the downward spiral began....

Bonds took over for Murcer in center field and even made the All-Star team, but an early season knee injury that got progressively worse reduced his defensive range to marginal levels for the position.[17] Though his offensive production was up to snuff (Bonds would place among the top five in slugging percentage, runs scored, and homers) the bottom line was that the Yankees finished a disappointing third ... and that's the only one that counted where a soon-to-be free agent was concerned.

The bicentennial season found Bobby back home (he grew up roughly 40 miles away) with the California Angels, who as a consequence of his acquisition believed themselves to be serious contenders in the AL West.[18] However, a chipped bone in his hand suffered during the preseason turned into ligament damage that furloughed the slugger after only 99 games and ten homers.[19] Bonds rebounded smartly in 1977 but the Halos finished fourth again when such acquisitions as Joe Rudi and Bobby Grich pulled up lame. Bobby's drive to become baseball's first 40/40 man (he ultimately fell three homers short) while the team was floundering led to a whisper campaign about his dedication to the team.[20]

Once again Bonds hadn't carried a team over the top and thus it was off to the south side of Chicago for 1978, where Bill Veeck was busily renting players on a one-year basis in the hopes of keeping his team in contention and financially solvent. The White Sox got out of the gate slowly, though, and with Bonds's contract demands being beyond anything Veeck could afford, he was dispatched to Texas after 26 games (in a priceless aside, Claudell Washington, the man Bonds was traded for, took four days to report to the White Sox. When asked why, he replied, "I overslept"[21]). Ranger owner Brad Corbett gave Bonds the long-term deal he was looking for and the slugger responded by belting 29 homers in 133 games ... but the team lost $800,000 despite setting a club attendance record and finishing with their second best won-lost mark ever.[22]

Two days after the season ended he was sent to Cleveland.

By this time Bobby was 33 and showing signs of becoming disinterested in the proceedings. The Indians weren't a bad offensive club (Toby Harrah, Mike Hargrove, Cliff Johnson, and Andre Thornton surrounded Bonds in the 1979 Tribe lineup. While none of those names save Grover's may ring a bell with modern fans each was an offensive force to be reckoned with at the time.) But with only two quality starters and a like number of bullpenners worth handing the ball to, the team clearly wasn't destined for glory. Thus, Bonds's game began to devolve into the look-at-me self-exhibition that critics had always claimed it was. He habitually skied his throws—center fielder Rick Manning claimed that "Bobby wouldn't hit the cut-off man if he were King Kong."[23] Bobby continued swiping bases despite a now-poor success rate. He tweaked the front office's noses by standing with doomed manager Jeff Torborg, simultaneously ingratiating himself with teammates by declaring in typical Bonds fashion, "If you don't have the horses, you can't pull the wagon."[24]

The last two years of his career would prove to be a sad coda of injuries and ineffectiveness. Traded to the Cardinals for the 1980 season, Bonds injured his wrist during the second week of the season and ended up hitting .203 in a half-season's worth of play with minimal power ("I don't know what's happened to him," St Louis manager Whitey Herzog said at year's end. "All those years he had 30 and 30 he had to be helping teams sometimes"[25]). Sold to the Cubs after the season, manager Joey Amalfitano made the now 35-year-old's status clear, reportedly telling Bonds, "Bobby, you know where you are. If you have any bullets left in the gun you'd better fire 'em."[26] Unfortunately, his wrist never quite came back, and after 163 largely futile at-bats the curtain fell on the career of a man who was tabbed with the dubious distinction of being "promising" virtually to the day he retired.

Like so many of us, Bobby Bonds' career was a continual procession of wrong places reached at the wrong time. It was his fate to play primarily for the kind of teams that were good enough to contend only if everything fell just right — then, as today, such clubs are the ones most likely to take on tarnished sluggers with big upsides. Their relative success in this endeavor can best be measured by the fact that between 1974 and 1980 every team that Bonds played on fired its manager midseason, which has got to be a record of some kind.[27] In such an environment a team's best players are forever under a microscope with every perceived shortfall or indiscretion magnified 1,000 fold — and Bobby, being just like the rest of us, had an ample supply of those.

The big money hit for Bonds at the time that his skills went into decline, thus turning the second half of his career into a constant shuffle by teams to get him off the roster. Bobby grew bitter and cynical as the years passed, suspecting the motives of virtually everybody he dealt with: when acquired by the Indians he initially refused to report, declaring, "I will never play for Gabe Paul" due to the team president's supposed role in Bonds's departure from New York.[28] He would even half-verify teammates' claims of self centeredness, stating that his 1979 Indians campaign was one of his most trying despite superficially impressive stats.[29]

It was a story that was novel and supremely aggravating to baseball fans of the day but strikes modern ears as ... well, somewhat ordinary. So Bonds spent his declining years as a bat for hire: isn't that what Don Baylor and Dave Winfield did? An overpriced player passing from hand to hand is a perfect description of Dante Bichette's final seasons, isn't it? Lengthen the career a little bit and change a few particulars and Bobby's story could easily double for that of Rickey Henderson. Or Bobby Bonilla. Or Brian Jordan. Does a suggestion of Andruw Jones's early career struggles waft through Bonds's early years? Jose Cruz Jr.? J.D. Drew?

There are those in stat geek circles who argue that Bonds Sr. could easily have ended up where Bonds Jr. will — i.e. Cooperstown — had people simply left him alone to do what he was good at. Perhaps that's so, but in most ways Bobby Bonds's story is one that every star of today can relate to.

It just came about some thirty years before its time.

11

Henry Aaron, Race, and the Record

Every society goes through an embarrassing moment of truth now and then — a point at which a problem that it believed was in the process of being addressed jumps up again and bites it in the behind. Mikhail Gorbachev's Soviet Union experienced theirs in 1991, when a cabal of Communist hardliners marshaled their waning power to overthrow the government ... and ended up bringing down the last vestiges of the worker's paradise in the process. The Japanese thought that they were the bee's knees in designing buildings to withstand earthquakes, then watched a substantial percentage of the city of Kobe disintegrate during a temblor that it should theoretically have withstood. The 1972 U.S. men's Olympic basketball team won their gold medal match against the Soviet Union twice — too bad it was the third try that ended up counting.[1]

Baseball's phoenix issue reared its head at what should have been a proud moment — the career home run crown's passage from a man/child who'd once dangled his manager out of a speeding train to a dignified individual whose life represented a triumph of will over the specter of bigotry. Instead, the battle for the new record dramatized the game's turbulent relationship with the phalanx of black and Latino stars who were taking over its upper echelons— and vice versa. The result was a bittersweet episode in which baseball and its fans were displayed at their best and very incredible worst, while the threats coupled with his generation's demons largely kept the man who would be king from savoring the fruits of his 20-year-long struggle.

At the center of this maelstrom was a reticent man from Mobile, Alabama, named Henry Louis Aaron.

Aaron in many ways was baseball's answer to Charles Lindbergh. Both were intensely private, almost withdrawn men, though Lindbergh was withdrawn because that was his nature while Aaron assumed that façade out of a sense of self-preservation. Both had a single-minded love for their profession, and both sacrificed much from a personal standpoint for that love. Both were dark horse entrants in historic races. Both reached the pinnacle of their professions despite a lack of formal training therein. Both grew to resent the spotlight their exploits drew, yet utilized the platform fame granted them to exspouse their beliefs—and both were reduced in the public mind for so doing. Aaron's psychological balance suggests that he will avoid the recluse-like existence of Lindbergh's final years, yet in the manner of Lucky Lindy, Henry has become something of an ethereal presence on the fringe of baseball society since his unevenly successful reign as Atlanta's director of player development in the 1980s.[2]

Of course, there is Hammerin' Hank's natural suntan to consider as well....

Somehow, the social history of black America as it tightrope-walked its way through the middle third of the 20th century is becoming blurred. While filmmakers like Alan Parker have captured the journey's highlights after a fashion in such works as *Mississippi Burning*, the grinding degradation of daily life — what Uncle Sam terms covert rather than overt activities— well, that isn't the stuff of $100 million box offices. In his autobiography, *I Had A Hammer*, Aaron detailed a sampling of the indignities that were part and parcel of getting along in his father's day:

> If you were in line at the grocery store, a white person could just step right in front of you and you couldn't say a thing. When you got paid at the end of the week, your salary was whatever they wanted to put in that envelope. Once when Daddy went into the courthouse to get a license, a deputy jumped all over him for not taking his hat off. Daddy told him that he was so scared he didn't know if his hat was on or off— which was exactly what the deputy wanted to hear. So the deputy got a big smile on his face and Daddy went about his business.[3]

The father's experiences as a boilermaker's assistant and sometimes moonshine purveyor[4] were a mere sideshow to Aaron's plight in the vanguard of an integration movement that for all its tentativeness was still a generation ahead of society in general. Some of the stuff that Aaron experienced seems almost comical in retrospect, such as the time when the management of a restaurant near Griffith Stadium in Washington broke all of the dishes that Henry and his Indianapolis Clowns teammates had just eaten off of.[5] Now there's a racist with conviction — a financially naive racist (one wonders why the restaurant bothered serving the team in the first place), but a man of conviction just the same. Some showed the lengths to which people would go to degrade others: according to Dodger great Don Newcombe, when St. Louis's Chase Hotel finally agreed to admit black players they were inevitably assigned rooms facing brick walls or service alleys to keep them from sneaking peeks at the white girls lounging around the pool.[6] Some were arguably committed with the best of intentions, as was Braves manager Charlie Grimm's affectionate likening of the 19-year-old Aaron to the bug-eyed 1930s character actor/ stereotype Stepin Fetchit.[7]

Add these experiences to Henry's quiet nature and the product was a modern day Sphinx — a man who gave away so little of himself that sports-writers couldn't (or couldn't be bothered to) develop a full-fledged portrait. Not that he was unappreciated as a ballplayer: Aaron received MVP votes every year he was a National Leaguer except his first and last, while gracing 21 consecutive All-Star teams.[8] Yet somehow the headlines always seemed to go to others whose essences lent themselves to easier caricature, such as the sunshiny Ernie Banks or the scowling brushback artist Don Drysdale or the mercurial yet cannon-armed Roberto Clemente.

And then, of course, there was Willie Mays.

Mays was already a sensation in the manner of promising young New York players from the days of Christy Mathewson on by the time Aaron reported for his first big league spring training camp in 1954. One MVP sea-son and a dramatic catch of a Vic Wertz drive later, Willie's persona was at such a level as to blot out whatever sun might have shone on quieter indi-viduals such as Aaron. While there was justification for the oversight (Mays through the mid-1960s was as consistent as Henry on offense and a Gold Glove center fielder to boot), there also was a jingoistic aspect to this bias as well. Willie was a talkative sort in a good-spirited, uneducated manner that readily lent itself to the demeaning "natural talent" label — a little slow per-haps, but plenty strong and capable under the tutelage of a wise old hand like Leo Durocher. Willie Mays — the kid who played stickball on the streets of Harlem, who when asked how the Wertz catch compared to others he had made, said, "I don't compare 'em, I catch 'em,"[9] the Say-Hey Kid — the good black boy.

It was a smugly appealing image, and one that was hung on virtually every black and Latino player of the era who did not otherwise protest. In Aaron's case, his thoughtful yet terse and sometimes less-than-articulate answers to reporters' questions made the "natural talent" label a ... well, nat-ural. One of psychology's main tenets is the principle of association — basi-cally, that people see what they expect to see — and in the case of sportswriters covering Aaron this tendency often manifested itself in a lack of customary editing of the things Henry would say. Atlanta *Journal* columnist Furman Bisher in a 1956 *Saturday Evening Post* article about the Braves' slugger chose to include such comments as "Nobody is hit .400 since Ted Williams." While probably Henry's exact words, such a remark might have been grammatically cleaned up in a piece about someone else. Bisher retained the lead-in word "man" for several Aaron comments, chose to hear the bastardized "dat" in another quote and topped it all off with his description of Aaron's "satchel posterior and shuffling gait" — the Stepin Fetchit characterization again.[10]

The point is not that Bisher was a racist or even particularly insensitive, but that it was perfectly acceptable in those days for the nation's largest weekly magazine to depict Aaron as a backwards kid who through some sort of cosmic fluke was blessed with great physical skill.

Yet over the years one thing became certain — for a fluke of nature, Hammerin' Hank was an amazingly consistent and persistent one. Between Aaron's broken-ankle-shortened rookie season and his late thirty somethings, his idea of an off season was what virtually everybody else would call a career year. Nominally speaking, 1968 looks like his worst campaign in that span, but then again 1968 was pitching's High Noon: Aaron's 29 homers and 86 RBIs that year ranked fifth and seventh in the league respectively, while his .498 slugging percentage was only exceeded by three others. Or maybe Henry's nadir was 1964, when he hit .328 but with only 24 round trippers and 95 RBIs. Of course, he was still in the top 10 in both of those power figures as well as batting average, runs scored, hits, on-base percentage, walks, and stolen bases.[11]

However, while Aaron's performance remained as consistent as the seasons, the stage upon which he performed was undergoing cataclysmic changes:

1. Overtly racist attitudes and practices came under siege by a coalition of minority activists, Baby Boomers less burdened by Jim Crow ideology than their forefathers, and lawmakers who recognized the potential value (as measured in votes) of those two groups. A lot of things, like refusing to serve people based upon their race, that had been OK for years were wiped from the scene by political mandate — and what's more, the government was utilizing its might to enforce the new standards.

   In many eyes (especially those covered by pale-colored lids), this effort represented a major step towards atonement for the previous 250 years of injustices ... and at the macro level it was. The problem with addressing social problems via canon law, though, is that the people being reformed never change as fast as the statutes do, often simply carrying on under a different guise.

   Such was the case with prejudice. While blatantly biased behavior may have been curtailed in the late 1960s, the parallel practice of covert bigotry died a much slower death. Sure, colored sections in Southern stadiums were eliminated, but that didn't keep people from referring to half the dark skinned Latinos that entered baseball in those years as Chico — literally "boy." Rico Carty was known as the Beeg Boy, partly because that's the way he referred to himself and partly because recording the moniker in that semi-illiterate manner was cuter and more endearing.[12] After having some "soul sisters" pointed out to him by a white teammate on the team bus, African-American infielder Leon McFadden wondered aloud, "Why do I have to have any special interest in the black girl? And why can't he be just as interested in the black girl? And why can't I be interested in a white girl?"[13]

2. Aaron's team was transplanted to Atlanta, which was about as close to the

racism battle's front lines as one could get without being on the business end of a nightstick. The Georgia capital was a paradoxical town in those days: at once the headquarters of Martin Luther King's Southern Christian Leadership Conference and the Ku Klux Klan-backed Governor Lester Maddox, a man who'd defiantly and publicly closed a restaurant he owned in preference to serving them coloreds.[14]

> Well, from a financial perspective it beats the heck out of breaking a set of dishes every time a black family shows up for a meal....

Not surprisingly, given the situation and Aaron's native caution, the future home run king's relationship with Atlanta was an ambivalent one. Henry publicly aired his lack of enthusiasm for Georgia prior to the Braves' move, and while a tour of the city assuaged those doubts somewhat,[15] he would always feel compelled to maintain as low a profile as possible given his contractual obligations as a ballplayer. This is not to suggest that Aaron refused to sign autographs or grant interviews with the working press, but he didn't go one step out of his way to initiate such events.[16] Given their limited access to Aaron the man, it is not surprising that Atlantans never really took him to heart — Henry simply didn't expose enough of himself to drive much emotion one way or the other.[17]

The move did have one significant benefit for Aaron from a historic perspective: it moved him from homer-stifling Wisconsin to the Launching Pad,[18] arguably the best pre-Coors Field hitter's paradise in the majors. The equation's latter half is well understood, but the preponderance of Gorman Thomases and Joe Adcocks that inhabited Milwaukee's environs over the years buried the former point under an avalanche of road kills. County Stadium and successor Miller Park are situated within spitting distance of Lake Michigan at roughly the same latitude as Mongolia — a combination that made for plenty of cold, dank evenings early and late in the season. As a result of this phenomenon, Aaron hit 15 percent more homers on the road than at home during his Milwaukee Braves days,[19] but that trend reversed with a vengeance once he came to Atlanta. The high altitude and pervasive warmth allowed Aaron to concentrate upon his power game for the first time, and as a result Henry's best five-year period for circuit clouts began in 1968 — when he was 35 years old.

3. While Aaron was getting his park-aided second wind, Willie Mays literally fell off the cliff, thus clearing some space in the limelight. Baseball fans 100 years from now are probably going to wonder what was so surprising about a decline from 52 homers, 117 RBI and a .317 average at age 35 to 33-104-.288 at 36 and 22-63-.263 at 37, and from an analytical viewpoint they are correct. Still, the idea that the Wonderful Willie could be mortal proved difficult for the public to accept: practically every baseball magazine of the late 1960s ran two or three articles a year on the likelihood of a Mays comeback.[20]

The result of this agonized hand-wringing was that it was 1970 before the average fan got over his fixation with Mays— and by that time Henry Aaron was sneaking up on all of us in a big way.

In the manner of most aging players, Aaron's skill set by the early 1970s was becoming severely restricted. Henry's conversion to dead pull hitting began to trigger Mark McGwire/Ted Williams-style defensive shifts. His basepath speed was history: Aaron led the league in doubles four times during his career and had 11 seasons in the top 10, but by 1972 Henry was down to 10 two-baggers in 449 at-bats. His range and arm declined to left fielder/first baseman grade.[21] Still, 40 homers a year is hefty compensation for a lost step or two, and Aaron's late life power boost came with increased walk totals that more than counterbalanced a modest decline in average (and the key word here is modest: Hammerin' Hank's average between 1969 and 1973 was .299).

As Henry's career numbers and profile within the sport began to reach historic proportions, he became more outspoken with the mainstream press on racial issues (his previous comments on the subject had been largely limited to black-targeted publications such as *Jet*). Like many of his generation Aaron harbored an esteem bordering on awe for Jackie Robinson[22] and he felt compelled to utilize fame's bully pulpit to further Jackie's works. At the same time, though, one gets the impression of a man sensitive to any comment that could even potentially smack of brawn-over-brains typecasting. When told that an unnamed Atlanta official attributed Aaron's late-career performance in part to his being "a smarter hitter than he ever was," the right fielder agreed … then quickly added with emphasis, "I never have been a dumb hitter."[23]

This new stridency in Aaron's tone was greeted with everything from shoulder shrugging surprise to mild distaste by the media and many fans. Few were prepared for the depth of Henry's emotions on the racial issue and fewer yet even cared — baseball, after all, is escapism for most folks and the average fan rarely canvasses the sports pages for a discussion of James Baldwin's works.[24] Still, Aaron's diatribes were relatively few in number … and another story involving baseball's most gargantuan figure loomed larger by the day.

America has always had a curious love affair with flawed personalities. Perhaps it's an offshoot of our egalitarian society, one in which (we believe) even the roughest roughneck can make it to the top if he wants it badly enough. George Patton, Frank Lloyd Wright, John Kennedy: all of these men achieved an icon status sufficient to eclipse contemporaries that were 99 percent as capable, yet each had weaknesses of intellect or character that made them … well, better in retrospect than they were in their time.

At or near the apex of that company stands Babe Ruth.

Henry Aaron is a "natural talent"? Well, what's the appropriate term for a man who set as many single season and career records as anybody, yet habitually called people he'd played alongside for years "kid" because he couldn't remember their names?[25] Yes, the Babe was a legitimate epochal figure in the sport and as wonderful an overgrown six-year-old as anyone would want to meet, but put that all together and the result is a baseball savant. Ruth was a man who acted as if rules were for losers, a conviction that allowed him to perform feats on the diamond that exceeded others' wildest dreams but also turned his extracurricular life into a circus of gluttony, tawdry hangers-on, and irresponsibility. It is good that modern observers view Ruth's profanity, vanity, and cavalier treatment of women in the context of his reformatory school upbringing, but that does not divorce those qualities from his character.

The cruel irony of the Aaron-Ruth duel was that, while the Babe was a man who excelled in the face of crippling limitations, Aaron was one who by and large overcame his on the road to greatness. Leave aside 755 versus 714, or the 2,000-plus additional at-bats it took Aaron to topple the Babe, or the relative playing conditions of their times: which one of these guys would the average Joe want his kids to emulate?

Yet in spite of (or perhaps because of) Ruth's flaws, baseball's reverence and affection for this most human of superhuman men has if anything become more tenacious over the years. Perhaps Ruth reminds us of simpler times, or we perversely admire his ability to indulge to excess with guiltless abandon, or his soft-heartedness towards ill and disadvantaged children still touches us. Whatever the reason, the specter of this man who has been dead for more than half a century maintains a tenacious grip upon the average fan's heartstrings to this day, and those who assault his records do so at their peril. This grip had proven sufficient to nearly crush a decent white guy like Roger Maris ... and he wasn't even skin tone challenged.

As the pivotal 1973 season unfolded, Henry Aaron was dropped into a pressure cooker existence that converted him into as much of a hermit as one can be when thousands pay to watch your daily exploits. Some 930,000 pieces of mail (Dinah Shore was second among non-politicians that year with 60,000), much of it laced with such erudite epithets as "nigger," "jigaboo," and "jungle bunny," gushed in.[26] Unnerving threats of bodily harm to Aaron and his family were daily occurrences; his daughter Gaile was stalked while taking her studies at Nashville's Fisk University.[27] Even the demands of well-wishers became a burden, with Henry being forced to sleep at the Astrodome during a 1973 trip to Houston after fans discovered his room number and knocked on his door for two days straight.[28]

All of this was bad enough, but what proved even more demeaning was the collective yawn with which Atlanta fans greeted Henry's run at immortality. Less that 10,000 people attended the typical Braves game in 1973; only the nearly bankrupt San Diego Padres, losers of 102 games while sporting the league's second worst ERA in a terrific pitcher's park, drew fewer patrons.[29] The Braves were anything but a dull team, even absent Aaron's duel with the Babe — the 1973 club featured the first ever 40-homer threesome (Aaron, Darrell Evans, and Dave Johnson)—yet the local attitude towards their favorite son was best summed up by the number 1,362. That's how many Atlanta fans bought tickets to witness Aaron's 711th home run.[30]

Frustration overtook Henry by the middle of the year. He issued a statement calling America a racist country and suggesting that Atlanta represented the nation's epicenter of hatred and intolerance. After thinking that one over for a few days, Aaron modified his statement to say that the only thing wrong with Atlanta was that it had Georgia sticking out of it.[31] He became more reclusive, rarely leaving his apartment except to go to the ballpark (Henry got to the point that he knew exactly how many times the hotel sign across the street blinked in an hour[32]). To taunt the ever-present pack of reporters, upon leaving the clubhouse Aaron would immediately go inside the foul lines where the press was not allowed—and then walk parallel to the line out to the outfield fence and along the warning track.[33]

In retrospect it is easy to see that Henry's reactions at this point represented the emotional equivalent of Roger Maris' celebrated hair loss. Yes, Aaron was subjected to a level of stress unknown since Jackie Robinson's first few turns around the league, but between the self-enforced isolation and his personal history, Henry came to see everything as a racial slight. The attendance situation is a case in point: in *I Had A Hammer*, Aaron forwards every explanation from local apathy to high ticket prices that excluded blacks from the proceedings for the Braves' poor 1973 attendance. This is all well and good, but one could also point out that:

• By midseason it was clear that absent some catastrophe, Aaron would ultimately break the Babe's record, and thus the immediacy of coming out to see him play was gone. Racism conspiracy theorists might also want to consider that only 23,154 Yankee fans bothered to haul themselves out on a warm Sunday afternoon to see Maris hit his 61st home run for a pennant-winning team.[34]

• If Atlanta blacks couldn't afford tickets they must have been very poor indeed, since the Braves were one of the two NL teams of the day to offer $1 general admission seats.[35]

• While the Braves had plenty of offensive punch, they were also saddled with a starting staff that suffered from injuries (Ron Reed, Gary Gentry), ineffectiveness (Pat Dobson), and inexperience (Ron Schueler, Roric Harrison). The bullpen, bled white by closer Danny Frisella's shoulder problems and the loss of Schueler and Harrison to the rotation, would lose 30 games in which the Braves were tied or leading after seven innings, inspiring General Manager Eddie Robinson to comment that 1973 "was a great seven inning year for us."[36] Add to that a porous defense (especially in the infield) and the result was more runs allowed than any other National League team and a fifth place finish 22½ lengths behind the division-winning Reds.[37]

Same thing with the mail: though Henry had every right to be upset with the number of juvenile and barbaric letters he received, the fact was that the majority of writers were supportive from the start, and that majority became a landslide when Aaron finally went public in May about the hate mail.[38]

Racists and wackos are the human incarnations of cockroaches: they feast on whatever is available, their boldness makes them seem more numerous than they are, and if a nuclear holocaust obliterated every other living thing there would still be a couple of them left to bicker over the remains. Yes, the overt bigots represented a larger minority in 1973 than today and yes, the non-actively racist majority had plenty to learn about human rights and tolerance and yes, nearly two decades later an agonized Rodney King would still be asking, "Can't we all get along together?" The point, though, is this: the vast majority of baseball fans voicing an opinion were supportive of Aaron's challenge, yet even 20 years after the fact Henry chose in his autobiography to focus on the empty portion of that particular glass.

Perhaps that's as far as Aaron's generation could go—expressing outrage at what they and their predecessors endured while demanding a better and more egalitarian future that (they believe) will not emerge in their lifetimes. That they should have been forced to struggle so mightily for that which others received as a birthright is a tragedy; that they could not find it within themselves to acknowledge and build upon what gains were actually achieved is sad.

Aaron's journey to 715 had one final ironic twist—or twist of knife in gut, depending on one's point of view. After finishing the 1973 season one homer short of the mark (what a winter that must have been), the Braves asked Henry to sit out 1974's initial series in Cincinnati so that the magic 714 and 715 could be hit in Atlanta if at all possible.[39] It was a request that had more than a slight tinge of green to it (one can imagine owner Bill Bartholomay salivating over the prospective 50,000-plus crowds) and one that would result in a less than optimal lineup facing a serious contender for the NL crown.

It was also something that Bowie Kuhn in his never-ending defense of "the best interests of baseball" could not condone.

Kuhn strongly suggested that the Braves should use Aaron in at least two out of the three Cincinnati contests,[40] a reasonable request assuming one overlooked the obvious alternative of manipulating the schedule so that Atlanta's initial 1974 games were at home. What followed was a cloudburst of controversy that nearly consumed the event at the center of it all—vitriolic articles suggesting that the Braves were selling out, threatened defiance from manager Eddie Matthews, counterthreats from the commissioner if Aaron was held out.[41]

Thus, Henry Aaron hit his 714th home run in Cincinnati, and Bowie Kuhn was addressing the Wahoo Club in Cleveland when number 715 flew into the Braves' bullpen in Atlanta four days later.

Kuhn portrays the decision to go to Cleveland in his book *Hardball* as a simple scheduling conflict involving a prior commitment,[42] a position that begs the question of

a) whether the Wahoo Club might have been prevailed upon to bump their meeting back a week or so under the circumstances, and
b) whether it had occurred to the commissioner at anytime during the previous eight months that it might be a good idea to build some slack into his early season schedule.

Aaron, for his part, chose to be offended by Kuhn's absence.[43] It was a wound that cut deeply enough for Henry to return the favor some years later by refusing to personally accept an award from Kuhn commemorating his 715th home run. In his place, he sent a representative with a prepared statement that said in part, "I understand that Mr. Kuhn requested that he presented me with the award for the outstanding moment of the 1970s in honor and recognition of the all-time home run record set on the eighth of April, 1974. However, looking back upon that time, I remember that the commissioner did not see the need to attend."[44]

It was a less than gracious response to Bowie's attempt to bury the hatchet and Henry was roasted by the press for it,[45] but how many of us can honestly say we would not have at least considered reacting in the same manner? After the decades of catcalls, threats, and snubs, can anyone be surprised that Aaron was not willing to forgive and forget on command? Exactly how many allowances would anyone make for a man that Marvin Miller one described as someone you didn't have to deal with for very long to be unimpressed by his height?[46]

Such is the legacy of racism, and such are the burdens that Henry Aaron will carry with him for the rest of his life. One hopes that Aaron was able to derive more pleasure from his career than his autobiography suggests — and that those who follow in his footsteps will have the capacity to grow beyond the specters that ultimately bound Henry to his past.

12

The Ten-Cent Beer Fiasco

The miracle of world-class fiascoes is how a slight miscalculation or two can transform a perfectly sound concept into the new Edsel. Take the Susan B. Anthony dollar: while its durability and functionality for vending machine use represented obvious advantages, the designers apparently forgot to consider that (1) nobody really wanted a dollar coin, and (2) they especially didn't want one that could be easily mistaken for a quarter.

There are those who argue that the designated hitter falls into this category as well, but for the real king of baseball bad ideas one has to look no further than 10-Cent Beer Night, the Cleveland Indians' 1974 ode to politically incorrect behavior.

The reader can probably guess where this one is headed already....

The '74 Tribe was in the midst of an upswing by the standards of the post-Rocky Colovito/pre-Jacobs Brothers era: Gaylord and Jim Perry represented a fine if superannuated one-two pitching punch while the offense featured three or four good young bats and Dennis Eckersley was just around the corner. Of course, a 77-85 finish would cause them to trade three of the four young bats for a collection of overrated players and has-beens while the Perrys would be history by the middle of 1975, but such was life in Cleveland baseball's fast lane for a quarter century. Anyway, with new ownership on site after a season in which a big 615,000 fans had filed into the Indians' Mistake by the Lake home, the situation was ripe for some heavy duty promotional effort to counteract what was likely to be a long campaign on the field.

Into this firmament someone in the Indians' front office decided to parrot a concurrent promotion run by the Minnesota Twins and Milwaukee Brewers[1] and offer patrons on selected nights the opportunity to buy their suds for only a dime. Cheap beer and baseball fans: a marriage made in heaven except for two miscalculations and one quirk of fate:

1. The Twins' and Brewers' customers were limited to two discount beers a visit via chips issued when they entered the park, a refinement that the Indians failed to pick up on.[2]

2. The Indians' rivals for the first 10-Cent Beer Night were the Texas Rangers. It was a logical enough choice given the Rangers' traditional futility (though Billy Martin would lead them to an 84-78 record that year) but an unfortunate one given that the two teams had engaged in an ugly brawl just six days earlier in Arlington.[3]

3. Nearly double the expected crowd (some 25,134 in number and thirst) showed up, stretching park security to the limit.[4]

Practically every inning was delayed by one or more youths running around the outfield, including a streaker who eluded security long enough to hop the right center field fence ... and land on the other side directly in front of a police officer.[5] An obviously inebriated woman wandered out onto the field and tried to kiss home plate umpire Larry McCoy.[6] By the seventh inning a mixture of beer and trash along with the occasional cherry bomb was raining down on the Rangers' dugout, prompting Martin to pull his team from the field for approximately 20 minutes until some semblance of order was restored.[7]

Team owner Vincent (Nick) Mileti, VP Ted Bonda, and General Manager Phil Seghi apparently witnessed all of this commotion from the owners' box. Exercising the foresight and judgment that was a hallmark of Indian management in those days, they concluded after the premature seventh inning stretch that everything was under control and thus left early, though Seghi would later say that he was in "constant contact" with the park.[8]

Ironically, in the midst of all of this mayhem, a pretty good game was going on. After falling behind early the Indians spent the latter portion of the night chipping away at the Texas lead, rallying to within two runs of the Rangers after eight innings. Four bottom-of-the-ninth singles tied the score and deposited the winning run at third base with one out,[9] but for reasons that had nothing to do with pitching or defense, that was as close as the Indians were fated to get.

The collective weight of the 65,000 beers served (or the collective loss of brain cells associated with consumption of same) finally overpowered any concept of sportsmanship or fair play. A group of fans took the field and headed for Rangers left fielder Jeff Burroughs, surrounding him and ultimately stealing his cap and glove. The Texas bench mobilized and came to Burroughs' aid, some understandably but unfortunately carrying bats. More fans left the grandstands, the Indian players came to the Rangers' aid, and it just escalated from there.[10]

Numerous fist fights broke out on the field, with crew chief Nestor Chylak suffering a cut on his forearm as a result of one and Texas outfielder Tom Grieve having his thumb jammed in another. Cleveland reliever Tom Hilgendorf was brained by a folding chair thrown out of the stands; fortunately, he escaped with bruises only. The Rangers and Indians were more or less forced to fight their way off the field, with Cleveland outfielder Alex Johnson clearing away several rowdies with an imposing bull rush and throw process (one would think given Alex's past that even these intelligence-starved people would have known better).[11]

After another 20 minute interlude to clear the field and get things back on the reasonably straight and something approaching narrow, Chylak had apparently had everything he was going to take that particular night. Thus, when a new fight broke out around the Texas dugout between fans and the Ranger players, the future Hall of Fame umpire barely drew a breath before forfeiting the game to Texas.[12]

In the following day's news conference Bonda and Seghi did exactly what the authors of such a debacle could be expected to do—they blamed everybody in sight for the "incident." According to them, the Rangers' bat wielding march across the field instigated the debacle. Chylak was faulted for forfeiting the game too quickly, with the Indian brain trust going to the extent of asking AL President Lee MacPhail to overturn his decision.[13] The Tribe's high command suggested that the situation in the park was thoroughly under control—an interesting observation given chief of stadium security Frank Ferrone's comment that the fans "were drunk all over the place. We would have needed 25,000 cops to handle it."[14] They even said that they intended to go on with three future Beer Nights as long as MacPhail did not overrule them.[15]

The Yiddish had a term for such behavior that has made its way into the English language—chutzpah. The 1974 Indians may not have been pennant contenders, but in the world of chutzpah their management were grand high llamas.

Well, it had seemed like a good idea at the time....

13

The End of the
Fireballer Epoch

Remember CB radios?

The primeval cell phone, the CB (citizen's band) radio was a transmitter-receiver that allowed communication with others within a 25 mile or so range. Previously the domain of police departments and long-haul truckers, the CB's emergency, information, and entertainment value made it for a time the "in" thing to equip one's mid-1970s Buick LeSabre with. Yet despite these advantages, CBs were not fated to become a ubiquitous feature of the American automobile. As practical as they were, people just didn't break down on highways in the middle of nowhere very often, and other than that all they offered was endless chatter about smokeys (police), choke 'n' pukes (diners), and seat covers (girls). The radios remain a law enforcement and transportation industry mainstay, but in popular circles the CB has become what $3,000 "professional" style stoves will be in due course.

Such was the fate of Sandy Koufax's progeny, the pure power pitcher. The unquestioned kings of the mid to late 1960s hill, this breed of 250-plus inning Supermen dominated the baseball landscape with an intimidating array of heaters and hard breaking stuff. Yet by 1975 the fireballer ranks had been whittled down to the occasional Nolan Ryan or J.R. Richard, while potential successors struggled to achieve the breaks that had once been as plentiful as dimpled chads on a Florida ballot.

A simple comparison dramatizes the changeover. The 1969 National League ERA leader board featured Juan Marichal, Steve Carlton, Bob Gibson, Tom Seaver, and Jerry Koosman — all power pitchers with the possible exception of Marichal, who threw every pitch known to modern man. Nine years later, the top six were Craig Swan, Steve Rogers, Pete Vuckovich, Bob Knepper, Joe Niekro, and Burt Hooton — one guy who threw pretty hard (Rogers), two others that relied on gimmick pitches (Hooton and Niekro), and three soft tossers.[1]

While the quest for arms capable of propelling baseballs through brick walls predates the era when Spalding was a pitcher rather than a glove, the convergence of a series of events conspired to turn the 1960s into power pitching's High Noon:

1. The spate of new stadiums that came into existence between 1958 and 1968 proved to be the types of places where fly balls go to die. Candlestick Park represented San Francisco's contribution to the Practical Joke Hall of Fame. The Astrodome featured 16-foot-high fences and the deepest power alleys in the majors.[2] Dodger Stadium was built in a natural hollow, Washington's D.C. Stadium in a swamp, and the Oakland Coliseum was counter-sunk into the ground within a mile of San Francisco Bay; heavy night air made all three especially poor offensive parks under the lights. The design of Shea Stadium's grandstand mandated unusually deep fences between the power alleys and the foul lines (roughly 370' within 30' of each foul pole),[3] while the Angels' Anaheim pad proved a pitcher's pal despite extensive pre-construction tests designed to assure a neutral offensive environment.[4]

2. Baseball's front line pitching ranks underwent a mass generational purge. Under normal circumstances baseball is a seamless sport: most eras will include roughly as many hotshot youngsters as wise old heads. For example, a list of 1970s pitchers who made a mark in the 1980s would include Nolan Ryan, Tom Seaver, Don Sutton, Steve Carlton, Phil Niekro, Ron Guidry, Charlie Hough, Bert Blyleven, Frank Tanana, Steve Rogers, Bob Forsch and probably a half dozen others.

   The JFK years, though, aren't like that: Don Drysdale and Jim Bunning are the only guys who truly span the era. Warren Spahn had one good post-1962 season left in him before succumbing to age. Whitey Ford posted a Cy-Young-type season and another decent one before the league caught on to his various mud and scuff balls. Early Wynn needed six tries to notch his 300th victory before retiring in 1963. Lew Burdette, Billy Pierce, Jack Sanford, Dick Donovan, Frank Lary ... some would poke along for awhile as middle relievers or spot starters, but by the mid-'60s they were pretty much consigned to history.

   Thus, the early 1960s represented an ideal time to come of age with a golden arm. Contemporary observers wonder if the 22-year-old (as of 2001) Rick Ankiel has been rushed into pressure situations, but Steve Barber went from leading the Alabama-Florida League in walks at 20 (1959) to being a contending team's ace at 22.[5] Gary Peters surrendered more than a hit an inning while going 33-29 with a pedestrian 3.86 ERA in his final three minor league seasons; in his first big league campaign Peters would work 243 innings and win the Rookie of the Year Award for the second place White Sox.[6] Dean Chance (a Bo Belinsky-class knight errant but forgiven for it because he walked the talk on the mound[7]) was a rotation starter at 21 and the youngest ever Cy Young recipient at 23.

3. Maury Wills and Luis Aparicio notwithstanding, baseball strategy by the new decade's dawning suffered from an advanced case of inertia. That's not surprising when one thinks about it: the rules had basically remained inviolate since the spitball's 1920 banishment while 12 of the 16 teams played in venues inhabited when Harding was president. Give Forrest Gump 40 years to adjust to a static set of circumstances and it's a pretty safe guess that he'd ultimately figure out the following formula: (a) little guy slaps ball into opposite field for single, then stands on base until (b) big guy hits ball over fence.

That's really all there was to it. Critics decry baseball's current offensive mono-dimensionality, but imagine what the 2001 National League season would have been like with roughly the same number of hits and walks but 20 percent fewer doubles and two-thirds as many steals.

Envisioning such a state of affairs will provide a clear image of the 1961 NL season.[8]

With fan interest in this battle of who has the best big guy/little guy combination stagnating, baseball's lords decided to tinker with the pitcher-batter balance that had driven the game for the previous four decades. The change they devised was a minor thing really—a simple reversal of a 1950 rule whose impact had been underwhelming.[9]

And thus the strike zone was expanded to encompass everything from the top of the batter's shoulders down to the bottom of his knees.

Combine these circumstances and ... well, it shouldn't take twenty guesses to figure out who will come out on top.

A veritable tidal wave of fireballers, many of whom had struggled mightily in the pre-1962 era, quickly came to the forefront. Bob Gibson, in his first season as a rotation starter (1961), led the NL in free passes—not surprising for a guy that practically threw himself off the mound at the batter. By 1968 Gibson, flailing follow-through and all, was down to 62 walks in 304 innings ... and was BOB GIBSON. Jim Maloney previous to 1962 sported an 8-13 career record with a 4.47 ERA due largely to the 96 walks he'd yielded in 158 innings. Under the 1963 conditions the 23-year-old Maloney magically matured, walking 88 men in 250 frames while winning 23 games with a 2.77 ERA.[10] Al Downing, Sam McDowell, a kid named Koufax—these were the type of men that reshaped the game in those years.

Mounds, theoretically 15 inches in height but practically impossible to measure,[11] grew into mountaintops to accommodate maximum effort motions such as Marichal's over-the-head leg kick. Workloads rose in accordance with the youth and apparent strength of these guys: prior to 1962, no one had worked as many as 300 innings in eight years, while between 1963 and 1966 that milestone would be surmounted eight times. The brushback pitch gained ferocity, with hit batsmen rising to levels (roughly one HBP for every two games played in 1968[12]) unseen in nearly a half century.

By decade's end virtually every rotation featured at least a couple of guys whose idea of finesse was setting up a 92 MPH fastball with an 87 MPH curve. Even with Koufax long gone and Drysdale on his last legs, the roster of 1969 National League aces (as measured by most starts) reads like a quasi-Cooperstown reunion. Gibson, Gaylord Perry, Ferguson Jenkins, Phil Niekro, and Tom Seaver were in their prime as staff leaders, while backing them were people like Marichal and Don Sutton, who qualify as number two guys despite pitching nearly 300 innings apiece. All of the above except Niekro were hard throwers, as were the majority of the non-Hall-of-Fame-but-plenty-good aces surrounding them, like:

- Bob Veale,
- Larry Dierker (with four good pitches and 55 wins under his belt despite military obligations, the most similar pitcher in baseball history to the then 23-year-old Dierker was Don Drysdale[13]), and
- Current Anaheim Angels' General Manager Bill Stoneman, whose 54-85 career record and 4.08 ERA may not look like much, but (a) he spent his entire career working in good hitters' parks, (b) his best seasons were spent with an expansion team, and (c) the man did throw two no-hitters.

Veale, though never at the top of the pack due to chronic back and elbow problems, was in many ways the generation's prototype. A huge man whose poor eyesight made his hard fastball and sharp breaking stuff even more terrifying,[14] the Pirate lefty was Ryne Duren in Technicolor less the predilection for booze. Like most guys with big-time heat, Veale progressed quickly through the Bucs farm system until he was one step from the top at 24: like many of his kin, he stalled there due to a lack of control that became near terminal when he blew his top.[15] By 1962 he was the ultimate enigma, at once:

- Too tantalizing to ignore (averaging ten strikeouts for every nine innings pitched over his minor league career),
- Too wild to use at a key point in the game (the K's came with nearly six walks per game),
- Too inefficient to work deep into the game as a starter, and
- Too old (27) to leave stewing on the farm indefinitely.

A more talent-laden organization might have dealt such a denizen of Prospect Hell away on general principles, but the Pirates' rotation by 1963 was basically Bob Friend and anybody with a pulse. With opportunity at his fingertips and the winds of change at his back, Veale's career gained traction: despite wearing the NL walk crown four times, Veale won 80 games between 1964 and 1968 while posting a 2.83 ERA and heading the list of those who could win 20, if only....[16]

Yet within two years this all-star-in-waiting was purged from the Pittsburgh rotation as he lost eight of ten down the stretch en route to a 10-16 record with a 3.92 ERA. On the face of it, Veale's decline is *de rigueur* for a 35-year-old guy with shoulder problems that was transplanted from pitching friendly Forbes Field to the more neutral Three Rivers Stadium. However, Veale simply represented the vanguard of what would prove to be baseball's equivalent of a lemming run.

Drysdale opted for retirement rather than shoulder surgery at 33. Marichal (31) would post a sub-.500 record after 1969 with an above-league average ERA. Maloney's 29-year-old wing and Achilles tendons had a mere 37 innings left in them. The 28-year-old Luis Tiant would require three years of rest and therapy to over-

The prototypical 1960s flamethrower, Bob Veale had somewhat suspect control that became even more threatening to hitters on hot days, when the big right-hander would forever be cleaning his Coke-bottle-bottom glasses trying to see the plate. (*National Baseball Hall of Fame Library, Cooperstown, NY*)

come a dead arm resulting from a May 1970 stress fracture of his rib cage before reemerging as the cigar smoking El Tiante who won on guile as much as stuff.[17] These losses among the one-time elite were bad enough, but even more devastating were the number of potentially fine careers that just never happened.

Larry Dierker began suffering from a Whitman's Sampler of arm ailments — shoulder pain starting in 1970, elbow problems that cost him half of the next season and a calcium deposit in his hand thereafter. The net result of all this pain was a future that would hold 3½ quality seasons and play out by Dierker's 30th birthday. Blue Moon Odom looked like a potential ace — despite suspect control Odom was a two-time All Star by the age of 24[18] — but as a result of a balky elbow was reduced to finesse pitching by his 25th birthday. He was out of the majors at 31. Bill Singer, known as the Singer Throwing Machine (a made-for-TV nickname if ever there was one), proved to be pitching's answer to Bob Horner — assembled with too many factory seconds body parts. The Bill Singer who won 20 in 1969 already sported three arm surgery scars, two of which were incurred while he was in the minors.[19] He would contract hepatitis in 1970, then be limited by shoulder problems and finger surgery to a 16-33 record over the next two campaigns. After winning 20 in 315 innings for the 1973 Angels, a ruptured disc permanently took the zip from Singer's heater,[20] forcing him from the scene within three years.

In essence, it was a dinosaur-like mass extinction: ruling the earth one minute, fossilized fodder for Steven Spielberg movies the next. One can, of course, make too much of this — Ferguson Jenkins and Steve Carlton turned out OK working under the same conditions — and it is possible that baseball's modern quest for the 32 start/190 inning nirvana represents such an overreaction. Still, the felling of so many mighty oaks in such a short period demands an explanation, and while one can never know for sure several common threads run through the dearly departed's biographies:

1. *Heavy workloads.* Ever notice how old fads are often revived the moment those who remember what it was really like the last time they were in the vogue pass from the scene? Junk bonds are a good example: a key contributor to the 1929 stock market crash, these high yielding but risky instruments made a comeback in the early 1980s — when those who actually remembered the Depression had passed into retirement. The Soviet Union began crumbling the moment those who lived through the Bolshevik Revolution keeled over, while today's fast track drug approval proponents are too young to remember what a Thalidomide baby looked like.

    Starter workloads have progressively declined as staffs first expanded in the 1890s in response to the 154 game schedule, then adapted to the lively ball (outmoding the Iron Man McGinnity throw-BP-style-pitches-until-someone-gets-on-base philosophy) and finally developed specialized roles. Occasionally, though, a Walter Johnson or Lefty Grove would emerge and warp reality through their unique ability to work oodles of high quality innings without collapse. If Johnson can work 350 innings without harm, why can't my Harry Coveleski or Jim Bagby do the same? Well, the answer is that they can ... for a few years. Bagby, for instance, would notch only 21 big league victories after working 339 innings and winning 31 in 1920. Coveleski, who at his peak was roughly as good as his Hall of Fame brother, was basically finished at 30 after serving up three consecutive 300-plus frame seasons.[21]

    By the time Koufax and Drysdale began their run of seven 300-inning campaigns in five years (1962-66) and captured the baseball world's imagination, the last such ironman phenom's (Bob Feller's) salad days were 15 years in the past. So too were memories of such contemporaries as Prince Hal Newhouser (chronic shoulder problems reduced him to spot starter status at 29[22]), the intimidating sidearmer Ewell Blackwell (tossed 23 complete games at 25 but only three after his 29th birthday), and Bobby Thomson's victim Ralph Branca.

2. *The slider.* The split-fingered fastball of the 1960s (Ted Williams once termed it the best pitch in baseball[23]), the so-called nickel curve is a cross between a fastball and a hook. Intended to be hit rather than missed, the slider's value lies in a late downward break which ideally results in either cue shots off the end of the bat or jam jobs.[24]

   In many ways the slider seems like an ideal choice for a young flame-thrower — easy to learn, controllable, and the harder it's thrown the more the ball breaks. Unfortunately, the slider's mechanics are an engineering nightmare, requiring an off-balance grip as well as a relatively stiff wrist action at release that Cookie Lavagetto likened to throwing a football.[25] Such a motion places a not insignificant stress on the elbow as well as any nearby associated tendons; those who remain in doubt are invited to try it a few times themselves.

   Like the splitter, the slider's effect on its practitioners has been the source of intense Hot Stove debate for years. The pitch's reputation was that of an arm shredder before George Blaeholder became the first to throw it regularly in the 1920s[26]; forty years later sliders were being promoted by such luminaries as Early Wynn as a relatively low impact offering.[27]

   OK, so Wynn tossed sliders until he was 43 and barely able to make it to the mound under his own power, but (a) Blaeholder was pretty much history at 30; (b) George Uhle, a fine contemporary of Blaeholder's who threw nickel curves until he was 37 admitted in later years to pitching in constant pain[28]; and (c) at least three of the late '60s slider throwers listed above had bone chips removed from their elbows at one time or another. None returned as anything more than a shadow of their previous selves. Is it enough evidence to convince a skeptic of the slider's potential danger? Hardly ... but by the late '70s the Mets organization for one was officially discouraging its use.[29]

3. *The historic distrust of pitchers for the medical profession.* From the third degree burns Dale Alexander received while using an early diathermy machine[30] to the vitamin-shot-induced abscess that knocked Mickey Mantle out of the 1961 World Series,[31] the supposed benefits of modern medicine were a mixed blessing to players for many years. Trainers and team doctors often provided perfunctory care at best[32] while a lack of consensus among even the most learned on how to treat basic maladies often drove players— especially pitchers with their fickle wings— into the world of voodoo medicine. Muscle warming liniments such as Heet and Atomic Balm are good examples: 1960s era arms were slathered with these treatments until the skin literally peeled off (a practice that we now know aggravates swelling and damage to joints).[33]

   Between the limited medical expertise and this penchant for home remedies, pain was seen as coming with the territory, while rehabilitation was along the lines of "if it doesn't hold up now, it never will." Rick Wise, for example, lost most of the 1974 season to tendonitis contracted during an April 13 nine-inning effort (the game was played in deference to NBC despite sleet and mid-30s temperatures[34]) and a broken finger. The next season, Wise worked 255 innings and hurled 17 complete games ... ... only to have his arm go sour again in 1977.

Under such conditions it's easy to understand why so many 1960s wun-

derkinds prematurely departed the scene — but what is striking at first glance is the paucity of similarly hot arms stepping forward to take their place. The 1965 season saw the debut of six pitchers (Steve Carlton, Ferguson Jenkins, Tug McGraw, John Hiller, Rudy May, and Skip Lockwood) who would work over 1,000 major league innings while striking out six or more men per nine innings pitched.[35] Seven years later Goose Gossage would be the only member of his 54-man freshman class to achieve that milestone, yet the Goose's contemporaries were anything but a bunch of wimps. Steve Busby was in that group: armed with a classic power pitcher repertoire of fastball, slider, and curve,[36] Busby walked 278 men in his first three seasons as a starter — but two of his seven shutouts were no-hitters. Mac Scarce's "hopping" fastball and nasty slider whiffed 98 men in 69 minor league innings as he jumped from Florida State University to the majors within a year and a half.[37] Elias Sosa was a Juan Marichal clone complete with high leg kick, grab bag of high velocity pitches, and a willingness to let his fastball sail in high and tight on occasion.[38]

Despite having an outstanding rising fastball, Jim Bibby was 28 before he could get himself established as a big league starter, needed several years to recover from a Herculean workload in pursuit of a pennant that couldn't be won, and was basically finished at 35 courtesy of a torn rotator cuff. His odyssey through the majors was symbolic of the hurdles power pitchers faced in the new era. (*National Baseball Hall of Fame Library, Cooperstown, NY*)

Ron Schueler, Tom Walker, Jim Bibby, Lynn McGlothen — all of these guys initially threw just as hard as their storied predecessors.

Yet while some would have their moments, only one other than Gossage was fated to record as many as 100 wins or last much past age 30. All except Busby (who broke down early) would be vagabonds: Sosa toiled for eight major league teams over his 12 year career, McGlothen six, and Walker five in six seasons (the Expos twice). Only Sosa and Bibby among the non-Geese were fated to see the postseason, and Elias was a fringe player when he hit paydirt.

What the heck happened?

In part, the game's mechanical requirements simply changed. The strike zone was restored to its pre-1963 armpit to top of knees range. The mound was reduced to 10 inches in height and, equally importantly, a mechanism was put in place to assure compliance. Pitching coaches urged their charges to truncate their motions in response to the running game's rebirth, ultimately dooming the classic pinwheeling wind-up as well.

Suddenly, a young power pitcher attempting to establish himself was confronted with a decreased margin for error around the plate as well as less leverage coming off the mound to make fastballs hop and sliders break. Strikeout rates for even the most powerful youngsters were a shadow of those recorded a few years prior: Busby, who threw as hard as anybody of his day, never struck out as many as 200 men in a season though his workload pushed 300 innings at his peak. Ross Grimsley, remembered nowadays as a puffball throwing flake, whiffed 162 men in 188 innings at Indianapolis (1970) and inspired umpire Chris Pelekoudas to comment that he "was throwing as hard as any lefthander since Sandy Koufax"[39] after a 1972 outing. Yet Grimsley would fan as many as 100 men only once in his big league career and averaged a mere 3.3 whiffs per nine innings pitched.

Simultaneously, the bullpen's heightened profile within the game made it an increasingly serious competitor for young arms — especially those that teams couldn't quite decide what to do with. Jim Kern's heater, curve and palm ball earned him the American Association's 1974 Pitcher of the Year honors (17-7, 2.52 ERAs, 202 strikeouts in 189 innings)[40] and should have been just the ticket for a Cleveland rotation featuring the Perry boys and a legion of guys collecting their last paychecks. Kern, though, wore a scruffy looking beard, was unconventional at a minimum (his nickname was The Emu[41]) and had an off-again on-again romance with the strike zone — those 202 K's came with 104 walks and 17 wild pitches. Thus, when Kern did not immediately excel in a starting role the Indians quickly shuttled him off to the bullpen; he would later comment that "they decided I wasn't smart enough to throw anything but fastballs."[42] While the conversion's results were impressive (Kern would be named to three All-Star teams and win the 1979 Rolaids Relief Award[43]) one wonders how far a man whose fastball was once compared favorably to Nolan Ryan's[44] could have gone had he been given a full shot at a starting role.

These changing winds of fortune along with the arm problems that young flamethrowers remained unduly susceptible to (Busby's career went AWOL after pitching a complete game on a cold April night when his arm didn't feel right[45]) ultimately resulted in something approaching a pattern of covert discrimination. The best example of this phenomenon is Jim Bibby, a huge righthander whose rising fastball would more than occasionally lose its way en route to the strike zone. As the song goes, Bibby was one of those guys who if it weren't for bad luck would have had no luck at all. He was initially signed in 1965 as a very raw 20-year-old by a Mets organization that was on the cusp of overflowing with hard-throwing talent. Almost immediately sent to Vietnam for two years, Bibby lost a third minor league season to back surgery at the time he was ready to emerge.[46] Off a so-so recovery campaign, he was sent as part of an eight-player cat and dog trade to another organization (St. Louis) that didn't need him any more than the Mets had.

Bibby was 28 before he got a chance to establish himself in the bigs, took several years to recover from a 264-inning workload he shouldered in pursuit of a divisional title that couldn't be won, and tore his rotator cuff one year after re-establishing himself as a full-time starter. His 111-101 career record and 3.76 ERA fairly represent how well he pitched when the heebie-jeebies or whatever weren't getting the best of him: a 1974 *Sporting News* piece by Randy Galloway stated that "every starting assignment for Bibby is an adventure, a mystery. Maybe you get a no-hitter, and again, maybe he doesn't last the first inning."[47]

Yet before we write Bibby off as yet another guy who couldn't harness his talent, consider the following comparison of his final minor league season (1972) to that of a man 11 years earlier:

	G	IP	H	BB	K	W	L	ERA
Bibby	27	195	155	76	208	13	9	3.09
Mr. X	28	201	169	92	208	14	11	2.55

The variance in runs allowed between Bibby and Mr. X is primarily due to the time and place that they pitched in — both were among the league leaders in ERA during their respective seasons. The two were also similar — one might say eerily similar — in other ways as well:

- Both were huge men — Bibby measured in at 6'5" and 235, Mr. X at 6'6" and 220.
- Bibby was born on October 29, Mr. X on October 28.
- Both were prototypical power pitchers, sporting an explosive fastball, curve, and slider. Neither man would have known what a change-up was if one bit them on the butt.
- Both were destined to bear the burden of talent unfulfilled for the major-

ity of their careers, each being labeled as a guy who could win 20 if he could just get over some ill-defined hurdle.

- Each would battle control problems throughout his career, though their size and relative wildness would give them the "intimidating" tag. Bibby would walk 3.8 men per nine innings pitched, Mr. X 4.0.
- Both would be plagued by back problems for most of their careers.
- Both spent their best seasons pitching for the same team.
- Mr. X would post his last good season at 34 and retire four years later; Bibby would enjoy his final big year at 35 and retire four years later.[48]

Yet when their big league careers are viewed in the encyclopedias, Bibby looks like a journeyman type while Mr. X appears to be in the Jose Rijo/Mario Soto class of guys that something just "happened" to:

	G	IP	H	BB	K	W	L	ERA
Bibby	340	1723	1565	723	1079	111	101	3.76
Mr. X	397	1925	1684	858	1703	120	95	3.08

And that's a fair approximation of how they were appraised in their day. Mr. X, though a moderate disappointment in many eyes, was the ace of his staff for five seasons and made two All-Star appearances, while Bibby spent only 2½ of his 12 seasons as a dedicated starter.

Yet for all of that, the difference between the two is primarily one of timing and circumstance. Bibby struck out fewer men than Mr. X because he worked in an era that was less conducive to big time strikeout totals, while his inferior won-loss record is primarily a factor of the teams he toiled for. Each allowed a nearly identical number of baserunners per inning, but Mr. X (a lefty) spent virtually his entire career in a home park that was among the toughest ever for a right-handed power hitter. Bibby on the other hand, plyed his trade for the most part in average venues.

Mr. X, for those who have not figured it out yet, is Bob Veale.

Could Bibby have had as impressive a career as Veale if the two had swapped places in the time-space continuum? From a durability standpoint perhaps not — everything about Bibby's career screamed, "Work this man over 210 innings and his arm is going to go south for the winter." However, if the question is whether Bibby could have been as effective when he did pitch, or could have posted as solid a set of ERAs, or struck out as many men per inning pitched given a couple more inches at the top of the zone to play with….

Well, let's just say that one would have to like his chances.

It was the fate of Jim Bibby and his heat-packing contemporaries to be the right men trapped in the wrong era. These pitching Adonises would to their (and everybody else's) astonishment be relegated to spectator status

while center stage held a potpourri of geezers, bionic wonders, and 5'11"
breaking ball pitchers that a generation before would have been career
AAAers. With the exception of an occasional Randy Johnson, today's pure
power pitcher is basically a bullpen dweller, and while their contributions in
that role are significant, they can be excused an occasional twinge of longing
for the days when their forefathers were the undisputed kings of the hill.

14

Steve Carlton's
Sounds of Silence

In any field of endeavor there are those who know how to "play the game" (i.e. say the "right" things, act the "right" way, drink the correct brand of booze) and those who don't. The so-called losers in this peculiar competition run the gamut from "in" crowd wannabes to iconoclasts who do things differently for the sake of being different. The most mystifying subset of this group from society's viewpoint, however, are those who refuse to acknowledge that a game is being played — the kind of person who wouldn't invite the boss over for dinner when a promotion was on the line because the guy is a bore.

Steve Carlton was such a person.

Carlton was a man who believed that the mental and physical aspects of pitching were just as important as the mechanical ones. That's not a concept that 1,000 other pitchers haven't voiced in varying degrees of seriousness, but Lefty really walked the talk. His physical regimen was strenuous in the extreme: he lifted weights at a time when such training was discouraged, was a martial arts devotee, and strengthened his pitching arm by using it to dig to the bottom of a barrel of rice.[1] On the intellectual side, Carlton was what would best be described as a disciple of the power of positive thinking. He was into metaphysics, meditation, and spirituality.[2] Tim McCarver said that his battery mate's pregame ritual included visualizing the black on each side of the plate as "fertile lanes" into which the ball was to be propelled.[3]

Given that discussions of Eastern philosophy and calisthenics are not what articles about 3-2 ballgames are typically made of, reporters would normally have relegated Lefty to the category of "kook good for a feature article on a slow news day." At a certain talent level, however, such considerations as whether a guy is a good interview or not fly out the window for even the most battle-hardened sportswriter — and Carlton exceeded that hurdle rate by as much as anybody of his era.

Armed with three quality power pitches (the fastball and curve yielded the majority of his outs initially, with a hard, biting slider becoming more prominent as the years progressed), Lefty generated comparisons to Sandy Koufax and was more than capable of justifying them at his best. His 1972 season, given the circumstances under which he labored, is among the most dominant ever: those who might doubt the veracity of such a statement are asked to consider Philadelphia's most-used lineup from that season:

		Age	G	AB	R	H	2B	3B	HR	RBI	AVG	OBP	SLG
C	John Bateman	31	82	252	10	56	9	0	3	17	.222	.246	.294
1B	Tom Hutton	26	134	381	40	99	16	2	4	38	.260	.354	.344
2B	Denny Doyle	28	123	442	33	110	14	2	1	26	.249	.295	.296
3B	Don Money	25	152	536	54	119	16	2	15	52	.222	.278	.343
SS	Larry Bowa	26	152	579	67	145	11	13	1	31	.250	.291	.320
LF	Greg Luzinski	21	150	563	66	158	33	5	18	68	.281	.332	.453
CF	Willie Montanez	24	147	531	60	131	39	3	13	64	.247	.320	.405
RF	Bill Robinson	29	82	188	19	45	9	1	8	21	.239	.258	.426

The Phillies were an organization in transition, one so focused on prepping for the future (they had Bob Boone, Andre Thornton, Jim Essian, and a fellow named Schmidt in the minors at that time) that they were throwing anybody who fit the uniform out there in the interim. The situation is even worse than it looks: in the time-honored tradition of installing fast middle infielders at the top of the lineup, manager Frank Lucchesi used Doyle and Bowa in the 1-2 spots for most of the season, thus robbing this offense of whatever spark it might have had. The outfield is horrible defensively with two stationary bodies bookending Montanez, a guy playing center because there wasn't anybody else on the roster even vaguely capable of doing so (the Phillies would be forced to deal away Oscar Gamble to remedy this problem over the winter).

The guys with gloves generally can't hit — the incredibly versatile Don Money is the exception to that rule, but 1972 was by far and away the worst of his career offensively. The guys with bats can't field. A couple of people can't do either. The team is slow, doesn't have enough pop to blow the top off a bottle of Budweiser, and is loaded with strikeout lions.

If that's possible, the pitching staff is even worse off. Remove Carlton from the mound corps and the Phillies' team ERA would have been more than four-tenths of a run higher than any other NL team save the Braves. The team's number two and number three starters were 25 and 24 respectively, which would seem like a reasonable basis for optimism until one realizes that both men would depart the majors before their 29th birthday. Mac Scarce, a hard-throwing young lefty whose professional resume prior to 1972 consisted of 28 Carolina League innings (and who would, in the manner of all too many such pitchers, throw his arm out by his 25th birthday), was the team's nominal closer ... he saved a big four games.[4] The guy amongst the non-Carltons with the best future in front of him was probably the 32-year-old Woodie Fryman, who would post a 70-78 record over the remainder of his career.

Yet somehow amidst this Hiroshima of a roster Carlton fashioned 27 victories for a team that had a .269 winning percentage with others on the mound; no man in the modern era has ever won a greater percentage of his team's games than Lefty's 45.8 percent that season. He set a Phillies record by running off 15 consecutive wins between June 7 and August 17 — the team went 10-38 in the other games during that span.[5] To assure as many of those hard-fought victories as possible, Carlton completed 30 of his 41 starts, averaging an incredible 8.44 innings per outing. Despite the questionable defense and fatiguing workload, Carlton led the NL with a 1.97 ERA while striking out 61 more men than anybody in the league and walking just over two batters for every nine innings pitched.

Given that, Carlton was one of the stories of the 1972 season from both an athletic and man against the odds point of view, and a reporter could write just so much about Charlie Finley's A's before requiring detoxification.

A veritable torrent of articles came out profiling the Phillies lefthander. Most featured discussions of Lefty's theories regarding conditioning and mental preparedness because that's what Carlton wanted to talk about, but many also went to incredible lengths to humanize him. Stories about Steve as a barefoot kid catching rattlesnakes in the Everglades made the rounds, along with his ability to hit birds with rocks[6] and his relatively late conversion to baseball (he was 12 before entering Little League for the first time).[7] Carlton would answer such questions in a not unfriendly but perfunctory manner ("If you could throw at all you were a winner in Little League" was his response to a query regarding his youthful successes[8]) and thus others would frequently be called upon to fill in the blanks.

It was the kind of arrangement that can work when a player is doing well, but circumstances would change as 1972's Superman act had less-than-savory aftereffects on Carlton's productivity. The 346 innings proved to be too much: Lefty lost enough velocity and command during his encore 1973 season to propel him to the NL loss lead while his ERA rose by nearly two runs per game. He inadvertently began tipping his pitches, bringing his glove back further when winding up to throw a breaking pitch than for a fastball.[9] It would be three years before Carlton would completely get his act back together, and during that time span reporters started asking different, more probing questions. People wanted to know if Steve's arm was hurting him, why his velocity was off, what had happened to the command of his devastating but tricky-to-control nickel curve....

... And the man simply chose not to answer for the most part.

Carlton was really serious about all of this stuff regarding attitude. To him, negativism was the biggest obstacle to future success, and talking about failure was the same as expressing negativism. The star's curse of having to answer the same questions over and over proved intolerable: as Steve once commented, "I would think a man coming to interview an athlete who's had as much ink as I've had in the past year would do his homework. Guys are wasting my time and theirs asking me where I was born, am I married, what's my best pitch, stuff that's available in the press guide."[10] Finally, Lefty had a stubborn streak: his unwillingness to bend in negotiations with the equally cantankerous Gussie Busch ("I don't give a damm if Carlton never pitches another baseball for the Cardinals," Busch said during Steve's 1970 holdout[11]) had greased the skids for his ultimate banishment from St. Louis.[12]

Reporters, however, are a creative breed, and if the horse's mouth wasn't emitting anything worth printing there was always a stable boy around that would. A cottage industry in Carlton observations sprung up among pitching coaches, teammates, and unnamed sources in the Phillies front office — one might even suggest that Philadelphia's 1976 acquisition of McCarver was as much to give Lefty a mouthpiece as a think-mate. Given the myriad axes that such a mixed crew had to grind, an estrangement between the tall left-hander and the Fourth Estate was inevitable, and after a couple of suspect 1978 articles Carlton broke contact completely. He would emerge from his self-proclaimed exile only after his 1986 release from the team, for which he had won 241 games and four Cy Young Awards.

Yet for all of that, Lefty's vow of silence came to be grudgingly accepted if not modestly admired by those who followed the Phillies. OK, so maybe they didn't really have a choice, but reporters for the most part came to recognize that the man's public reserve wasn't a sheer act of defiance à la George Hendrick. Carlton lived in a condominium complex near Philadelphia's Rittenhouse Square for a decade, yet many of his neighbors were skeptical that he had ever been amongst them.[13] His relationship with teammates was cordial yet distant: when Lefty won his 300th game he poured a glass of champagne for every player, said "All right, everybody. Let's drink up," then retired in solitude to the trainer's room.[14] Even after 14 seasons with the Phillies organization, ex-manager/GM Dallas Green doubted that Carlton had the rapport with anybody in the front office to tell them that he was retiring. If push came to shove, "He'll go to (manager) Paul Owens and say, 'Pope, I'm hanging it up.'"[15]

Steve Carlton's rift with the press was in many ways a historic chasm, a milestone in the transformation of sports reporting from the accurate recording of events to an arcane art rife with third person innuendo and amateur psychology. That the man at the eye of this particular hurricane cared little about the storm that ranged around him made his stance all the more ironic, since the flow and tenor of articles about Carlton remained more or less unchanged during his years of silence. People read into his motives, analyzed his actions, and speculated about his physical soundness in the same way they would have if he'd been devoting an hour a day to press relations.

Not a bad bargain, when one stops to think about it.

15

Messersmith and McNally: The Guys Who Fought the Law and Won

One of the basic principles of military strategy is called strategic disengagement. According to this theory, if the tide of battle appears to be going against an army, its commanders should immediately break off the fight, regroup, and have at it another day rather than risk total defeat in an unfavorable position. Pride being what it is, the concept is easier to discuss than it is to execute, but strategic disengagement has been at the heart of more than one against-the-odds victory — the American Revolution being an excellent example.

It was a lesson that baseball's ownership cabal would have been well advised to heed in the case of its hallowed reserve clause.

By 1974, Major League Baseball Players Association chief Marvin Miller was in a serendipitous position. Miller's negotiation skills and acumen in uniting the players over his eight years at the MLBPA helm had resulted in significant advances in the areas of pension benefits and health care coverage, plus a near doubling of the minimum wage. This was all well and good and Miller's members revered him for his efforts, but the union chief recognized that the real brass ring — achieving true market value wages for his members via elimination of the reserve clause — was as remote as ever. With *Flood vs. Kuhn* standing as conclusive evidence that no help was forthcoming from the legal arena, player leverage in salary negotiations was effectively limited to the "cut off your nose to spite your face" threat of sitting out.

Furthermore, while the 1972 strike had demonstrated the players' ability to unite for shared goals, the reserve clause was, on the face of it, a one-on-one issue. Contracts were offered to players individually, making a Curt Flood's negotiation woes seem somehow separate from those of other players. If the benefits from establishing an auction market for their services seem obvious to us today, keep in mind that the typical 1975 player was a high school graduate lacking professional representation of any kind — agents and business managers were strictly for the superstar class in those days. While Miller's words carried considerable weight with these people, so too did those of the owners with whom they had had a long and rewarding relationship, and these knowledgeable folks were predicting the end of life as we know it if the clause was tampered with in any way.

With Flood's frontal attack on the clause having proved unsuccessful, Miller began to look for alternate approaches. His first step in this direction was an innocuous amendment to the 1970 basic agreement that established a binding arbitration process to address future disagreements between the owners and players.[1] A common practice in industrial circles, the cornerstone of this process was a three-man panel consisting of one owner-selected member (initially John Gaherin, chairman of the owners' Player Relations Committee), one chosen by the players (Miller), and one approved by both sides. Since the owners weren't in the mood to arbitrate anything, this "impartial" third member would represent the deciding vote in all disputes.[2]

A simple substitution of one type of judge for another on the face of it, binding arbitration effectively divorced management from the judicial system that had consistently ruled in their favor. Furthermore, arbitration by its nature assumes two concepts that were anathema to the owners:

1. Compromise by both parties. The idea behind any arbitration system is that negotiations between two parties will often bog down over one or two relatively minor items out of twenty that were originally under dispute. With the majority of the contract agreed to by both sides, the arbitration panel's job is to decide on those few small issues, with a "split the child in half" approach normally employed to give each side a portion of what they wanted.

2. The issuance of specific decisions that ignored concerns about what was "good for the game." In the business world, rulings typically do not end the arbitration cycle: the assumption is that negotiations will continue to determine how edicts will be enacted. Thus, arbitrators rarely concern themselves with the practicality of their judgments, assuming that the two parties will work such things out between themselves.

Next, Miller went to the trouble of reading the standard player contract. Contrary to popular belief, the hallowed clause incorporated therein was an amorphous thing, the key to which resided in paragraph 10a: "If prior to March 1, the Player and the Club have not agreed upon the terms of the contract, then on or before 10 days after said March 1, the Club shall have the right by written notice to the Player to renew this contract for the period of one year."[3]

What that obviously means is ... well, whatever one would care for it to mean. The owners interpreted paragraph 10a as saying that a player who did not sign a new contract could be retained under the terms of his previous agreement for as long as his team wanted him. That's not an unreasonable reading, though one wonders why the owners didn't just come out and hang the two words "in perpetuity" onto the end of that sentence if that's what they really meant. Given the clause as written, though, a disinterested party could just as easily read it to say that a player refusing to sign a contract was bound to his team for one additional year only. Since the contract doesn't specify what happens after the year is up, the assumption is that the player is welcome to do whatever he wants at that point—like sign with whoever pays him the most money, for example.

Regardless of how one interpreted the scenario, it was clear that players were not required to sign contracts before setting foot on the field, and thus with Miller's tacit urging a new phenomenon was unleashed upon the baseball world. Yankee pitcher Al Downing was the first to report to spring training sans contract in 1969,[4] with Ted Simmons becoming the first man to play in a regular season game under a renewed deal three years later.[5] Sparky Lyle and Bobby Tolan would follow Simmons down the renewal trail in subsequent years, but both of these men would agree to new deals just before the end of their respective seasons—surprisingly lucrative ones, in fact.[6]

At this point an interesting question poses itself: if the reserve clause was rock solid, why were clubs so paranoid about enacting it for a second season? Why would an injury-diminished problem child like Tolan receive a big raise plus a loan for a house he wanted to buy on the last day of a season in which he had hit .266 in 95 games? Exactly how valuable is a speed merchant who had stolen seven bases in 16 attempts?

Apparently valuable enough to avoid risking the entire reserve system over ... at least until a righthander from Toms River, New Jersey, named Andy Messersmith came along.

A product of the California Angels' organization, Messersmith had spent five solid seasons with the Halos before being sent cross town for a couple of guys (Bill Singer, Bobby Valentine) that had broken down before becoming as good as the Dodgers had thought they were going to be. Messersmith was supposedly shocked by the deal[7] (one wonders what game Andy had grown up playing) and apparently resolved to do whatever he could to preclude such arbitrary moves in the future. Thus, when Messersmith's contract expired after a 1974 season in which he finished second in the Cy Young Award balloting, Andy asked for the inclusion of a novel feature in his new deal—baseball's first limited no-trade clause.[8]

The Dodgers summarily rejected the offer with owner Walter O'Malley allegedly telling Messersmith that the league wouldn't allow him to sign such an agreement,[9] an ironic remark given that in many ways O'Malley *was* the National League. For years this jowly, almost elfin man with the bottom-line mentality had been the driving force behind the senior circuit's positions on

Andy Messersmith simply wanted to stay in Los Angeles. When the Dodgers refused his request for a no-trade clause, Messersmith inadvertently became the point man in the MLBPA's quest to breach baseball's reserve clause — and the man who ushered in the free agency era. (*National Baseball Hall of Fame Library, Cooperstown, NY*)

expansion, the DH, franchise moves ... in short, everything from A to Z. That O'Malley would be concerned about the league's reaction to anything he did was an absurdity.[10] What he was really saying was that the man who'd traded the aging Jackie Robinson to the Giants wasn't about to give up his rights to do what he wanted when he wanted.

In short, Walter O'Malley wouldn't let Walter O'Malley agree to a no-trade clause.

With no agreement in sight the righthander's contract was renewed for the 1975 season, one in which Messersmith strengthened his bargaining position by winning 19 games, leading the league in innings pitched, and making his third All-Star appearance. As negotiations heated up again towards the end of the season, Andy naturally saw no reason to moderate his demands while O'Malley proved flexible on salary, length of contract ... anything save the no-trade clause.[11]

In light of what will happen, it is important to note that the Dodgers' stance in regards to Messersmith's request is by no means off the wall. Keep in mind that:

1. This was a time in which player negotiation rights were similar to those enjoyed by Kunta Kinte,
2. The Dodgers had such talents as Rick Rhoden, Rick Sutcliffe, Charlie Hough, and the surgically repaired Tommy John waiting in the wings for rotation spots, and
3. The now 30-year-old Andy had put 864 innings on his arm over the past three seasons.[12]

From Marvin Miller's point of view, O'Malley's apparent obstinacy was a godsend, but the opportunity to challenge the reserve clause remained moored to a leaky platform. Messersmith still wanted to settle if at all possible: the money gap between the two sides was narrowing, and if the Dodgers would just come around on the no-trade clause ... well, Los Angeles was where he wanted to be.[13]

Thus into the fray entered a Billings, Montana, Ford dealer named Dave McNally.

McNally had been one of the American League's top pitchers during the Nixon years as well as a man obsessed with money — his spring training holdouts were an Orioles staple.[14] Showing signs of age by 1974, McNally was dealt along with 24-year-old center fielder Rich Coggins to the Montreal Expos for Ken Singleton and Mike Torrez, one of those legendary trades that by the middle of the next year was a total washout for one side. Not being particularly enthused about Canada or the money the Expos were offering, the left-hander began the season without a contract; after 12 unimpressive starts neither side was interested in further formalizing the arrangement. Convinced that he was through, McNally announced his retirement in mid-season, walking away from $85,000 or so that the Expos were contracted to pay him and making contract discussions moot.[15] Thus, by the end of 1975 McNally had gone a full year without agreeing to a new deal — making him, by Miller's standards, a free agent.

Uncertain as to whether Messersmith would stay the course and convinced that now was the time to act, Miller enlisted McNally as Alternate Plan A in case Andy were to reach an agreement with the Dodgers. McNally, a staunch union man and former player representative, was enthusiastic about the idea in the manner of someone who had no intention to pitch again anyway and thus couldn't be harmed by an adverse ruling.[16] As for Messersmith, adding McNally to the case doomed any chance (small as it might have been) of achieving his no-trade guarantee, but that's what happens when one tangos with a Walter Reuther-style unionist.

By the time Messersmith's and McNally's grievances were filed on the last day of the 1975 season, the owners were in agreement on one thing: they did not want the reserve clause's future hanging on the whims of the arbitration board. Since 1973 the committee's swing vote had been in the hands of Peter Seitz, a veteran industrial arbitrator who had previously worked on contract disputes with the NBA but had no background in baseball matters.[17] Seitz's decisions to date had betrayed no particular bias, but his 1974 vote to grant Catfish Hunter free agency over what a more sympathetic ear might have termed procedural errors in the funding of an annuity rankled baseball's establishment, and that made him a risk worth avoiding if possible.[18]

To this end, the owners filed suit in Kansas City's U.S. District Court (chosen because Kansas City's Ewing Kauffman was the point man on this one) to keep the arbitration board from hearing the case. It was a reasonable move given baseball's historically good reception before the bar, but one that collided with a fact of judicial life: judges' caseloads are too heavy to take on issues that can be dealt with otherwise. Thus, District Court Justice John Oliver refused to enjoin the board, reasoning that the owners were welcome to appeal any decision rendered but that the system baseball had set up for this purpose was going to be used.[19]

With the legal avenue cut off for the time being, baseball reverted to form. Several weeks before the arbitration hearing was to commence, Dave McNally received a drop-in visit from Expo General Manager John McHale, who apparently just happened to be passing through Billings in mid-November. McHale also (wonder of wonders) had a deal in tow for McNally's consideration: $25,000 for showing up at spring training camp to see if he had anything left in his arm, and $125,000 more if he made the team. The combined figure represented more than the lefthander had ever earned before, and at worst the $25,000 consolation prize for soaking up a few weeks of Florida sunshine would be a nice going away present.

Ever the union man, McNally turned it down.[20]

Though it took three days and generated 842 pages of testimony (Seitz commented during the deliberations that "Whole hillsides are being decimated for the exhibits in this case"[21]), the players' and owners' positions as presented in the arbitration hearing could be summarized succinctly:

• The players saw paragraph 10a as binding them to a team for one year beyond the last one for which they performed under contract.

• The owners argued that baseball's viability would be threatened if the meaning of paragraph 10a were altered from what it had meant (i.e. lifetime bondage to one club) for the previous 75 years.

From the arguments expressed above, one can be excused for wondering if baseball was engaging in a legal matter or a philosophical debate. The union's position was as anal retentive as possible in contrast to the I-am-a-man/wave-the-flag argument that had sunk Curt Flood four years previous. Simultaneously, the owners were offering the kind of plea that James Earl Jones might have made if the hearing had been spliced into *Field of Dreams*. Forget about what the clause might be interpreted to say, forget about whom such a reading might injure; focus on the maintenance of baseball as we know it.

Having said that, implicit in the owners' argument is a point

Having lost his last six decisions while sporting a 5.26 ERA, Davis McNally walked away from $85,000 by quitting the Expos at mid-season 1975. His staunch support of the MLBPA, along with the fact that he had been playing under a renewed contract, would turn the Billings, Montana, car dealer into the union's backup position should Messersmith opt out. (**National Baseball Hall of Fame Library, Cooperstown, NY**)

with true legal power. A fundamental principle of business law is that if two people act like they have a contract, they have one in fact regardless of what a piece of paper says or doesn't say. In terms of paragraph 10a this means that the reserve clause's abstract meaning is immaterial — what matters is that both sides had interpreted it the same way forever and now the players were trying to back out of their side of the bargain.

Two problems occur with this argument in the eyes of the law. One is that the owners drafted the agreement in the first place — if they really meant to say that players were bound to their teams forever, why hadn't they just come out and said it? The other is that the point remained implicit because management spent the bulk of its time talking about the calamities that would befall the game if the reserve clause was eliminated.[22] It was an interesting (and accurate as it would turn out) appraisal, but one that had nothing to do with the issue at hand.

Still, this presentation did not necessarily spell doom for the owners. Arbitration, as mentioned above, is as much about negotiation as confrontation, and to this end Seitz wrote an eight-page memo to Gaherin and Miller encouraging both sides to reach a compromise on 10a's meaning.[23]

The owners, though, would hear nothing of it.

To Marvin Miller and perhaps the average layman as well, this seems like a preposterous stance given the legalistic weakness of management's argument. However, such an interpretation by its nature assumes either delusion or idiocy on the opposite side of the table, and morons don't build brewing empires or publish newspapers. Thus, let's consider some rational reasons that management might have had for remaining resolute at this critical point:

1. *They thought that they were going to win.* Let's face it: this line of reasoning, shaky as it might be, had carried the day against Flood. Thus, for those not closely following matters the idea that such an argument would win again was not that much of a stretch.

2. *They planned to appeal a negative ruling.* The owners had clearly signaled this from the start and Judge Oliver had in a backward way encouraged them to do so. Thus no matter how Seitz ruled, the owners could always return to the scene of their previous successes.

3. *They had no choice but to fight it out.* The idea that the owners' fears of ruination were well founded is roundly criticized by latter day observers conscious of today's multi-billion-dollar horsehide colossus. Miller wonders with unbecoming amazement how the owners could predict disaster when the day's headlines were full of stories about attendance records and megadollar TV contracts.

OK Marvin, suppose some Mr. X owns a business in a rapidly growing industry. The company has revenues of $10 million per year and profits of $1 million so he should be feeling really flush, right? Driving a Mercedes with a house in the Hamptons, right? Why not — he's got $1 million a year to spend, doesn't he?

Well, no, because the industry is expanding and Mr. X's company will become the next Visi-Calc if he doesn't expand with it. He'll have to buy equipment to maintain market share, hire additional people to keep up with the increased volume, invest in research that may take years to bear fruit but will drive the next generation's sales. In short, every penny of that $1 million plus whatever Mr. X can beg, borrow, or steal goes straight back into the business.

Soon the company is generating $100 million in revenues and $10 million in profit, but Mr. X is driving a '73 Pinto because this Godzilla of an enterprise is still consuming every penny he can throw at it and then some. Furthermore, sleep becomes elusive as the realization that everything he owns is tied up in this leveraged-to-the-teeth business becomes omnipresent. What happens if something goes wrong?

This was the situation dot-commers faced on their meteoric run up and down the hill, and it was the one that baseball ownership feared with the advent of a higher wage scale. The sportsmen and retired executives that traditionally backed teams were into estate planning, not risking everything on some temperamental superstar's hamstring. Lacking the cash flow from outside businesses to feed this 600-pound gorilla, these people knew it would only be a matter of time before they were squeezed out of an uncontrolled market. Sure, they would get a good price for their clubs, but the big money would end up going into deeper pockets. Thus the gulf between the owners' and players' positions remained inviolate, a situation that both amazed and frustrated Seitz.[24] This wasn't the way arbitration procedures were supposed to work: in most industries people understood the meaning of memos addressed to one side urging further negotiation. The concept of taking an activist approach was foreign to Seitz, while the lack of movement on either side suggested that nothing would be gained by allowing further time for deliberation. Constrained by the owners' obstinacy and the limits of his mandate as he saw it, the arbitrator was left with no alternative but to decide one way or the other.

On December 23, 1975, Seitz in a 64-page opinion sided with the players, opening the door for free agency for anyone who cared to play out his contract and stick around for one more season[25]— and all hell broke loose.

Oddly enough, nobody really wanted unlimited free agency. The owners' reasons were obvious, but Miller recognized that a scenario in which everybody came available within two years was one that would yield less than optimal prices, especially at the lower talent levels where players were largely interchangeable.[26] If three teams need a 20-homer-a-year outfielder and only one is available, somebody's going to end up buying that man a condo on Waikiki Beach. If ten 20-homer-a-year outfielders are available along with a dozen or so first sackers with similar offensive abilities ... well, how much of a premium will the average Joe pay for Coke when there's a full display of lower-priced Pepsi sitting next to it?

The owners, however, persisted in believing that this genie could somehow be stuffed back into its bottle. As expected, they skedaddled to court in the hopes of invalidating Seitz's ruling ... and were turned down. They appealed the decision ... and were turned down again. They opened negotiations with the union ... but were merely willing to "consider" changes in the reserve clause. Finally, they came up with an offer: players would be reserved by the teams for nine seasons, with free agency granted after the tenth (renewed contract) year unless the club offered a new contract worth $30,000 or more. Oh, and any club signing a free agent would have to compensate the team losing said player.[27]

OK, let's see ... the potential free agents under this plan are so-so players in their early- to mid-30s that other teams want so badly they are willing to pay a competitor for the privilege of signing them.

Heck, tons of people should have qualified for that one....

Given that Seitz's ruling made nearly unlimited free agency the status quo, management's offer seems laughable, yet this borderline insulting proposal served a very tangible purpose. The basic agreement between the players and the owners expired on December 31, 1975, lumping the Messersmith-McNally ruling's fallout into the negotiations for a new pact. In the business world companies have to negotiate with labor regardless of how ticked off they are at their workers — ongoing talks and an occasional proposal or two must transpire to keep the Feds happy. As long as these so-called good faith offers are being made and responded to, negotiations continue and employees generally remain at work under the covenants of the old contract. However, if a point is reached at which no progress is being made management has the legal right (though it's not highly thought of in political circles) to tell its employees to not come to work — a "lockout."

That, on March 1, 1976, was what the owners initiated.

To an extent, one wonders why the owners even bothered trying this gambit. A lockout's goal is as subtle as a sledgehammer: a worker sans paycheck has added motivation to listen to management's offers. The strategy can work assuming either the union is relatively weak, or management has the resources and willpower to stay idle for a long time. One would have thought that any illusions about the MLBPA's solidarity would have been dashed by the 1972 strike, but the players' show of solidarity and even militarism during the lockout made any thought of a quick cave-in ludicrous. A number of players that had arrived in Florida before the lockout was announced attended negotiation sessions in St. Petersburg — as the spectacle unfolded before them they began to occasionally heckle the owners' representatives. Some such as Johnny Bench even began participating in the deliberations, once asking incredulously, "How can you say that a player must play ten years to be a free agent? Only four percent of major leaguers ever play that long!"[28]

Given that players typically receive a low per diem pay rate during spring training (contracts normally don't kick in until the regular season begins) the lockout appeared to be more of a shot in the dark than a serious union-busting tactic. Perhaps management's idea was that there was no harm in trying a lockout as long as the regular season wasn't imperiled. Perhaps the players might not comprehend free agency's value and thus would not be willing to risk much for its preservation. Perhaps rising salaries had made the players fat, dumb, and happy.

Perhaps cows will grow wings.

Ever the realist, it quickly became clear to Walter O'Malley that the MLBPA wasn't going to cave in to strong-arm tactics any time soon. Though in many ways the catalyst of the current dilemma, O'Malley recognized that the lockout was coalescing resistance to management demands across the board: basic agreement negotiations could be imperiled if baseball remained unwilling to face facts. Via some strong-arming of his own, O'Malley got Bowie Kuhn to re-open the camps on March 17, after which Gaherin and his team were sent back to the bargaining table for serious negotiations.[29]

It was slow going, with the owners contesting every point in the manner of a defeated army covering its retreat. It was the day before the All-Star Game when the two sides finally settled on the following:

1. Free agency for every eligible player at the end of the 1976 and 1977 seasons, regardless of their length of service (which, due to Miller's efforts, included nearly half of all then-current major leaguers)
2. Free agency for future major leaguers at the end of their sixth major league season
3. The right of a player with five seasons of service to:
   - Demand a trade
   - Make of a list of teams that he could not be traded to (a limited no-trade clause)
   - Become a free agent if the demanded trade did not occur by March 15.[30]

One of the misconceptions about this process is that the reserve clause was ripped out of baseball's loins in the manner of Patrick Henry being given liberty at the potential cost of death. Such was not the case, though: paragraph 10a remains part of the standard player contract to this day. What changed in those momentous nine months was a century-old mindset in which players had been accorded the status of animated property. Within the relative twinkling of an eye baseball's labor contingent became a dynamic part of the business scene, more partner in the game's future than employee.

As with many revolutions, the marquee figures would not fare as well as the revolt itself. Serving at the leisure of both the owners and the union, Peter Seitz was fired within minutes of issuing his fateful order.[31] John Gaherin's inability to get the players to accept the owners' borderline ludicrous offers would result in his early 1977 "retirement."[32] Marvin Miller's stature reached its zenith during the crisis: once the agreement was signed his control over the players would be slowly eroded by the Frankenstein's monster that his efforts had helped create — the agent. Dave McNally returned to selling cars in Billings— he'd never really stopped, in fact, having had little to do with the case other than lending his name to it.

As for Andy Messersmith, the half-unintentional protagonist of this ordeal, time would prove the Dodgers correct in not acceding to his demands. Messersmith's arm would go sour before the ink was dry on his three year, $1 million deal with the Atlanta Braves. After working 321 innings in 1975, Andy would log a total of 394 innings in the remaining four seasons that he was destined to play. In an ironic twist, the final 62 1/3 innings of his career would be spent with the Dodgers, the team whose refusal to grant him a no-trade clause had directly led to baseball's world being turned upside down.

As with the American Revolution, the death of the reserve clause as it had been known throughout professional baseball's first century of operation was probably inevitable. However, management's inability to see this inevitability, coupled with the organized efforts of a determined opposition, made this eventuality come about more quickly and disastrously for the owners' standpoint than it might have otherwise. While the game itself would survive this seismic upheaval, baseball as it had been, as well as those who had shaped it, would be swept away as a result of this near-sightedness.

16

The Potential Immortality
of Marvin Miller

There is a difference between technical expertise and true greatness. Bert Blyleven, for example, equipped himself with the outstanding curve ball of his era: it was the pitch that everybody associated with him.[1] Thrown with a deceptively easy motion, the key to Blyleven's yakker was a late sideways break that turned many a batter's front leg into Jell-O. Yet despite that ability and the 287 career wins that resulted from it, Blyleven has to this point in time been passed over for the Hall of Fame because ... well, throwing a great curve is not exactly the same as being a great pitcher. It's a decent leg up on being one, but there is a little more to it than that.

This is exactly the dilemma that the Hall of Fame finds itself in when considering Marvin Miller's merits.

A minor movement is underway to get Miller's visage enshrined alongside those of Kenesaw Mountain Landis, Connie Mack, and all the other movers and shakers of baseball history (not to mention the mere players like Ruth, Cobb, etc.). The rationale for this effort is easy to understand. Clearly Miller was a titan of his time, his efforts vastly improving the playing class' lot while coincidentally setting off the economic avalanche that would bury the majority of his adversaries while paving the way for the business of baseball as it exists today. Perhaps there were some unfortunate side effects that resulted from his work, but Marvin's impact on the game is undeniable and there are plenty of Cooperstown residents whose legacy is mixed at best.

In an odd way, the Miller supporters' argument is similar to that of Pete Rose's fans: Pete may or may not have engaged in some risky behavior after his playing days were over, but 4,256 hits is a lot to overlook.

While all of the above is true, it misses the point about what a Hall of Fame is. The general concept behind honoring people is that their successes did so much to improve our lives that the money they received for their efforts is insufficient—we bestow immortality on them as a psychic reward above and beyond the financial gains from their labor. In short, the real question that must be asked of any potential Hall of Famer is whether he improved the game, moved it forward in a positive manner from where it was before he came on the scene. Chick Gandil's impact on baseball was huge via his ringmaster role in throwing the 1919 World Series, but nobody's going to put him in the Hall of Fame for that, are they?

Marvin Miller should not, of course, be considered in the same breath with Gandil: Miller was an honorable man who served those who hired him with distinction, producing results far beyond anything that they had ever dreamed of. Furthermore, as detrimental as his efforts might have been to certain facets of the game (like family ownership of teams, the building of dynasties via the farm system, etc.) the flat fact of the matter is that the MLBPA chief's impact on baseball was essentially neutral. Despite skyrocketing player-related costs, the game not only survives but continues to increase its popularity and revenue base to this day, a point Marvin has repeatedly made in defense of his actions. It may be controlled by different people and operated in a more impersonal manner than before, but baseball is still baseball — the sport itself is simply too great and adaptable to have been destroyed by such machinations.

All of which brings us back to our original question: sure, Miller changed the game, but what did he do to help improve it? Not what did he do to improve the lot of the players, but what did the man contribute to making baseball the great game that it is today?

The answer to this question, obviously, is nothing ... nor should anyone have expected such from him. The thing that Miller's fans and detractors fail to understand is that: (a) the man had no responsibilities towards baseball as a whole; and (b) given what his function was nobody should have expected anything else from him.

Marvin was a hard case labor leader, period: he made it clear to everyone from the start that his relationship with the baseball establishment would be purely adversarial.[2] As far as Miller was concerned his duty began and ended with the people who employed him. Baseball's financial success was important to the MLBPA chief, but only to the extent that the game's cash flow represented a pot of gold from which his clients could draw. Beyond that ... well, it was the owners' job to get the fans into the stadiums.

Miller's position was incomprehensible to the Bowie Kuhns of the world because baseball to them was as much labor of love as business. Anybody other than a media/entertainment mogul who "invests" in the game is a fool — even Kuhn himself, though hardly the most adept lawyer in the Wall Street jungle, could have netted many millions more if he'd limited his baseball cravings to a box seat at Yankee Stadium. Charlie Finley perhaps said it best: after pointing out that he only held 30 percent of A's stock in his name and could be fired at any time, Finley observed, "But where would they find someone else to do all this work for no salary?"[3]

Immortalizing Marvin Miller is about the same as paying homage to Gussie Busch for all the $3-a-cup beer he produced to quench fans' thirsts. A reasonable case can be made for either man (frankly, Busch is probably the superior potential honoree given his long-term ownership of the Cardinals) but one wonders if either Marvin or Gussie expected such accolades for what he did or would have even have cared if such were tendered. Each received their money, the psychic payment of recognizing that they had done their job well, and the gratitude of those who worked alongside them — and that's probably enough.

Should Miller have his face immortalized in bronze? Sure — but the people who should do it are the players, those people who owe their millions to his tireless efforts. As for the rest of the world, well, it's hard to see how we owe Marvin Miller anything.

After all, he didn't work for us, did he?

17

The Big Red Machine
and the End of an Era

Dinosaurs have gotten a bad rep in modern society. To be called a dinosaur is something close to the ultimate insult: in order to achieve such status one has to be:

1. Big (preferably as the result of the sweat of some industrious ancestor's brow),
2. Ponderous,
3. Not very bright, and
4. On the road to extinction.

While there is some justification to this viewpoint of dinosaurs, the term has become corrupted much in the way that the word "mediocre" has (for those who don't know, the dictionary definition of mediocre is to be slightly above average). What dinosaurs really were was a highly evolved life form, one that was strong enough to completely dominate its era — and if an ice age or two hadn't intervened in the interim, they'd probably still be king.

That's the Big Red Machine in a nutshell.

The mid-1970s Cincinnati Reds in many ways represented the ultimate refinement of the pre-free-agent era baseball organization. They were a team that required every tool in the box to produce: savvy amateur signings, a willingness to gamble on unproven but promising talent, perceptivity in discerning less-than-obvious strengths and weaknesses, diligence (though not brilliance) in the trade arena and patience when patience was needed. Yet within a year of their peak, the Reds' formula would be as anachronistic as their college-style player rules (no overlong stirrups of the style first popularized by Frank Robinson, no facial hair, solid black spikes only, jackets and ties on all public occasions) and clubhouse *joie de vivre*.

That fact, however, in no way diminishes the stature of general manager (GM) Bob Howsam's creation, though some have claimed that it was as much accident as design. Start with three Hall-of-Fame-type players in their prime (Johnny Bench, Tony Perez, Pete Rose), add another (Joe Morgan) via a lopsided trade, get lucky (George Foster) and add a few quality youngsters (Dave Concepcion, Ken Griffey Sr., Don Gullett) — what's so magical about that? Heck, give the 1998 Kansas City Royals a healthy Kevin Appier and Jose Rosado plus a Jermaine Dye and Mike Sweeney who matured on schedule and the unlamented Herk Robinson could have been the exact same kind of genius.

Of course, the Reds' metamorphosis was anything but easy or painless. It was a sometimes frustrating one-step-forward-two-steps-back process that took a good seven years to reach maturation — but when it did, the result was one of the greatest teams of all time.

While Howsam often receives the lion's share of the credit for Cincinnati's mid-1970s success, the story really starts with predecessor Bill DeWitt, a man whose name evokes mixed emotions among the Cincinnati faithful to this day. A battle-hardened GM-owner (he'd once operated the St. Louis Browns, and if that wasn't the financial equivalent of hand-to-hand combat nothing is), DeWitt had shocked the baseball world by turning a sub-.500 squad into pennant winners in his first (1961) season at the helm. Though the Reds had failed to scale the heights since then, they had by and large remained a formidable squad due to DeWitt's three ironclad operating rules:

1. Build through the farm system as much as possible,
2. Don't worry if the organization develops too many of the same types of players: a quality prospect can always be dealt away for need,
3. Trade anybody — anybody — once he reaches 30. Keep a man too much longer after that and the club ends up paying top dollar for declining productivity.

It was that last rule that secured DeWitt's place in Cincinnati's Hall of Shame — the Reds missed out on the second half of Frank Robinson's career because of it — but the other two resulted in a strong talent base that fueled Rhineland success for years to come. Pete Rose, Tony Perez, Johnny Bench, and Gary Nolan were all products of the DeWitt regime, and many of the key acquisitions that would follow (Joe Morgan, Jack Billingham, Bobby Tolan) were paid for with pre-1967 acquired personnel.

Still, as Howsam discovered upon assuming the Cincinnati helm, there's a big difference between an undifferentiated talent blob and a team. To the casual observer, the 1967 Reds seemed to be on the verge of putting it all together. They could hit, had a reasonable mix of youth and experience (though only center fielder Vada Pinson's hairdresser knew for sure just how old he really was[1]), and the front end of the pitching staff seemed strong if a bit problematic with the 19-year-old Nolan, noted right-hander/clubhouse lawyer Milt Pappas,[2] one-time staff ace Jim Maloney, and reigning Fireman of the Year Ted Abernathy.

The problem was that these strengths were basically the same ones that had characterized Cincinnati teams for years—and none of those squads had won anything either.

It was the less-than-apparent stuff that kept holding the Reds back. The defense was a delightful mix of iron gloves, people playing out of position, and guys who didn't make errors but weren't making plays either. The 1967 squad was eighth in runs scored despite good power and a favorable home park because virtually nobody on the roster believed in taking walks—Pete Rose was the only member of the team to draw as many as 50 free passes, and the trio of Pinson, Lee May, and Tommie Helms combined for a mere 69 in over 1,600 plate appearances. The pitching staff couldn't stay healthy and was destined for an early demise—Gary Nolan was the only pitcher on the Reds' staff who would be active five years hence, and none of the young guns would remain effective past their 30th birthdays.

It was Howsam's job to turn this classic profile of a fourth place team into a powerhouse—and to continue to do so even after his best-laid plans went awry.

The aforementioned starting rotation/MASH unit became the prime example of Howsam's persistence in the face of repeated setbacks: in fact, the first two years of his regime reads like some sort of voodoo ritual performed by an angry witch doctor whose bill wasn't paid. After logging 226 innings in 1967, Nolan worked a total of 259 over the next two seasons due to a combination of arm miseries that included a strained forearm suffered when his spikes caught while pushing off the Fulton County Stadium mound during an early 1969 game.[3] Tony Cloninger, a one-time 24 game winner imported from Atlanta to take up the slack created by Nolan's on-again, off-again presence, lost contact with his control. George Culver, acquired to fill Sammy Ellis's spot in the rotation, produced one OK season and then contracted hepatitis.[4] Maloney, who at his peak was something akin to a mirror image of Sandy Koufax, was finished—like Koufax—at the ripe old age of 31.

No quitter he, Howsam ordered up replacements: Jim Merritt, a 27-year-old lefty with pinpoint control and just enough of everything else to get by; Jim McGlothlin, a 26-year-old pitching coaches' nightmare (he threw everywhere from sidearm to straight over the top[5]) who'd led the AL in shutouts just two seasons prior; and an out-of-nowhere (he'd posted a 4.89 ERA while leading the International League in losses the previous year[6]) prospect/suspect named Wayne Simpson. These three guys and a healthy Nolan were enough to carry the Reds to the 1970 World Series, but within two years:

1. Simpson had come down with circulation problems in his pitching shoulder and was diagnosed with an irregular heartbeat.[7] He would win 22

games over the remainder of his career, posting a sub-4.00 ERA only once (and that in a 31-inning 1975 season).

2. Merritt, the first Reds lefthander to win 20 games in over 40 years, felt an ominous pop in his left elbow in late August 1970.[8] Elbow problems, of course, are the kiss of death for breaking ball pitchers: with marginal heat to begin with and now less bite on his trademark curve, Merritt fell to 1-11 in 1971 and would win only seven games before hanging 'em up.

3. McGlothlin's availability would be limited first by elbow problems and then by a rare disease that would ultimately take his life in 1975.

4. Nolan's arm gave out again, causing him to miss the majority of the 1973 and 1974 seasons.

It was enough to turn any GM's hair white, yet Howsam simply reloaded with a combination of:

- Prospects (Don Gullett, Ross Grimsley),
- Acquisitions, some of which worked (Jack Billingham, Fred Norman), some of which worked for a little while (Clay Kirby), and some of which flopped (Roger Nelson), and
- Rubber-armed relievers (Clay Carroll, Pedro Borbon, Tom Hall) to take on what the chronically stamina-challenged starters couldn't.

... And Cincinnati was back at the top of the heap in 1972.

Bobby Tolan initially was a steal; one of the shrewdest acquisitions Howsam made. Liberated from the Cardinals, where he'd been acquiring splinters watching Curt Flood play center field, Tolan blossomed into a terrific offensive player and prolific base stealer (he could have paid more attention to Flood's defensive technique, though) for a couple of years. However, a torn Achilles tendon cost him the 1971 season and a prolonged slump two years later frustrated Tolan to the point where his Dick Allen gland spontaneously triggered.[9] At 28, Tolan had improbably become a has-been as well as a royal pain in the posterior, but Howsam had an alternative available — Cesar Geronimo, a fine defensive center fielder who was tossed into the Joe Morgan trade because his bat just wasn't good enough to shove Cesar Cedeno aside. Geronimo may not have been an ideal choice — Tom Goodwin is probably every bit as good — but he did fill a definable role and hey ... the man does own two world championship rings.

Speaking of Morgan, plenty of eyebrows were raised when the Reds deported the left side of an infield (Lee May and Tommie Helms) that had taken them nearly all the way just a year earlier plus Jimmy Stewart for Little Joe, Geronimo, Billingham, Denis Menke, and Ed Armbrister. With 20/20 hindsight it's easy to wonder what Houston GM Spec Richardson could possibly have been thinking, but keep in mind that Morgan was a .263 career hitter at that point with a heck of a lot less power than Lee May had. Billing-ham had been posting league average ERAs over the previous three seasons in a ballpark that represented Houston's ode to the Dead Ball era. Menke sure looked like he'd hit the wall (well, Richardson was right about that one), and the other two guys were nothing to get choked up about. Yes, there are some misconceptions cleverly interwoven amongst those truths, but the fact of the matter is this: the deal just wasn't that unbalanced.

Sure, Morgan won a couple of MVP Awards en route to Cooperstown's doorstep, but Lee May was a very fine player — good enough to play over 1,300 games and hit 207 home runs for three divisional champions after the trade. Jack Billingham may have won 87 games for the Reds, but after 1973 he really was nothing more than the average pitcher he'd always been, while Tommie Helms gave the Astros three fine seasons before Father Time and the injury bug caught up to him. If Ed Armbrister hadn't stumbled into Carlton Fisk's way in Game 2 of the 1975 World Series nobody would remember him, and as for Geronimo, well ... there are probably ten career minor leaguers today who are every bit as good as he was. It was simply Cesar's good for-tune that the Reds didn't happen to have any such people in their system at the time....

... Which was exactly the point of the trade. Geronimo may have been a nothing-special offensive player, but the Reds had adequate punch even without May: what they needed by 1973 was a good defensive player who could keep his mouth shut and hit something over .206. So maybe Billing-ham was Stan Bahnsen with better taste in baseball teams, but there have been plenty of clubs laden with booming bats (see the 1960s San Francisco Giants for details) who have fallen short for want of 200 "he kept us in the game" innings. As for Morgan and Menke, the level of improvement they represented over May and Helms is debatable: after all it was the Astros, not the Reds, who led the majors in runs scored in 1972[10] (now there's a piece of trivia guaranteed to win a beer at any bar).

Yet Howsam recognized that nothing can thwart a team's power like a sub-.300 on-base percentage (May's) and that Tony Perez's career could be derailed if they kept forcing him to make a fool of himself at third. Thus, by adding Morgan's strike zone judgment and a real third baseman while turn-ing the defensively-challenged hot corner incumbent into an above-average first sacker, Cincinnati went from the outhouse to the penthouse in both on-base and fielding percentage — and the rest is history.

Not that Howsam was an infallible dealmaker or talent judge, mind you. Sure, the Morgan deal worked out great — but swapping the 23-year-old Hal McRae for Roger Nelson and Richie Scheinblum pretty much washes that one out.[11] His passion for spit-and-polish types forced a couple of useful guys (Grimsley and Bernie Carbo) out of the nest prematurely. Howsam bailed too quickly on Tommie Harper, who had a 34-home-run season and a cou-ple of stolen base crowns in front of him, as well as a cameo role (meaning that he didn't shoot enough beaver to be worthy of much comment) in Jim Bouton's *Ball Four* world.

The point of all this is that any organization of the day was capable of building a great team so long as it accurately identified its needs, was persistent at solving them, and caught a lucky break here and there. Of course, once Andy Messersmith and Dave McNally were done with the system two other factors—having the requisite amount of scratch and structuring the club's contract situation properly—entered the picture....

... And the Reds' way of doing business was obsolete.

As some may have noticed, Cincinnati's path from contender to champion was liberally strewn with discarded bats and arms. Some fell by the wayside as their fortunes changed, but many departed simply because they didn't fit Howsam's plans quite as well as an alternative might—and in a system where players were animated baseball cards that could be swapped at will, that was a reasonable strategy. Simultaneously, the Reds maintained a veteran core of outstanding and increasingly high-priced players for extended periods and through varying twists of fate. Under current rules Tony Perez would have been eligible for free agency after the 1971 season, a year in which the Reds finished 79-83 as the rotation imploded and Perez's productivity was severely impacted by a wrist injury. With May still a season away from free agency, would Howsam have chosen to resign the future Hall of Famer, or would he have kept May, let Perez walk, and spent the money saved on whatever big-time pitcher was available?

Consider the 1975 Cincinnati Reds in modern terms. Eight members of that squad (Johnny Bench, Jack Billingham, Clay Carroll, Clay Kirby, Joe Morgan, Gary Nolan, Tony Perez, and Pete Rose) had six or more big league seasons under their belt and thus would be playing under a market value contract. Five others (Pedro Borbon, Dave Concepcion, Don Gullett, Fred Norman, and Merv Rettenmund) would have been in their super-arbitration seasons and eligible for free agency at year's end. In short, every key player save George Foster and Ken Griffey's dad would either be making big bucks or on the verge of doing so for a team with questionable pitching (healthwise) that had fallen four games short of an up and coming Dodger club the prior year.

How many modern general managers would have the intestinal fortitude to commit the $95 million or so it would take to keep that group together under those competitive circumstances? How sensible would it be to do so in the NL's smallest market, one where the current-day Reds are keeping afloat by trading everyone the moment that they come within spitting distance of free agency?

Of course, the Big Red Machine's payroll wouldn't have been that high, since Morgan, Billingham, and Geronimo almost certainly wouldn't have been with the team....

Joe Morgan in 1971 would (under the terms of our scenario) have been

A Big Red Machine with interchangeable parts: only five of the players in this 1975 photograph were on hand to grace Cincinnati's 1970 team photograph. (*National Baseball Hall of Fame Library, Cooperstown, NY*)

a couple of years into a contract that he'd have signed after the 1969 season. That year, 1969, was something of a low point for Morgan—Joe was rusty both at the plate and with the leather (he endured a 14-game experiment in center field) after missing virtually the entire 1968 season with a broken leg. There is no way that anybody this side of Scott Boras could have negotiated a big-bucks agreement under those circumstances, and thus Little Joe probably would have been quite a bargain by the fall of 1971. The same would have held true for Billingham (still a couple of years away from free agency) and Geronimo (who wouldn't have even been eligible for arbitration, had such a concept existed at the time). Menke would in all likelihood have represented a salary dump, but overall the Astros' side of the package in current terms would have been very lucrative indeed.

What did the Reds have to offer in return? A guy who would be eligible for free agency at the end of the next season (May), a guy who was eligible for free agency now and was thus nil in terms of trade value (Helms), and a guy who at his age (32) and talent level would be signed on a year-to-year basis and thus had no value either (Stewart).

In short, there would have been no deal—and since the Reds' farm system wasn't particularly productive at this point in time, there weren't many alternative faces available for inclusion.

Could the Reds have won anyway? Well:

• They'd probably have resigned May and accepted Perez's defense at third,
• Doug Flynn would have taken over at second as Helms aged,

- Howsam would have learned to live with Ross Grimsley's hair, and
- A Cesar Geronimo-like outfielder would have been acquired to hold down center field until Ken Griffey came of age.

They'd probably have won a divisional crown or two, though the Dodgers would have taken them in 1973 and pushed them to the wall three years later. From there ... well, as it was the Reds needed every bullet in the gun to get past the 1975 Boston Red Sox, and the 1976 Phillies won 101 games with a young and exceptionally well-balanced team.

The Big Red Machine was a highly evolved life form — a dinosaur, if you will — that through brawn, skill, and timing was able to rule the baseball world for a period. Like all such creatures their time soon passed, yet the fact of the dominance remains — and should be appreciated for what it was.

18

Pete Rose in Full Bloom

People's images have a remarkable way of changing over time, especially when latter day events intercede to cast earlier accomplishments in a different light. William Jennings Bryan is a perfect example of this phenomenon — a true man of the people who according to a lot of folks should have been president, The Great Commoner's image today is that of the doddering geezer who prosecuted John Scopes for teaching the theory of evolution. While America's penchant for long-term memory loss may benefit some — Earl Warren's Supreme Court tenure overshadowed his role in the internment of Japanese-Americans during World War II — for every Warren there is a Richard Nixon whose career will forever be viewed through Watergate-tinted glasses.

To put perhaps too literal a point on it, Pete Rose has evolved over the years into baseball's answer to Richard Nixon — a man whose indiscretions (or, in Rose's case, alleged indiscretions) obscured what had once been a sentinel life force within the game.

Man is by nature a retrospective beast, endlessly rehashing the past in an attempt to comprehend a confusing and scary future. It is this preoccupation that has converted Rose's win-at-all costs mentality into the manifestation of a reckless spirit fated to go astray when his ability to achieve such goals on the playing field was gone. The once perversely appealing braggadocio is now seen as self-aggrandizement, his quest of Ty Cobb's hit record self-centered, and his lust for respect via money (in the late 1960s practically every Rose interview mentioned Pete's goal of becoming the first $100,000 per year non-home-run hitter[1]) utterly crass. Taken by current attitudes, one could be excused for wondering what our antecedents could have seen in this modern day Neanderthal.

Well, in all honesty, there was quite a lot to see.

Lost in the debate over whether Rose's 4,256 hits, 17 All-Star appearances, three batting titles, and MVP Award are enough to parole him out of baseball's holding cell is the fact that the man was a moderately gifted athlete. Pete wasn't a big guy (5'11", 180 in his salad days) and his crouching stance with bat held flat across his shoulder eliminated any chance of getting much loft on his drives. He was never particularly fast, though like John Kruk Rose possessed the gift of looking like he was really motoring even when he wasn't. Quickness and agility in the field weren't highlights of his resume either — Pete's difficulties turning two forced him to third base when Tommy Helms came up in 1966, then to the outfield when Tony Perez proved more capable at the hot corner (think about that one for a moment…). His arm was never particularly strong and by the early 1980s it was strictly Rickey Henderson grade.

Yet statisticians 100 years from now will heartily debate each of the afore-mentioned points because Rose's statistical record gives few of these physical shortcomings away. Despite the crouch, Rose hit as many as 16 round-trippers in a season and for a time in the '70s was number three on the all-time homer list for switch hitters behind Mickey Mantle and Reggie Smith. Though less than speedy, Pete stole as many as 23 bases in a season with a fine success rate. His earlier failure notwithstanding, Rose possessed enough agility or whatever to make a successful conversion to third base in his mid-30s. While his arm may well have been mediocre, it apparently wasn't enough of a handicap to keep Charlie Hustle from winning a Gold Glove during his years as a right fielder.

As third base coach Alex Grammas commented early in the 1973 season, "If Pete gave the Reds any more than he does now, we'd have to take blood from him."[2]

This ability to continuously redefine himself in light of his team's needs and his own changing skill set was a Rose trademark. As rookies there was little to separate Pete and Steve Sax save speed — and Sax had the better of that comparison. Within three years, however, Rose had accented his offensive game with enough average and power to make a conversion to the outfield feasible, whereas Sax was forced to confront his bout of Chuck Knoblauch Disease in order to stay in the league. When the over-the-fence power began to wane in his early 30s, Rose focused on stroking the ball into the gaps (he'd record as many as 51 doubles in a year[3]) along with improved plate discipline that allowed him to record 90 or more walks in four separate seasons. As for Sax, he pretty much continued to be what he'd always been, and once his speed was gone at 32 Steve was quickly ushered from the game.

Capping it all was the intensity, the Charlie Hustle attitude that made Pete run full speed to first base after every free pass ("Pete Rose just beat out a walk," Dodger announcer Vin Scully deadpanned one night[4]), go in head-first whenever a slide was called for, and play in four amateur basketball leagues during the off season to stay in shape.[5] It was a characteristic that drew him oodles of admiration from the hustler and hard hat strata of baseball society. Leo Durocher was a particular admirer; he once said that he would willingly trade six of his Cub regulars to acquire Rose.[6] Steve Garvey praised Rose several times in his book (published a couple of years before Pete's gambling and tax problems became public knowledge), characterizing Charlie Hustle as perhaps "the greatest player of our time, the one who, more than any other, has caused his team to win."[7] Perhaps that's a part of Pete's current troubles— neither The Lip nor Garvey would be what anyone would call a good character witness nowadays.

The best way of understanding the transformation in Pete Rose's image is to consider his 12th inning leveling of Ray Fosse en route to scoring the 1970 All-Star Game's winning run. Nowadays the play is seen in many circles as a cheap shot, a needlessly brutal move in a meaningless game that commenced Fosse's downhill slide from serious contender for the mantle of the AL's best catcher to a brittle journeyman.[8] The play takes on an especially nasty taste in conjunction with the rolling takeout block that Rose levied on Mets shortstop Bud Harrelson in Game 2 of the 1973 NL Playoffs.[9]

Yet what is forgotten is that the sequence was one of the most exciting and dramatic (if not the most exciting and dramatic) in the history of the all-too-often uninteresting Midseason Classic. The crowd went bananas when they saw it (OK, so the game was staged at Riverfront Stadium; it was a thrilling play just the same) and the collision is to this day a primary image in any All-Star Game montage even though we know what Fosse's ill-fated future would hold. Furthermore, if the game is really meant to be a glorified photo op in which the Larry Walkers of the world bat right-handed with their helmets on backwards, why was Ray Fosse blocking the plate in the first place? If people really want to see their heroes operating at 85 percent of capacity, why invite Pete Rose? After all, someone with 85 percent of Charlie Hustle's natural talent would be lucky to earn a California League tryout....

Future Hall of Fame sportswriter Dick Young perhaps stated it best: "Sure, Pete Rose could have slid around Ray Fosse. And Derek Sanderson could skate around people instead of banging them into the boards. And Jimmy Brown could have tried to out-nifty more guys instead of running over them. A man must play it his way, right now, in the split-second of decision."[10]

That was Pete in a nutshell—doing it his way in a manner that would have made Ol' Blue Eyes proud. His real and alleged transgressions are likely to fade from the collective conscience over time: heck, if Joe Jackson can become the subject of public sympathy there's got to be hope for Rose. Baseball can only pray, though, that the image of Pete Rose the ballplayer is not forced down history's drain along with the less savory images.

19

The Rotation Revolution

One of psychology's basic tenets is that change is normally a product of desperation. Consider the annoying co-worker with the hourglass-shaped wife, *Father Knows Best*-style kids, and Beemer in the driveway. Now, what pair of birds in the bush could be enticing enough to risk THAT lifestyle for? Put him in a situation where Repo Man is after the Beemer while his wife is making eyes at the pool man, though, and suddenly those "get rich quick by selling herbal products" commercials that run at 3 a.m. look mighty interesting.

That's where baseball's brain trust was by the mid-1970s in terms of rotation pitching talent. The double whammy of the power-pitching generation's premature demise along with the bullpen's rapid rise produced a tremendous talent vacuum, turning one-time desperation moves into business as usual for even the most prestigious organizations. Men whose fastballs wouldn't be ticketed for speeding in a school zone became valued members of expanded rotations. Decade-long minor league veterans whose skills had been sneered at a few years earlier were suddenly making World Series starts. Pitchers with once-debilitating injuries were given second and even third chances to reclaim their previous glory.

Out of such chaos, though, came order ... an order that challenged thought patterns ingrained in the game's psyche since the days when balls were thrown underhand. It was a hit-and-miss evolution for the most part and not altogether a logical one, but the results of this seismic change in philosophy reverberate through the game to this day.

The initial salvo in this revolution would be fired from the smoggy hillsides of Southern California.

The year 1971 was the best and worst of times for the Los Angeles Dodgers. After being devastated by Sandy Koufax's and Don Drysdale's premature demises plus a series of less-than-inspired trades, the Dodgers had ridden a rag-tag group of 1960s holdovers and reclamation projects to respectability while fiendishly building the real team of the future in the minors. With the Steve Garveys and Bill Buckners just entering the picture, the Dodgers' path was obvious: work the kids into the lineup as much as possible while patching whatever holes might spring up in the meantime with any old Duke Sims or Pete Mikkelsen that might come to hand.

As baseball fate has a tendency of doing, though, several events intervened to complicate matters:

1. The Cincinnati Reds went into hibernation for a year (Sparky Anderson would quip towards the end of this most undistinguished season, "Last year they called me 'Sparky Who?' Now they call me 'Sparky Why?'"[1]),
2. Al Downing, a once-fireballing lefty acquired for a half-time outfielder, improved his control in the face of decreased arm strength and won 20 games, and
3. The other Dodgers starters (particularly Bill Singer) began having enough health issues to create ongoing work for another man.[2]

Finding themselves in the midst of an unexpected pennant run, the Dodgers plucked a 20-year-old control artist named Doyle Alexander out of their minor league system. Utilizing him as the designated replacement for whoever needed extra rest, manager Walter Alston now found himself with five active starters on his staff (Alexander, Downing, Singer, Don Sutton, and Claude Osteen), each capable of getting the team into the eighth inning. Oddly enough, Doyle himself did not pitch particularly well (6-6 with an above-league average ERA in a pitcher's park)—but the team got hot within five seconds of his arrival and that's enough to launch a new paradigm in any self-respecting league.

Well, maybe not so new....

Some 40 years previous the carrying of six or even seven starters was standard operating procedure for many teams. Given that the concept of devoting valuable arms to career bullpen work was unfathomable, a team's key hurlers would often split their duty between starting and closing tight games. Since pitchers of the era were no more supermen than those of today, most clubs would add somebody capable of holding his own against the weaker teams or (if they were lucky) a still-crafty veteran no longer capable of shouldering a true front line workload to their rotations. In the manner of Nolan Ryan some 50 years later, longtime White Sox workhorse Ted Lyons evolved by his early 40s into the Chisox's Sunday starter: his success and fame in the role were ultimately rewarded with a Cooperstown plaque.[3] Though the practice went into decline with the development of the specialized bullpen, traces of it remained for many years afterwards—Casey Stengel kept somewhere between five and eight starters busy on his 1950s Yankee teams.

Furthermore, it wasn't as if other contemporary teams didn't employ the practice from time to time, though such a setup was more likely to be an act of improvisation rather than design. The early 1970s Big Red Machine frequently utilized five men in their rotation, but that was because half the staff was inevitably succumbing to or battling their way back from arm miseries. The 1972 Houston Astros featured a quality quintet of Don Wilson, Larry Dierker, Jerry Reuss, Dave Roberts, and Ken Forsch, but over the winter Reuss and Roberts were traded to shore up the infield. The New York Mets that year added the promising young lefty Jon Matlack to four-fifths of their Miracle staff (Seaver, Koosman, Gary Gentry, and Jim McAndrew), yet by the next year Gentry had returned to the minors while McAndrew was converted to bullpen duty.

The Dodgers thus became the first to intentionally revive this archaic practice, and given the organization's resources and needs, they were the obvious ones to do so. Though deep in quality arms, several key staff members were in precarious straits: Singer was coming off a 10-17 season, Downing's surge would prove to be more last hurrah than revival, and Claude Osteen was beginning to wind down at 32. However, with a minor league system rife with guys like Charlie Hough and Doug Rau, the Bums were both capable of maintaining an elongated rotation and needing to do so in order to season the young arms properly.

Thus, when Alexander was traded to the Baltimore Orioles for the player that used to be Frank Robinson, the Dodgers quickly turned around and imported another veteran starter (Tommy John) to perpetuate the five man rotation. With only a minor interruption during the 1975 season, the Dodgers became firm proponents of the art form, and given their long-term success, other teams began to follow their lead. There were some holdouts, of course — Earl Weaver would say to the end that it was easier to find four good starters than five[4] — but the trend towards longer rotations was clear by the end of the decade.

To have a Big Five, however, a team must first come up with five guys it wants to use — an easy proposition perhaps for the pitching-centric Dodgers but a little trickier for the average team.

With that old standby (the fastball) in increasingly short supply, a new generation of pitchers entered the scene that by the standards of the previous decade would have been given scant consideration for a rotation assignment. Fred Norman was the poster child for this trend — armed with an OK screwball and grade B heater, Norman spent the 1960s developing into the quintessential AAA starter: crafty enough to get by at a lower level, but lacking the true out pitch that spells major league success. Input from Tulsa manager Warren Spahn during the 1971 season sharpened his scroogie and yielded impressive results (6-1 with a 2.18 ERA and 72 K's in 62 innings),[5] but Norman was nearly 29 and his bread and butter pitch was an odd one for a lefty to throw (the screwball is basically a curve that breaks in the opposite direction, giving the person who throws it a reverse platoon differential.[6] Thus, Norman represented a conundrum — a southpaw who wasn't particularly effective against lefties). Furthermore, he was a two trick pony in a world where the dogma said that a minimum of three pitches were necessary to succeed.

A two-pitch pitcher whose minor league career stretched back to the Eisenhower years, 29-year-old Fred Norman finally caught his break with the 1971 Padres. Despite a 1-7 start two years later, Norman would net San Diego the defending American Association batting champ plus another player and cash. (*National Baseball Hall of Fame Library, Cooperstown, NY*)

In short, as of June 10, 1971, Fred Norman was indistinguishable from twenty other AAA hurlers who were probably good enough to pitch in the Show but were never going to get the chance ... and then lightning struck. He was traded to the San Diego Padres, who at the time were locked in a fight to the death with the Cleveland Indians for the title of worst major league team.

To a typical regular, such an assignment would be akin to being sentenced to Devil's Island. For someone whose biological clock was ticking loudly in AAA, though, a bad team represents salvation — even one drawing 5,000 fans per game whose owner was on the IRS's hit list[7] (according to then GM Buzzie Bavasi, things got so tight that the Padres couldn't come up with an additional $2,000 to sign Doug DeCinces, who went on to a storied career with the Baltimore Orioles and California Angels.[8] The shortfall was probably as unfortunate for DeCinces as it was for the Pads: if he'd latched on with San Diego, Doug wouldn't have spent the first half of his career explaining why he wasn't Brooks Robinson). Under such circumstances anybody with a pulse would get a shot, and with the addition of a slider courtesy of pitching coach Roger Craig,[9] Norman became one of the Padres' most effective pitchers over the next year and a half. In 1973, however, the little lefty got off to a 1-7 start with a 4.26 ERA, the kind of numbers that normally spell banishment to the bullpen for a 30-year-old guy with marginal stuff and a career 17-35 record.

Instead, Fred was one of the hottest tickets around. The Giants, doggedly chasing the Dodgers with a rotation of Jim Barr, Juan Marichal's corpse, and one-year wonder Ron Bryant, were interested.[10] The Astros, just a step behind the Giants at the time with two lefties (Dave Roberts and Jerry Reuss) who would win 33 games for them already on their staff, were also in touch with Bavasi.[11] Cubs manager Whitey Lockman, his team leading the NL East but possessing only one potential lefty starter (the not-yet-ready-for-prime-time Larry Gura), quizzed ex-Padre manager Preston Gomez at length about Norman.[12]

The ultimate winner of the Norman Conquest was the defending NL Champion Cincinnati Reds. They offered up reigning American Association batting champ Gene Locklear *and* a 23-year-old reliever who'd recorded a 2.27 ERA in 107 AAA innings the prior season *and* cash for a guy who two years earlier had been indistinguishable from 20 other AAA starters....

... and the move was an absolute steal for the Reds.

Though never good for more than 25 to 30 starts per season, Norman would become the Reds' winningest pitcher in their most successful decade ever. He would always be described as a "competitor,"[13] as "gutting it out with limited stuff,"[14] as showing (according to Sparky Anderson) "that there's more to pitching than sheer strength"[15]— yet despite the backhanded compliments Norman would rack up 104 major league victories and pitch in five postseason series.

Former Arizona State All-American Larry Gura's heater was never much more than major league average for sizzle, thus forcing him to rely on a five-pitch arsenal (two fastballs plus a curve, slider, and change) buttressed by excellent command.[16] This precarious mix caused Gura to spend most of his mid to late-20s bouncing between the majors and minors: to Royals GM Joe Burke the then 28-year-old lefty's 1976 acquisition was initially just a byproduct of getting Fran Healy off the roster.[17] Yet in nine Kansas City seasons Larry would ride that repertoire to 111 wins and three top-10 finishes in the Cy Young Award balloting.[18] Wilbur Wood was a pot-bellied 29-year-old knuckleballer with thinning hair who seemed destined for middle relief oblivion after losing his closer job to Terry Forster in the spring of 1971— or at least he did until longtime White Sox mainstay Joel Horlen injured his knee.[19] Once inserted in the rotation, Wood reeled off 84 wins over the next four seasons while shouldering a gargantuan 1,500-inning workload. Jim Rooker was a 30-year-old converted outfielder plagued by conditioning,[20] control,[21] and attitude problems when the Pirates got hold of him after the 1972 season.[22] Yet when Steve Blass came down with his now famous disease, Rooker's average stuff and 21-44 career record were judged worthy of another shot ... and he rewarded them with 67 wins and a 3.00 ERA over the next five seasons.

As with the five man rotation, there was nothing particularly revolutionary about the concept of resurrecting bodies from blown prospect hell. It was simply the sheer scale of the effort, the fact that pennant-winning teams such as the Reds, Pirates, and Royals were dipping into this well on a regular basis, that gave the trend special meaning.

Yet simultaneous to this massive Lazarus act, a real revolution was occurring in the operating room.

Marvin Miller, in his book *A Whole Different Ball Game*, remembered visiting the National League clubhouse after the 1966 All-Star Game and seeing Sandy Koufax's left arm swollen up like a balloon. When Miller expressed concern, Koufax told him not to worry, noting that "it always blows up like this after I pitch."[23]

At a time in which doctors removed calcium deposits with a chisel and mallet,[24] torn rotator cuffs, ruptured tendons, and strained ligaments were things to be lived with until the point at which one's arm either locked up or fell off. The stories of guys like Freddie Fitzsimmons having their hands disappear up the sleeves of their jerseys as the innings rolled on are legion: it was said that an ex-pitcher on the street could be easily identified by the rolling gait his permanently crooked arm induced.[25] Such legends continue on to this day, as witnessed by John Smoltz's pain-induced alteration of his pitching motion down the stretch in 1999 that helped the Braves over the top but forced the righthander's conversion into the Dennis Eckersley of the new millennium.[26]

In those days, the prescription for anything that couldn't be splinted or

A three-time 20-game winner after undergoing the surgery that now bears his name, Tommy John wasn't the first guy to come back after going under the knife, but he was the first to return and be really successful. His story would be crucial in sports medicine's elevation from something to be avoided at all costs to a near-normal part of a player's physical conditioning regimen. (*National Baseball Hall of Fame Library, Cooperstown, NY*)

sewn back together again was simple — rest, and if rest didn't work, perhaps pain medication or another line of work. All of that changed as a result of Tommy John's experiences.

That's an oversimplification of course, but John did become the poster boy for what was possible in the realm of corrective surgery. A lefty who combined a repertoire of breaking pitches with just enough heat to get by, John had racked up a typical resume of arm maladies (well, maybe not quite typical — a fight with Dick McAuliffe once tore ligaments in Tommy's shoulder[27]) before tearing his medial collateral ligament (MCL) while throwing a curveball during a May 20, 1976, game.[28] The MCL is an itty-bitty thing roughly the diameter of a pencil, its small size being a byproduct of the fact that typical humans don't ask it to do very much beyond aiding them in grasping items with their hands. Pitchers, though, make their living by endlessly repeating an unnatural motion, and that movement appears to be one that often imperils this tiny but essential muscle.[29]

In previous times such an injury would have represented a one-way ticket to insurance sales, but John was the kind of guy who was full of faith in God as well as downright stubbornness. Thus, Tommy went to Dr. Frank Jobe, a guy who'd been performing various sports surgeries for years and had an idea as to the potential for transplanting tendons....

And baseball history was made.

The point wasn't that John was the first guy to return from surgery, but that he was the first guy to return and have a really successful career afterwards — and better yet to do so without enduring incredible amounts of pain. In fact, one can make a case that T.J. returned from the operation an even better pitcher than he'd been before:

- Prior to 1976, John had topped 200 innings pitched in five of his first 12 major league seasons; he would exceed that level in each of the five seasons immediately after the operation.
- John's career high in wins before the injury was 16 — afterwards he was a three-time 20 game winner.
- In the five years prior to the injury, John had hurled 33 complete games; in the five years afterwards, he would record 57.

While John is the era's most famous guinea pig, he was far from the only one. Plenty of other guys whose careers might otherwise have been little more than footnotes were posting good and occasionally distinguished seasons after going under the knife. Mike Caldwell, a sinkerball-throwing lefty whose ultra-combative nature and perpetual scowl earned him the nickname Mr. Warmth (to emphasize the point, Caldwell wore a shirt emblazoned "Mr. Fucking Warmth"[30]), appeared finished after undergoing reconstructive elbow surgery during the 1974-1975 off-season. Yet with the bionic joint and a new emphasis on changing speeds (as well as, some whispered, a spitball[31]) Caldwell would record 91 victories for the Milwaukee Brewers over a six-year period and finish second in the 1978 Cy Young Award balloting. A 1977 Achilles tendon tear appeared to signal the end of the line for the then 33-year-old Ferguson Jenkins: after off-season surgery Jenkins won 18 games with a 3.04 ERA for the Texas Rangers, reestablishing himself on a road that would lead to Cooperstown immortality.[32] Soon teams were even sending prospects to the hospital: a 23-year-old AA pitcher named Tom Candiotti had his elbow rebuilt by Dr. Jobe in 1981[33]—within two years Candiotti commenced an 18-year big league career in which he would record 151 wins.

The net result of this infusion of long-term minor leaguers and bionic arms was a Darwinian nightmare. Unlike Col. Steve Austin of *Six Million Dollar Man* fame, this new generation of pitchers was anything but faster, stronger, or better than their predecessors from a physical standpoint. Strike-out rates plunged throughout the decade: a typical American League ace in 1979 fanned 18 percent fewer men per inning than his counterpart of ten years earlier, a difference dramatized by Larry Gura's feat of leading a quality Kansas City Royals staff in K's that season with 85.[34] Starter workloads were simultaneously being chopped by 11 percent, in part because of the bullpen's development, but also because of a significant graying of the talent pool. Only two aces of 1969 senior circuit staffs were significantly over the age of 30 (Bob Gibson and Bob Veale); ten years later only one ace (Pete Vuckovich) was significantly *under* that age.[35]

Simultaneously, the elevation of back-end rotation slots from blown prospect wasteland to strategic weapon began drawing quality hurlers who would devote lengthy, productive careers to those roles. Scott Sanderson was just embarking on his 19-year journey through both leagues as a number four starter: a litany of elbow, back, shoulder, thumb, and knee problems would limit him to fewer than 210 innings in all but two seasons, yet Sanderson would win 134 games and make four postseason appearances. Mike Krukow had a 20-win season in front of him but would average only 175 innings a year over the next decade. Don Robinson, Steve Renko, Eric (no, Harry ... no, Eric) Rasmussen, Dick Ruthven—none of these guys would ever highlight anyone's rotation, but all were solid, dependable members of more than one successful staff.

Evolution is one of the most misunderstood theories active today. Using the taken-out-of-context "survival of the fittest" cliché as a guidepost, the layman's concept of evolution is a process by which superior entities (be they plants, animals, or businesses) dominate the world while inferior ones are forced out of existence. That isn't what Charles Darwin or those who followed in his footsteps had in mind, however: they saw evolution as a process by which organisms became better adapted to the situations under which they existed. Successful species don't necessarily become bigger, stronger, or more agile—the eyes of fish that live in subterranean caves, for example, have evolved away over the centuries—but they do become more specialized as a rule, developing sometimes odd capabilities to exploit whatever their assigned ecosystem has to offer.

Thus it was with this new wave of factory second starters. The typical rotation member's workload declined by approximately 7 percent between 1969 and 1979,[36] an unsurprising result given the kind of talent and health histories that were increasingly being tapped for the role. Yet, having said that:

a)   The decline in workload was probably as much a function of the improved relief options at the typical manager's disposal as it was due to any weakness on the part of early inning hurlers, and

b)   The relative effectiveness of these men in the innings they worked appears to have changed very little as this trend accelerated. In 1979 starter ERAs, for example, were approximately 3 percent higher relative to the game as a whole (after taking DH impacts into account) than those of a decade before.[37] Now a differential of three percentage points is very real — plenty of pennants have been decided by lesser margins — yet keep in mind that this variance was derived over a period in which
     • Two new and at that time very raw teams with marginal rotations had been added to the mix,
     • The disco generation was playing its games in six new ballyards as well as three others that had been significantly remodeled, and
     • More frequent mid-inning pitching changes increased opportunities for the ultimate starter's nightmare to be played out (i.e. a new guy comes in and allows all the runners he inherited to score).

In short, given the outside influences, a 3 percent nominal difference isn't anything worth gambling one's life on.

Thus by the end of the '70s a new stasis regarding rotational talent had been reached, one that with evolutionary modifications remains intact to this day. Whether the craft as a whole was improved by this new order is open to question, but regardless of the movement's rationality, there was something undeniably heartening in the sight of the Fred Normans and Mike Caldwells of the world having their day in the sun.

At least it was a change from all those clean-cut fireballers who reminded us of our snotty neighbor with the Beemer and the cute wife....

20

Consistency and Wit
in the Shadows

The American Diamond is a stage specifically designed to highlight dramatic moments. In comparison to continuous action sports like basketball or hockey, baseball's interludes produce a *Mission: Impossible*-style tension at key moments that brand each clutch home run or spectacular catch indelibly in onlookers' minds. As a result of this natural theatricality, a Joe Rudi (on an average day the left fielder version of J.T. Snow) can achieve folklore status—and that's one of the game's more endearing aspects.

Unfortunately, baseball's collective conscience, like that of every other activity under the sun, has a finite capacity. Our recollection of the Joe Rudis and Bucky Dents come at a price, and that is the diminution of those with quieter abilities. Not that the talents of a Roy White or Freddie Patek are completely wiped from memory, but White and Patek were at a minimum the equals of Rudi and Dent ... yet it would be a promotion for the former pair to be half as famous as the latter two today.

This sense of collective amnesia can even throttle memories of those with Cooperstown qualifications, as witnessed by the fate of one Donald Howard Sutton.

For a man with 324 career wins and a devastatingly wry sense of humor, Sutton possessed an amazing ability to fade into the woodwork, yet when one examines Don's career as well as the goings-on around him, it is easy to see why. His consistency denied him the drama inherent in the return-from-nowhere stories surrounding Tommy John and Al Downing. He reached the 20-win plateau only once in his career, which meant that he normally seemed like a second banana alongside a parade of Claude Osteens, Bill Singers, and Andy Messersmiths—in fact, Sutton would lead the Dodgers in victories only twice during the 1970s. Heck, Sutton was rarely top dog in anything, his 23 years of toil resulting in one ERA crown (1980) and a single seat atop the shutout heap (1972).[1] As for his sense of humor ... well, imagine competing with the tidal wave of Frank Sinatra stories emanating from Tommy Lasorda's office, not to mention the well-oiled publicity machine surrounding Steve Garvey.

Yet Sutton in his own way was a (if not *the*) critical cog in the 1970s model Dodger machine—a man who brought home the bacon every year while doing his bit to keep the clubhouse loose.

Let's play GM for a moment. Suppose a hypothetical organization possessing a Grade A crystal ball was offered a pitcher that they knew would win 166 games over the next ten seasons while posting a 3.06 ERA. No question that the team would be interested in the guy, but suppose their fortune-telling capabilities were refined enough to further disclose that:

- He would never win fewer than 12 games in any of those ten seasons
- He would never work fewer than 226 innings in any campaign and would be among the top ten in innings worked seven times
- His ERA would exceed 4.00 only once ... and he'd still post a winning record that year
- He would be among the league leaders in strikeouts every year but one
- He would be among the leaders in (fewest) runners allowed per nine innings pitched nine times during that span
- He would rank among the top ten Cy Young Award vote-getters for five consecutive seasons in the heart of that time frame.[2]

In short, one sweep of the pen will not only solve 20 percent of the team's pitching problems, it will do so in a way as to make that roster spot a strength *every year*. Now how badly will this hypothetical GM want this guy?

Steve Carlton won 168 games during the 1970s and posted two Cy Young Award seasons during that span, but he also led the league in losses twice and posted ERAs over 3.55 five times (Sutton did so twice). Now Lefty was a great pitcher capable of turning a contender into a champion—but he was also capable of kicking out a 10-19 season if overworked or hurting or having problems concentrating. Furthermore, when Carlton ran into trouble, it was oftentimes difficult to get him back on track because Steve was roughly as communicative as Helen Keller when times were bad.

Sutton, on the other hand, always had something to say—tinged with a touch of acid perhaps, but generally coated by a self-effacing humor that made his double entendres easier to swallow. After a protracted contract battle in which Don had gone as far as supplying the Dodgers with a list of teams that he wanted to be traded to,[3] he was queried about his loyalty. "I'm the most loyal player money can buy,"[4] Sutton quipped, which produces a smile but also answers a question or two that nobody asked. Occasionally the acid would run a little heavy, as it did in 1978 when he characterized Steve Garvey as "a Madison Avenue image" and stated that Reggie Smith had been the team's best player over the previous two seasons.[5] That broadside led to a scuffle with Garvey in the visitor's clubhouse at Shea Stadium,[6] but ... well, Smith probably *was* the most valuable player on those Dodger teams.

As Sutton aged he began doctoring the ball a bit ... ok, maybe more than a bit, given opposition pitching coach Ray Miller's comment that the righthander should have gone to the mound with a tool kit attached to his belt.[7] It was an image Don reveled in, seizing every opportunity that came along to enhance it.[8] Doug Harvey (the closest thing to a god that the umpiring profession has produced since Bill Kelm) tossed Sutton from a 1978 game after three balls showed signs of mutilation; Don threatened to sue the National League for interfering with his ability to make a living.[9] When asked if he used foreign substances on the ball, Sutton slyly replied, "Vaseline is made right here in the USA."[10] He took strong exception to Bobby Valentine's claim that all Dodgers pitchers during his tenure with the club sandpapered the ball, pointing out that "Al Downing never uses it."[11]

So Sutton never sent the electric shock of a no-hitter through our veins—he won eight 1-0 games during the first half of the decade (Carlton won only four such contests during that period)[12] and that's enough to get any fan's pulse racing. So he only pitched in four All-Star Games—he didn't yield a single run in any of his midsummer appearances and was the MVP of the 1977 contest.[13]

And what the heck ... there has to be space in our collective memory bank for a guy who, when told that he had just passed Sandy Koufax as the Dodgers' all-time strikeout king, said, "Comparing me with Sandy Koufax is like comparing Earl Scheib with Michelangelo."[14]

21

The Evolution of the Bullpen

The road from idea to finished product is often a torturous one filled with false starts, dead ends, and intermediate decisions that may represent the one step back rather than the two forward. Consider automobiles: the seemingly organic combination of power, shape, and ergonomics that today's car represents was anything but a done deal for many years. Steam, for example, was an accepted power source for engines until the mid-1920s. The latter half of the Eisenhower years witnessed the sprouting of gargantuan tail fins that were as much a stylistic statement as an attempt to improve automotive aerodynamics. It only took 25 years of fast food, singed crotches, and stained seat covers for automakers to provide a holder for that morning cup of McCoffee.

So it was with automobiles and so it was in baseball's Last Frontier, the bullpen.

Through the years, relief pitching had evolved from a refuge for blown prospects and old pros on their last legs to … well, a refuge for blown prospects and old pros on their last legs that was becoming really important. As the 1970s dawned, there were only two things that baseball people agreed upon when it came to relievers: they were necessary, and nobody had a clue as to what made a good one.

Actually, that's not quite fair: the collective mind-set did know a thing or two about relievers—or at least they knew something about closers—but some of their conclusions might come as a shock to modern day observers.

Take, for example, the average fireman's pitching repertoire. At a time when fireballers such as Nolan Ryan, Tom Seaver, and Bob Gibson terrorized the baseball world, it may surprise today's fans to discover that virtually none of the best closers were particularly hard throwers. This is not to insinuate that people like Tug McGraw and Ron Perranoski were wimps: these guys could and did throw hard enough to effectively set up devastating breaking pitches. Still, that's what the typical closer's fastball (assuming he had one) was—something to show the hitter while setting him up for whatever it was that he threw for dough.

The reason for this void was simple: teams still inevitably earmarked their best arms for the starting rotation. Yes, a few fireballers like Dick (The Monster) Radatz and Billy McCool found their way into the fireman ranks during the mid-1960s, but keep in mind that:

- Radatz was 22 before he even signed a professional contract
- McCool was wilder than a Detroit teenager on Hell Night, and
- Both were finished before their 30th birthdays.

While the Radatzes and McCools were flaming across the sky, guys like Hoyt Wilhelm, Don McMahon, and Lindy McDaniel who could barely throw hard enough to break glass were racking up tons of impressive-looking seasons. Most of these guys were destined to weave their magic far from the madding pennant race, but all were still standing at decade's end and ... well, there's something about a 1.64 ERA that tends to capture the imagination of even the most hidebound GM.

Actually, calling them soft tossers is a bit of a misnomer: what each was really armed with was a trick pitch or delivery. Wilhelm, of course, was a knuckleballer. Stu Miller threw an assortment of off-speed pitches that died from exhaustion upon arrival at the plate. McDaniel rode a screwball to 18 seasons of major league paychecks, while Ted Abernathy's submarine delivery was a remedy for early career elbow problems.[1] Since this foursome plus Perranoski represented all of the closers of the 1960s who were both good and long-lived, it was natural that the class of 1970 would largely emulate them. Tug McGraw and Jim Brewer were both screwball practitioners à la McDaniel, and both would prove to be among the most consistent relievers of their time. Wayne Granger and Joe Hoerner were sidearmers in the Abernathy mode, while Wilbur Wood threw the knuckler and Phil Regan offered up ... well, suffice it to say that a lot of people thought the Vulture's success was one part talent and one part Vaseline.[2]

What strikes a modern observer is that none of these people were throwing anything a quality pitcher would serve up nowadays—a fact that severely impacted their job stability. Wilhelm posted some eye-popping statistics over a 21-year career that is immortalized in Cooperstown — yet he toiled for nine different teams during his career. McGraw kept bouncing between New York and AAA Jacksonville early on because first pitching coach Warren Spahn and then manager Gil Hodges didn't like his scroogie: after being sent down in 1968 Tug abandoned the screwball for the curve ... and damaged his arm.[3] Abernathy led the 1968 NL in appearances while finishing 10–7 with a 2.46 ERA and 13 saves; he was traded that winter for a career backup catcher (Bill

Hotter than a pistol for one turn around the league, Detroit closer Tom Timmermann would record a 6.51 ERA over the last two and a half months of the 1970 season — and still be named "Tiger of the Year." (*National Baseball Hall of Fame Library Cooperstown, NY*)

Plummer), a future batting coach (Clarence Jones) and a minor league pitcher.

The reason for this seemingly random scattering of dictatively fine talent was that the funky deliveries and pitches that brought these guys success made them a risk in their overseers' views. Then, as now, the fastball was the number one pitch, with a breaking pitch (either curve or slider) ranking second in importance and effective off-speed stuff coming in third. Some combination of that repertoire was thrown by 95 percent of baseball's pitchers, and as a result those pitches were the ones best understood by the managers and pitching coaches of the time. It was easy to counsel a kid whose curveball kept ending up in the dirt, but what do you tell a submariner who is leaving his pitches up in the zone? How could a coach who probably hadn't seen five quality knuckleballers in his life get a Wilhelm turned around?[4] Could a manager of a contending team afford to have a key pitcher that couldn't be helped if he went sour?

The answer to that final question was whenever possible a resounding no.

Like it or not, though, teams often found themselves resorting to these guys with the odd deliveries because they didn't have an alternative. As difficult as it might be for the modern mind to conceive, nobody — literally nobody — was training young pitchers with talent to be relievers at the time. It's amazing in a sense: twenty years after a fireman (the overaged Whiz Kid Jim Konstanty) was deemed worthy of the Most Valuable Player Award, closers were still primarily being selected from the pile of factory second starters and career minor leaguers.

Typical of this breed was Tom Timmermann, a Tiger farmhand whose sinking fastball wasn't nearly as big as his person.[5] Like most pitchers with OK heat and decent control, Timmermann blew through the lower minors (he led the Northern League in wins in 1961[6]) but hit the wall in AAA as his lack of a strikeout pitch resulted in too many opposition hits. Stuck in the

AA Southern League at 25, Timmermann even quit baseball for a time to go to college but was talked back into the game by Detroit farm director Don Lund.[7] Armed with a new dedication, Timmermann's control sharpened to the point where by 1969 he received a shot with the parent club as the Tiger bullpen struggled to cover for Joe Sparma's collapse and Don McMahon's departure. He did as well as anyone could possibly have wanted (a 2.75 ERA in 31 appearances), yet on a staff that was loaded with younger, more promising talents the 29-year-old Timmermann found himself back in the minors as the 1970 season started.

Then Denny McLain got suspended while Earl Wilson ran out of gas at 35 and Detroit needed every able body they could get their hands on.

Now, even with the drain on their pitching resources, the Tigers had a number of good possibilities available for the closer job. John Hiller was in the 1970 bullpen — after recovering from a heart attack[8] he'd save 100 games and win 58 more in six seasons as the Detroit closer. Fred Scherman was a younger Timmermann, while Mike Kilkenny was a good looking prospect who'd posted a 1.66 ERA with 73 strikeouts in 76 innings as a minor league reliever just two seasons prior.

Yet after considering the available options, Detroit manager Mayo Smith put Kilkenny in the starting rotation (where he'd record a 5.16 ERA), used Hiller as a middle reliever/spot starter and anointed this journeyman with no out pitch as his closer. Timmermann's results were as anyone would have expected — he was hotter than a pistol for one turn around the league, then posted a 6.51 ERA over the season's final 2½ months as the Tigers finished under .500 for the first time in eight years and Smith lost his job.

None of which kept Detroit writers from selecting Timmermann as "Tiger of the Year" in a postseason poll.[9]

There were tons of people like that running big league bullpens in those days— Jerry Johnson, Claude Raymond, Ken Sanders, Ken Tatum — and as one might expect virtually none of them lasted more than a year or so as firemen. It isn't that these guys were bad pitchers either — Timmermann, for example, would be the number three starter for the Tigers' 1972 divisional championship team. However, once the age, resume, and stuff of these hurlers was factored into the equation ... well, it would have been a major upset if they had been anymore successful or long-lived in such a high profile role.

Unfortunately, that type of pitcher was all that most systems had to offer. The American Association (AAA) save leaders for 1970 were future Yankee pitching coach Art Fowler and Garland Shifflett, each of whom was 35 or older and hadn't pitched in a major league stadium in six years. Bob Duliba and Hal Reniff were two-three in the International League (both had left the majors for good in 1967), while ex-Phillie Jack Baldschun and Reniff's Yankee teammate Jim Coates (once described as the guy on the iodine bottle[10]) were top dogs in a pair of Pacific Coast League pens. The phenomenon even extended further down the minor league chain: Don Nottebart, who'd thrown a no-hitter for the Houston Colt 45s in 1963, tied for the Texas League lead in saves as San Antonio's 1970 closer.[11]

If all of this sounds haphazard and chaotic, it was: each spring training inevitably became an open casting call in the majority of major league bullpens. Yet it would be a mistake to judge the era's managers and executives too harshly in this area. Keep in mind that "modern" relief pitching as such had only been around for 25 years or so at this point — before World War II starters on their days off had typically closed out the key games. Thus, relief pitching in 1970 was basically at the same developmental level that the game as a whole had been in the days when first basemen played on the bag with a runner on base, the fielding glove was a disdained innovation, and most pitching staffs consisted of one guy. Think about trying to make sense out of a situation where

- A 35-year-old Mudcat Grant could save 24 games with a 1.87 ERA while striking out fewer than four batters per nine innings,
- A 26-year-old Dick Selma could save 22 games with a 2.75 ERA in 1970, yet post a 5.34 ERA over the remaining four years of his career, or
- A 30-year-old Dave Giusti could go from being a mediocre starter (47-52 with a 4.02 ERA in the Astrodome) to a dominating fireman (saved 127 games with a 2.80 ERA in his five seasons as the Pirate closer).

It would be enough to drive anyone nuts.

The first person to bring some sense to these proceedings was Rollie Fingers. A failed starter who transitioned into the fireman role over a three-year period, Fingers brought a heretofore unknown level of consistency to closing. He was *numero uno* in whatever bullpen he inhabited for 13 consecutive seasons, posting only one subpar campaign during that time frame — and two years after that he was the AL's MVP. Yes, Hoyt Wilhelm is in the Hall of Fame alongside Fingers, but Hoyt went through a very fallow period in the mid-1950s and was sporadically relegated to second fiddle status behind people like Eddie Fisher and Bob Locker throughout the 1960s. Ron Perranoski was a terrific go-to guy as well ... but Bob Miller and Phil Regan were the top bullpen dogs on the last two Dodger pennant winners that Perranoski was associated with.

The reason for Fingers's consistency, of course, was that he was a legitimately good pitcher. Armed with a hard slider and a fastball good enough to change speeds off of effectively, Rollie had been a quality minor league starter, never posting an ERA over 3.00 while allowing 7.65 hits per nine innings pitched and striking out more than twice as many men as he walked.[12] He reached the majors for good at 21, then "failed" in 35 starts scattered over the next three seasons—campaigns in which Fingers was posting league average ERAs while giving up less than a hit an inning and striking out more than twice as many as he walked.[13]

Fingers would tend to pooh-pooh his capabilities as a starter once he'd hit fireman pay dirt, claiming that he'd overanalyze his starts in advance and would consequently be too tense and tired when game time came around.[14] That may well be true (one hesitates to doubt that which comes from the horse's mouth), but on closer examination a couple of other possible reasons for his relative lack of success present themselves:

1. With people like Catfish Hunter, Vida Blue, Blue Moon Odom, and Chuck Dobson at the A's disposal, Fingers would probably have had to go 35-0 with an ERA the size of Osama bin Laden's conscience to garner much attention.

2. Rollie hadn't demonstrated much stamina as a minor league starter after a horrific 1967 injury.[15] At a time when an unholy mix of rookies and down-on-their-luck veterans composed the nether reaches of most pitching staffs, starters were expected to regularly work into the eighth inning. On the 1971 A's staff, for instance, Odom was the only man with 20 or more starts to work less than six frames per start[16]—a workload that Fingers had never successfully shouldered in any of his minor league seasons.

Thus, the A's found themselves with an obviously talented pitcher who wasn't as capable of working deep into games as the guys that they already had. That their answer to this dilemma seems obvious today should not obscure the creative arrogance it took to refrain from trading Fingers to some needy team ... or stretching him beyond his physical resources ... or simply consigning him to the Twilight Zone of middle relievers and blown prospects.

As hidebound as baseball people are in certain areas (such as dressing their players in knickers 75 years after they went out of style), show them an idea that helps a rival three-peat and they'll dump decades of tradition without a second thought. Fingers's icon status quickly elevated the closer role to something that a team could gamble a quality arm on without being roasted in the press or by its peers—or at least a quality arm that was struggling in the rotation. As a Midwest League starter in 1971, the 19-year-old Goose Gossage posted a 1.87 ERA while working 7½ innings per outing; after thrashing about for three years in a swing role Gossage became a full-time fireman at 23, recording numbers that may yet propel him through Cooperstown's doors. Al Hrabosky was an undersized lefty with a terrific fastball but marginal control of his breaking stuff as a starter—once converted to closing, he became "The Mad Hungarian." The flamethrowing wild man (in more ways than one) Jim Kern was the American Association's 1974 Pitcher of the Year as a starter; by 1976 he was arguably the most intimidating closer in the American League.

What these four men collectively represented was the first wave of orthodoxy in the fireman profession. Unlike their forebears, these men by and large had conventional stuff and pitching motions that their coaches could under-

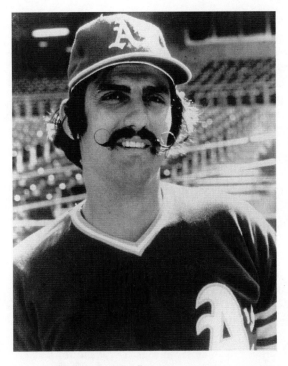

A quality pitcher who had a phobia about starting, Rollie Fingers brought a heretofore unknown
level of consistency to relief pitching. In thirteen
seasons as the closer for three different teams, Fingers would post only one sub-par season ... and
would win the Cy Young Award two years after
that. (*National Baseball Hall of Fame Library,
Cooperstown, NY*)

stand and critique if need be.
The value of such potential
help (some might call it meddling) remains speculative to
this day, but the bottom line
was that contending teams
felt more comfortable with a
standard guy throwing standard stuff out there in key situations. As a result, this new
generation of closers became
pennant race and postseason
fixtures, moving the profession out of the second division shadows that had often
obscured its best practitioners. Wilhelm, McDaniel and
McMahon worked a com-
bined 61 big league seasons
and pitched in two World
Series: Fingers, Gossage, and
Hrabosky would pitch in 15
October series during their
combined 51 years.[17]

As ex-starters these peo-
ple had another distinct
advantage: they had a reasonable chance of holding up
under the 120-plus inning
workloads that firemen were
typically expected to shoulder in the days before the rotator cuff became a
permanent part of baseball's lingo. Of course, as in everything else having to
do with closers in those days, there were exceptions to this rule: Earl Weaver,
for instance, won a world championship with a lefty-righty closer duo (Eddie
Watt and Pete Richert) that rarely worked more than an inning per appearance. On the flip side, though, were organizations that remained unconvinced
(and not totally without reason) that a workload 60 percent of the one routinely endured by front line starters represented the limit of a fireman's productivity.

At the apex of this experiment in human endurance was Mike Marshall.
Baseball history is loaded with people who are dedicated to conditioning, visions of Mickey Lolich and Cecil Fielder to the contrary — a late 1970s
commitment to weight training transformed a once pudgy White Sox catcher
named Brian Downing into someone who, with the proper pigmentation,

Mike Marshall (shown here preparing to throw one of his trademark screwballs) was a conditioning fanatic and baseball's resident intellectual snob. Marshall holds the seasonal record for appearances in each league, yet despite his success under seemingly Herculean workloads, baseball largely chose to ignore his trailblazing efforts. (*National Baseball Hall of Fame Library, Cooperstown, NY*)

could have served as a body double for Dick Allen. Marshall was one of those guys, but with a twist: possessing a doctorate in physiological psychology, Iron Mike was a health nut who really knew what he was doing. His studies in kinesiology yielded an individualized training program that Marshall insisted was too difficult for the layman to understand, along with the conviction that consistent work (he'd note that the body is a muscle that atrophies without regular use) was not only possible but desirable.[18]

And when Iron Mike said regular, he meant regular....

After a late start that was due to four years of toil as a minor league shortstop as well as a personality that caused three successive organizations to dump him, Marshall became pitching's answer to Cal Ripken upon linking up with the down-and-out, nothing-to-lose Montreal Expos. Armed with a killer screwball (yup, another oddball pitch) plus a slider and sinker for variety, Marshall logged a respectable 111 1/3 innings while posting a 5 — 8 record with 23 saves in his first season as the Expos' closer ... and that was only the beginning. From there, Iron Mike's workload increased to 116 innings in 1972 and a staggering 179 frames the following season, a year in which he went 14-8 with a 1.78 ERA and finished in the top five in both the Cy Young and MVP balloting.

On the basis of such a record one might think that Marshall was well on his way to becoming a Montreal icon ... but public adoration (or even indifference) was never one of his goals. A blunt man by nature, Marshall's apparent lack of concern over the impact of his words created numerous tempests with management, teammates, and sportswriters. When asked once about Montreal's infield defense, Marshall allowed as how it stunk, singling out second baseman Ron Hunt (who in all fairness had nothing wrong with him that a new body wouldn't have solved) in the process.[19] He refused the team's MVP award and accompanying cash prize, noting his disdain for such competitions — then complained when the cash award didn't go to the charity he specified.[20] An impolitic comment to one sportswriter resulted in Marshall being served with a lawsuit by a rival writer while sitting on the Expos' bench.[21]

Thus, in a trade that should strike a chord with current Expos fans, Marshall was dispatched to the Los Angeles Dodgers for the aging Willie Davis — and finally found the stage upon which he was meant to perform. With longtime closer and fellow screwballer Jim Brewer battling arm and back problems, while the 23-year-old Charlie Hough struggled with command of his knuckleball, Marshall became the man supporting a 1974 Dodger rotation primarily comprised of young pitchers whose arms were still in the seasoning process.

This combination of pitching paternalism with Marshall's conditioning principles and ego produced a seasonal record that is inconceivable to modern fans. Working in the late innings of virtually every close game, Marshall racked up a phenomenal 108 appearances (Kent Tekulve is the only other pitcher in major league history to top 90 in a season[22]) and 208 innings of work. The bottom line results were equally impressive: 15 victories, 21 saves, and a 2.42 ERA along with a trip to the World Series and the Cy Young Award to add to Marshall's trophy case.

This proved to be the high water mark of relief pitching workloads, and while there are some good and compelling reasons for that fact, it's hard to understand why there was virtually no attempt to follow through on Marshall's accomplishment. While Iron Mike faded quickly after 1974, it was primarily back problems from a childhood injury that triggered his demise[23] — once Marshall got past those he recorded a couple of fine seasons with the Minnesota Twins before time and the ailments caught up with him again. Still, 150-plus inning efforts declined rapidly after 1974, and no pure reliever has worked as many as 130 innings since 1985. Even stalwarts such as Fingers saw their workloads progressively reduced over the years for no particularly good reason — he went in steps from 120 innings a season in the mid-1970s to 75 or so by the early 1980s, while his strikeout, walk, and health data remained constant.

Perhaps Marshall's status as baseball's resident intellectual snob had as much to do with it as anything. In a game where Pedro Guerrero achieved star stature without the mental capacity to use a checkbook, Marshall's intelligence and frequently against-the-grain comments branded him as a kook — someone who could be ridiculed or ignored as needs be. Compounding this problem was an attitude that neither suffered fools gladly nor left any doubt that Marshall often considered himself surrounded by nothing but fools.[24] Though Iron Mike would claim that his early career difficulties were the result of managers resisting his screwball, keep in mind that this was a man who micro-managed his appearances to the point of shifting his infielders around on a hitter-by-hitter basis.[25] Between this and Marshall's *enfant terrible* cameo role in Jim Bouton's *Ball Four* world, one gets the impression that the man's difficulties stemmed from a perception that he'd do whatever he wanted whenever he wanted and to heck with everyone else. Maybe this is an incorrect interpretation, but somehow a 24-year-old pitcher who posted a 1.98 ERA with ten saves down the stretch ended up not being invited to spring training the following year.[26]

Think about that one for a moment....

For whatever reason, baseball decided to march en masse away from Marshall's accomplishments ... and the wisdom of that decision is open to debate. For all the things Iron Mike might have been he was an expert in his field, and while recent findings on repetitive stress injuries might temper his training program today, his theories remain plausible in the main and are not inconsistent with the performance of his peers. Even if Marshall is written off as a fluke, what about Fingers, who worked an average of 125 innings per year between 1969 and 1978? Or John Hiller, who put out 118 innings per season in the five years immediately following his heart attack? Or Kent

Tekulve, who toiled 269 innings in 1978-1979 yet remained a top reliever for another ten years? Sure, a bunch of guys weren't able to endure that kind of workload — but does that mean that baseball has to cut every reliever's innings?

Rollie Fingers worked 1,701 innings in a 16-year career that lasted until he was 39 years old. Take a current mid-career closer at random — say, Robb Nen. As of the end of the 2000 season the 31-year-old Nen had spent eight seasons in the majors, working a grand total of 563 2/3 innings or just a little over 70 per season. OK — who exactly has benefited from the 35 or so fewer innings per season that Nen has worked on average? His teams certainly haven't; they have been forced to use lesser pitchers in the eighth inning to protect a pitcher's future that will go to the highest bidder come free agency time. It's doubtful that Nen has either: he'll clearly never reach Fingers's career numbers and even with the reduced workload has already endured two elbow surgeries.

Is it possible that Nen's effectiveness (and dollar value) has been artificially constrained by relegating him to a lesser role during his prime seasons than he could otherwise have handled?

Well, we'll never know for sure ... but clearly the emphasis after 1974 began to turn towards maximizing the impact of the innings a closer worked. An indirect effect of this movement was the emergence of a new reliever strain — the man who had the stuff but not the stamina to work those back-breaking inning counts. These guys ran the gamut from youngsters like Bob McClure, who had run into arm and shoulder problems early,[27] to veterans such as Ron Reed, who kept breaking down at about 200 innings or so.

Which brings us to a kid out of Moline, Illinois, with unusually long fingers[28] named Bruce Sutter.

Sutter, like many of his predecessors, came armed with a trick pitch — in his case, a forkball that by utilizing the thumb for additional power[29] was transformed into the first split-finger fastball (sorry, Roger Craig fans: he learned the pitch from Sutter[30]). However, what Bruce also had was a fragility that manifested itself early in his career (his adoption of the splitter was the direct result of an elbow injury) and would ultimately result in 11 operations to various and sundry body parts.[31] As a result of this, the Chicago Cubs were essentially forced to limit Sutter to something approximating a modern relief role, rarely calling for him before the eighth inning was in progress and normally only using him in the ninth frame. It was a difficult lesson to absorb, but one that Sutter would inevitably reinforce by either breaking down in the stretch or simply running out of gas.

But when he was on ... man, he was on.

Pitching first in the Friendly Confines and then at Busch Stadium, Sutter established a level of dominance that remains unparalleled among closers. He led the league in saves in every season but one between 1979 and 1984 — and if Rollie Fingers hadn't spent a couple of years in San Diego's bullpen it

Blessed with exceptionally long fingers yet cursed with questionable durability, Bruce Sutter became the ultimate tactical weapon. In mostly ninth inning appearances, Sutter's split-fingered fastball would limit opposing batters to 5.95 hits per frame in his 1979 Cy Young Award season — and that wasn't even Bruce's best year. (*National Baseball Hall of Fame Library, Cooperstown, NY*)

would have been seven out of eight. At his peak Sutter was virtually impossible to reach base against: during his Cy Young Award winning 1979 season, Bruce allowed 5.95 hits and 2.84 walks per nine innings pitched while striking out 110 batters in 101 1/3 innings — in Wrigley Field.[32]

What's more, that wasn't even his best season....

Through his sheer dominance and the impact that his trademark pitch made on those subjected to it, Sutter became a milestone in the evolution of relief pitching. The first thing he proved was that ironman workloads weren't necessary to have a big impact on the outcome of a game — or for that matter to be the best pitcher in the league. The second and more subtle point Sutter's success made apparent was that fireman duty was a unique craft best practiced by people trained specifically for that purpose as opposed to the failed starters and midseason crapshoots that had previously been the norm.

Once again, this was a lesson that baseball people were quick to follow up on. Dan Quisenberry, whose first pro season coincided with Sutter's major league premiere, would never start a game in his career at either the minor or major league level. Rawly Eastwick, a fireballing contemporary of Sutter's who posted a couple of fine seasons before arm problems and temperament got the best of him, would open only one game. This wasn't an instantaneous or total conversion of course — people as unlikely as Jesse Orosco, Dave Righetti, and Terry Forster (best remembered today as the butt of David Letterman's "tub of goo" jokes) would still occasionally undergo starter conversions — but the game's future course was clearly set.

After a century of experimentation and false starts, the closer had within the space of one decade evolved from an amorphous life form to something approximating the role as we know today. Firemen as well as those surrounding them (who would move into the developmental spotlight during the next decade) still had many twists, turns, and tail fin eruptions to overcome before reaching their present, highly evolved state, yet for all of that the modern mechanism was in place....

... Not that that's 100 percent logical or reasonable, mind you.

22

The Aborted Sale
of Vida Blue

There's an old saying that goes something along the lines of "you need to be nice to the people you meet on the way up because they'll be the same ones you'll see on the way down." Somewhere alongside it in the realm of familiar quotations is another one: be careful what you wish for, because you might just get it.

Those two statements aptly sum up the confrontation between Charles O. Finley and Bowie Kuhn in the fall of 1976. By trying to sell three of his biggest stars—Vida Blue, Joe Rudi, and Rollie Fingers—Finley crossed over into the realm of "we don't have to do this for you if we don't want to" ... and quickly learned what payback is. At the same time, by deciding to clip Charlie's wings while he had the chance, Kuhn altered baseball's economic structure in ways that reverberate to this day—and unwittingly drove the final nail into the coffin of those he sought to serve.

A casual fan might wonder exactly how such a calamity could so quickly befall the most successful franchise of the early 1970s. Didn't the A's win three consecutive world championships? Wasn't the roster liberally seasoned with Hall of Fame and near-HOF-type players? Weren't the Mustache Gang and their flamboyant owner on virtually everybody's lips?

One of the things forgotten about the early 1970s A's is that the team drew very poorly. There were a number of reasons for this:

- The A's had a Johnny-come-lately/second city status in the Bay Area,
- The park itself (partially countersunk into the ground within a half mile of San Francisco Bay, the Coliseum was and is nippy on all but the warmest summer afternoons), and
- Neither Finley nor the majority of his bickering minions were particularly easy to love even under the best of circumstances.

Whatever the reason for it, the A's drew a big 2.76 million fans during their 1972-1974 championship run, or just a little over 11,000 per game to see a team that is on virtually everybody's all-time top 20 list. Sure, attendance figures all over the American League were stuck in neutral at the time, but by way of comparison Oakland's 1974 World Series opponents, the Los Angeles Dodgers, garnered 2.63 million admissions in that season alone.[1]

It was kind of an odd situation for an inveterate promoter to be in, but Charlie's promotions too often possessed either an ulterior motive or the subtlety of a sledgehammer.[2] Thus, at a time when ticket sales and concessions were still the primary drivers of club income, the A's found themselves in an uphill battle for solvency despite their success on the field — and Finley was no Phil Wrigley when it came to patience or bankroll size.

The first shot across Charlie's bow occurred prior to the start of the 1974 World Series. A clause in Cy Young Award winner-to-be Catfish Hunter's contract stated that half of his $100,000 annual salary was to be paid to him during the season, with the other half going into a deferred annuity.[3] The annuity turned out to be the tricky part for some obscure reason that probably hinged on Finley's well-known weakness for any stray buck that was within radar range of the straight and narrow. Charlie's efforts to avoid funding the annuity until the last possible moment thus dissolved into a montage of claims and counterclaims surrounding lost documents, stuff that wasn't delivered, concerns about the agreement's tax consequences and the like.[4]

It was a typical Finley performance, but one that was apparently pulled on a man who was apparently fed up with Charlie's shenanigans, and had a lawyer who could read a contract.

Thus, when Finley predictably failed to purchase the annuity by the deadline stated in Hunter's contract, players association general consul Dick Moss had a little surprise ready for the owner of the A's. Citing section 7A of Hunter's standard player contract (which states that a player could terminate his contract if his club defaulted on payments to him and failed to remedy the situation within ten days of written notice), Moss declared Catfish a free agent....

... And Peter Seitz, the chairman of baseball's arbitration panel and the only guy whose opinion mattered (the other two members, Marvin Miller and John Gaherin, chairman of the owners' Player Relations Committee, voted their respective party lines as usual), agreed with him.[5]

Given Seitz's "a contract is a contract" view of the world, it's hard to find fault or bias in his ruling. Still, the general impression at the time was that the hammer was being dropped awfully hard for what was basically a minor infraction — after all, the team's owner did attempt to hand Hunter a check for $50,000 to settle the matter but was rebuffed.[6] Of course, Finley only did that after Moss had notified him of the default and Hunter's free agency, but the general consensus was that A) somebody else might have gotten off a bit easier, but B) it didn't really bother anybody that much given who the injured party was.

A more sensitive individual might have been given pause in light of the Hunter debacle — but then again sensitive individuals are rarely drawn to baseball ownership, and few of those would name the team mule after themselves. In any event, with a Hall of Famer having flown the coop, Dave Hamilton and Glenn Abbott unable to plug the resulting hole and Blue Moon Odom's elbow shot, Finley had a real challenge on his hands as the 1975 season opened. In the grand tradition of operators with limited bankrolls who are this close to the pennant, he went out and acquired an All-Star staff ... circa 1968, that is. Sonny Siebert, Dick Bosman, Gaylord Perry's now superannuated brother Jim, Stan Bahnsen — all things considered, the 351 innings of mediocre baseball this quartet gave Finley in the league's best pitcher's park was something of a minor miracle.

Yet mediocre can get the job done if there are enough horses around to do the heavy work — and if there's one thing the A's had, Hunter or no Hunter, it was plenty of horses. Such talents as Reggie Jackson, Gene Tenace, Sal Bando, Joe Rudi, and Bill North led an offense whose potency was obscured somewhat by the park — for all the Bash Brothers hype, the 1973 squad is still the only Oakland team to lead the AL in runs scored.[7] Vida Blue and Ken Holtzman were arguably the best 1-2 rotation punch in the league, while Rollie Fingers headed up a solid bullpen.

Even better, there was oodles of quality talent waiting in the wings. Phil (Scrap Iron) Garner and Claudell Washington kicked off 1,800-plus game careers with the '75 A's: while neither may be a Hall of Fame candidate, both were key members of contending teams for a long, long time. Behind them was the outfield that would propel Oakland to its next post-season appearance (Rickey Henderson, Dwayne Murphy, and Tony Armas) as well as a bunch of people like Mitchell Page, Wayne Gross, Mike Norris, and Steve McCatty, who would have their moments. Heck, guys like Chet Lemon (he went in the Bahnsen trade) and Denny Walling were being more or less casually kicked out of the nest amidst the bounty.

Still, Finley had significant issues to address if the A's intended to stay ahead of an up-and-coming Kansas City Royals team. Bert Campaneris was 34 and seemed to be losing a half step of range a season in the field, while Rudi had already collided with one outfield wall too many and the back end of the roster was seriously clogged with old guys collecting their last paycheck.

Thus, the owner of the A's found himself at a crossroads in the fall of 1975. Should he clear space for the young talent and resign his ego and wallet to several .500 seasons while everyone matured, or continue on the veteran importation treadmill until it inevitably broke down?

It's hard to guess what Finley would have done under ordinary circumstances (though combining the concepts of "Finley" and "ordinary circumstances" is ludicrous in and of itself), but the events of December 23, 1975, turned normality upside down. Given the pressures (financial and otherwise) that the team's owner faced once the Messersmith-McNally decision was handed down, Charlie's subsequent moves were perfectly logical — brash perhaps, but that was the nature of the man. Think about it: Finley had

- A strong farm system capable of restocking the team within a couple of years,
- A bunch of peak and past-peak players who would be heading for the free agent hills as soon as their contracts ran out,[8]
- No hope of retaining the current squad or financing any acquisitions beyond the journeyman outfielder level given his current cash flow situation, and
- No great love for most of the incumbent players anyway.

One doesn't have to effect the morally calloused viewpoint of legendary Sunbeam CEO "Chainsaw Al" Dunlop to know what has to happen under such circumstances. It's a simple choice really: drain the bread-and-butter insurance business in the name of sportsmanship, or take a chance on becoming baseball's answer to Bob Vila.

Oh, and for those who might be wondering, a teardown-rebuild strategy with an in-their-prime team was not unprecedented either in baseball history or the Athletics franchise's annuals.

Sixty-some odd years before, Connie Mack faced a similar problem when the Federal League's rise engendered a parallel salary escalation spiral. Like the current A's, Mack's men had been the AL's dominant team over the past five seasons. Like the latter team, the 1914 A's featured a couple of Hall of Famers in their prime (Home Run Baker and Eddie Collins), and several other guys who were almost as good (Chief Bender, Wally Schang, Bob Shawkey, and Stuffy McInnis). Like Finley's squad they had young talent (future Hall of Famer Herb Pennock, Bullet Joe Bush, Shawkey, and McInnis were all 23 or younger) and impending holes (shortstop Jack Barry hit the wall at age 28, Rube Oldring at 30, and while still pitching well Eddie Plank was 38) in abundance.

And, like the Mustache Gang, Mack's Athletics hadn't been drawing well. Despite a widely acclaimed ballpark and four pennants in the preceding five seasons, attendance had fallen to just under 4,400 fans a game, a total that was fifth in the eight-team American League.[9] Mack and his partner Ben Shibe had borrowed heavily to construct their stadium and simply didn't have the funds to outbid the Federal League for top talent — furthermore, the outbreak of World War I in Europe cast a shadow over the game's immediate future. Could they survive if the U.S. was drawn into the conflict and play was suspended?

Mack simply couldn't afford to find out. Thus, he sold his key players — Shawkey went to the Yankees for $18,000, Collins to the White Sox for $50,000, Schang, Bush, and Amos Strunk to the Red Sox for $60,000 and three players, Barry to Boston for $8,000, Eddie Murphy to the White Sox for $13,500, and Home Run Baker to the Yankees for $37,500.[10] These were tremendous figures for the time, and the money did see Mack through until the next round of young talent manifested itself in the mid-1920s—but the short term result was a truly sad team, one that would be mired in the AL cellar for the next six seasons. But Mack not only survived; he built an even greater powerhouse from the ashes with such players as Mickey Cochrane, Jimmie Foxx, Lefty Grove, Bucketfoot Al Simmons, Eddie Rommel, and George Earnshaw.

Whether Finley was aware of this history on a conscious level is speculative—frankly, the man doesn't strike one as the reflective type—yet there is no question that his subsequent moves followed Mack's precedent nearly to the letter. The trade of Jackson and Holtzman for Mike Torrez, Don Baylor, and Paul Mitchell was a reasonable attempt to cut payroll while building for the future, but by the June 15 trading deadline Finley decided to cut his losses. Thus, in the grand tradition of Mr. Mack, the team's most salable assets went under the hammer: Vida Blue was sold to the Yankees for $1.5 million, while Joe Rudi and Rollie Fingers went as a package deal to the Red Sox for $2 million.[11]

Well, at least they were sold for the twenty-minute period before Bowie Kuhn found out about the deal....

In the discussion that is to follow, it is important to keep the commissioner's historic frame of reference in mind. Kuhn, you see, reached professional maturity during the heady New Frontier/Great Society era of the early 1960s, when America at its zenith suddenly developed a social conscience. For those accustomed to the "what's in it for me" outlook that has characterized much of the last two decades, it's difficult to recapture the near religious fervor of service to others that pervaded even the basest, most money grubbing activities of the time. Millions of all-electric "Medallion" homes were constructed not because utilities had lots of unused power capacity available (which they did) or because electricity was cheaper than gas (it wasn't and isn't) but because they were clean, safe, and "modern." Fast food was an inexpensive time saver rather than a nutritional nightmare/money machine, while anti-ballistic missiles weren't intended to bomb our enemies to Kingdom Come—they protected democracy.

Pretty much every endeavor in those days was seen though glasses tinted with concepts of the public trust, and baseball à la Kuhn was not immune to such aspirations. To Bowie, the Eisenhower years of Yankee dominance had been akin to a modern Dark Age where money and influence had doomed seven cities to perpetual second-class status, while the inauguration of the amateur draft represented a ray of hope for fans everywhere. Yet in a veritable moment, all of that progress was being threatened, first by the Hunter-Messersmith/McNally doubleheader and then by this "bully and cheapskate" who "could hardly face up to a world where the hired hands had the better of him."[12]

That's what Kuhn the human being really thought of Charlie O, as he makes abundantly clear in his book *Hardball — The Education of a Baseball Commissioner.* Within *Hardball's* pages Finley's voice is characterized as having a "rasping, low, nervous quality,"[13] his choice of beverages is appraised as "horrid,"[14] his eyes are seen as "dark, riveting, cold."[15] According to Bowie the man possessed "a gift for embarrassing and demeaning people," "treated players like plantation hands," and made "pigheaded remarks."[16] In other words, it's obvious by the end of the book that these two guys aren't going to be rooming together in school next year.

Thus, it should surprise no one to discover that Kuhn's unilateral rejection of Finley's sales took on a casual, almost off-hand aspect given the enormity of the issue being decided. The word "unilateral" is key since the evidence is that more than a few baseball executives were skeptical of Bowie's decision and a vote would probably have been a contentious affair.[17] Yet Kuhn's authority to act as he did under the Major League Agreement would ultimately be borne out in federal court and the Oakland owner would bear the brunt of resentment from fellow owners for precipitating this indirect assault on the reserve clause.[18]

Of course, from Finley's point of view Kuhn's dismissal of his fund-raising activities were anything but a trivial slight[19] — yet if there's one thing that Charlie's personal history clearly establishes, it's that the man was bull-headed … er, persistent … in the pursuit of his goals. Thus, within a week after his suit over the voided Blue/Rudi/Fingers deals was dismissed, Finley was on the Let's Make a Deal trail again, selling Paul Lindblad, a fine veteran reliever, to the Texas Rangers for $400,000.[20]

It is from such small acorns that giant oaks grow, and in this case Finley unwitting begot a real Rosemary's Baby.

When the deal finally came across Kuhn's desk (Finley by this time wasn't in the mood to give the commissioner the normal courtesy of informing him beforehand[21]) he decided to uphold it — with a Machiavellian caveat reminiscent of Chief Justice John Marshall's decision in *Maubury vs. Madison.* Those who have taken high school civics courses may vaguely remember the case: it was nominally about a guy who was trying to take over a job that he'd been appointed to by the outgoing John Adams administration, but James Madison (the new secretary of state) refused to commission him. The case wasn't a big deal in and of itself, but once Marshall got done with it … well, it had become the legal basis for the Supreme Court's authority in American government.[22]

Thus, Kuhn ruled that $400,000 would from here on represent the maximum amount that any sale could be consummated for. In *Hardball* Kuhn refers to the figure as if it were a matter of convenience rather than the product of some sort of rational analysis — the number simply seemed about right, so that's what he chose for it to be. Furthermore, the commissioner made his decision by edict once again, confident in the perspicacity of his decision but knowing darned well that "too many clubs would put their own self interest ahead of what was best for the game" if it were to have come to a vote.[23]

Thus with an offhand move Kuhn wiped away an operating tactic that had been a cornerstone of franchise operations for roughly eighty years—and could have been a critical lifeline for small market owners struggling to cope with the economics of the free agent era.

Bowie the human being harbored a belief Curt Flood would have thoroughly appreciated: that there was something unseemly about selling players as if they were used cars. That's a noble sentiment, but the problem is that such a theory flies directly in the face of baseball's economic realities. The flat fact of the matter is that a team's worth lies primarily in the value of the players that it owns via contractual agreements—always has and always will—and as salaries and the game's revenue potential spiraled upwards that inherent value grew by leaps and bounds. Yet without the ability to realize the value of excess talent via cash sales, the less affluent team becomes trapped on an increasingly precarious financial tightrope.

Consider the Oakland A's as a business enterprise. In the terms by which accountant types evaluate typical organizations the A's aren't worth Cactus Jack Garner's pitcher of warm spit. They own virtually nothing of tangible value (the ballpark they play in was leased from Alameda County) and possess no unique patentable processes. The club's value is primarily derived from four sources:

1. Its membership in the American League, which provides organized competition to play against,
2. Its good name (a somewhat humorous concept in this team's case) and reputation within the community for playing exciting baseball, which is the source of attendance and sales of concessions, souvenirs, logoed merchandise and the like,
3. The value of the broadcast rights to the club's games (some of which come under master agreements drawn up by Major League Baseball), and
4. The value of the player contracts they own at the major and minor league level.

That final category's the big number, given the players' ability through their relative success or failure to influence items two and three, but it's also kind of tricky to get one's arms around. Obviously, changes in on-field performance can dramatically impact an individual's worth relative to his paycheck, but there are other, more subtle influences as well:

1. How long the player has been in the major leagues. Claudell Washington in 1976 was 21, fast, capable of playing all three outfield positions, and already had an All-Star appearance under his belt. Obviously destined for

a lengthy career, Washington as a second year major leaguer nonetheless fell under the tenets of the Collective Bargaining Agreement, which effectively capped his earning potential for the next four years.

OK, so Claudell wasn't destined to be a superstar — actually, his destiny was to be an amazingly frustrating talent tease for six future teams.[24] Still, how valuable would a .278 career hitter with speed and some power have been to the St. Louis Cardinals, a team with plenty of financial backing and a number of fine players in their prime (Keith Hernandez, George Hendrick, Ted Simmons, Garry Templeton, Bob Forsch) that nonetheless spent the late 1970s stuck in neutral due in part to a couple of outfield holes that stubbornly defied filling?

2. Whether the team could utilize the talent it has to its maximum potential. With Sal Bando, Wayne Gross and a bevy of young and established outfielders, the 22-year-old Denny Walling's value to the A's organization was minimal at best. Yet Walling was anything but a useless player: after being sent with cash to the Houston Astros in exchange for the last 59 games of Willie Crawford's career, Denny went on to post a workmanlike 18-year career as a platoon regular/jack of all trades/pinch hitter extraordinaire. In other words, Walling was a valuable player — but like Sandy Alomar Jr. in his Padre days (he was blocked by Benito Santiago), his worth lay more in what he might be able to do for someone else.

3. The desperation factor of teams that are this close to the top. A good example of this phenomenon occurred during the 2000 season, when the New York Yankees found themselves in the thick of the pennant race without an adequate left fielder. To plug the gap they acquired David Justice, an injury-prone 34-year-old DH with two shot knees who was having a nothing-special season at the time of the trade and was way overpriced at $7 million a year. In fantasy baseball terms Justice was probably a replacement level player — to a second division team his contract and health status made him less than worthless. Yet to the Yankees at that time and in a world where their options were severely limited, Justice was worth whatever it was going to cost to get him.

OK, so the A's have player assets, some of which are worth a lot more than the club is currently paying for them. Now, given that: the team's pockets aren't nearly deep enough to buy the additional talent necessary to move back atop the AL West; and the attendance base didn't respond all that resoundingly when the team was in the catbird seat.

One hundred professional managers out of 100 would have immediately engaged in what is euphemistically referred to nowadays as a "strategic retrenchment"— that is, selling off assets and hunkering down until things get better. It's a tactic that is engaged in by businesses every day and one that does cause social distress— inevitably, "retrenchment" results in some life-blood-of-the-community factory being shut down — but in the long run society grudgingly accepts such episodes as an unfortunate byproduct of the free enterprise system.

However, as should be abundantly clear by now, baseball was anything but a free enterprise operation and Bowie Kuhn was a man who refused to acknowledge unfortunate byproducts.

Once Kuhn removed the cash sale option, Finley was reduced to making the kind of deals that we are familiar with today: trading his proven veterans for packages of young, speculative talent. While such moves can prove beneficial for the occasional Jerry Reinsdorf with deep pockets and a barren farm system, the A's were already hip deep in good looking fuzzy faces. What they really needed was money, cash, scratch, bread, and bucks to see them through the next couple of years.

Consider the trade that Finley finally engineered for Blue: just before the 1978 season, Vida was dispatched to the San Francisco Giants for seven players and $390,000.[25] On one level it wasn't that bad a deal: everybody Finley received played in the majors, most were under 25 and all of them at least had some promise of becoming quality players. Yet as is the case in most such deals, none were true Grade A prospects, and thus they were steamrolled by hotter talents. Of the seven, all were destined to become fringe players: the best of the bunch was probably John Henry Johnson, a lefty with control but no out pitch who posted one good season as a rotation starter before fading into the middle reliever Twilight Zone.

What's more, the problem with player contract values would only escalate as time went on. With free agent prices increasing at double-digit rates, the real value of a team's players under contract was skyrocketing as well. That's no problem for those who could realize this value either by winning a pennant or selling out, but for an out-of-the-running organization, the situation becomes a treadmill to nowhere. To maintain any semblance of a competitive position ownership is forced to continuously pour incremental money into these illiquid assets regardless of the results at the gate — a problem that was dramatized in Jerry Colangelo's calls for more money from his limited partners at the end of the 2000 season.

Thus, once a financially prudent operator falls out of the running both on the field and at the box office, he is left with two options. He could reduce his payroll to a level that his reduced revenue stream can support and hope for lightning to strike (we'll call this the Carl Lindner solution). Or, he could stop beating his head against a brick wall by selling out to someone with fresh cash.

The latter course was the one that Finley finally chose in 1980 — but by that time it was anything but a road not taken. Baltimore's Jerry Hoffberger completed the sale of his team as it was driving towards the 1979 pennant.[26] Philadelphia's Carpenter family had owned their franchise since World War II and were fresh off a world championship. No matter, though: they were out of the game by the end of the 1981 season.[27] Bill Veeck, Texas' duo of Brad Corbett in Arlington and Roy Hofheinz in Houston, and even Kuhn's old boss Calvin Griffith were ultimately dislodged by the economic whirlwind.

As we've seen before, there were plenty of reasons for this massive disembarkation — but the inability to convert assets into cash was definitely one of the more prominent ones.

In fairness to Kuhn, the previous discussion is one of economics and business, two areas in which Bowie, a lawyer by trade, was not schooled. Furthermore, there is no question that the ongoing cost spiral that characterizes MLB salary negotiations to this day was above and beyond anything that anyone forecasted at the time. Yet Kuhn somehow failed to realize that much of Branch Rickey's success in bringing the Brooklyn Dodgers back from the brink of bankruptcy in the 1940s was funded by his selling of excess talent.[28] Or that his erstwhile first employer Griffith was characterized by Bill Veeck as the kind of operator who for $100,000 in cash would have readily sold his two best players to the Tribe.[29] That Connie Mack's Philadelphia A's had eventually arisen from their 1914 funeral pyre with a team that many consider to be one of the greatest of all time.

In short, Kuhn's decision to stop Charlie Finley's sales unintentionally turned out to be the death knell for a generation of owners that he was not only supposed to protect, but also liked and admired. It was also the catalyst for the big market/small market conundrum that the game struggles with to this day.

As the saying goes, be careful what you wish for, because you might just get it.

23

A Paradox in Action

It is to baseball's detriment in many ways that the tornado of activity and damage potential that was Charlie Finley is no longer with us. The man was a living, breathing paradox, at once brilliant and obtuse, caring and brutal, generous and stingy — heck, take any two emotional opposites and Finley probably embodied them at one point in time or another. A five-foot shelf of books couldn't contain all of the off-beat, crazy, insane, sometimes thoughtless but occasionally prescient things Finley said and did, but to give the reader further insight into this madcap idea man, the following is a Whitman's Sampler of Charles O. Finley in action:

- Prior to the beginning of the 1971 season, Finley made his mark as a champion of equality by hiring the first ball girls to retrieve fouls hit down the left and right field lines. One of his selections would prove inspired in retrospect: Debbi Sivyer, the 13-year-old daughter of an A's secretary, would go on to become Debbi Fields of Mrs. Fields cookie fame.[1]
- Finley hired a team astrologer, Laurie Brady, in the mid-1970s. When asked what her qualifications for the job were, Brady replied that she had predicted the date of her divorce upon marrying her former husband. Her confidence stemmed from the fact that they "were not a mix. He was my son in a previous life."[2]
- To visually distinguish them from the players, Oakland's coaching staff wore a different color cap (white with a green bill rather than green with a gold bill) and uniform (solid white at home with a gold A's logo on the front).
- In the true spirit of thrift, A's players were issued a grand total of two caps a season. Uniforms were worn until they fell apart: Reggie Jackson remembered starting the 1975 season wearing vintage 1972 pants and a jersey from 1974[3] — and this was when the A's were coming off three straight world championships.
- As the 1970s wore on, the Athletics' back-of-the-house staff steadily declined under the combined weight of firings and people looking for

more congenial and lucrative livelihoods. The team's scouts were gradually let go,[4] and by 1976 the administrative operations were reduced to such a skeletal level that when Don Baylor went looking for the business offices, he couldn't find them. He asked then-manager Chuck Tanner where they were ... and Tanner didn't know either.[5]

• Ever a sucker for self-promotion, Finley biographies and full-page pictures were routinely featured at the front of A's yearbooks and scorecards.[6] When *Time* ran a feature story on Finley in 1975, he dispatched his front office employees throughout the East Bay to buy up every copy they could find. Each A's player was treated to one that night[7] (Yankee manager Billy Martin examined Finley's batting grip in the front cover photo and remarked, "He'll never get the bat around holding it that way"[8]).

• One of Finley's more interesting ideas was the so-called "alert orange" baseball. It was an idea he promoted endlessly: "Someday this colored ball will be standard because it's easier for the hitters to see and the fans to follow."[9] The logic was there (try buying a white tennis ball nowadays) and the baseballs were even used in an exhibition game or two,[10] but the subtlety of its advantages plus the general distaste for Finley among his fellow owners stilled the project before it gained much momentum.

• In commemoration of having seven of his A's selected to the 1975 All-Star team, Finley strolled onto the County Stadium field in Milwaukee wearing his trademark green sports jacket along with a yellow shirt, green tie, black slacks, white shoes, and a green cowboy hat. He was accompanied in his box by four blondes wearing A's uniform jerseys and several cartons of the orange baseballs bearing the motto "approved and recommended by Charles O. Finley."[11]

• Finley's relationship with the city of Oakland was an ongoing melodrama. His continuous attempts to break his agreement with the Coliseum Commission and his ire at the team's poor attendance led to some uniquely embarrassing moments. San Francisco Mayor Joseph Alioto was tabbed to throw out the first pitch at one of the team's postseason games, an honor that no Oakland mayor ever received.[12] Finley initially announced that the postseason headquarters for the 1971 playoffs would be at San Francisco's Mark Hopkins Hotel—civic indignation caused him to move the headquarters across the bay at the last moment.[13] The A's Booster Club along with city of Oakland and its port authority plus the chamber of commerce once scheduled a luncheon to honor the A's—when the team fell short of one million attendees despite running away with the AL West crown, Charlie had his players boycott the affair.[14]

• When the team's press office received a request for a picture of Catfish Hunter to use in the production of his 1973 All-Star Game portrait, they responded with what they had—a five-year-old photograph of their ace sans mustache, long hair, and current uniform.[15]

Charles O. Finley as *The Sporting News'* 1972 Man of the Year. A copy of this cover was included as the first inside page of Oakland's 1973 team yearbook. (*The Sporting News*)

- Never missing a trick, Finley had manager Dick Williams wear a green and gold tam-o'-shanter out to the plate in Chicago when delivering the lineup cards on September 6, 1972. The idea was to promote Finley's Memphis Tams basketball team, but the timing was unfortunate to say the least — September 6 was the day after 11 Israeli athletes were murdered by Arab terrorists at the XV Summer Olympiad in Munich, West Germany. The A's Jewish players plus Reggie Jackson were wearing black armbands, Williams a green and gold tam....[16]
- The highlight of many players' careers is the receipt of a world championship ring — it's a symbol of athletic excellence that reminds even the lowliest utility infielder that he had a part in producing a champion. Thus, it was a big deal when the A's players received their 1973 world championship rings and discovered that the one karat diamond that had adorned the 1972 models had been replaced with a synthetic emerald, cutting their appraised value from $1,500 to $400 apiece. Not being stupid, Finley delegated the responsibility for handing out the rings to traveling secretary Jim Bank (Finley himself had presented the previous year's model).[17]

Like Sam Goldwyn, Lyndon Johnson, and Vince Lombardi, Charles O. Finley's eccentricities are a heck of a lot easier to chuckle at in retrospect than they were at the time. Still, baseball lore in the *All in the Family* era would be far less entertaining if this incredible man had not chosen to associate himself with the game.

Of course, those who actually dealt with him may be excused for having other feelings....

24

The Commissioner

Ever hear of Walter Mitty?

The name is probably vaguely familiar to most Americans over the age of 40: James Thurber's semi-downtrodden Everyman character who incessantly daydreams of greatness while slogging his way through a mundane life became something of a cliché in postwar America. What those who haven't read Thurber's work or seen the movie version may not know is that Mitty actually becomes involved in a real life drama surrounding the Dutch crown jewels—and in the process concludes that fantasizing about having a big red S is superior to donning one.

That was Bowie Kent Kuhn in a nutshell.

Those familiar with the era may wonder why Kuhn's name has not figured more prominently in this narrative. Contemporary observers certainly considered him to be a pivotal figure, and the man's name was connected — sometimes less than favorably — with everything from Aaron's 715th home run to the initiation of nighttime World Series games (even the coldest of which he would pointedly sit through sans overcoat[1]), yet his impact on the course of events is remarkably slight. Only in the case of Charlie Finley's attempted fire sale of the aging Mustache Gang did Kuhn make an enduring mark on the game, and the wisdom of that particular decision is highly debatable.

An inveterate fan (he was the Griffith Stadium scoreboard operator for a time in the 1940s[2]), Kuhn's route to baseball supremacy came in a manner that is pretty common in business circles: he was a lawyer with Willkie, Farr & Gallagher, the National League's counsel. Kuhn was never *the* guy representing the NL, mind you, but he did have nearly twenty years of experience working on baseball matters, most notably defending the league against the State of Wisconsin's efforts to keep the Braves in Milwaukee.[3]

Say the word "lawyer" to the average American and one image inevitably materializes: Raymond Burr. Unfortunately for the romantic in all of us, Bowie Kuhn's type of law has about as much in common with Perry Mason as Roy Hobbs does with Albert Belle. Corporate lawyers are primarily document drafters—the incomprehensible agreement that accompanies new Visa cards is a prime example of their output. A dynamic persona or gift of gab is not required here: in fact, many corporate lawyers make terrific livings without ever setting foot in a courtroom. It's a world where guilt and innocence are abstract concepts, where appearances often speak as loudly as actions, and where one clear word is usually inferior to ten that can be interpreted as needs be.

Anyway, by late 1968 Kuhn was enough of a baseball fixture to have a second row seat at the San Francisco execution of William "Spike" Eckert, a retired Air Force general who, to the amazement of virtually everybody, had become baseball's fourth commissioner following Ford Frick's 1965 retirement. Labeled "The Unknown Soldier" by media wags, Eckert really didn't know much of anything about baseball (a flaw that was repeatedly exposed during press conferences[4]) and suffered from a heart condition to boot, but he was an ex-general, though possibly not the right ex-general. According to Bill Veeck, the search committee's initial choice was General Curtis LeMay (one chuckles at the idea of LeMay and Marvin Miller seated across from each other at the bargaining table). Uninterested in the job, LeMay recommended Eckert, his ex-procurement officer. The committee, mistaking Eckert for the recently retired Secretary of the Air Force Eugene Zuckert, agreed heartily.[5]

Having said that, however, Eckert did have the dual qualities of being available and without enemies in the game, and thus was installed in baseball's New York headquarters where he presided over the game for three years like ... well, like someone with a heart condition. With the MLBPA chief's image becoming ever larger in baseball's rear view mirror, however, the owners by the fall of 1968 decided that they needed someone more vigorous than a guy who was destined to drop dead on a tennis court in a little more than two years.[6]

Once the ex-general had gone quietly into the night, it became clear that baseball's owners had fallen into a trap that often befalls businessmen desperate to shake things up: they had fired Eckert without having the faintest idea of who would replace him. New York Yankees' president Mike Burke, Horace Stoneham's son-in-law Chub Feeney, Montreal Expos president John McHale, Supreme Court Justice Byron (Whizzer) White—baseball went through these names and more in a mind-numbing 13-hour marathon meeting that was adjourned with no decision reached after 19 ballots.[7]

(By the way, don't scoff at the idea of White, the 1938 NFL Rookie of the Year, as a viable candidate for baseball's top job. Before selecting Eckert in 1965, the game's power elite had also toyed with the idea of Richard Nixon as commissioner. Imagine what fun that one would have been.[8])

After a follow-up meeting held a couple of months later deadlocked once again, the owners found themselves between the proverbial rock and hard place. Spring training camps would open in less than a month, Miller was making noises about calling a strike over the pension agreement that was due to expire on March 31,[9] neither league would accept a figure from the other

Bowie Kuhn (center) meets with White Sox manager Chuck Tanner (left) and GM Stu Holcomb while making his spring training rounds in 1972. Kuhn would often note the cordial response he'd receive during these outings, but according to Marvin Miller, "All I got from the players were comments such as 'What a stuffed shirt'." (*The Sporting News*)

as commissioner and nobody was really wild about taking the job. Four years earlier, a similar set of circumstances had begot the hapless Eckert; now the owners gave their unanimous approval to this tall, vaguely Rotarian looking man who stated in his first press conference that Kenesaw Mountain Landis had been one of his boyhood heroes.[10] While that pithy little statement probably sent a collective shudder through the shoulders of those owners in attendance, they could comfort themselves with the fact that Kuhn had only been given the title of interim commissioner, as in "just hold the fort for us while we look for a real number one man." Furthermore, he'd surely been around long enough to know that baseball's power elite — his employers — had no desire for another Landis.

Little did they know that Kuhn would be "holding the fort" for the next 15 years, and that he really meant it about Landis.

Despite contemporary dismissals of Kuhn as something of a Prince Charles-like upper crust bumpkin (FYI folks: morons don't usually graduate cum laude from Princeton[11]), it quickly became apparent that Bowie had a well-thought-out plan for achieving Landis-like power. The new commissioner understood that his position as it stood had about as much authority as a referee at a WWF event — yet he also realized from his years of dealing with the National League's labor problems that the owner-player relationship was rapidly moving towards deadlock.

In this, Kuhn saw an opportunity — one that might take a while to materialize but with enough patience and political savvy might just pan out. By positioning himself as an impartial figure that was above the fracas, Kuhn thought that he could ultimately become the arbitrator for baseball's labor woes ... and by extension the determiner of where the game would go. To accomplish this, though, Bowie would first have to prove himself to be a viable leader in the more mundane operational areas of the job, like levying fines and disciplining wayward players and owners. The new commissioner thus became a flurry of activity, visiting training camps to personally meet with the players, making himself accessible to the press, and taking an activist stance towards practically everything that crossed his desk.[12]

It was this frenetic desire to put his personal stamp on every issue large and small that got Kuhn into trouble. It wasn't that Bowie made particularly poor decisions, but like veteran politicians who run for the presidency after thirty years in Congress, Kuhn quickly reached the point where everybody simply knew too much about him. Every wart, imperfection, and flaw was given multiple opportunities to shine during his tenure — and few escaped exposure.

Consider Kuhn's penchant for discovering fine distinctions that were invisible to the average onlooker. George Steinbrenner's two-year suspension from baseball in the wake of his Watergate-era conviction on illegal campaign contribution charges became a prime example in many eyes of how the commissioner was able to manipulate the rules to achieve personal motives.

Before buying the Yankees in consort with 15 limited partners in January 1973, Steinbrenner was the CEO and majority owner of American Shipbuilding, a New York Stock Exchange-listed company that sounds more impressive than it really was. Cut away the hoopla and what remained was a smallish outfit in an embattled industry beset with contentious unions, astronomical labor costs, and a veritable bumper crop of profit-draining regulations. It's the kind of business where a 100 percent honest buck is virtually impossible to turn.

Take all of the above factors into account and ... well, it would have required a lot more character than the Boss ever exhibited to refrain from contributing as much as was economically (if not legally) feasible to those who might help him. In earlier days such contributions were commonplace if never condoned; Steinbrenner's mistake was to drop his money in the collection plate of Richard Nixon and his Keystone-Kops-style operatives. By raising dirty tricks and ineptitude to an art form, these men so thoroughly enraged the public that everything and everyone they touched had to be brought down to quell the uproar — and George happened to be one of the guys left without a chair when the music stopped.

It was a felony conviction, but within the hierarchy of perjurers, burglars, and unindicted co-conspirators that were flowing through the court system like unprocessed waste from a flooded sewage treatment plant, Steinbrenner was decidedly small potatoes. As a result, he received a chump change fine and that was that....

Except where Bowie Kuhn was concerned.

The commissioner zeroed in on the word "felony" and apparently couldn't get over it. To Kuhn's way of thinking, dishonesty in non-baseball matters was just a hop, skip and jump away from a direct attack on the game's integrity. Thus, such people had to be purged for a suitable time from baseball management ("suitable" being a flexible concept — Kuhn was prepared to ban Steinbrenner for life if he'd gone to jail[13]).

Now all of the above represents a perfectly reasonable rationale for the commissioner's actions — assuming that one was uninviting a loud-mouthed neighbor from his next cookout. However, the concept of arbitrarily depriving someone of the right to operate his business (in effect instituting a punishment above and beyond that meted out by the court system) is a distinctly slippery slope. To reuse a metaphor, once this principle is established it's just a hop, skip and a jump to the idea that any behavior that is believed to negatively reflect on baseball is fair game for disciplinary action.

Once that has been rationalized, lots of stuff is possible — such as the suspension of addled old women with warped views of the Third Reich (Marge Schott) and redneck relief pitchers naive enough to air their prejudices in *Sports Illustrated* (John Rocker). The point isn't whether Rocker's, Schott's, and Steinbrenner's actions were morally reprehensible, it's whether their Constitutional rights can be breached for what Kuhn was fond of calling "the best interests of baseball."

Furthermore, in the commissioner's world there seemed to be a fine distinction between felons.

Shortly before Steinbrenner's shenanigans came to light, Houston Astros center fielder Cesar Cedeno had been involved in an O.J. Simpson-type affair in which he, his gun, and a 19-year-old girl had rendezvoused in a motel room, and only Cesar and the gun had come out alive. After some adroit legal maneuvering Cedeno got off with an involuntary manslaughter conviction and a small fine,[14] yet Cesar was allowed to continue plying his trade without so much as a dollar sacrificed or a game lost to suspension.

For whatever reason, the stink that Cesar Cedeno had made on baseball's crowded elevator was somehow more tolerable to Kuhn than the one that George Steinbrenner had begot ... and nobody could exactly get their arms around why that was so.

Kuhn made lots of decisions like that. He was an outspoken opponent of the mixing of gambling interests and baseball, a sensible posture for a man with a strong sense of the game's history to assume. In that light, his actions to force three Atlanta Braves executives off the board of directors of Parvin-

Dohrmann Corporation (operators of three Las Vegas casinos) made perfect sense,[15] as did his opposition to Edward DeBartolo's (owner of three race-tracks) attempt to buy the Chicago White Sox.[16] Yet the idea that Willie Mays was somehow tainted by taking a nonoperational (public relations) position with Bally's[17] seems a bit much, and exactly how much worse was DeBartolo than Pittsburgh's Galbraith family (who had a small interest in Churchill Downs) or the mighty Steinbrenner (who owned half of Tampa Bay Downs)?

The commissioner's ongoing attempts to keep Mr. Charles Oscar Finley on the reasonably straight and something approaching narrow frequently neared the level of a 1930s screwball comedy. Given Finley's blind spot where rules and ethics were concerned, repeated collisions between him and whoever was in authority at the time were inevitable. Furthermore, some of Kuhn's decisions regarding Charlie's more egregious moves (most notably his attempt to cut Mike Andrews from the 1973 World Series roster after the infielder committed a pair of errors that led to the Mets' Game 2 victory) were obviously correct. Still, Bowie used Finley's eccentricities and unpopularity among his fellow owners as excuses to place virtually every move the man made under a microscope. We have already examined the long-term implications of Finley's attempt to revive Connie Mack's 1914 "fire sale" strategy, but there were other dubious interventions as well:

- Sending a sulking young player to the minors for a few weeks of "reality therapy" was and still is an accepted tool in baseball's psychology kit. Yet when the names involved were Reggie Jackson and Charlie Finley the result was, according to Kuhn, conduct "motivated by personal reasons unrelated to Jackson's ability."[18]
- As the 1972 season dawned Vida Blue was 22, loaded down with the 1971 MVP and Cy Young Awards, and demanding a $100,000 raise after his first full season in the Show. When Finley refused to budge from his $50,000 offer (which was not unreasonable by then-current standards), Kuhn decided to step in, citing an action that Landis had taken some thirty years earlier when the Cincinnati Reds had refused to negotiate "in good faith" with star pitcher Paul Derringer.[19]

  Well, yes, Derringer was a precedent — but so was the duo holdout of Sandy Koufax and Don Drysdale prior to the 1966 season. As sensational as that one was (the two pitchers involved were Hall of Fame-bound and had claimed three of the previous four Cy Young Awards), the commissioner's office had not deemed it necessary to get involved ... and nobody needed a baseball encyclopedia to refresh their memories on those events.

Then there was Joe Reichler. Reichler had been an Associated Press sportswriter for years before signing on with the commissioner's office as public relations director during Eckert's reign. Kuhn kept him on and apparently grew fond of the man — from what one can surmise Reichler was engaging company in a "hale fellow well met" manner and he was something of a walking encyclopedia on the game.[20]

What he wasn't, however, was particularly well off financially. The way the story goes, Reichler had built up a reasonably impressive collection of baseball memorabilia in his garage, which just happened to be next to some similar stuff that was on loan to the commissioner's office from the Baseball Hall of Fame. The two piles of items became intermixed in the way that such things will and as a result Reichler ended up mistakenly selling Cooperstown items for his own benefit.

At least that's how Reichler told it, and the whole thing could have been just that innocent … assuming that one ignored the property stamp prominently affixed to each Hall of Fame-owned item.[21]

Yet for whatever reason — be it loyalty to a long-time associate and friend, compassion for a man who was already suffering from the heart problems that would take his life less than five years hence,[22] or embarrassment that a guy who was enshrined in Cooperstown (Reichler had been the 1980 recipient of the J.G. Taylor Spink Award[23]) could end up illegally converting items ("stealing" is the more common term) from that institution — Bowie decided not to act against good ol' Joe. Reichler remained vice president and general manager of baseball's film division as well as Kuhn's special assistant to the very end.

With that kind of "consistent without being truly consistent" record, it is not surprising that the commissioner was never called upon to play more than a cameo role in the struggles with the MLBPA. Not that baseball lost out on much: Bowie's assessment of Marvin Miller as calculating, unscrupulous, and disinterested in the game's overall welfare[24] (which was at a minimum two-thirds accurate) colored both his attitudes towards the labor chief as well as his assessments of Miller's successes and failures. From the players' perspective Marvin's activist stance eliminated the need for a surrogate Big Daddy appointed by The Oppressors,[25] while a growing (but politically important) minority of owners found it difficult to stomach a man who was seemingly forever ruling against their best interests.[26]

Thus, Bowie Kuhn was in effect a man waiting for a train that never arrived.

So maybe it isn't much of a heritage … yet when reviewing the cast of characters Kuhn's standards become obvious: by and large he decided in favor of the good guys and against the bullies and braggarts. Yes, he was unduly harsh with Finley, but Charlie O. was the kind of man who merited a roughing up now and then on general principles. Perhaps Steinbrenner didn't deserve the suspension, but given the number of ulcers he's induced in very fine people over the years, any injustice done probably didn't result in too many sleepless nights. In fact, if a man can be best judged by his enemies, a casual scan of Kuhn's list suggests that he must have been a very fine person indeed.

And you know what? He was a fine man — perhaps not much of a commissioner of baseball, but a fine man just the same.

First and foremost, Kuhn loved the game. Perhaps the one dose memory, one dose fantasy baseball world he envisioned was terminally at odds with the "me" generation, but that's the type of human failing that even the greatest moguls periodically fall prey to. Consider the commissioner's attitude towards Jim Bouton and his landmark book *Ball Four*. Looked at today, *Ball Four* reads like a PG-rated version of *Animal House*. Kuhn, though, wasn't a PG kind of guy at heart: he wanted the game to be viewed as wholesome family entertainment. Thus, Bowie's efforts to coercing Bouton into renouncing the book were natural if almost hilariously futile and naïve — but his error was human rather than malicious.

Secondly, he was an intelligent, farsighted man, a fact that was overlooked (sometimes malevolently so) by virtually every observer of his day. Kuhn takes a lot of flak for underestimating Marvin Miller's penchant for wreaking havoc, but name one of the commissioner's contemporaries — including the members of Miller's own union — who accurately anticipated what was to occur. If Kuhn's initial reaction to the Flood suit was just as ostrich-like as everybody else's, at least he was quick to recognize the prescription for disaster inherent in the owners' stubborn unwillingness to bend.[27] He was 25 years ahead of everybody else in suggesting that the league offices be abolished, he was a fervent supporter of the DH rule, and he advanced the game to within a light year of the NFL in terms of marketing.

Finally, he had the courage of his convictions and was willing to accept tremendous amounts of ridicule to see them through. Kuhn's dismay at Bob Short's decampment from Washington and his subsequent long-running efforts to return baseball to the District of Columbia[28] have been dismissed as amateur political posturing by many, but the fact of the matter was:

- Kuhn was a long-time Senators' fan (remember the boyhood scoreboard experience),
- He honestly believed that forsaking the nation's capital was a bad idea for any game whose key underpinning (baseball's anti-trust exemption) existed at the leisure of Congress,[29] and
- He was 100 percent against the movement of franchises under any event.[30]

It was a costly (Jerry Hoffberger, whose Baltimore Orioles struggled at the gate throughout the 1970s despite the Senators' demise and a string of divisional championships, became an arch-enemy as a result of Kuhn's stance[31]) and somewhat quixotic stance — yet the commissioner continued agitating for Washington to the end.

Like most men Kuhn favored certain types of people over others, and like most his tastes were somewhat idiosyncratic. He never connected with the flamboyant Bill Veeck, partially because he felt that the White Sox owner was out of touch with the times, partly because he viewed Veeck as a quick buck artist, and partly because the man had an almost impish penchant for tweaking authority's nose whenever possible.[32] Yet Kuhn was able to find room in his affections for such characters as the somewhat boozy and ineffectual Horace Stoneham[33] as well as Walter O'Malley, the man who wrote the book on how to strong-arm partners and abandon loyal fans.[34] Of course Stoneham had been in the game forever, O'Malley had developed the charm that aging reprobates often do, and Kuhn was a hero-worshipper at heart, so....

He believed heavily in image — a not surprising trait for a Wall Street lawyer. Kuhn was a sensitive, introspective man: he took incredible pains to assure that nothing he said caused either undue pain or a potential lawsuit. As a result, Bowie's speeches and press conferences tended to take on a pro-fessorial tone that strikingly contrasted with the "let the chips fall where they may" attitude of so many of those he was surrounded by. Kuhn seemed stodgy, colorless, and perhaps a bit obtuse by comparison, and he suffered mightily for that image.

Hardball is a melancholy book in many ways, with Kuhn portraying him-self as a George Bailey whose guardian angel was waylaid by Potter en route to Bedford Falls. Four years after his dismissal (the book was originally pub-lished in 1988), Bowie seems profoundly dismayed and puzzled by his vilified stature in the public conscience. It's the kind of book that a non-Watergate-despoiled member of the Nixon White House might have written. Kuhn often wonders aloud what he could have done differently given the constraints he was operating under, as well as why the sporting press was so vicious and how the best efforts of so many could have resulted in such chaos.[35]

At base, Bowie Kuhn was, like Walter Mitty, an ordinary man who was called upon to perform an extraordinary function. Those who criticize his achievements or lack thereof miss the point: *there really wasn't any other alter-native.* Keep in mind that the job Kuhn inherited was the baseball equivalent of being Britian's Prince Phillip — he may look formidable, but it's the per-son on his left who has all the power. It wasn't the kind of job that was going to attract anyone with big-time prospects in front of them, and thus it shouldn't be much of a surprise that it ultimately fell to an anonymous lawyer with few qualifications other than a love for the game. Perhaps Kuhn wasn't the best (or even a good) choice for the job, but he gave it an honest effort and comported himself with dignity throughout.

And, in the final analysis, the game not only survived but prospered on his watch. Perhaps Kuhn had little to do with that, and maybe he was even counterproductive at times, but hey ... Calvin Coolidge wasn't much of a president either, and that didn't stop the 1920s from roaring.

During the 1970 debate over G. Harrold Carswell's ultimately doomed nomination to the Supreme Court, Nebraska Senator Roman Hruska unintentionally drove a nail into the nominee's coffin by stating that "there are a lot of mediocre judges and people and lawyers … and they are entitled to a little representation, aren't they?"[36]

That was Bowie Kuhn: a Walter Mitty trying to fill a big man's shoes.

25

The Bird

Baseball at its root is a kid's game, and every so often a certifiable inno-cent will amble out of nowhere to remind us all of that fact. Their ranks have included everything from the manchild Rube Waddell to the infinitely lov-able Kirby Puckett, but each in his own way has charmed us with their com-bination of eye-catching ability and willingness to humanize these sometimes all-too-solemn proceedings. Turk Wendell is the breed's current (2002) poster boy, but Wendell is a peripheral player whose career is winding down. The lack of such a specimen at center stage is arguably one of the biggest issues baseball is facing today.

Back in 1976, though, the game more or less bumbled across one of the all-time greats in a pencil-thin righthander with a high, piping voice who was once described as looking like a cross between Harpo Marx and rubber-jointed baseball clown Max Patkin[1] — one Mark Steven Fidrych.

The Bird (supposedly nicknamed for his resemblance to the Sesame Street character[2]) almost defied description: he was equal parts flower child, four-year-old on his first trip to Disneyland, and Bellevue escapee. He exuded enthusiasm, applauding his infielders after every out and once running out to center field to hug and kiss the man who made the last catch in a pennant-clinching game.[3] He acquired few of the accouterments of fame, driving a subcompact car and dressing whenever possible in a motley collection of T-shirts, jeans, and sneakers.[4] In an era when players were becoming increas-ingly reticent with the press, Fidrych was something of a modern Dizzy Dean, firing off triple entendre after triple entendre. When asked about his house-hold habits, Fidrych replied, "Sometimes I get lazy and let the dishes stack up. But they don't stack up too high. I've only got four dishes."[5]

But it was his antics around the mound (accomplished in dead earnest) that were the most hypnotic part of the Bird's act. Fidrych, you see, believed each horsehide had a karma, and that by discussing his plans with the ball it would be aided in its mission to elude the evil hitter and his barbaric club. Mark would often show the plate to the ball while talking to it, mimicking the erratic trajectory that he wanted it to take in its journey to the safety of the catcher's mitt.[6] Once while Fidrych was conducting his deliberations with the ball, Yankee third baseman Graig Nettles stepped out of the batter's box and gave his bat an impromptu pep talk. "Now don't you listen to that ball," Nettles told his bat. Helpfully pointing to the right field seats, he said, "When it comes in here you hit it right up in that upper deck up there."

After popping up, Nettles discovered the error in his strategy. "I just realized I was using a Japanese bat. Doesn't understand English."[7]

That was the way the entire 1976 season went for Fidrych. Opponents got so caught up in the Bird's shtick that they lost their concentration. "I've never seen anything like it," Rico Carty once commented. "In the dugout everyone kept saying, 'Let's get this guy: let's get him.' But we were too concerned about that and we didn't pay attention to our hitting. Sometimes I was almost laughing. How can you hit when you're laughing?"[8]

Fans responded in droves to Fidrych. Over 600,000 fans came out to Tiger Stadium to witness the Bird's 21 starts there,[9] a real windfall for a fifth place team that finished 24 games behind the Yankees and had drawn just over one million fans for its entire 81 game home schedule the previous season. Fidrych's act played just as well on the road, aided largely by his willingness to sign thousands of autographs at such events as Mark Fidrych Autograph Day at Anaheim Stadium.[10]

Yet for all of the hoopla that surrounded him, the Bird's performance on the mound was arguably more spectacular. Incapable of fanning anybody due to the lack of a true out pitch, Fidrych nonetheless rode a bevy of breaking pitches thrown with impeccable control to the American League ERA crown. A gawky-looking beanpole (6'3", 175), the Bird nonetheless had the stamina to complete an astounding 24 of his 29 starts, leading the league in that category despite not joining the Tigers rotation until 1½ months into the season. He was the hands-down choice as Rookie of the Year and finished second in the Cy Young Award race.

Yet by the next spring, it was all over.

Loosening up in the outfield one day Fidrych tore cartilage in his knee while chasing a fly ball, thus missing the first third of the season. He pitched well for a couple of months thereafter, even making his second All-Star team, but began suffering from tendonitis and on August 24 was forced to pack it in for the remainder of the year.[11] Returning too quickly in 1978, he injured the arm again, and from there on would never be able to stay healthy. By age 25 he was history, though outwardly as cheerful and grateful for his moment of fame as ever.

A long-running debate has centered over this man in Hot Stove circles. Some have suggested that Fidrych could have been Hall of Fame material had Fate and his body had not conspired otherwise. Others point out with lots of statistical backing that virtually nobody who strikes out 97 men in 250 innings is successful in the long run.

Both arguments miss the point, which is that the Bird was probably with us as long as he should have been. Fidrych's song and dance act was that of a young man — had he continued on into middle age the eternal smile would probably have faded, the discussions with the ball discarded as passé, and we probably would have found something about him to dislike anyway. As tragic as his ending was, there is something pleasant in the fact that we were all spared the spectacle of a crippled John Kennedy turning 70 — if the back problems hadn't confined him to a wheelchair by then the Addison's Disease almost certainly would have. Instead, our mind's eye remembers only the young Kennedy, vibrant and full of life, and that's really the way he should be thought of.

The same holds true for Mark Fidrych. While his career was (like the best parties) all too short, the Bird managed to pack more living into his year and a half at the top than many of his more starchy contemporaries accommodated in decade-long careers. That he found his way to the stage at all was a miracle for both himself and baseball as a whole, and latter day fans can only hope that they will in time be as fortunate as their forebears.

26

George Steinbrenner's
New Economics

Some people in this world are destined to be typecast — no matter what else they do in life, some image (appropriate or not) becomes a cross that they are destined to bear for the rest of their lives. Say "Mickey Mantle" to a modern fan and the image of a career tragically shortened by injury and intemperate living materializes. Mention Roger Maris and the number 61 immediately comes to mind. For Bill Buckner it's a twisting ground ball going through the wickets (sorry, Bill).

Now all of these images do have some truth attached to them, yet keep in mind that:

1. His aches and off-field escapades notwithstanding, Mantle was a durable player; he still ranks among the top 100 all time in number of games played and answered the bell 140 or more times in 12 of his 18 big league seasons.[1]

2. Maris never hit more than 39 homers in any other season of his career,[2] and

3. While Buckner was never the slickest fielding first baseman around (Bill led the league in errors twice), his teams didn't view him as a defensive liability either. Despite knee and ankle problems that required him to wear special orthopedic high top shoes, Buckner even in his later years was considered to be "a fine first baseman, especially adept at saving errant throws from landing in dugouts or bouncing off railings."[3] Furthermore, despite after-the-fact memories of Buckner as a guy who was often substituted for defensively in his later years ... well, it just didn't happen that much. In 1985, for example, Buckner appeared in all 162 games as a first baseman for the Red Sox, while everybody else on the team made a total of nine appearances at the position.[4]

Thus, the most obvious images can sometimes be deceiving or at least they can obscure some of the basic truths about a man — which brings us to one of the most misunderstood figures in baseball both then and now, Mr. George Steinbrenner III.

That's right — somebody actually used the words "Steinbrenner" and "misunderstood" in the same sentence.

At a basic level Steinbrenner is Fidel Castro subscribing to *Forbes* magazine — loud, arrogant, frenetic, and as cynical as a streetwalker pushing 40. To those who buy this image The Boss is at once mighty overlord and buffoon, a well-to-do blind squirrel that nonetheless has more than his share of acorns. Get underneath that veneer, though, and a more multi-dimensional character appears. He was half throwback to an era when baseball was a business because it couldn't afford not to be, and half trailblazer for the "sports as business" men who would follow in his footsteps.

In short he's an ugly American entrepreneur, capitalism's answer to hot dogs (you're better off not knowing what's inside). That Steinbrenner is popularly viewed as a borderline evil character is natural given America's odd willingness to embrace the Christian belief that poverty is somehow associated with virtuosity. Yet while the man's methods may represent a real stretch of the term "sportsman," in business circles they are nothing extraordinary — and that was what baseball was fated to become once free agency turned the game into a B-school case study.

Consider Steinbrenner and the partnership group that he led into Yankee Stadium. Though once involved in college football (the mind boggles at the thought of Steinbrenner pacing the sidelines as an assistant coach at Northwestern and Purdue[5]) and possessing some sports ownership experience,[6] George at that time had no baseball background other than a failed 1970 attempt to purchase the Cleveland Indians.[7] Furthermore, beyond veteran GM Gabe Paul and Mike Burke, the CBS vice president who had served as the deal's Mr. Inside (and would be fired 19 games into the 1973 season[8]), Steinbrenner's partners were by and large non-New Yorkers with no particular sporting bias either. The most noteworthy members of the group from veteran columnist Jerome Holtzman's point of view were Thomas Evans, the deputy finance director for the Committee to Re-Elect the President (a connection which foreshadows Steinbrenner's future campaign contributions tribulations) and James Neiderlander, a Broadway producer and theater chain owner.[9]

Well, maybe that was Holtzman's idea of the syndicate's key members, but several other names jump out at the latter day observer. One is Lester Crown, a well-heeled venture capitalist who would provide the initial funding for some of the most successful technology startups of the 1980s and 1990s. The name Thomas Evans means little unless one knows that his middle name is Mellon, as in Mellon Bank and the secretary of the treasury under Harding, Coolidge and Hoover — he'd turn plumbing manufacturer Crane Corporation into a multi-billion dollar conglomerate. Nelson Hunt from Dallas was a scion of that Hunt family, while John Z. Delorean had a "back to the future" car and numerous exotic business dealings on his personal horizon.

These people couldn't have cared less about baseball per se — the Yankees might as well have been a chemical company from their point of view. The attraction to them was the $10 million bargain basement price[10] (the lowly Cleveland Indians had changed hands for $9 million a year earlier[11]) and the latent capital gains potential in such a well-known brand name. It was Steinbrenner's duty as the general partner to take the steps necessary to unlock that latent value ... and Ruth and Gehrig be dammed if need be.

Under such circumstances the front office purge that followed Steinbrenner's assumption of the Yankee throne was a natural. Well, perhaps the word "purge" is less than fair: let's just say that within a year or so of The Boss' ascension a bunch of long-time employees magically came to the conclusion that selling insurance would be a more rewarding occupation. At the apex of this exodus was Lee MacPhail, a second generation general manager who from society's standpoint was a major step forward on the evolutionary scale from his brilliant but volatile father, but from a baseball perspective....

MacPhail had cut his operational teeth working in and then heading the bountiful postwar Yankee farm system before migrating to Baltimore, where he learned how to assemble a competitive roster without the benefit of big-time bucks. By the time MacPhail returned to New York in 1966, his *modus operandi* had evolved into three basic principles:

1. Build a strong minor league system and use its progeny,
2. Plug holes that the young talent can't fill with castoff-for-castoff trades (in this respect one wonders how this particular apple could have fallen so far from the MacPhail family tree), and
3. Have plenty of patience.[12]

By most standards MacPhail's tenures in Baltimore and New York were successful: both teams improved under his stewardship and entered golden eras shortly after his departure. Still, the phrase "after his departure" appears to be the key one from this vantage point. MacPhail seems to have been incapable of pulling off the big deal, instead clogging his teams' arteries with C-home grown players who never quite became what the organization needed them to be. The Yankees in the early 1970s were loaded to the gunwales with these guys— Bobby Cox, Jerry Kenny, Frank Tepedino, John Ellis, Steve Whittaker, and Rusty Torres were just some of the more prominent names. Even worse was that the presence of this AAAA player mass led to the squandering of some other fellows with real careers in front of them (Rick Dempsey, Tippy Martinez, Charlie Spikes) before informed decisions could be made on them.

This was not the kind of philosophy that was going to play well with an ownership group married to the profit motive; thus, within a year MacPhail chose the better part of valor by taking Joe Cronin's vacated seat in the AL president's office.[13] He was replaced — not coincidentally, one supposes — by Gabe Paul, an inveterate trader at heart who may or may not have been an improvement over MacPhail but was action-oriented and fully understood the concept of providing positive returns to his fellow partners.

MacPhail basically was out the door before Steinbrenner got his seat warm — it took longtime manager Ralph Houk an additional year to get the message.

Houk is something of an enigma among baseball's long-lived figures — the medieval Tom Kelly perhaps. Like Kelly, Houk's reputation was made early in his managerial career and survived largely intact through the years of mediocre performance that would follow. Like Kelly, Houk was a field general in the Omar Bradley mold, insisting on professionalism over color, regimentation over individuality, and the team over the individual — just the type of squad leader one would want hitting the beach at Guadacanal.[14] Like Kelly, the caliber of talent that Houk had to work with in his later years was suspect, but also like Kelly he seemed unusually capable at getting a good season or two out of players who hadn't looked like they were going to be much of anything. He'd spent 35 years working for the Yankees organization (Kelly spent 32 years with the Twins) as everything from a slap-hitting catcher to the team's general manager and as a result of this believed strongly in the concept of Yankees *uber alles*. However, after one year of The Boss, Houk opted for retirement, manfully accepting blame for the club's lackluster performance as he did.

For about two weeks, that is, after which he signed a three-year deal with the Detroit Tigers.[15]

Now there are lots of juicy possibilities and intrigues wrapped up in those two departures, but let's set aside the Peyton Place stuff for a moment and consider the situation from a business perspective. Houk and MacPhail had been running the Yankees for seven years as the 1972 season closed — the team had finished in the first division once during that time frame. Though the Yankees's farm system had been reasonably productive (Stan Bahnsen, Thurman Munson, Bobby Murcer, Fritz Peterson, and Roy White) they seemed incapable of developing the kind of impact players that take a team to the next level. MacPhail's December 1972 deal for Graig Nettles may well have provided a critical component of the future champion,[16] but the five seasons between Clete Boyer's departure and Nettles's arrival were mighty long ones around third base at Yankee Stadium. Houk's insistence on placing Horace Clarke (a player whose name, to paraphrase Gene Mauch's description of Bob Bailey, meant leather rather than wood) in the leadoff spot did little to aid a power-starved lineup in its quest for runs.

In business-ese terms, these guys simply didn't meet their performance standards. Nobody doubted that they were hard-working, upstanding men of character who had achieved a measure of success, but the bottom line was that their job was to win pennants and it didn't happen. Sure, that's a tough goal that the vast majority of teams won't achieve in a given year, but does Microsoft reward people for developing software that ranks second in its marketplace? Does anybody remember the names of the Apollo XII crew, the second group of men to set foot on the moon? What's Al Gore doing nowadays?

With Bill Virdon assuming Houk's dugout role, the focus turned to the diamond where the Bronx Bombers fielded a respectable team — not great, but respectable. Here's the lineup as it stood at of the end of the 1972 season:

		Age	G	AB	R	H	2B	3B	HR	RBI	AVG	OBP	SLG
C	Thurman Munson	25	140	511	54	143	16	3	7	46	.280	.343	.364
1B	Felipe Alou	37	120	324	33	90	18	1	6	37	.278	.326	.395
2B	Horace Clarke	32	147	547	65	132	20	2	3	37	.241	.315	.302
3B	Celerino Sanchez	28	71	250	18	62	3	3	0	22	.248	.292	.304
SS	Gene Michael	34	126	391	29	91	7	4	1	32	.233	.290	.279
LF	Roy White	28	155	556	76	150	29	0	10	54	.270	.384	.376
CF	Bobby Murcer	26	153	585	102	171	30	7	33	96	.292	.361	.537
RF	Johnny Callison	33	92	275	28	71	10	0	9	34	.258	.299	.393
DH	Ron Blomberg	23	107	299	36	80	22	1	14	49	.268	.355	.488

		Age	G	GS	IP	H	ER	W	L	SV	ERA	BB	K
SP	Mel Stottlemyre	30	36	36	260	250	93	14	18	0	3.22	85	110
SP	Fritz Peterson	30	35	35	250 1/3	270	90	17	15	0	3.24	44	100
SP	Steve Kline	24	32	32	236 1/3	210	63	16	9	0	2.40	44	58
SP	Mike Kekich	27	29	28	175 1/3	172	72	10	13	0	3.70	76	78
SP	Rob Gardner	27	20	14	97	91	33	8	5	0	3.06	33	58
CL	Sparky Lyle	27	59	0	107 2/3	84	23	9	5	35	1.92	15	11
RP	Lindy McDaniel	36	37	0	68	54	17	3	1	0	2.25	11	7

Though never a serious threat, this team had managed to stay within hailing distance of the Orioles all season before slumping in the final weeks to finish at 79-76. In retrospect it's clear that the Yankees' 1972 performance is about as good as anyone had a right to expect from this bunch, but that's not to say that there aren't some positives here. The front line pitching is strong, the defense just this side of exceptional and there's enough pop to get by in a tougher-than-people-think-it-is hitter's park. Alongside those strengths, however, stand some rather nasty limitations — the infield is an offensive wasteland, Alou and Callison were over the hill, the back end of the roster was overloaded with stiffs, and Munson and Lyle are the only guys on the team with much upside.

In the pre-free-agent era, the 1972 Yankees represented the classic profile of a .500 team that's destined to stay at .500 for the foreseeable future. It's the kind of club that's just good enough to convince someone (as it apparently did MacPhail) that it's just a trade and one hot rookie or two away from the top when in reality the leaks are destined to spring up just as fast as management plugs them. The talent core simply isn't strong enough to take the team much of anywhere no matter how many supporting players are piled atop it, and the Yankees' farm system has little excess talent to offer up for the necessary impact players. Still, given enough time and amateur drafts plus a lightning bolt or two on the trade market, who knows?

Steinbrenner, though, didn't think that way. It was clear early on that ownership of the Yankees was a first step towards a sports-based colossus rather than an end in itself. Unlike the typical operator who regarded baseball ownership as a prestige thing or the CBSes or Ted Turners that at least initially saw baseball as an adjunct to their primary broadcasting business, Steinbrenner envisioned the Yankees as a foundation from which an entertainment empire could be built. Pay per view, broadcast rights, merchandise sales—all of them would be coordinated around the Yankees' recognizable logo and image.

Of course, to accomplish this Steinbrenner would need big guns of a type that were difficult to obtain without the kind of top-drawer young talent that was the coin of the realm in the reserve clause days. Thus, The Boss' early team enhancement efforts were for the most part restricted to the Never-Never Land of old pro/reclamation project types who are always available for cash. Jim Ray Hart (Hart's nickname—Old Crow—was derived from the brand of booze he drank, which may help explain Jim Ray's early decline[17]), Matty Alou, Sam McDowell, Wayne Granger—for a couple of years the Yankees liberally loaded up on these throwbacks to a bygone era....

... And they did so successfully—at least at first blush. By 1974 Virdon was Manager of the Year, leading the temporarily transplanted Bronx Bombers (they were playing in Shea Stadium while the House that Ruth Built was being refurbished) to 89 wins and an unobstructed view of the Orioles' tail feathers with the following lineup:

		Age	G	AB	R	H	2B	3B	HR	RBI	AVG	OBP	SLG
C	Thurman Munson	27	144	517	64	135	19	2	13	60	.261	.316	.381
1B	Chris Chambliss	25	110	400	38	97	16	3	6	43	.243	.282	.342
2B	Sandy Alomar	30	76	279	35	75	8	0	1	27	.269	.302	.308
3B	Graig Nettles	29	155	566	74	139	21	1	22	75	.246	.316	.403
SS	Jim Mason	23	152	440	41	110	18	6	5	37	.250	.302	.352
LF	Bobby Murcer	28	156	606	69	166	25	4	10	88	.274	.332	.378
CF	Elliott Maddox	26	137	466	75	141	26	2	3	45	.303	.395	.386
RF	Lou Pinella	30	140	518	71	158	26	0	9	70	.305	.341	.407
DH	Roy White	30	136	473	68	130	19	8	7	43	.275	.367	.393

		Age	G	GS	IP	H	ER	W	L	SV	ERA	BB	K
SP	Pat Dobson	32	39	39	281	282	96	19	15	0	3.07	75	157
SP	Doc Medich	25	38	38	279 2/3	275	112	19	15	0	3.60	91	154
SP	Dick Tidrow	27	33	25	190 2/3	205	82	11	9	1	3.87	53	100
SP	Rudy May	29	17	15	114 1/3	75	29	8	4	0	2.28	48	90
SP	Mel Stottlemyre	32	16	15	113	119	45	6	7	0	3.58	37	40
CL	Sparky Lyle	29	66	0	114	93	21	9	3	15	1.66	43	89
RP	Cecil Upshaw	31	36	0	59 2/3	53	20	1	5	6	3.02	24	27

Does this team represent a marked improvement from the 1972 squad in anything but the won-lost record? Hard to say — Nettles is admittedly a whole staircase above Celerino Sanchez and the offense has gotten younger in general, but other than that it's hard to see much progress. The starting outfield hit 17 homers per position in 1972 — they now contributed a total of 22 in 180 more at-bats. Of the various cash acquisitions Sandy Alomar, Elliott Maddox, and Rudy May are the only ones making a significant contribution, and Maddox is a role player having his career year. The emergence of Doc Medich along with Pat Dobson's rebirth have negated Mel Stottlemyre's premature aging and the disintegration of Steve Kline's elbow, while Dick Tidrow is the only one of the starting quintet destined to play any role in the glory days to follow. In short, the 1974 Yankees were basically as good as they'd ever been — capable of winning if everything fell into place and nobody else was having a good season, but otherwise destined to be a bridesmaid....

... Until the Catfish Hunter Follies changed the game's economics forever.

At the time Hunter's five-year, $3 million deal was widely decried as extravagant in the extreme,[18] but even a cursory running of the numbers suggests that ... well, the term "slam dunk" comes to mind. The Yankees attracted just over 1.2 million fans into their temporary home in 1974, a season in which the Los Angeles Dodgers were once again proving that attendance figures of 2.5 million and more were possible in an area 60 percent the size of the New York megalopolis. Figure: an average $4 ticket price per incremental admission that was pure gravy from a profit standpoint, and $3 or so in concession sales per new body at a 50 percent margin.

And Steinbrenner was looking at $4.4 million in potential bottom line growth if the Yankees only reached the two million mark — and that was before any increase in the value of television rights or merchandise sales was figured in. Against that, Hunter's $600,000 or so annual paycheck was veritable peanuts. Heck, a team could even afford to stock up on Hunter-like players so long as they staked their claim before everybody else ran the numbers through their adding machines.

That of course was what the Yankees did, and by so doing a team of second banana types became world-beaters. Reggie Jackson and Don Gullett rapidly followed Hunter into pinstripes, and the benefits this troika brought to New York extended beyond their on-field performance. By acquiring premium talent in areas where they were already strong, the Steinbrennerians were able to deal now-excess bodies to fill holes that couldn't be addressed through the free agent market. The Jackson signing, for example, made possible the acquisitions of Ed Figueroa, Mickey Rivers, and Bucky Dent: without Reggie, the Yankees would have been compelled to hang onto Bobby Bonds and possibly Oscar Gamble as well. Pass on Gullett and Doc Medich stays in the Bronx while Willie Randolph becomes a Pittsburgh legend upon succeeding Rennie Stennett.

Sure, Paul made some good trades (most notably obtaining Chambliss and Tidrow from the Indians for four guys who promptly hit the wall[19]), but on the whole the organization paid mightily for the pieces obtained via trade. Add Larry Gura, Lamarr Hoyt, Scott McGregor, and Medich to Ron Guidry and the directionless Yankee teams of the early 1980s would have boasted a fine rotation. Instead, they were scattered to the winds for such talents as Dent (the definition of a mediocre shortstop, playoff homer or no playoff homer) and the aging Carlos May. Sure, moves like that are ones that even the most level-headed general manager is prone to when the scent of the pennant is in his nostrils, but still....

Between the ongoing body turnover and the assembly of so many big-time egos on one team, a certain amount of unrest would have been expected under any event, but season that mixture with baseball's answer to Donald Trump (Steinbrenner), Muhammad Ali (Reggie), and Paranoia (Billy Martin), and Yankee Stadium became the site of the sauciest soap opera in Creation.

The various feuds surrounding this triumvirate have become legendary. The Boss' legendary tirades and willingness to deceive his minions (most notably Sparky Lyle and Thurman Munson) to get what he wanted was a source of constant turbulence, misunderstandings, and dismay. His predilection for toying with a manager who was dangerously close to the end of his emotional rope under normal circumstances bordered on the sadistic.[20] Martin's ongoing feud with Jackson turned the Yankee clubhouse into baseball's equivalent of Northern Ireland: we might be under a cease-fire now, but God only knows what tomorrow — or five minutes from now — might bring. This emotional carousel was a sensation at the time and still plays well today as Steinbrenner approaches three decades in the game, yet transplant this song and dance routine to the executive suite of a major corporation and ... well, nobody would bat an eye.

A sad fact of life is that people generally don't get to the top in business (or sports, for that matter) by being reasonable, pleasant, or well-balanced in the way they approach life. Mega-success in any enterprise is a long shot proposition that requires an unhealthy amount of dedication, avarice, and ego: those who desire a family life, friends, and leisure time activities need not apply. Multiply that level of intensity and alienation from one's fellow

Recognizing a good buy when he saw one, George Steinbrenner purchased the Yankees in early 1973 for $3 million less than CBS had paid for the team nine years earlier. Within four years he would have the Bronx Bombers back on top via a spending-based paradigm that doomed many of his fellow owners. (*National Baseball Hall of Fame Library, Cooperstown, NY*)

man by a factor of 20 and the result is the entrepreneurial life, the most against-the-odds existence imaginable.

An entrepreneur makes it to the top by trusting his own judgment — those of similar talent who follow the conventional wisdom end up managing Burger Kings — and thus their organizations tend to be filled with henchmen rather than associates. The driving personality, impatience, and seemingly idiosyncratic decisions that raise an organization from the dust require a continuing importation of new blood at premium prices to replace those who fall by the wayside due to burnout or hurt feelings. Furthermore, the kind of guys that entrepreneurs typically attract fall into three categories: (a) those who have few attractive alternatives and know it (Martin), (b) those with bullet-proof egos (Jackson), and (c) those with personality quirks that might lessen their desirability to other operators (the manic-depressive Munson).

Yet having said all that, the entrepreneur remains human at his core, and that streak of humanity often comes back to bite him. In Steinbrenner's case it was a weakness that he shared with Franklin Roosevelt: the inability to tell people things that they didn't want to hear. The insecure Thurman Munson, for example, believed that The Boss had promised that he'd always be the highest paid Yankee. The signing of Reggie Jackson to a $3 million deal fermented a grudge that Munson carried to his grave, yet the idea that anyone would make such a promise to a guy who may or may not have been one of the ten best players of his time is absurd. In all likelihood, Steinbrenner said things in a one-on-one conversation with the All-Star catcher that were calculated to salve his feelings. Munson *interpreted* these comments to mean that he would be the highest paid Yankee in perpetuity because that's what he wanted to hear, while the boss did nothing to dissuade him from that line of thinking because he wanted Thurman to leave happy.

This is business in the fast lane — perhaps not the kind that had historically been practiced in baseball's executive suites, but one that is very familiar to anyone who has worked for a proprietor owned and operated firm. The infighting, snap decisions, relegation of talented employees to menial jobs by whim — and occasional dose of humanity — are permanent (if overstated) parts of the business landscape. After all, how long has Mr. Dithers been badgering Dagwood Bumstead?

Yet even after Charlie Finley's histrionics in Oakland, baseball seemed incapable of getting the message that modern business mores (no matter how distasteful) and deep-pocketed moguls (ditto) would chart the game's future course. Perhaps they were hoping that Steinbrenner would ultimately run out of cash or people willing to accept his abuse as Finley did. Perhaps they hoped that the fans would stop responding to such a star-crossed franchise as the Oakland fans ultimately did. Perhaps they were hoping that cows would sprout wings and fly to the moon.

Yet the fans did respond in a way that no owner could ignore. Once the team returned to their Yankee Stadium home, attendance soared past the two million mark, remaining there until age and the 1981 strike year caught up with them. Money literally gushed into Yankee coffers, financing further free agent signings under the "if a little is good more must be better and a lot must be great" theory, as well as a sports empire that now includes cable TV operations, the New York Nets and Madison Square Garden.

In short, Steinbrenner had perfectly taken the measure of his market. He intuitively recognized that in a town where calling someone a SOB is a term of endearment, a few heated words and fist fights would be no big deal. Winning was the number one priority and he had built a winner; color was the number two priority and God knew the Yankees had more than enough of that. Thus, by catering to his audience's needs, Steinbrenner had built a money machine the likes of which no one had ever seen before, and thus the blueprint for the modern baseball organization was hatched.

Of course Steinbrenner didn't have all the answers: no one ever does, and even if they do for an instant, the rules of the game inevitably change. Over time The Boss began to believe that purchasing talent was the only sensible way to compete, which made sense in the early days when bodies were relatively cheap but became a problem as more and more owners jumped on the free agency bandwagon. Steinbrenner's selection criteria slid to the point that acquisitions like Dave Collins and Dave LaPoint were clogging the Yankees' roster with tons of mediocre, overpaid players on the shady side of 30. As The Boss' success grew so did his ego, to the point where he basically destroyed an organization that was more valuable than he initially imagined.

Still, such is the evolutionary process of most businesses. That George Steinbrenner was so successful given his volatile personality and operating style was something that, in retrospect, should have surprised no one save those who were blinded by the stereotypes surrounding him and baseball ownership....

... And harboring such illusions was something baseball owners increasingly did at their competitive peril.

27

Rod Carew and Ted Williams–Style Greatness

In baseball, greatness can neatly be divided into two categories: Mickey Mantle great and Ted Williams great. Mickey Mantle-type greatness comprises the ability to do everything well: latter day memories of Mantle's myriad injuries obscure the fact that the young Mick was one heck of an outfielder and baserunner — essentially Larry Walker without the need for Rocky Mountain High air. Ted Williams, on the other hand, possessed at best league average speed and was an OK but nothing special left fielder, yet his ability to out-hit anyone this side of Ruth has placed him alongside if not slightly above Mantle in baseball's Pantheon.

With this in mind we take up the case of Rod Carew, the Hall of Fame second baseman of the Minnesota Twins … except that he played more games at first than he did at second… and he wasn't that great a second baseman anyway, and … well, you get the idea.

A lean, athletic-looking man with 20-10 eyesight who projected a sense of total concentration on the field, Carew was arguably his generation's greatest student of the art of hitting. One of the most difficult things to do on a baseball field is to play within yourself, recognizing the fine line between stretching one's capabilities and attempting that which is impossible; the failure to recognize this distinction probably cost Fred Lynn a Cooperstown plaque. Carew excelled at knowing what he could and couldn't do and working within that framework, an understanding that reached the height of expression at the plate.

A man who considered feeling too strong to be his greatest threat,[1] Carew concentrated on hitting each ball where it was pitched while adjusting his stance from at-bat to at-bat. Against Nolan Ryan, for example, Rod would assume a crouch to neutralize The Express's terrific rising fastball. He'd open his stance when the (at the time) hard-throwing lefty Frank Tanana was on the mound — Tanana's tendency was to bust balls in on people's fists. Rod would shift his weight backwards against soft tossers, and move up in the box when a curveballer was on the mound: Dick Williams once said that pitching to Carew over the course of a nine-inning game was like working to five different guys.

He utilized an unorthodox style (gripping the bat normally rather than with hands spread) to become one of the best bunters of his era. Picking out a spot on the third base line, Carew would drop bunt after bunt during batting practice until he could regularly stop the ball where desired.[2] Ex-Angel reliever Dave LaRoche told of four consecutive bunt singles Carew dropped in front of Ken McMullen, a third baseman who would have won a Gold Glove or two had Brooks Robinson not been in the league. After the third bunt, McMullen simply threw his glove in the air.[3]

Rod Carew was the Ted Williams of his era in terms of his approach to the art of hitting. He adjusted his batting stance to accommodate each pitcher he faced. A's/Angels manager Dick Williams once said that pitching to Carew over the course of a game was like working to five different hitters. (*The Sporting News*)

The payoff for all this dedication was a run at the top of the batting charts unmatched by anyone this side of Ty Cobb. Between 1972 and 1978 Carew won six batting championships, and if a couple extra drives had dropped in during the 1976 season, it would have been seven in a row. Though the contact hitting credo depresses walk totals (his theory was "if the ball is around the plate and you think you can get wood on it, I don't see why you shouldn't swing"[4]), Rod was among the AL's top ten in reaching base every year he played regularly after 1971. He was a fine, aggressive baserunner in his prime (setting a major league record by stealing home seven times during the 1969 season[5]), remarkably consistent at the plate, and capable of adjusting his game when circumstances demanded it. As Minnesota's power waned in the latter part of the decade Carew focused on driving the ball more, with the result that this once and future slap hitter finished second to Jim Rice in slugging percentage during his 1977 MVP season.

In short, with the wood in his hand Carew was the Tony Gwynn of his generation. Having said that, however, you've pretty much said it all....

Defensively Carew was an enigma. His good lateral range was compromised by a penchant for backhanding grounders rather than camping in front of them. A decent arm was betrayed by a tendency to nonchalantly flip the ball to—and sometimes over the head of—the first baseman.[6] Carew seemed to be mastering the double play pivot prior to a 1970 knee injury (he and Leo Cardenas had led the majors in twin killings the previous season[7]), but his totals fell off rapidly thereafter. By 1976 Rod's defense had regressed to the point that manager Gene Mauch moved the perennial batting champ to first base, where he developed a reputation as a man who never went one step out of his way to make a play.

Moody and shy early on (Twins' manager Sam Mele was going to return him to the minors in 1967 based on his reputation before then-coach Billy Martin intervened[8]), Carew matured into a terse if not blunt man who refused to back down from a statement once it had been made. His annual salary negotiations with Twins' owner Calvin Griffith were often tense—an unsurprising development given that Griffith was at the save-a-buck-at-any-price stage of his operating life. He threatened to bolt the Twins upon learning that Griffith was refusing to even consider signing free agent closer Mike Marshall despite manager Gene Mauch's recommendation; shortly thereafter, Marshall was signed to a three-year $850,000 deal.[9] After observing that the second year Seattle Mariners—a team fated to lose 104 games—didn't look particularly good to him, Carew's every move was booed in a subsequent three-game series. He added fuel to the fire by tipping his hat or bowing to the crowd after every foul ball: "They don't realize I'm beyond that" was Carew's reply when asked about the booing and his response.

Of course, the fact that he got five hits in his first seven at-bats of the series didn't help matters either.[10]

Intensely private yet cock-sure of his capabilities (when comparing himself to the Cobbs, Williamses, and Hornsbys, Carew said, "I don't put myself second to anybody when it comes to hitting"[11]), Rod was often referred to as possessing a regal bearing[12] that was mildly off-putting to teammates and reporters alike. He'd occasionally squawk about the resulting dearth of media attention that came his way, but:

a) His matter of fact comments made him a less than ideal interview under any event,

b) The Twins were rarely more than fringe participants in the pennant race during his prime seasons, and

c) Newspaper reporters are like the rest of us: if they have a choice between a story that writes itself and one that requires a lot of intensive interviewing and research ... well, the country never does get tired of hearing about Tom Seaver, does it?

Attempting to rank him among the all-time greats is an equally thankless task. Glove and all, Carew as a second baseman has to rank among the ten greatest of all time, but he spent just a shade less than half of his career in the middle of the infield. As a first sacker Rod doesn't match up particularly well with anybody that's played since the Dead Ball Era, but if push came to shove that portion of Carew's career would probably fall somewhere between Wes Parker and Mark Grace.

So where should two parts Frankie Frisch to one part Mark Grace and one part Wes Parker fall on the greatness meter?

Carew is in many ways the infield version of Al Oliver, the Pittsburgh Pirate gardener of the same era. Like Carew, Oliver was a consistent high average contact hitter — a Pittsburgh doctor once confided that Oliver possessed the highest level of hand-eye coordination he'd ever seen.[13] Like Rod, Al had a less-than-stellar defensive rep, though Carew earned his by being an obvious second baseman who couldn't master the position while Oliver became a center fielder because the other options were Willie Stargell and Richie Zisk. Like Carew, Oliver played for a small market team and may not have received the attention his efforts deserved, though like Rod he brought some of it on himself by not being much of an interview. Like Carew he was prone to complaining when things weren't going his way, though such was never a real problem in either case.

Now, Carew is in the Hall of Fame while Oliver probably has a long wait in front of him — and the reason for that boils down to the 154 hits that Oliver fell short of 3,000 and the 53 by which Carew exceeded the mark. Yes, Carew won an MVP Award and Oliver didn't, but Al was almost as fast as Rod in his prime, played better D at his position (and was a good left fielder when given the chance), hit .311 lifetime, and was on a different plane in terms of power.

Yet, of course, that isn't all of it.

Rod Carew made the All-Star team in every season he played save his last; Al Oliver played in four mid-season classics. Carew won the 1977 MVP Award and was in the top 10 in the balloting five other times; Oliver placed in the number ten spot once.

In short, Rod Carew's excellence at the plate (in real and perceived value) was great enough in the public mind to overcome his fielding difficulties, lack of media attention, and battles with ownership. This is an inevitable consequence of our inability to adequately measure the impact of defense and character on a team's success — yet it is undoubtedly easier to exploit a player who does one thing very well as opposed to someone who is decent but nothing special in every area. Edgard Clemente is probably twice the athlete that Ben Grieve is, but Grieve's bat appears good enough to assure a long and prosperous DHing career while Clemente is an outfielder who lacks the power to play the corners and the speed to hold down center.

Was Rod Carew a great player? Well, he did an outstanding job of doing what he was capable of doing for a long time ... and heck, there never are enough Mickey Mantles to go around.

28

Contending on the Cheap

One of the melancholy things about both baseball and romance is how often a well-stocked bank account (or nowadays a Platinum Visa card with a 1.9 percent introductory interest rate) can overcome even the gravest deficiencies in character, taste, or judgment. Donald Trump, for example, may well be a terrific guy when he's not trumpeting every successful business deal he's ever made, but the subways are lousy with blue-suited forty something guys who don't get to date a steady string of supermodels. Actions more complex than wearing a uniform overloaded with medals appear challenging to Prince Charles, yet that didn't keep him from attracting the closest thing to a babe that aristocracy has bred in 500 years. Federal Reserve Chairman Alan Greenspan's marriage to NBC reporter Andrea Mitchell should probably not be interpreted as a signal that 75-year-old economists are a hot item on the dating scene.

As art imitates life, so too does baseball. Brewery-earned riches allowed Colonel Jacob Ruppert to purchase Babe Ruth and transform the so-so Highlanders into the formidable Yankees. Having the reasonably enthusiastic backing of the Brooklyn Trust Company[1] allowed Branch Rickey's Dodgers to construct the mother of all farm systems, while a short personal bankroll caused Rickey to be squeezed out before the fruits of his labor fully flowered.[2] Cable TV riches buoyed Atlanta's Ted Turner through a decade of Nick Esasky-style free agent buys and Brett Butler plus Brook Jacoby for Len Barker trades en route to building the Regular Season Team of the 1990s.

As for postseason play, well....

The story of the 1970s to this point has largely been told in terms of dollar signs. Players wanting a bigger piece of the pie, owners humping cash-strapped municipalities for new stadiums, owners of "modest" means being replaced by nouveau riche tycoons ... seems just like modern times if one thinks about it. Yet even in today's $10-for-a-beer-and-a-dog world is evidence that money does not conquer all (especially if spent as the Los Angeles Dodgers have recently) and conversely that modest means and attendance figures need not be a bar to postseason play (see Oakland for details).

The original blueprint for the latter situation was drawn up on the shores of another bay some 3,000 miles and 30 years distant.

After developing a late 1960s powerhouse featuring oodles of Hall of Fame or near-Hall of Fame caliber talent, Jerry Hoffberger's Baltimore Orioles endured a decade that no baseball fan would have wished on anyone this side of Scott Boras. Key players aged prematurely, the club's brain trust hemorrhaged talent, and when free agency threatened to rob Baltimore of its progeny, mediocre attendance figures left them powerless to respond. Thus, an outfield where Don Buford, Paul Blair, and Frank Robinson once roamed was by decade's end populated by Al Bumbry, Gary Roenicke, Ken Singleton, and a bunch of guys who could just as easily have been on someone's AAA roster as not.

Yet this seeming Bataan Death March led to the most improbable of destinations—five divisional titles and the AL's best winning percentage for the decade as a whole. Between a veritable geyser of minor league talent in which solid pros like Bumbry and Rich Dauer represented the factory seconds, a constant inflow of flawed yet valuable if used properly players, and the ability to mold these disparate and sometimes ill-fitting pieces into a team, the Orioles crafted baseball's answer to the assembly line: a machine that melded interchangeable parts into a product of remarkable precision … if debatable charisma.

It was a franchise that had never been to the manner born. As the St. Louis Browns, the team endured 52 largely futile and unprofitable years (at the bottom of the Depression only about 800 hardy souls were attending the typical Browns game[3]) only to achieve its defining moment when then-owner Bill Veeck sent a midget up to bat.[4] While the team's subsequent sale to minor beer baron Hoffberger and move to Baltimore improved matters, the Orioles were never fated to be a big bucks operation, a fact which comparative sales of Hoffberger's National Brewing Company products with Gussie Busch's Budweiser made obvious.

Under the stewardship of first Paul Richards and later Lee MacPhail, the O's built a cost-effective farm-based operation, plugging the gaps with players like Jim Gentile and Gus Triandos whose paths in their current organizations were blocked by the likes of Gil Hodges and Andy Seminick. A natural consequence of this operating philosophy was the development of a cadre of talented managers and coaches, one of whom was an ex-minor league second baseman named Earl Weaver.

Weaver was one of those people who was just a little short (no offense, Earl) all the way around of being a major league player. A sure-handed defender who lacked the range and arm for a utility role, a .260ish leadoff man that had trouble handling good breaking stuff, Weaver still was probably equal to Buddy Biancalana or 100 others who have enjoyed the stub end of a major league career. However, it takes an unbroken string of luck and happenstance to elevate a Biancalana to 15-minutes-of-fame status: a com-

Earl Weaver in the mid-1970s. (*National Baseball Hall of Fame Library, Cooperstown, NY*)

bination of ill-timed injuries, slumps, and comments wiped out any Warhol-esque fantasies that Weaver might have harbored by his 24th birthday. Showing uncommon rationality in the face of this disillusioning fact, Earl committed to the managerial course early on with an intensity and attention to detail that would become his trademark.[5]

Weaver was what is popularly called an "out of the box" thinker nowadays. Most managers counseling a slumping player will tell him to crowd the plate or whatever and cross his fingers: Earl utilized lessons gleaned from Dale Carnegie's *How to Win Friends and Influence People* to sell his advice.[6] He referred Paul Blair to a hypnotist after a horrific 1970 beaning by Ken Tatum had left the center fielder tentative at the plate.[7] Noting the inordinate trouble some players had correcting the most obvious flaws in their game, he gave everybody IQ tests ... and in so doing discovered that the legendary fireballer/wild man Steve Dalkowski was essentially incapable of learning anything. Utilizing this knowledge, Weaver reduced Dalkowski's training regimen to the absolute basics—i.e. throw strikes—and Dalkowski reportedly responded by allowing only one run in 57 innings while striking out 110 (yes, he really was that dominant) and walking 11.[8] The next spring Dalkowski hurt his arm when another manager decided that he needed to learn how to throw a curve and that was that.

What really set Weaver apart from his brethren, though, was a hellbent desire to win. Though victory as such is seen as a desirable result, many front offices (and fans for that matter) view the minors in the way the Nazis viewed the concentration camps: as a no-cost laboratory for even the most outlandish experiments. Think Jeff Burroughs might make it at third base? Why not give it a shot — who cares that his team (the 1970 Denver Bears) was locked into a tight pennant race while Burroughs was posting an .857 fielding percentage in 28 games.[9] Want to try Richie Hebner at shortstop? So what if he commits 13 errors in four games and his team loses the 1968 IL pennant by ½ game—it isn't as if he did that with the Pirates, is it?[10] Try picturing Steve Garvey as a second baseman—yup, he really played eight games at the position for Spokane in 1970, but they won the PCL pennant by 26 games anyway.[11]

Earl didn't see it that way: to him, utilizing a player in a sub-optimal position was blasphemy, especially when a league title was on the line. When ordered to play Pete Ward—a fine defensive third baseman and future Rookie of the Year who nonetheless wasn't going to shove Brooks Robinson aside—in the outfield during the heat of the 1960 Three I League pennant race, Earl complied—for the one inning necessary to have Ward listed as having played left field in the next day's box scores.[12]

This driven nature and near-total confidence in his own judgment made Weaver just this side of insufferable in many eyes, a facet of his personality that has largely been rewritten into cute crustiness since Earl's elevation to Hall of Fame icon status. Read the reports of the time, though, and the picture that materializes is one of the know-it-all next door neighbor from a 1950s sitcom—a guy who continuously says "I told you so" when he's right and blusters when he isn't. Weaver's 1982 autobiography, *It's What You Learn After You Know It All That Counts*, provides numerous cases in point. He devotes the better part of a chapter to describing what a jerk Earl Williams was,[13] repeatedly boasts about his championing of Ellie Hendricks,[14] and basically blames umpires Shag Crawford and Lou DiMuro for the Orioles' 1969 World Series defeat.[15]

Like all such portraits, there is truth and falsehood in both the contemporary reports and Weaver's after-the-fact reminiscences. His difficulties with the umpiring fraternity were a natural offshoot of Earl's belief that everybody should be as dedicated to the pursuit of excellence as he was. Weaver's celebrated feud with Ron Luciano stemmed from a not totally unfounded belief that the arbiter's shtick was taking precedence over the proper calling of balls and strikes—yet Earl's provocative response to Luciano's 1977 league mandated apology[16] served to exacerbate the situation. Similarly, in the manner of many self-made men, Weaver's hardscrabble life on the road to managerial greatness left him less than tolerant of the whiny Jim Palmer—an intolerance that appears to have fermented into bitterness as a 2000 incident with Palmer at a celebrity roast clearly illustrates.[17]

Because (and in spite) of these qualities, by 1968 Weaver reached the majors as a coach on an Orioles team that under MacPhail's successor Harry Dalton had gotten over the top two years prior by adding Frank Robinson to their cadre of homegrown players. Thereafter, though, the team had drifted as

1. Robby's propensity for bulldozing basepath obstacles caught up with him (he would suffer from double vision for most of the 1967 and 1968 seasons after a collision with Al Weis[18]), and

2. Manager Hank Bauer proved to suffer from that most human of managerial maladies: the inability to cast adrift those who had helped him win
the 1966 Series, regardless of their current capabilities.[19]

Promoted to the manager's post at midseason, Weaver stepped into a
situation tailor made for a bright, action-oriented guy who had come up
through the ranks. Quality bats, gloves and arms were already there in quantity: all Earl needed to do was relieve the tension of Bauer's final months, sort
out the talent (much of which he had helped develop), and help the youngsters mature. By doing these basic yet "tougher than you think they are to
pull off" things, the Orioles took the league by storm in 1969 and stayed at
the top of the heap for three seasons.

And Earl Weaver looked like an absolute genius.

What's interesting about this period is how little bearing it has on
Weaver's image as it exists today. His first 3½ years working with the team
that Bauer had assembled would spawn three pennants and Earl's only world
championship — yet it is the remaining 11 seasons in which the Orioles would
win only one title that have cemented Weaver's reputation as a Hall of Fame
manager.

The real story of Weaver and the Orioles commences after the 1971 World
Series, when he was confronted with the following roster:

		Age	G	AB	R	H	2B	3B	HR	RBI	AVG	OBP	SLG
C	Ellie Hendricks	30	101	316	33	79	14	1	9	42	.250	.334	.386
C	Andy Etchebarren	28	70	222	21	60	8	0	9	29	.270	.321	.428
1B	Boog Powell	29	128	418	59	107	19	0	22	92	.256	.379	.459
2B	Davey Johnson	28	142	510	67	144	26	1	18	72	.282	.351	.443
3B	Brooks Robinson	34	156	589	67	160	21	1	20	92	.272	.341	.413
SS	Mark Belanger	27	150	500	67	133	19	4	0	35	.266	.365	.320
LF	Don Buford	34	122	449	99	130	19	4	19	54	.290	.413	.477
CF	Paul Blair	27	141	516	75	135	24	8	10	44	.262	.306	.397
RF	Frank Robinson	35	133	455	82	128	16	2	28	99	.281	.384	.510
OF	Merv Rettenmund	28	141	491	81	156	23	4	11	75	.318	.422	.448

		Age	G	GS	IP	H	ER	W	L	SV	ERA	BB	K
SP	Mike Cuellar	34	38	38	292 1/3	250	100	20	9	0	3.08	78	124
SP	Pat Dobson	29	38	37	282 1/3	248	91	20	8	0	2.90	63	187
SP	Jim Palmer	25	37	37	282	231	84	20	9	0	2.68	106	184
SP	Dave McNally	28	30	30	224 1/3	188	72	21	5	0	2.89	58	91
SW	Grant Jackson	28	29	9	77 2/3	72	27	4	3	0	3.13	20	51
CL	Eddie Watt	30	35	0	39 2/3	39	8	3	1	11	1.82	8	26
RP	Pete Richert	31	35	0	36 1/3	26	14	3	5	4	3.47	22	35

By any standards, the table above portrays a tenuously balanced situation. The rotation was obviously outstanding, but keep in mind that this foursome was composed of:

a. A 34-year-old guy (Cuellar) whose pre-1969 health history under heavy use was less than sterling.[20]

b. Another pitcher (Dobson) who had gone 14-15 with a 3.76 ERA in San Diego the prior season and had a reputation as a big mouth. While with the Tigers, Dobson had characterized his infielders as "hippety-hop" players "... they need five hops to reach a ground ball or it's a hit."[21]

c. A third man (Palmer) who two years previous had been virtually worthless due to arm problems,[22] and

d. A lefty (McNally) whose strikeout rate was edging precariously close to what is now known in Baltimore as the Jeff Ballard Zone (i.e. he can't throw anything past me, so let's keep fouling them off until he serves up something I can rip).

Backing these guys was a relief corps whose occupants were, by modern standards, permanently encased in rust. The eight men other than Grant Jackson who served time in the bullpen logged a combined 257 innings, a usage more reminiscent of the 1940s than the Age of Aquarius. Given Weaver's care in the construction of other portions of the roster, his bullpens uncharacteristically seemed an afterthought for years. Though its performance when given a chance was probably a touch above average, the 1971 relief squad was overloaded with people like the 40-year-old Dick Hall: fine in a limited role, but nobody who could step in if Jim Palmer's (or even Eddie Watt's) arm went south again.

The offensive situation was even more critical. Frank Robinson's $130,000 contract and declining productivity were shipped to the Dodgers for Doyle Alexander (his career dimmed by contract squabbles and ill-timed moves, Alexander is the prime example of why players should employ agents[23]). Don Buford would inexplicably crash and burn at 35, and the majority of the remaining players would age poorly. Boog Powell's early career numbers appear Cooperstown-bound — unfortunately, Boog's waistline was growing apace of his stats and he would post only one good season after age 30.[24] Dave Johnson in 1971 was Bret Boone without the overswing and had a 43-homer season in front of him, but to hit those taters Johnson would trade defensive range for bulk.[25] Paul Blair never really recovered offensively from his beaning and gradually slipped into a subsidiary role.

This scenario of latent problems and unanticipated declines is one that championship teams often face: the Atlanta Braves at the time of this writing seem to be making an annual habit of it. The Orioles, however, had several major advantages in dealing with this dilemma:

1. The perennially productive farm system was on the verge of kicking into overdrive. Eddie Murray, Bobby Grich, Don Baylor, Doug DeCinces, Mike Flanagan, Al Bumbry, Rich Coggins (Al Bumbry Lite on the playing field, the prototypical Hip Black Dude from an episode of *Kojak* off it[26]), Wayne Garland (looked for a moment there like the successor to Dave McNally — won 20 games in 1976, then tore his rotator cuff and was essentially finished at 27[27]) and Enos Cabell would all emerge from the Oriole system over the next five seasons. That's quite a haul — so good, in fact, that a guy like Bumbry (.281 career average over a 14-year career, good plate discipline, ran like a wounded deer even though he didn't have the instincts to play center field) tends to fade into the mental wallpaper.

2. Frank Cashen, an ex-sportswriter and National Brewing Company executive who was thrust into the GM position when Gene Autry's loaded saddlebags enticed Dalton westward, proved adept at the time-honored Oriole art of body scrounging. Tommy Davis, for example, had been kicking around both leagues for years as a high-average hitter for hire with marginal power, patience at the plate, speed (the result of a 1965 broken ankle), and defensive skills. At 34 and bitter over his vagabond existence,[28] Davis represented a riddle that most organizations couldn't be bothered to decipher. Used as a DH, though, in a park that neutralized power somewhat with a left-handed thumper (Terry Crowley) backing him on the bench … well, you just might have something there.

Ex-NL batting champion Tommy Davis had been released or traded six times in five years prior to latching on with the Orioles in 1973. Despite limited power and plate discipline, plus a glove that was best kept on the bench, Davis gave Baltimore four quality seasons in the DH role … with judicious assistance from Terry Crowley, among others. (*National Baseball Hall of Fame Library, Cooperstown, NY*)

Acquiring people with perceived shortcomings became something of a cottage industry in Baltimore.

• Ken Singleton was a .300 hitter whose batting eye in a 1978 poll was ranked among the top five in baseball,[29] but marginal fielding skills and less than prototypical corner outfielder power made Singleton an expendable commodity in soon-to-be outfielder-rich Montreal. For the price of Coggins and the aging and money-centric McNally, the Orioles acquired Singleton plus Mike Torrez — and added a long-term middle-of-the-order hitter plus a 20-game winner to their 1975 roster.

• Lee May was a capital class slugger who had the misfortune of being the marquee guy in a trade (the fabled Joe Morgan deal between the Astros and Reds) that had largely backfired. He moved in mid-career to a park that artificially depressed his numbers, thus making him look like he'd prematurely lost and he was a key player on a team that had first disappointed its fans, then slid into the second division.

May had some real limitations as a player (he didn't believe in ball four and wore a glove only to be fashionable), but at 32 he was remarkably level-headed (when asked for his reaction upon being traded by the Reds, May replied "I play for money and they pay money in Houston"[30]) and pretty much the same player he'd always been.

To the suddenly power-starved Orioles, that was a very attractive package.

• Ross Grimsley was a fine young left-hander with a Cincinnati Reds team that needed every healthy arm they had. However, his irreverent lifestyle and attitude were too much for a management obsessed with basic black shoes and close shaves,[31] and thus Grimsley became available for Merv Rettenmund, a terrific platoon outfielder who, as Champ Summers would a decade later, loudly aspired to be more than what he was.

Grimsley would win 50 games in four seasons with the Orioles, while after hitting .227 in 396 at-bats over two seasons, Rettenmund would be dealt to the Padres for a minor league shortstop and cash.

Not every move panned out, of course, the Orioles subjected themselves to two years of Earl Williams, a power-hitting catcher who wasn't wild about blocking balls in the dirt, participating in pregame drills, or doing much of anything that inconvenienced him.[32] Still, Cashen's (and successor Hank Peters's) ability to turn Baltimore's odd and ends into productive players was a key ingredient in the team's ongoing success.

3. Weaver was intellectually flexible enough to mold whatever he was given into a team. Consider Baltimore's outfield situation as camp opened in 1973 — Frank Robinson gone, Buford reduced to ineffectiveness, Baylor still a work in progress, Blair erratic at the plate, Rettenmund proving incapable of handling full-time play, and the only options being two rookies (Bumbry and Coggins) who were both left-handed hitters, had limited power, and lacked the defensive skills to play center field.

It was an outfield with all of the earmarks of qualifying for disaster relief funds, and a quick review of the quintet's 1973 stats would tend to support that idea. None of the five hit more than 11 homers that season ... or drove in as many as 65 runs ... or scored more than 73 times.[33] In short, these guys individually came off as the half players they were — but put them all together, and the result was:

- a .296 average with 15 homers and 78 RBIs per position;
- 107 runs scored per position by virtue of a .363 on-base percentage;
- havoc wreaked on the basepaths (a combined 102 steals in 150 attempts), plus
- fine defense if optimally aligned, though the arms at the corners were somewhat weak.

For a man supposedly wedded to the three-run homer, Weaver put together a lot of arrangements like that. The 1975 Oriole offense finished seventh in runs scored and looked worse; Belanger, Blair, and Brooks Robinson were pretty much hopeless by that time, while the catchers (Dave Duncan and Ellie Hendricks) were about as valueless as a platoon that contributes 20 homers and 79 RBIs can be. The defensive backup on the bench was spotty at best, with Doug DeCinces as the key utility infielder (one involuntarily smiles at the thought of DeCinces playing shortstop). The pitching after Jim Palmer and Mike Torrez was undistinguished, and Palmer would be the only staff member to have his mug grace the 1979 pennant winners' team photo.

Yet for all of that, the 1975 Orioles won 90 games, finishing a respectable second to the Red Sox while posting the AL's best record from the middle of May on. The reason for this success was simple: though deficient in big fly potential, everybody did something to help the team win. While the back end of the lineup was offensively challenged, it did provide Gold Glove defense — and did so at key defensive positions. The pitchers other than Torrez were stingy with free passes, a trait that when coupled with the gloves behind them resulted in the fewest runs allowed of any AL team.[34] The five key hitters complemented each other well, while a couple of bench guys (Jim Northrup and Tony Muser) came up big.

The miracle of it all was that Weaver was able to adjust his approach to such a changing and disparate group of cast members and continued to do so successfully as the farm system's output quality slid towards the end of the decade. Make no mistake about it: the system continued to belch forth talent, but the prize pupils were now guys like Rich Dauer, a typical old-school second baseman (sharp on the double play, good range, could poke enough singles to keep from being a black hole, finished at 32). More common were players like Kiko Garcia, Andres Mora, Tom Shopay, Dave Skaggs, and Larry Harlow — OK, perhaps, but nothing that wasn't readily available on the waiver

The 1975 Orioles were a good young team that finished within four games of the pennant-winning Red Sox. Yet only five of the players in this picture (well, six if you count Ellie Hendricks's one 1979 at-bat) would still be with the team when it hit paydirt four years later. (*National Baseball Hall of Fame Library, Cooperstown, NY*)

wire. However, the point about these players was that they didn't cost additional money to utilize, and each could do something.

A key problem most baseball teams face is the man who performs at a C to C+ level in every facet of the game. Baseball is lousy with guys like this; we'll use Craig Paquette as an example, but virtually every team has someone like this on their roster, and it's nothing personal, Craig. Anyway, Paquette has power but not enough power to be useful in the middle of the lineup, hits for a decent average but doesn't walk enough to be an on-base threat, and can play some D but lacks the range for a middle-of-the-diamond position or the brilliance to plant at a corner spot given his offensive productivity.

In short, Paquette is virtually impossible to utilize effectively. He's marginal at best in a starting role, lacks the versatility to be much of a utility player, and lacks the power or average to be an effective pinch hitter. In short, he's just there — a player who does everything well enough to say that he does it but nothing in a big enough way for anyone to really want him to do it for them.

Weaver didn't believe in that type of player and in point of fact went out of his way to clear guys like Enos Cabell and Bob Bailor off of his roster in favor of the Larry Harlows and Tom Shopays. Now, on a straight talent basis, these moves were less than 100 percent efficient — Cabell and Bailor were certainly superior overall to Larry Harlow, a .248 career hitter with minimal power and a so-so arm. The difference, though, is that while Cabell and Bailor spent their careers as men without a position, Harlow actually could do certain things well — he could take a walk, steal a base on occasion, cover center field adequately enough to be useful in the late innings. In short, Harlow was a valuable guy for a team needing those qualities ... or one headed by somebody with the patience to construct a role for him.

The result of these machinations was an against-the-odds success story that gave heart to the small-market teams throughout the league ... or at least it would have if the resulting financial picture had not been so bleak.

The dark side of the Orioles' 1970s success story lay in the public's anemic response to the team's on-field triumphs. Baltimore attendance numbers ranked in the bottom half of the league for seven consecutive seasons; the 1973 division winners, for example, outdrew only three of their AL competitors.[35] The reasons for this apathy started with Memorial Stadium itself, an improvised/compromised structure and wildlife sanctuary (the stories of skunks, feral cats, and other animals making their way onto the field during games are legion[36]) remote from the city's center. By the early 1970s, the park's inadequacies had become so profound that even Weaver's vibrant tomato plants in the Orioles' bullpen[37] couldn't cover them. A $44 million price tag to renovate the then 20-year-old structure was only $7 million shy of what a new downtown domed stadium on the site of the B&O rail yard was estimated to cost.

That proposed site was a place called Camden Yards.[38]

The imbroglio over the Camden Yards project would engulf the city of Baltimore and the state of Maryland for the next two decades. Like many eastern metropolises, Baltimore was hemorrhaging its populace and tax base — the city would lose 15 percent of its residents during the 1970s.[39] Thus, local authorities of necessity looked to the state to foot the majority of the stadium/convention center's bill — an interesting proposition given then Governor Marvin Mandel's promise that the project would not cost "one red cent" of taxpayer money.[40] The result of this dichotomy was a situation that in certain ways presages San Diego's current travails with its downtown stadium: calls for abolition of the overseeing Maryland Sports Complex Authority, demands for statewide referendums on the question, even concern from the city's comptroller about the legality of the Authority's proposal.[41]

And like the modern-day Padres, Jerry Hoffberger and the Orioles were caught in the middle.

Yet having said that, there is some evidence that the club was a victim of its unique approach to empire building. Though applauded by aficionados for their meticulous construction, the 1970s Orioles often lacked two of the key elements that attract the casual fan — well-known stars and players with lengthy histories in the organization. The 1971 Orioles finished third in AL attendance with a roster loaded to the gunwales with guys that fit those qualifications to a T, while the 1977 squad on which only one key player had been with the team for more than three seasons would be outdrawn by nine others.[42]

Thus despite Baltimore's on-field success, the organization often found themselves shut out in free agent negotiations for their progeny. Don Baylor and Mike Torrez (both in their final year before free agency) were dispatched to Oakland for Reggie Jackson: after one OK year, Jackson was on his way to the Big Apple and postseason fame.[43] Despite his obvious potential and Baltimore's crying need at the time for infielders who knew what a bat was for, the club never really had a shot at retaining Bobby Grich, who ultimately signed a five-year, $1.75 million contract with the California Angels.[44] Economics forced the Birds to choose between Wayne Garland and Mike Flanagan[45]; that they made the right choice in this case does not negate the agony inherent in having to make such a decision in the first place.

Yet for all of that, the 1970s Baltimore O's remain a monument to what can be done with a short bankroll. It is surprising in a sense that so few teams have chosen to revisit the Orioles' formula in recent years—but then again, the formula requires more than a little work, diligence and patience to yield fruit.

In short, it's just a whole heck of a lot easier to have money.

29

Bill Veeck's
South-Side Wreck

There's an old joke that ends with the punch line "The patient's been dead for six months and doesn't even know it."

That line aptly sums up the plight of major league baseball's less affluent owners in the aftermath of the Messersmith-McNally debacle. With payrolls growing at rates greater than 20 percent every year between 1976 and 1982[1] people who had entered the game for high-minded reasons found themselves immersed in an increasingly cutthroat business in which they were forever running harder just to keep up. Though expanding television revenues and gate sales were sweetening the overall pot, the relative differential between the haves and have-nots was growing ever wider. Attendance figures vividly depict the widening gap; while home attendance for baseball's five worst draws rose by 8.1 percent between 1968 and 1979, crowds for the five most popular teams increased nearly 40 percent.[2] Put those numbers against the player salary gains, and ... well, it doesn't take a Ph.D. to know where the talent was going to flow.

In short, the rotisserie owner's dream of turning a beleaguered franchise into a champion without the injection of Bill Gatesian-type scratch was progressively becoming more of a mirage ... and the object example of this phenomenon was acted out on the south side of Chicago.

As the 1975 season came to a close, the White Sox franchise was in the final throes of executing an ominous double play: the team was simultaneously broke and awash in mediocre players. Take a typical 75-win team — say, the 2001 Anaheim Angels. One look at the Angels' stats makes it obvious why the team had an upper deck view of the Seattle Mariners' rumps: a couple of proven players had off years, the Halos got zip from their DHs and first basemen, and the rotation was a couple of studs short. Thus GM Bill Stoneman first dipped into the Disney vaults to sign a couple of free agents (Brad Fullmer, Aaron Sele), then traded for another guy (Kevin Appier), crossed his fingers that the two stars (Darin Erstad, Tim Salmon) would snap out of it, and chose to platoon at first. These moves bore spectacular fruit in the form of the 2002 World Series crown. The Angels identified their problems, addressed them, and thereby produced a basis for fan optimism about the upcoming season.

The Pale Hose couldn't do that, due largely to the fact that they didn't have any blatant weaknesses. Take the situation at third base: Bill Melton had been a terrific player in the early 1970s, the first league home run champ ever to come from the South Side and an acceptable defender.[3] By 1975, though, back problems had reduced Melton's prowess on both sides of the ball while limiting him to 120 games or so a season.[4] Yet he retained decent power and a keen batting eye, while behind him the Chisox had Bill Stein, a 28-year-old third baseman with limited sock and a marginal arm ... but Stein could hit .270 and accepted his life on the fringes of baseball society. Thus when Melton was healthy, the Sox were OK at third, and when he wasn't — well, a team could do worse.

The team was loaded with players like that. Second baseman Jorge Orta's speed and ability to hit for average would land him in the Mexican League's Hall of Fame,[5] but poor defensive instincts along with a lack of other offensive capabilities would make his career on this side of the border a catch-as-catch can affair. Shortstop Bucky Dent was 23, played decent defense and could hit .260, but his 1978 playoff homer notwithstanding, Dent's .260 was roughly as valuable as Rey Ordonez's .260 today. Carlos May (Lee's brother) had some speed, some power, would take a walk, and wasn't impossible in the field — but a weak throwing arm (hampered by a thumb reduced to a stump in a 1969 mortar accident[6]) limited him to positions at which a team needed more than that. They had Ken Henderson, a .260s-hitting center fielder with adequate speed capable of producing maybe ten homers and 60 RBIs a season. They had Pat Kelly, a marginally powerful, fast guy who never quite figured out how to use his speed to full advantage, playing right field. Behind the outfielding regulars stood Jerry Hairston, a man who could hit .280 in his sleep and would take a walk but lacked the power to hold down a corner spot and the arm to play anywhere else. The situation wasn't completely bleak, with Goose Gossage and Terry (not yet the tub of goo) Forster in the bullpen, while 20-year-old center fielder Chet Lemon was at the outset of a 16-year career as an accomplished defender, fine hitter, and excruciatingly bad base runner.[7] Still, the White Sox' 75-86 record was a fair reflection of what they were: a team just good enough to look noble in defeat.

The team's owner at the time was John Allyn, a patrician man who had been a silent partner in the team for a decade before assuming full control in 1969.[8] Allyn was in many ways the prototypical team owner — an investment broker by trade with a significant family fortune backing him and an aversion to rancorous confrontations. When then-GM Stu Holcomb first played hardball in contract negotiations prior to the 1973 season, then released some people he couldn't sign, a couple of fringe players and manager Chuck Tanner squawked publicly, and Holcomb unexpectedly "resigned" on July 27.[9] To appease Dick Allen, the White Sox carried his brother Hank (a weak-hitting outfielder who'd been out of baseball for a year) on their roster for two seasons—he went seven for 60 and didn't drive in a run.[10] When Melton, Henderson, and Tanner suggested that announcer Harry Caray's criticism was damaging the players' on-field performance, Allyn fired the popular broadcaster, categorizing him as a "disruptive influence."[11]

After losing an estimated $2 million during the 1975 season[12] Allyn found himself unable to make his final payroll,[13] and in that failure his fellow owners saw an opportunity to resolve one of their longest-standing headaches. The city of Seattle had been suing the American League ever since the Pilots were spirited away to Milwaukee in 1970; if Allyn offered the Sox to a Seattle group, the league would provide a $500,000 bridge loan to tide him over until a deal could be completed.[14] Though the scheme made perfect sense for everyone involved, it was a bitterly ironic pill for Allyn to swallow given that he had originally bought control of the Sox to keep them from being moved to Milwaukee (the team had played 11 "home" games at County Stadium in 1969).[15] Still, with no alternatives in sight....

It is out of desperate situations that miracles spring forth, and in this case an unlikely savior arose from the shores of Chesapeake Bay—one William Louis Veeck, Jr.

A legendary operator in his time, Veeck had driven the 1959 White Sox and 1948 Cleveland Indians to pennants and attendance records with a mixture of promotional flair and savvy deal making. He'd pioneered the idea of Ladies' Day,[16] built scoreboards that shot off fireworks and played Handel's *Messiah* (you know—"Hal-ley-loo-yeah, hal-ley-loo-yeah, hallelujah, hallelujah, hal-ley-LOO-OO-OO-YEAH!") after a home run,[17] and once allowed 500 fans seated in a special section of the stands to manage his team for a day.[18] Veeck was Charlie Finley save the terminal cheapness and meanness of spirit (Finley's original *modus operandi* was actually modeled on Veeck: Charlie would drive then GM Frank Lane nuts by responding to his suggestions with "I wonder what Bill Veeck would think of that?"[19]), which proves how cornball some of Bill's ideas could be and how tough it is to keep good-natured fun from turning into vulgarity.

Both visionary and impatient, Veeck was not a man to let traditions or others less gifted stand in his way, and thus he was (to put it mildly) less than well loved by the league's vested interests. At the pinnacle of that antipathy mountain was the commissioner, who, as it was his duty to tell people that they couldn't do things, was in constant conflict with the wily Veeck, who saw rules as things that simply made the trip to what he wanted to do more torturous. Between that antipathy and ongoing ill health, Veeck had been out of baseball proper for 13 years, though he had maintained his gadfly status via a biting syndicated column plus testimony for the "wrong" side in both the Curt Flood and Milwaukee vs. the Braves cases.[20]

Such stances would cost Veeck dearly, as his initial application to buy the White Sox was turned down by a resounding 10-3 vote on December 3.[21]

One can only speculate as to the degree of payback incumbent in the owners' decision, but regardless of that there was also a practical reason for the AL's hesitation. Veeck's proposed financial structure was exceedingly debt-heavy (better than a 10-1 debt to equity ratio[22] — the kind of financing that made dot-coms what they are today) and thus dependent on his intangible marketing and horse-trading skills. Ten years earlier such a bid would probably have been accepted with little more than a raising of eyebrows, but by the winter of 1975 baseball was hip-deep in financial crises. The San Francisco Giants' plight had filled the season with elements of melodrama, skullduggery, and low comedy. Various rumors had owner Horace Stoneham unable to pay the rent on Candlestick Park,[23] selling to Canada's Labatt Breweries, who would then transfer the team to Toronto,[24] selling to unnamed Japanese investors, who would move it to Tokyo[25] — hell, they could have ended up anywhere. Downturns in Judge Roy Hofheinz's Astrodomain conglomerate had caused him to cede control of the Houston franchise to a creditor-dominated three-man board at midseason.[26] A 46 percent year-to-year attendance decline was about to drive the Atlanta Braves into the arms of "internationally known yachtsman" Ted Turner.[27] Even a consistently successful team like the Baltimore Orioles was apparently available for the right price: prior to his White Sox foray, Veeck had made an offer for the O's that received serious consideration from owner Jerry Hoffsberger.[28]

Under normal circumstances that would have been that, but the AL owners recognized that slam-dunking a public icon was a less than PR-sensitive approach. Thus after three hours of further discussion, the league decided to take the gentlemanly way out by announcing that it would reconsider Veeck's bid if certain conditions were met. Naturally, the conditions were deal breakers — elimination of the debenture/stock grouping that was the key to potential profits for his backers along with the raising of an additional $1.5 million — but hey, it wasn't as if they weren't giving him a chance, was it?

And oh, by the way Bill, take all the time necessary to get the deal done — we're giving you seven days.[29]

The problem with taking the gentlemanly (read: easy) way out of a situation is that if the other guy proves more tenacious than expected, you've painted yourself into a corner, and that's exactly what happened to the American League in this case. At enormous personal cost, Veeck reconfigured his offer, finding seven new investors (no sweat for a man who once wrote a book called *The Hustler's Handbook*), then basically tossing his share of the equity into the pot to keep the deal on track. His wife, Mary Frances, summed the situation up perfectly: when informed that her husband would be more

Bill Veeck had been out of baseball for more than a decade when his group purchased the Chicago White Sox in late 1975. Despite a deft marketing touch and an improbable 1977 pennant run, Veeck's second go-round on the South Side would founder in the economic tidal wave of baseball's new era. (*National Baseball Hall of Fame Library, Cooperstown, NY*)

employee than owner of the restructured group, she said, "What you are telling me is that it isn't an investment any more; it's a vendetta."[30]

Despite meeting the onerous qualifications, Veeck was still one vote short of approval when his revised offer was brought back in front of the AL elders, a result that left Detroit's John Fetzer somewhere between unhappy and incensed. A man who believed in stability (GM Jim Campbell, for example, had been with the Tigers since 1949 and would still be around as CEO when the 1990s dawned[31]) and decorum, Fetzer was the antithesis of Veeck in many ways. Yet Fetzer believed that a deal was a deal; the league had set conditions for Veeck, he had met them, and that was that. "Look, I don't like it any more than you do that we're allowing this guy in here," Fetzer reportedly said, "But gentlemen, we're just going to have to take another vote."[32]

This time Veeck received ten affirmative votes and admission to the pantheon.[33]

He immediately began operating in typical fashion, commandeering an alcove in the lobby of the hotel where baseball's winter meetings were being held and erecting a hand-painted "Open For Business: By Appointment Only" sign announcing his willingness to wheel and deal.[34] Bowie Kuhn and several owners considered the display to be gauche in the extreme[35] (Milwaukee owner Bud Selig likened it to a meat market[36]), but they missed the point. Onlookers were stopping by to watch the proceedings (a cheer was let out when Veeck completed a deal minutes before the trading deadline[37]), while newsmen were standing there pen in hand — in short, Veeck was generating publicity, getting people to talk about the White Sox.

What's more, despite the distaste that his fellow owners may have felt over the spectacle, Veeck did get four deals done ... and not surprisingly, one of those trades sent Ken Henderson to Atlanta while another made Melton the property of the California Angels.[38] Tanner was ousted within a week despite having three years left to go on his contract, while Caray turned out not to have been fired after all, the now minority holder Allyn remarking that "I would assume that if (Veeck) wants Harry, he can have Harry."[39]

Thus began a reign of marketing terror the likes of which baseball hadn't seen since — well, since the last time Veeck had owned a ball club.

The first salvo was fired shortly after the club changed hands. A diehard opponent of artificial turf ("When you go to a ballgame, you are entitled to smell grass freshly cut; it is part of the atmosphere, part of the escape."), Veeck invited the fans to come out and help him eradicate the synthetic blight from Comiskey Park. Some 3,000 potential ticket buyers responded to his call to arms, taking away everything from postage-stamp sized clumps to room-sized rolls of the not-so-hallowed stuff.[40]

When the owners decided to lock the players out of spring training in 1976, Veeck followed the edict to the letter even though he'd voted against it — but since the lockout order applied only to those on major league rosters, he opened a camp for non-roster players and free agents.[41] From a practical viewpoint, nothing much came of the camp (onetime Met Cleon Jones parlayed his attendance into 40 regular-season-at-bats), but from a publicity angle ... well, if a team holds a camp when no one else is and does so at a time when Florida was crawling with idle sportswriters, it's only natural that the name "Chicago White Sox" will start popping up in lots of articles.

On opening day, the peg-legged Veeck, along with business manager Rudie Schaffer and manager Paul Richards, dressed as the three minutemen of the famed "Spirit of '76" painting (as Veeck put it, "If you've got the guy with the wooden leg, you've got the casting beat"[42]). In a tableau dripping with symbolism and schlock, this trio of White Sox veterans from the glory days of the 1950s marched in from second base to home plate, where Richards (he was the one carrying the flag) solemnly recited the fourth stanza of "The Star Spangled Banner."[43]

Why the fourth stanza? Well, those who've considered the words they sing prior to the start of a baseball game will immediately realize that the initial stanza (which is all anybody plays) simply asks if the flag is still there. It's the fourth stanza that proudly proclaims, "And the Star-Spangled Banner in triumph shall wave o'er the land of the free and the home of the brave."[44]

This oversight had driven Paul Richards nuts for years, so given that it was the bicentennial year, the third largest opening day crowd in Comiskey Park history on hand, fathers and sons standing side by side in Norman Rockwellesque fashion....

Heck, what red-blooded American could pass up such an opportunity to stir the hearts of his fellow men and the country's progeny?

The "nights" staged by the Sox ranged from the eclectic to the bizarre. Shakespeare Night featured vignettes performed on the field by a local troupe of Bard devotees[45] — exactly how many of those have appeared at ballparks recently? On Band Night, anybody with a musical instrument was admitted free of charge (several young women brought a player piano; they and the piano were admitted) and were led in a rendition of "Take Me Out to the Ballgame" by the associate conductor of the Chicago Symphony Orchestra.[46] Veeck came up with the idea of beer case stacking as a sport, holding a series of elimination rounds that pitted three-man teams against one another in a contest to see who could stack flats of suds the highest and fastest....

... and if a stack would occasionally topple and spray gallons of beer on the contestants, well, so much the better.[47]

His most famous—er, infamous—event was the brainchild of a well-known local DJ. An outspoken foe of the then popular disco genre, he and Veeck devised a promotion called Disco Demolition Night. Everyone who brought a disco record to a July 12, 1979, doubleheader with the Detroit Tigers would be admitted for 98 cents, with the between-games entertainment being the destruction of the collected pile of records by the disc jockey with the aid of a suitably impressive plunger.

It was an interesting, if somewhat offbeat, promotion sure to garner local and national attention for the team. The only problem was that some 70,000 fans/disco haters responded to the call to arms[48] (another 20,000 were reportedly stuck in a massive traffic jam on the Dan Ryan Expressway), which wouldn't be any big deal except for the fact that Comiskey Park's capacity was a little under 45,000. Thus at the end of the first game (ominously lost to the Tigers 4-1), there were some 50,000 paid admissions in the stands along with 5,000 gate crashers and another 15,000 or so milling around outside the park with nothing to do. In was a situation ready to (excuse the expression) explode, and when the records went up, general mayhem erupted. Some 7,000 people made their way onto the field, dragging the batting cage into the middle of the field and destroying it. A fire was set in the center field bleachers. A banner on the left field foul pole was set ablaze as well. It took 20 minutes, the mounted police, a SWAT unit and the fire department to restore order — and to add insult to injury, once the field was cleared, the umpires declared it unfit for play, forfeiting the second game to the Tigers.[49]

Yet for all of his promotional exploits, Veeck fully understood that in the long run "there is no known substitute for winning and no known cure for losing."[50] People might make their way to the park a bit earlier or stay later to see a fireworks display (and, not incidentally, buy another beer and hot dog in the process), but as he wrote in his autobiography, *Veeck as in Wreck,* "We are dealing here only with remedial action. It has always been my belief that you have three years to produce a winning team once you come to town. If after that time you haven't come through, I suspect that the value of entertainment and publicity and promotion will fall off very substantially."[51]

His initial machinations on the team development front proved uninspiring, though in fairness nobody that Veeck dealt that winter had much of a future in front of him. Melton's demise netted the White Sox Jim Spencer, a fine defensive first baseman whose offensive capabilities could best be described as Mark Grace suffering from anemia. Being of the era in which bullpen duty was considered to be a waste of a good arm, Veeck and Richards decided to turn Gossage into a starter[52]; this allowed them to convert 20-game winner Jim Kaat into Ralph Garr, essentially the outfielder version of Jorge Orta. With Orta relegated to DH duty and a couple of good field/no hit rookies plugging the holes at second and third, the White Sox were transformed from a team with decent defense, no power, and no speed to one with good speed, no power, and outfielders who made errors *really fast*. Add to that Wilbur Wood's shattered kneecap[53] and the inability of Gossage and Forster to adapt to starting roles, and the White Sox finished 1976 with their second worst record in 26 years.

To neatly top the situation off with a cherry:

a. Veeck's two most marketable talents (the Goose and the future tub of goo) were, as a result of the Messersmith-McNally decision, destined to become free agents at the end of the 1977 season.
b. The team's finances had quickly deteriorated to the point where each check that cleared the bank was a cause for celebration.

It was a desperate situation, and in the spirit of a man with nothing to lose, Veeck embarked on what at first glance would seem to be a foolhardy course: he rebuilt the Sox as a power-hitting team with a short fuse. Gossage and Forster were dealt to the Pittsburgh Pirates for free agent-to-be Richie Zisk, a quality hitter with marginal defensive range whose fate it was to succeed Roberto Clemente as the Bucs' right fielder and be endlessly reminded that he wasn't as good as the man he replaced. Bucky Dent was sent New York-ward for Oscar Gamble, a grade B power hitter who would also reach free agent nirvana at the end of the '77 season, a kid pitcher named Lamarr Hoyt, and the cash to help the team meet its first payroll.[54] Finally, Veeck raided the free agent market's bargain basement, signing the 27-year-old ex-Twin (Minnesota was the Aberdeen Proving Grounds for future free agents even then) Eric Soderholm, a pretty good defensive third baseman with power ... or at least he'd been good before knee surgery KOed his 1976 season.[55]

The philosophy at work here is one that should be familiar to fans of the 1997 Florida Marlins. What Veeck had devised is commonly referred to today as the rent-a-player strategy, i.e. trying to get over the top with people too expensive to keep past season's end. The goal is to generate enough riches with the stacked team to retain one or two hired guns capable of keeping the franchise respectable until a youth movement is ready to take over. It's a risky strategy, as Wayne Huizenga and the fans of Florida baseball would learn some two decades later, but in 1977 it paid off as well as anyone could possibly have expected for Veeck.

The White Sox came out of the moves as anything but a balanced team. The infield defense was horrible; Soderholm never really recovered from his knee problems, shortstop Alan Bannister led the league in errors, and Gamble's arrival plus the maturation of Chet Lemon forced Jorge Orta back to second base. The starting rotation was overflowing with retreads (Wood, Steve Stone, Steve Renko) and young guys with less than distinguished futures in front of them (Chris Knapp, Dave Frost, Francisco Barrios). With the departure of Gossage and Forster, the bullpen talent was so thin that the closer role fell to journeyman Lerrin LaGrow, a onetime Tiger starter who'd spent the majority of the 1976 season in the minors posting a 6-10 record with an above-league-average ERA.

Yet out of that unholy mess improbably emerged a contender. The Pale Hose hit 192 homers that season, second only to the Red Sox and 54 more than the previous club record.[56] Before injuring his knee in the second half, Zisk was a legitimate MVP candidate; as it was, he hit .290 with 30 homers and 101 RBIs. Spencer and Lamar Johnson, a barrel-chested right-handed hitter with glacial speed and defensive range who, like Greg Colbrunn today, was too good for a part-time role and not good enough to play regularly, produced 34 homers as they shared first base. LaGrow came up with a career year, saving 25 games while posting a 2.46 ERA. Boosted by such strong production, the White Sox stunned the baseball world by winning 90 games and leading the AL West for six weeks in the heart of the season.[57]

And the fans responded.

Over 1.6 million admissions made their way into Comiskey Park in 1977 to witness the homers, milking contests, errors, and nights honoring every ethnic group in creation (fans on Mexican Fiesta Night saw Chicago baseball legend Minnie Minoso in full matador regalia taming an ersatz bull[58]). Though that number may not seem high by current standards, the attendance figures at the time represented a new record for the franchise and were within 18,000 of the all-time Chicago record. It was a young crowd, too, one that would invent the curtain call for a player who hit a home run,[59] the first to stand and applaud the closer as he worked to what everyone hoped would be the final opposing batter,[60] the first to sing "Take Me Out to the Ball Game" with Harry Caray.[61]

Yet it wasn't enough.

Zisk was out the door after receiving a ten-year, $2.955 million offer from the Texas Rangers.[62] Veeck had expected that — the guy he wanted to keep was Oscar Gamble, the Afro-topped left-handed slugger (Gamble's hair was so big that it would on occasion pop the batting helmet off of his head[63]) who'd hit .297 with 31 homers. He offered Gamble $350,000 per year for three years—and was outbid by San Diego's Ray Kroc, who doled out $2.85 million over six years with a $150,000 bonus.[64]

And that, in essence, was the end of the game.

Though Veeck would control the club for three more years, the Sox would not top .500 again. Attendance declined by over 40 percent as the team fell out of contention, but even worse was that the Chicago slide was occurring at a time when the American League as a whole posted a 14 percent gain in admissions.[65] In short, the White Sox were not only losing revenue, their relative position vis-à-vis the rest of the league was declining even faster.

This was the exact situation that Charlie Finley was facing in Oakland, and Calvin Griffith was facing in Minnesota, and the Mariners' ownership group (which included Danny Kaye) was facing in Seattle, but with the difference that *Veeck was basically doing everything right*. His trades were decent; he may have given up on Brian Downing too early, but the Downing trade netted Bobby Bonds along with Richard Dotson, a hot pitching prospect who became a key member of the Sox' 1983 divisional championship staff. Veeck did a good job identifying and developing young talent; an organization whose four minor league teams had all finished last in 1975 within five years boasted such talents as Hoyt, Dotson, Britt Burns, Steve Trout, Harold Baines, and Ron Kittle. From a promotional point of view, the effort was unsurpassed.

Yet all that effort and creativity was for naught, and the worst part of it was that Veeck didn't even come particularly close to achieving success.

Remember the Edsel, the "distinctive"-looking Ford Motor Company car of the late 1950s whose name has become synonymous with failure? What most people don't realize about the Edsel is that the car made a heck of a lot of sense when it was first proposed in 1954. A significant price differential existed between plain-Jane Fords and top-of-the-line Lincolns at the time, and the Edsel was designed to bridge that gap. Extensive market research showed that potential buyers wanted more convenience features in their cars; thus Edsels were loaded with every gadget known to modern man. Finally, the country was in the middle of an economic expansion, and when things are going good everybody wants bigger cars, better cars, flashier cars....

By the time the Edsel hit the market in the fall of 1957, though, the world had changed. The price gap in Ford's lineup had been filled by the Mercury division, while the post-Korean War boom had given way to a recession—and in tough times, people discover that they can live without such niceties as push-button chassis lubricators, electric trunk openers, and Teletouch transmissions. Thus a car projected to sell over 200,000 units in its first model year racked up less than 63,000 sales in that time frame[66] and would be gone from the scene entirely (along with $250 million of Ford's money[67]) by the end of 1959.

Such was the story of Bill Veeck's second fling on the South Side of Chicago. The Sox' decline and eventual sale to Jerry Reinsdorf and Eddie Einhorn represented the final confirmation of the Messersmith-McNally decision's cataclysmic effect on baseball's operating environment. Though money was pouring in (as Marvin Miller was quick to point out on any occasion), the fact that it was going out just as fast became the death knell for a whole generation of moguls lacking the deep pockets necessary to ride out the current storm.

Veeck put up a titanic and highly entertaining struggle to save his team and place in baseball's hierarchy. Too bad that all of the fireworks were shot off after his dream was already dead....

30

Vern Rapp and Management 101

It is the sad fate of many people to have their time pass before they ever get a chance to shine. Perhaps the best example of this is Herbert Hoover, our country's 31st president and butt of jokes to this day about the Great Depression. Despite his popular reputation, Hoover was a legitimate Renaissance man, one who built railroads in China in his 20s, headed commissions after both world wars to assure that a decimated Europe got fed, and served with distinction as Secretary of Commerce. He was The Great Engineer, everybody's choice to succeed the taciturn Calvin Coolidge as chief executive.

Then the stock market crashed, and Herbert Hoover became a synonym for futility. Nothing in his background remotely prepared him for dealing with the Depression — not that anybody else would have done a whole lot better. Had he come along as little as ten years earlier, Hoover could easily have gone down in history's annals as a fine president instead of the man for whom the 1930s shantytowns, called Hoovervilles, were named.

Alongside Hoover in baseball's annals stands one Vernon Fred Rapp, who in one year-plus at the St. Louis Cardinals' helm became the managerial racket's monument to the dream gone wrong.

A catcher whose bat went AWOL by the time he reached the high minors, Rapp's transition into the coaching ranks commenced relatively early in life. By his mid-30s he was a manager, by age 40 a successful one, having led an Arkansas Traveler (AA) team whose best offensive player was Boots Day (a prototypical number four outfielder who got in enough time with the Expos to earn a pension) to the league's best record.[1] From there he jumped to the Cincinnati Reds' AAA farm team at Indianapolis, where he put the final touches on such men as 1969 American Association batting champion Bernie Carbo, Dave Concepcion, Wayne Simpson, and Frank Duffy (hey, the Giants gave up George Foster for him).[2]

237

The 1976 Minor League Manager of the Year, Vern Rapp brought a spit-and-polish attitude to his new job as the St. Louis Cardinals' skippr — then had the club revolt on him by the middle of his first season. (*National Baseball Hall of Fame Library, Cooperstown, NY*)

When the parent club fired Dave Bristol that fall, Rapp was rumored to have the inside track on the Cincinnati helm. For whatever reason he was bypassed in favor of Sparky Anderson, a 36-year-old ex-second baseman whose record was roughly equivalent to Rapp's save a year on the San Diego Padres' inaugural coaching staff.[3] It's an odd thing, really; given the similarities in attitude, strategy, and disposition between Rapp, Anderson, and Bristol, one wonders why GM Bob Howsam even bothered to make a change.

Anyway, it didn't happen for Rapp, and thus he continued to shape the Big Red Machine's future mainstays. Tons of quality major leaguers such as Joaquin Andujar, Ross Grimsley, Pedro Borbon, Rawly Eastwick, Pat Zachry, Milt Wilcox, Ray Knight, Dan Driessen, Joel Youngblood, and Ken Griffey Sr. passed through his sphere of influence. In light of future events, it should be noted that several of these guys represented managerial challenges.

- Andujar was already demonstrating the Jekyll and Hyde temperament that would ultimately lead to his celebrated meltdown in Game 7 of the 1986 World Series, though it also yielded a pair of 20-win seasons along the way.

- Borbon once did a Mike Tyson on Pirate pitcher Darryl Patterson's ear during an on-field brawl.[4]

- Eastwick was so full of himself that he would ultimately categorize Cincinnati management as "a bunch of backstabbers."[5]

Yet somehow Rapp dealt with this witches' brew of talent successfully, contributing what he could towards molding them in the spit and polish image that the Cincinnati Reds exuded in those days.

That's what it was, too—a spit and polish image reminiscent of college football. Players were expected to wear coats and ties on road trips, no facial hair allowed, stirrups were to be short (oddly enough, it was ex-Red Frank Robinson who had begun the fashion trend of long stirrups), cleats solid black. The idea, loosely stated, was that conformity fostered the self-sacrifice that made teams successful while "doing your own thing" risked the cohesion necessary to keep a team going through the inevitable slumps and injuries. It was an against-the-grain stance that Howsam went to extravagant lengths to maintain (Grimsley was practically given away to get his attitude off the roster), but as the record amply shows, it was a more than successful one.

It was also the environment in which Vern Rapp received his graduate training.

When Reds third base coach Alex Grammas landed the Brewers' managerial post in the winter of 1975, Rapp was passed over again in favor of Russ Nixon, a longtime big-league catcher who had been managing the Reds' Florida State League team for the past five seasons.[6] This, in business world lingo, is referred to as a wake-up call. Despite having nothing left to prove, it was clear that Rapp was going no further in the Reds' organization, and at 48 the clock was ticking loudly on his chances for a big-league assignment anywhere. After thinking things over carefully, he decided to give it one more try, accepting the helm of the Montreal Expos' top farm team in Denver.

And lightning struck.

The 1976 Denver Bears were a very talented team stocked with the key members of the cast that would lead the Expos to the brink of postseason glory a few years later. Andre Dawson, Ellis Valentine, and Warren Cromartie would within two years be the parent team's starting outfield. A minor league superstar named Roger Freed led the league in homers, RBIs, and total bases; Freed was one of those guys who might have had a career had he caught his break with a better team than the early '70s Phillies. Despite a pitching staff of fringe major leaguers and guys on their way down, the Bears ran roughshod over the league, winning the American Association championship and earning Rapp accolades as Minor League Manager of the Year.[7]

That got his telephone ringing. A couple of major league teams wanted him to coach for them; Rapp had actually accepted a slot with the expansion Blue Jays before a fateful call came from the St. Louis Cardinals. Having jettisoned Red Schoendienst after a disappointing 72-90 campaign, the Cards were looking for someone who could bring more intensity and a disciplined approach to the manager's office. Rapp was a St. Louis native, he'd spent four seasons managing in the Redbirds' system, and the Cardinals were committing themselves to a youth movement. All in all it seemed like a match made in heaven.

The Cardinals organization, after their El Birdos run in the late 1960s, had developed the deadly habit of being satisfied with third-place finishes. It was one of those phenomena that was everybody's and nobody's fault at the same time. A number of fine players like Joe Torre, Matty Alou, Dick Allen, and Reggie Smith passed through the scene during those seasons, but for all of that the Cardinals' roster typically had an unfinished aura. The 1971 team, for example, got an MVP season out of Torre, saw the emergence of Ted Simmons as an All-Star-caliber catcher, sported an outfield of Lou Brock, Jose Cruz, and Alou, and had a rotation of Bob Gibson, Steve Carlton, Jerry Reuss, and Reggie Cleveland. Yet with all of those positives, the Cards still fell seven games short of the Pirates as the latter two starters were still learning their craft, the bullpen was full of guys collecting their final paychecks, and the people alongside Torre in the infield couldn't stay healthy. Within a couple of years the pitching had matured, but Torre and Gibson were getting old, Cruz hadn't developed, and the team suffered from a near terminal lack of power that limited them to a .500 record. Recognizing the problem, Cards GM Bing Devine acquired Reggie Smith from the Red Sox for Rick Wise — then saw the Cards fall two games short of the Phillies as nobody stepped forward to claim Wise's number two spot in the rotation.[8]

Compounding the problem was the number of characters who flowed through the team's locker room in those days. Allen, Smith, Reuss, Willie Davis, Jose Cardinal, Bernie Carbo, Moe Drabowsky — none of these guys save Allen was a real problem child per se, but all of them were people who from time to time required special handling.[9] Being from the "play hard and I won't bother you" school, Schoendienst got what he could out of these people, yet in so doing fostered a less than ideal nursery for the Simmonses, Hraboskys, Bake McBrides, and John Dennys who were going to matter in the long run. As a result of this, practically every key member of the roster was a pop-off, a flake, or a social renegade by the time Rapp arrived on the scene, a fact that had not escaped the attention of Devine and owner Gussie Busch.

With a clear mandate from his management, Rapp set about remolding the Cardinals like a man possessed. Fielding drills along with bunting, hitting behind the runner, and other technical aspects of the game, received a new emphasis in the Cardinals' St. Petersburg camp.[10] Ted Simmons was told to lose ten pounds.[11] Then there were the rules: no blue jeans, no drinking in the hotel bar, strict curfews, no long or facial hair.[12]

Characters are one of the most endearing elements of sports, with baseball characters the most endearing of all due to their physical ordinariness. For 1970s fans, Al Hrabosky was the classic character — a guy who looked and acted like a junior member of the Mongol horde. Each Hrabosky delivery was a mini-drama commencing behind the mound with either a moment of serious contemplation or an animated self-argument depending upon the game situation.[13] Once this hellishly introspective ritual was completed, he'd vigorously pound the ball into his glove, stomp back up the hill, and stare in at

A relatively clean-shaven Cardinals team surrounds Rapp in this 1977 photograph. Al Hrabosky (second from left in the top row) had fired the first salvo against Rapp's old-style rules in spring training: still sporting his trademark Fu Manchu mustache and beard in this photograph, the Mad Hungarian's facial hair would be gone in a subsequent retake that graced the *Official Baseball Guide*. Yet it would be an altercation with the hard-bitten, win-at-all-costs Ted Simmons (third row, second from right) that led to the manager's ouster. (*National Baseball Hall of Fame Library, Cooperstown, NY*)

the plate with what one reporter called an "evil leer [that] would transfix the Exorcist."[14] Between the act, a Fu Manchu mustache and long hair billowing wildly in his wake, the Mad Hungarian looked intimidating, powerful, and more than a little nuts. It was a performance ideally suited for opposition stadiums where, as Hrabosky put it, "my greatest ambition is to get a standing boo."[15]

Shave off the mustache and trim the hair, though, and the result was a man of medium stature who could easily pass for that slightly harried junior executive working in the next cubicle.

Whether the Mad Hungarian gig psyched out opposing hitters was beside the point — what mattered was that Hrabosky felt more hittable without the Mongol look and self-hypnotic pep talks.[16] He thus defied Rapp's edict for a time while hinting that he wasn't the only one having problems with the new manager. The statement seems prophetic with the passage of time, but nobody at the time stepped forward to support Hrabosky's claims, and he ultimately chose to apologize to the team. "Maybe I was a little selfish and a little childish about the matter," Hrabosky commented in his mea culpa. "I accept [the hair code] now."[17]

Ever read *The Caine Mutiny*, Herman Wouk's tale about a ship's officer corps that relieves the mentally shaky Captain Queeg in the middle of a typhoon? It's the kind of story that takes two readings to thoroughly comprehend, but after the second go-round one gets the feeling that Queeg might have been a decent commander if his crew had ever cut him any slack. Instead, a series of rookie mistakes by the new commander predispose the *Caine's* officers against Queeg, causing them to place every future decision under a microscope. Given the cold shoulder by practically everyone on board, Queeg's crack-up is a self-fulfilling prophecy ... and it's the well-meaning men around him who unwittingly cause his downfall.

That in a nutshell is what the 1977 season turned into for Vern Rapp. Rapp may have come on too strong early on, but his players would never let him forget it and thus interpreted every move in the worst possible light. 1976 ERA champion John Denny, for example, complained about being lifted from games too early,[18] a reasonable statement given that Denny worked less than six innings a start at a time when top pitchers were putting in seven-plus. However, when one considers that Denny's 1977 ERA was a full run higher than the league average in a pitchers' park[19] ... well, just how long should Rapp have gone with a moody guy posting those kinds of numbers?

Lots of stuff like that landed on Rapp's doorstep. Bake McBride was supposedly traded for surreptitiously letting his trademark mutton chops grow back[20] ... which could be true, but keep in mind that the 25-year-old ex-Denver Bear Tony Scott looked at the time like McBride with a batting eye. Third baseman Ken Reitz raged about the lack of a set lineup,[21] but with seven of the eight regulars playing at least 138 games that season,[22] one wonders how much more "regular" they could have been. Lou Brock added his name to the list of doubters after being pinch hit for by Mike Anderson, a .246 career hitter with minimal power. A silly decision on the face of it, but when one considers that Brock was 38 and by this point didn't have any power himself, Anderson, a right-handed hitter, was being brought in to replace the lefty-swinging Brock against a left-handed pitcher, and Anderson had been the team's best pinch hitter in 1976 and would go a respectable five for 20 this season,[23] the move makes a bit more sense.

Naturally, Anderson rose to the occasion by grounding into a double play.[24]

Taken individually, none of these comments were anything out of the ordinary. Brock's sentiments were those of 1,000 other veterans on their final downhill run. Denny's complaints are nothing that scores of young pitchers who are going badly and don't know why haven't uttered. Reitz's likely memory of a day or two when the lineup was jumbled categorizes him with someone attempting to estimate a tree's height by looking up from its base. Al Hrabosky simply wanted to maintain what he thought of as a competitive edge.

This brave new world where the questioning of authority was seen as a God-given right was not one that Vern Rapp's experiences had prepared him for. Perhaps fittingly, it would be the most symbolic of his rules that would start his downhill slide.

Despite the simmering clubhouse turmoil, St. Louis was within five games of the division-leading Cubs as July opened, though the Cardinals' relatively lofty position was as much a matter of lackluster starts by the favored Phillies and Pirates as any Redbird brilliance. Thus, a 3-8 road trip replete with late-inning losses,[25] along with some lengthening hairlines, caused Rapp to call a July 14 team meeting in Philadelphia. One thing led to another, and the meeting was degenerating into something of a bitch session when Lou Brock spoke up. The players were willing to work with Rapp in the achievement of his major goals, Brock said, if he'd just bend a little on some of the petty stuff.[26]

Now, there are several ways to take that. One could see Brock as the voice of practicality, or at least as a well-meaning man who was somewhat misguided about the importance of that "petty stuff." Rapp, however, chose to see Brock's statement as a figurative gauntlet thrown down by one of his most respected players, who, incidentally, was a coach as well. To Rapp's way of thinking, the "petty stuff" was a critical component of his organizational blueprint, tried and true philosophies that were being questioned by people who, frankly, had not proven themselves worthy of doing so.

Rapp simply told the assembled, "I'm not going to change" and walked out of the clubhouse.[27]

The battle lines were irreversibly drawn at that moment. Roger Freed, who had come with Rapp to the Cardinals and was making a name for himself as a pinch hitter extraordinaire, reformed the meeting after Rapp's departure and spoke up for him. The support he received was lukewarm at best,[28] and after an ironic extra-inning victory Al Hrabosky went on the Cardinals' postgame show with announcer Jack Buck, leaked the meeting's highlights, and announced his desire to be traded. Buck, though in the main defending Rapp after Hrabosky's interview, characterized the Cardinals' manager as "a one-dimensional man."[29]

Yet in postgame discussions with the media, Rapp was anything but recalcitrant. "I've said it before," Rapp told reporters. "I didn't come here to be liked. I'm not trying to treat them like little kids. It's just that they haven't been accustomed to discipline. Today it's do your own thing, be a free soul, live for today because tomorrow may never come. But reality has got to come sometime."[30]

Upon returning to St. Louis, Rapp met with Busch and Devine to sort out what had occurred. Out of that meeting came three key results:

1. The hair policy (which Hrabosky had threatened to challenge via a grievance) was suspended for the balance of the season in as condescending a manner as possible. "I intend to call your bluff," Busch said in a post-meeting statement aimed at the Mad Hungarian. "You said in the newspaper that you can only get batters out by being psyched up with your mustache and beard. Then go ahead and grow it. But boy, are you going to look like a fool if you don't get the batters out."

2. To reemphasize the point that discipline was to be maintained, Rapp's contract was extended through the 1978 season.

3. The club committed to trade Hrabosky (who was suffering through a miserable season and had previously earned himself a two-day suspension by refusing to meet with Rapp in his office) over the winter.[31]

In short, order was restored inasmuch as any edict could. However, it was up to Rapp to maintain that order and ultimately win the respect of his charges ... and that clearly was not going to happen.

The St. Louis papers for the remainder of the season were loaded with innuendo, comments from unnamed sources, and informed speculation about the status of the Cardinals' clubhouse. The team drifted slowly out of competition; as Keith Hernandez characterized the situation some years later, "I wouldn't say that we had a negative attitude; rather, we didn't have the positive attitude of 'Let's *play* for this guy.'"[32]

In the end, though, the Cardinals posted as good a season as anyone had a right to expect. The team won 83 games despite off years from Hrabosky and Denny, Scott's mid-August leg injury, and elbow problems that limited Larry Dierker to 39 innings of work. Garry Templeton recorded 200 hits at age 21 while showing terrific range (if an erratic glove) in the field. The 27-year-old Bob Forsch won 20 with a fine change-up and curve to work off a "moving" (coachspeak for not good enough to win with by itself) fastball[33]; the converted third baseman would ultimately win more games for the Cardinals than anyone not named Bob Gibson or Jesse Haines. Denny was just 24 and still had that marvelous curve, while a 22-year-old right-hander named John Urrea had shown a good mix of stuff and poise in 12 late-season starts. Mark Littell was a young (24) flamethrowing replacement for the not so dearly departed Hrabosky, and behind him were 1976 co-Rookie of the Year Butch Metzger, veteran Clay Carroll, and an out-of-nowhere 26-year-old lefty named Buddy Schultz.

It was a seductively positive outlook for those unacquainted with the day-to-day situation (*The Sporting News* would name the Cardinals as favorites to win the 1978 NL East[34]) yet even a cursory look at the roster should have given cause for concern. Despite finishing fourth in runs scored, the 1977 roster consisted of three players with real offensive roles (Simmons, Templeton, and Hernandez) and a bunch of number seven hitters. The lineup had no real power other than Simmons, the fast guys had trouble leveraging their speed on the basepaths, and Ken Oberkfell was the only bench rider with much of a future in front of him. Though deep and young, the pitching staff was heavy on fragile arms and light on fastballs, a pair of phenomena that 99 times out of 100 do not bode well for a team's future development.

In short, the Cardinals were perched upon a tightrope, with high expectations tied to a volatile chemistry likely to explode the moment something didn't happen according to plan ... yet like the *Titanic* steaming towards the iceberg, nobody realized it.

- Gussie Busch would tell the players in spring training, "I've got every confidence in the world in you. I think you can go all the way."[35]
- Bing Devine observed, "We're 10 to 15 percent stronger than 1977 because of a year's familiarity with our players for Rapp."[36]
- The team itself had come to believe in its future. An April 5 article in the St. Louis *Post-Dispatch* was entitled "Cards Pick Themselves to Win."[37]

Rapp relaxed both his spring training regimen and his demeanor somewhat, saying, "I think now that we understand each other better, the players and I."[38] The team would even start the season off in reasonable fashion, poking their noses above .500 after Bob Forsch's April 16 no-hitter against the defending champion Phillies.[39]

Yet the wheels would come off in short order after that highlight moment. Demonstrating the emotional balance that would cause him to be shipped to a psychiatric hospital after flipping off the Busch Stadium crowd in 1980, Garry Templeton got into a screaming match with Rapp after publicly criticizing one of his coaches. As Buddy Schultz was leaving the mound during a pitching change, Rapp reportedly made a sarcastic remark about his performance; Schultz twirled around and screamed at the manager. Rapp lost his cool twice during postgame interviews.

All of the above happened within the space of six games.

The final straw came on April 24 in Montreal. After a tough loss, Ted Simmons turned up the clubhouse stereo in violation of the age-old decorum under which losers must contemplate their failures in stony silence. Rapp chewed Simmons out for the breach of clubhouse etiquette and then made a fatal error — he called the local hero "a loser."[40]

Rapp probably recognized his mistake the instant the comment came out of his mouth; though Ted Simmons was prone to talking out of turn, he was obsessed with winning in the manner of a star player who hadn't won anything yet and was the number two guy at his position.

Though Rapp quickly apologized to Simmons for his remark, word of the comment reached Jack Buck, and when Rapp begged off a postgame show appearance, Buck reported the faux pas to the Cardinal Nation. He wasn't trying to get Rapp fired, Buck would say in future days ... all he was doing was his job as a journalist.[41]

Vern Rapp was canned the next day. After returning to the Expos organization as one of Dick Williams's coaches, Rapp would have one final shot as a major league manager with the 1984 Cincinnati Reds—and would be dumped after 121 games for the ultimate prodigal son, Pete Rose.[42]

To modern ears, Rapp's story plays like something out of the Stone Age, and most after-the-fact comments have emphasized the martinet aspects of his reign. Yet what people with selective memory tend to forget is that the Cardinal manager's modus operandi had been the standard just a few years before. So Rapp demanded short haircuts and clean faces— Sparky Anderson did too in his early years, and that idiosyncrasy didn't keep him out of the Hall of Fame. His tendency to chew people out publicly is nothing that Billy Martin didn't pull on a regular basis. Rapp's PR difficulties were tepid compared with Earl Weaver's; prior to Earl's becoming a certified genius, fans could count on reading at least one "the problem with the Orioles is Earl" article a month.[43]

In most ways Weaver is a fine parallel for Rapp, though Vern lacked the obsession with roster design that characterized his Baltimore rival. Both were ex-minor leaguers who turned to the coaching ranks at a relatively early age. Both were very successful managers in the minors, yet each man's journey to the Show took longer than one would have normally expected it to. Both were control freaks by nature, possessed by the fits of anger and nervous habits (Weaver was a chain smoker who could hit the booze hard on occasion[44]) that such men often exhibit. Both eschewed personal relations with their players, and both were less than popular as a result (a fact that has been increasingly forgotten since Weaver's plaque has been hung at Cooperstown).

What gave Weaver a long career was timing. He came along at a time when the alternative to putting up with Earl's shtick was a career in computer maintenance. He could continue in that manner after Marvin Miller had made players aware of their rights because by then Weaver was a proven winner — a player donning a Baltimore uni might take a lot of guff, but doing so yielded a better than average shot at winning it all. By the time Rapp came along, new managers were required to earn the right to behave like a firebrand before a clubhouse would allow him to do so with impunity. Sure, to this day a Larry Bowa will rise up every now and then to try it, but exactly how long has Larry lasted in any of his jobs?

Al Hrabosky would tell Bill James late in the 1978 season that Rapp was one of the most insecure people he'd ever met.[45] OK, Al — exactly how secure is someone being subjected to sniper fire from everybody in their corner of the world supposed to be? Vern Rapp, like Howard the Duck, suddenly found himself living in a world he'd never made, and the price of that was rigidity.

Could Rapp have been a Hall of Fame manager had he, rather than Sparky Anderson, gotten the call to run the Reds in 1970? Probably not, but one would have to have liked his chances of having a long and successful career given a good team and a couple of years to get his feet under him before the winds of change became apparent. Like Herbert Hoover, it was a mere pittance of time that made the difference between crowning success and abject failure for Vern Rapp — and his experience served as a monument to the enormous changes of his times.

31

Steve Garvey and the Essence of Fame

Statistical analysis has significantly altered the average fan's view of baseball in recent years, and this impact is most clearly displayed in the actions of the National Baseball Hall of Fame. Early in its existence, the Hall of Fame was just that — a place dedicated to honoring people whom everybody remembered. As time passed and our methods of measuring performance were refined, it became clear that those we waxed nostalgic over weren't necessarily the best players of their era. Tommy McCarthy wasn't half the player George Van Haltren was, but McCarthy had the memory hook of having popularized the hit and run play and thus he's in. Roger Bresnahan supposedly was the first catcher to wear shin guards, and the addition of that factoid to his longtime association with John McGraw cast his visage in bronze — but Bresnahan probably was no more than the third best catcher of his era. There are probably a half-dozen pre-1900 shortstops who were every bit as good as Hughie Jennings, but Jennings was the colorful one who played with the right team (the Baltimore Orioles).

With our increased understanding of how games are won and lost, a welcome dose of rationality has entered the immortality selection process. Given the mindset of 40 years ago, Paul Molitor's injury record and small-market resume might well have stalled his Hall of Fame entry for a number of years, while under current conditions it is all but certain that Molitor will be a first-ballot selection. On the whole that's a good thing, but this trend towards performance *uber alles* in the selection of Cooperstown honorees begs the question of what importance actual fame should play in the selection process. After all, it is a Hall of Fame, isn't it?

All of which brings us to one Steve Garvey.

In the tumult over this onetime All-American boy's sex life, marital problems, and business practices, the image of Garvey the player and Garvey the icon as he existed in the 1970s has been severely muddled. That's too bad, because for six or seven years there he really was something special on the field, and he really was a cultural icon as well, not because people in those days were stupid or gullible but because ... well, they wanted him to be one.

But now we are getting ahead of the story.

A Tampa, Florida, native who in his youth served as a Dodger spring training batboy (his father drove the team bus[1]), Garvey was an only child who grew up serious and goal oriented in the way such kids often do. He wore neatly pressed button-down shirts and slacks,[2] kept track of his batting averages to the point that he could recall them twenty years later,[3] and routinely rejected any behavior that might even possibly jeopardize his goal of an athletic scholarship ... in short, a real fun-time kind of guy. Yet the same single-mindedness that probably made him seem like a bit of a prig to his contemporaries also drove him to continue playing baseball after going zero for his first season of Little League play.[4] It was the drive that caused Garvey in his preteen years to commence the weight training regimen that would ultimately build his forearms to blacksmith proportions. It gave him the inner strength to maintain focus in the face of his early career throwing problems at third base (courtesy of a shoulder injury suffered while playing football at Michigan State[5]). It helped him accept the sometimes acid-tongued advice of batting coach Dixie Walker and refine his offensive game by learning to hit the ball to all fields.

Garvey would in his salad days occasionally identify Pete Rose as his on-field role model[6] (drips with irony, doesn't it?), and his approach to baseball was often reminiscent of Charlie Hustle's. Like Rose, Garvey wasn't a particularly large man (he stood 5'10" and weighed 192 in his prime) and thus worked hard to develop the kind of power that first basemen traditionally provide. As Steve aged, his training regimen became even more comprehensive, emphasizing diet (lots of fruit, vegetables, fish, chicken and complex carbohydrates), stretching (40-45 minutes a day) and aerobics along with the weight training and alternate sports like golf and tennis that he'd always indulged in.[7]

At the same time Garvey (again like Rose) had a yearly goal of 200 hits, and in typical fashion he had a detailed blueprint of how they were to be gained. He knew how many bunt singles he intended to get (people forget that Steve possessed good speed early on), how many doubles, how many homers—the man kept a list of these things and checked it constantly to assure that his production in each area stayed on track.[8]

Talk about discipline with a capital D ... yet the results were enough to turn any sinner into a saint. Between 1974 and 1980, Garvey averaged 23 homers, 104 RBIs, and a .311 average, but the more remarkable thing about his productivity was its consistency. In that seven-year span, he missed a grand total of six games—all of those in his first (MVP) season. His lowest average during the period was .297. He connected for 200, 210, 200, 192, 202, 204, and 200 hits. He recorded 56, 62, 54, 61, 66, 61, and 54 extra-base hits.

Perhaps the numbers seem mundane in the current context, but they were good enough to place Garvey among the league leaders in most key offensive categories every season[9] and it is virtually impossible to understate the value of having a team's stars be stars year in and year out.

Especially during an era in which baseball's, and the nation's, stability was being sorely challenged.

Keep in mind that Garvey's prime spanned the period in which baseball players were first flexing their economic muscles. The fact that strikes and abrupt changes of scenery were incumbent in this process was not the players' fault per se, but the result was a sense of alienation that imperiled the game's relationship with its fan base. People were looking for old-time heroes, guys who embodied the idealized ethic of hard work that seemed to be missing in baseball as well as in the society in general. Someone who stood for integrity in a sea of Watergaters and Reggie Jacksons forever pursuing power and/or the wayward buck.

Steve was young, handsome, dedicated to his work, intelligent (in a 1978 poll of players, managers, sportswriters, and broadcasters, Garvey was named as the game's best managerial prospect[10]), and inordinately capable of giving the right answer with style while the flashbulbs popped. His self-promotional/bottom line orientation could be offputting; one Dodger told a San Bernardino *Sun-Telegram* reporter in 1975 that the first baseman "doesn't have one friend on this team" while second baseman Dave Lopes stated in a subsequent postgame interview "… the other eight starters look at baseball as a game. Garvey thinks of it more as a business."[11] Yet in an organization that extolled the concepts of family values and teamwork, Steve's All-American persona found its natural showcase — and the result was a veritable feeding frenzy of exploitation.

High schools were named for Garvey. Product endorsement opportunities were so numerous that the income derived from them nearly eclipsed Steve's baseball salary.[12] He made numerous television appearances and even starred on a talk show with his wife, who became a minor TV celeb on his coattails.[13] People discussed the possibility of running Garvey for the U.S. Senate — and it wasn't just idle talk (in a 1988 poll the ex-first baseman garnered one-third of the vote for a city council seat in the district in which he resided … and Steve wasn't even running[14]). Perhaps the best example of the public attitude towards Garvey was portrayed in a Los Angeles *Times* cartoon drawn after the Dodgers got off to a slow start one season. The Little Old Lady in Tennis Shoes is talking to Big Dodger in the Sky:

Little Old Lady in Tennis Shoes: "Big Dodger in the Sky, why are you persecuting the Dodgers so?"

Big Dodger in the Sky: "Well, I have to be fair to everybody."

LOLITS: "But they are such nice men … Lopes, Cey, Yeager, GARVEY!"

Big Dodger in the Sky thinks about that one for a moment.

BDITS: "I'll see what I can do."

Perhaps Garvey should have known that his private life would ultimately be exposed, but keep in mind that he was a young man at the time as baseball players inevitably are. Readers in their 40s and 50s can reflect back on how worldly they really were back in the days when, as Will Rogers once put it, they looked at their fathers and said, "There goes dear old Dad — how did he live so long and know so little?" Think about it: a man in his mid-20s is subjected to adulation beyond his wildest dreams, complete with people clamoring for his autograph, wanting to give him things, asking him to endorse products — all of it aboveboard and honest. Who this side of Ghandi could turn down such manna from heaven? How many of us would honestly turn our backs on such riches and opt for the pseudo-monastic route Steve Carlton took?

In their infinitely analytical manner, the Dodgers organization sensed early that Garvey would not age well and thus allowed him to be snatched away in the winter of 1982 by the San Diego Padres in what was to that time the biggest free agent deal in baseball history. His over-the-fence power declined precipitously once he passed his 32nd birthday; in an attempt to maintain it, Steve threw plate discipline to the winds as his on-base percentage fell to .304 over his last three seasons as a regular.[15] By the Padres' 1984 World Series appearance, serious fans were openly questioning Garvey's value, and after a desultory 1987 campaign in which he first lost his starting job then tore a tendon in his right biceps, the All-American Boy was history.[16]

From a purely statistical prospective, Garvey's career wasn't of Hall of Fame caliber — Paul O'Neill was every bit as good a player, and unless Cooperstown intends to annex Middletown to handle the overflow, there simply isn't enough room available to commemorate all such talents. Yet Steve is not all that far from having Hall of Fame-like credentials (a couple more good seasons would have been enough), and the man was a genuine cultural phenomenon. In his era there weren't three players of greater renown in society as a whole, and none of those other guys stood for anything in particular ... or at least anything that anyone would want to stand for. Perhaps our ancestors were naïve in their adulation of this "as flawed as the rest of us are" man, but that's 20/20 hindsight ... and one can bet that many of today's heroes will over time prove to be less than we think they are today.

Maybe fame isn't everything, but is being arguably the most noted player of one's time frame enough to make up for two years of missing performance? Or have we come to the point at which the statistical record rules all?

Consider Bid McPhee, a recent Hall of Fame inductee who was a fine second baseman for the Cincinnati ball clubs of the 1880s and 1890s. According to the numbers, McPhee was a wizard with the leather as well as a better than fair offensive player — think Bill Mazeroski with more plate discipline, and you get the general idea. One might question the caliber of competition he faced (professional baseball was still in its infancy and McPhee spent much of his career in the weaker of the two then-"major" leagues), but Bid was clearly a fine player and perhaps even an excellent one.

The problem is, however, that virtually nobody remembers anything about the man himself. Nearly a whole page is devoted to McPhee in the excellent *Baseball: The Biographical Encyclopedia*, yet only a small fraction of the commentary concerns the second baseman as a person.[17] No comments from his contemporaries are included for the simple reason that they don't exist as part of the common lore. McPhee left the game in 1902 and died while MacArthur was island-hopping in the Pacific; virtually nobody in baseball had given the man a second thought before sabermetrics came along to cast a new light on his achievements.

In short, what the Cooperstown voters chose to salute was a set of statistics.

While the two are difficult to compare directly, it is probably fair to say that Garvey was the superior player at his peak; one assumes that if Bid McPhee had been seen as an MVP-type player, a story or two about him would have filtered down through the years. Similarly, McPhee maintained a high level of performance for a significantly longer period of time than the Dodger/Padre first baseman did — before 1973, Garvey was a marginal defensive third baseman struggling for playing time, while after 1980 he quickly devolved into the primeval Rico Brogna. One can make arguments for either one, but for the sake of this discussion let's say that McPhee comes out slightly on top from a straight value perspective.

But then there's the fame aspect to consider....

It isn't just that Steve Garvey was arguably the best-known player on the planet (especially in non-baseball circles), it's that Bid McPhee is both totally anonymous and impossible to recapture as a person at this late date. What little we know about McPhee suggests that he was a nice guy, but in an era of non-investigative reporting, Garvey would have come across as a hell of a fellow too.

In the final analysis, McPhee may well have been a great player and a hale fellow-well-met, but we can't pretend to honor him now because he, in a very real sense, no longer exists.

McPhee, though, is just the tip of the iceberg; the real problem comes with those of the modern era whom we are belatedly appreciating for what they were. Take Harold Baines: at his peak nearly as good as Garvey (Baines was a "mobile, graceful outfielder" equipped with a "powerful arm [that] discourages most notions" before his knees gave out[18]) and lasted much longer, but how much imagery does Baines's name evoke in the average fan's mind? How much does that fan remember about Al Oliver, or Lou Whitaker, or Darrell Evans, or what will he remember about Paul O'Neill in a few years' time? Some of the aforementioned players were a bit better than Garvey, some a bit worse — but all were and are every bit as good as plenty of Cooperstown residents....

… And none of them were ever considered to be senatorial candidates.

Steve Garvey had a seven-year run as a fine player and supposed paragon of virtue … and no after-the-fact episode can change that or his effect upon the game of his times.

32

Being Without a Chair
When the Music Stops

It is human nature to simplify matters. Life is too complex to take in all of the details associated with a happening — thus, what we do is to eliminate "extraneous" matters and glean the event down to one or two images that capture its essence. Charles Lindbergh is thus remembered as the first man to fly across the Atlantic when he was actually number 23: Lindy's feat was to be the first to do it solo. Every school kid knows that Christopher Columbus discovered America even though extensive evidence exists that the Vikings were prowling around Canada 400 years earlier (not to mention all those Native Americans who didn't know they needed to be discovered). While the Volkswagen Beetle may be the biggest selling car model of all time, try fitting parts from a 1949 VW onto a 1969 Bug sometime....

Much to the agony of long-suffering Boston Red Sox fans, such is the image that the 1978 American League East pennant race has taken on in the public mind. Ask a typical baseball fan about the events of that season and what he or she will probably come up with are two images:

1. The three-run fly ball homer by Bucky Dent that won the playoff game for the Yankees.
2. That the Red Sox choked down the stretch, surrendering a 14½ game lead to the Bronx Zoo gang in a mere six weeks.

OK, so maybe the more sophisticated fan adds a third element to explain the disaster — that Red Sox manager Don Zimmer rode his starting nine to the point of exhaustion. The Bosox front liners played an average of 147 games that season[1] with a litany of broken fingers (George Scott), rib injuries (Carlton Fisk), and dizzy spells (Dwight Evans)[2] that were topped off by the elbow problem that converted third baseman Butch Hobson into a trivia question.

You know the one: who was the last man to play as many as 100 games at a position during a season and record a fielding percentage under .900?

Now all of the above is true — Dent *did* hit the homer, the Red Sox *did* go cold in the heat of the pennant race, and the Bosox did log 200 more games played out of their regulars than any other AL team.[3] Having said all of that, the 1978 season was one filled with an unusually large number of potential heroes and goats — the Red Sox simply happened to be the ones without a chair when the music stopped. Thus, before we consign them to the same level of hell inhabited by the 1951 Brooklyn Dodgers, let's take a closer look at the race as it developed.

The first thing to keep in mind is that the Red Sox did not enter the 1978 season as the favorites to take the AL East. That honor was reserved for the two time champion Yankees — and why not? Despite allowing 17-game winner Mike Torrez to walk over the winter, the team was loaded to the gunwales with quality starters like Don Gullett, Catfish Hunter, Andy Messersmith, Ken Holtzman, Ed Figueroa, and a diminutive lefty curveballer named Ron Guidry who had come out of nowhere the prior year. A bullpen featuring Cy Young Award winner Sparky Lyle and guys like Dick Tidrow and Jim Beattie who would have been rotation starters elsewhere had been bolstered over the winter by the free agent signing of Goose Gossage, giving the Yankees a potent lefty-righty closer combo. Offensively the New York lineup was nearly flawless, featuring leadoff speed (Mickey Rivers and Willie Randolph), middle of the order thump (Thurman Munson, Reggie Jackson, Graig Nettles, and Cliff Johnson), and bottom of the order guys who were far from worthless (Chris Chambliss, Lou Pinella, and Bucky Dent). The defense was tight, the bench filled with old warhorses with mileage left on them, and as for the management situation ... well, it couldn't possibly be any worse than it had been in 1977, could it?

As for the Red Sox, they had the prototypical Boston team: power-laden, slow, and just long enough on the mound to challenge if everything broke right.

The offense was hard to argue with, featuring two Hall of Famers (Fisk, Carl Yastrzemski), another that might make it yet (Jim Rice), one who would have save a penchant for beating himself up (Fred Lynn) and a bevy of guys who while not Cooperstown quality were plenty good in their own right. The off-season addition of California Angel second baseman Jerry Remy represented a significant upgrade on both sides of the ball from the departed Denny Doyle,[4] while the outfielders were all rangy at this point in their careers. The bench seemed solid with long-time Cleveland second baseman Jack Brohamer providing infield D while the left-handed hitting Bernie Carbo supplied punch.

On the mound, the Sox had taken significant steps to shore up a pitching staff that had had trouble staying healthy the prior year. Boston had been the recipient of Torrez, a veteran workhorse whose four quality pitches had produced 15 or more wins in each of the previous three seasons but whose tendency to nibble had caused him to win them for three different teams.[5] The back end of the 1977 rotation plus a couple of people the Red Sox weren't going to use were shipped to Cleveland for the hard throwing, hard drinking 22-year-old Dennis Eckersley.[6] Add to those guys the aging Luis Tiant, the one-time flamethrower now finesse pitcher in training Reggie Cleveland, and resident lefthander/oddball Bill "Spaceman" Lee and the result would be either a starting rotation or a disaster area. Recognizing the risks inherent in that scenario, the Red Sox had gone so far as to convert promising young sinkerballer Bob Stanley into a set-up man behind 1977 Fireman of the Year Bill Campbell, who'd logged a Mike Marshallian 147 appearances and 308 innings over the past two seasons.[7]

Put it all together and a serious contender emerges—maybe. Even if everybody did what they were supposed to do, the Sox were clearly going to need some luck both within their own ranks and in the Bronx to get over the top.

Thus, in many ways the miracle was that Zimmer's charges came as close as they did to pulling it off.

After breaking evenly the Red Sox got blazing hot in May, seemingly hitting on every cylinder. The team's batting average was close to .300 as Rice began putting together what would prove to be the best individual offensive season in two generations. Eckersley would win 10 of 11 decisions beginning on May 4 while demonstrating a penchant for developing slang terms, some of which (yakker for curve, cheese for fastball) remain part of baseball's lexicon today.[8] Stanley stepped into the breach when Campbell's arm started acting up: he would win 11 straight games over the next three months and not blow a save opportunity until the last day of August.[9] There were some warning signs amid the euphoria—Campbell's difficulties, George Scott's sidelining, Hobson's sailing throws—but such matters were trivial in comparison to the wild ride that the Yankees were about to be launched on.

The defending champions more or less kept pace with the Red Sox through the end of May, but as June began the Yankees began losing ground under the accumulated weight of

- Injuries—a hairline fracture in Mickey Rivers' hand, knee problems for Willie Randolph, a hamstring pull for Bucky Dent.[10] If the key to defense is held by those who play at the center of the diamond the Yankees were in serious need of a locksmith.
- Several problems that had been overlooked in all of the pre-season optimism.

First off, many of those reassuringly Big Men on the Mound proved incapable of staying healthy. Andy Messersmith fell while racing to cover first during a spring training game and separated his shoulder—the instigator of the free agency era would pitch only 22 1/3 innings for the Yankees.[11] The rotator cuff problems that would end Don Gullett's brilliant career after this year sidelined him for the first half of the season.[12] Catfish Hunter's shoulder was so stiff by the middle of May that he reportedly couldn't throw the ball to home plate on the fly.[13]

Then, of course, what Yankee season would be complete without personality problems? Despite the rotational holes Ken Holtzman was rarely used, on orders from owner George Steinbrenner: Holtzman, you see, had committed the cardinal sin of invoking his contract's no-trade clause to nix a deal with the Texas Rangers.[14] The lefty-righty closer duo had quickly dissolved into Goose Gossage doing the closing and Sparky Lyle in middle relief, a situation that left Lyle depressed and caused third baseman Graig Nettles to comment that the lefthander had "gone from Cy Young to sayonara."[15] Thurman Munson was wracked by insecurity (when asked if Munson was moody, Lyle once said, "Thurman's not moody. When you're moody, you're nice sometimes. Thurman's just mean"[16]), Mickey Rivers along with half of the others were upset about money....[17]

... And finally there was Reggie Jackson.

It was once said of Theodore Roosevelt that if he were ever to write an autobiography, every page would consist solely of the personal pronoun "I." That was Jackson in a nutshell: though he'd insist that his fateful "I'm the straw that stirs the drink" comment to *Sport* magazine writer Robert Ward was born of naiveté and paraphrased,[18] it just *seemed* so vintage Reggie. A truly great player (something that people to this day grant only grudgingly) who was confident of his greatness, Reggie often seemed unaware of the impression that his comments made on others and was genuinely baffled when things he said were taken the wrong way.[19]

Many of Jackson's problems during his New York stint were a direct consequence of this tendency to display confidence bordering on arrogance. After the *Sport* article was published, Reggie was by his own admission pretty much alienated from everyone on the team save reserve catcher Fran Healy.[20] Furthermore, his bold comments melded with the media hype that any Big Apple figure generates to create an image that anybody not wearing a big red S across their chest would have found impossible to live up to.

As a great player Jackson was equally confident of what his role within the Yankee hierarchy should be: he was to hit fourth in the lineup, play right field every day, and receive the respect such a player was due.[21] Manager Billy Martin, on the other hand, saw Jackson as a direct challenge to his control of the team as well as a player who fell into horrendous slumps and was sometimes less than fully engaged in the field but, via his pipeline to the owner, was above discipline.[22] As a result the two men were increasingly at loggerheads with one another,[23] with Reggie's July 17 decision to "prove that he was a team player" by striking out attempting to bunt in the 10th inning of a game against the AL West-leading Royals proving to be the proverbial last straw[24], no pun intended.

The collective problems as well as the stress incumbent in not meeting Steinbrennerian expectations had taken a tremendous toll on Martin, an insecure man whose self-identity was seemingly hogtied to the Yankee organization. With the team losing, the clubhouse in an uproar, and the Boss continuously undercutting him on personnel decisions, Martin had begun to crack physically and emotionally.[25] The situation came to a head when Billy suspended Jackson for five days without pay over the bunting incident. When Reggie subsequently jumped the team, Steinbrenner agreed to allow him to come back without paying the fine if he kept quiet about the whole thing,[26] which — given the two participants in that conversation — was akin to telling a starving dog not to eat a nearby steak. Being shown up yet again, Martin, his speech slurred by drink, approached two reporters at an O'Hare Airport newsstand on July 23 and made the fateful comment that Jackson and Steinbrenner "deserve each other. One's a born liar, the other's convicted."[27]

And thus ended the not so short, not so happy life of Billy Martin in pinstripes … or so it seemed at the time.

It was the kind of soap opera-ish episode that breaks 99 out of 100 teams, and thus it would become with the aid of 20/20 hindsight the turning point in the AL East race. It probably would have broken the Yankees as well under normal circumstances— Sparky Lyle's memoir of the 1978 season, *The Bronx Zoo*, doesn't betray much confidence in the budding New York miracle until early September.[28]

Independent of any Bronx goings on, however, the chinks in the Boston armor were rapidly becoming apparent.

On the day of Martin's firing/resignation, the Red Sox were busy dropping their fifth consecutive game to the Minnesota Twins. Though Stanley remained excellent and veteran Dick Drago posted a fine season in long relief, the bullpen was proving too shallow to provide the kind of support that the problematic starting rotation required. Bill Lee would not win a game after July 15 because of shoulder problems dating back to a 1976 Graig Nettles body slam[29] as well as a long-running personality clash with Zimmer.[30] Things got so bad that Alan Ripley, a 25-year-old finesse pitcher who'd gone 2-2 with a 5.59 ERA at AAA Pawtucket, was called up at midseason to make 11 starts down the stretch. At least Ripley was consistent: he ended up 2-5 with a 5.55 ERA for the Bosox.[31]

The team's offensive output was becoming more erratic as the realization set in that the Red Sox had nine players worth using and that was about it. With the probably personality-driven early season sale of Carbo to the Indians (Bernie was a member in good standing of a moderately subversive clubhouse clique called the Loyal Order of the Buffalo Heads. By the beginning of the 1979 season all five Buffalo Heads would be in other uniforms[32]) the 1978 Boston bench became as weak as any that ever supported a contending team. It consisted of:

- Brohamer, a 28-year-old zero offensive value utility infielder who was rapidly approaching the point at which he was too slow to man second or short any more.
- Frank Duffy (a.k.a. the guy the Giants traded George Foster for), a three year older version of Brohamer who would be finished after six 1979 appearances.
- Garry Hancock, a 24-year-old outfielder with so-so power and a marginal glove.
- Fred Kendall, a 29-year-old catcher (and daddy of Jason) who'd been a decent player for the Padres four or five years back but had zip power and only 65 games in his future.
- Bob Bailey, a once-fine hitter who at 35 had hit the end of the line, posting a .191 average in 94 at-bats.

OK, exactly which of those guys should Zimmer have sat Jim Rice to play? Fred Lynn spent much of the season battling back problems,[33] but there isn't a backup center fielder among that bunch — in fact, things got so bad that the 38-year-old Yaz played eight games in center that season.[34] Rick Burleson answered the bell at short, bad ankle and all, 144 times because erstwhile replacement Duffy made seven errors in the 21 games he played at the position while making one play less per game.[35] Those who wonder if Bailey (who played 1,194 career games at third base) could possibly have been any worse than Hobson are offered Expos manager Gene Mauch's appraisal of the man's fielding prowess: "Bailey means wood. Bailey doesn't mean leather."[36]

And by 1978 he didn't even mean wood....

There wasn't even anything in the minors for Zimmer to scoop up and add to his bench. Hancock and a kid named Sam Bowen (six at-bats) were the ones tried: the best AAA prospects were people like Dave Stapleton (a first baseman who didn't hit enough to play first) and International League MVP Gary Allenson (would hit .221 in over 1,000 major league at-bats). Wade Boggs was at AA Bristol, but it would take four years for the Red Sox to figure out that he was a ballplayer.[37]

Given the options that Zimmer had at his command, what would any manager with a smidgen of self-preservation running through their veins have done? Would anyone in his right mind have sat Dewey Evans down the stretch with the Yankees playing .733 ball for a guy (Hancock) who recorded three extra base hits—all doubles—all season?

Thus, the Red Sox began to slowly fade in the AL East. The key word, though, is *slowly*—the team would play better than .500 ball after the All-Star break and in their worst month (July) would only be two games under the break-even point.

Simultaneously, though, the Yankees got about as hot as any team ever has down the stretch.

Two events turned the Yankees' season around. First, the replacement of the hypertense Martin with the laid back to the point of catatonia Bob Lemon cleared the stress from the clubhouse,[38] while secondly (and probably more importantly), the team got healthy — or at least as close to healthy as it could. Catfish Hunter, for example, gathered himself together for one last push down the stretch and pitched magnificently, winning 10 of 13 decisions.

Yet for the most part it was simply a matter of people playing the brand of baseball that they were capable of. A look at the 1978 Yankee roster shows virtually nobody save Guidry, Ed Figueroa, and the Goose having particularly good seasons. Lou Pinella had a fine year as a semi-full-time outfielder hitting .314 — but six homers and 69 RBI from a corner outfielder/DH is nothing special. Jackson's 27 homers represented his lowest full season production between 1972 and 1983. Chris Chambliss's 12 homers and 90 RBI were basically the kind of season Chambliss posted every year between 1971 and 1983.

Closely shadowing all of this activity was the Milwaukee Brewers, the forgotten team of the 1978 pennant race. Historically living off others' leftovers, the Brewers had finished last or next to last in every season of their existence prior to 1978. Tired of his team's also-ran status, owner Bud Selig had first dove headlong into the free agent market (hard to believe but true), then hired one-time Baltimore GM Harry Dalton out from under the California Angels.[39] Dalton's natural first move was to hire tons of Oriole vets including pitching coach George Bamberger for the manager's chair vacated by Alex Grammas (first baseman Mike Hegan's assessment of his ex-skipper: "Alex Grammas is a nice guy, but as a manager he makes a good third base coach"[40]).

Having finished 11th in runs scored and ERAs the previous season, the Brewers had plenty of room for improvement on both sides of the ball, yet save the acquisition of free agent slugger Larry Hisle, Dalton's and Bamberger's moves were anything but revolutionary. A 28-year-old left-handed hitting platoon slugger named Ben Oglivie was acquired from the Tigers in exchange for the previous year's ace (and All-Star representative before melting down in the second half) Jim Slaton.[41] Number one draft pick Paul Molitor was rushed to the majors after 64 games of A ball.[42] A bear of a man/poster boy for intemperate living named Gorman Thomas, who in four previous big league trials had hit .193 with 227 strikeouts in 668 at-bats, was installed as the new center fielder.[43] On the pitching side the cast remained pretty much the same save Slaton and Moose Haas, who missed virtually the entire season due to a torn muscle near his right elbow.[44]

Yet in the magical way that such things happen every so often, this seeming shuffling of deck chairs produced a significant uptick in Brewer fortunes. Oglivie had been slowly gaining on a regular job for years: in Milwaukee he finally got a full shot at it and proved that he could indeed hit those lefties.[45] Molitor had a fine (though in a foreshadowing of future events, injury prone) rookie year, winning *The Sporting News'* Rookie of the Year Award. Robin

Yount began to mature into the Hall of Famer that he would become. Mike Caldwell, a left-handed soft tosser who had been a long man in the Cincinnati bullpen at the start of the previous season, won 22 games with what was commonly believed to be a newly learned spitball.[46]

In a sense, one could make an argument that the Brewers were 1978's true chokers. They outscored the Red Sox (804-796) while allowing fewer men to cross the plate (650-657), yet never mounted a serious charge and ended up 6½ games out.[47] The Brewers never played badly, posting winning records in every month after April, but a bullpen too shallow to adequately support the back end of the rotation[48] kept them from ever getting anything going on a prolonged basis. In essence, the situation comes down to this: nobody grills a consensus fifth-place choice that ends up winning 93 games ... even if they actually were every bit as good as those in front of them.

In retrospect, the defining moment of the season was played out in Fenway Park over the weekend of September 7-10. While the Red Sox had dropped their last three contests (including two to an Oakland A's team that went 14-42 after August 1[49]) Boston still had a four-game edge on New York as the series started. At the same time, the Yankees, though having won 13 of 15, were headed into a stadium in which they had lost seven of their last nine games.[50] In the first game of the series, the Red Sox had ex-Yankee Mike Torrez ready to go against Catfish Hunter, the Boston ace versus a guy who six weeks earlier was having trouble shaving.

Torrez didn't make it out of the second inning as the Yankees connected for 12 runs in the first four frames en route to a 15-2 victory.[51]

For Game 2 the Yankees had to resort to Jim Beattie, a 23-year-old curveballer who'd bounced back and forth between New York and AAA Tacoma. No matter; Dwight Evans's ongoing dizziness resulted in a dropped fly ball, while Pudge Fisk's broken ribs probably contributed to two throwing errors. Between those injury-related miscues and a couple of more conventional boots by Burleson and George Scott, the Yankees cruised to a 13-2 victory that would have been a shutout save a dropped popup with two outs in the ninth.[52]

That simply delayed the whitewash job for one day.

Ron Guidry vs. Dennis Eckersley. A guy who would end up 25-3 with a 1.74 ERA versus one who would go 20-8, 2.99 in a better hitter's park. A tough, close game, right?

Wrong. Eckersley was knocked out in the fourth as New York turned four walks, five hits, a boot and a wild pitch into six runs ... all with two outs in the inning. Final score: Yankees 7, Red Sox 0.[53]

In the final game of the series, the Red Sox were down to using Bobby Sprowl, a 22-year-old lefty who'd been called up after posting a 4.15 ERA in 15 appearances (11 starts) for a AAA Pawtucket team that had posted an overall 3.55 ERA.[54] The Yankees scored five runs in the first two innings en route to 18 hits on the day and an easy 7-4 win.[55]

And there goeth the lead....

With 20-20 hindsight, this manic weekend has become the metaphorical turning point of the season, the time at which the Yankees were magically transformed from pretenders to the chosen ones. However, let us move forward to September 22, when the Red Sox were two and a half games out and though they had stabilized after their heartbreaking slide appeared to be dead in the water.

Somehow the team that from a historical prospective is doomed, the one whose starting lineup was half incapacitated, picked that point in time to fashion a season-ending eight-game winning streak. Yes, the tear included five victories over the hapless Blue Jays (Tornoto closed its season with four wins in their last 26 games[56]), but by any measure the Bosox played like true champions. A staff that had spent most of September getting the bejeesus beaten out of them tossed four shutouts in those eight games,[57] two against the better than fair Tigers.

In the meantime, the Yankees split six games with a 69-90 Cleveland Indians team that finished tenth in runs scored and 11th in ERA. In the 162nd game of the season, the one that could have clinched the pennant for the Bronx Bombers, Catfish Hunter couldn't get out of the second inning while a 26-year-old lefty finesse pitcher named Rick Waits held the Yankees to five hits en route to a 7-2 victory.[58]

Thus we come to that incredible 163rd game and the legend of Bucky Dent.

It was a contest filled with undercurrents and second-guessable moves. Take the starting matchup: Ron Guidry vs. Mike Torrez, a logical pairing of the eventual Cy Young Award winner versus the man who'd made the most starts for the Red Sox that season. However:

- Guidry was working on three days' rest for only the second time that season, mostly because the only alternative would have been Dick Tidrow, who had gone 7-11 with a 3.84 ERA in 25 starts.
- Torrez had lost seven of his previous eight decisions (though his most recent outing was a 1-0 shutout of the Tigers) and was going on short rest as well.[59]

Both lineups showed signs of the wear and tear that a 162-game season imparts on the body. Willie Randolph was finished for the season with a hamstring pull, leaving the second base chores to a combination of Brian Doyle and Fred "Chicken" (alluding to his straight-backed, head-up running style[60]) Stanley. Reggie Jackson had torn a fingernail off a couple of days earlier and was DHing as a result,[61] leaving the right field chores to Lou Pinella. On the Red Sox side, the .234-hitting Jack Brohamer would start the game at third base as Hobson's elbow problems relegated him to DH duty while Dewey Evans's dizziness had finally forced him to the bench.[62]

The first two-thirds of the game were reminiscent of the twelfth round of

Bucky Dent was allowed to hit his famous home run (with Mickey Rivers's or Roy White's or somebody else's bat) in the 1978 playoff game against the Red Sox because the Yankees were out of middle infielders. Though his clout would be remembered as the contest's decisive blow, in reality it came with one out in the seventh inning to give New York a one run lead ... and Boston would score twice more before the game ended. (*National Baseball Hall of Fame Library, Cooperstown, NY*)

a championship prize fight. Both starters struggled with their pitch placement, though a moderately stiff wind blowing directly in the hitters' faces served to hold up most everything headed for the fences until an outfielder could get under it.[63] After six innings, the Yankee ace had the worst of it, giving up a second-inning line-drive homer to Carl Yastrzemski on a fastball that didn't get far enough under Yaz's hands[64] and another in the sixth on a single by Jim Rice. Then with one out in the top of the seventh, the Yankees got a pair of singles from Chris Chambliss and Roy White, bringing Dent to center stage. It may seem odd that a .243 hitter with no power and a mere 23 walks in 402 plate appearances would be used in such a situation, but with Doyle having already been lifted for a pinch hitter, Lemon had no choice; he was out of middle infielders.[65]

Torrez's first pitch was a nasty slider that Dent fouled off of his foot, at which point the legends begin:

• According to third base coach Dick Howser, Dent hobbled over to him to him and said, "If that son of a bitch comes in there again with that pitch, I'm going to take him into the net."[66] That's pretty bold talk for a man who'd hit five home runs that season and would hit four more in the remaining five years of his career.[67]

• As recalled by others, Torrez became annoyed as the Yankee trainer spent what seemed to be inordinate amounts of time ministering to Dent. Thus angered, he ended up grooving a fastball to Dent on the next pitch.[68]

• Finally, Mickey Rivers, in the on-deck, supposedly saw that Dent had cracked his bat (how the man himself didn't realize this is left unanswered). Rivers went back into the dugout and got a new one of his own for the Yankee shortstop to use[69]— or maybe it was one of Roy White's.[70]

Regardless of what skullduggery took place, the results were the same — a three-run homer, a 3-2 lead, and the satisfying triumph of an Everyman in the midst of all those superegos.

Yet the game was far from over. Remember, there's only one out in the top of the seventh as Dent's ball clears the Green Monster; the Red Sox still have three at-bats to go and only one run to make up. Well, by the time they got going it was actually a three-run deficit, as Thurman Munson doubled in Rivers later on that inning and Reggie Jackson hit a shot into the right field stands to open the Yankees' half of the eighth.

Now things got really interesting.

The Red Sox put up a two-spot in the bottom of the eighth on four hits against Goose Gossage, who was perhaps running low on gas in the aftermath of a season in which he'd worked 134 innings. Yet with the previous season's Cy Young Award winner in the bullpen and a couple of left-handed hitters due up in the ninth, Bob Lemon stuck with Gossage ... and almost got burned for it.

With one out in the bottom of the ninth, the Goose walked Rick Burleson, bringing the left-handed-hitting Jerry Remy to the plate. Having gone against the platoon percentages, the Yankees were rewarded with a liner hit almost directly at right fielder Lou Pinella. A hard but easy out, assuming that Pinella was tracking the ball.

With the sun directly in his eyes, Lou lost sight of Remy's drive almost immediately after it came off the bat. Showing the presence of mind that would make him a successful manager, Pinella acted as if he would make a routine catch, thus freezing Burleson between first and second. It was only at the last moment that he threw his arms out wide in the hope that the ball would at least hit him rather than bound past into the depths of Fenway's cavernous right field.

The ball bounced once and hit Pinella directly in the glove, forcing the Rooster to stop at second.[71] This fake-out/stroke of luck would immediately loom large as Jim Rice's fly ball on the next pitch backed Pinella to the warning track, more than deep enough to score Burleson had he been on third.[72]

With two out and the Red Sox shortstop belatedly ninety feet away, the left-handed-hitting Carl Yastrzemski strode to the plate. The left-handed Lyle was ready in the bullpen, Gossage had given up two runs on five hits in his two innings of work, the Red Sox had been splattering most everything the Goose has served up — and Lemon never made a move off the bench.

Yastrzemski popped up to third baseman Graig Nettles.[73]

Now, exactly how many potential heroes and goats reside in that sequence? Had Lou Pinella or Bucky Dent or Goose Gossage or Bob Lemon not gotten lucky, the Yankees would be the team remembered as 1978's choke artists. One can easily write the scenario: a preseason favorite to win it all that first self-destructed, then rallied, only to blow it in the last week and a half of the season. As for the Red Sox, they would have been regarded as a gritty team that overcame severe weaknesses, crippling injuries, and a ferocious charge by the defending champs to win when they had to.

Yet it was not to be, and thus a blown 14 ½-game lead, a third baseman airmailing throws into the stands, and a lazy fly ball arching over a high green wall on an Indian summer afternoon would be the images carried by a generation of fans. They would also be the ones that the Red Sox faithful would add to their already overstocked suitcase of woes....

... And keep in mind that Bill Buckner was still a first baseman with the Cubs at that time.

33

The Stolen Base Revival

One of the problems with the mad rush to modernity that has often characterized American history is that some good stuff inevitably gets tossed out with the bad or outmoded. Cloth upholstery in cars gave way to solid vinyl in the 1950s due to the latter material's durability and resistance to stains; a few million first degree burns on hot summer days later, cloth made a comeback and is now the material of choice once again. After two centuries of headlong migration towards urban areas, Americans are repopulating ex-urban and rural enclaves in search of a simpler life. Urban railway systems, art deco, and Harry Truman are all once-passé things rediscovered by a society that has come to the realization that Dear Old Dad may not have been as dumb as he seemed.

Baseball is not a particularly introspective sport — given its proclivity for living in the past it has little need to be — but even the denizens of our sometimes hidebound National Pastime will occasionally pull a forgotten strategy out of the archives and give it a try. Sometimes the results bring a smile to the face, as did Yankee pitcher Steve Hamilton's resurrection of Rip Sewell's "eephus pitch,"[1] while in others such as the Casey Stengel-driven rebirth of platooning a team achieves a competitive advantage over its brethren. Only on rare occasions, though, has the game's complexion been changed by the dusting off of a bygone strategy — and the 1970s rekindling of baseball's romance with the stolen base was one of those cases.

The decade witnessed a rise in thievery that ultimately reached proportions unseen since the days when Ty Cobb's flashing spikes reigned supreme. The Joe Adcocks and Boog Powells that had clogged basepaths for generations gave way to a deluge of Omar Morenos and Rick Mannings who could fly but needed a 100-MPH tailwind to hit the ball 400 feet. Even the new breed of power hitters were liberally seasoned with people like Bobby Bonds, Dave Parker, and Dave Winfield who could steal 20 bases a season while covering half the Australian Outback in the field. This addition of speed turned the more static game of the immediate postwar years upside down, as organizations were forced to rethink some of their most hallowed axioms regarding talent … and rethink them … and rethink them….

Though Luis Aparicio's and Maury Wills's late 50s/early 60s exploits rekindled interest in the stolen base as an art form, it was the 1963 strike zone expansion which ushered in the game's second Dead Ball Era that initially sparked the stolen base revolution. Caught flat-footed (literally) with legions of Frank Howard-like behemoths well equipped to do war in the power-driven 1950s game but poorly suited for moving runners along with outs and executing the humble sacrifice bunt, baseball's scouting apparatus was sent scurrying to uncover talents capable of exploiting the new realities. In the meantime, though, the game was forced to make do with what it had — and "make do" was definitely the operative phrase.

Mid-1960s baseball is a monument to evolution theorists: an era in which man, having descended from the trees but now faced by a saber-toothed tiger, turns to swing up out of harm's way with the tail that had heretofore been a nuisance ... only to discover that it had evolved away. The problem was especially acute in the National League, where venues such as Crosley Field, ivy covered Wrigley, Sportsman's Park in St. Louis, and Atlanta's Fulton County Stadium had pushed the power-hitting culture to greater heights than were ever seen in the junior circuit. Even after five years of practice the NL's 1969 stolen base figures documented an exercise in futility: a league-wide 59.4 percent success rate; Johnny Bench attempting 12 thefts; and Orlando Cepeda, to whom knee cartilage was just a fond memory, coming within two bags of leading the Atlanta Braves in steals.[2]

While all of this may sound like low comedy, keep in mind that by the 1960s nobody other than Casey Stengel could remember the days when the stolen base had last been an effective weapon — and Casey was kind of on auto-pilot by that time. Given the virtually nonexistent experience base, it is not surprising that few offensive strategies of the era included baserunning as anything more than a sideshow element or that many young players with speed remained unschooled in the craft. The 1959 rookie crop included some of the biggest stars of the following decade (Willie McCovey, Billy Williams, Tim McCarver, Zoilo Versailles) — yet only one player from that group other than Wills would steal as many as 100 bases in his career (Tommy Davis). Curt Flood was one of the fastest men in baseball in the 1960s, yet he recorded only 88 steals over his 15-year career. Cookie Rojas was a mobile second baseman who prior to 1970 had stolen a grand total of 28 bases — but had been caught 34 times.[3]

With the 1969 pitcher's mound and strike zone revisions restoring conditions to those of the Ozzie and Harriet days, one might have expected this mania for thefts to quickly return to its dusty place in baseball's attic, but the force of several other epochal shifts intervened:

1. After decades of neglect, college talent began to make its presence known in a big time way. The Oakland A's were transformed in the span of three years from laughingstock to serious contender on the shoulders of such

college-bred talent as Reggie Jackson and Rick Monday, and between this spectacular reversal of fortune and the principals' "understated" natures, the implications were unignorable. The advantages of the college player were many and varied, but the key one for this discussion was their command of the game's finer points. As intelligent men college players were naturally biased towards maximizing their physical gifts; as products of a fundamentals-driven system (the back end of most college rosters, then and now, are pretty weak by professional standards) they were compelled to hone little ball skills along with the classic uppercut swing.

Many high profile players of the 1970s emanated from the college ranks, and the baserunning skills that these men brought to the game along with their other talents were a revelation to front offices accustomed to speed coming only in whippet-like bodies. Ohio University graduate Mike Schmidt was a huge man (6'4", 195 even in his early days), yet he averaged 15 steals a season between 1974 and 1981. Dave Winfield was even bigger than Schmidt, yet he posted similar swipe totals into his mid-30s. Jackson, Monday, Toby Harrah, Dave Lopes: each struck a different balance between power and speed, but all of them experienced success in both venues—and each was a college attendee.

2. The first large-scale wave of Latin American talent was entering the game at this time, and more often than not speed was a key element of their game. Bolstered by active public interest in their home countries, Latino players, like their college brethren, were entering organized baseball with highly developed skill sets and thus were able to make big time impacts at an age at which their wheels were still in prime condition. Not only did many of these players possess excellent speed, their judgment on when to run was often exceptional. Dave Concepcion stole 220 bases in the '70s with a 78 percent success rate. Cesar Cedeno swiped as many as 61 in a season while being caught less than one time in four. Omar Moreno would lead the league in steals for three consecutive seasons. Jose Cruz (or Jose Cruuuzzz for those who recall his Astrodome PA system intros[4]) overcame a slow start in the Cardinals system to become a fine power-speed combination in his 30s—he'd probably have hit 20 or 25 homers a season to go with his 35 steals in any other park.

Cruz points out an important fact to remember about these people, Latino and college men both: by and large they were multi-faceted players whose baserunning acumen represented just another piece of shrapnel in their talent hand grenade. Take away Maury Wills's basepath prowess and what remains is a below-average defensive shortstop with no power and minimal plate discipline; take away Mike Schmidt's speed and you still had three MVP awards. Cedeno's combination of five Gold Gloves and 20-plus homers per season in the Astrodome would have made him one of the league's better (if most frustrating) players even if he hadn't been swiping 45 bases a year. Winfield played so long after his

speed had departed that today's fans could be excused if they have trouble visualizing him as a lithe speedster ... but he was.

3. Finally, the advent of artificial turf was rightly or wrongly changing per-
ceptions of the game's requirements, especially in the senior circuit. The
National League's early-decade building boom combined with the plastic
salesmen's success in converting existing fields resulted in a game that by
1977 was being played more than half the time on fields that no self-respecting cow would feed off of. The speed with which balls squirted between
outfielders to the fence was obvious to even the most casual observer —
and brought into high relief the defensive inadequacies of the dinosaurs
that had traditionally guarded the outfield corners.

In the years since Red Sox owner Harry Frazee had discovered *No No
Nanette* and sent Babe Ruth New York-ward, the outfield had progressively
become a dumping ground for power hitters who couldn't play other positions. Even center field, once the bastion of the Terry Moores and Sam Chap-
mans who could track down anything that didn't make it over the fence first,
was becoming clogged with guys who had reliable gloves and good bats but
limited range and nonexistent arms.

Swapping one outfielder for another with half a step less range is a subtle thing, something that probably doesn't cost a team five plays a season —
but keep making substitutions like that for 50 years or so and the numbers
can become staggering. In 1949 six of the eight National League center fielders
accepted 2.5 or more chances per game: twenty years later, Curt Flood was
the only NL outfielder to accept that many.[5] Greg (The Bull) Luzinski's range
was so poor that the Phillies had him set up facing the left field line: center
fielder Garry Maddox was expected to track down everything hit more than
a step or two to Luzinski's left.[6] The powerful but erratic Mack Jones spent
three seasons as a starting center fielder, and in two of those years his cohort
in right (Henry Aaron) actually made more plays per game than he did.[7]

Thus, baseball found itself on the horns of a dichotomy, with the promise of easy offense conveyed by the lowered pitcher's mound and decreased
strike zone on the one hand, but dynamics that dictated a speed-based game
of the type traditionally associated with "grind it out" strategies on the other.
As in so many things, there never was any point at which a conscious decision was made to resolve this dilemma, just as there had never been one made
to sacrifice 15 percent of an average outfielder's range to get another Hank
Sauer in the lineup. Yet when the myriad decisions made by front offices and
managers were taken together the drift was clear: speed was in, while power
was ... well, if not out at least no longer the be-all and end-all.

In baseball as in life, trendsetters inordinately come from the ranks of
the young — those unencumbered by their elders' physical and emotional
investment in the status quo. Unlike life, though, a veteran player can't just
buy a shotgun and move to Wyoming (Cleveland was the baseball equivalent

in those days) when unpleasant new realities intrude: they must adapt or ... well, buy a shotgun and move to Wyoming. Since most players choose to stay in baseball until the last GM drags them out of the last locker room, the importation of all of this speed had an interesting secondary effect as veterans adapted their games, and perhaps to their surprise found themselves adept at thievery.

Vada Pinson had ranked in the top five in steals from 1959 through 1963, but by 1969 recurring hamstring problems had pushed him from center field to right while reducing his basepath exploits to a meager four thefts in eight attempts. Magically, by 1974 Pinson was back to stealing 21 bases in 26 attempts at an age that was somewhere between 35 and 39, depending on who one believed. Between age 21 and 25 (1965 to 1969) Joe Morgan stole 112 bases in 569 games: between age 33 and 37 (1977 to 1981) he swiped 134 in 643 games. Even Cookie Rojas got into the act — after going 28 for 62 in the 1960s, Rojas would steal 18 bases in 22 attempts as a 34-year-old Kansas City Royal.[8]

All of which was peanuts next to Lou Brock, baseball's poster boy for adaptation in the face of declining skills.

Brock was essentially Rickey Henderson without the fanatical affinity for ball four: a good to very good average, surprising power, fine base running instincts, prone to the dropsies in the field ("Brock as in Rock" was a popular chant during his Cub days[9]). He inherited Maury Wills's base stealing crown in 1966 and wore it for the remainder of the decade, but by the early 1970s two key elements of Brock's game — foot speed (in a 1974 interview Lou admitted that he was a half second slower to first than in his salad days[10]) and power (Brock hit 36 homers in 1966-1967 versus 34 in his final nine seasons) — were in serious decline. Perhaps recognizing that the life expectancy of a 30-something left fielder with no thump and suspect defense is typically measured in weeks, Brock reinvented himself as Henderson would a couple of decades later. He became a slap hitting on-base machine, topping .300 six times between 1970 and 1977. Lou took more walks in the decade's first five years than he had in the entirety of the 1960s. As for his work on the basepaths ... well, one wonders if a Joe Hardy-like deal with the Devil wasn't struck.

OK, so Lou's on first base 50 to 60 more times per season than in his younger days but is a couple of steps slower than he used to be between bases. Explain exactly how the man:

a)   Led the league in stolen bases for four consecutive seasons in his early-to mid-30s against the likes of Cedeno, Morgan, and Bobby Bonds,

b)   Stole 371 bases between age 32 and 36, his seasonal average during that period matching his previous career best set in 1967,

c)   Capped his run as NL stolen base king with a Norm Cash-like 1974 campaign in which he pulverized Wills's mark with 118 thefts, and

Though by his own admission a half-second slower to first than in his salad days, the 34-year-old Lou Brock obliterated Maury Wills's single season stolen base record in 1974. He is shown here garnering the then–record-setting steal number 105 against the Phillies. (*National Baseball Hall of Fame Library, Cooperstown, NY*)

  d)   improved his effectiveness in the process (Brock was successful 78 percent of the time between 1971 and 1976 as opposed to a 75 percent career rate). Maybe it was something in the air.

By 1975 this revolution in stolen bases had created a philosophical diversity in strategic circles, the likes of which is rarely seen in baseball. There were teams stealing 168 bases in a season with an 82 percent success rate while others swiped 66 with a 53 percent success rate — and those two clubs (the Cincinnati Reds and Boston Red Sox) met in the World Series.[11] Seven of the top eight qualifiers for the AL batting title that year stole ten or more bags and lest one wonders about their overall quality, the list includes such names as George Brett, Rod Carew, Jim Rice, Fred Lynn and Hal McRae.[12] Outfielder range factors soared (Chet Lemon's 536 chances handled in 1977 is the fourth highest seasonal mark of all time[13]) as even decent defenders like McRae and Oscar Gamble were pushed into DH-hood to accommodate the speedy throng.

One of the most American of concepts is the idea that if a little bit of something is good, more is better and a lot must be great, and baseball's love affair with beating feet would be no exception. The logical conclusion to this trend surfaced in Oakland (where else?) where track star Herb Washington would "play" in 105 games as baseball's first designated runner.[14] While Washington was an Olympic class sprinter (he once held the world indoor track record in both the 50 and 60 yard dash[15]) he was coming off a 1½ year stint as a sportscaster and, more interestingly, hadn't played baseball since high school. Still, Charlie Finley was confident that, when armed with a six-day cram course from Maury Wills,[16] the Michigan State education grad would, according to an A's press release, "be directly responsible for winning ten games this season." Well, maybe not that confident: Finley apparently felt the need to add some weight to his appraisal and thus added manager Alvin Dark's name to it without his knowledge. When told of this, after stating that he didn't know how many games Washington would impact, Dark, ever the company man, replied, "I guess that's how many."[17]

Let's see ... the A's had won 94 games the previous season, and Finley was saying that a guy who couldn't hit or field was worth ten victories all by himself. Makes one wonder what he thought the value of the other 24 guys was, doesn't it?

While Washington wasn't particularly effective in his limited role (Herb's defining moment came in Game 2 of the 1974 World Series when he was picked off first with the A's down by a run in the ninth[18]) he was symbolic of a baseball-wide rethinking of what it took to be a big league player. After starting the decade as an important enhancement to a player's game, speed had risen in the pantheon of abilities to become the featured skill on many resumes. The impact of this attitude adjustment became most apparent with fringe players—those guys who were on the dividing line between the Show's bright lights and the minor league Twilight Zone.

The 1977 high minors' scene provides an excellent example of this phenomenon. During that season, there were ten players in the three U.S. AAA leagues (American Association, International League, and Pacific Coast League) who hit 25 or more homers. Not surprisingly, these guys by and large were neither particularly young nor terribly hot prospects (they'd have been called up long before amassing those big time power numbers otherwise) and thus their future performance as a group was nothing special. Two of the ten (Lance Parrish and Gorman Thomas) became quality players, while a couple of others (Dave Revering, Terry Crowley) stuck around long enough to be remembered and Randy Bass was destined to become a Japanese legend after enduring six seasons of half-chances with five teams. Four of the remaining five, though, would never get anything more than a cup of coffee in the majors for their efforts and two would never again see the inside of a big league park from the dugout.

Contrast the experience of the people mentioned above with that of the 17 men who stole 35 or more bases that season at the AAA level. Proportionally, this group did just about as well as the sluggers in yielding long-lived players (Julio Cruz, Lonnie Smith and Willie Wilson were the speedsters who would play 1,000 or more big league games), but take a step down the quality ladder and the comparison changed dramatically. Only one of the 17 would fail to make the bigs, and many of the remaining names would be recognizable to moderately serious fans of the era: U.L. Washington, Rafael Landestoy, Joe Simpson, Pepe Mangual, Bobby Brown, and Horace Speed (a member of the Razor Shines All-Cool Name Team).[19]

What was most conspicuous about these guys was what they weren't. As a group they had very little power, many finding themselves at pains to crank out the occasional double or triple. Few believed in taking walks and their defensive skills were surprisingly undistinguished — Smith, for example, was famous for his pratfalls in the pursuit of elusive fly balls.[20] In short, most of these people had little to recommend them outside of their quickness on the basepaths — yet roughly two-thirds of the 17 would make it into baseball's pension system.

This phenomenon extended further up baseball's food chain as well. Frank Taveras was a career .255 hitter who never took more than 44 walks in a season and had mediocre defensive instincts: he would rank last or next to last among shortstops in chances accepted per game every season he was a regular except one.[21] Yet despite these apparent handicaps, Taveras would craft an 11-year big league career, and one has to think that his 1977 stolen base crown had a lot to do with that. Jim Wohlford possessed limited range in right field and wasn't even that successful as a base stealer — in his four best seasons Wohlford would steal 67 bases and be caught 52 times — but he lasted for 15 seasons.[22] Miguel Dilone was a marginal center fielder who in his career year went homerless while drawing 28 walks in 528 at-bats — the combination of a .341 batting average and 61 steals, though, were enough to keep his career going for another five years.[23]

Even quality players not blessed with speed or thievery instincts caught the stolen base fever, and some of the numbers they put up bordered on the draconian. Chet Lemon was a fine center fielder and offensive player over a 16-year career, yet his base running efforts are notable for their persistence in the face of futility: Lemon would be thrown out in more than half of his 217 career stolen base attempts.[24] Ivan DeJesus is probably best remembered as the man the Phillies gave up Ryne Sandberg for,[25] but he was a solid all-around shortstop in his own right — except when it came to base stealing, where he would be thrown out in 126 of 268 career attempts. John Stearns set a record for catcher steals in 1979 and was thrown out half the time in the process (thanks John).[26]

The net result of all of this turmoil was a radically changed offensive climate ... but one that didn't initially yield any results on the scoreboard. Doubles and triples per game played jumped by 20 percent to 30 percent over the course of the decade as a byproduct of all of this added speed, while round-trippers declined by 25 percent after 1974 for pretty much the same reason. The bottom line was that batting, slugging, and runs scored levels (adjusted for the DH in the American League) would basically end the decade where they began — down about 5 percent to 10 percent from the days when everybody liked Ike for the first time.[27]

Yet the fans loved it.

This may not surprise modern day baseball aficionados upon reflection, but for all of the old-timers' love for pitching duels and defense, major league attendance has generally been controlled by a simple formula: more bop equals more butts in the seats. People will suggest that Babe Ruth was the big reason behind the growth in baseball attendance in the 1920s and in certain ways he was—but if the Babe was the primary draw, why did National League attendance increase at a greater rate than did AL turnout during the decade? Sure, the Depression was the key driver of the 1930s downturn that coincided with a gradual decline in scoring levels, but what about the attendance declines during the good times that coincided with the Dead Ball Era? Or the American League's 27 percent drop from 1960 to 1965 in the midst of one of the greatest economic expansions in history?[28]

This time, however, was different. With no real offensive growth to fuel it, baseball nonetheless witnessed sustained attendance growth of a type associated with dot-coms from 1975 through the end of the decade, with senior circuit per game figures rising 27.5 percent while the American League's numbers jumped nearly 45 percent. Yes, there were other reasons for the gains—an improved economy, stronger ownership, and a series of good pennant races—but the biggest statistical change of all between the 1969 game and that of a decade later was the increase in stolen bases of more than 60 percent. Furthermore, this pattern of increased speed without inflating run totals would persist well into the next decade — and attendance would grow another 19.4 percent during that period.[29]

When asked by an American journalist what it was like to become an overnight sensation, British comedian Benny Hill replied that it was wonderful ... especially considering the fact that it had taken him 35 years to achieve such quickie fame. Like Hill the speed game base required an extended gestation period to emerge as a revolutionary force, but once embraced, Ty Cobb's trademark strategy became a staple of a refreshed, revitalized National Pastime.

Guess those Dead Ball Era geezers did know a thing or two after all.

34

Dave Kingman: Master of the Homer and the Big Breeze

It is some people's fate in this world to never get "it"—whatever "it" might be. Bowie Kuhn, for example, tried to be the new Kenesaw Mountain Landis to the very end despite the fact that (a) nobody (owners or players alike) wanted a new Landis, and (b) contrary to popular opinion, few had been all that wild about the original model anyway. Ralph Houk spent the vast majority of his managerial career laboring under the illusion that speedy middle infielders represented leadoff hitter nirvana regardless of how often they reached base.[1] Denny McLain seemed to think his misadventures with various lowlifes and shady businessmen didn't matter, right up to the moment that Commissioner Bowie Kuhn suspended him for half of the 1970 season—and beyond, given his pair of post-career criminal convictions.[2]

And Dave Kingman believed that the home run conquered all.

Kingman at the plate was one of the most awe-inspiring sights of his era. A very tall (6'6") man whose height was accentuated by a lean, athletic frame, Kingman towered over any umpiring and catching duo stationed alongside him. His swing was something that Mighty Casey would have favored—a lengthy, swooping affair that featured a massive yet surprisingly graceful and controlled uppercut. Astro/Dodger center fielder Jim Wynn's cut is the only contemporary that rivaled Kingman's in terms of trajectory, and Wynn swung so hard that he practically screwed himself into the ground. To heighten his swing's drama Kingman adopted a more or less upright stance and set his bat on a arc-like trajectory down and up through the zone: he frankly looked like a guy knee-deep in sand swinging a nine iron.

When bat met ball solidly on that flight path, the result was often majestic. If Dave ever hit a line drive that sneaked over the 330 sign it wasn't recorded—what he specialized in were towering shots that cleared light standards, streets, and nearby office buildings. Mark McGwire specials if you will, or more properly, McGwire hit Kingmaneqsue drives. Like McGwire 20 years later, everybody seemed to have a story about some Kingman shot, like the one he hit on the roof of a house across Wayland Avenue one day in Chicago, or the 500-foot jobber that busted a fan's windshield in the parking lot at Shea Stadium.[3]

One evening during Kong's first tour of duty with the Mets, teammate Joe Torre found the cover of a baseball near the batting cage. "Kingman must have hit this one," Torre said. "The inside of this cover is probably in the Hudson River."[4]

The problem with all of this, though, is it's tricky getting the bat to meet the ball squarely when the ball is traveling on a more or less level plane and the bat is moving upwards at a 45-degree angle. Be just a little late on the pitch and an elevator shaft home run is sent towards the shortstop; be a little early and a routine grounder results instead. Be more than a little early or late and the result is big breezes of a type that Dave produced in gargantuan quantities. The man known as K-K-K-Kingman during his San Francisco days[5] was among the league leaders in whiffs in every full season he played except his last.

The strikeouts, though, were just the tip of the iceberg — Dave's real problem was that he didn't do much of anything except hit homers. A typical season for Kingman would yield 30 homers but only 18 other extra base hits. His career batting average was .236, which would be livable under normal circumstances but Kingman was unexceptional in his ability to work pitchers for a walk. Though surprisingly fast and agile, he was a horrific fielder who once confessed that his defensive position was "standing around with a glove in my hand."[6] In watching the man go through his paces one wondered whether Rod Deadeaux, the legendary USC coach who'd converted Kingman from the mound, ever issued grades to his charges.

Kong's ability to not only sustain his career in the face of such limited talents but thrive to point of knocking down $1 million-plus per year in the days when that was a more than respectable figure represented a turning point in baseball's attitudes towards whiff-prone players. Consider Dave Nicholson, an Orioles/White Sox/Astros outfielder of the previous decade. Playing through the gut of baseball's second Dark Age in two of the worst hitter's parks going, the St. Louis native nonetheless belted 61 homers (one of which cleared the left field roof at Comiskey Park[7]) in 1,400 at-bats. Despite a .212 career average, Nicholson's penchant for free passes produced a league average on-base percentage to go with the power — yet excessive strikeouts finished his big league career at 27.

Now Nicholson *really* struck out (his 175 1963 K's were a major league record until Bobby Bonds came along) and was an awful outfielder to boot (his fielding exploits inspired a coach to comment one spring that while Nicholson hadn't caught a ball just yet, he was at least getting closer to them).

Dave Kingman's long, swooping swing was reminiscent of a golfer standing knee-deep in a sand trap. Among the league leaders in whiffs virtually every season he played regularly, Kingman nonetheless connected often and spectacularly enough to open the door for a new breed of big-breeze, low-average sluggers. (*National Baseball Hall of Fame Library, Cooperstown, NY*)

Still, a guy capable of producing ten homers in 280 at-bats along with a .356 on-base percentage for the 1966 Astros ... well, let's just say that one wouldn't normally expect him to be history after a mere 25 plate appearances the next season.[8]

During and after Kingman's reign, however, such players began making extended runs in the Show: these men's existences may have been precarious, but some would play key roles on quality teams. There was Steve (Bye Bye) Balboni, a first baseman who ranked near the top of the K charts in three of his four seasons as a regular and possessed limited defensive range, yet was a critical member of the Kansas City Royals' 1986 world championship team. Rob Deer whiffed in 36 percent of his big league plate appearances and hit .179 in 448 at-bats for the 1991 Tigers, but Deer's 25 homers and 89 walks that season were enough to keep him going as a regular for a couple more seasons. Gorman Thomas led three minor leagues in strikeouts, yet despite a .225 career average and 1,339 major league punch-outs, Thomas would for five years represent the power core of a Milwaukee team that would ultimately make its way into the World Series, twice receiving significant MVP support in the process.[9]

If Kingman ever perceived his position as baseball's reigning homer/strikeout king as being precarious he never betrayed it. The USC alum's comments were forever centered on his homers, how many he could hit, and how far they traveled. "It's a thrill to really get into one," Kingman once confessed. "You can feel the bat bend in your hands. It's a great feeling to just stand there and watch the ball instead of running for first base. That's the one thing I always thought of, the one thing I never got tired of: watching the ball go over the fence."[10]

It bugged Dave endlessly that people didn't always have the same level of appreciation for his taters and would periodically bench him, as the Giants did in 1973 when Kingman hit .203 and made 18 errors in 54 games at third base. He'd regularly ask to be traded and thus played for eight teams (the Mets twice) during his career. Not that anybody in the locker room was disappointed to see him go, mind you: Bill Caudill commented after Kong's departure from the Chicago Cubs that "having him leave was like having an aching tooth pulled. It was painful at first, but once you get past that things are a lot better."[11]

Having said all of that, Dave wasn't really the bad guy that such comments and his late career escapades with rats (he sent a dead one while with the A's to a reporter named Susan Fosnoff[12]) would lead one to believe. A loner at heart, Kingman simply never connected with the cutups and overgrown frat boys who dominated most major league locker rooms or the people who recorded their efforts.[13] A typical article about this larger-than-life man left the reader with the impression that, like Dick Allen, Kong thought baseball would be a lot more fun if all of the fans and reporters were eliminated from the proceedings.

He may not have been a great player (his 442 homers are likely to remain the highest total for a non-Hall of Famer, Jose Canseco haters notwithstanding), but he was a major presence on the baseball scene for 16 years and very few can say that. His advantages may have been as ethereal as the memories of his clouts will prove to be in time, but for all of that Dave Kingman was a real character — something of a negative image of Babe Herman, perhaps. Yet had Kingman ever gotten "it" ... well, add 25 points to his career average plus four or five walks a month, and the result is Frank Howard's spitting image. Frank isn't a Hall of Famer, of course, but Howard didn't finish second in the AL in homers during his final season, either.

Not that anybody would really have wanted to see Kong's visage in bronze, mind you.

35

Power to the Umpires

Many of history's pivotal events have their roots in small issues that flew under the historical radar of the time. The Munich Beer Hall Putsch of 1923, for example, was a Keystone Kops-like affair authored by a bunch of right-wing fanatics overwhelmed by their own rhetoric; within a decade the putsch's leader, one A. Hitler, was Germany's chancellor and in the early stages of executing *Mein Kampf*— "my plan." The Boston Massacre, a watershed event on the road to the American Revolution, took about five minutes from start to finish and claimed a grand total of two lives. World War I's genesis was due in part to the shooting death of a playboy archduke who wasn't in line for the Austro-Hungarian throne by a somewhat addled anarchist.

Out of such acorns occasionally sprout mighty oaks, and such was the case with the 1979 umpires' strike. This vaguely remembered (even Ken Burns couldn't find time to mention it in his 18-hour *Baseball* opus) 45-day walk-out represented a turning point in the relationship between baseball and the men in blue—one that would ultimately spawn such 1990s staples as personally defined strike zones, on-field heart attacks by 300-plus-pound physiques (John McSherry), and a growing sense of *hubris* that would reach its logical conclusion with an ill-considered resignation ploy that would destroy much of what the arbiters had built.

All of this would sprout from a humble work action initiated by a bunch of guys who, in the midst of escalating player salaries and owner bankrolls, were making less than $30,000 a year on average.

Umpiring has been a tough occupation since that fateful day when Abner Doubleday crawled out of his cave and hit a rock his neighbor Oog threw at him 450 feet ... only to have the blind SOB standing behind him call it a ground-rule double. Obscenity-laden tirades, having dirt kicked on one's clothes and the occasional physical assault (the four-in-hand knot became a sartorial no-no in arbiter circles after Brooklyn Dodgers pitcher Johnny Allen utilized George Barr's neckwear as an impromptu Alcatraz Ascot) had been part and parcel of the man in blue's experience for years, but by the early 1970s relative poverty was taking its place alongside these qualities in the umpiring pantheon. Only incorrigible baseball fanatics and the chronically unemployable need apply; for those who beg to differ, consider the steps Ron Luciano endured on the road to becoming the unofficial Clown Prince of Arbiters:

1. Completing a six-week self-paid course at one of the two umpiring schools extant at that time. Essentially the profession's version of boot camp (complete with barracks-style accommodations, mess hall dining and drill sergeant-style direction),[1] umpiring school provided the basics of technique and attitude, but little else; in terms of jobs, the students were strictly on their own. This was not a matter of callousness so much as one of simple mathematics. Both schools were of equal size and prestige in Luciano's day (1965), so based upon his graduating class of 58 we can estimate that roughly 115 prospective umpires were descending each spring on a professional structure that employed fewer than 200 arbiters in total—and many of those spots were in short-season leagues. Even given the high dropout rate among umpires low on the totem pole and the potential for work in the amateur and collegiate ranks, a school system that graduates enough men to completely repopulate its profession every two years is unlikely to be particularly active in the job placement arena.

2. Spending four years working his way up through the minors. For those who shudder at the petty indignities of a player's life as portrayed in *Bull Durham*, consider the umpire's lot:

   - Afterthought dressing room facilities (Durwood Merrill told stories of snakes, black widows, and other various elements of wildlife sharing dressing rooms with him[2]).
   - Rowdy fans who would think nothing of slashing a ump's tires or locking him in the dressing room after a tough loss.[3]
   - No equipment men or chartered buses to get them from town to town.
   - The kind of salaries (around $500 a month including food and lodging subsidies for a five-month season at the A level[4]) that are sure to breed that classic "African kid in the middle of a drought" look in one's dependents.

Furthermore, four years was how long a prospective big league umpire spent in the minors if he was really good and really lucky. Ken Kaiser weathered 13 seasons on the bush league trail before getting the call, while Angelo Guglielmo would spend nearly 40 summers in the business—only one of which was in the bigs (1952, in which he became the first umpire to throw Jackie Robinson out of a game[5]).

For those few fortunate men in blue who were judged to be of major league caliber (remember, there are three umps in the minors at any given time for every one in the Show), there was fame and ... well, certainly not fortune. An eight-year veteran in 1968 earned $12,000 for the six-month regular season[6] plus $30 per day for hotels, meals and transportation[7] — a livable sum assuming a decent off-season job, a preference for Motel 6 and a spouse with marketable skills. However, once the continuous travel (umpire Lou DiMuro's son once told his classmates that his father worked at the airport[8]), lack of in-season vacations, and opportunity to see one's mistakes replayed endlessly were factored into the mix, the arbiter's life was something akin to Karl Marx's wet dream.

The 1979 action traces its origins to the 1968 firings of Al Salerno and Bill Valentine, two veteran American League arbiters active in efforts to organize their brethren (the NL umps had formed their own union in 1963 and not surprisingly enjoyed higher wages and better benefits[9]). According to AL president Joe Cronin, the decision to not offer the pair new contracts was an idea that had been "kicked around" for some time, though to their colleagues the announcement's timing (a mere 48 hours after Salerno attended a meeting of the National League Umpires' Association and announced that the AL arbiters wanted to join them[10]) was, shall we say, more than a little suspect. Whether junior circuit umps at that time were as solidly in favor of uniting with their NL colleagues as Salerno intimated is debatable, but once he and Valentine were tossed, there was no doubt where the AL men stood. Action built upon action like a mushrooming thunderhead; a boycott of the 1968 World Series was narrowly avoided, the two leagues' arbiters amalgamated themselves into what would become the Major League Umpires Association (MLUA), and when Cronin refused to rehire Salerno and Valentine, a spring training strike was threatened.[11] For their part, the two ousted men quickly filed a grievance with the National Labor Relations Board (NLRB) a move that indirectly threatened baseball's antitrust exemption, and would ultimately sue the game for $4 million.[12]

Like Hitler in Munich, though, the Salerno-Valentine affair proved to be too much too soon. The spring training walkout never came to pass and was later dismissed by veteran columnist Jerome Holtzman as "an idle threat."[13] Salerno and his attorney rejected several proposals from the league that would have led to his reinstatement with back pay under the theory that big bucks were just around the corner — then was astonished as the NLRB ruled against him and Valentine twice.[14] The umpires' joint civil suit was dismissed (translation: it isn't even worth our time and effort to hear the case) at the district and appeals court level. Bill Valentine became a tragic figure; he'd begged Salerno to settle prior to the NLRB hearing (even offering Salerno a portion of his share of the proceeds), cried when describing his dismissal to the board and ultimately wrote an impassioned — but futile — letter to Cronin begging for reinstatement.[15]

Though in the end Salerno and Valentine stayed fired, their martyrdom served to unite their umpiring brethren for the first time, and in so doing they recognized their combined strength. Significant pay and benefits gains were racked up by the new union in its early years of operation, and after an impasse was reached in negotiations over All-Star Game and playoff remuneration, the association proved cohesive enough to strike the first game of the 1970 playoffs despite some internal opposition. Once it became clear that virtually every stadium worker in heavily unionized Pittsburgh would honor the umpires' picket lines for the second game of the playoffs, talks were quickly resumed, with the arbiters ultimately winning a 15-plus percent pay increase for working those marquee games.[16]

These were heady gains, but while the representatives of the men in blue would continue to make progress throughout the 1970s, there was a feeling that plenty was still being left on the table, especially in the areas of fringe benefits and work rules. For example, an umpire with 20 years of major league service who retired at age 55 in 1974 was eligible for a pension of slightly less than $10,000 per year.[17] That's OK at a time when the average production worker was making $4.24 an hour,[18] but with the value of the dollar fated to decline by one-third over the next five years ... well, one hopes that the retired ump had a good-paying job on the side. Per diems rose to $51 per day by 1979, yet remained so scanty in relation to the actual cost of travel and lodging that Bruce Froemming estimated that it cost him $3,000 annually in additional out-of-pocket expenses to adhere to his assigned schedule.[19] In-season absences for any reason remained a Bozo no-no; when AL umpire Durwood Merrill once asked for leave to attend his son's high school graduation, supervisor of umpires Dick Butler asked, "What do you need to do, Durwood? Help him across the stage? Can't he pick up the diploma by himself?"[20] Even the MLUA itself was a compromised duck, collectively bargaining with the owners on the one hand while its members were bound by individual "at will" contracts on the other. Ron Luciano considered the association's efforts so valueless that he refused to join for a number of years.[21]

Enter one Richie Phillips.

Phillips shared certain traits with Player's union chief Marvin Miller — a professional lawyer, a longtime union organizer, not particularly interested in baseball per se. However, if Miller's image was that of labor leader as pseudo-Captain of Industry, Phillips represented the Jimmy Hoffa version (sans the underworld connections): brash, argumentative, a born gambler — the kind of guy who could knock back a few brewskis with the boys at the bowling alley and not look out of place. It was perhaps this somewhat casual, crude air that fostered baseball's initial underestimation of Phillips; Bowie Kuhn barely mentions the man in *Hardball*, and when he does the union chief is depicted as something of a gadfly riding on Miller's coattails.[22] Such a reading, however, overlooked the spectacular gains Phillips had won for the NBA's referees, who after ten years of experience were making 38 percent more for working an 81-game season than an equivalent MLB umpire was for a 162-contest campaign.[23]

Initially, Phillips was operating under a significant handicap: his predecessor had negotiated a basic agreement with the owners covering wages, benefits and work rules that extended through the 1981 season. Strikes based upon issues that were ostensively agreed to a few months before tend to be viewed in an unfavorable light by the law, and thus a Phillips-engineered 1978 walkout was terminated by a federal restraining order after one day.[24] However, in reviewing the arbiters' situation, Phillips discovered an incongruity: while the MLUA was a trade union at heart (i.e. its members' pay rates, unlike that of the players, were based primarily on seniority), the umpires' real bind to baseball was a standardized annual contract. Every arbiter was hired on an "at will" basis—if the league didn't want an umpire back, it could simply fail to offer him a new contract (this is essentially what happened to Salerno and Valentine; they weren't fired, they simply weren't offered the chance to continue working).

AL umpires Al Salerno (pictured) and Bill Valentine were fired for incompetence shortly after attempting to organize their junior league brethren. Though the league would attempt to settle with the two umpires on several occasions, Salerno held out for big bucks—then came away with nothing as the NLRB rules against him. (*The Sporting News*)

However, if baseball wasn't required to send contracts out to every umpire, the arbiters weren't required to sign what they received, either.

From this realization, a strategy emerged. Suppose that none of MLB's umpires signed new contracts one spring. Under those circumstances, the men in blue wouldn't really be striking per se, yet the effect would be the same. Furthermore, such an action (or really such a series of actions by individuals who refused to agree to the terms offered to them) had nothing to do with the collective bargaining agreement as such, thus cutting off the owners' likely court injunction response.

Of course, such a strategy called for each umpire to individually reject his contract in the hopes that his comrades would do the same, and Valentine's and Salerno's fates represented a still-fresh example of what happened to people who stuck their necks out. While this fear factor certainly was on the arbiters' minds as they contemplated their 1979 agreements, there were a couple of other factors at play as well:

1. Phillips was (and is) a very persuasive man.
2. Despite the previous decade's gains, the umpires, unlike the players, still didn't have all that much to lose economically even under the worst-case scenario. Sure, $17,500 for six months' work by a first-year ump was hardly starvation wages for the time, but midlevel corporate managers who weren't anywhere near the top 52 in their profession could easily match that and have a family life to boot. Furthermore, the $39,000 base rate for arbiters[25] with 16 or more years of experience was roughly what a journeyman welder at GM with similar seniority could pull down — and those guys only had one supervisor screaming at them.

Under those circumstances, it should come as no surprise that 51 of the 52 men in blue chose to turn their contracts over to Phillips when the moment of truth arrived.[26]

Baseball's response to this boycott was more or less along the lines of a parent dealing with a recalcitrant six-year-old. A February 2 letter to each umpire stated that he would not be allowed to work spring training games and was risking his job by not returning the contract,[27] a tactic popularly known in business circles as the "my way or the highway" strategy. The two leagues conceded little in negotiations with Phillips because they didn't feel that they had to— after all, if the union held firm, baseball could always return to federal court and get the previous summer's restraining order reinstated. As a symbolic cherry on top of the matter, when baseball did decide to go the court route in mid-March, it added a $10,000-per-day fine onto the complaint against the MLUA.[28]

As any management guru will verify, a hardball tack such as this has two possible outcomes:

1. One's opponents will knuckle under ... assuming that you have the power to back the threats up.
2. Those opponents will become the modern equivalent of the Crusaders: 100 percent convinced of their righteousness and absolutely unwilling to settle for anything less than whatever their demands were before plus a 25 percent annoyance tax.

As Phillips had chopped the legs out from under baseball's court strategy (an injunction was denied on March 26 by the same judge who had handed down the previous year's restraining order[29]), baseball's tough love tactics played straight into his hand. Only one of the 51 arbiters broke with the union in a March 30 vote, and, as Phillips announced after the meeting, "I believe the umpires feel more pride in their decision to see this through as a unit than they have ever felt."[30]

With the initial negotiation-by-judo strategy having blown up in their face, baseball moved on to Plan B — the hiring of AAA umpires as crew chiefs with local amateurs utilized to round out the staffs. In effecting this plan, however, the leagues discovered a phenomenon that would be reenacted during the 1994-1995 players' strike: the majority of the AAA guys initially approached refused the assignment despite the dangling of two- and three-year guaranteed contracts in front of their noses. One look at the list of arbiters that passed on the offer (Drew Coble, Balkin' Bob Davidson, Gerry Davis, Mark Johnson, Randy Marsh, Dan Morrison, Rocky Roe, and Charlie Williams) makes the reason for this rejection of a seemingly golden opportunity obvious. By and large these guys were on the verge of making the Show anyway (all but Morrison would be in the majors by 1983) and knew it; thus the prospect of being branded with the Scarlet S (scab) in exchange for a few fewer miles on the minor league trail was less than enticing.

As a result of this, baseball opened the season with:

- The two umpires (Ted Hendry and Paul Pryor) who had crossed the line.[31]
- An assortment of first- and second-tier AAA guys whom AL president Lee MacPhail said "probably will be as good as the bottom half of the ones we have regularly"[32] (now there's a ringing endorsement). Probably the most famous (or notorious, for those who are Pete Rose fans) of these guys was Dave Pallone, the first admittedly gay umpire who would be fired for incompetence — maybe — by NL president Bart Giamatti after a turbulent ten-year big-league career.
- A motley crew of local and amateur umpires.

As one might expect, a plethora of controversies swirled around the decisions or non-decisions that these guys made. A quartet assigned to a Mets-Giants game at Shea Stadium in late April reversed themselves twice en route to a compromise solution that caused both managers to protest the game.[33] May 9 was a seminal day: four managers, a coach, and five players were ejected as the result of a series of debatable calls and indecision.[34] Comments from players and managers about the problems jammed baseball's airwaves, and a crisis mood seemed to be descending upon the game.

Yet when viewed from a distance, the replacement umpires' impact on the game, detrimental or otherwise, is difficult to get a handle on — assuming that such an effect exists at all. The April 1979 batting and pitching statistics for both leagues are virtually identical to those in prior and succeeding seasons: no inordinate spikes in strikeouts, errors, or walks jump out at the modern day observer.[35] Perhaps the various and sundry rhubarbs seemed worse because people thought that they could latch onto a reason for them; in point of fact, the number of ejections and protested games did not increase while the fill-in umps were on the job.

When the leagues had mailed out their initial warning letter to the men in blue, MLUA president Luciano commented, "I guess they figure that we're all expendable and that they can walk into any bar, round up 52 guys and say, 'Hey, here's a blue suit, how about working our games?'"[36] Well, in essence that's exactly what baseball had done (and ironically what NL president Chub Feeney would say at a later date[37]) — and from an on-field perspective, they were getting by with it.

The public relations battle, though, was another matter altogether.

Phillips was not sitting idle as the season progressed without his men. Appreciating the strength that resides in numbers greater than 50, the association chief began contacting the local and national leaders of sister unions in search of support. It was a decidedly uphill battle. Labor leaders are pragmatic by nature — a sympathy strike for a handful of guys wearing nice suits who work six months out of the year is a tough sell to someone who's struggling to keep 10,000 Joe Lunchboxes in line and paying dues into a depleted strike fund. Recognizing this, Phillips made sure that his members were out on the picket lines and signing autographs whenever possible ... and if "whenever possible" meant "whenever the game in question was on national TV," well, so be it.

For those raised on yuppie dreams and dot-com-style workdays, unionism's tenacious hold on the minds and hearts of the era's common workingman is difficult to comprehend at anything beyond the stereotypical level. Our modern "through the looking glass darkly" view of organized labor at high noon tends to characterize its charges as lazy, casual about the quality of their work, and antagonistic towards anyone who worked in an office and wore a suit. There is some truth to these allegations, but at the same time:

• The typical yuppie might be amazed at exactly how fatiguing eight hours of frequently anaerobic labor in awkward positions is.
• The stuff they turned out may not have been as good in all cases as others may have wished, but it was apparently more than adequate to serve as the foundation for the economic boom that would take up most of the next two decades.
• The struggles, deprivations, and occasional physical pain that had been endured to obtain from companies such basic benefits as restroom breaks, an eight-hour workday, and machinery that didn't actively try to kill people were anything but ancient history to these folks.

Banding together, not extra effort or ingenuity, had won a lifestyle for common workers that their parents (many of whom had labored for the same companies in identical positions) could only have dreamed of. The changeover was just this side of miraculous to many and confirmed long-held suspicions about the so-called Captains of Industry for whom they toiled. Obviously, these guys had been holding out on their employees for years, the common wisdom held, and only unified action and a hard-nosed attitude had compelled them to share a modicum of the wealth. Furthermore, with news reports trumpeting ever-higher corporate profits, the potential pot for employees was seemingly bottomless.

Yet by late in the decade, this workers' utopia was in serious jeopardy for reasons that were as hazy and misunderstood as those that had brought about its rise. Inflation (which was really just the effect of one man paying for someone else's pay raise) had turned many work actions into rearguard attempts to maintain jobs and purchasing power. Wage hikes had often come at the expense of reinvestment (U.S. Steel in the late 1970s was still utilizing furnaces built by Andrew Carnegie some 80 years previous), and thus an increasing number of products and the jobs that went with them had effectively been exported to countries that had once been hard pressed to build a decent transistor radio. Whole communities were torn asunder as the jobs and public services that had emanated from the local mill as reliably as that odd yellowish dust that the company said was harmless began to slowly trickle away.

Organized labor's answer to this threat was to draw closer together, and as a result the 1970s had become the second "golden" era of the strike. Over 260 million man-days of labor were lost to work stoppages during the decade,[38] and many of them (like the four-month-long action against General Motors in 1970) had reached levels of ugliness not seen since the Depression.

These people represented the core of MLB's fan base, especially in the heavily industrialized cities of what would soon become known as the Rust Belt. By presenting themselves as regular working stiffs who were only asking for a modest pay hike and the opportunity to see their kids a couple of times during the season, Phillips's men were hitting the average fan/laborer with an easy-to-understand message, one that superseded any qualms about the tag that 50,000 people in the stands saw clearly but that blind SOB in blue somehow missed.

Attendance levels, especially in the heavily unionized cities of the East and Midwest, fell precipitously. A Saturday afternoon helmet giveaway in Pittsburgh attracted just 10,950 fans after local union presidents exhorted their members to not attend Pirates games.[39] A contest in Detroit was almost canceled after electricians and other tradesmen refused to cross the umpires' picket lines—a relenting by the picketing arbiters "for the good of the game" allowed it to go on.[40] Two local umpires' associations refused to provide its members for major league games.[41]

Despite occasional rumors to the contrary, owners are highly practical people. Recognizing that 50 men asking for $10,000 a year in raises represented peanuts in comparison to the sudden wave of empty seats, the two sides finally hammered out an agreement on May 17 that was more or less a capitulation by the owners. Phillips basically came away with everything he'd asked for: pay gains averaging $7,000 per man, an immediate 31 percent increase in hotel and meal money, two weeks' paid vacation after the first year of service, higher spring training per diems, improvements in the pension plan and more.[42]

The AAA guys who answered the call won as well, though theirs would be a bittersweet victory in certain ways. The new vacation schedule created the need for four additional umpires per league to cover the midseason absences, and these men were the ones chosen to fill the new positions. However, any illusions that their arbiter brethren would let bygones be bygones were quickly shattered: the Ostracized Eight, as they came to be known,[43] would suffer petty and not so petty indignities for years. Other umpires shunned them away from the diamond, delighted in reporting every slip-up they made to league headquarters, and left them strictly on their own in on-field disputes.[44] The Scarlet S would be attached to their names for years, and God help them if their equipment was left unguarded or arrived before they did.[45]

From baseball's perspective, the loss represented another bewildering example of how the inmates were increasingly taking over the asylum, but by the standards of their recent bouts with the players, the owners came out just fine, thank you. The incremental financial cost of the new contract wasn't huge (about $2.5 million over the pact's three-year life span[46]), and if the umpires and fans were happy, what was the big deal?

Well, of course it was a big deal for two reasons:

1. As a result of the negotiations, the individual contracts that had sparked the action in the first place were replaced with a pattern agreement with salaries based solely upon seniority—in other words, a traditional industrial setup where the operators effectively "hire" the union to provide employees. Under such a structure, an employer's ability to unilaterally discipline or fire workers is severely constricted; pretty much everything has to be done in conjunction with a union representative whose business is to keep his guy employed and paying his dues.

    It's easy to see where this argument is going. With an aggressive negotiator like Phillips in the union's corner, baseball's ability to deal with even the most obviously recalcitrant arbiter came to a standstill. Under such circumstances, growing waistlines, strike zones in the eye of the beholder, and personalities that impacted on-field decisions were a natural.

2. One man's chump change can often represent another's banquet, and whoever lines up that feast is immediately in line for demigod status. The 52 arbiters' annualized gains were barely enough to cover Rod Carew's new

contract with the Angels, yet the $10,000 increase in total benefits that Phillips negotiated for the umpires represented a 25-30 percent boost for most of these guys ... and that's real money in anybody's league. As a consequence of this, the union chief developed a following among umpires that was just this side of fanatical. Men like Eric Gregg, Richie Garcia, and Country Joe West, whose names would figure prominently in the 2000 strike, were veterans of the 1979 action, and their devotion to the union chief was made clear both in their public utterances and their actions.

Perhaps the strike's greatest impact was on Phillips himself. From a financial perspective, his activities on behalf of the umpires turned out to be something of a minor bonanza. Normally speaking, a union leader is hired by the members at a fixed price, in essence becoming an employee of the association. Phillips, however, took the arbiters' cause on a contingency basis, accepting 5 percent of whatever he got for them as a fee — which turned him a tidy $250,000 payday over the contract's three-year duration.[47]

From a psychological standpoint, his 1979 experiences appear to have strongly — and irreparably — shaped Phillips's outlook on the game in general and his adversaries in particular. Like many old-school trade unionists, Phillips believed that an adversarial relationship with management was the ticket to extracting the maximum amount of benefits. It was also apparent that the owners viewed his members as small potatoes in the grand scheme of things, meaning that further large concessions both in economic and psychological terms were attainable as long as everything stayed within limits.

It was this final point that would ultimately trip the MLUA up. As the song says, "The times they are a-changin," and in point of fact Phillips's action was initiated at virtually the last possible moment at which it could have been received so well. The unions and the companies that they served were (to maintain the musical motif) fighting the Law — that is, the law of global economics— and during the early 1980s, the Law won with a vengeance. Union rolls would decline by nearly three million members over the next decade[48] as members' job migrated first to Japan, then Korea, then to a spectrum of Southeast Asian nations where three squares a day and running water represented a middle-class lifestyle. Baseball's fan base metamorphisized as well, with rising ticket and concession prices driving Joe Sixpack out of the stands in favor of the suburban professional and his kids— in short, the oppressor whom workers were perpetually trying to rebel against. Caught in a John L. Lewis-style time warp, Phillips's tactics began to seem more bombastic, arrogant, and counterproductive, though in reality they were exactly the same ones he'd utilized two decades before. The umpires' final fall in 2000 was lauded by virtually everyone in a manner that surprised no one but the arbiters themselves ... yet for five years and more, such an ultimate fate had been obvious to all but the most casual observer.

Still, all of this turmoil was far in the future. For now the umpires had broken free from the chains that had bound them to the owners' whims since the game's creation. As with Hitler in Munich, only the most prescient observer could have forecast the two decades of heady times, swelling salaries, and inflated egos that would follow — along with the faint, distant storm clouds that would signal their ultimate demise.

36

The Roman Umpire

The 1970s were the golden era of the anti-whatever. Anti-war, anti-establishment, anti-nuke: everybody seemed to be hellbent to break out of whatever molds previous generations had made for people of their ilk. Clint Eastwood achieved a huge international following as an anti-hero willing to bend the law and morality into pretzels as the mood struck him. Jimmy Carter ran counter to every presidential prototype: he was Southern with a capital S, lacked political experience at the national level, donned sweaters and blue jeans whenever possible, and seemed kindly whenever he wasn't talking about whipping Ted Kennedy's ass.

In the umpiring business, the Jimmy Carter of the 1970s was an ex-Detroit Lions linebacker named Ron Luciano.

The so-called Roman Umpire was everything that arbiters were not supposed to be. A naturally gregarious man, he was constantly doing things that made him part of the scene while prompting memos from the league office to the effect that fans did not come out to see Ron Luciano arbitrate.[1] His method of "shooting" players out (adopted to compensate for a mental block regarding Royals outfielder Amos Otis[2]) rather than giving them the traditional thumb was both distinctive and controversial, with Kansas City shortstop Freddie Patek, among others, feeling "shown up" by the amateur theatrics.

Never at a loss for a gesture, Luciano began calling Patek out by lobbing phantom hand grenades at him.[3]

As the second base umpire one night, he positioned himself in short center field with the goal of talking good guy center fielder Mickey Stanley out of retiring.[4] He would chat with fans between innings, accepting food and soft drinks from them. On one memorable occasion the inning started with Luciano by the stands with a hot dog and soda in hand. Upon noticing that the game had resumed, the arbiter ran back to his position, made a call on a close play at third—and in so doing tossed his soda all over the front of George Brett's uniform.[5]

An ejection machine in the minors,[6] Luciano mellowed by the time he'd

Opposite and above: In yet another rendition of what he called, in his book *The Umpire Strikes Back,* "La Ballet de l'Umpire," Ron Luciano struts his stuff during a Red Sox vs. A's game in the mid-1970s. (*The Sporting News*)

reached the Show to the point that he was anything but the typical overblown authority figure that fans and players have grow to know and loathe. If long-time National League umpire Doug Harvey was known as God, Luciano was Puck — above the realm of normal humankind, but with an impish streak that probably got him sent to stand in one of Valhalla's corners from time to time. He was constantly talking with players during the game, chatting about restaurants (a favored topic that began to tell in his later years), the opposition, what a jerk the manager was— he'd even do it while they were at bat, which had to be wonderful for the ol' concentration.[7] When a manager would come out to argue a call, the Roman Umpire would affect the same manner-ism, turning a potential thumb into an animated (from the fan's point of view) discussion about the weather, inflation, hunger in sub-tropical Africa, whatever.[8] On days when he was having trouble calling balls and strikes,

Luciano would address the problem by having the catcher do so; an immediate throwback to the pitcher was a ball, holding the horsehide for a split second longer was a strike.[9]

Above all else, Luciano delighted in furnishing reporters with an interesting quote or two or ten. Despite the jovial Friar Tuck image painted in his books, the burly umpire was not above holding a grudge or letting everybody know which ones he held. He thought Alex Johnson should have been banned from the game ("He came up to home plate one time and said 'My gawd, what an awful smell' and then he looked right at me"[10]). Bill North was "a definite black hat, because no matter where the pitch is, if he doesn't swing at it, it's a ball." Jim Palmer was what he termed "a surveyor ... as he lets go of the ball, he starts peering down at us suspiciously, and we haven't even called the pitch yet. If you call it a ball, he gives you that dying swan act."[11]

Then there was Earl Weaver.

Ron had a mutual abomination society going with the Baltimore manager. He couldn't stand Weaver's frequently spit-laced tirades (Luciano once commented that Earl "knows every word in the English language that starts with a 'P'"[12]) as well as his penchant for crowd-inciting histrionics. In this Luciano was merely echoing the sentiments of virtually every other umpire in Creation; after all, it's tough to admire a man who routinely entertained the Memorial Stadium faithful with such antics as theatrically shredding a rule book, then sprinkling the remains at the umpires' feet.[13] Weaver, for his part, felt that Luciano was an unprofessional arbiter who spent too much time talking and not enough concentrating on getting into position to make good calls[14]—a sentiment that was not unheard of among other managers either. The difference was that both of these men were prone to say whatever came into their heads at any time, and thus the Luciano-Weaver feud spilled into the national press.

Weaver was quoted as saying that Luciano was the most inept umpire in the majors.[15] Luciano countered by saying that every umpire in the AL hated Weaver and looked for excuses to thumb him. Hypersensitive to the slightest hint of conspiracy,[16] Weaver countercharged that the umpires, and Luciano in particular, biased their calls against the Orioles.[17] Luciano said that he never slanted his decisions against anyone, while adding, "I don't care who wins the pennant as long as it isn't Baltimore."[18]

Ultimately the press war devolved into a bare-knuckle battle, with each man screaming at the other. Ron was ultimately taken off of Baltimore games, and Weaver cemented his reputation as "the worst enemy umpires ever had."[19]

Luciano's ability as an umpire is a matter of some debate. In a 1974 player survey, the Syracuse University grad was one of two AL umps to receive an "excellent" rating, yet the man's skills were obviously impacted by Eric Gregg/John McSherry disease (Ron admitted to carrying 300 pounds on his 6'4" frame) in his later years.[20] Durwood Merrill believed that the strain of keeping up the act and umpiring at the same time ultimately became too much — "It got to where the fans expected a circus performance every night out of Ronnie," Merrill wrote in *You're Out And You're Ugly Too*.[21] Continuously in hot water with the league office (the fact that he was MLUA president during the 1979 strike probably didn't help matters any) Luciano was essentially forced to retire at 42.

His after-umpiring life has the melancholy overtones that so many athletes' lives have. Luciano became a color commentator for NBC but was fired after one season, his lack of discipline being just as obvious in the broadcast booth as it was on the field.[22] He wrote a series of books about his and fellow arbiters' experiences, continuing to do so until he ran out of anecdotes. Finally, on January 18, 1995, the self-anointed Roman Umpire went into the closed garage of his Endicott, New York, home and started his car, ending his life via carbon monoxide poisoning at the age of 57.[23]

His legacy in the game, like that of many pioneers who were in reality regular guys that just happened to wander away from the pack, is paradoxical. To an extent, one could argue that union chief Richie Phillips's drive to wrest control of the arbiters' futures from the leagues was inspired by Luciano's experience — clearly, outspokenness, unorthodox methods of umpiring, and expanding waistlines became more accepted in the years following the Roman Umpire's demise. Yet, sadly, the man's sense of humor and natural liveliness were discarded in the translation, making the succeeding generation's errors of the mouth, eye, and flesh even more insufferable to fans and management alike.

Look at it this way — Jimmy Carter lasted only one term himself....

37

Willie Stargell and the Evolution of the African American Player

Some baseball players achieve greatness through titanic home runs, lofty batting averages, and clutch performances at key moments in their teams' histories. A select few of those bring an innate humanity and dignity to the game as well, elevating their team's play while enriching the lives of those they come in contact with. In the highest and most hallowed pantheon, though, are the men who reach the pinnacle of athletic and spiritual excellence — and then find a way to exceed even that.

Wilver Stargell was one of those men.

He's the kind of guy who historians a century from now are going to have a tough time getting a handle on. An unemotional review of his statistics suggests he is someone who, while qualified for Hall of Fame enshrinement, simply isn't the slam-dunk first ballot guy that Wilver was in 1988. Sure, Stargell won an MVP Award, was named to seven All-Star teams, led the league in homers twice plus slugging percentage, doubles, and RBIs once apiece, but so what? Jim Rice did that and more while playing a superior left field (at least superior to Stargell), and nobody's etching his visage in bronze just yet. The only categories in which Stargell ranks among the top 25 all-time are homers and strikeouts— and with Jeff Bagwell, Frank Thomas, and Juan Gonzalez hot on his tail, Pops' top drawer dinger status won't last too much longer.

Furthermore, Willie's 1979 MVP is more than a little squirrelly. OK, so his team won and he was a terrifically motivational guy, but let's get real: Stargell was a 39-year-old defensive zero who may have been terrific with the wood (32 homers, 82 RBIs in 424 at-bats) when available but couldn't answer the call 30 percent of the time. That such a player could be superior to the in-their-prime Steve Garvey (.315 28 110) and Dave Winfield (.308 34 118) is prima facie absurd, not to mention co-MVP Keith Hernandez (.344 11 105) or Cy Young Award winner Bruce Sutter (a 2.23 ERA in Wrigley Field plus 37 saves). Heck, with the pre-drug inhibited Dave Parker's bat (.310 25 94) and arm in right field, it's questionable whether Pops was even the best player on his own team.

Having said all of that, there is still something decidedly right about Stargell's preeminence in both the 1979 and 1988 balloting. While the Angry Men in many ways embodied the worst of baseball's "coming of age" experience in the 1970s, Stargell represented the best: a man who out of adversity achieved a level of personal development that exceeded all expectations. Perhaps it was primarily a personal triumph (his "Pops" act, however inspirational it was, didn't keep the Bucs from ultimately losing their way in a drug induced haze) and certainly not as heroic as the struggles of those who came a generation before him. Yet in a quiet way Willie's capacity to grow beyond what his forebears were capable of conceiving reflected a new maturity in this sometimes-troubled game — a beacon, if you will, that others could follow.

Of course, it didn't start out that way....

Part African-American, part Native American (now there's a combination sure to tickle any bigot's fancy), Stargell was born in Oklahoma but raised in Alameda, California, alongside such future big leaguers as Frank Robinson, Joe Morgan, Vada Pinson, Curt Flood, and Tommy Harper.[1] It was a good place for a black kid to grow up, granting that the meaning of "good place" was relative amidst the escalating racial tension that characterized the *Leave it to Beaver* days. Demonstrating a typical level of sensitivity for the era, the Pirates first assigned this scrawny (Willie didn't become the big bopper we remember until 1962[2]) kid to a league that covered New Mexico and West Texas. While not possessing the Deep South's *Mississippi Burning* reputation, indignities like segregated hotels and restaurants, slurs casually tossed off the lips of upstanding citizens, and the occasional shotgun pointed at your head[3] were part and parcel of life in those parts — and such experiences nearly broke the young Stargell.

There were basically two ways for an African-American to make his way under such circumstances: stand up for his rights and humanity until he ended up on the business end of a tire iron, or maintain as low a profile as possible in the hope that at least some of the yahoos will fail to notice him.

Wilver, having the prerequisite number of brain cells firing at the same time, chose the latter course, as did most promising young black men of his day regardless of whether reticence was a natural personality characteristic. Branch Rickey's "turn the other cheek" admonishment to the young Jackie Robinson is well known, but it may surprise some to know that Frank Robinson was considered to be a very soft-spoken fellow until about 1970 — tough as nails on the field perhaps, but a real model citizen off it. Bob Gibson, who privately seethed at every slight,[4] was seen as quiet to the point of near-obtuseness before winning the 1968 Cy Young Award. Bill White was a reticent man while active on the field, Maury Wills was known as "The Mouse" before he discovered Doris Day,[5] and Henry Aaron's trials have already been discussed. The point is that none of these guys were understated by nature, yet they adopted such a front (and exacerbated their frustration with the world in the process) because that's the price people with natural suntans paid in those days for success.

Thus, the young Stargell became something of a pacifist — an attitude that may have eased his way through life but had a limiting effect on his baseball career. Not that Wilver (note the name: that's how Stargell signed it at the time, as if using the diminutive Willie would have represented a self-imposed slight) didn't put plenty of effort into the game. It's just that his regimen mirrored that of Boog Powell: play hard during the season, relax after it, and never pass up a wayward piece of pie. Excess tonnage and less than stellar defensive instincts left Stargell mightily stretched to cover Pittsburgh's cavernous left field, thus forcing him to repeatedly sacrifice his body for the play too far. The physical cost was horrendous: two ruined knees and a series of bumps, strains and breaks (he nearly lost his eyesight running face first into the Forbes Field scoreboard[6]) that kept him from ever playing as many as 150 games in a season.

Offensively, his early seasons were a succession of prodigious hot streaks followed by incredible slumps. A left-handed muscleman in one of the toughest parks ever constructed for a hitter of his type, Stargell's game made two-steps-forward-one-step-back-or-vice-versa headway during the late 1960s. He was easy pickings for southpaws (Stargell once commented that he was one for nine against sidearmer Joe Hoerner — one hit in nine seasons[7]), his huge swing produced monstrous strikeout totals, and with Willie's wheels it took two hits and Don Baylor's throwing arm to get him home from first.[8]

The Pirates' clubhouse leader in those days was Roberto Clemente, a man whose reputation (like that of Elvis Presley, John F. Kennedy, and the Studebaker *Avanti*) has benefited from the fact that he died before his time. Not that Clemente wasn't a truly great player or a humanitarian on a level that few even aspire to, but ... well, let's just say that personality wasn't necessarily one of Roberto's strong points. A man of stereotypical Latino passion and temperament, Clemente had a volcanic way of expressing his grievances that was, to put it mildly, off-putting to many reporters.[9] As a consequence of this, the Pirate right fielder consistently received bad press: he was lazy, not team oriented, a whiner who milked every injury and injustice for all it was worth.

With thirty years of perspective we understand (or believe we understand) the tremendous professional, cultural, and personal pressures that Clemente was under and thus characterize these contemporary evaluations as the petty railings of a Neanderthal press corps. Still, these people were not predisposed against Latino superstars; they simply weren't crazy about being loudly berated at the drop of a less-than-fawning question. They didn't like habitually being accused of racism. They found it tough to admire a man who considered anyone who didn't think he was the greatest player on Earth to be an SOB.[10]

Yet for all of that, Clemente was anything but another Angry Man. He cared deeply about the game as well as his performance, and thus maintained a rigorous training regimen (some of which was just this side of witch doctory[11]) to his dying day. Many contemporaries' anger at injustice drove them to despair and bitterness; Roberto's made him charter the DC-7 that was supposed to fly relief supplies to earthquake-stricken Nicaragua but instead became his tomb.[12] No one was quicker to provide kind words or solid advice as necessary to young Pirates.

It's hard to tell exactly how much Willie gleaned from this turbulent role model, but there is evidence that Clemente's act — for better or worse — at least partly rubbed off on the younger man. Between Roberto's example and

A mature Willie (no longer Wilver) Stargell in the days of the Fam-i-lee. (*National Baseball Hall of Fame Library, Cooperstown, NY*)

talks with such luminaries as Aaron and Willie Mays, Stargell's dedication and intensity level rose dramatically: the former was a good thing, the latter a mixed blessing. He started to keep his up-to-date offensive statistics in his helmet, referring to them before each at bat.[13] He became touchy when people asked him about his weight or his troubles with lefties. When a trio of white guys won MVP Awards while Stargell was producing back-to-back-to-back seasons that were just about as good as anyone could possibly want (averaging 42 homers, 119 RBIs and a .296 average in a pitcher's era), Willie bitterly played the race card.[14] It was a performance that few of the reporters in attendance would soon forget. Sure, Stargell's comments were nothing compared to the vitriol that Dick Allen would spout off whenever things seemed too comfortable around him, but there you have it: yet another Angry Man in the making.

To compound the matter, Stargell's professional and personal lives were about to go into a tailspin. Wrist and shoulder problems took a big bite out of Willie's power in 1974, while a broken rib did much the same the following year. In May 1976 Stargell's wife Delores was diagnosed with a blood clot on the brain; the next season he was limited to 63 games by a pinched nerve in his elbow suffered while breaking up an on-field fight.[15]

Under similar circumstances, a Dick Allen might well have unloaded his tension on whomever or whatever was handy. A Reggie Jackson would attempt to obscure his emotions within a fog of bombast and bluster. A Henry Aaron would redouble his efforts to become Jackie Robinson's successor. As for Stargell, he somehow found the strength to bury the racial hatchet without the lingering anger that characterized Clemente, embrace the team captain role that he'd balked at after the Hall of Famer's death, and overall become something more than what he had been.

There was nothing radical or particularly noteworthy about this transformation; certainly the qualities that characterized the elder statesman had always been in evidence at some level. Yet in a game where the cry of "what's in it for me?" was being uttered all too often, a man who was obviously comfortable with himself and his place in the world was of immense value both for the Pirates and baseball as a whole.

Willie became more accepting of his own weaknesses, more willing to tease and be teased (in honor of his mammoth strikeout totals the Pittsburgh writers presented a smiling Stargell with a bat that had a hole in the barrel[16]), and more accessible to young players facing the pressures of sudden stardom. He became "Pops": one would have to believe that the younger Wilver might have rolled his eyes (privately, of course) at such a figure ... but then again maybe not, as the older man was in fact hatched from the younger one.

And God knows that the Bucs needed that kind of leadership.

The Pirates in the late 1970s had become baseball's answer to the Molotov cocktail — an unholy mix of attitudes, kooks, and "delicate" types who played poor fundamental baseball, viewed Pittsburgh management with barely disguised contempt, and comported themselves like something out of *Animal House*. The number of "handle with kid gloves" types bordered on the ridiculous: John Candelaria, Jerry Reuss, Terry Forster, Goose Gossage, Bert Blyleven, Al Oliver, Bill Madlock, Dave Parker. The bench was filled to overflowing with one-time regulars on their last legs (Bobby Tolan, Jim Fregosi, Tommy Helms, Ed Kirkpatrick), and the effects of age and several heart attacks had noticeably slowed longtime skipper Danny Murtaugh.

It was the kind of situation that cried out for a Gene Mauch-type of manager, someone with

1. Enough of a disciplinary streak to get the team focused on the job at hand (though the Pirates would have revolted if a Dick Williams had taken the reins),
2. The ability to sort out the talent and utilize it within its capabilities, and
3. A strong tactical sense and attention to detail.

Instead, they got the Good Humor man.

Chuck Tanner was a terrifically nice fellow and a decent manager when given a roster where the decisions about who was and wasn't going to play were clear-cut. However, Tanner's Dick Allen experience had amply demonstrated that he wasn't anybody who was going to tell people to lose weight, or send a kid with an overactive mouth to the minors for reality therapy, or threaten a veteran with professional extinction if he didn't shape up. A Dale Carnegie poster boy-type, Tanner's philosophy was to send his eight best horses out there as often as their health permitted, and if they had a good year they'd win, and if not — well, at least they'd have fun.

Given that the Pirate players were already having enough fun to place their livers and other sundry bodily organs in grave danger, this was an obvious recipe for disaster — yet, after pushing the Phillies to the wall in 1978, the Pirates somehow managed to win it all the next season.

The 1979 Pirates were in many ways an odd team. Pittsburgh led the league in runs scored despite having no one who drove in as many as 100 runs and only two guys who topped 80. Nobody on the staff won as many as 15 games though six guys had ten or more victories and winning records. Heck, none of the key players except Kent Tekulve even had a particularly good year by their standards. But, nobody stunk up the joint and the bench (headed by John "The Hammer" Milner who cranked out 16 homers in half-time play) was superb. The bullpen was deep in quality pitchers having good seasons. And just coincidentally, Willie Stargell had his last reasonably healthy season.

How much additional value, if any, did this moderately overweight, middle-aged black guy who pinned stars on people's caps possess vis-à-vis some anonymous player who could hit 32 homers in 424 at-bats plus five more in the postseason? The typical "buy me some peanuts and Cracker Jack" fan would probably argue that Stargell's emotional impact was immense given that the Pirates collectively tanked once Pops' body started giving out in 1980. The more sophisticated *Baseball Tonight* crowd would counter by saying that a club with the oldest roster in the majors and enough head and nose cases to fill a ward at Bellevue was destined to crash and burn no matter how many Sister Sledge albums anybody played for them.

Well, there is plenty of truth in the old adage that intangible benefits usually are that way because they really don't exist ... but it is also true that there's normally something to even the hairiest old wives' tale. While the Fam-i-lee was an old team with several key players (Stargell, Bill Robinson, and Jim Rooker) on their last legs:

- Mike Easler (a career .293 hitter with power and walks) and Lee Lacy (would hit over .300 in four of the next five seasons) were on the 1979 bench.

- Rick Rhoden (he'd win 79 games for the Bucs over the next seven seasons) was cooling his heels in the bullpen.

- Johnny Ray (a very fine but virtually forgotten second baseman who hit

.290 lifetime and finished in the top 10 in hits four times) and Tony Pena (a five time All-Star and four time Gold Glove winning catcher) were a year or so away in the minors.

What's more, the majority of the roster — old or not — had plenty of quality miles left. The pitching staff had an eyelash shy of 600 wins in front of them which, while nowhere near a record, is a more than respectable total. As for the offensive players: Bill Madlock had a couple of batting titles in his future; The Cobra (Parker) had over 200 homers and an MVP near miss ahead of him; Scrap Iron Garner would make a couple of All-Star appearances and become a valuable member of Houston's 1986 division-winners; and as we've already seen, there was plenty of quality talent either riding the pines or about to emerge.

Yet despite all of these assets, this incarnation of the Pirates would never seriously challenge again. Yes, the recreational substance use had something to do with it, but pretty much every team had a drug problem by this time — the Bucs simply came equipped with the biggest mouths. In terms of clubhouse harmony, half the Yankee roster at this time was slipping bombs into the pockets of the other half and it didn't stop them from winning a championship or two. As for Tanner, if someone like Harvey Kuenn could take the Milwaukee Brewers to the Series, well....

Yes, a number of issues conspired to sidetrack Pittsburgh after 1979 — and yes, and the lack of a true clubhouse leader (someone who could be depended upon for equilibrium as well as a key hit) was definitely one of the most important.

In the bittersweet way of most icons, Stargell's post-career years were anticlimatic. Willie drifted into coaching, ultimately tagging along with Tanner to Atlanta once the Pirates had crashed and burned. For whatever reason, Pops never quite clicked in the role, perhaps because the boundary line between "veteran leader" and "old fogey" is a perilously thin one. Willie's wife, whose near-death experience had conspired to ruin his 1976 season, left him. Finally, he returned to the Pirates as a vice president of nothing in particular and came down with a kidney ailment that rendered him inactive for the last couple of years of his life.

Even then, the man's positive demeanor and dignity shone through: despite being obviously ill Stargell never struck people as a man who either wanted — or more importantly, needed — their pity.

In many ways Wilver Stargell wasn't that titanic a figure. His contributions outside to the statistical record are the types that do not lend themselves to easy comprehension or praise. At base, he was simply a man who combined maturity, grace and physical skill at a time when baseball's on-field supply of the former two qualities was in perilously short supply. In a turbulent, troubled game, that was a significant accomplishment — and one that functioned as a ray of hope for the game's future.

Epilogue: August 9, 1979

Some eras die before they officially end. The Roaring '20s, for example, came to a screeching halt with the stock market crash of October 29, 1929. Though the decade had two months to go, the "brother can you spare a dime" '30s were officially under way as of that moment. Marilyn Monroe faded from the scene with 1960 filming of *The Misfits*, given that the remaining two years of her life would produce little more than a semi-scandalous appearance at President Kennedy's 1961 birthday party. One could almost feel the air come out of the Oakland A's after Kirk Gibson's ninth-inning homer in Game 1 of the 1988 World Series. While the series would drag on for four more games, there was no subsequent moment at which any onlooker really got the feeling that the A's were going to get back into the affair.

Thus it was not surprising (and mildly ironic) when on August 9, 1979, a page of baseball history was turned, not on some emerald playing field, but in a Rochester, Minnesota, hospital room.

It was in that room that Walter Francis O'Malley drew his last breath.

O'Malley had made it to 75 before succumbing to cancer, a miracle given the man's passion for cigars and his family's predilection for the dreaded disease. Yet what passed simultaneously with him was the last major link to a more genteel (if robber-baronish) era of baseball management, one where contract negotiations had been 30-minute affairs, attendance drove financial success, and a healthy minor league system was the cornerstone of successful operations.

It was a game the Dodger panjandrum had played better and more aggressively than anyone else. He grasped early on the demographic shifts that would ultimately have turned his quaint Ebbets Field home into Brooklyn's answer to Fort Apache — The Bronx. He leveraged his franchise's marquee value to build a stadium on 351 prime acres overlooking the center of Los Angeles at minimal out-of-pocket cost (with a big assist from the city and a $10 million advance from Union Oil[1]). He'd pushed for baseball's initial expansion to ten teams, then profited mightily by assessing a $350,000 fee on the expansion Angels for "playing rights to the Los Angeles market."[2]

He was legendarily tight where salaries were concerned. Two decades before Andy Messersmith asked for a no-trade clause, O'Malley had gazed out his office window and told raise-seeking ticket manager Harold Parrott that "a lot of 46-year-old guys down there wouldn't mind having your job."[3] After an O'Malley comment to the effect that he'd lost $2 million since Buzzie Bavasi had forsaken the Dodgers for a partial ownership position in the San Diego Padres, Buzzie smiled — he knew that Walter's "loss" was actually just $2 million less profit.[4] Walter Alston managed the club to seven pennants and four world championships in 23 years, each under a one-year contract.[5]

Yet at the same time O'Malley was squeezing his employees, the man was forever reinvesting in his business. The Dodgers were the first team to own an airplane. Dodger Stadium was kept immaculate and advertising-free save the obligatory Union 76 signs on the scoreboards. The farm system was heaped with benefits by the standards of the day, both in terms of young players and state-of-the-art facilities.

Yet the Walter O'Malley who contemplated death on that August day must have been somewhat amused (O'Malley was far too shrewd and realistic to have anything surprise him) by the changes that had overtaken the game to which he had given so much and received so much back from in return.

Baseball's newly high-powered economics had driven an almost complete turnover of the cast that had assembled in Bal Harbor some ten years earlier. Horace Stoneham, the often inebriated Giants owner whose willingness to move with O'Malley spurred the game's westward migration, had effectively been in semi-retirement for years (allowing a cabal of Irish cronies to run the team) before selling out to real estate magnate Bob Lurie in 1976. Joan Payson, whose money filled the void O'Malley and Stoneham had left behind in New York, had passed away in 1977; her daughter, Lorinda DeRoulet, headed the team for a couple of years before passing the helm to printing magnate Nelson Doubleday. Both C. Arnholdt Smith and Roy Hofheintz had bankrupted and run afoul of the law in the process (Smith, known as Mr. San Diego, was a minor character in the Watergate scandals). Even where the name was the same, the face had changed; while a Galbraith still ruled in Pittsburgh, a Wrigley in Chicago, and a Carpenter in Philadelphia, it was the next generation that was now running the show — and all of the above would sell their teams within two years.

Assuming their thrones was a core of hard-case businessmen: the bombastic Steinbrenner, the perpetual-motion machine Ted Turner, cable TV pioneer John McMullen in Houston (Doubleday was about to make moves in that direction as well), McDonald's architect Ray Kroc, Texas oilman Eddie Chiles. Waiting in the wings were Oakland's Haas family (Levi-Strauss) and the Chicago *Tribune*. In operational terms these men were the literal descendants of Walter O'Malley, yet for all their similarities there were two significant differences between this new ownership generation and the old lion who lay dying in Rochester:

1. O'Malley's end was baseball, while the new generation saw the game as a means to an end. Previous to buying the Braves for $12 million prior to the 1976 season, Ted Turner knew virtually nothing about the game save the fact that it provided three-plus hours of programming 60 days a year to his WTCG (now WTBS) UHF station. What he did know, however, was that he had been paying $600,000 a year for the right to broadcast those games,[6] and as expensive as that was, relatively speaking, sports represented first-run entertainment at a fraction of the cost of having Norman Lear invent a series. In addition, with no competing franchise within 400 miles, the Braves had an opportunity to become a regional ratings powerhouse ... assuming that Turner could get his station's signal out to those prospective fans in the hinterlands.

   A 1972 FCC ruling that allowed cable television operators to import signals from selected stations in the nation's top 100 television markets provided the opportunity,[7] while an explosion in available satellite capacity for forwarding a station's signal economically and reliably represented the means to exploit the FCC edict. By 1979, two-thirds of WTCG's audience resided outside of Georgia, and Turner's reach was growing by an estimated 100,000 households per month.[8] The problem, from baseball's standpoint, however, was that many of those new potential viewers resided in traditional feeder markets for other teams.

   The superstation/cable TV battleground would become one of the major points of contention within ownership ranks during the 1980s. Baseball's attitude towards broadcast rights had traditionally been bifurcated, with revenues from local broadcasting accruing solely to the individual club while national monies were distributed evenly. The rapid expansion of local cable TV operations along with their voracious appetite for programming, however, made this distinction obsolete: clearly, any signal that was offered for free (as Turner's was) was going to be welcomed with open arms in Tupelo, Tacoma, or wherever. As a result of this conundrum, Commissioner Kuhn would forge an unholy alliance with other sports, the big three networks, and Hollywood to try and gain control of superstation transmissions via a requirement that their consent be given before such programming could be distributed.[9]

   Kuhn's stance was honorable and even visionary to an extent, but a course of action that pitted the game against its largest and most influential backers was nearsighted at the least. Clearly the commissioner didn't intend to grant consent for any transmissions outside a team's geographical market without compensation to the other teams, a nightmarish stance from a morality/PR viewpoint that allowed the Turners and *Tribunes* of the world to position themselves as defenders of a free and unfettered media.[10]

   It also, though Bowie apparently refused to recognize the fact for some time, served as the final nail in his baseball stewardship's coffin. Kuhn's

actions over the years had produced an enemies list that ran the gamut
from Steinbrenner (the commissioner had suspended him twice) to Baltimore's Edward Bennett Williams (Bowie's outspoken desire to return
baseball to Washington was unlikely play well with someone who owned
a franchise 35 miles up the road). Adding Turner and his ilk to that list
resulted in an insurmountable obstacle when the commissioner's contract came up for renewal in 1983.[11]

The disproportionate influence of television revenues on certain teams'
bottom lines would contribute mightily to the spiraling salary inflation
that plagues baseball to this day. In any business the most profitable
operators are the ones who can spread their costs over the largest number of units—in fact, if a company's scale of production is large enough,
they can even get away with an Edsel-sized goof or two and come out
just fine. Conversely, one could also make the argument that as a result
of their increased market, each machine, player, or whatever that a large
operator obtains is more valuable to him than to a mom-and-pop business. Even if the big guy does overpay a bit, his scale of operation is such
that he can accept a lower margin per admission/cup of beer/logoed T-
shirt and still come away with a bigger pile of bucks due to his volume.

2. Though intelligent, action-oriented, and quick on the draw with a checkbook, the new breed had a lot to learn about operating baseball teams.
The Yankees' early success in the free agent market had turned the annual
reentry draft into something of a circus, with even the most dubious of
players receiving enormous sums as teams tried to improve themselves
without expending talent to do so.

Consider the 1979 draft: 44 players went the free agent route that season, running the gamut from superstars (Nolan Ryan) to decent veterans (Bob Watson) to guys on their last legs (Don Kessinger). It was
anything but a deep talent pool: other than Ryan, the best pitchers in
the draft were a couple of closers (Al Hrabosky and Don "Stan the Man
Unusual" Stanhouse) plus Dave Goltz, a 30-year-old Twins right-hander who was the Brad Radke of his era. The offensive pickings were even
leaner, with the aging sluggers Watson (a onetime catcher who'd evolved
into a Tino Martinez-type first baseman) and Tony Perez representing
the best catches, along with Greg Gross, a slap-hitting outfielder who
lacked the arm to play center.

In short, not a lot to get excited about, yet given the financial standards
of the time, some of these people made out like bandits.

• John Curtis, a 31-year-old left-hander who'd improbably won 10 games
while posting a 4.17 ERA as a hybrid starter/reliever in Candlestick Park,
received $1.8 million for five years from the San Diego Padres. No mat-
ter that the man had a 67-72 career record or that he'd never been able
to hold a rotation spot for more than a season and a half; the magic
words were *free agent* and *left-handed*.

The $1.8 million lavished on Curtis would buy 22 wins over the next five seasons for the Padres and Angels.

- Milt May, a 28-year-old catcher who'd stayed healthy enough to play as many as 120 games once in his ten-year career, got $1.4 million from the Giants over five years. May would catch an average of 102 games a season for the Giants over the next three years before falling into backup catcher limbo. Offensively, he'd give them an average of six homers and 38 RBIs per season through 1982.
- Rudy May, yet another southpaw (ah, to be born left-handed) who'd been pitching since 1965 and had posted 93 2/3 quality relief innings for the Montreal Expos, knocked down $1 million from the Yankees for three years with a $250,000 signing bonus.[12] May did give the Bronx Bombers one good season as a spot starter, but after that ... well, the man was 35, so what did George really expect?[13]

Ironically, it was O'Malley's Dodgers— or at least his son's Dodgers— who were fated to make the biggest splash in this winter's free agent market. With the old man buried, the organization loosened the purse strings to the tune of $3.1 million for Goltz's services over the next six seasons and $2.1 million for Stanhouse over five years.[14]

Unfortunately for the Dodgers, this initial foray into the free agent market was fated to be a flop of *Heaven's Gate* proportions. Goltz's 1979 double booby prize of leading the American League in hits allowed while his ERA jumped by over a run and a half foretold of a fastball that was losing velocity; he would post a 7-11 record in 1980 with a 4.11 ERA and never regain his effectiveness. Stanhouse would fare worse due to the funky mechanics that had caused him to spend seven seasons bouncing between the minors and majors before getting it together as a closer with the Expos.[15] Under pressure to perform, his motion came undone again — trying to bull his way through the problem, Stan the Man Unusual's back and shoulder gave way.[16] As a result, Stanhouse would work only one inning at the major league level after 1980.

Alarmed by this overwhelming lack of performance for higher pay, baseball's ownership cabal began searching for opportunities to stuff the free agency genie back into its bottle as the current Basic Agreement drew to its conclusion. Their initial proposal as presented to the players in November 1979 was a straightforward attempt to gut the Messersmith-McNally decision. The owners wanted to do away not only with salary arbitration but indeed with the whole concept of individual contracts, substituting a fixed salary scale that in essence said that if the players really were a union, they should be paid in the manner of a union. If putting them on a pay scale didn't adequately dampen their urge to change teams, management also wanted to compel an organization acquiring a free agent to give the losing club compensation in terms of major league-caliber players.[17]

The game's Player Relations Committee almost certainly wasn't deluded enough to expect that all or even a significant percentage of these goals were achievable. Given how the talks went, their tactics appear similar to those used by Dwight Eisenhower during World War II: Ike would propose grandiose schemes only to strike a conciliatory pose by conceding point after point in negotiations ... but never one that was critical to his bottom line aim.

Given baseball's pregame moves, such a hardball stance at the negotiating table was anything but surprising. Upon the 1978 pseudo-retirement of John Gaherin as their chief negotiator, baseball had selected Ray Grebey, a tough-minded, expletive-oriented industrial relations expert from General Electric, as their new advocate.[18] Knowing that their goals as well as Grebey's hard-nosed advocacy would inevitably lead to strife, the owners took out a $50 million strike insurance policy while establishing a $7 million contingency fund for helping out weaker owners in the case of a lengthy work stoppage.[19] Finally, a somewhat draconian owner discipline committee was established and armed with the authority to dole out fines of up to $500,000 for those fraternity members who talked out of turn during negotiations— a move that belied latent fissures within the ownership ranks.[20]

Thus the essence of the coming owner-player conflict would revolve around baseball's inability to resolve its own structural problems, a battleground that has become all too familiar to modern-day fans. The negotiations that opened in late 1979 would ultimately lead to a calamitous 1981 strike that would rip 50 days out of the gut of the season and turn the Cincinnati Reds into the only team to lead its league in winning percentage but not qualify for postseason play. Though victory claims (or at least suggestions that the other side suffered more) would come from both camps as the 1981 agreement was inked, speculation quickly commenced in many quarters as to what (if anything) the owners had come away with. Free agency remained intact, compensation was limited to a pool of players from the back end of each team's 40-man roster (a system that was abandoned in 1985[21]), and salary growth continued at double-digit rates through the mid-1980s.[22] In short, the brave new inflationary world pioneered by Marvin Miller was here to stay, and the owners would have to find another method by which to address their financial problems.

That method, as it turned out, would be collusion.

As player relations and management control over its workforce eroded, another specter threatened the remaining shreds of baseball's once clean-cut image. Less-than-prescription drug use had long been a factor in the game; Jim Bouton and his *Ball Four* cohorts discuss greenies (amphetamines) in such a causal manner that the reader knows without being told that players had routinely used such substances for years.[23] While baseball's Mahogany Row thought it had dealt with the issue via a drug education and prevention program initiated in February 1971,[24] the problem had simply migrated into the shadows. Los Angeles Dodgers pitcher Bob Welch would be the first to come forward, admitting in early 1980 that he had spent five weeks the previous winter at an Arizona substance abuse clinic for alcohol dependence.[25] Royals catcher Darrell Porter shortly thereafter left training camp to enter the same facility for alcohol and drug abuse treatment,[26] and the rush was on.

The team physician for the Phillies' AA team was indicted on 223 counts of prescribing amphetamines without physically examining the patients; among those he OKed drugs for were Pete Rose, Steve Carlton, Larry Bowa, Greg Luzinski, and Tim McCarver.[27] On August 25, Rangers pitcher Ferguson Jenkins was arrested by police at the Toronto airport — in his possession were two ounces of marijuana, four grams of cocaine, and two grams of hashish.[28] A year and a half later, Padres outfielder Alan Wiggins was arrested for cocaine possession.[29] Shortly after his arrest, Dodgers reliever Steve Howe would begin an odyssey of drug abuse and sporadic rehabilitation efforts that would span the better part of two decades.[30] Four Kansas City Royals (Willie Aikens, Vida Blue, Jerry Martin, and Willie Wilson) were sent to prison on drug charges — singled out, as stated in the opinion handed down by District Court Judge J. Milton Sullivant, because of their role model status.[31]

Baseball's response to the drug abuse scandals was strangely restrained, in large part due to the animosity between the players' union and the game's ruling class. In a sense, it was the Alex Johnson argument come full circle: if mental illness was a sickness akin to an injury, then so too was substance abuse. Bowie Kuhn attempted to suspend Jenkins when he refused to answer questions regarding his drug arrest — baseball's three-member arbitration panel overturned the ruling two weeks later.[32] The commissioner supposedly sidelined Wiggins without pay for thirty days, yet the Padres continued issuing him regular checks on the sly.[33] Steve Howe was initially banned for a year as a result of his repeated fallings off the wagon, a penalty that was ultimately mitigated to placement on the inactive list so that Howe could continue to accrue time towards pension benefits.[34] Aikens, Martin, and Wilson were originally kicked out for a year as well — the arbitration panel pared the suspension to six weeks.[35]

In short, the game that the old man dying in Rochester contemplated was teetering on the brink of calamity ... yet at the same time was in the midst of a period of unprecedented prosperity. A new television contract with NBC and ABC would net nearly double the revenue (some $175 million over its four-year life span) of the previous pact.[36] Attendance records continued to fall despite all of the turmoil; baseball's 26 teams recorded over 43 million admissions in 1979, with eight teams topping the two million level.[37] Of the top 25 single-season team attendance marks, six were recorded in 1979 and 19 had been posted within the decade.[38]

A tidal wave of historic milestones was being achieved, in part due to improved conditioning but also partially due to a higher salary structure that made it more profitable for aging players to stay in the game. Lou Brock and Carl Yastrzemski stroked their 3,000th hits during the 1979 season — of the then 15 members of the 3,000 hit club, seven had reached the threshold during the decade.[39] Six eventual 300-game winners (Don Sutton, Tom Seaver, Steve Carlton, Phil Niekro, Gaylord Perry, and Nolan Ryan) were both active and among the Show's elite. Three future 500-homer men were around too (Reggie Jackson, Eddie Murray, and Mike Schmidt), and all of them figured in the 1979 MVP balloting.

It had been a tremendously diverse decade. The all-time home run leader had shared the field with the all-time stolen base king. An era in which strikeouts had continuously decreased spawned both the single-season (and ultimately all-time) strikeout king as well as the batter who amassed the most whiffs in a season. Rod Carew hit .388 in 1977, while Ron Guidry posted a 1.74 ERA the next season.[40]

In short, baseball was still baseball — the arguments and problems might have morphed somewhat, but the game continued to endure. Willie Stargell hatched the idea of awarding stars to teammates for superior plays, and the supposedly jaded millionaire athletes surrounding him fought over them like they were penny candy. Billy Martin returned to the Yankees in midseason, punched out a marshmallow salesman and was fired again on October 28.[41] After allowing Nolan Ryan to go the free agent route, Angels GM Buzzie Bavasi made the immortal comment that the 16-14 Ryan could be replaced by two 8-7 pitchers.[42]

As fine a year as 1979 was for rookie ballplayers, it would still go down as one that could have been a whole lot better if fate hadn't intervened a time or two. Not that elements of that season's kiddie corps wouldn't put together lengthy careers; in fact, three 1979 freshmen (Rickey Henderson, Tim Raines, and Jesse Orosco) remained on the baseball scene as the 2001 season closed. 1988 World Series MVP Kirk Gibson, whose broad skill set, gritty determination, and perpetual five o'clock shadow made him the grunge movement's answer to Mickey Mantle, was a late season callup as well that year. Yet the roster of talents betrayed is in many ways even more impressive, including:

- Dickie Thon, a shortstop whose 1983 season in Houston's Astrodome compares well with anything Derek Jeter has ever put up on the boards. Just 25 at the time, Thon seemed headed for stardom before an April 1984 beaning by Mike Torrez knocked him out for the season with headaches, blurred vision, and nausea.[43] While Dickie fought his way back and was able to play for another eight seasons, he was never again a serious offensive force.

- 1984 Cy Young Award winner Lamarr Hoyt, a fine left-hander who could change speeds with the best of them yet met his Waterloo in recreational drug use.

- John Tudor, the primordial Bret Saberhagan. A tall, lean left-hander, Tudor's whipping three-quarters motion was reminiscent of Ewell Blackwell ... as was his surgical history. Still, even in 1990 when Tudor's heater

Walter O'Malley (right), who reigned for two decades as baseball's king among kings (though he would regularly deny it) is pictured with manager Tommy LaSorda (center) in this 1977 photograph. O'Malley's death two years later due to cancer would bring to an effective and symbolic end to the era as Baseball Lord. (*The Sporting News*)

was barely able to break 80 MPH, he went 12-4 with a 2.40 ERA — and quit baseball due to the pain.[44]

- Mike Scott, who took six long years to get going but became in his early to mid-30s what Dwight Gooden could have been had Doc kept away from the fast friends and controlled substances.

- Dan Quisenberry, a sidearming reliever whose major league career wasn't curtailed but whose life sadly was. A witty man with a natural gift of gab and zany sense of humor, Quiz was the logical candidate to become the Joe Garagiola of his generation before a brain tumor tragically ended his life in 1998.[45]

At the same time, 1979 represented the coming of age or high noon for a number of bigger-than-life characters. There was American League home run champion Gorman Thomas, a bear of a man who could have given Kirk Gibson lessons on scruffiness[46] but managed to play a creditable center field and be a major offensive force despite a beer-barrel physique and bushels of whiffs. There was James Rodney Richard, a 6'8" mound behemoth who combined great power stuff with dazzling control. Until a stroke suffered during a 1980 pregame workout nixed his career,[47] people were comparing J.R. to Sandy Koufax with zero irony. Ozzie Smith was in his second season of turning cartwheels for the San Diego Padres; already known as "The Wizard of Oz," Smith's chances prior to the 1978 season had seemed so dim that he hadn't been included in the team's press guide.[48]

No one can know what the Dodgers' aging baron was thinking as he lay there in his final moments of life. Probably his contemplations, such as they were, were of a more personal nature. But if Walter O'Malley reflected upon the game that had so dominated his life, he probably did so with satisfaction … limited satisfaction perhaps, since O'Malley was not a man to be complacent with anything, but satisfaction just the same. Whatever its future course, though, this most rational of men surely realized that baseball itself would survive his absence, just as it had weathered everything from gambling scandals to one-armed men playing during World War II.

Of course, if he'd just thought to tell his kid not to put out big-time money for Stanhouse and Goltz....

Chapter Notes

INTRODUCTION

1. Holtzman, Jerome, "Two Divisions, Rules, Player Demands, Etc.," *1970 Official Baseball Guide*, pp. 300–301. Eight months in the making, the Wharton report envisioned among other things the combining of the National and American League umpiring staffs into one, interleague play, and the elimination of the individual league presidents.

2. Giles had been a serious candidate to succeed Happy Chandler as commissioner after Chandler's 1951 resignation, but withdrew from the race when he and then–NL president Ford Frick deadlocked in the balloting (see *Baseball: The Biographical Encyclopedia*, p. 412 for details). According to Jerome Holtzman ("Expansion, Canadian Club, Feature 1968," *1969 Official Baseball Guide*, p. 187) Feeney received support from 17 of the 24 clubs in his drive to replace Gen. William Eckert. The voting rules, though, required Feeney to secure three-fourths of the vote from each league, leaving Chub out in the cold when a bloc of AL owners refused to back down from their support of Yankee president Mike Burke.

3. Brunet is the guy in Jim Bouton's *Ball Four* world who doesn't wear undershorts (see *Ball Four*, p. 307), but his durability and longevity south of the border are worthy of a book in and of themselves. In 1980, for example, the then 45-year-old left-hander led the Mexican League in innings pitched (177) and shutouts (8) en route to an 11–10 record with a 2.61 ERA for an Aguila team that came within one and a half games of the Western Division crown.

4. Marvin Miller, *A Whole Different Ballgame*, p. 99, and Holtzman, "Two Divisions, Rules, Player Demands, Etc.," *1970 Official Baseball Guide*, p. 302.

5. Holtzman, "Two Divisions, Rules, Player Demands, Etc.," *1970 Official Baseball Guide*, pp. 266–267. Santo went so far as to say that he would be in uniform on March 1 whether an agreement had been reached or not. "Mr. Wrigley [Cubs owner Phil Wrigley] has been good to me," the All-Star third baseman commented in a manner that would seem almost childishly naïve within a couple of years, "and I'm going to be good to him."

6. Miller's invitation to the commissioner was, however, ominously less than cordial. See Bowie Kuhn, *Hardball*, pp. 80–81 for details.

7. Holtzman, "Two Divisions, Rules, Player Demands, Etc.," *1970 Official Baseball Guide*, p. 304.

8. *1969 Official Baseball Guide*, p. 171, and *1970 Official Baseball Guide*, pp. 630–631.

9. *Ibid.*

10. Holtzman, "Two Divisions, Rules, Player Demands, Etc.," *1970 Official Baseball Guide*, pp. 281–284.

11. Sean Forman, *Baseball-Reference. com.*

12. *Ibid.*

13. Bucek, Jeanine (ed. dir.), *The Baseball Encyclopedia* (1996 ed.), pp. 499–501.

14. Kuhn, *Hardball*, pp. 38–39.

15. An interesting illustration of this phenomenon can be seen in the *Cincinnati Reds '71 Yearbook Magazine*. On page 57 of

that publication are photographs of the Reds' front office staff save general manager Bob Howsam, who is pictured with the team's "officials" on page five. The arrangement of the staff portraits makes it clear that there are two levels of senior executives in the Reds' hierarchy. Tier 1 contains assistant GM Dick Wagner (nicknamed "The Field Marshal" by baseball insiders, Wagner's name was often pronounced in the manner of the German composer who was Hitler's favorite), director of player personnel Chief Bender, and special assistant for scouting Rex Bowen, while the second rank contains ten others with titles that nominally sound just as impressive. The final person listed in that second group is promotions and sales director Sonny Tate, which is just a quirk of alphabetical fate but seems prophetic when a survey of the worker-bee level below him reveals six ticket department employees, two accountants ... and one sales and promotions guy.

Tate's position within the Reds' hierarchy is actually superior to that of New York Mets promotion director Arthur Richman. Richman is listed twentieth among the Mets' top executives in the *1970 Official Baseball Guide* (p. 113), six slots below the team's controller and two below the ticket manager.

A second point to ponder: though the concept of marketing as a discipline had been codified into the American business scene for nearly two decades by the dawn of the 1970s, no senior baseball executive had the term in his title at that time.

16. David Pietrusza et al. (ed.), *Baseball: The Biographical Encyclopedia*, p. 501.

17. This suggestion was actually tried in a 1969 A's preseason game. The result was 18 walks.

18. An entertaining account of AL president Joe Cronin's reaction when he found himself on the receiving end of one of Finley's harangues can be found in Kuhn, *Hardball*, p. 126.

Kuhn suggests (p. 24) that Walter O'Malley's steadfast opposition to the DH rule was in part due to his detestation of Finley and his tactics.

19. *1970 Official Baseball Guide*, pp. 110–116.

20. Leo Durocher with Ed Linn, *Nice Guys Finish Last*, p. 54.

21. George McCormick, "Denny McLain and His Feuds with the Tigers," *All-Star Sports*, September, 1970, p. 26.

22. Kuhn, *Hardball*, p. 74. In fairness to Cannon, it should be noted that he intended to retain his seat on the U.S. Circuit Court in Milwaukee while taking care of MLBPA business in his off hours. However, given his demand for a $50,000 annual salary — roughly what a senior vice president at a Fortune 500 company was pulling down in those days — one would think that the players could have received something more than part-time attention (Miller, *A Whole Different Ball Game*, p. 8).

23. This issue was under negotiation at the time, but would become part of the new Basic Agreement which was finalized on June 8, 1970 (Jerome Holtzman, "Players, Umpires, Books, Lawsuits...," *1971 Official Baseball Guide*, p. 291).

24. *1979 Official Baseball Guide*, pp. 8–21, 130–41.

CHAPTER 1

1. Uncredited, *Sport World*, October, 1968, p. 40.

2. Curt Flood with Richard Carter, *The Way It Is*, p. 157.

3. *Ibid*, p. 4.

4. Holtzman, "Players, Umpires, Books, Law Suits...," p. 275.

5. This rather straightforward six-paragraph decision (Federal Base Ball Club of Baltimore, Inc. v. National League of Professional Base Ball Clubs et al [259 U.S. 200]) has somehow become one of the most misunderstood/misrepresented treatises in American History. Holmes' opinion is generally referred to as the "baseball is a sport, not a business" decision, a definition that as eminent an observer as Marvin Miller accepts and goes to some lengths to decry (*A Whole Different Ball Game*, pg 42).

In fact, Holmes said nothing of the sort: his opinion simply states that baseball was not engaged in interstate commerce, which is what the Sherman Act regulated, and therefore was not subject to the strictures of that law. This may seem like a quaint position to modern observers, but keep in mind that club revenue in those days was primarily driven by sales of tickets, concessions, and the like to local fans. If you are in the business of selling stuff to people who don't generally cross state lines to receive it federal law doesn't apply — didn't then and doesn't now.

Still, the decision is on the face of it a suriously nit-picky one as Bill James noted in *The New Bill James Historical Baseball Abstract* (pg l06). In that discussion, James suggests that the era in which the opinion was handed down (the appeals court hearing which the Supreme Court would ultimately affim began only three weeks after the Black Sox scandal first hit the papers) may have heavily influenced Holmes' thinking. It's a reasonable rationale, but a more likely factor in The Great Dissenter's decision was his monumental disdain for the Sherman Act, which he "regarded as one of the worst and certainly most poorly written pieces of federal legislation to be enacted in his lifetime." (Henry J. Abraham, quoted by John Bowen at www.ripon.edu) That Holmes would choose not to extend the reach of a law that he once derided as "dammed nonsense" is anything but suprising.

6. *Flood vs. Kuhn's* precursor was *Toolson vs. New York Yankees, Inc.*, 346 U.S. 356 (decided in 1953). George Toolson was a somewhat pudgy swingman who had the misfortune, from his perspective, of finding himself in the talent-laden Yankee farm system. Exactly how good a player Toolson was is a matter of debate; according to Miller (*A Whole Different Ball Game*, p. 174), the right-hander "probably could've caught on with another team," but a review of his record suggests the most marginal of major league skills. In the two seasons prior to Toolson's 1950 refusal to report to Class A Binghamton, the right-hander had posted a combined 9–15 record with a 5.05 ERA for the top Red Sox (Louisville) and Yankee (Newark) farm teams while allowing nearly 15 base runners per nine innings pitched (figures courtesy of Pat Doyle, *Old-Time Data*, Shawnee Mission, KS). In fairness, many hurlers of Toolson's day walked 40 percent more men than they struck out, but ... well, there had to be a dozen guys pitching alongside him who were every bit as good and never saw the lights of a big league park either.

Still, he represented a decent safety net if somebody on the parent club got hurt and thus wasn't going to be traded or released so that he could pursue his career with a sec-

ond-division organization that might be more likely to give him a shot at the Show. Rather than accept his fate, however, Toolson chose to sue baseball under the premise that the Yankees' retention of his contract represented a violation of the Sherman Antitrust Act. Toolson's case might have made for a good argument except for two small problems:

1. Holmes had said *specifically* that baseball was not subject to the Sherman Act.
2. A House Judiciary Committee report issued the previous year had said in part that "the overwhelming preponderance of the evidence established baseball's need for some sort of reserve clause" (H.R. Rep. No. 2002, 82nd Congress, 2nd Session, p. 220).

Thus, a seven-man majority rejected Toolson's claim with a short *per curiam* (that's judge talk for "this case isn't worthy of a full-fledged opinion") which stated that it was up to Congress to decide whether baseball was a sport or not — and until they did, Holmes's decision would stand.

Miller (*A Whole Different Ball Game*, p. 174) terms this logic "fuzzy at best" while claiming that "Neither [Congress or the Supreme Court] had the slightest concern for the rights of employees— the players. Both always have had great concern for the 'property' rights of owners."

7. Miller, *A Whole Different Ball Game*, p. 181.

8. *Ibid.*, pp. 187–189.

9. Flood with Carter, *The Way It Is*, p. 161, suggests that Quinn's impression may have been driven by an offhand comment Flood made to a well-wisher at an adjoining table indicating that "I'm with them [the Phillies] now."

"The flat assertion may have signified more to Quinn than it did to me," Flood wrote. "It may have accounted for his perplexity when I filed suit. He had thought that I looked upon myself as a Phillie."

Well, yes ... that plus the fact that Flood spent four hours that evening discussing contract details with Quinn down to the point that a specific salary and reimbursement package totaling over $100,000 was placed on the table by the Philadelphia GM.

10. Excerpts from a joint statement by AL President Joe Cronin and NL prexy Chub

Feeney are recorded in Holtzman, "Two Divisions, Rules, Player Demands, Etc...," pp. 306–307. Cronin and Feeney stated in the letter that "professional baseball would simply cease to exist" if Flood's suit was successful. "When a player refuses to honor an assignment," the communiqué continued, "he violates his contract, in which he agrees that assignment may be made, and he violates the fundamental baseball rules, including the reserve clause, which experience has shown to be absolutely necessary to the successful operation of baseball."

11. Typical of the comments were those of Cardinals third baseman Joe Torre, long a prominent voice in player matters. Torre voiced his support for Flood in this manner: "It is only right for us to back him because we believe the reserve clause *should be modified*" (*Ibid.*, p. 306). Cubs player representative Milt Pappas, apparently unaware of the thrust of Flood's argument, would comment after the Supreme Court reached its final verdict, "The players were not looking to make utter chaos, which complete elimination of the reserve clause would do. What we are still going to seek at the bargaining table is an agreement that will give veteran players some freedom in negotiating." (Merrell Whittlesey, "Did High Court Err? Everybody Has Opinion," *The Sporting News*, July 8, 1972, p. 5.)

Even Bill Veeck, who testified for Flood in the District Court trial, stopped short of endorsing elimination of the clause, suggesting instead either

a) A motion picture–style contract in which players would be bound to their teams for a fixed period of time with guaranteed raises or

b) A form of professional football's option system, where a team losing someone who has played out his option would be compensated by the team signing the player. For baseball's purposes, Veeck suggested cash compensation rather than replacement players.

Spoken like a man used to operating with a short bankroll ... (Holtzman, "Players, Umpires, Books, Lawsuits...," *1971 Official Baseball Guide*, p. 277).

Veeck, by the way, would comment after the final judgment was handed down that the players had erred in pinning their hopes on the high-salaried, controversial Flood (Whittlesey, "Did High Court Err? Everybody Has Opinion," p. 5).

12. *Ibid.*, pp. 276–278.

13. "I spent six weeks in New York during the trial," Flood recalled years later, "and not one player came to see what was going on. All right, I had all the news media there; that was cool. There were ex–baseball players who came and said how they got ripped off. But not one baseball player who was playing at the time came just to see — I didn't want them to testify — just to see what was going on because it involved them so dramatically. But no one came just to sit and say 'Hey, this is pretty important. It concerns me and my wife and my kids and, if they ever play baseball, their kids." (Murray Chass, "Curt Flood: Baseball's Forgotten Pioneer," *Baseball Digest*, January, 1977, p. 63.)

14. Holtzman, "Players, Umpires, Books, Lawsuits...," *1971 Official Baseball Guide*, pp. 276–277. Garagiola opened his testimony with a joke and kept them coming hot and heavy throughout his 13 minutes of "testimony." It was a highly irreverent performance for a courtroom, but Judge Cooper had set the trial's tone from the outset by characterizing himself as "a man in blue" who would "call them as I see them." (*Ibid.*, p. 274.)

15. *Ibid.*, p. 276.

16. "Judge Points the Way," *The Sporting News*, August 29, 1970, p. 16. According to Cooper, "Baseball remains exempt [from the antitrust laws] ... unless and until the Supreme Court or Congress holds to the contrary."

17. Holtzman, "Players, Umpires, Books, Lawsuits...," p. 278.

18. *Ibid.*, p. 277. Flood made this comment while testifying in his own behalf.

19. Miller, *A Whole Different Ball Game*, p. 188. Goldberg served as general council for the Steelworkers' Union and the CIO in the 1950s, but he'd been in the political arena ever since John Kennedy had named him Secretary of Labor in 1961. Goldberg had spent less than a year in private practice when Flood and Miller showed up on his doorstep.

20. Holtzman, "'71 Saw Gate Up, Short Move, Alex Angry," p. 297. Flood's financial problems pretty much started the day he filed the suit. As early as August 1970, the IRS was seizing equipment from his photographic business to satisfy tax liens.

21. Flood, *The Way It Is*, p. 180.

22. Holtzman, "'71 Saw Gate Up, Short Move, Alex Angry," p. 296.

23. Merrell Whittlesey, "Problem-Pressed Flood Seeks Haven in Europe," *The Sporting News*, May 15, 1971, p. 5. Flood sent the following wire to Short from New York's Kennedy Airport before departing on a flight to Lisbon and Barcelona: "I tried. A year and a half is too much. Very severe personal problems are mounting every day. Thanks for your confidence and understanding."

Bowie Kuhn in *Hardball* (p. 87) mentions running into Flood (then an Oakland A's broadcaster) at a 1980 party held in George Steinbrenner's office at Yankee Stadium. Kuhn shook hands with the ex–center fielder and assured him that he harbored no hard feelings. "But," he told Flood, "you were wrong to walk out on Bob Short in 1971 after taking his money" (p. 90).

24. Bob Woodward and Scott Armstrong, *The Brethren*, p. 190. To Associate Justice Potter Stewart, the senior member of the majority voting against Flood, the two prior cases upholding Holmes's ruling made *Flood vs. Kuhn* "a case of '*stare decisis*' double dipped"—in layman's terms, open and shut.

25. *Ibid.*, pp. 189–192. Associate Justice Harry Blackmun apparently took the selection of the players he chose to include in the opinion's first section very seriously. When asked jokingly by one of Justice William Rehnquist's clerks why former Washington Senators pitcher Camillo Pascual wasn't included amongst the list of greats, a Blackmun clerk replied, "The Justice recalls seeing Pascual pitch and remembers his fantastic curveball. But he pulled out his [*Baseball*] *Encyclopedia* and looked up his record. He decided Pascual's 174 wins were not enough. It is difficult to make these judgments of who to include, but Justice Blackmun felt that Pascual is just not in the same category with Christy Mathewson's 373 wins. I hope you will understand."

According to Woodward and Armstrong, calling Blackmun's chambers to request that a favorite player be included in the opinion became a favored pastime among Supreme Court clerks.

26. In Stan Isle, "Kuhn Hails Supreme Court Decision," *The Sporting News*, July 1, 1972, Bowie is quoted as saying, "The decision opens the way for renewed collective bargaining on the reserve system after the 1972 season. I am confident that the players and the clubs are in the best position to determine for themselves what the form of the reserve system should be.... Any desirable changes should be the product of mutual agreement, so that there will be assurance that all concerned are prepared to live with and support the result."

"There is one thing that is especially good in the 5–3 decision against Flood," a July 8, 1972, *Sporting News* editorial claimed ("Flood's Loss Is Baseball's Gain," p. 14). "It will serve as an incentive to the club owners and the players to get together and hammer out some kind of agreement on the reserve clause."

27. Murray Chass, "Curt Flood: Baseball's Forgotten Pioneer," *Baseball Digest*, January, 1977, p. 61.

28. Pietrusza et al., *Baseball: The Biographical Encyclopedia*, p. 366.

CHAPTER 2

1. Kuhn, *Hardball*, p. 73.

It's difficult to tell from either Kuhn's memoirs or Bouton's book (Jim Bouton and Leonard Shecter, *I'm Glad You Didn't Take It Personally*, pp. 67–79) exactly what the commissioner's goal was in his meeting with the Astros knuckleballer. Bouton clearly feared a repeat of the "informal" February get-together between Kuhn and Denny McLain, which resulted in the pitcher's suspension, and thus brought Marvin Miller and MLBPA counsel Dick Moss along with him, a move that may well have put a crimp in Bowie's pontifical game plan. According to both Kuhn and Bouton, the commissioner's concerns revolved around the veracity of his observations and whether the revealing of such was in baseball's best interests, the inference being that Bowie was looking for some way to put the genie back in the bottle. Bouton, backed by Miller and Moss, would have none of it; he asserted that the book "gives an accurate view of what baseball and baseball players are like" and that *Ball Four* would actually stimulate interest in baseball by bursting the game's "phony goody-goody image." (*I'm Glad You Didn't Take It Personally*, p. 70.)

The result of the meeting was a three sentence statement by Kuhn in which he "advised Mr. Bouton of my displeasure with these writings and have warned him against any future writings of this character." This imprecise and vaguely ominous proclamation was manipulated by *Ball Four's* publishers into the tagline "The Book Baseball Tried to Ban," helping to boost sales of the memoir to over 100,000 copies in 1970. (Holtzman, "Players, Umpires, Books, Lawsuits, Etc.," p. 302.)

Bouton fully recognized his indebtedness to the commissioner. While presenting an award to Twins pitcher Jim Perry at a Baseball Writers Association of America dinner in 1971, the now ex-pitcher acknowledged those on the dais with him, including "Bowie Kuhn — and we all know what *he's* done for me."

Unfortunately, "For some reason, my friend Bowie Kuhn just sat there, staring straight ahead, purple rising up his neck." (Bouton and Shecter, *I'm Glad You Didn't Take It Personally*, p. 68).

2. Bouton devotes a chapter in *I'm Glad You Didn't Take It Personally* (pp. 92–124) to player reactions to *Ball Four*. Many of the most vehement comments apparently came from those who either didn't read the book or limited their perusal to the excerpts published in *Look* magazine. Perhaps the most priceless response came from Billy Martin, who proclaimed *Ball Four* to be "a horseshit book. I didn't read it, but I know it's horseshit. My wife read it. She thought it was great" (p. 104).

3. Edgar Munzel, "Hard-Nosed Ron Santo: Modern Gashouser," *The Sporting News*, September 6, 1969, p. 3. The assessment of Santo is Munzel's rather than Durocher's and stands in stark contrast to Leo's comments in *Nice Guys Finish Last*, where he categorizes the Cubs third baseman as a guy who "tried too hard. He'd get into a slump and press so bad that he became helpless. And then the fans would get on him and his fielding would fall apart too. A very emotional kid."

One has to believe that Durocher's characterization of Santo as someone who "is going to come up with the game on the line and nine times out of ten he's going to kill you" is a key reason why Santo's face has not been immortalized in Cooperstown bronze (pp. 363–364).

4. Jerome Holtzman, "'Santo's Our Guy!'

Cubs' Fans Chorus," *The Sporting News*, June 23, 1973, p. 3.

5. Sparky Lyle and Peter Golenbock, *The Bronx Zoo*, pp. 47–48. "Until the press ruined it for me, the thing I enjoyed more than anything was sitting on cakes," the lefty reliever admitted. Yankee pitching coach Jim Turner loved cake and would forever try to get a piece before Lyle made his two-point landing, but "he never beat me to the cake. Not once."

CHAPTER 3

1. Comiskey Park, Fenway Park, and Tiger Stadium all predated World War I, while Yankee Stadium opened in 1923 and Cleveland's Municipal Stadium hosted its first big-league game on July 31, 1932 (though the Mistake by the Lake would not become the Indians' full-time home until 1947).

2. Bob Broeg, "Three Rivers Stadium — Ball Park With Perfect Name," *The Sporting News*, July 27, 1974, p. 4.

3. The incline, roughly thirty feet wide along the left field foul line and gradually tapering away to nothing in left center field, is plainly visible in Lowell Reidenbaugh, *Take Me Out to the Ball Park*, p. 88.

4. Oscar Palacios, Eric Robin and STATS, Inc., *Ballpark Sourcebook: Diamond Diagrams*, p. 138. Ironically, though, the park did end up falling prey to a fire set in the press box by a couple of stepbrothers roughly a year after the Phillies abandoned it. The August 20, 1971, blaze caused the grandstand roof along the first and third base lines to collapse and litter adjoining 21st Street with debris. (Allen Lewis, "Connie Mack Stadium Destroyed by Blaze," *The Sporting News*, September 11, 1971, p. 13).

5. Reidenbaugh, *Take Me Out to the Ball Park*, p. 214.

6. Bill James, *The Bill James Baseball Abstract* (1984 ed.), p. 82.

7. Chris Rowe and Dick Kaegel (eds.) *1968 Baseball Dope Book*, pp. 63, 77, 81.

8. Walt Hoffman, "D-Day in South Philadelphia," *1972 Philadelphia Phillies Yearbook*, p. 5.

9. Forman, Baseball-Reference.com.

10. Reidenbaugh, *Take Me Out to the Ball Park*, p. 210.

11. *Ibid.*, p. 221.

12. Bill Veeck and Ed Linn, *Veeck as in Wreck*, p. 17.

13. Reidenbaugh, *Take Me Out to the Ball Park*, p. 149.

14. Peter Golenbock, *Bums*, p. 19. Despite the area's unpretentious nature, it took Ebbets three years to acquire the parcel from the 40 people who either owned portions of the land or had taken possession via squatter's rights.

15. Milton Gross, *Baseball Digest*, September, 1971, p. 36.

16. Palacios, Robin, et al., *Ballpark Sourcebook: Diamond Diagrams*, p. 150. The distance to the backstop at Forbes Field, by the way, was a massive 120 feet for most of its life.

17. A diagram of Crosley Field's layout in its later years is depicted in *Baseball Digest*, October, 1975, p. 16.

18. Palacios, Robin, et al., *Ballpark Sourcebook: Diamond Diagrams*, p. 171.

19. Reidenbaugh, *Take Me Out to the Ball Park*, p. 167. The three tape measure jobs were hit by Joe Adcock, Lou Brock, and Henry Aaron. Interestingly, the final two occurred on consecutive days.

20. *Ibid.*, p. 214.

21. Richard Piellisch, "Do Artificial Surfaces Help or Hinder the Game?" *Baseball Digest*, June, 1980, pp. 45–46. The seven stadiums were Pittsburgh's Three Rivers, Busch in St Louis, Olympic Stadium in Montreal, Veterans in Philly, Riverfront Stadium in Cincinnati, Houston's Astrodome, and Candlestick Park on San Francisco Bay. This majority rule for synthetic turf would not last long, however, as the City of San Francisco would remove Candlestick's Astroturf in 1978 at the behest of the football 49ers.

22. Chris Rowe and Dick Kaegel (eds.). *1970 Baseball Dope Book*, p. 103.

23. Chris Rowe, Joe Marcin, and Larry Wigge (eds.). *1972 Baseball Dope Book*, p. 103.

24. *Ibid.*, p. 81.

25. *Ibid.*, pp. 108, 122.

26. Pat Calabria, "Greg Luzinski: The Maturing of a Major League Slugger," *Baseball Digest*, November, 1975, p. 47. The Bull's drive was estimated at 500 feet.

CHAPTER 4

1. Andy O'Brien, "Ron Hunt: No. 1 on the Majors' Hit Parade," *Baseball Digest*, August, 1972, p. 32.

2. Ian MacDonald, "Hunt Makes 'Hit' as Expos' MVP," *The Sporting News*, October 16, 1971, p. 40.

3. Earl Lawson, "Today's Reds—Greatest in Rhineland History?" *All-Star Sports*, November, 1970, p. 42 (photo).

4. Ian MacDonald, "Hunt, Pitchers' Favorite Target, Says Hurlers Are Much Too Wild," *The Sporting News*, September 4, 1971, p. 22. "My hitting style is to lean towards the pitcher," Hunt commented in the same article. "If I pull back, I sacrifice some of my hitting area and I can't afford that. I won't do it.

"Some guys give that up, but I can't."

5. O'Brien, "Ron Hunt: No. 1 on the Majors' Hit Parade," p. 34.

6. Jack Zanger, *Major League Baseball 1970*, p. 133.

7. MacDonald, "Hunt, Pitchers' Favorite Target, Says Hurlers Are Much Too Wild," p. 22.

8. *Ibid.*

9. According to the *1967 Los Angeles Dodgers Yearbook*, p. 25, "Hunt volunteered to go the club's Florida Instructional League camp on a conditioning and weight control program" upon joining the Dodgers as a result of the Tommy Davis trade. It would not be the only time.

10. Mets outfielder Ron Swoboda once quipped, "When Hunt got traded, he was the only player who ever was sent to a new club with batteries and a complete set of instructions on how to assemble." (Maury Allen, Untitled, *Baseball Digest*, September, 1972, p. 16.)

11. Ian McDonald, "Expos' Hunt Handles Bat Like Baton," *The Sporting News*, August 5, 1972, p. 16.

12. In O'Brien, "Ron Hunt: No. 1 on the Majors' Hit Parade," pp. 31–32, Hunt commented on his breaking of the then 75-year-old record, "It's taken all that time to find somebody as stupid as Jennings."

But then again, perhaps Hunt didn't break Jennings's record. With the increased effort in recent years to verify old statistics, Jennings is now credited with 51 HBP in 1896 according to Sean Forman's *Baseball-Reference.com* website, leaving Hunt as the "modern" (post–1901) record holder.

13. Ian MacDonald, "Hunt Makes 'Hit' as Expos' MVP," p. 40.

Perhaps Pappas would have used a bit more discretion with his words if he'd known Hunt's history. After having a tooth loosened by Padres pitcher Steve Arlin's second errant toss of the day, catcher Bob Barton jumped up and began debating Hunt's "talent" with the second baseman at top volume. Hunt raised the catcher's mask and punched him in the nose, noting that "I had to leave the game anyway because I was bleeding and groggy."

Once he made his way back into the locker room, club trainer Joe Liscio suggested that a dentist be called to look at Hunt's mouth and noted that there was one handy — Arlin, the guy who had administered the *coup de grace* (and who was, in reality, a dentist). Hunt promptly threw Liscio into the whirlpool bath (O'Brien, "Ron Hunt: No. 1 on the Majors' Hit Parade," pp. 32–33).

Maury Wills in *on the Run* (Wills and Mike Celizic, p. 117) claimed that Hunt had a trick of coming down with his knee on a sliding runner's thigh when covering second on an attempted steal; if the runner slid head first, Hunt would land on the man's collarbone instead.

14. Forman, *Baseball-Reference.com.*

15. MacDonald, "Hunt, Pitchers' Favorite Target, Says Hurlers Are Much Too Wild," p. 22.

16. In a Michigan State University alumni magazine article that came out after the 1973 season's conclusion, Marshall was quoted as being critical of the Expos' defense in general and Hunt in particular. In a later interview with L.A. sportswriter Ross Newhan, however, Marshall insisted his comments had been taken out of context. "What I said to him," Marshall explained, "was, 'Just between you and me, the problem with the Expos was that the defense was terrible.' It was just terrible to see Ron Hunt have to play on one knee in a position where you have to have tremendous agility."

Well, perhaps that's better ... (Ross Newhan, "Iron Mike — What's Behind Brilliant Record?" *The Sporting News*, July 27, 1974, p. 3).

17. Pat Frizzell, "Hunt Sets N.L. Plunk Mark," *The Sporting News*, August 1, 1970, p. 8.

CHAPTER 5

1. Allen and Whitaker, *Crash*, p. 12. Dick

stated many years later that his assignment to Little Rock was part of a hidden agenda on the Phillies' part to break the color barrier in Arkansas. He blamed the team for not properly preparing him for what was to come. "Maybe if the Phillies had called me in," Allen said, "man to man, like the Dodgers had done with Jackie, and said, 'Dick, this is what we have in mind, it's going to be very difficult, but we're with you'— at least then I would have been better prepared."

In an interesting side note, *Arkansas Gazette* reporter Jim Bailey was told by his editors to downplay the fact that Allen was the first black Traveler. "The paper had won two Pulitzer Prizes for editorial writing during the Central High crisis in '57," Bailey said. "But the paper was still reeling from the fallout of all that.... The editors decided we'd be better off not getting things all stirred up again." (*Ibid.*, p. 23.)

2. *Ibid.*, p. 18.

3. *Ibid.*, p. 15.

4. *Ibid.* The Phillies found housing for Allen with a family in the "colored" section of Little Rock, and that was that. This was a pretty standard arrangement for young black players in those days, but it didn't make the young Wampum native feel like part of the Travelers'— or Phillies'—family. "I didn't live near the other ballplayers, and I didn't dare visit them — and I guess the white players didn't feel comfortable visiting me," Allen remembered a quarter-century later.

"I got lonely fast."

5. Elias Sports Bureau, *Who's Who in Baseball* (1971 ed.), p. 38.

6. Jim Scott, "Alex Johnson vs. Ron Johnson — A Study in Moods," *Super Sports*, June 1971, p. 25. "I don't think I've ever been scared pitching batting practice behind a screen before," Angel coach Rocky Bridges admitted, "but this man is something else. You can throw to certain areas against other hitters and know where they're going to hit it, but with Alex you just fire and fall back. It's like being caught on a rifle range during target practice."

7. Miller, *A Whole Different Ball Game*, p. 138. Ironically, it was Angels general manager Dick Walsh who provided this observation at Johnson's arbitration hearing.

8. David Fink, "The Other Side of Alex Johnson," *Baseball Digest*, June, 1974, p. 28.

9. Jim Hawkins, "Alex Johnson: A De-

fiant Champion," *Baseball Digest*, July, 1971, p. 78.

10. *Ibid.* The reference to bragging represents Hawkins's interpretation of his interview with Johnson. While on-the-spot impressions should not be discounted, Alex's comments in retrospect seem more like those of a salesman talking about a minor deal that didn't happen; he seems more analytical about the situation than enthused or frustrated. "They just used a little common sense," Johnson added regarding to the Cardinals' decision to trade him for outfielder Dick Simpson. "When they realized I wasn't going to do what they wanted me to do, they got rid of me. I made them.

"I came to this game to play baseball, not to oppose people. But any time anybody tells me to do something that's abnormal to me, then that's distasteful to me. St. Louis wouldn't listen to my reasoning."

11. John Wiebusch, "'I Lead Two Lives' ... by Alex Johnson," *The Sporting News*, June 27, 1970, p. 9.

12. Scott, "Alex Johnson vs. Ron Johnson — A Study in Moods," p. 23.

13. *Ibid.*, p. 50.

14. Dick Allen and Tim Whitaker, *Crash*, p. 105. According to Allen, "To Alex Johnson, baseball was a whole world of dickheads. Teammates, managers, general managers, owners. Everybody was a dickhead to him. That was just his way. But it scared the front office guys to death. They'd walk into the clubhouse to say hello, and Alex would say, 'How ya doin', dickhead?' Just like that. The front office types would take it personally. But then again, maybe Alex hit a nerve."

Yes Dick, that's probably a fair assumption.

15. Bill James, *The New Bill James Historical Baseball Abstract*, p. 759.

16. Hawkins, "Alex Johnson: A Defiant Champion," p. 80.

17. *Ibid.*

18. Si Burdick, *Baseball Digest*, October, 1971, p. 38.

19. Ross Newhan, *The California Angels: The Complete Story*, p. 118.

20. Miller, *A Whole Different Ball Game*, p. 132.

21. Newhan, *The California Angels: The Complete Story*, p. 118.

22. *Ibid.*

23. *Ibid.* In Scott, "Alex Johnson vs. Ron Johnson — A Study in Moods," p. 50, it is said that no Cincinnati beat writer approached Johnson for an interview during the entirety of a 1969 season in which Alex hit .315 with 17 homers and 88 RBIs.

24. John Wiebusch, "'I Lead Two Lives' ... by Alex Johnson," *The Sporting News*, June 27, 1970, p. 9. The legend on the drawing had the catcher saying to the pitcher, "Why not do us both a favor and let him hit it?"

25. Hawkins, "Alex Johnson: A Defiant Champion," p. 76. Hawkins went on to characterize Johnson as baseball's answer to Sonny Liston, boxing's primordial Mike Tyson. Scott ("Alex Johnson vs. Ron Johnson — A Study in Moods," p. 24) draws the same parallel.

26. Hawkins, "Alex Johnson: A Defiant Champion," p. 76.

27. Newhan, *The California Angels: The Complete History*, p. 119.

28. Russell Schneider, "Alex an Early Arrival in Tribe's Overhaul," *The Sporting News*, October 23, 1971, p. 22. Johnson's fines totaled $3,750, or just over 7 percent of his $52,500 salary for the season.

29. Holtzman, "'71 Saw Gate Up, Short Move, Alex Angry," p. 284. The quote is from a letter presented to Alex by Walsh at the time of his suspension.

30. Dick Miller, "Hard-Luck King? Angels May Qualifies Easily," *The Sporting News*, July 10, 1971, p. 13.

31. Dick Miller, "Angels Perform Like Demons with Sulking Alex on Bench," *The Sporting News*, June 26, 1971, p. 25.

32. *Ibid.*

33. Dick Miller, "Alex Johnson's Dogging It Leads to Angels' Doghouse," *The Sporting News*, June 5, 1971, p. 8. With Johnson on the bench that day, the Angels produced their biggest hit and run totals of the season to that point, beating the White Sox 10–5.

34. Allen and Whitaker, *Crash*, p. 106.

35. Fink, "The Other Side of Alex Johnson," p. 27.

36. Allen and Whitaker, *Crash*, p. 106.

37. Scott, "Alex Johnson vs. Ron Johnson — A Study in Moods," p. 50.

38. Miller, *A Whole Different Ball Game*, p. 134.

39. *Ibid.*, p. 135.

40. Scott, "Alex Johnson vs. Ron Johnson — A Study in Moods," p. 22.

41. Newhan, *The California Angels: The Complete Story*, pp. 117–118.

42. Holtzman, "'71 Saw Gate Up, Short Move, Alex Angry," p. 288.

43. Jerome Holtzman, "Chisox' Allen Swings Hot, Heavy Bat," *The Sporting News*, June 29, 1974, p. 22. Dick used a 40 ounce bat in his prime as opposed to the 31–33 ounce models preferred by most players of the day.

44. Holtzman, "The Year of the Player Strike," *1973 Official Baseball Guide*, p. 295. Allen received 21 of the 24 first-place votes that season (the other three writers pegged him at number two).

In the kind of interesting irony that often plagues MVP balloting at the "he's not going to win so it's OK if we make a statement" level, Yankee relief ace Sparky Lyle finished third in the 1972 MVP balloting, handily outpolling Cleveland ace/slimeballer Gaylord Perry and White Sox knuckleballer Wilbur Wood, who finished 1–2 in the Cy Young Award sweepstakes.

45. Forman, *Baseball-Reference.com*.

46. Allen and Whitaker, *Crash*, p. 12. In an interesting display of sensitivity by Travelers management, Orval Faubus, the one time Arkansas governor who had defied the federal government in an attempt to keep black children out of white schools, was invited to throw out the first ball at the team's season opener. "I knew who he was," Allen said, "and I sure as hell knew what he was famous for, but I didn't know what he was doing there."

47. Allen and Whitaker, *Crash*, p. 59.

48. *Ibid.*, p. 65.

Allen never completely regained feeling in the ring and middle fingers of his right hand after the accident. "On cold and rainy days my hand feels like it has pins and needles in it," Dick commented some years later (Dave Nightingale, "The Human Side of Richie Allen," *Baseball Digest*, July, 1972, p. 18), "but otherwise there is no sensation. I could burn the fingers with a cigarette and not feel it. In fact, I've done just that."

49. Nightingale, "The Human Side of Richie Allen," p. 17.

50. Allen and Whitaker, *Crash*, pp. 71–74.

51. *Ibid.*, pp. 77–78. Allen termed his writings "dirt doodling" and would use them for everything from getting points across to management (Dick once wrote OCT 2 in the dirt to commemorate his prospective last day as a Phillie) to saluting

friends (PETE was for Philadelphia clubhouse man Pete Cera). Umpire Lee Weyer once got into the act as well: when Allen wrote LEE with his spikes, Weyer returned the favor by etching RICHIE ALLEN #15 on the Connie Mack Stadium infield.

When Allen reminded Weyer of his dislike of the cutesy first name, Weyer rubbed it out.

52. *Ibid.*, p. 129.

53. *Ibid.*, pp. 165–166.

54. *Ibid.*, p. 16. To show how stories sometimes don't get better with age, consider the version Allen told to Dan Berger ("How Richie Allen Finally Became a Complete Ball Player," *All-Star Sports*, September, 1971, p. 56):

"My locker consisted of a nail in the wall. When I finally moved my things to a locker in the equipment room, the papers reported that Allen had gone off on his own, that he had turned his back on his teammates.

Well, one of my teammates moved his locker at the same time I moved mine. He was fined $100; I was fined $500. Does that sound like two sets of rules?"

Well, perhaps ... but:

1. Does anyone believe that the Phillie players were really hanging their clothes on nails in 1969? Sure, Connie Mack Stadium was outmoded by that time, but contemporary photographs of the locker room depict something a bit more advanced than the *Bull Durham*–esque environment Allen refers to.

2. Dick, your teammate simply moved from one place to another within the locker room — you rejected the company of your teammates in total to dress behind closed doors. There is a difference.

55. *Ibid.*, p. 79.

56. *Ibid.*, p. 152. "This is hard for me to say," Allen told his assembled teammates. "I've never been happier anywhere but here. You're still going to be a good ballclub without me. You've got a good manager in this guy...."

At this point Dick pointed at Tanner, found himself unable to continue, and ultimately walked out of the White Sox clubhouse, never to return.

57. Bill James, *The Baseball Book 1990*, p. 211.

58. Allen and Whitaker, *Crash*, p. 169. "Before I joined the A's," Dick recalled in an

interview with collaborator Tim Whitaker, "I told Finley I wouldn't agree to being the team's designated hitter. As far as I was concerned, the DH was the worst thing that had happened to baseball in my lifetime."

59. James, *The Baseball Book 1990*, p. 212. For Allen's part, he remembered the Oakland owner as "a liar, as in l-i-a-r.... The man was always working a scam. He said he was going to make us a winner. He was going to trade for this guy and that guy. Got me fired up. But all he did was make everybody feel like a loser." (Allen and Whitaker, *Crash*, p. 169.)

60. *Ibid.*, p. 34.

61. Reggie Jackson with Mike Lupica, *Reggie*, pp. 28–30.

62. Dennis Bretz in *The Great American Stat Book* (1987 ed.), p. 267.

63. Ron Bergman, "Moody Jackson: A Fascinating Riddle," *The Sporting News*, April 13, 1974, p. 3.

64. Jackson with Lupica, *Reggie*, pp. 50–65. From the "the more things change, the more they stay the same" file, Jackson tells a story about innocently going to a restaurant that apparently had yet to be reached by the actions of the federal government or the words of Dr. Martin Luther King. Reggie ordered a steak, only to have the waiter present him with a half-cooked piece of meat a few minutes later that he promptly dropped on the table from a height of three feet or so.

"Nigger," the waiter said, "don't you *ever* come back here."

Jackson said "Yes sir" and literally ran the six blocks or so back to the colored hotel at which he was quartered.

65. *Ibid.*, p. 61.

66. *Ibid.*, p. 63.

67. Jim Scott, "Is There a New Reggie Jackson?," *All-Star Sports*, July, 1971, p. 12.

68. *Ibid.* Reggie was fined $200 for the rankly insubordinate act of playing baseball while he wasn't under contract. (Scott, "Is There a New Reggie Jackson?" p. 12.)

69. *Ibid.*

70. Ron Bergman, "Reggie and Charlie Kiss and Make Up, or Do They?" *The Sporting News*, September 26, 1970, p. 19.

71. Kuhn, *Hardball*, p. 127.

72. Bergman, "Reggie and Charlie Kiss and Make Up, or Do They?" p. 19. In a precursor of things to come, the platooning reportedly ended as a result of a long telephone conversation between Reggie and Finley during the 1971 All-Star break.

73. Scott, "Is There a New Reggie Jackson?" *All-Star Sports*, July, 1971, p. 13.

74. *Ibid.*, p. 13.

75. *Ibid.*, p. 12.

76. Jackson and Lupica, *Reggie*, p. 89.

77. *Ibid.*, p. 74. Scott, however, in "Is There a New Reggie Jackson?" says Jackson's 1971 contract was identical in terms to his pervious year's deal.

78. Scott, "Is There a New Reggie Jackson?" *All-Star Sports*, July, 1971, p. 12.

79. Allen and Whitaker, *Crash*, p. 111.

CHAPTER 6

1. Geoffrey C. Ward and Ken Burns, *Baseball: An Illustrated History*, pp. 121–123. Initially founded by David Fultz, the Fraternity's goals were twofold: to eliminate the reserve clause and to increase salaries. Fultz made limited headway at first, but as the upstart Federal League began to draw a significant number of start quality players under its banner, some of his initiatives began to bear fruit. Players were no longer required to buy their uniforms. Outfield fences were painted dark green to provide a better backdrop for hitters. Veterans of ten or more major league seasons gained a very limited form of free agency (basically, they could ask for their release if their team was through with them), and such players could not be optioned to the minors without their consent (Bill James, "A Decade Wrapped in Greed," *The Bill James Historical Baseball Abstract*, p. 110). Most importantly, salaries skyrocketed: Ty Cobb's paycheck, for example, rose from $12,000 to $20,000 in one season.

The problem was that all of this largesse had less to do with union might than it did with the fact that there was now a third major league out there that was trying to hone in on the baseball pie. Once the Federal League threat passed, American League President Ban Johnson simply announced that the agreements signed with the Fraternity were no longer in effect—faced with a 1/3 decline in the number of major league teams to ply one's trade with, the players acquiesced with barely a whimper. As a *New York Sun* reporter noted, "When Ban Johnson ... turned the hose on the Fraternity, it vanished like old newspapers on the way to a sewer."

2. Chicago *Tribune* sports editor Arch Ward dreamed up the All-Star Game as an opportunity to boost attendance at Chicago's Century of Progress World's Fair as well as a way to help former players down on their luck as a result of the Depression. Baseball's Executive Row was less than enthusiastic about the idea, agreeing to the game as an one-year-only event and insisting that the *Tribune* pick up all expenses if the game were rained out, a guarantee Ward granted without consulting his bosses. A crowd of 47,595 fans jamming Comiskey Park at a time when World Series games were barely drawing 30,000 admissions, however, quickly assured the All-Star Game's perpetuation.

Of the $52,000 raised by the initial game, $45,000 was donated to needy ex-players. ("A Tried and True Showcase," *The Sporting News*, July 29, 1972, p. 18.)

3. Miller, *A Whole Different Ball Game*, p. 156.

4. *Ibid.*, p. 64.

5. *Ibid.*, p. 338.

6. The Pasquels, armed with a fortune estimated between $60-$100 million, offered $15,000 salaries plus bonuses and fringe benefits (when ex-Giant second baseman George Hausmann needed a haircut, Bernardo Pasquel offered the services of his personal barber) to gringo major leaguers willing to make the jump. Several quality players, including Mickey Owen, Sal Maglie, and Max Lanier, took the bait, as well as a dozen or so lesser lights.

The Pasquels' league had an interesting operating structure. Players were signed by the commissioner's office and assigned to the various teams with an eye towards equalizing the talent distribution: individual teams were not allowed to buy, sell, or draft players. Gate receipts were not split between the home and visiting teams as was (and is) the case in U.S. baseball; they were sent to league headquarters, which then paid out monthly operating fees to each club. Any monies left over at the end of the season after expenses were deducted were to be divvied up among the teams according to their home attendance.

It was this egalitarian split of revenues that ultimately doomed the Mexican League. The teams with the high-priced major league players found themselves unable to cover

their higher salary costs, and thus by August 1946 the league began to come apart. The "jumping beans," as Giants manager Mel Ott termed them, were informally blacklisted from playing in the majors for several years, but the ban was lifted by commissioner Happy Chandler in 1949 to fend off a proposed suit by ex-Giant outfielder Danny Gardella (Lewis F. Atchison, "How Mexican Raids Threatened to Ruin Majors 25 Years Ago," *Baseball Digest*, July, 1971, pp. 72–75).

7. Miller, *A Whole Different Ball Game*, p. 87. The owners had even footed the bill for Miller's predecessors J. Norman Lewis (served 1954–60) and Robert Cannon (1960–66). As a result of this symbiotic relationship, Lewis's early successes in negotiating improved pension benefits for the players probably led to his demise. In early 1959, management suggested in a stage whisper to the players that Lewis should be replaced, and the player representatives (who incidentally were chosen by club management) predictably took this advice to heart.

8. Miller, *A Whole Different Ball Game*, p. 46.

9. *Ibid.*, pp. 3–5.

10. *Ibid.*, pp. 51–52.

11. *Ibid.*, p. 206.

12. Jerome Holtzman, "The Year of the Player Strike," *1973 Official Baseball Guide*, p. 267.

13. *Ibid.*

14. *Ibid.*

15. Miller, *A Whole Different Ball Game*, pp. 204–205.

16. Holtzman, "The Year of the Player Strike," p. 268.

17. Holtzman, "'71 Saw Gate Up, Short Move, Alex Angry," pp. 308–309.

18. Spink, *1973 Official Baseball Guide*, p. 110.

19. Holtzman, "The Year of the Player Strike," p. 269.

20. Miller, *A Whole Different Ball Game*, p. 212.

21. Holtzman, "The Year of the Player Strike," p. 273.

22. *Ibid.* Parker wrote a letter to Miller after the strike ended, saying in part, "Though I may have misinterpreted your position, I have never doubted your sincerity or your ability as a negotiator and clear thinker. I think that your advice and leadership throughout [the strike] was sound."

Marvin Miller suggests (*A Whole Different Ball Game*, p. 209) that Parker may have sacrificed much for his advocacy of management in the strike. The Dodgers' vote on giving strike authority to the Executive Committee was 21–4, with Parker as one of the dissenters. At a subsequent meeting with the MLBPA leader, Walter O'Malley asked who the four naysayers were; when Miller refused to tell him and asked why he wanted to know, O'Malley replied, "A baseball team is only as good as its unity. I don't want players that cast themselves as management tools on my team. Don't get me wrong; I'd prefer the players to vote unanimously not to strike, but if the majority decides to walk out, I don't want dissenters on my club opposing their teammates. A winning club is united, not split."

According to Miller, the four who stood with management were Parker, two other veteran stars, and a utility catcher ... and two of the four retired at season's end (one being Parker), while the other two were traded.

Well ... maybe that's true and maybe it isn't. Parker, a Gold Glove first baseman with marginal power but good strike zone judgment, was 32 in 1972 and had Steve Garvey and Bill Buckner breathing down his neck — these were the reasons he gave for his retirement at the time. Still, neither Buckner nor Garvey was quite ready for prime time (Garvey representing a particular risk coming off a season in which he'd hit .269 with 17 walks in 294 at-bats), while Parker was probably just as good offensively as either one and a superior gloveman.

Was Wes Parker given a helping hand into retirement? Only Wes knows for sure.

23. Miller, *A Whole Different Ball Game*, p. 209.

24. Major League Baseball Players Association Player Representatives, *1973 Official Baseball Guide*, p. 67.

25. Holtzman, "The Year of the Player Strike," p. 273.

26. Some comments from *A Whole Different Ball Game*:

On Angels player rep Bob Rogers's admission that he had been pressured by fellow players to publicly criticize Miller shortly after his election to the MLBPA helm in 1966: "A more perceptive or intelligent man would have said, 'The players in management's pocket put a lot of pressure on me'" (p. 44).

On Fred Lynn and Carlton Fisk, who be-

came free agents after the 1980 season despite the best efforts of their agent (Jerry Kapstein) to deprive them of that right: "Both Lynn and Fisk had been poorly served by Kapstein, and the union rescued them.... And, worst of all, neither player was perceptive enough to understand what had happened, even though the facts stared them in the face."

On the lack of support by current players for Curt Flood: "... the fact that not one player showed up at the trial to demonstrate his support highlighted the 'me first' attitude that, regrettably, has always been a part of the game and perhaps a major element in our society as well. Because in the final analysis, the Flood case was the players' case, and *some* of them should have been there."

27. Holtzman, "The Year of the Player Strike," p. 277. This calculation is based upon the ultimate settlement, which called for $500,000 of the pension surplus to be reallocated for payment of retirement benefits plus $490,000 in increased health care costs/savings that would now accrue to the players divided by the 600 players on major league rosters at the time.

28. Kuhn admits in *Hardball*, p. 106, that "The PRC strategy was to stand fast on what it felt was a fair offer. Among the club executives there was a divided view as to whether Miller was bluffing. Some felt that if Miller called a strike their players would not comply."

29. Miller, *A Whole Different Ball Game*, p. 209–10.

30. Holtzman, "The Year of the Player Strike," p. 276. The Towers, Perrin, Foster and Crosby report was never made public — in fact, the owners were forced to return their copies at the end of the April 4 meeting at which the analysis was presented.

31. Spink went so far as to question whether "the whole idea of pensions for major league players may have been a mistake growing out of a misconception of what constitutes a career." (Miller, *A Whole Different Ball Game*, p. 215).

32. Holtzman, "The Year of the Player Strike," p. 274.

33. *Ibid.*

34. *Ibid.*, p. 277.

35. *Ibid.*

36. *Ibid.*, p. 278.

37. *Ibid.*, p. 277.

38. There was amazingly little comment

about this obvious injustice at the time, perhaps because Detroit took two out of three from Boston in the season's final series at Tiger Stadium. Yet such is not to say that emotions didn't run high: Carl Yastrzemski wept openly in the dressing room after the Bosox were eliminated, saying that the 1972 pennant race "meant more to me than 1967." (Larry Claflin, "Kasko Finds 2-Year Contract In Midst of Bosox' Flag Ruins," *The Sporting News*, October 21, 1972, p. 17).

39. Holtzman, "The Year of the Player Strike," p. 279.

40. Forman, *Baseball-Reference.com*.

41. Holtzman, "The Year of the Player Strike," p. 279.

42. Ted Simmons, for example, said in reference to the MLPBA chief on the eve of the 1981 strike, "All I need to know is what he wants done." (*A Whole Different Ball Game*, p. 303) Miller portrays this as being a "for the fans" type of comment and he may well be right about that, but consider Ferguson Jenkins's claim on the same page that "We [the players] would be lost without the Association. We're like a bunch of foundering idiots without it."

43. Robert L. Burnes, "Season's High, Low Spots," *Baseball Digest*, January, 1973, p. 78.

44. Miller, *A Whole Different Ball Game*, pp. 240–241. During the grievance hearing, Cincinnati GM Bob Howsam claimed that that the club had been unable to contact Tolan during his suspension because "he was shacking up with a white woman." Howsam's comment was ultimately stricken from the record.

Having said that, Tolan's trade was as much a result of a nightmarish season (.206 with only 15 steals and 27 walks in 457 at-bats) and the concurrent emergence of Ken Griffey Sr. as it was due to any off-field shenanigans. Still, an August 23 shouting match with director of player development Sheldon "Chief" Bender was probably the final nail in Bobby's Cincinnati coffin. Complaining of back problems, Bender scheduled an 8:30 a.m. appointment with team physician Dr. George Ballou — when Tolan complained about the early hour, one thing led to another and a couple of players ended up having to separate the two before fists flew.

After failing to keep the appointment the next day, Tolan was placed on the disabled list, prompting him to unleash a verbal tirade at Bender in a follow-up telephone call that cost him $250 (Bobby was fined an additional $100 for missing the appointment). (Earl Lawson, "Tolan Barks Once Too Often, Winds Up in Red Doghouse," *The Sporting News*, September 15, 1973, p. 14.)

Though Bowie Kuhn and Chub Feeney overturned the disabled list move under the premise that Tolan was declared unfit before being examined, the center fielder was hardly used down the stretch and would be the only player on the roster not to see action in the 1973 NLCS against the Mets (Bucek [ed.], *The Baseball Encyclopedia* [Tenth Edition], p. 2920).

45. Joe McGuff, "Royals' Fans Expect Tallis to Swing a Big Deal," *The Sporting News*, November 25, 1972, p. 41. No formal complaint was filed after Lemon was hired as a special assignment scout by the club at his managerial salary.

Kauffman's "younger man" comments were in part spurred by a John Hall column in the Los Angeles *Times* in which the one-time Indians hurler was quoted as saying, "For the first time I'm glad I'm old…. I'm just a couple of years away from retirement and I'm going to get out as fast as I can run…. I'm going to take my wife and we'll settle on some remote island. I'll buy a little beer bar and just sit there and think. I hope we don't even have any customers." (Joe McGuff, "Slowdown at Gate Could Speed Lemon's Exit From Kansas City," *The Sporting News*, October 14, 1972, p. 8).

46. "Major League Attendance for 1972," *1973 Official Baseball Guide*, p. 350.

47. "Major League Attendance for 1968," *1969 Official Baseball Guide*, p. 171.

48. Holtzman, "The Year of the Player Strike," p. 279.

CHAPTER 7

1. Phil Elderkin, "The Fireball Who Survived A Flameout," *Baseball Digest*, November, 1978, p. 38. The two state championship no-nos were back-to-back a la Johnny Vander Meer.

2. In an article by Jack Lang ("Majors Draft Record Low of 785 Prospects," *The Sporting News*, June 23, 1973, p. 5), it is mentioned that "According to major league

scouts, Clyde not only was the best prospect in the country, but there was a sharp drop in talent after Clyde."

The number three draft pick that year was held by the Milwaukee Brewers, who used it to select a Woodland Hills, CA shortstop named Robin Yount, while the San Diego Padres at number four settled for a University of Minnesota outfielder/first baseman/pitcher named Dave Winfield.

3. Jerome Holtzman, "Expansion, Canadian Club, Feature 1968," *1969 Official Baseball Guide*, pp. 203–204. According to Bowie Kuhn (*Hardball*, p. 93), Short's $9.4 million bid aced out an attempt by comedian and longtime baseball fan (he'd been a minor partner in Bill Veeck's Cleveland Indians partnership in the late 1940s) Bob Hope to purchase the team.

4. Bowie Kuhn in *Hardball* (p. 94) recounts a rambling late-night telephone conversation with the then-Senators owner in which he threatened everything from setting up shop alongside Calvin Griffith in St. Paul to selling manager Ted Williams to Boston. "No one can keep me in Washington," Short declared, "not Nixon, not Cronin, not Kuhn…. I'll go elsewhere before I'm forced into bankruptcy like Seattle."

5. Elderkin, "The Fireball Who Survived a Flameout," p. 38.

6. Randy Galloway, "Ranger Clyde Sweeps in Like Texas Tornado," *The Sporting News*, July 21, 1973, p. 17.

7. *Ibid.*

8. *Ibid.* Short's cut of the concession sales represented an additional (though difficult for outsiders to determine) windfall.

9. Merle Heryford, "To Find Rangers, You Have to Visit Infirmary," *The Sporting News*, August 11, 1973, p. 18.

10. *Ibid.*

11. Galloway, "Ranger Clyde Sweeps in Like Texas Tornado," p. 17.

12. Randy Galloway, "Ex-Whiz Kid Clyde Facing Fight to Regain Ranger Job," *The Sporting News*, September 27, 1975, p. 12.

13. Chris Roewe, "Pitching Averages—Including Games of August 23," *The Sporting News*, September 8, 1973, p. 23, Forman, *Baseball-Reference.com*.

14. Randy Galloway, "Teen-Ager Clyde Taming Hitters with Wise Pitches," *The Sporting News*, June 1, 1974, p. 8.

15. Elderkin, "The Fireball Who Survived A Flameout," p. 37.

16. Swioff (ed.), *Who's Who In Baseball* (1980 edition), pp. 127–128.

17. Elderkin, "The Fireball Who Survived A Flameout," p. 39. Haddix went on to characterize Clyde as "one of the nicest and most receptive kids I've ever worked with…. Physically I think he probably was ready for the big leagues at 18, but he wasn't ready mentally."

18. *Ibid.*

19. Randy Galloway, "Rangers Flash Slowdown Sign to Eager Young Clyde," *The Sporting News*, March 30, 1974, p. 42.

20. Merle Heryford, "Short Sells Rangers to Texas Group," *The Sporting News*, April 20, 1974, p. 16. "I just wish I could have done better myself," Short said after consummating the deal, "but I did everything I knew how, financially and otherwise, to make this team a success."

His sale to Corbett did not completely remove Short from the baseball scene, however; the ex-DNC chairman retained a 14 percent interest in the Rangers as a minority member of Corbett's group.

21. Galloway, "Rangers Flash Slowdown Sign to Eager Young Clyde," p. 42. "We had to stay after him," pitching coach Art Fowler added, "because he was forcing everything. I told him no less than two dozen times to just relax, to let everything come naturally.

"He wants to do so well that he has a tendency to overthrow every pitch."

22. Forman, *Baseball-Reference.com*.

23. In Pietrusza, et al., *Baseball: The Biographical Encyclopedia*, p. 1039, Phillies manager Eddie Sawyer is quoted as saying "Simmons had a great arm; he could really fire. His problem was that he had received too much well-meaning advice. He had been overcoached more than any pitcher I ever saw. Everybody and his brother had tried to straighten him out…."

24. Furman Bisher, "Hank Aaron Tells a Secret," *Baseball Digest*, November, 1971 includes an interview with Curt Simmons. Simmons's shoulder and elbow problems stemmed from a habit of striding slightly towards first base during his delivery, forcing him to throw across his body. This placed an enormous stress on his arm, and by the late 1950s the power curve that had propelled him

through the Phillies' minor league system in four months was gone. Reborn as a puffballer with the St. Louis Cardinals, Simmons recorded 78 victories and made two World Series starts after losing his Grade A stuff.

CHAPTER 8

1. Bill James, "A History of Being a Kansas City Baseball Fan," *The Bill James Baseball Abstract* (1986 Edition), pp. 40–41. Johnson's business dealings were intertwined with those of Yankee co-owners Dan Topping and Del Webb on a number of levels. Before entering the game, Johnson had partnered with the two men in a number of non-baseball businesses. He also was Webb and Topping's landlord, having purchasing Yankee Stadium as well as Kansas City's Muehlebach Field with the aid of a $2.9 million second mortgage from the team and then leasing the ballparks back to the Bronx Bombers. Not coincidentally, Webb's construction company was commissioned to build the new Kansas City Municipal Stadium.

Veeck once overheard KC general manager Parke Carroll confidently state to a group of baseball men, "I don't have to worry. Weiss has promised to take care of me," which pretty much characterizes the A's/Yanks relationship at the time. (Veeck with Linn, *Veeck as in Wreck*, pp. 267–269).

2. Dave Condon, "Charlie O.: Amazing Sports Maverick," *The Sporting News*, January 6, 1973, p. 29.

3. Veeck and Linn, *Veeck as in Wreck*, p. 324.

4. Bill James, *The Bill James Baseball Abstract* (1986 edition), pp. 41–45 gives a good overview of Finley's years in Kansas City.

5. "Draft History: 1965–1969," *CBS Sportsline.com*. The Athletics would net an impressive ten future major leagues in the inaugural draft.

6. To help close the deal with 1965 number one draft pick (number two overall behind Steve Chilcott) Reggie Jackson, Finley invited the ASU slugger and his father out to his gentleman's farm near Laporte, IL. Charlie cooked breakfast for the Jacksons that morning ... and had Reggie under contract before the meal was completed (Jackson with Lupica, *Reggie*, pp. 51–52). Simi-

larly, in the midst of romancing young right-hander Blue Moon Odom, Charlie donned an apron and cooked a fried chicken dinner for the Odom family in their kitchen (Kuhn, *Hardball*, p. 129).

7. Ron Bergman, "Hunter Dropped His Hands to Raise Win Total to 20," *The Sporting News*, October 2, 1971, p. 8.

8. Wells Twombly, "Cause For Concern — A's Seem Too Peaceful," *The Sporting News*, April 26, 1975, p. 20.

9. Charlie O. was actually a gag gift from the governor of Missouri during the team's Kansas City days. (*1973 Oakland A's Yearbook*, p. 48).

According to Catfish Hunter the mule traveled everywhere with the team, oftentimes even residing in the same hotel as the players. As Charlie O. got older he began losing his hair in the way of all mules, compelling Charlie O. (the human) to have an ersatz mane and tail made for him. (Lyle, *The Bronx Zoo*, p. 83.)

10. Ron Bergman, "Green Right at Home as A's Moving Man," *The Sporting News*, November 25, 1972, p. 47.

11. Jack Murphy, Untitled, *Baseball Digest*, June, 1972, p. 58. "Vida was my father's name, the Spanish word for life," the A's left-hander explained. "Now that he's dead, I honor him every time the name Vida Blue appears in the headlines."

12. Bergman, "What Happened to the Mustache Gang?" p. 17.

13. Kuhn, *Hardball*, pp. 134–137. Andrews was reinstated to the Oakland roster by Kuhn and, in an act of defiance by manager Dick Williams (who would resign at series end) sent up as a pinch hitter in the eighth inning of Game 4. The second baseman received a standing O from the Shea Stadium crowd, and in true storybook fashion ... grounded out.

What escaped much comment at the time was the question of why Williams chose to put Andrews out on the field in the first place. True, the other A's second basemen had a horrible series at the plate (they went a combined one for 19), but Andrews was brought in to pinch for Ted Kubiak with two out and nobody on base in the bottom of the eighth inning ("1973 World Series," *1974 Official Baseball Guide*, p. 229). Mike had shown virtually no defensive range in the nine regular season games he'd played at the position for the A's that season (his all-too-real back problems, by the way, were common knowledge at the time). Though he'd been a fine hitter earlier in his career, Andrews had posted a .200 average with no homers in 180 at-bats in 1973 — numbers that were virtually identical to those of the man he was replacing.

In all likelihood Williams simply ran out of ideas. Down two runs near the end of a game that the A's had seemingly already booted away (Oakland reliever Darold Knowles had given the Mets their lead via a wild throw to the plate in the sixth inning), he exchanged a potential single for placing his worst defensive second baseman on the field at what (with luck) could be a crucial moment. That Finley might go a bit bonkers as a result of such a move is, shall we say, less than surprising.

14. Bouton, *I'm Glad You Didn't Take It Personally*, p. 15. At the 1970 All-Star break, Bouton, who was sporting a 4–6 record with a 6.05 ERA, was offered a five-year contract to do the evening sports reports for WABC's *Eyewitness News* at $40,000 a year to start. Naturally, the Houston knuckleballer turned down the offer ... even though he'd be sent to the minors in less than three weeks (*ibid.*, p. 66).

15. Ron Bergman, "Tenace Size-Up of Blue—'Mentally Still Not Ready,'" *The Sporting News*, July 7, 1973, p. 10.

16. Baylor with Smith, *Nothing but the Truth: A Baseball Life*, p. 98.

17. Bergman, "Heavy Frost Killing Good Will in Finleyland," p. 5.

18. Ron Bergman, "Athletics Avoid Deep Water When Horacio Is on Bridge," *The Sporting News*, May 19, 1973, p. 13.

19. Ron Bergman, "Heavy Frost Killing Good Will in Finleyland," *The Sporting News*, May 4, 1974, p. 5.

20. Chris Rowe, Joe Marcin, and Larry Wigge, *1973 Baseball Dope Book*, p. 62. At a time at which a fan could cop a bleacher seat at Cleveland's Municipal Stadium for $0.50, Finley was charging $2.

21. Forman, *Baseball-Reference.com*.

22. Bergman, "Heavy Frost Killing Good Will in Finleyland," p. 5.

23. Ron Bergman, "Girls Swoon, Batters Fade When A's Put Rollie on Hill," *The Sporting News*, September 8, 1973, p. 8.

24. John Kuenster, "The Mad, Mad World of the Oakland A's," *Baseball Digest*, November, 1974, p. 8.

25. Ron Bergman, "Finley Blisters A's After Jackson-North Bout," *The Sporting News*, June 22, 1974, p. 13.

26. Ron Kroichick, "'Blue Moon' Risen: Ex-A's Pitcher Says He's Now a Better Man," *The San Francisco Chronicle*, October 14, 2001, p. C-2. Odom sprained his ankle as well in the melee.

27. Ron Bergman, "A's Charge Double Standards in North Case," *The Sporting News*, June 9, 1973, p. 16.

28. Bergman, "Finley Blisters A's After Jackson-North Bout," p. 13.

According to Dick Young ("Fights Routine With A's," *The Sporting News*, June 22, 1974, p. 14), while Jackson and North were duking it out Ken Holtzman, Rollie Fingers, Dick Green, and Darold Knowles were playing bridge across the room. The quartet "didn't look up: never missed a trick," according to Young. "It was just a routine day in the A's locker room to them."

Ray Fosse's injury was basically the beginning of the end for his career. Despite the diminishment of skills that had resulted from his celebrated run-in with Pete Rose at the 1971 All-Star Game as well as other less publicized collisions, Fosse had caught 120 or more games in each of the four seasons leading up to the Jackson-North bout. He would never play regularly after 1974, however, and a 1978 spring training injury essentially finished his career at age 30.

29. Bergman, "Heavy Frost Killing Good Will in Finleyland," p. 5.

30. Ron Bergman, "Mincher Weary of Bench Duty, Retires as 200-Homer Belter," *The Sporting News*, January 13, 1973, p. 44.

31. Maury Allen, Untitled, *Baseball Digest*, January, 1972, p. 39.

32. In the September 16, 1972 edition of *The Sporting News*, Bergman included a note at the end of his article ("Sharp Bullpen Halts A's Skid—Offsets Anemic Bat Production," p. 30) that read as follows:

"Listening to the A's play-by-play announcers, you get the impression that they're in some sort of contest to see which one can make the most complimentary remarks about Owner Charlie Finley."

One can't blame Charlie for taking exception to such a comment, but in typical Finley fashion he immediately turned a throwaway line that no more than one *TSN* reader in 50 probably caught and turned it into a cause celebre. Bergman was banned from traveling with the team on its charter flights, with the A's owner going so far as to instruct road secretary Tom Corwin to physically throw the Oakland *Tribune* writer off the plane if he tried to board. Corwin was told not to be seen talking to Bergman, nor was he to make his hotel reservations as had been previously the custom (the *Tribune* paid for Bergman's room and airplane seat).

Bergman's reply to Finley (published in "Bergman Bounced by Finley," *The Sporting News*, September 23, 1972, p. 7) was to the effect that the A's broadcast crew of Monte Moore, Jim Woods, and Jimmy Piersall would "be better if they didn't mention your name eight times every minute."

33. Ron Bergman, "Peace Reigns Briefly, Then A's Blow Stacks," *The Sporting News*, April 27, 1974, p. 5. "I want to play all nine innings of all 162 games," an agitated Rudi stated after the game. "When they take you out for a pinch runner, it makes you look like half a player." According to manager Alvin Dark, though, the move had nothing to do with Rudi's ability on the basepaths; he was simply under orders to get pinch runner Herb Washington into each of the season's initial three games.

In the final game of that mandatory appearance streak, Washington would record his first stolen base attempt of the season ... and be picked off by the Rangers' Jim Merritt.

34. *Ibid.* "I knew Alvin Dark was a religious man," Vida Blue noted after being pulled in the fifth inning of the season's third game, "but he's worshipping the wrong god — C.O.F."

35. Ron Bergman, "Bando's Outburst Just the Tonic A's Needed," *The Sporting News*, July 13, 1974, p. 7. After making the final out in an extra-innings loss to the Red Sox, Bando kicked a trash can ("I picked the largest one I could find to make sure I'd hit it," the 0-for-4 Bando said later) and exclaimed, "He couldn't manage a [expletive deleted] meat market!" Naturally, he — meaning Dark — was standing right behind Bando at the time, along with a couple of reporters.

36. Ron Bergman, "Athletics' Sizeup of Rudi: Greatness Without Glamour," *The Sporting News*, June 8, 1974, p. 5.

37. Forman, *Baseball-Reference.com*.

38. Don Baylor with Claire Smith, *Nothing But the Truth: A Baseball Life*, p. 99.

39. Sal Bando had an interesting slant on the Andrews affair — at least for public consumption. "Aw, that stuff about Mike Andrews was actually good for us in the end," Bando commented afterwards. "You know what it did? For two whole days it made us completely forget the fact we had to face [Tom] Seaver.

"How can the opposition psyche you out when you're too busy fighting among yourselves to notice?" (John Kuestner, "A's At Their Best When Fighting," *Baseball Digest*, January, 1974, p. 5).

40. Forman, *Baseball-Reference.com*.

41. John Kuestner, "Added Pitching Bolsters Dodgers and Astros for Coming Pennant Scramble," *Baseball Digest*, February, 1980, pp. 18–19. According to first baseman Dave Revering, the A's of those days had "about five men who can play every day in the majors."

CHAPTER 9

1. Reiderbaugh, *Take Me Out to the Ball Park*, p. 52.

2. Peter Golenbock, *Bums*, p. 98. Rickey received 20 percent of the profits on the players he sold on top of his $65,000 annual salary as Dodgers president. While working under a similar deal with the St. Louis Cardinals, Rickey had earned $88,000 from player sales in 1941.

3. *Wall Street*, Twentieth Century Fox Film Corporation, 1997.

4. Forman, *Baseball-Reference.com*.

5. Jerome Holtzman, "Summation of Year's Activities," *1974 Official Baseball Guide*, p. 288.

6. "Major League Attendance for 1972," *1973 Official Baseball Guide*, p. 350.

7. Forman, *Baseball-Reference.com*.

8. *Ibid.*

9. Bucek (ed.), *The Baseball Encyclopedia* (Tenth Edition), pp. 3000–3001.

10. *Ibid.*

11. *Ibid.*, p. 2636. The Giants apparently figured that the 35-year-old Stu Miller was finished after a poor 1962 season and thus sent him, McCormick (who had fallen into a long relief role after leading the league in homers allowed in 1961) and Johnny Orsino (a right-handed-hitting catcher made ex-

pendable by the presence of Ed Bailey) to Baltimore for Fisher, veteran swingman Billy Hoeft, and catcher Jimmy Coker.

The deal was a disaster for the Giants and was a factor in their passing of the NL crown to the Dodgers. Miller, as it turned out, had four more quality seasons in him, while San Francisco would play Russian Roulette with a series of hurlers before Frank Linzy stepped forward in 1965. Hoeft came down with arm trouble and was a throw-in in a trade with Milwaukee the next winter, while Fisher's performance (6–10, 4.58 ERA) was enough to get him sold to the Mets at season's end.

12. By 1971 Yankee Stadium was severely outmoded—the park had no escalators or elevators, minimal parking was available adjacent to the stadium (fans coming out to nighttime games were often forced to park their cars blocks away on dimly lit side streets in the days when the Bronx was the Bronx), and chunks of concrete would occasionally fall from the facades. It would take two years and $100 million to get the stadium and its surrounding infrastructure back in shape (Lee MacPhail, *My Nine Innings*, pp. 122–124).

By the mid-1970s, Metropolitan Stadium had the reputation of being one of the worst facilities in baseball. The upper decks behind home plate had been built on the cheap in the late 1950s to lure a major league team and thus were short on amenities such as leg room and easy access. The predominant view outside the stadium was that of acres of surface parking, while Calvin Griffith's shallow pockets and the ongoing attempts of the co-tenant Minnesota Vikings to abandon the Met led to peeling paint and disintegrating masonry (STATS, Inc., *Diamond Chronicles 1999*, p. 16–7).

The Mall of America, by the way, now stands on the site of Metropolitan Stadium. Though some may wax nostalgic over the loss of the old Met, the Mall of America's 35 million annual visitors is some ten times greater than what the Twins and Vikings drew (Palacios et al., *Ballpark Sourcebook: Diamond Diagrams*, p. 114).

13. Consider Orioles special assistant Jim Russo's 1974 assessment of the leagues' competitive situation from the vantage point of a super scout who frequented ballparks in both leagues: "The one thing that hurts the AL is that we haven't kept pace with the Na-

tional League in upgrading our parks. The newer stadiums in the NL tend to attract more fans because of their very newness and the greater comfort they provide in the way of seating accommodations and other facilities." (C.C. Johnson Spink, "We Believe...," *The Sporting News*, August 24, 1974, p. 16).

14. Palacios, Robin, et al., *Ballpark Sourcebook: Diamond Diagrams*, p. 51.

15. *Ibid.*, p. 32.

16. *Ibid.*, p. 24.

17. *Ibid.*, p. 178.

18. "Population of 100 Largest U.S. Cities," *The World Almanac* (1996 Edition), pp. 390–391.

19. *Ibid.*

20. Reiderbaugh, *Take Me Out to the Ball Park*, p. 73.

21. Three consecutive seasons of sub-700,000 attendance (Marcin, et al. [eds.], *1976 Baseball Dope Book*, p. 52) would force Short to sell his Rangers to Brad Corbett in early 1974. Griffith became so tightfisted with a buck that seven members of a reasonably young 1977 Twins team that won 84 games and appeared to be on the rise opted for free agency that winter (Bob Fowler, "Free Agent Losses Crippled Twins in '78," *1979 Official Baseball Guide*, p. 61). Allyn would be unable to meet his payroll by the end of the 1975 season (Veeck with Linn, *Veeck as in Wreck*, p. 381). Finally, two consecutive seasons of $1 million-plus negative cash flow bred a palace revolt in which Mileti was ousted by his partnership group in favor of parking magnate Alva T. (Ted) Bonda (Unattributed, "Mileti Out and Bonda In," *The Sporting News*, September 22, 1973, p. 14).

22. Holtzman, "Summation of Year's Activities," p. 288.

23. Randy Galloway, "Superstitions Are Still Part of the Major League Scene," *Baseball Digest*, October, 1979. Carty developed the habit as a teenager fresh out of the Dominican Republic. With American dollars scarce where he grew up, Rico didn't trust anybody with his cash ... and still didn't 20 years later.

24. Prominent on the list is Hal King, a 25-year-old catcher who suffered from John Russell disease, his glove inadequate for regular use behind the plate, while despite having led the Carolina League in homers in 1967, his bat wasn't quite good enough to transfer to another position. Frank Tepedino, a once-hot Yankees prospect who

became the quintessional AAAA player of his era, saw significant time in the role as well.

25. Charley Feeney, "Robertson's Home-Run Barrage Just a Mirage?" *The Sporting News*, June 22, 1974, p. 12. "I just need steady play," Robertson told Feeney after a mini-outburst in which he hit six homers in as many games. "When I play every day, I develop a short stroke. That makes all the difference. Without it, I'm lost."

Well, sure, Bob ... but given the fact that Robertson was coming off a two-season stretch in which he'd hit .219 with 26 homers in 706 at-bats, while Willie Stargell ground away what cartilage remained in his knees attempting with indifferent success to play left field, one wonders exactly how much more regularly then-manager Bill Virdon was supposed to utilize Robertson.

"I don't know what the hell is going on," the first baseman said late in the 1973 season, "but sitting on the bench like this is a very, very uncomfortable feeling. I feel like I have too damn much talent to be sitting on the bench. And I've kept my mouth shut long enough." (Unidentified, "Robertson Has Doubts, *The Sporting News*, September 15, 1973, p. 17).

26. *1969 Official Baseball Guide*, pp. 301–308, *1970 Official Baseball Guide*, pp. 402–408, *1971 Official Baseball Guide*, pp. 409–416.

27. Holtzman, "Summation of Year's Activities," p. 287.

28. *Ibid.*, p. 281.

29. *Ibid.*, p. 287. "I'll be able to stay stronger during the game because I won't have to come to bat and run the bases," Lolich said in a manner calculated to generate an unintended smile or two, adding that "I'll get a lot more rest between innings."

30. *Ibid.*, p. 281. "I think baseball is a very good game and has been successful," the Baltimore skipper stated, "and I don't think it has to have any changes. I might be from the old school, but I don't think baseball needs saving."

31. Harold Kaese, "It Won't Be Baseball — It'll Be Dumbball," *Baseball Digest*, April, 1973, p. 43. Yaz continued on to say, "It's legalized manslaughter. The only thing preventing pitchers from throwing at hitters now is that they must come to bat themselves."

32. *Ibid.*, p. 45.

33. Holtzman, "Summation of Year's Activities," pp. 282–283.

34. Forman, *Baseball-Reference.com*.

35. "Major League Attendance for 1972," *1973 Official Baseball Guide*, p. 350, and "Major League Attendance for 1973," *1974 Official Baseball Guide*, p. 183.

36. Forman, *Baseball-Reference.com*.

CHAPTER 10

1. Forman, *Baseball-Reference.com*.

2. Roth (ed.), *Who's Who In Baseball* (1970 edition), p. 9.

3. Forman, *Baseball-Reference.com*.

4. Dick Joyce, "They Can Cram the Money!" *All-Star Sports*, June, 1979, p. 33.

5. Pat Frizzell, "Gilt-Edged Bonds Supporting Giants' Flag Bid," *The Sporting News*, June 26, 1971, p. 7.

6. Phil Elderkin, "Bobby Bonds Pays Off with Speed and Power," *Baseball Digest*, December, 1977, p. 94.

7. Pat Frizzell, "Bonds Rates as Giants' No.1 Candidate for Laurels as MVP," *The Sporting News*, October 2, 1971, p. 16.

8. Not that Bonds was the only Giant having problems with Fox, mind you. During a 1973 spring training brawl between San Francisco and the California Angels, a voice could be clearly heard above the din exhorting the Angels to "Get Fox! Get that [expletive deleted]!."

That voice belonged to Giants third baseman Al Gallagher, who was sold to the Halos a month later (Wayne Lockwood, "The Funny Side of Baseball Brawls," *Baseball Digest*, August, 1973, p. 37).

9. Dan Schlossberg, "How the Players Rate Their All-Stars," *Baseball Digest*, July, 1972, p. 52. Henry Aaron was pretty much a first baseman by that time and made the players' All-Star team at that spot. Had Aaron still been considered a right fielder, Bonds would have dropped to the number two spot.

10. Ross Atkin, "Bobby Bonds Takes a Giant Step Forward," *Baseball Digest*, October, 1973, pp. 21–22.

11. *Ibid.*, p. 24.

12. Zander Hollander, *The Complete Handbook of Baseball* (1975 Edition), p. 93.

13. Forman, *Baseball-Reference.com*.

14. Joyce, "They Can Cram the Money!" p. 33. The New York Yankees hired a private investigation agency to check out Bonds's past before trading for him.

15. Pietrusza, et al. (eds.), *Baseball: The Biographical Encyclopedia*, p. 103.

16. Joyce, "They Can Cram the Money!" p. 54.

17. Phil Pepe, "Bonds Promises Gilt-Edged Payoff Next Year," *The Sporting News*, October 4, 1975, p. 9. Bonds suffered cartilage damage in his right knee as the result of a game-saving catch on June 7 in Chicago. Forgoing knee surgery until season's end, Bobby had trouble getting started quickly both in the field on the basepaths for the remainder of the 1975 campaign. He also was unable to pivot at the plate, which strongly affected his offensive numbers. After 51 games, Bonds had cracked 15 homers and driven in 41 runs; over the remaining 111 contests, he would produce 17 taters and 44 RBIs.

18. Manager Dick Williams said during spring training that the 1976 Halo squad was the best he'd ever managed (Ross Newhan, *The California Angels: The Complete History*, p. 146). That sounds like hype for public consumption, but owner Gene Autry's "I honestly believe we'll go into the 1976 campaign as a contender" assessment ("More Power to the Rabbits," *Baseball 1976*, p. 49) was anything but a minority opinion. Most preseason publications rated the Angels a respectable third behind the A's and Royals.

In the aftermath of an altercation with Bill Melton on the team bus, Williams was fired on July 23 with the team 20 games under .500.

19. Joyce, "They Can Cram the Money!" p. 54. The chip was suffered during a Freeway Series collision with Dodger catcher Steve Yeager, but the Angels' team doctor wasn't able to detect the bone fragment until June.

20. *Ibid.*, p. 32.

21. John Kuenster, "It's Been A Wild and Cra-a-zy Sort of Season in the Majors!" *Baseball Digest*, October, 1978, p. 17.

22. Joyce, "They Can Cram the Money!" p. 56.

23. Pietrusza, et al. (eds.), *Baseball: The Biographical Encyclopedia*, p. 104.

24. Byron Rosen, "Rebellion by Indians Socks it to Boss Paul," *The Washington Post*, July 4, 1979, p. D4. In a simultaneous act of defiance against team president Gabe Paul, Torborg and a number of Indian players pulled the legs of their uniform pants down to the point that they covered all of the stripes on their leggings. "To hell with the stripe," Torborg declared in a manner that inspired joking comparisons to the infamous 1940 Cleveland "Crybaby" revolt against manager Ossie Vitt.

25. George Vass, "Five Biggest Surprises, Disappointments of 1980," *Baseball Digest*, December, 1980, p. 34).

26. Bill James, *The Baseball Book 1992*, p. 256.

27. For the record, the midseason fires (Bucek [ed.], *The Baseball Encyclopedia* (Tenth Edition), pp. 522–560) were Charlie Fox (San Francisco, 1974), Bill Virdon (Yankees, 1975), Dick Williams (California, 1976), Norm Sherry (California, 1977), Billy Hunter (Texas, 1978), Jeff Torborg (Cleveland, 1979), and Ken Boyer (St. Louis, 1980).

28. Joyce, "They Can Cram the Money!" p. 56.

29. Pietrusza, et al. (eds.), *Baseball: The Biographical Encyclopedia*, p. 104.

CHAPTER 11

1. Howard Cosell gives a cohesive account of the game's multiple endings in *Cosell*, pp. 42–43.

2. As Aaron points out in his book (Hank Aaron with Lonnie Wheeler, *I Had A Hammer*, p. 309), his record looks worse than it is because many of the quality guys they came up with like Brett Butler, Brook Jacoby, and Steve Bedrosian went out the door before they reached anything approaching their potential. Still, the Braves won an average of 65 games a season during the final half-decade of Henry's regime and did so with more home-grown talent than people tend to remember them having. For example, five of the eight regular position players and the four top starters on the 1988 team that lost 106 games were home grown, and while Tom Glavine, Ron Gant, and Zane Smith had careers in front of them, the other six were basically fringe players.

3. Hank Aaron with Lonnie Wheeler, *I Had A Hammer*, p. 18.

4. *Ibid.*, p. 9.

5. *Ibid.*, p. 34. Henry was aware of the irony even as an 18-year-old kid—"If dogs had eaten off those plates, they'd have washed them."

6. *Ibid.*, p. 90. Newcombe got even, though: "But what he [the hotel manager]

didn't know was that I had women in my room all the time. Black women, white women, all kinds. That bigot should have come to my room one night and seen what was going on."

7. Aaron with Wheeler, *I Had A Hammer*, p. 85. Perhaps even more telling was an ensuing headline from the Milwaukee *Journal*—"Aaron Has Nickname of Stepanfetchit, Because He Just Keeps Shuffling Along."

8. Forman, *Baseball-Reference.com*.

9. Durocher and Linn, *Nice Guys Finish Last*, p. 315.

10. Aaron with Wheeler, *I Had A Hammer*, pp. 112–113.

11. Forman, *Baseball-Reference.com*.

12. Ron Hudspeth, "Rico Carty: He's No Longer the 'Beeg Boy'," *Baseball Digest*, February, 1973, pp. 74–76. Carty was really two men in one, a public character with a perpetual smile on his face and a private one who called other black players "nigger" because he considered himself to be Spanish.

"Man, you look like you're from Newark to me," catcher Earl Williams told Carty after being informed of the difference.

A compulsive needler, Carty was generally disliked by his teammates and would fight with them on occasion; Hank Aaron once put his fist through an airplane luggage rack trying to hit the Beeg Boy after Carty had called Henry a "black slick." Still, he was a man who could easily be sympathized with — he lost a season to tuberculosis, was beaten up by three Atlanta policemen who only stopped when they recognized him, and watched his largely uninsured barbecue restaurant burn to the ground.

Though Hudspeth referred to Rico as having "a lot of ham and a little con artist in him," one has to give some credit to a man who overcame so much adversity and was thought of highly enough to be made an honorary general in the Dominican army.

13. Bouton and Shecter, *Ball Four*, p. 372.

14. Hal Jacobs, "Lester! The Strange but True Tale of Georgia's Unlikeliest Governor," *Creative Loafing*, March 20, 1999, p. 29. "By not serving blacks in his restaurant," Jacobs wrote, "Maddox says he was merely exercising one of the rights of private ownership guaranteed all Americans by the Constitution. When he closed the restaurant rather than integrate under a federal injunction, he said that 'my President, my Con-

gress, and the Communists have closed my business and ended a childhood dream.'"

Considering Martin Luther King to have been "an enemy of our country," Maddox refused to close state governmental offices or even attend an Atlanta funeral for the slain civil rights leader that drew 200,000 mourners. The governor even considered personally raising flags outside the capitol building that were flying at half-mast — according to journalists, only the presence of news cameras at the scene dissuaded him.

15. Aaron with Wheeler, *I Had A Hammer*, p. 183.

16. *Ibid.*, p. 185.

17. In some ways the best expression of this ambivalence was demonstrated in the response to a proposed exhibition game pitting the home run king and his new team, the Milwaukee Brewers, against the Braves in Atlanta on July 19, 1975. Only 200 Atlantans were interested enough to buy tickets for the contest, forcing the teams to cancel what had to have seemed like a good idea at the time. (Dick Young, "Young Ideas: Braves' Fans Snub Aaron," *The Sporting News*, July 5, 1975, p. 12.)

18. Longtime Braves starter Pat Jarvis bestowed the nickname upon Atlanta-Fulton County Stadium in the early 1970s. Riding into town on the team bus after an early-season road trip, Jarvis introduced the park to the new Atlanta staff members. "There it is, boys," Jarvis said as the stadium came into view. "Welcome to the Launching Pad. You might as well get used to it. The ball really jumps outta there." (Ed Hinton, "Why Hitters Call Atlanta Stadium The 'Launching Pad,'" *Baseball Digest*, July, 1981, p. 27.)

19. Bill James, *The Bill James Historical Baseball Abstract*, p. 619.

20. As late as 1972, *Chris Schenkel's Sportscene* chose Mays as one of the National League's All-Star outfielders for the coming year over such players as Willie Stargell, Pete Rose, Billy Williams, Cesar Cedeno, and Bobby Bonds. "Willie Mays could still do it all," the publication stated in defense of its choice. "He did last season in directing the Giants to the Western Division pennant in the National League."

Willie Mays in 1971 hit .271 with 18 homers and 61 RBIs in 136 games. With Willie McCovey only sporadically available during the season's second half due to torn cartilage in his left knee (Pat Frizzell, "Giants Put It All Together in '71," *1972 Official Baseball Guide*, p. 45), Mays frequently took over Stretch's duties at first base ... and produced a grand total of four dingers in 191 at-bats down the stretch.

Make no mistake: Mays posted a terrific season for a 40-year-old guy, one that merited selection by Bill James in his 1986 *Baseball Abstract* (p. 325) as the best ever by a man of his age. Still, the idea that such a season could rank ahead of the 48 homers, 125 RBIs and .295 average posted by Stargell that year demonstrates the amount of sentimentality that surrounded Mays and his performance in the early 1970s.

And oh yes, didn't Stargell's team win the world championship that year?.

21. Forman, *Baseball-Reference.com*. Aaron began having problems with his right knee after an inopportune slide into home plate against the Giants in July, 1970. Refusing to have the damaged joint operated on, Henry would have the knee drained a half dozen or so times a season and wear a brace for the remainder of his career.

22. Aaron refers to Jackie as "the man whose judgments I valued more than anybody's" (Aaron with Wheeler, *I Had A Hammer*, p. 116). "He [Robinson] made a special point of talking to the players he thought would be stars, because he knew their voices would be heard over the others'. I was honored that he pulled me aside a few times." (*Ibid.*, p. 115.)

23. Kenneth Reich, "Hank Aaron in Countdown on Ruth Mark," *Baseball Digest*, January, 1972, p. 44.

24. Aaron and Wheeler, *I Had A Hammer*, p. 168. "Baldwin wrote about the waiting and more waiting that American black people had done for generations," Aaron wrote. "I agreed with him that the waiting period was over."

25. Durocher and Linn, *Nice Guys Finish Last*, p. 55.

26. Aaron and Wheeler, *I Had A Hammer*, p. 242. Some "good" examples of the type of mail Henry received follow:

Dear Nigger,

You can hit all dem home runs over dem short fences, but you can't take dat black off yo face.

Dear Hank Aaron,

How about some sickle-cell anemia, Hank?

Dear Black Boy,

Listen Black Boy, We don't want no nigger Babe Ruth.

27. *Ibid.*, p. 235. Federal protection for Aaron and his family increased markedly after this incident. "There were FBI agents all over the campus, disguised as yardmen and maintenance men," Gaile Aaron recalled years later. "The whole year at Fisk, I was never by myself. It was pretty frightening, and I know my father was worried sick about it. He flew to Nashville to visit me almost every time he had an off day."

28. Wayne Minshew, "Evans's Batting Feats Lost in Aaron's Shadow," *The Sporting News*, August 18, 1973, p. 13.

29. "Major League Attendance for 1973," *1974 Official Baseball Guide*, p. 183.

30. Aaron and Wheeler, *I Had A Hammer*, p. 250.

31. *Ibid.*, p. 232.

32. *Ibid.*, p. 239.

33. *Ibid.*, pp. 249–250.

34. Veeck with Linn, *Veeck as in Wreck*, p. 242.

35. Chris Rowe, et al. (ed.), *1973 Baseball Dope Book*, p. 74.

36. Wayne Minshew, "Braves Bats Boom; Pitching Falters," *1974 Official Baseball Guide*, pp. 151–152.

37. Bucek (ed.), *The Baseball Encyclopedia* (Tenth Edition), pp. 518–519.

38. Aaron and Wheeler, *I Had A Hammer*, pp. 241–242.

39. *Ibid.*, p. 258. "If the Braves wanted me to hit the home runs there [Atlanta], I didn't have any objections," Aaron stated. "I sort of liked the idea of being able to show my grandchildren the spots where 714 and 715 landed."

40. Kuhn, *Hardball*, pp. 119–121. While Bowie's request wasn't exactly an order, the difference was minor: Kuhn threatened to make out the Braves' lineup card himself if Bartholomay refused to comply.

The two out of three game minimum was based upon the 108 games that Aaron had played in 1973.

41. Mathews called a press conference prior to the second game in the Cincinnati series and said that the Braves "had been fair enough" after Henry had hit number 714 in the opener against Cincinnati's Jack Billingham and thus Aaron would not play until the team's first home game three days later. "Right or wrong, this is Eddie Mathews' de-

cision," he said in summation. (Kuhn, *Hardball*, pp. 122–123).

"That's when the commissioner got pissed," Mathews remembered some years later. "And I mean pissed. He was gonna suspend me, suspend the owners, the integrity of baseball was at stake, blah blah blah. So I had to play him Sunday" (Aaron with Wheeler, *I Had A Hammer*, p. 266).

42. Kuhn, *Hardball*, pp. 123–124. Twenty-plus years after the fact, Kuhn goes somewhat out of his way to express no regrets about being absent from Fulton County Stadium when Aaron hit number 715. He points out correctly that there was no telling when Henry was going to uncork the climatic clout and that his duties as commissioner precluded him from becoming a camp follower for the indefinite future. "By hindsight, would I have opted for Cleveland or Atlanta?" Bowie asks his readers. "The answer is Cleveland, but how I wish I could have been two people in two places that night."

On the face of it, that comment seems reasonably gracious, but … ah, Bowie: you mean to tell America that if you'd known Aaron was going to break Babe Ruth's record that night you would *still* have addressed the Wahoo Club? That the symbolism of an exemplary individual of African American decent breaking one of baseball's most hallowed records in the heart of Dixie wouldn't have been worth a look-see? That showing up for the Braves' home opener (a team that, at the time, was in as precarious a financial position as the Indians) just to tip your hat to the future home run king wouldn't have been a wise idea in any event?

43. Aaron and Wheeler, *I Had A Hammer*, p. 267. The new home run king's dissatisfaction with Kuhn stemmed from Bowie's failure to be in attendance when Aaron copped his 3,000th hit in 1972 as well as the lack of so much as a telegram when Henry hit his 700th round-tripper off of Ken Brett in July. "I was deeply offended that the commissioner of baseball would not see fit to watch me try to break a record that was supposed to be the most sacred in baseball," Aaron wrote. "It was almost as if he didn't want to dignify the record or didn't want to be part of the surpassing of Babe Ruth. Whatever his reason for not being there, I think it was terribly inadequate."

Not surprisingly, Aaron saw Kuhn's snubs, if that's what they were, as racially motivated. "I believed he would have showed more interest in the record if a white player were involved and I also believed it was my duty to call attention to discrimination in baseball." (*Ibid.*, p. 247.)

44. Kuhn, *Hardball*, p. 125. Kuhn gives the impression that the rift with Aaron was mended during a 1981 luncheon when he and Henry shook hands and embraced, but the home run king makes it clear in *I Had A Hammer* (written four years later) that such was not the case. "I would have felt like a hypocrite receiving an award from Bowie Kuhn for the best moment of the decade," Aaron said in his book (p. 319).

45. Aaron and Wheeler, *I Had A Hammer*, p. 319.

46. Miller, *A Whole Different Ballgame*, p. 87.

CHAPTER 12

1. "Beer Bust or Ball Game?" *The Sporting News*, June 22, 1974, p. 14.

2. *Ibid.*

3. Russell Schneider, "Incident or Riot? That Depends on Who's Talking," *The Sporting News*, June 22, 1974, p. 5.

4. *Ibid.*

5. *Ibid.*

6. *Ibid.*

7. *Ibid.*

8. *Ibid.*

9. 6/4/74 Texas at Cleveland game summary, *The Sporting News*, June 22, 1974, p. 28.

10. Schneider, "Incident or Riot? That Depends on Who's Talking" p. 5.

11. *Ibid.*

12. *Ibid.* Chylak in "Beer Bust or Ball Game" described the fans who poured onto the field as "uncontrollable beasts."

13. *Ibid.*

14. "Beer Bust or Ball Game?" *The Sporting News*, June 22, 1974, p. 14.

15. Schneider, "Incident or Riot? That Depends on Who's Talking," p. 5.

CHAPTER 13

1. Bucek (ed.), *The Baseball Encyclopedia* (Tenth Edition), p. 498, 551.

2. Palacios, et al., *Ballpark Sourcebook: Diamond Diagrams*, pp. 80–83.

3. *Ibid.*, pp. 122–123.

4. Situated so the prevailing wind would blow out, air density and wind tests were run daily at the typical starting time for afternoon (1 p.m.) and evening (8 p.m.) games during construction of the Big A. The results from these tests determined the completed park's dimensions in the power alleys (Braven Dyer, "The Big A: A Dream Stadium Comes True," *All About The Angels* [1967 yearbook], p. 54).

5. Roth, (ed.), *Who's Who In Baseball* (1968 edition), pp. 74–75.

6. *Ibid.*, p. 111.

7. Chance, an intimidating right-hander who began his delivery with his back to the plate a la Luis Tiant, ran with Belinsky for as long as both were with the Angels. According to Angels traveling secretary Tommy Ferguson, "By far the most compatible [road roommates] I ever had were Bo Belinsky and Dean Chance. They were both deranged."(Untitled, *Baseball Digest*, May, 1977, p. 85.)

"Nobody made it with girls the way Bo did," Chance recalled after his career had run its course. "I never learned his secret, but I enjoyed trying." (Newhan, *The California Angels: The Complete Story*, p. 42, 49.)

8. Forman, *Baseball-Reference.com.*

9. "Major Changes in Baseball Playing Rules," *Baseball Digest*, April, 1973, p. 47. According to Sean Forman's *Baseball-Reference.com* website, the average 1950 National League team scored 4.38 runs per game in the four years prior to the change, 4.66 runs in 1950, and 4.49 runs on average in the four succeeding seasons. The junior circuit's run production jumped by more than .6 runs per team in 1950 from the 1946–49 average ... and then fell slightly *below* the immediate postwar level over the next four seasons.

10. Roth (ed.), *Who's Who In Baseball* (1968 Edition), p. 101.

11. Bill Veeck used to have the mound at Cleveland's Municipal Stadium tailored to the day's pitching matchup. When Yankee lefty Ed Lopat (who preferred a low, flat mound) went up against the flamethrowing Bob Feller, "we'd make it so high that if he [Lopat] had fallen off he'd have broken a leg" (Veeck with Linn, *Veeck as in Wreck*, p. 160).

12. Bill James, *The Bill James Baseball Abstract* (1985 Edition), p. 133.

13. Forman, *Baseball-Reference.com.*

14. Maury Wills and Mike Celizic, *On the Run*, p. 179. Veale would either intentionally or unintentionally reinforce this image by constantly wiping the sweat from his Coke-bottle glasses while on the mound.

15. "The 1968 Who's Who in the Majors," *Sport World*, October, 1968, p. 63.

16. Forman, *Baseball-Reference.com.*

17. Dick Young, "The Comeback of Luis Tiant," *Baseball Digest*, December, 1972, p. 32.

18. Forman, *Baseball-Reference.com.*

19. Mike Littwin, "Pitching Arms Should Get Special Care," *Baseball Digest*, September, 1977, p. 69. "It's hard to believe that a team will pay so much for a player, then send him to the minors where there's no trainer and bad coaching," Singer said in his final days as a Toronto Blue Jay. "I've seen a few careers ruined. Can you imagine a big company doing something like that? But baseball never seems to want to change."

20. Dick Miller, "Singer Undergoes Surgery," *The Sporting News*, June 29, 1974, p. 18.

21. Forman, *Baseball-Reference.com.*

22. *Ibid.*

23. Bob Ryan, "An Analysis of the Fine Art of Pitching," *Baseball Digest*, November, 1977, p. 37.

24. Robert Riger, "The Pitch That Changed the Game," *Baseball Digest*, February, 1972, p. 57.

25. *Ibid.*, p. 59.

26. Pietrusza et al. (eds.), *Baseball: The Biographical Encyclopedia*, p. 92.

27. Riger, "The Pitch That Changed the Game," *Baseball Digest*, February, 1972, p. 60.

28. Uhle was the subject of an extensive interview in Richard Bak's *Cobb Would Have Caught It: The Golden Age of Baseball in Detroit*. According to his account, Uhle came up with the pitch more or less by accident during a workout with Harry Heilmann. "I just happened to turn a ball loose a certain way," The Bull recalled, "and it sailed. I said to Heilmann, 'I've got a new one!' So I threw another one that way, and it sailed. I started using it in ballgames. When I first started using it with Detroit, the batters would call time and want the umpire to look at the ball, like I had roughed it up."

Exactly how much of an impact the slider had on Uhle's career is difficult to determine, given that the right-hander had already experienced arm trouble in his years with the Senators. However, it should be noted that after working 488 innings in his first two campaigns throwing the nickel curve, Uhle would record only 444 additional frames in the remaining five seasons of his career.

29. Ryan, "An Analysis of the Fine Art of Pitching," pp. 37–38.

30. James, *The Baseball Book 1990*, p. 200. Alexander nearly lost his leg in the incident, which may or may not have terminated his big-league career as well. A lifetime .331 hitter and the previous year's batting champion, Alexander was let go after the 1933 season by the Boston Red Sox when he didn't hit after returning from the scalding. Given the Big Ox's career average and the fact that he was a quality minor league hitter for nearly a decade after leaving the Show, one might assume that a potential Hall of Fame career was sacrificed on the altar of medical science on that May day in 1933. However, do keep in mind that:

1. Alexander was 30.
2. He was a poor defensive player (after a 1931 season in which he'd hit .325, Alexander was benched by the Tigers in favor of a guy named Harry Davis, who would hit .264 with minimal power while finishing third in [most] errors committed by an AL first baseman).
3. He was as fast as 6'3," 215 guys normally are even before the injury.
4. After hitting 45 homers in his first two seasons, the Big Ox had connected for only 16 in the three following campaigns (1,222 at-bats).

31. Pietrusza, et al. (eds.), *Baseball: The Biographical Encyclopedia*, p. 705. The doctor even sent Mantle a bill for his "services."

32. Jim Bouton tells a wonderful story (Bouton and Shecter, *Ball Four*, p. 46) about a 1965 visit to Yankees team physician Dr. Sidney Gaynor when Bouton's arm problems were beginning. After having Bouton go through some stretching exercises, Gaynor said, "You got a sore arm."

Bouton: "Yeah, I know. It hurts when I throw."

Gaynor: "If it's sore, don't throw."

Bouton: "For how long? A day, a week?"

Gaynor: "I don't know. When it starts feeling better, then you can start throwing again."

"I believe Dr. Gaynor was actually offended when you came to him with an injury," the knuckleballer-to-be wrote. "You were imposing on his time. I'm sure there were a lot of guys who chose not to go to him with injuries because they didn't want to take his guff. I know I did."

33. *Ibid.*, pp. 45–46.

34. Peter Gammons, "Spear-Carrier Guerrero? He's Bosox Beaut at Short," *The Sporting News*, May 4, 1974, p. 4. The visiting Detroit Tiger relievers resorted to lighting a bonfire in their bullpen to keep warm. "I once played in a snow and ice storm in Wisconsin Rapids," Boston catcher Bob Montgomery said after the game. "The only reason this was any better was that it was played in Boston, not Wisconsin Rapids."

35. Forman, *Baseball-Reference.com*.

36. Sid Bordman, "'I Hope I'm Never Satisfied'— Busby," *The Sporting News*, August 3, 1974, p. 3. Busby, however, didn't consider himself a power pitcher — "I can't throw the fastball up very often and not get hit," he commented when asked about the classification.

Busby already had a history of health problems by the time Bordman's article came out; a knee injury had cost him a big bonus from the Giants out of high school, while surgery to relocate his pitching arm's ulna nerve had pretty much wiped out his sophomore year at USC. Steve felt that his heater was still rebounding four years later and that he hadn't completely regained the touch on his curve.

37. Ray Kelly, "Quakers Miffed by Scarcity of Mac's Headlines," *The Sporting News*, June 8, 1974, pp. 3–4.

38. Melvin Durslag, "A Duster Artist," *The Sporting News*, August 25, 1973, p. 7.

39. *1973 Cincinnati Reds Yearbook*, p. 39. Houston manager Harry Walker said after Grimsley's performance, "He may be the best left-hander in the league with the exception of Steve Carlton."

40. *1975 Official Baseball Guide*, p. 385.

41. Peter Gammons, "Jim Kern: Best Reliever in the American League," *Baseball Digest*, September, 1979, p. 76. Though people sent Kern dozens of emu pictures, ex-roommate Dennis Eckersley's moniker. "The Air-

head Master"—seems like a more fitting tribute. Kern apparently had a thing about setting people's shoes on fire: a pair of Danny Darwin's shower clogs were once sacrificed to the gods because of their bedraggled look. While with the Indians, Kern ran a contest to see who could raise the biggest spider in Municipal Stadium's decrepit bullpen (Paul Hagan, "Rangers' Bullpen Takes a Zany Road for Relief," *Baseball Digest*, June, 1980, p. 76).

42. *Ibid.*, p. 77.

43. Forman, *Baseball-Reference.com*.

44. *Ibid.* Rangers outfielder/teammate Al Oliver made the comment, further stating, "When he's pitching the way he has, it's like having a vacation in the outfield."

45. Bill James, *The Bill James Guide to Baseball Managers*, p. 147.

46. Randy Galloway, "Who's Jim Bibby? The Rangers' New Mound Whiz," *The Sporting News*, August 4, 1973, p. 18. "There were times during that recuperation period of 1970 when I wondered if it was worth it," the then 28-year-old rookie said. "I thought maybe it just wasn't meant for me to play baseball, that maybe I should quit and get into something else. But I guess I had something to prove. I pushed myself into coming back for more."

What Bibby had to prove, by the way, may have had as much to do with living up to the family athletic tradition as it did with achieving his own potential. Jim's younger brother Henry was the UCLA and New York Knicks' star.

47. Randy Galloway, "Bibby on Hill, Anything Can Happen," *The Sporting News*, August 10, 1974, p. 14.

Rangers manager Whitey Herzog in Galloway, "Who's Jim Bibby? The Rangers' New Mound Whiz," p. 18, noted that "What interested us about Bibby was the fastball. I'd say only Nolan Ryan throws consistently harder in this league. And since this is a breaking-ball league, we felt that if Bibby could get the ball over the plate, he might be successful."

48. Forman, *Baseball-Reference.com*.

CHAPTER 14

1. Pietrusza, *Baseball: The Biographical Encyclopedia*, p. 172.

2. John Flynn, "Steve Carlton: At Last, a Winner for the Phils," *Baseball Digest*, November 1972, p. 41. Carlton's uncles originally introduced him to metaphysics as a kid.

3. Pietrusza, *Baseball: The Biographical Encyclopedia*, p. 172.

4. Forman, *Baseball-Reference.com*.

5. *1973 Official Baseball Guide*, pp. 164–165.

6. Gary Ronberg, "Steve Carlton: Pitcher with the Classic Style," *Baseball Digest*, December, 1977, p. 27.

7. Flynn, "Steve Carlton: At Last, a Winner for the Phils," p. 42 gives a good capsule biography of Carlton's early years.

8. *Ibid.*

9. Gary Ronberg, "From the Archives: A New 'Interview' With Steve Carlton," *The Philadelphia Inquirer*, September 26, 1983, p. 8 (Sports Section). Carlton sparked a minor war in 1973 when he decked Expos pitcher Bailor Moore with a nasty beanball after realizing that the Montreal hitters were reading his curve with confidence.

10. Ronberg, "From the Archives: A New 'Interview' With Steve Carlton," p. 8 (Sports Section).

11. Neal Russo, "Steve Ditches 'Made in Japan' Slider," *The Sporting News*, May 8, 1971, p. 3.

12. Carlton's contract expired at the end of the 1971 season and by the middle of February 1972, the Cards and their erstwhile left-hander were still $15,000 apart (Flynn, "Steve Carlton: At Last, a Winner for the Phils," p. 44). "I guess, really, this thing was generated by our differences with Carlton two years ago," Cards GM Bing Devine stated when the deal that sent Lefty to Philadelphia for Rick Wise was announced. "We could sense a similar situation developing. We decided it would be better to trade him." (George Vass, "Spite Trades Can Ruin Flag Hopes," *Baseball Digest*, July, 1972, p. 30).

13. Robert Seltzer, "Unheard, Unseen Dorchester Neighbors Knew Little of Carlton," *The Philadelphia Inquirer*, June 27, 1986, p. C03. According to building staff members, friends who came to pick Carlton up at the Dorchester would wait outside the building with their car doors open to facilitate quick departures.

"I've never seen him, and I've lived here

ten years," one building resident said. "I don't even have any idea what floor he lives on. I've often wondered if he really does live here."

14. Jayson Stark, "The Door Remains Shut As Carlton Toasts 300," *The Philadelphia Inquirer*, September 25, 1983, p. E01.

15. Bill Conlin, "Lefty Says Goodbye," *Philadelphia Daily News*, June 26, 1986, p. 104.

CHAPTER 15

1. Miller, *A Whole Different Ball Game*, p. 97.

2. Holtzman, "Summation of Year's Activities," *1975 Official Baseball Guide*, p. 293.

3. Uniform Player's Contract, paragraph 10a.

4. Miller, *A Whole Different Ball Game*, p. 240. When Downing arrived at the Yankees' Fort Lauderdale camp that spring, New York GM Lee MacPhail informed him that he couldn't work out with the team until he signed a new deal. Pointing out that the reserve clause tied him to the team whether he had a new pact or not, Downing explained to MacPhail that keeping him from performing his duties under the contract would represent a breach on the Yankees' part, making Al by default a free agent.

Downing signed a slightly enhanced deal a few days later and was traded at season's end.

5. Simmons ultimately signed a two-year deal for $75,000 in early August. After earning $17,500 in his first full big-league season (and hitting .304 with seven homers in 133 games), the Cardinals catcher was looking for $35,000, while the Cardinals, citing federal wage controls stemming from President Nixon's 1971 wage-price freeze, were offering $25,000. Though Ted stated that he'd considered a Curt Flood-style suit if the impasse with the Redbirds had not been broken, he quickly added that such a move had never been a serious notion. (Neal Russo, "Cards Finally Sign Simmons," *The Sporting News*, August 12, 1972, p. 13).

6. At the end of a season in which Sparky went 9–3 with a 1.66 ERA and 15 saves, he received a deal calling for $87,500 in the about-to-be-completed 1974 cam-paign and $92,500 for 1975; by way of comparison, Rollie Fingers had received $65,000 from an arbitration panel that spring. Tolan earned $76,000 (an $11,000 raise over his 1973 pay rate) for his 1974 efforts plus $84,000 for the coming year, while Joe Rudi took home $55,000 for a season in which he'd finish second in the AL MVP race. (Holtzman, "Summation of the Year's Activities," *1975 Official Baseball Guide*, pp. 301–304).

7. Bob Hunter, "Swap to L.A. Gives Andy 'Good Feeling,'" *The Sporting News*, January 6, 1973, p. 31. Messersmith learned about the trade by listening to the radio in his camper while snowbound near Yosemite National Park. The more he thought about the situation, though, the happier he was. "It's tough getting motivated when you're fighting only for fourth place and drawing 6,000 fans," Andy commented regarding to his Angel years some time later.

8. Jerome Holtzman, "Summation of Year's Activities," *1976 Official Baseball Guide*, p. 286.

9. Miller, *A Whole Different Ball Game*, p. 242.

10. "The game the owners play is with or against each other," columnist Jerome Holtzman noted in regards to the turbulence surrounding Bowie Kuhn's 1975 re-election. "Twenty-four men, all with dukedoms. But for the last two decades, there has been only one king.... When O'Malley speaks, the dukes listen." (Jerome Holtzman, "Charlie-Jerry vs. Establishment," *The Sporting News*, August 2, 1975, p. 18).

11. *Ibid.*

12. Forman, *Baseball-Reference.com*.

13. "I like it here and I want to stay," Messersmith said late in the season, though he added ominously, "I don't know what's going to happen with the contract and I can't say I'm going to test the option because I don't know how it's going to go." (Gordon Verrell, "Messersmith Heads an Elite Corps of Dodger Hill Artists," *The Sporting News*, October 18, 1975, p. 39.)

14. Earl Weaver (Weaver and Stainback, *It's What You Learn After You Know It All That Counts*, pp. 221–222) characterized McNally as "the toughest negotiator I knew among the players," while Jim Palmer termed him "the number one mercenary." "Every spring McNally was a holdout for ten

to fifteen days," Weaver recalled, "and every day George Bamberger and I would collar [GM Harry] Dalton and say, 'For God's sake, Harry, give McNally what he wants. We can't afford to lose a 20-game winner and you know it.'.

"McNally would be in Key Biscayne playing golf, refusing to even talk until Dalton agreed to discuss Dave's figure. McNally was the only player I knew who could consistently bring Harry Dalton to his knees. Dalton never once got Dave to come down even a nickel below what he felt he was worth."

15. Miller, *A Whole Different Ball Game*, p. 243.

After starting the season 3–0, McNally had dropped six consecutive decisions while watching his ERA balloon to 5.26 at the time of his decision. "It got to a point where I was almost stealing money," the veteran lefty said at the time. "If I was throwing the ball well and wild, or throwing it well and making bad pitches, I could correct that — at least I feel I could. But I just was not throwing the ball well enough. I don't think I'd have gotten by even if I was making good pitches, with the stuff I had."

Still, as was often the case with McNally, contract issues were lurking in the background of his decision. Upon arriving in Montreal, McNally had, like Messersmith, asked for a baseball first — a no-cut contract. When Expos GM Jim Fanning balked on the novel concept, talks quickly broke down, ultimately forcing invocation of the renewal clause in Dave's contract to get him to camp. While the left-hander felt that the team had backed water on a promise made at the time of the trade that reaching agreement on contract terms wouldn't be a problem, it was clearly the no-cut demand that caused the impasse. McNally reduced his salary demands by over $30,000 from what the Expos had promised him over time without any sign of interest from the other side.

A point that would become more significant as time progressed: McNally neglected to sign voluntary retirement papers upon leaving the club. "They're putting me on some other list," he said, "a list that enables them to put another player on their 25-man roster, and that doesn't thoroughly throw me out yet." (Bob Dunn, "McNally Declares His Decision to Retire Is Firm," *The Sporting News*, June 28, 1975, p. 17.)

16. Miller, *A Whole Different Ball Game*, p. 243.

17. *Ibid.*, pp. 245–246.

18. Marvin Miller points out (*A Whole Different Ball Game*, pp. 245–246) another reason for the owners to have pause regarding Seitz. In an opinion written about an NBA dispute, Seitz had referenced a 1969 California Court of Appeals ruling that had found that the standard basketball contract permitted the renewal of an existing player contract for one year only. Since the NBA's "reserve clause" was essentially copied from baseball's standard contract ... well, let's just say that the MLBPA chief saw an opportunity.

Kuhn notes in *Hardball* (pp. 155–157) that a November 12 Player Relations Committee meeting was held to determine whether Seitz should be fired before the Messersmith-McNally question was brought before him. The vote was 6–1 to retain the grandfatherly arbitrator, with only Montreal's John McHale in dissent; Bowie's analysis of the matter was that the PR fallout from firing a guy who had achieved a modest amount of renown for his decision to free Hunter was unacceptable to the PRC.

Perhaps that's true, but a more likely explanation is that firing Seitz at that point would have looked too much like an attempt to get rid of someone certain to rule against ownership, thus calling into question any future ruling in which baseball prevailed. In short, gambling on Seitz seemed superior to having every newspaperman in the country questioning any affirmative decision a new arbitrator made.

19. Jerome Holtzman, "Summation of Year's Activities," *1976 Official Baseball Guide*, p. 287.

20. Miller, *A Whole Different Ball Game*, pp. 244–245.

21. *Ibid.*, p. 248.

22. Bowie Kuhn delivered a statement in which he claimed that "Without a reserve system, our vast array of minor leagues would hardly survive," while suggesting, "It is not hard to imagine that we could even lose a major league."

Seitz responded by reminding the commissioner that "the arbitrator's function is very limited. I'm not empowered to seek solutions to collective bargaining problems, merely to interpret the contract." (*Ibid.*, p. 248.)

23. *Ibid.*, pp. 248–249.

24. *Ibid.*, p. 251.

25. Jerome Holtzman, "Summation of Year's Activities," *1976 Official Baseball Guide*, pp. 288–290. The decision was common knowledge by that time, however; Messersmith had leaked the result to Bob Hunter of the Los Angeles *Herald-Examiner* a couple of days earlier.

Seitz emphasized in his opinion that "this decision strikes no blow emancipating players from claimed serfdom or involuntary servitude such as was alleged in the Flood Case.... It does no more than seek to interpret and apply provisions that are in the agreements of the parties." He goes on to say that his decision "does not condemn the reserve system currently in force" or even require that it be changed at all.

This is literally true, of course — the players and owners could have negotiated a Paragraph 10A that said in fact what everybody had thought it had said for 75 years — but in real life Seitz's statement represented either extreme naiveté or unseemly buck passing on the arbitrator's part. What Seitz ignores in his dissertation is that while everybody is free to negotiate what they want, the de facto situation has been radically changed; as a result of his ruling no reserve system exists beyond the one option year. The owners are now dealing from a position of weakness, attempting to regain advantages they are no longer entitled to under Seitz's interpretation of Paragraph 10A.

None of this, of course, means that Seitz's ruling was either wrong-headed or unfair: simply that the arbitrator would have been more worthy of the accolades that have been showered upon him if he'd been willing to face up to the implications of his decision.

26. Miller, *A Whole Different Ball Game*, p. 267.

27. *Ibid.*, p. 256.

28. *Ibid.*, p. 261. One wonders if Bench received some statistical help on that one.

29. *Ibid.*, p. 264. At least that's the way Miller was told that the decision came down. Bowie Kuhn (*Hardball*, pp. 162–164) tells a different story in which he played the key role in deciding to open the camps and O'-Malley is not mentioned. While Kuhn's version may indeed be the correct one, the idea of Walter O'Malley being disconnected from

any major decision regarding baseball is prima facie absurd.

30. Holtzman, "Summation of Year's Activities," *1977 Official Baseball Guide*, pp. 291–292.

31. Miller, *A Whole Different Ball Game*, pp. 250–251.

32. Kuhn (*Hardball*, p. 163) recalls Gaherin's departure and farewell luncheon fondly, while Miller (*A Whole Different Ball Game*, pp. 275–276) has the ex-negotiator commenting, "They [the owners] naturally want to hold on to as much as they can for as long as they can. In my judgment it was time for compromise. I think baseball would be better off today if we'd taken that route. My advice was ignored and a hard-line strategy was adopted."

Gaherin was a jovial Irishman with extensive labor negotiation experience in the airline and newspaper industries, but he was also a man who spoke his mind often and loudly while making little attempt to hide his true feelings on strategies he didn't agree with. As a result of this he made enemies (Baltimore's Jerry Hoffberger being the most vocal) among baseball's elite and according to Kuhn became more defensive in his dealings with the owners as time progressed.

Chapter 16

1. As early as 1973, Orlando Cepeda termed Blyleven to be "the greatest curveball pitcher I've ever seen" (Bob Fowler, "Bert Blyleven — the Touch of a Dutch Master," *The Sporting News*, August 4, 1973, p. 3). His hook was a virtually unanimous choice as the junior circuit's best in a 1975 poll (Larry Bortstein, "How 14 Leading Hitters Rate Best Pitchers," *Baseball Digest*, January, 1975, pp. 47–48) — "It's common knowledge," according to Rod Carew.

In a similar poll conducted three years later, the Holland-born right-hander was deemed after one senior circuit season to possess the NL's best breaking pitch. "It seems that throwing a good curve is becoming a lost art in the majors," one voter noted. "The slider is the big pitch now. But Blyleven has a fantastic curve, in fact two of 'em. He throws the nickel curve and a strike-

out curve that breaks with good spin on it."
(John Kuenster, "How Major League Play-
ers Are Rated in Special Talent Categories,"
Baseball Digest, April, 1979, p. 18).

2. In Miller, *A Whole Different Ball Game*,
p. 47, Marvin set the tone for his tenure in
comments to the California Angel players
made while stumping for his election early
in 1966:

"I want you to understand that this is
going to be an adversarial relationship. A
union is not a social club. A union is a restraint on what an employer can otherwise
do. If you expect the owners to like me, to
praise me, to compliment me, you'll be disappointed. In fact, if I'm elected and you
find the owners telling you what a great guy
I am, fire me! Don't hesitate, because it can't
be that way if your director is doing his job."

3. Condon, "Charlie O.: Amazing Sports
Maverick," p. 29.

CHAPTER 17

1. Pinson was, if you will, the primordial
Rafael Furcal. While most sources still list
Pinson's birthdate as August 11, 1938, it is
now commonly accepted that he was a couple of years older than that.

2. Leo Durocher with Ed Linn, *Nice Guys
Finish Last*, pp. 376–378. According to
Durocher, Pappas "was always agitating. He
became the player representative when
Randy Hundley quit, a job nobody else
wanted and Milt always loved. He had also
been the player representative at Baltimore,
Cincinnati, and Atlanta. Once he was the
player representative, he was holding meetings all the time. Practically overnight, all
harmony disappeared from the Chicago
clubhouse."

That paragraph tells the reader as much
about Leo and management attitudes of the
day towards vocal players as it does about
Pappas himself.

3. Earl Lawson, "Arms, Arms, a Red
Kingdom for an Arm," *1970 Official Baseball
Guide*, pp. 153–155.

4. *Ibid.*, p. 155.

5. Jack Zanger, *Major League Baseball
1970*, pp. 36–37.

6. Roth (ed.), *Who's Who In Baseball*
(1971 Edition), p. 121.

7. Brenda Zanger and Dick Kaplan,
Major League Baseball 1971, pp. 35–36.

8. *1971 Cincinnati Reds Yearbook*, p. 27.

9. Earl Lawson, "Tolan Barks Once Too
Often, Winds Up in Red Doghouse," *The
Sporting News*, September 15, 1973, p. 14.

10. Bucek (ed.), *The Baseball Encyclopedia* (Tenth Edition), p. 514.

11. The young Hal McRae's speed was
comparable to that of his son, but a 1969
ankle injury reduced his wheels to major
league average or perhaps a touch below.
Lacking good defensive instincts ("If we had
two platoons in baseball, I'd be a superstar,"
Hal said at the time) McRae languished in a
spare-parts role with the Big Red Machine.
By 1972 McRae began undercutting the
Reds' All-American credo by letting his hair
grow longer, leaning against the dugout rail-
ing while the National Anthem was being
played, and generally "making myself obnoxious"—and was gone that winter. ("Hal
McRae: A Premier Designated Hitter," *Baseball Digest*, July, 1977, pp. 50–51.)

CHAPTER 18

1. Cooper Sanders, "Inside Pete Rose,"
All-Star Sports, August, 1970, p. 55. Rose announced his goal immediately after winning
the 1963 Rookie of the Year Award. The article is interesting in the fact that it is based
around a rundown of Rose's salaries to date.
At a time at which the size of a player's paycheck was not normally a topic of general
discussion, we are told that Rose's 1965
breakout season (.312 with 11 homers, 81
RBIs, and 117 runs scored) earned him a raise
to $30,000 for the following campaign. From
there he went to $40,000 in 1967, $85,000 for
1969, and the magic $100K in 1970.

"Talk with Pete for five minutes and I'll
bet you'll be talking about money," former
Reds manager Dave Bristol said in a comment that means more now than it probably
did at the time. "He's infatuated with it."
(*Ibid.*, p. 72.)

2. Earl Lawson, "Reds' Rose Still Has
Rifle Arm, Foes Discover," *The Sporting
News*, April 28, 1973, p. 7.

3. Hustle, not surprisingly, was at the
heart of Pete's mid-career extra-base renaissance. "I've led the league in doubles for

three straight years," Rose commented after the 1976 season's conclusion, "and half of them were singles." (Maury Allen, Untitled, *Baseball Digest*, January, 1977, p. 43).

4. Jim Murray, "Murray's Best: Rose Is Red-Hot Item," *The Sporting News*, September 5, 1970.

5. Earl Lawson, "Hustler Pete Rose: Baseball's Best Ad," *The Sporting News*, July 18, 1970, p. 3. Rose played in as many as four amateur leagues at one time during the off season.

Ultimately, Reds management financed a team featuring Rose, Johnny Bench and Jim Maloney as a PR effort. Having said that, there was even more method to GM Bob Howsam's madness: he figured if some of his biggest stars were going to play basketball anyway, "I'd rather have them playing against high school faculties than in organized leagues. There was a lot less chance of them getting hurt."

6. Paul Donley, "The New Challenge Facing Pete Rose," *Sport World*, April, 1969, p. 8.

7. Garvey with Rozin, *Garvey*, p. 134.

8. In reference to the infamous Jim Gray interview before Game 3 of the 2000 World Series, Oscar Palacios commented in *Diamond Chronicles* (2000 Edition), p. 85, "Gray's interview [of Rose] was selfish. As selfish as dislocating a catcher's shoulder in an All-Star Game." Similarly, Geoffrey C. Ward (Ward and Burns, *Baseball: An Illustrated History*, p. 439) referred to the "savagry" of Rose's play.

9. Joe Marcin, "Mets Unseat Reds in Turbulent Series," *1974 Official Baseball Guide*, p. 211. Though Rose and Harrelson began duking it out after the play was finished, neither was ejected from the game for his actions.

Some years later, Rose and Harrelson would be teammates with the Phillies. "Bud's a good guy to have on the club," Rose said. "I like him, even though I did have to knock him on his butt in the playoffs that time."

Harrelson, dressing in the next locker stall, retorted, "What do you mean? I won that fight. I hit you in the fist with my eye." (Ray Didinger, Untitled, *Baseball Digest*, September, 1979, p. 62.)

10. Dick Young, "Young Ideas: Rose Does His Thing," *The Sporting News*, August 1, 1970, p. 16.

CHAPTER 19

1. Unattributed, *Baseball Digest*, September, 1971, p. 65.

2. Bob Hunter, "Dodgers' Ailing Hurlers Look Sharp in Action," *The Sporting News*, July 3, 1971, p. 18. Bill Singer's career between his 20-win seasons of 1969 and 1973 was one that according to columnist Dick Miller made the right-hander "the poster kid for the American Medical Association." Singer lost half of the 1970 season to a combination of hepatitis and a broken finger (the resulting surgery shortened the first digit on his throwing hand), missed significant time in 1971 to pulled groin and back muscles, then broke several bones in his hand just as he seemed to be rounding into form the following year. (Dick Miller, "Angels Hailing Zing in Singer's Fast Ball," *The Sporting News*, June 30, 1973, p. 20).

3. Pietrusza, et al. (eds.), *Baseball: The Biographical Encyclopedia*, p. 688.

4. Daniel Okrent, *Nine Innings*, pp. 40–41.

5. Roth (ed.), *Who's Who In Baseball* (1972 Edition), p. 117. One of the six wins was a no-hitter against the Cincinnati Reds' Indianapolis farm club.

"He taught me the mechanics and psychology of pitching after all those years," Norman would later say of Spahn (Bill Braucher, "Fred Norman's Long Search For Big League Stardom," *Baseball Digest*, June, 1975, p. 59).

6. Bob Ryan, "An Analysis of the Fine Art of Pitching," *Baseball Digest*, November, 1977, p. 38.

7. In August, 1973, Padres' owner C. Arnholt Smith received notice from the Internal Revenue Service that liens were being placed on his properties in association with $22.8 million in back taxes and interest owed since 1969. Leveraging his longtime relationship with President Nixon, the Padres' owner got the IRS to back off for the time being — a move that would suck him into the ever-widening Watergate gyre (Phil Collier, "IRS Could Nip Padre Plans to Move," *The Sporting News*, August 25, 1973, p. 12).

8. Buzzie Bavasi with John Strege, *Off the Record*, p. 145. The Padres offered DeCinces a $4,000 bonus; however, the future All-Star

third baseman held out for $6,000, a sum adequate to finance his college education.

9. Phil Collier, "Zimmer's Goal: to Vacate Dungeon," *The Sporting News*, October 7, 1972, p. 18.

10. Earl Lawson, "Reds Offer Thanks to Padres After Early Norman Conquests," *The Sporting News*, July 14, 1973, p. 22.

11. *Ibid*. Astros coach (and ex–Padres manager) Preston Gomez told skipper Leo Durocher, "Norman can be a good asset on a good club. The guy's a great competitor. In fact, he's a good all-around athlete. He has a good move to first, he can run and he can hurt you with his bat on occasion."

Even better, according to Gomez, was the fact that given the Padres' operating situation he was sure that the little lefty would be available for the right price.

12. *Ibid*.

13. *Ibid*.

14. Cord Communications Corporation, *Major League Baseball 1975*, p. 146.

15. Lawson, "Reds Offer Thanks to Padres After Early Norman Conquests," p. 22.

16. Jerome Holtzman, "Gura Geared for Spring Assault On Spot as Cub Mound Regular," *The Sporting News*, December 23, 1972, p. 45.

17. Joe McGuff, "Royals Find Bullpen Help in the 'Hall-Way'," *The Sporting News*, June 5, 1976, p. 3.

18. Forman, *Baseball-Reference.com*.

19. Edgar Munzel, "Wood's Knuckler a Mystery to A.L. Batters," *The Sporting News*, June 2, 1973, p. 3.

20. Joe McGuff, "Royals Flush a Quartet of First-Rate Starters," *The Sporting News*, September 6, 1969, p. 18. "I had him in my office the other day to talk about his future," then-manager Joe Gordon said. "I told him of the opportunity he has if he'll just bear down a little more on physical conditioning.

"The way he has been pitching, he'll go along real good and then run out of gas."

21. Paul O'Boynick, "Rooker Curbs Wildness, Saves Job," *The Sporting News*, August 23, 1969, p. 16.

22. Brenda Zanger and Dick Kaplan, *Major League Baseball 1971*, p. 211.

"Too much nitpicking goes on over there," Rooker said several years after leaving the Royals' organization. "When Kansas City shipped me out the last time, I couldn't

understand it.... Bob Lemon was managing Kansas City and he said the reason I was being farmed out was because I couldn't get left-handed hitters out. That was a joke. He brought me into a game only once to face a left-hander, and I got him out and pitched three more scoreless innings." (For the record, Rooker's 4.38 1972 ERA was the second highest of all Royals pitchers working 50 or more innings.)

Not that moving to Pittsburgh changed him all that much, mind you. After an unlucky early 1974 stretch in which he went 2–2 in six starts despite a 1.65 ERA, the left-hander was quoted as saying that "I'm not sore at anybody right now, but if I continue to pitch with consistency and find myself a .500 pitcher in July, I'm going to be mighty upset." (Charley Feeney, "Rooker Feels Cheated: Low ERA, Few Victories," *The Sporting News*, June 8, 1974, p. 18.)

23. Miller, *A Whole Different Ball Game*, p. 79.

24. A good description of the relatively crude state of orthopedic work in those days can be seen in Doctor X, *Intern*, pp. 251–305, a journal written by a young doctor who is rotating through the various medical services at a hospital in a medium sized southwestern city. The specific reference to mallet and chisel work is on pp. 297–298.

25. Durocher and Linn, *Nice Guys Finish Last*, p. 143.

26. John Dewan (editor), *The Scouting Notebook 2001*, p. 364.

27. Tommy John with Dan Valenti, *T.J.: My 26 Years In Baseball*, pp. 107–108. The White Sox team doctor advised surgery to reattach the ligaments, but John opted instead for a regimen suggested by a Palm Springs orthopedist that featured carrying his golf bag on his left shoulder. The shoulder healed on its own by the end of the year.

"It's a good thing we didn't operate on it, now isn't it?" the Chisox' doctor exclaimed after examining John the following spring.

28. *Ibid*., p. 143. According to John, the MCL tear occurred over a two-pitch sequence to Expos first baseman Hal Breeden. "My first pitch to Breeden was strange," John would recall. "As I came forward and released the ball, I felt a kind of nothingness, as if my arm wasn't there, then I heard a 'pop' from inside my arm, and the ball just blooped up to the plate."

After releasing the next pitch, "I heard a slamming sound, like a collision coming from inside my elbow. It felt as if my arm had come off."

29. Dr. Mike Marshall (yes, that Mike Marshall), "Pitchers and Injuries: Tommy John Surgery," *WebBall.com.*

30. Daniel Okrent, *Nine Innings*, p. 81.

31. *Ibid.*, p. 82. Brewers manager and ex-Orioles pitching coach George Bamberger helped Caldwell perfect his spitter, which earned him a berth on Lee MacPhail's widely ignored list of pitchers suspected of doctoring the ball.

32. Jenkins spent eight weeks in the hospital with four different casts on his leg, then underwent a physical therapy regimen that included electric shock treatments to get back on his feet. (George Vass, "Fergie Jenkins Wants to Go Out a Winner," *Baseball Digest*, August, 1979, p. 44.)

33. Pietrusza, et al. (eds.), *Baseball: The Biographical Encyclopedia*, p. 166.

34. Forman, *Baseball-Reference.com.*

35. *Ibid.*

36. *Ibid.*

37. *Ibid.*

CHAPTER 20

1. Forman, *Baseball-Reference.com.*

2. *Ibid.*

3. Robert Markus, "Don Sutton: Will He Be the Best Dodger Pitcher Ever?" *Baseball Digest*, May, 1977, p. 36, The four teams were Boston, Kansas City, Philadelphia, and the New York Yankees.

Why those four? "Well, remember this was at the beginning of last year [1976]," Sutton said. "Where did those teams end up? Kansas City, Philadelphia, and the Yankees made the playoffs. And Boston is always a good place to play ball."

4. Pietrusza, et al. (eds.), *Baseball: The Biographical Encyclopedia*, p. 1105.

5. Steve Garvey with Skip Rozin, *Garvey*, p. 101. The passage quoted was from an article by Thomas Boswell in the *Washington Post.*

6. *Ibid.* According to Garvey, the fight ignited over comments Sutton made about Garvey's wife Cyndy when the first baseman confronted him several days after the Boswell article ran.

7. Pietrusza, et al. (eds.), *Baseball: The Biographical Encyclopedia*, p. 1105. The comment has been attributed to Billy Muffit as well.

8. In Ross Newhan, "Do Dodgers' Hurlers Cheat? A Silly Question!" *The Sporting News*, May 25, 1974, p. 20, Sutton comments, "Why should I admit that I do or don't do something to the ball? Let 'em guess. It gives them one more thing to think about."

9. Burt Solomon, *The Baseball Timeline*, p. 811.

10. Pietrusza, et al. (eds.), *Baseball: The Biographical Encyclopedia*, p. 1105.

11. Newhan, "Do Dodgers' Hurlers Cheat? A Silly Question!" p. 20.

12. Chris Roewe, "32 1–0 Tilts in Majors — Drop of 24 From '69," *1971 Official Baseball Guide*, p. 349; "'70 1–0 Games in '71, 38 More Than in '70," *1972 Official Baseball Guide*, p. 350. "Angels Participants in Most 1–0 Games," *1973 Official Baseball Guide*, p. 337. "Mets, Matlack Busiest in 1–0 Games," *1974 Official Baseball Guide*, p. 330. "Heroics Punctuate A.L. 1–0 Games," *1975 Official Baseball Guide*, p. 336.

13. Joe Marcin, "First-Inning Explosion Ignited N.L. Triumph," *1978 Official Baseball Guide*, p. 300. Even as the game's MVP Sutton found himself overshadowed, as the game marked Tom Seaver's return to New York (it was held in Yankee Stadium) after the infamous June 15 trade that sent him to the Cincinnati Reds. Seaver received a standing ovation from the crowd and had to acknowledge it three times before the tumult subsided.

14. Pietrusza, et al. (eds.), *Baseball: The Biographical Encyclopedia*, p. 1105.

CHAPTER 21

1. Bill James, *The Baseball Book 1990*, p. 171.

2. "Phil Regan had a thick layer of grease on his forehead," Steve Barber claimed in a 1972 interview ("Should The Spitball Be Legalized?" *Baseball Digest*, December, 1972, p. 41). "If he saw an ump coming, he'd just wipe it off with his sleeve."

3. Pietrusza, et al. (eds.), *Baseball: The Biographical Encyclopedia*, p. 753.

In the grand tradition of bullpenners with odd pitches, McGraw was a free spirit at heart. After he'd passed on to the Phillies, Tug was asked how he intended to spend his then more than ample $75,000 salary. "Ninety percent of it I'll spend on good times, women, and Irish whiskey," the reliever said. "The other ten percent I'll probably waste." (Joe Falls, "Now It's Time for a Few Laughs," *The Sporting News*, May 17, 1975, p. 32.)

4. Pitching coaches, of course, weren't the only ones who had problems dealing with Hoyt's specialty. In the days when the Atlanta Braves were blessed/cursed with the presence of both Wilhelm and Phil Niekro on their staff, coach Charlie Lau opined during a seminar for the organization's catching prospects that "There are two theories on catching it [the knuckleball]. Unfortunately, neither of them works." (Wayne Minshew, Untitled, *Baseball Digest*, July, 1977, p. 64).

5. Watson Spoelstra, "Timmermann a Blue Chip Reliever," *The Sporting News*, October 3, 1970, p. 10. "I'm not the overpowering type," Timmermann observed near the close of the 1970 season. "I never have been. Check my strikeout ratio and this shows up. I figure if I lose a little off my fastball in the next couple of years, my ball will sink better."

6. Roth (ed.), *Who's Who in Baseball* (1971 edition), p. 123.

7. Spoelstra, "Timmermann a Blue Chip Reliever," p. 10.

8. "I was at home at the time having a cup of coffee," Hiller remembered some years later (Craig Stolze, "A Pitcher With a Heart — That's John Hiller," *Baseball Digest*, March, 1974, p. 38). "It felt like someone was sitting on my chest. I couldn't breathe. Pain shot up and down my arm." Though the left-hander quickly called a doctor, "I still had to unload a snowmobile before I could drive in to town."

The heart attack was basically a turning point in Hiller's life. Before the January, 1971, near-death experience he was a pudgy (carrying 220 pounds on his 6' frame), sometimes obnoxious guy who would routinely shove autograph seekers aside and toss fan mail in the trash. He lost 55 pounds after the attack via a training regimen that got him out of bed at 7 every morning ("At first I thought it [the early wake-up habit]

was from being in the hospital so long," Hiller said. "You know, they wake you up at six in the morning to stick a needle in your butt...") while becoming one of the most accommodating Tigers to fans and reporters alike.

"If I hadn't been able to play ball again, I'd probably be selling furniture in Duluth, Minnesota right now. That isn't the worst thing in the world — but it isn't the same as playing ball." (Jim Hawkins, "John Hiller: Tigers' One-Man Bullpen," *The Sporting News*, June 1, 1974, p. 3).

9. *1971 Detroit Tiger Yearbook*, p. 14.

10. Bouton and Shecter, *Ball Four*, p. 55.

11. Spink, *1971 Official Baseball Guide*, pp. 396–473. Hot on the heels of Fowler, Shifflett, and a guy named Bob Stickels in the American Association save race was 31-year-old ex-Yankee Dooley Womack and the well-traveled 36-year-old Danny Osinski. Neither would ever see the inside of a big-league stadium again.

12. *Who's Who In Baseball* (1973 edition), p. 98.

13. Forman, *Baseball-Reference.com*.

14. Ron Bergman, "Fingers Points Way for Athletics," *The Sporting News*, August 19, 1972, p. 21.

15. Fingers took a line drive in the face on opening day, then vomited through his teeth for three days (Rollie's jaw was wired shut) as he proved spectacularly allergic to a medication administered at the hospital. The right side of Fingers's face had to be reconstructed with wire after the accident.

In "more characteristic than people like to remember" fashion, Charlie Finley called Fingers and his wife shortly after his discharge from the hospital and told them to go anywhere they wanted in Florida for a delayed honeymoon (they'd been married nine days before the season started) with all expenses paid. (Ron Bergman, "Rollie's Follies Real Oakland Thigh-Slapper," *The Sporting News*, March 3, 1973, p. 3.

16. Forman, *Baseball-Reference.com*.

17. *Ibid.*

18. Newhan, "Iron Mike — What's Behind Brilliant Record?" p. 12.

19. *Ibid.*, p. 3.

20. *Ibid.*

21. Newhan, "Iron Mike — What's Behind Brilliant Record?" p. 12. The writer, J.P. Sarault, published the entire text of his suit

against Marshall in his paper's sports section the next day.

22. Bucek (ed.), *The Baseball Encyclopedia* (Tenth Edition), p. 36.

23. Pietrusza, et al. (eds.), *Baseball: The Biographical Encyclopedia*, p. 714. The then 11-year-old Marshall was riding in a car driven by his uncle when a train hit the vehicle. Mike's uncle was killed in the accident, while Marshall's injuries drove his interest in human anatomy.

24. Ted Blackman, "Mike Marshall: The Pitcher Nobody Wanted," *Baseball Digest*, December 1973, pp. 32–34 contains a series of comments — few flattering — about practically everybody Marshall had worked with at the big-league level. Ex-Expos catcher John Bateman, for example, is skewered for his "horsebleep" pitch calling early in the 1971 season, which may be true but given that Bateman was retired by then and not in a position to defend himself, one wonders if Iron Mike's memories might have been spiced up just a bit.

25. Newhan, "Iron Mike — What's Behind Brilliant Record?" p. 3. "After all, I have a general idea where the ball is likely to be hit according to what type of pitch I'm throwing," Marshall pointed out, "and I want my men standing in a spot so that potentially we would not be vulnerable."

26. Blackman, "Mike Marshall: The Pitcher Nobody Wanted," p. 32.

27. McClure, though remembered nowadays as a short reliever who was around forever, had been a hot enough prospect in the Royals' system to be a key figure in the deal that brought Darrell Porter to Kansas City. He'd had shoulder problems in the minors, however (missing most of the 1975 season as a result), and a 1981 rotator cuff tear coupled with habitual trouble in getting right-handed hitters out would ultimately turn him into one of the pioneering "situational" pitchers. (Okrent, *Nine Innings*, pp. 7–9 gives a decent overview of McClure, though his early history of health problems is overlooked.)

28. Bob Rubin, "Trick Pitches Spell Success in the Major Leagues," *Baseball Digest*, November, 1978, p. 71.

29. Phil Elderkin, "Master of the Game's Best Split-Fingered Fastball," *Baseball Digest*, December, 1979, p. 76.

30. Pietrusza, et al., *Baseball: The Biographical Encyclopedia*, p. 1103.

31. *Ibid.*

32. Forman, *Baseball-Reference.com.*

CHAPTER 22

1. "Major League Attendance for 1972–4," *1973 Official Baseball Guide*, p. 350. *1974 Official Baseball Guide*, p. 183. *1975 Official Baseball Guide*, p. 202.

2. In the latter category were such promotions as Bald Head Day, Hot Pants Day, Poison Pen Day, the selection of San Jose mayor Norman Mineta to throw out the first ball of the 1974 season rather than Oakland chief John Reading, etc. (Bergman, "Heavy Frost Killing Good Will in Finleyland," p. 5.)

3. Jerome Holtzman, "Summation of Year's Activities," *1975 Official Baseball Guide*, p. 284.

4. *Ibid.*, pp. 290–291.

5. *Ibid.*, pp. 292–293.

6. *Ibid.*, p. 287.

7. Bucek (ed.), *The Baseball Encyclopedia* (Tenth Edition), p. 521.

8. Baylor with Smith, *Nothing But The Truth: A Baseball Life*, pp. 98–99. Finley more or less assured this result by cutting the salary of every man electing to play out his option the maximum 20 percent allowed under the basic agreement between the owners and players.

9. Forman, *Baseball-Reference.com.*

10. Bucek (ed.), *The Baseball Encyclopedia* (Tenth Edition), p. 2517, 2519, 2547, 2650, 2685, 2690.

11. Kuhn, *Hardball*, p. 174.

12. *Ibid.*

13. *Ibid.*, p. 128.

14. *Ibid.*, p. 176.

15. *Ibid.*, p. 128.

16. *Ibid.*, pp. 130–131.

17. Both AL president MacPhail and NL prexy Feeney as well as Tigers owner John Fetzer advised Kuhn to let the sales stand (Holtzman, "Summation of Year's Activities," *1977 Official Baseball Guide*, p. 296). Even Chicago's Phil Wrigley, normally reticent in public on baseball matters, wondered "why the commissioner got mixed up in this in the first place."

A *Sporting News* poll conducted at the time found only 12.7 percent of its readers agreed with the commissioner's move.

18. Kuhn, *Hardball*, pp. 141–142.

19. It was this incident that would inspire Charlie's famous characterization of Kuhn as "the village idiot" (Holtzman, "Summation of Year's Activities," *1977 Official Baseball Guide*, p. 298).

20. Jerome Holtzman, "Players, Lawyers Gained, Attendance Up," *1978 Official Baseball Guide*, p. 334.

21. *Ibid.* "Kuhn can read about it in the papers," Finley defiantly declared as the deal was being announced.

22. Samuel Eliot Morrison, *The Oxford History of the American People*, p. 363.

23. Kuhn, *Hardball*, p. 184.

24. Washington was a strapping six-footer who according to one Indians player "looks like a yield sign from the back" when wearing a yellow A's jersey. Employed as a janitor when A's scout Jim Guinn came across him [Ron Bergman, "A's Discover Mr. Kleen in SuperWash," *The Sporting News*, August 9, 1975, p. 3], Claudell hadn't played baseball since his preteen years and thus was unschooled in the game's finer points when called up during the 1974 stretch run. It was a shortcoming that in many ways he was unable to overcome.

Despite his obviously powerful physique, Claudell would never connect for more than 17 homers in a season. Though possessing outstanding speed (he stole 312 bases during his career with a good success rate and was considered the fastest A when he first came up), Washington's poor defensive instincts precluded him from playing center field on a regular basis. He struggled against lefties for much of his career, essentially being limited to platoon duty in his later years.

Yet you could never tell with Washington. The 17 home runs he clouted in 1984 were accomplished in 416 at-bats—prorate that over a 550 at-bat campaign (Claudell played in only 120 games that year) and you get 22 dingers (Bucek [ed.], *The Baseball Encyclopedia* [Tenth Edition], p. 1717). Though primarily stationed in right in the Show, he was a well-regarded center fielder in his minor league days and logged 103 games at that position for the 1988 Yankees with above-average range (Forman, *Baseball-Reference.com*). After hitting .299 with some power against lefties in 1984 (Bill James, *The Bill James Baseball Abstract* [1985 Edition], p. 150), Washington plummeted to just .206

with one homer against southpaws in 1985 (Bill James, *The Bill James Baseball Abstract* [1986 Edition], p. 249) ... then came back to hit .361 with a .475 slugging percentage against them in limited (61 at-bats) 1987 action (Bill James, Don Zminda, and Project Scoresheet, *The Great American Baseball Stat Book* [1988 Edition], p. 449).

25. Bucek (ed.), *The Baseball Encyclopedia* (Tenth Edition), p. 2525.

26. Hoffberger had been trying to sell the Orioles for five years before prominent attorney Edward Bennett Williams finally agreed to buy the club for $12.3 million on August 2. The fear in Maryland circles was that the Washington-based Williams would move the team to the nation's capital: the team's lease on Memorial Stadium had one year to go at the time and only guaranteed that the Orioles would play 68 games per season there. The late-decade attendance uptick, both around the league and in Baltimore specifically, convinced the lawyer to keep the team in Maryland. "So long as the people of Baltimore support the Orioles, they will stay there," Williams announced upon formally taking over the reins on November 1 (Katchline, "Ump Walkout, Yanks' Troubles Dominate," *1980 Official Baseball Guide*, p. 325).

27. Kuhn, *Hardball*, pp. 224–225. Despite the fact that the sale was consummated in the aftermath of the 1981 players' strike, the Phillies fetched $30 million from a group headed by GM Bill Giles.

28. A good (and humorous) overview of Rickey's techniques in turning players into dollars is in Durocher with Linn, *Nice Guys Finish Last*, pp. 221–224.

29. Veeck with Linn, *Veeck as in Wreck*, p. 138. Veeck was at the time after the then 28-year old Early Wynn as well as star first basemen Mickey Vernon. "I knew that Griffith had no great resistance to money," Veeck noted. "If I had been able to sit down alongside Griff and show him, say, $100,000 in cash, I had no doubt that — once he had been revived– he would have reached automatically for a pen."

Both Wynn and Vernon would ultimately wear the Cleveland colors.

CHAPTER 23

1. Burt Solomon, *The Baseball Timeline*, p. 709. A good photograph of Mrs. Sivyer,

who worked in the A's ticket department and was one of the many early 1970s departees, can be seen in the *1973 Oakland A's Yearbook*, p. 66, while Debbi and her cohort Mary Barry are on page 48.

2. Ron Bergman, "Diary of Defeat — A's Were Losers Even in Bus League," *The Sporting News*, June 12, 1976, p. 10. On May 21, Ms. Brady predicted an Oakland victory the following Sunday ... and was wrong twice as the A's dropped both ends of a doubleheader to a White Sox team that go on to post its second worst record since 1950.

3. Jackson and Lupica, *Reggie*, p. 71.

4. Though the team would continue to make use of bird dogs, the A's organizational roster in the *1979 Official Baseball Guide* (p. 18) list no full-time scouts.

5. Don Baylor with Claire Smith, *Nothing But the Truth: A Baseball Life*, p. 98.

6. The first page of the 1973 yearbook, for example, contains a recreation of the January 6, 1973, *Sporting News* cover on which Finley was proclaimed Man of the Year along with ten other photographs of the A's owner. In the 1974 edition, Charlie is the subject of a two-page bio complete with six pictures, two of which are in color — the only two color photos (other than ads and the team centerfold) in the entire magazine.

7. Ron Bergman, "Injury to Rudi's Thumb Darkens A's Prospects," *The Sporting News*, August 30, 1975, p. 36.

8. Ron Bergman, "Bando Bat Mark Plummets, Worst Season for A's Star," *The Sporting News*, September 6, 1975, p. 8.

9. Condon, "Charlie O.: Amazing Sports Maverick," p. 32.

10. Kuhn, *Hardball*, p. 54.

11. Ron Bergman, "A Strutting Finley Hogs The Spotlight — As Usual," *The Sporting News*, August 2, 1975, p. 19.

12. Kuhn, *Hardball*, p. 120.

13. *Ibid.*, p. 130.

14. Ron Bergman, "Fan Appreciation Day Revived," *The Sporting News*, October 2, 1971, p. 8.

15. Ron Bergman, "Series Still the Big Thing to 20-Win Holtzman," *The Sporting News*, September 22, 1973, p. 8.

16. Ron Bergman, "A's Sit Quietly, Awaiting Bando Bat Boom," *The Sporting News*, September 23, 1972, p. 7.

17. Ron Bergman, "'Call Me Dumb, Not Cheap,' Fumes Finley in Ring Furor," *The*

Sporting News, March 23, 1974, p. 33. After the rings were presented, Reggie Jackson confidently predicted that the A's would go on to win a third World Championship in 1974. Why? "We've got the turmoil going already, the undercurrent."

CHAPTER 24

1. Pietrusza, et al. (eds.), *Baseball: The Biographical Encyclopedia*, p. 629.

2. Kuhn, *Hardball*, p. 15. Kuhn carried a Social Security card for many years afterward that named Senators owner Clark Griffith as his employer.

3. *Ibid.*, pp. 21–22. According to Bowie, his later problems with legendary sportswriter and native Wisconsin Red Smith stemmed from Kuhn's representation of the National League against the City of Milwaukee's complaint. Whether this is true or not is speculative: a liberal by nature, Smith was much closer in outlook to MLBPA chief Marvin Miller and as a result was one of the few sportswriters of any stature to give the union chief a sympathetic ear. One wonders how close anyone who sided with Miller could have been to the epitome of the Establishment, Kuhn.

4. Kuhn, *Hardball*, pp. 29–30. Eckert admitted prior to his election as commissioner that he hadn't seen a game in ten years.

5. Veeck with Linn, *Thirty Tons a Day*, pp. 8–9. Lee MacPhail sort of half-denies the story in *My Nine Innings*, p. 97.

6. Pietrusza, et al. (editors), *Baseball: The Biographical Encyclopedia*, p. 327.

A month or so after Eckert's death, Detroit Tigers owner John Fetzer penned a defense of Eckert that ran in *The Sporting News* on May 29, 1971 ("Fetzer Fires a Rebuttal at Critics of Gen. Eckert," p. 5). Whether Fetzer's essay is a defense of Eckert or an apology for the circumstances that brought him to the forefront is debatable. The basic thrust of Fetzer's article was that a hopelessly deadlocked ownership council decided to bring in a non-baseball man as a figurehead commissioner with a deputy (ex-Orioles GM Lee MacPhail) to be the de facto chief. Fetzer and Pittsburgh's John Galbreath screened 100 or so names that had been suggested for the vacant post, ultimately narrowing the list to 12 — of which only three or four were even interested in the job given the limitations to be placed upon them. From that short list Eckert was chosen.

In short, what Fetzer was saying was, "Sure, Eckert wasn't any good, but under the circumstances who could we have gotten that was any better?.."

7. Holtzman, "Expansion, Canadian Club, Feature 1968," p. 187.

8. MacPhail, *My Nine Innings*, p. 95 (note).

9. Roughly 125 players met in New York City on February 3 (the night before Kuhn's affirmation), deciding without dissent not to sign contracts for the 1969 season or to attend spring training camps until an agreement was reached on an upgraded pension program. The MLBPA's resolve was never really tested as an agreement was reached on February 24; however, early indications were that a number of players (though few of the game's stars) were prepared to report to camp by the official March 1 opening date (Holtzman, "Two Divisions, Rules, Player Demands, Etc.," *1970 Official Baseball Guide*, pp. 266–268).

10. Kuhn, *Hardball*, p. 35. Bowie also established his credentials as a die-hard fan by reciting the 1944 St. Louis Browns' starting lineup.

11. *Ibid.*, p. 16. Kuhn's undergraduate degree was in economics.

12. Kuhn, *Hardball*, pp. 37–62.

13. *Ibid.*, p. 202. Kuhn's puritanical nature shows strongly in his discussion of Steinbrenner's campaign contribution fiasco. "By merely imposing a fine," Kuhn noted, "the court had pretty well precluded a permanent suspension by me, perplexed though I was by the court's leniency."

14. Joe Heiling, "Cedeno's Life Periled by Pittsburgh Caller," *The Sporting News*, August 3, 1974, p. 7. Cedeno paid a 100 peso (about $7) fine for "negligence in allowing the girl to handle the gun that discharged."

15. Kuhn, *Hardball*, pp. 50–51. The Parvin-Dohrmann episode also represented an opening salvo in what would become a long-running war between Kuhn and Charles O. Finley. Though not a board member, Finley did own a minor stake in the casino operator and was forced by Bowie to divest himself of it.

16. *Ibid.*, pp. 214–220. DeBartolo had a couple of other strikes going against him as well; he wasn't a Chicagoian (after Bob Short's exodus to Texas, Kuhn had promised himself that no team would be sold to non-local owners), and he was brought to the table by Bill Veeck, a man for whom Bowie had little regard.

17. *Ibid.*, pp. 323–330. The fact that Kuhn devotes a full chapter to this episode speaks volumes about his opposition to so much as the slightest hint of gaming interest.

18. *Ibid.*, p. 127.

19. *Ibid.*, p. 131.

20. *Ibid.*, p. 42.

21. An overview of the Reichler incident can be found in Bill James, *The Politics of Glory*, pp. 295–298.

22. *Ibid.*

23. *National Baseball Hall of Fame* website.

24. Kuhn, *Hardball*, pp. 76–80, contains a wide-ranging and largely negative portrait of the MLBPA chief. The key to Miller from Kuhn's perspective is his mistrust of practically every baseball person he came in contact with. "There was about Miller the wariness one would find in an abused animal," Bowie wrote in describing the union president. "It precluded trust or affection. It set up a wall against any kind of close approach. I doubt that St. Francis could have surmounted the barrier."

25. "He couldn't seem to accept the idea that he was *not* the players' representative," Miller wrote in *A Whole Different Ball Game* (p. 106), "no matter how badly he wanted to think of himself as such and no matter how many times he said so publicly. Further, he had no inkling of how to relate to players and had nothing to offer them except the clichés and bromides of the bosses.

"Kuhn's talent for self-deception was amazing. He told everyone, including me, about his great reception by the players [this was during the era in which Kuhn was visiting each camp during spring training], but all I got from the players were comments such as 'What a stuffed shirt,' and questions like 'Is he for real?' and 'Does he take us for dumb kids?' and 'Do we have to go to those meetings and listen to that crap?'"

26. For a full discussion of Kuhn's opponents and their rationales, see Kuhn, *Hardball*, pp. 144–153 and 366–403. The reader is advised to note the not so subtle shift in

anti-Kuhn rhetoric between his first (successful) reelection attempt in 1976 and his second (unsuccessful) one in 1983. In the earlier round concerns regarding Bowie's stewardship of the game on the field were paramount, whereas by the early 1980s his stances regarding baseball's economic future reigned supreme. Charlie Finley opposed Kuhn in 1976 because the commissioner had blocked Mike Andrews's deactivation during the 1973 World Series: Nelson Doubleday went thumbs down on him seven years later due to Bowie's support of revenue sharing.

27. Isle, "Kuhn Hails Supreme Court Decision," p. 8. After praising the Court for "its recognition that baseball has developed its present structure in reliance on past court decisions," the commissioner stated, "The decision opens the way for renewed collective bargaining on the reserve system after the 1972 season. I am confident that the players and the clubs are in the best position to determine for themselves what the form of the reserve system should be and that they will both take a most responsible view of their respective obligations to the public and to the game.

"Any desirable changes," Kuhn continued, "should be the product of mutual agreement, so that there will be assurance that all concerned are prepared to live with and support the result."

"Far from claiming victory," Bowie pointed out in *Hardball* (p. 89), "I was exposing collective bargaining as the road for change in the reserve system. The last thing I wanted was the clubs to view the Flood decision as an excuse for doing nothing.... All we had was breathing time."

28. Kuhn, *Hardball*, pp. 96–103. Bowie was the man (with an unlikely assist from Orioles owner Jerry Hoffberger) who came up with Washington supermarket chain owner Joseph Danzansky. Danzansky would make two runs at purchasing a major league club, first attempting to purchase the Senators to forestall Bob Short's move to Texas in 1971 and then entering into a July, 1973, agreement to buy the San Diego Padres and transplant them to the nation's capital. Though he came close twice (Topps even produced an early run of their 1974 baseball cards with the Washington caption for Padres players), both deals failed due to Danzansky's inability to get all of his finan-

cial loose ends tied up in time. Normally a day or two wouldn't have been a problem, but given the owners' antipathy towards a market that had yielded as many as one million admissions once in 71 seasons, their willingness to cut Danzansky only as much slack as they had to is unsurprising.

29. *Ibid.*, p. 95.

30. In explaining his opposition to Short's move, Kuhn wrote, "If baseball was going to repair its wounded image, the time had come to stop moving franchises. We had moved enough of them in the last two decades to make a troop of gypsies jealous. If the fans were going to start believing in us again, they had to be convinced we were intent upon franchise stability." (*Ibid.*)

31. Hoffberger was at the center of a "Dump Bowie" group that attempted to derail Kuhn's 1976 reelection bid and would be one of the two owners (Charlie Finley was the other) to ultimately vote against him that year (*Ibid.*, p. 151). When he finally decided to put the Baltimore franchise on the market in early 1978 the Orioles patriarch had one qualification for any prospective buyer — he or she could not be recommended by the commissioner (*Ibid.*, p. 228).

32. *Ibid.*, pp. 212–213, 220–221. It is to Kuhn's credit that amidst his all-too-real complaints about Veeck's methods he is able to effect something approaching a fondness for the man in the narrative's quieter moments. "For all his self-confessed faults, Veeck was more rogue than scoundrel," Bowie wrote. "He reminds me for all the world of what Bugs Baer wrote about Ping Bodie as a base stealer: 'He had larceny in his heart, but his feet were honest'."

33. *Ibid.*, p. 211. According to Kuhn, Stoneham came to the 1968 National League meeting that addressed expansion firm in his conviction that Buffalo should join Montreal as the senior circuit's newest cities. Whenever anybody even looked like they were going to propose San Diego as the second franchise, a well-fortified Stoneham would roar "San Francisco votes no!" which, as Kuhn wryly recalls "certainly saved calling the roll." Horace left during the lunch break, and his son-in-law Chub Feeney cast the vote that made the San Diego Padres a reality.

The number of "Stoneham under the influence" stories in circulation during the

1970s boggle the mind: see Durocher and Linn, *Nice Guys Finish Last*, pp. 288–289 and Miller, *A Whole Different Ball Game*, pp. 49–51, for two more examples.

34. Kuhn, *Hardball*, pp. 238–241.

35. On his treatment by the press:

"In my summing up of things, I cannot conclude that my faults warranted the kind of treatment which *generally speaking* I received from the writers. I think too many of them fell prey to their own built-in bias towards someone of my background, made me the scapegoat for their rage against the growing domination of television and took offense at my unvarnished willingness to stand for moral issues at a time in our culture when such a posture was unpopular. I suspect that Kenesaw Mountain Landis would have come a cropper too in the press climate of my time in office. I draw some, but not much, solace from that conclusion." (Kuhn, *Hardball*, pp. 301–302.)

On the 1976 junior circuit decision to earmark an expansion franchise for Toronto rather than Washington:

"What I found hard to forgive was the opportunism of the quality American League owners. Where were the good guys? Where were the guys I thought I could count on when decency and the general good of the game were at stake?" (*Ibid.*, p. 194.)

From a speech given at baseball's 1982 winter meetings approximately five weeks after Bowie's reelection attempt had been spurned:

"Over the last fourteen years, I have often been asked why I was prepared to accept the aggravations of the job, given the fact that other career opportunities were open to me.

"The answer is simple: I love the game, I love its sights, its sounds, its rhythm, its tradition, even its boisterousness and yes, its people...."

36. Woodward and Armstrong, *The Brethren*, p. 75.

CHAPTER 25

1. Jim Hawkins, "The Bird Amuses Tigers, Befuddles Enemy Swingers," *The Sporting News*, June 5, 1976, p. 8.

2. Larry Eldridge, "Mark (The Bird) Fydrich: A New Folk Hero Arrives," *Baseball Digest*, October, 1976, p. 20.

3. Hawkins, "The Bird Amuses Tigers, Befuddles Enemy Swingers," p. 8. Before the game, Fydrich told manager Fred Hatfield that he should order a case of champagne, stating confidently, "Tonight we celebrate."

Just as emphatically, Hatfield replied, "Tonight, I'll break every bottle over your head if we don't win."

4. Jerry Green, "Will Mark Fydrich Defy The 'Sophomore Jinx'," *Baseball Digest*, April, 1977, p. 57. During his magical 1976 season Fydrich was pulling down the $16,500 major league minimum, prompting a Michigan state legislator to sponsor a resolution aimed at getting the Bird a midseason raise.

"I'm satisfied," the Bird said of his salary. "If they give me a raise it might go to my head and I'd start losing" (Eldridge, "Mark [The Bird] Fydrich: A New Folk Hero Arrives," p. 22).

5. Pietrusza, et al. (eds.), *Baseball: The Biographical Encyclopedia*, p. 354.

6. Hawkins, "The Bird Amuses Tigers, Befuddles Enemy Swingers," p. 8.

7. Bill James, *The New Bill James Historical Baseball Abstract*, p. 286.

8. Hawkins, "The Bird Amuses Tigers, Befuddles Enemy Swingers," p. 8.

9. Jim Hawkins, "Fydrich Brightens Tiger Picture," *1977 Official Baseball Guide*, p. 153.

10. Pietrusza, et al. (eds.), *Baseball: The Biographical Encyclopedia*, p. 354.

11. John Kuenster, "Prediction: Mark Fidrych and Dave Kingman Will Make Big News in '78," *Baseball Digest*, April, 1978, p. 14.

CHAPTER 26

1. Forman, *Baseball-Reference.com*. Mantle ranked 66th in games played (2,401) as the 2002 season began and also sat out fewer than ten contests in eight consecutive seasons (1954–61).

2. *Ibid.*

3. *Bill Mazeroski's Baseball '86*, p. 29.

4. Forman, *Baseball-Reference.com*.

5. Jerome Holtzman, "Review of 1973," *1974 Official Baseball Guide*, p. 269.

6. *Ibid.* Steinbrenner had owned the Cleveland Pipers of the American Basketball League, an Abe Saperstein-orchestrated

concept that lasted two seasons, and had a minority stake in the NBA's Chicago Bulls.

7. *Ibid.*

8. *Ibid.*, p. 270. Burke didn't come out all that badly, though; three months later he became president and CEO of Madison Square Garden.

9. *Ibid.*, p. 269.

10. Jack Lang, "Fabled Yanks Sold for Cut-Rate $10 Million," *The Sporting News*, January 20, 1973, p. 39. "The Yankees were the best buy in sports today," Steinbrenner said at the January 10, 1973 press conference announcing the sale.

One certainly couldn't argue with the numbers: nine years earlier, CBS had spent $11.2 million to purchase 80 percent of the Yankees from construction/casino magnate Del Webb and his partner Dan Topping, acquiring the remaining interest over the next two years for an additional $2 million.

11. Holtzman, "The Year of the Player Strike," p. 285. Ironically, the Indians had come very close to being purchased by Steinbrenner previous to their 1972 sale to an eight-man group headed by millionaire Nick Mileti. The Boss had thought the deal done before Tribe owner Vernon Stouffer backed down at the last minute (Lang, "Fabled Yanks Sold for Cut-Rate $10 Million," p. 39).

12. "There are no short cuts to building a ball club," MacPhail told the assembled reporters upon taking over the Yankee helm in December, 1966. "I would say that it will take a minimum of five years to put the Yankees back in contention." (Jim Ogle, "Yanks' Rebuilding Job Is Ahead of Schedule," *The Sporting News*, June 27, 1970, p. 15).

"MacPhail is the low-key executive who just keeps making a move here and a move there," Ogle continued, "and suddenly he has made enough moves to have a contending team. It worked that way in Baltimore; now he's repeating the process in New York. There have been no headline-making deals since MacPhail came to town, but Lee has made a few swaps with spectacular results."

So that one may judge from themselves, the deals that Ogle presents as proof of MacPhail's prowess yielded Lindy McDaniel (an admittedly good move), Mike Kekich, Jack Aker, Ron Woods, Curt Blefary, Danny Cater (well, he was good enough to draw Sparky Lyle from the Red Sox), Bill Klim-

kowski, Terry Bongiovanni, and Rich Bladt....

13. One of MacPhail's first moves as AL president was to signal the beginning of the end for the custom of operating leagues as if they were home businesses by relocating the junior circuit's headquarters from Boston (Joe Cronin's adopted hometown) to New York. The wandering league office was a time-honored tradition that National League prexy Chub Feeney had indulged in by relocating his offices from Cincinnati (Warren Giles's old stomping grounds) to San Francisco, where his father-in-law had set down roots back in 1958. With MacPhail in Manhattan and Bowie Kuhn pushing for a centralized management structure, however, Feeney would finally be forced to move east in 1976.

Of course, the fact that MacPhail already lived in New York may have made his decision a bit easier ... (Lee MacPhail, *My Nine Innings*, p. 129.)

14. Jim Hawkins ("Tigers Purr Happily Under Houk's Easy Leash," *The Sporting News*, April 6, 1974, p. 8), utilized words from Bill Veeck's book *The Hustler's Handbook* to characterize Houk's leadership style:

"As a combat leader," Veeck wrote, "Houk would study the terrain, absorb the intelligence reports, map the battle plan, and attack. If the battle plan called for him to take a machine gun nest, you could be confident that he would either take it or go down moving towards it. You could be equally confident his men would follow him every step of the way."

15. Holtzman, "Summation of Year's Activities," *1974 Official Baseball Guide*, pp. 277–280. Houk's forsaking of New York for Detroit would become entangled with Dick Williams's celebrated parting of the ways with Charlie Finley after the 1973 World Series. The seemingly available Williams was Steinbrenner's choice to replace Houk, but when Finley demanded compensation from New York (Williams was still under contract to the A's), Steinbrenner turned around and demanded similar reparations for Houk, who still had a year to go on his New York deal.

The ultimate decision handed down by AL president Joe Cronin was an odd duck. The Tigers were not required to compensate the Yankees for Houk because he supposedly had a verbal OK to strike a new deal, whereas Steinbrenner would have to meet Finley's price because Williams did not have such approval.

16. Bucek (ed.), *The Baseball Encyclopedia* (Tenth Edition), p. 2653. Nettles was acquired from the Indians along with catcher Gerry Moses for one legitimate prospect (Charlie Spikes) and a trio of onetime phenoms (John Ellis, Jerry Kenney, and Rusty Torres). The deal looks as bad to modern eyes as it did at the time; of the first 100 callers to the Cleveland *Plain Dealer* after the trade was announced, 82 opposed it — after which the newspaper's staff stopped keeping count (Russell Schneider, "Nettles Fires Departing Salvo at Pilot Aspro," *The Sporting News*, December 30, 1972, p. 35).

Having said that, the trade could easily have worked out well for Cleveland had Spikes been able to live up to his potential. "A mass of muscle" according to the 1975 *Complete Book of Baseball* (p. 116), Spikes hit 45 homers in his first two seasons as an Indian, but his laid-back attitude ran afoul of manager Frank Robinson's intense nature. Robinson designated Charlie as a "special project" upon taking over the Cleveland reins in 1975, a dubious accolade made even more poignant by the emergence of Rick Manning, a legitimate center fielder and Pete Rose-style hustler. The 24-year-old Spikes responded to the challenge by hitting .229 in 111 games; he would never play regularly again. (*BaseballLibrary.com.*)

17. Wills and Celizic, *On the Run*, p. 176.

In the late stages of the 1962 season, Dick Allen was in a race with Hart for the Eastern League batting title. Never adverse to a drink himself, Allen seized on the idea of inviting Hart out for a libation or two or ten to perhaps gain a little edge in the chase. He invited Jim Ray out to a Williamsport, Pennsylvania, bar, slapped a twenty on the bar, and told him that they weren't leaving until money had run out.

Once the two had absorbed 20 dollars' worth of booze into their systems (and this was back in the days when $20 represented the better part of a typical day's pay), Hart reached for his wallet saying "Let me return the favor"... and slapped another one on the table. "Next day, I go to the park, all hung over," Allen recalled some years later. "First person I see? Old Crow, he's out at third base

fielding ground balls. Gives me a big wave and a loud hello."

After winning the batting title that day, Hart approached Allen waving a 20-dollar bill and asking Dick where he wanted to go to celebrate. (Allen and Whitaker, *Crash*, p. 105–106).

18. White Sox owner John Allyn's comments were typical. "I've been sitting here getting a lot of laughs out of the whole thing," Allyn said, further opining, "No player is worth that much money." (Holtzman, "Summation of Year's Activities," *1975 Official Baseball Guide*, p. 299.)

Interestingly enough, most of the angst at the time regarding to Hunter's deal was directed at the pitcher himself rather than Steinbrenner ... who, after all, was the guy who offered Catfish the money in the first place.

19. Phil Pepe, "Gabe Defends Hefty Outlay of Talent to Get Chambliss," *The Sporting News*, May 18, 1974, p. 5. The deal was quite controversial at the time. A team loaded to the gunwales with first baseman types such as Ron Blomberg, Mike Hegan, and Bill Sudakis added another along with a guy sporting a 5.19 ERA and a reliever on his last legs (Cecil Upshaw) for two once-quality pitchers (Fritz Peterson and Steve Kline) plus a couple of prospects (Fred Beene and Tom Buskey). The Yankee clubhouse went thumbs down on the deal from the moment it was announced in the way players often do when guys they know are traded for ones they don't, with Mel Stottlemyre's "You just don't trade four pitchers" response being typical. Yet:

1. Kline's arm would never recover from 1973 elbow problems.
2. Peterson would be through by the 1976 All-Star break.
3. Beene would post a 5.71 ERA in two seasons for the Tribe before passing from the scene.
4. Despite initial success as the Tribe's closer, Buskey developed back problems that would turn him into Cleveland's answer to David Clyde: the Tribe's throw-in in the John Lowenstein for Willie Horton deal.

From the Belaboring The Obvious Department: "When you get a chance to get a player like (Chambliss), you have to jump at it," Paul said when the deal was announced.

"As much as I'd have liked to keep Beene, I'm not going to let Fred Beene stand in the way of getting a hitter like Chambliss, who is one of the best hitters in the league and will prove himself as that type hitter many times over for us."

For those who don't know, Fred Beene was an undersized (5'9", 160) 31-year-old right-handed swingman who'd spent seven years kicking around the Orioles' minor league system before the Yankees purchased his contract in January 1972 (*Who's Who In Baseball* [1974 Edition], p. 86). While he'd pitched well for the Yankees in limited use (159 innings over two and a quarter years) … well, it's unlikely that anyone else would have let such a player stand in the way of acquiring a 25-year-old ex-Rookie of the Year who'd developed into a quality regular either. (Forman, *Baseball-Reference.com*.)

20. The intimidation had started with Martin's contract, which included special clauses pertaining to Billy's conduct, potential statements regarding club operations, and availability to discuss things with management on a moment's notice. (Billy Martin and Peter Golenbock, *Number 1*, p. 15.)

Then there was the list that Steinbrenner circulated to reporters in July 1977 of seven criteria that the Boss supposedly used to determine whether he'd fire Martin or not at any given moment. The list was as follows:
1. Win-loss record.
2. Does he work hard enough?
3. Is he emotionally equipped to lead the men under him?
4. Is he organized?
5. Is he prepared?
6. Does he understand human nature?
7. Is he honorable?

"I dare anyone else in the world to work under the conditions I was working under," Martin said (*Ibid.*, p. 127). "Here was a felon setting himself up as judge and jury to decide whether I was good enough, moral enough, and a good enough student of human nature to manage his team."

Chapter 27

1. Mark Heisler, "Why Rod Carew is Best Hitter in the Majors," *Baseball Digest*, July, 1979, p. 32.

2. Phil Elderkin, "Rod Carew: 'Homers Don't Interest Me,'" *Baseball Digest*, August, 1973, p. 21.

3. George Vass, "Are Major League Batting Championships Overrated?" *Baseball Digest*, June 1975, p. 23.

4. Jim Hawkins, "Rod Carew: He's in a Class by Himself," *Baseball Digest*, December, 1975, p. 39.

5. Melvin Durslag, "Carew admits stealing home is one feat that turns him on," *Baseball Digest*, July, 1979, p. 34. New manager Billy Martin felt that the Twins' offense need more spark and thus got Carew working on the art of stealing home in the spring. Amazingly, his seven thefts came in only eight attempts.

6. Bob Fowler, "Critics Take New Look, Salute Clouting Carew," *The Sporting News*, July 7, 1973, p. 21.

7. John Kuenster, "Double Play Kings of the Majors," *Baseball Digest*, March, 1974, p. 10.

8. Moss Klein, "When Billy Martin 'Went To Bat'" for Rod Carew," *Baseball Digest*, March, 1978, p. 38.

9. Kuenster, "It's Been A Wild and Cra-a-zy Sort of Season in the Majors!" p. 17.

10. Heisler, "Why Rod Carew is Best Hitter in the Majors," p. 30. It is apparent that the Rod Carew in Heisler's article is still smarting from his acrimonious departure from the Twins. Continuing to comment on his experiences in Seattle, Carew commented, "Every time I fouled a pitch off, I turned around and looked at the crowd, like I was saying 'Hey people, I've got it under control'. I tipped my hat, gave them a little bow. It tees them off."

11. Hawkins, "Rod Carew: He's in a Class by Himself," p. 38.

12. Heisler, "Why Rod Carew is Best Hitter in the Majors," p. 34.

13. Richard Justice, "Al Oliver's Inside Tips on Hitting," *Baseball Digest*, July, 1979, p. 37.

Chapter 28

1. Golenbock, *Bums*, p. 84. Over 60 percent of the money that the partnership of Rickey, Pfizer Corporation president John L. Smith, and lawyer Walter O'Malley used to buy the Dodgers came from the bank,

which four years earlier had been on the verge of foreclosing on the team.

2. *Ibid.*, pp. 250–251.

3. Forman, *Baseball-Reference.com.*

4. Veeck and Linn, *Veeck as in Wreck*, pp. 11–22, contains a highly entertaining version of the Eddie Gaedel caper.

5. The first move Weaver made as a manager was to bench himself. "Although I was hustling as usual, I wasn't hitting," Earl states matter-of-factly (Earl Weaver with Berry Stainback, *It's What You Learn After You Know It All That Counts*, p. 100). "The kid I put in was no terror with a bat, either. But he *might* have a future on the playing field. I sure as heck didn't."

6. *Ibid.*, p. 121.

7. Lou Hatter, "Blair Regains Star Route With Aid of Hypnotist," *The Sporting News*, July 14, 1973, p. 21. *Ibid.*, pp. 124–125. Blair, an outstanding defensive center fielder with decent power at his best, had subconsciously backed himself off the plate as a result of the Tatum beaning. After one 1973 session with Dr. Jacob Conn, a Baltimore area hypnotist, Blair regained his confidence at the plate and recorded his best season offensively since the beaning.

The visits were costly, though, and according to Weaver (*It's What You Learn After You Know It All That Counts*, pp. 124–125) when the center fielder began publicly pooh-poohing the value of hypnotism, Dr. Conn wouldn't see him any more. How much of an impact hypnotism had on Blair's performance is anybody's guess, but his hitting did fall off rapidly after 1974.

Hatter, by the way, credits Baltimore *News-American* writer Chan Keith with the suggestion.

8. *Ibid.*, pp. 128–129. To give the reader some idea of how hard the 5'8", 170-pound Dalkowski threw, it is said that the ricochet from one of his heaters that hit a batter on the helmet flew over the pitcher's head and landed near second base.

9. 1970 American Association Statistics, *1971 Official Baseball Guide*, p. 402.

10. 1968 International League Statistics, *1969 Official Baseball Guide*, pp. 301, 306.

11. 1970 Pacific Coast League Statistics, *1971 Official Baseball Guide*, p. 437.

12. Weaver with Stainback, *It's What You Learn After You Know It All That Counts*, pp. 113–114. Earl was tripped up when the Ori-

oles sent a scout to see how Ward's outfield conversion was progressing.

13. Williams, originally signed as a pitcher by the Milwaukee Braves in 1965, had spent his minor and early major league career as a man without a position before being moved behind the plate in 1971 by Braves manager Luman Harris (Brenda Zanger and Dick Kaplan, *Major League Baseball 1972*, p. 7). The move made sense theoretically—Williams had agility, soft hands and a good arm—but ran headlong into the fact that Earl didn't want to catch and wasn't particularly interested in learning any of the subtleties of the position. Still, since he caught 72 games while winning the 1971 Rookie of the Year Award, the concept that Williams was a catcher took hold in the collective psyche, and it was on this basis that the Orioles traded Pat Dobson and Dave Johnson, among others, for him after the close of the 1972 season.

Williams set the tone for his Baltimore tenure early by catching spring training games from his knees rather than in a crouch—anything that was more than a foot or so off the plate was guaranteed to go to the backstop. (Weaver and Stainback, *It's What You Learn After You Know It All That Counts*, p. 206.) Earl wouldn't warm up pitchers, wouldn't take infield practice, and began missing signs, batting practice, and the team bus. When called on the mat for his behavior, the erstwhile catcher would typically apologize and promise to do better, then quickly relapse into his old ways. (*Ibid.*, pp. 206–210.) "Still," Weaver noted in a 1974 interview, "we can't give up on him. You can't get rid of a guy that young and with that much potential. Anyway, we don't have any top catching prospects in our farm system." (Doug Brown, "Earls of Baltimore Having Their Problems," *The Sporting News*, June 29, 1974, p. 13.)

That was the bottom line with the Orioles—Williams was to be a catcher whether he wanted to be or not. When Earl produced two mediocre seasons while making no progress behind the plate, the Os essentially gave him back to the Braves for cash and a stringbean left-hander named Jimmy Freeman who would never again pitch in the majors. Williams's career quickly devolved from there; branded as a troublemaker, he was unable to get a full shot with anyone and thus couldn't get his bat going again. Released by the A's at the end of the 1977 season, Williams's stock had sunk to the point where his mother put an ad in the paper in an attempt to get him a roster spot; when the Expos responded, Earl missed the tryout and was finished at 28. (Pietrusza, et al., *Baseball: The Biographical Encyclopedia*, p. 1231.)

Despite all of the comments about Williams's lackadaisical attitude, one wonders if he couldn't have become a quality player if Weaver or somebody had just given in and let him play first base. Earl had come within six RBIs of winning the 1969 Western Carolina League's Triple Crown (*1970 Official Baseball Guide*, p. 566); sure, that was just an A league, but within two years he'd blast 33 homers in the Show while finishing in the top ten in slugging percentage. Earl was 25 when his Oriole career came to an end — the player in baseball history with the most similar stats at the same age was Miguel Tejada. (Forman, *BaseballReference.com*.)

Good defensively at first and passable at third, Earl Williams should have at least had Eric Karros's career, but it didn't happen ... and while Earl's attitude may have been less than perfect, his manager in Baltimore certainly didn't help matters any.

14. When Hank Bauer suggested that Hendricks be sent "back to the Mexican League or wherever he came from" at the end of the 1968 spring training season, Weaver stuck up for him to the point that Earl was more or less banished from the coaches' table at a Miami restaurant. "You shouldn't get rid of a guy who can hit like Hendricks," Weaver stated before retiring to another table. "I'm telling you I had him in Puerto Rico and he hit some tough major league pitchers, and he'll do that for us and he's the only left-handed-hitting catcher we got, and that's all I have to say."

"I went home to Mariana [Weaver's wife] with tears in my eyes," Earl recalled. "I couldn't help crying over the mistake we were making." (Weaver and Stainback, *It's What You Learn After You Know It All That Counts*, p. 144.)

While Weaver's assessment proved out and Hendricks did give the Orioles three quality seasons as a platoon backstop, it is also true that Earl eventually became blind to Hendricks' abilities or lack thereof. A mediocre defensive catcher at best with some power and a decent batting eye but little else, Hendricks evolved into the primeval Mark Parent: a guy with enough power to tantalize you, but not enough of anything else to *really* be worth playing. After 1971, Ellie posted a .193 average with generally poor defensive stats ... yet thanks largely to Weaver kept his career going until he evolved into a full-time bullpen coach at age 38. (Forman, *Baseball-Reference.com*.)

15. Weaver and Stainback, *It's What You Learn After You Know It All That Counts*, pp. 173–178.

16. Luciano and Fisher, *The Umpire Strikes Back*, pp. 205–206. During spring training that season, Luciano was asked whom he thought would win the American League divisional races and stated that he didn't care who won in the East "as long as it isn't Baltimore."

Not a good thing for an impartial arbiter to say, but when a press conference was arranged several months later for Ron to apologize, Weaver was in attendance and publicly badgered the Roman Umpire. When Luciano admitted his error but suggested that the Orioles manager may have said a few things in his lifetime that he'd regretted, Weaver replied, "No. I'm not sorry about anything I ever said about you or to you. I've meant every word of it."

The press conference soon devolved into a shouting match, and Luciano was thereafter removed from Orioles games.

17. Joe Strauss, "Palmer, Weaver Burn Roast," Baltimore *Sun*, November 4, 2000, p. 1C.

18. Alan Goldstein, "Frank Robinson's Dream: Can He Ever Reach It?" *All-Star Sports*, April, 1969, p. 31. "He just couldn't get himself untracked in '68," Brooks Robinson observed. "I definitely feel that Frank wasn't seeing the ball as well — not picking up the spin or having the depth perception he had before the accident."

19. Weaver with Stainback, *It's What You Learn After You Know It All That Counts*, pp. 142–143. "Loyalty is a good trait," Weaver wrote, "but it is not a good job-keeping trait if it results in your staying with players who can no longer do their jobs on the ball field as well as they had in the past. As a manager, your obligations are to the team you work for and the hell with the people who did

things for you yesterday. A manager must live by that hard-hearted cliché: What have you done for me today?."

In an ironic twist, Earl quickly follows this comment with a discussion of his soon-to-be-realized plan to integrate the newly acquired Don Buford into the Oriole lineup. Though Buford would post four outstanding seasons as the Orioles' offensive spark plug, Weaver would ultimately fall into the same trap Bauer did in evaluating his 5'7" leadoff man. In 1972 the by-then 35-year-old Buford had as grotesque a season as any plate setter has ever had, batting .206 in 408 at-bats with virtually no power (a total 13 extra-base hits all season after polling 19 dingers the year before) and sharply reduced speed.

"I'd drive home after a game thinking: I play Terry Crowley in left tomorrow. Or Tom Shopay. Or Don Baylor. Anyone except Buford," Weaver recalled. "Then I'd get home and think about all the hits Buford had gotten in other years off the next day's scheduled pitcher. I'd recall the season in which, with a man on third and less than two out, Donny had driven home the runner nineteen times in a row! I'd dream about Donny getting on the next day, stealing second, and scoring the winning run on a sacrifice fly.

So I kept playing Donny, and he kept failing. Try as he might, somehow he'd lost it at the plate." (*Ibid.*, p. 201.)

20. Cuellar, a Cuban native, went 13–12 with a 2.77 ERA for the Havana Sugar Kings in 1958, yet wasn't able to establish himself as a major league starter until 1966 because he simply didn't have the stamina to consistently work deep into games. Whenever his teams pushed him, he broke down. After working 433 innings for the Sugar Kings in 1958-9, Cuellar would post no more than 155 frames in any of the following five seasons. Once the Astros plugged him into their rotation he shouldered a regular workload for two years ... then missed the first third of the 1968 season with arm miseries (Allan Roth [ed.], *Who's Who In Baseball* [1970 edition], p. 84).

Those who look to Weaver and pitching coach George Bamberger for the answer to the riddle of how Cuellar became such a big-time inning eater in his early to mid-30s may be overlooking the true reason for his

success: Mike's impressive collection of rituals and homages to the gods of fate.

Baseball players are a superstitious bunch by nature, but Cuellar was a grand high llama of the black magic art. His rituals started in the training room, where he always sat on the "lucky side" of the table while trainer Ralph Salvon worked on his arm. Only coach Jim Frey was allowed to catch his pregame warmup tosses, though backstop Elrod Hendricks did have a role — he stood at the plate for a specified period of time simulating a batter. The Cuban lefty not only indulged in the traditional phobia of stepping over the foul line while exiting the field, he hurdled the top step of the dugout for good measure.

Cuellar's most distinctive eccentricity, not surprisingly, revolved around the humble horsehide with which he made his living. Mike, you see, believed that it was bad luck for anyone to throw him the ball at the beginning of an inning; his ritual was to pick it up from the ground, circle around to the back of the mound and ascend from that direction.

Alex Johnson, well aware of Cuellar's habits, decided to put them to the test during a May 26, 1972 game. After catching a fly ball to end an inning, Johnson jogged in slowly, timing it so that he reached the infield as Mike was approaching the mound. He nonchalantly tossed the ball to the Orioles lefty, who ducked just in time to spare himself a fate-displeasing catch.

The loose ball was retrieved by a batboy who helpfully threw it back ... only to have Cuellar squirm out of its path again. The baseball came to rest near first baseman Boog Powell, who momentarily forgot who he was dealing with and fired a strike to Mike, who caught the ball in self-defense.

No problem, though — Cuellar immediately tossed the now cursed sphere to home plate umpire Bill Haller and asked for another....

... which was then thrown back to the mound and avoided by Mike. It was second baseman Bobby Grich who finally retrieved the ball and properly rolled it back to the mound so that the game could resume.

Undeterred, Johnson attempted the same stunt at the end of the next inning. Cuellar, however, refused to leave the dugout until Alex had flipped the ball to Powell, who completed the cycle by rolling it to the mound (Lou Hatter, "Cuellar Authority on Whammies and Hoodoos," *The Sporting News*, August 5, 1972, p. 7).

21. Bob Sudyk, "The Travels and Travails of Pat Dobson," *Baseball Digest*, January, 1977, p. 76.

22. In *Palmer And Weaver, Together We Were Eleven Foot Nine* (Jim Palmer and Jim Dale, pp. 9–17) the three-time Cy Young Award winner suggests that the biceptal tendonitis that would cause him to fall as low as the Florida State League was the result of painting his daughter's bedroom. Things got so bad that during an early 1967 Fenway Park start, Jim's first three pitches were hit for a double, single, and home run.

When Orioles manager Hank Bauer came out to the mound and asked catcher Andy Etchebarren how Palmer was throwing, Etchebarren replied "How would I know? I haven't caught one yet."

Palmer's arm magically snapped back while pitching winter ball in Puerto Rico the next winter, and he was on his way.

23. Bill James, *The Baseball Book 1990*, pp. 200–202.

24. Forman, *Baseball-Reference.com*.

25. Weaver and Stainback, *It's What You Learn After You Know It All That Counts*, pp. 203–204.

26. *Ibid.*, p. 223. Coggins, who favored pink suits with a boutonniere in the lapel and large straw hats, ended up joining the FBI after his career ran its course.

27. George Vass, "Here Are The Six Biggest Free Agent Flops!" *Baseball Digest*, May, 1979, p. 52.

28. Doug Brown, "Orioles' Tommy D. Looks Back in Anger," *The Sporting News*, August 11, 1973, p. 22.

Davis's anger at this point stemmed from two things: first, that he was traded or released six times in a five-year period, and secondly that his salary had dropped from $70,000 to $25,000 over the same period. Tommy's average is discussed frequently throughout Brown's article, and in fairness it should be noted that Davis hit a combined .281 in the period between 1969 and 1972, but that .281 was accompanied by:

- Little power: on a 550 at-bat-per-season basis, Davis's 1969–72 numbers translate to 28 doubles, two triples, and seven homers per season.
- No great affinity for ball four, as witnessed by 32 walks per 550-at-bat season.
- Terrible defense at any spot: primarily stationed in left field or at first base during this period, Tommy combined poor range with 22 errors in 332 defensive games played (Bucek [ed.], *The Baseball Encyclopedia* [Tenth Edition], p. 947).

"A club doesn't release a .324 hitter, even if he's put in jail over the winter," Davis bitterly remarked about his 1972 spring training release by the Oakland A's. Well, yes, Tommy, a .324 average is hard to turn down, but in a game with no DH, 33-year-old corner outfielders with little power or defensive range generally have career expectancies that can be measured in weeks. This is especially true for those who are pulling down above-average salaries (Davis was making $37,000 at the time) while playing for pinch-penny organizations that aren't drawing well.

29. Eric Siegel, "Ken Singleton: He Tries to Get on Base Any Way He Can!" *Baseball Digest*, February, 1979, p. 43.

30. Bob Hertzel, "How About Some Recognition For Lee May?" *Baseball Digest*, August, 1979, p. 26.

31. Brodie Snyder, "Ross Grimsley: Master of the Changeup," *Baseball Digest*, September, 1978, p. 56. Grimsley's problems with the Reds began in 1970, when after leading the American Association in ERA he was bypassed for a late season call-up in favor of Milt Wilcox (who, in all fairness was the right-hander the parent club needed at that moment and finished second to Grimsley in ERA). "The next year," Grimsley recounted, "I had an outstanding spring and should have made the club and they sent me down. I was 6–0 at Indianapolis and they called me up after a month and I won ten games. The next spring they sent me down again. I flew off the handle.

"I said 'Hey, you know, if you've got somebody else that can do the job, then you get me the hell out of here. I don't have to stay here and take this.' They wanted you to run a certain way, wear this a certain way, associate with these people. I just wouldn't run and jump every time they snapped their fingers....'"

Grimsley was compelled to make four

trips to a barber shop near the Reds' Tampa, Florida camp one spring before his hair length met club specifications. (Earl Lawson, "The Reds' Pitching Staff Went That-A-Way!" *Baseball Digest*, April, 1979, p. 50.)

32. Weaver and Stainback, *It's What You Learn After You Know It All That Counts*, pp. 204–217.

33. Forman, *Baseball-Reference.com*.

34. "Official American League Pitching Averages," *1976 Official Baseball Guide*, p. 205.

35. "Major League Attendance For 1973," *1974 Official Baseball Guide*, p. 183. Interestingly enough, despite their success in the standings, the Orioles weren't particularly good draws on the road either. The 1,185,247 fans who came to road games involving the Os were fifth among the twelve junior circuit teams and just 17,000 more than was drawn by an 81–81 Minnesota team that finished 13 games out of the AL West lead while never mounting a serious challenge.

36. In *Wild World of Sports Bloopers: The Best of Baseball* (Madacy Entertainment Group Inc., 1996), a cat that obviously knows every nook and cranny of the stadium first tries to climb over the left center field wall into the Orioles' bullpen, then attempts to escape behind the left field tarpaulin (being dissuaded, perhaps, by the rats that according to Boog Powell lived there and occasionally came out to scavenge spilled popcorn during games). The speedy feline finally found refuge by crawling through a hole in the visitors' dugout.

In another vignette, an animal of unknown species scatters Oriole players as it climbs the home team dugout wall to make its way into a ventilator duct (at least the wildlife wasn't showing any favoritism).

37. Thomas Boswell, "Certain Ballparks Have Their Own Special Charm," *Baseball Digest*, August, 1979, p. 64.

38. Lou Hatter, "Giant Pleasure Dome In Baltimore Future," *The Sporting News*, June 23, 1973, p. 13. The total cost of the Camden Yards project, which was also to include a 4,500-space garage and an adjacent convention center, was estimated at $114.1 million and was to be completed by late 1976.

By the time it opened in 1992, Oriole Park at Camden Yards—sans the roof, parking, and convention center—ended up costing taxpayers $105 million.

39. Lou Hatter, "Study Indicates Face-Lifting Could Save Oriole Park," *The Sporting News*, January 20, 1973, p. 34.

40. Hatter, "Giant Pleasure Dome In Baltimore Future," p. 13.

41. *Ibid.*

42. "Major League Attendance for 1977," *1978 Official Baseball Guide*, p. 343.

43. According to Reggie (Jackson and Lupica, *Reggie*, p. 139), the Orioles did ultimately offer him a contract substantially similar to the five-year, $2.96 million deal he accepted from the Yankees. However, the offer was made at the eleventh hour, and by that time Jackson was enamored with the idea of playing in New York.

44. Holtzman, "Summation of Year's Activities," *1977 Official Baseball Guide*, p. 301.

45. Well, maybe. Flanagan did end up being a lot cheaper ($800,000 for five years) than Garland (he got $3 million for ten seasons from the Indians), but Garland's mid-1976 statement that he would resign with the Orioles only if Rochester manager Joe Altobelli replaced Weaver may have had a little something to do with the move too. (Weaver and Stainback, *It's What You Learn After You Know It All That Counts*, p. 241.)

CHAPTER 29

1. Kuhn, *Hardball*, p. 169. Total player payroll (per statistics supplied by baseball's Player Relations Committee) rose from $31 million to $159 million annually over that period.

2. Spink, *1969 Official Baseball Guide*, p. 171, and *1980 Official Baseball Guide*, p. 394.

3. While Bob Roth (1915) and Gus Zernial (1951) did lead the AL in homers during seasons in which they played with the Chisox, both spent time with other teams during their league-leading campaigns. Melton was the first to win a dinger crown while spending the entire season in Comiskey Park. (Jerome Holtzman, "Chisox Quaff Champagne—Toast Homer Champion Melton," *The Sporting News*, October 26, 1971, p. 33.)

The third baseman's defensive prowess had been a catch-as-catch-can thing earlier in his career. "I once picked up one of those little magazines that had a rundown of the prospects of all the 24 clubs," Bill remembered in late 1971. "When they came to me, the write-up read, 'A below mediocre third baseman'."

Though that epithet would spur Melton to improve his aggressiveness and lateral movement on defense, the road to fielding competency was anything but smooth. After committing ten errors in his first 24 1970 games, Melton had suffered the ultimate indignity of having his nose broken when a foul pop that he was camped under found its way between his hands and smacked him in the face. (Jerome Holtzman, "Bill Melton ... From Agony to Ecstasy," *The Sporting News*, September 4, 1971, p. 3.)

4. Melton lost most of the 1972 season to a herniated disc originally suffered when he fell off the roof of his house the prior winter. Rather than submitting to surgery, the Chisox third baseman had the disc injected with an experimental enzyme treatment designed to reduce the swelling. Nominally, the treatment worked — Melton resumed his career the next season and never did go under the knife — but he sacrificed a good portion of his power in the process as well as significant range in the field. (Edgar Munzel, "Chisox to Make Stretch Bid Minus Melton," *The Sporting News*, August 12, 1972, p. 13.)

5. Pietrusza, et al. (eds.), *Baseball: The Biographical Encyclopedia*, p. 854.

6. *1970 Chicago White Sox Yearbook*, p. 26. While swabbing out the firing tubes of 81mm mortars fired by his Marine Corps unit at Camp Pendleton, CA, Carlos came across one whose shell hadn't been fired. Ramming the swab down the tube pushed the projectile against the firing pin, shooting it out of the tube but not detonating it. "I'm lucky," Carlos said later. "I might have had my head blown off."

7. "I don't understand the criticism of my base running," Lemon stated in a 1981 interview. "My favorite players, Willie Mays and Roberto Clemente, played like that. If you put chains on me, then you're making me scared." (Phil Hersh, "Chet Lemon: The Struggle for a Spot In The Sun," *Baseball Digest*, June, 1981, p. 63.)

Admittedly, Lemon's base running was intermittently curtailed by leg problems early in his career ("I shy away from stealing because of injuries," he said. "How can you steal when you start the season with a pulled muscle?"). OK Chet, perhaps that does explain the 18 steals over three seasons (1978–80), but as for the 18 caught stealings during the same time frame ... well, let's just say that's a far cry from Mays's (82 percent) and Clemente's (79 percent) success rates — and those guys played through a pulled muscle or two in their day as well.

8. Holtzman, "Two Divisions, Rules, Player Demands, Etc.," pp. 279–280. Allyn's father had been part of the three consortiums Bill Veeck had put together to purchase major league teams in the 1940s and 1950s while the family holding company had bought out Veeck when he fell ill in 1962.

9. From the "the more things change, the more they stay the same" department, Allyn had supposedly backed Holcomb during a July 17 meeting with Tanner in Boston. "It was strictly a matter of principle," Allyn said later. "We had to decide just what we would do financially in each case and when that line was reached, that was it." (Edgar Munzel, "Allyn Backs Holcomb Against Non-Signers," *The Sporting News*, August 4, 1973, p. 21).

Within ten days, however, Holcomb had handed in his resignation, noting that his decisions both at the major and minor league level were subject to the approval of Tanner and personnel director Roland Hemond. "The reason I'm leaving is Chuck Tanner," Holcomb announced, ignoring Hemond's role. "It's not so much what Tanner has said about our operation, but what he hasn't said." (Jerome Holtzman, "Holcomb Quits Chisox, Hemond Replaces Him," *The Sporting News*, August 11, 1973, p. 10.)

10. According to Jerome Holtzman ("Holcomb Quits Chisox, Hemond Replaces Him," *The Sporting News*, August 11, 1973, p. 10), the decision to invite Allen (who needed 90 additional days on a big-league roster to qualify for a pension) to spring training in 1973 and keep him on the roster was Tanner's, based upon a request from Hank's brother (and resident Chisox superstar) Dick. "There was absolutely no deal with Richie," the manager said. "Hank Allen had a great spring and earned a spot on the club."

FYI: the 33-year-old Hank had hit .273 that spring with a homer and three RBIs in

44 at-bats. (Edgar Munzel, "Initial Allen Proves Super, So White Sox Go for Two," *The Sporting News*, April 21, 1973, p. 7.)

11. Jerome Holtzman, "Disappointing White Sox Make Changes," *1976 Official Baseball Guide*, p. 177. When asked if he held a personal grudge against Caray, Tanner dismissed the idea out of hand. "He is just a front-running second-guesser, that's all," was Chuck's analysis of the White Sox broadcaster. (Falls, "Now It's Time for a Few Laughs," p. 32.)

According to Caray (Harry Caray with Bob Verdi, *Holy Cow!*, pp. 200–202), he learned about his impending dismissal from a Chicago *Sun-Times* columnist who was watching an interview with Allyn on TV. Harry takes an ecumenical approach towards the whole thing in his book, saying, "I think Allyn knew he was going to sell the Sox, knew he wouldn't be returning in 1976. And I'm sure he wanted to go out a hero with Chuck Tanner and his players. What better way to make points than to say, basically, 'See fellas, if I'd been there, I would have gotten rid of Harry Caray.'"

One gets the impression that time and judicious editing have mellowed Harry's memories to a significant degree. *Holy Cow!* is one of those books that rightly or wrongly seems homogenized to the point that the traits that made the central character worth writing a book about are lost. Harry's tumultuous final days in St. Louis (during which he was photographed drinking a can of Schlitz beer) are virtually ignored. A volatile one-year tenure in Oakland in which he occasionally forsook the action on the field to recite poetry for innings at a time is reduced to a semi-fawning character study of Charlie Finley. His six seasons with the Cubs (the book was published in 1989) are telescoped down to 14 pages, five of which have to do with Ronald Reagan's cameo appearance at the end of the 1988 season.

At the time of his firing by Allyn, Harry characterized the White Sox owner as "stupid" and constantly manipulated by Tanner and Hemond (Holtzman, "Disappointing White Sox Make Changes," p. 177).

12. *Ibid.*, p. 175.
13. Bill Veeck with Ed Linn, *Veeck as in Wreck*, p. 381.
14. Jerome Holtzman, "Doc Veeck to Try

His New Theories on an Old Patient," *The Sporting News*, October 18, 1975, p. 25.

15. Holtzman, "Two Divisions, Rules, Player Demands, Etc.," pp. 280–281. Allyn's brother Art, who had been running the club, received a $13.7 million offer for the team during the summer of 1969. Though this was more than double what the brothers had paid for the team seven years earlier, half-owner John was unwilling to sell ... which was probably a moot point anyway, since a straw poll of the other AL owners indicated that they would have voted against a move.

16. Bill Veeck with Ed Linn, *Veeck as in Wreck*, pp. 125–127.

17. *Ibid.*, pp. 342–344. First built in 1960, the exploding scoreboard was still there (though it had stood mute for several seasons) when Veeck repurchased the club in 1975. Immediately pressed back into duty, the scoreboard was replaced by a modernized version in 1983.

One of the original pinwheels from the exploding scoreboard is still in service, though in an ironic place. This symbol of South Side success is presently stationed atop a private residence across from Wrigley Field, lighting up whenever a Chicago Cub hits a home run (Palacios, Robin, et al., *Ballpark Sourcebook: Diamond Diagrams*, p. 49).

18. *Ibid.*, pp. 219–221.
19. Condon, "Charlie O.: Amazing Sports Maverick," p. 32.
20. "I see where Bill Veeck, the ex-owner, etc. is writing a newspaper column again," Jerome Holtzman commented in an August 12, 1972 *Sporting News* article (p. 12), "which is fine because I like to see everybody gainfully employed. But all I can say is that Veeck is prolonging his all-time record for long-distance second-guessing."

Bowie Kuhn used to rib Bud Selig about his use of Veeck as an expert witness in the Milwaukee case. "Veeck gave a performance that left us lawyers on the other side virtually tumbling over one another to cross-examine him," Bowie recalled. "I cannot recall ever seeing such a lust to examine a witness."

Veeck, however, "conveniently" left town before Bowie had his opportunity (Kuhn, *Hardball*, p. 213).

21. Jerome Holtzman, "Disappointing White Sox Make Changes," *1976 Official*

Baseball Guide, p. 178.

22. Veeck's standard financing *modus operandi* is described in *Veeck as in Wreck*, pp. 88–89.

23. Art Spander, "Giants Discover Landlord Camped on Their Doorstep," *The Sporting News*, July 12, 1975, p. 25. The Giants' agreement with the City of San Francisco called for the team to pay 5 percent of their prior season's gate receipts or $125,000, whichever was less, every February. By mid-July the rent was still unpaid (Stoneham owed only the minimum based upon the Giants' 1974 attendance of 519,991), though according to Recreation and Parks Department assistant business manager Glenn Beauchamp, the team was staying up to date on its other bills such as utilities and the like.

Not surprisingly, the money crunch was making itself felt in operational areas as well. While San Francisco was playing practically anyone who could fit into a uniform at third base, the Expos had Bob Bailey, a certified hitter if not a glove whiz, sitting on their bench. A deal was worked out to send the onetime Pirate bonus baby to the Bay Area ... but was nixed at the last minute because Stoneham couldn't afford to pay Bailey's $80,000 salary.

24. Kuhn, *Hardball*, p. 190. An injunction filed by the City of San Francisco effectively put the kibosh on the $13.5 million sale announced on January 9, 1976. Less than three months later, the brewery would pay $7 million for the right to become one of the two 1977 American League expansion teams.

25. Art Spander, "Rumors Fly, Fans Flee as Giants End Season," *The Sporting News*, October 11, 1975. Perhaps the crowning insult to the deal, which was to have been financed by Japan's Seibu group, was that company president Yoshiaki Tsutsumi was reportedly more interested in the Giants' real estate holdings in Arizona and Minnesota than he was in the team itself. According to Spandler, Tsutsumi "finally decided the value of the real estate was insufficient to overcome the problems he foresaw in taking over the Giants."

26. Harry Shattuck, "Soaring Debts Pick Hofheinz Off Astro Perch," *The Sporting News*, July 12, 1975, p. 15.

27. Holtzman, "Summation of Year's Activities," *1977 Official Baseball Guide*, p. 284.

The fact that Turner owned an entity called Turner Communications was relegated to the second line of Holtzman's announcement.

28. Holtzman, "Doc Veeck to Try His New Theories on an Old Patient," p. 25. The collapse of that deal led to a lawsuit by Veeck against Hoffberger (Bill claimed that the Baltimore owner had guaranteed that a sale would be consummated) that was still pending as the White Sox offer became public.

29. Veeck and Linn, *Veeck as in Wreck*, p. 381.

30. *Ibid.*

31. "Strong Hands Guiding Tigers," *1976 Detroit Tigers Yearbook*, p. 4. Tiger Board of Directors, *1990 Detroit Tigers Yearbook*, p. 4.

32. Veeck and Linn, *Veeck as in Wreck*, p. 381.

33. Holtzman, "Disappointing White Sox Make Changes," p. 178.

34. Veeck and Linn, *Veeck as in Wreck*, p. 382.

35. Kuhn, *Hardball*, p. 214.

36. Veeck and Linn, *Veeck as in Wreck*, p. 382.

37. *Ibid.*

38. *Ibid.*, p. 383.

39. Holtzman, "Doc Veeck to Try His New Theories on an Old Patient," p. 25.

Harry and Jimmy Piersall would combine to make an outstanding broadcast team for most of Veeck's tenure in Chicago. The two had an edgy, lay-it-all-on-the-line attitude towards the game, the White Sox, and each other that is fondly remembered by many longtime Chicago fans. Some typical by-play between the two:

Caray: "Hey! It's a beautiful night for a ballgame!"

Piersall: "It is? Where?"

Caray: "C'mon Jimmy, it's been a nice day in Chicago today."

Piersall: "When we have a nice day in Chicago, send me a wire."

Caray: "Are you kidding? I walked all over the city today."

Piersall: "You look like it." (John Kuenster, "Brock and Grich: Top Candidates to Win 'Comeback Player' Awards," *Baseball Digest*, September, 1979, p. 16.)

40. Piellisch, "Do Artificial Surfaces Help or Hinder the Game?" p. 44.

41. Veeck and Linn, *Veeck as in Wreck*,

pp. 384–385.

42. *Ibid.*, p. 385.

43. *Ibid.*

44. *The World Almanac* (2001 edition), p. 473.

45. Veeck and Linn, *Veeck as in Wreck*, p. 393.

46. *Ibid.*, pp. 393–394.

47. *Ibid.*, p. 393.

48. "Long before the first pitch, I knew we didn't have your typical baseball crowd," umpire Durwood Merrill recalled (Durwood Merrill with Jim Dent, *You're Out and You're Ugly Too*, pp. 256–257), "because instead of families and kids, I saw a bunch of hard rockers with long hair and spacey-looking eyes. I could smell marijuana from the moment I walked onto the field and wondered if you could get high from secondhand smoke."

49. Veeck and Linn, *Veeck as in Wreck*, pp. 394–395.

50. *Ibid.*, p. 120.

51. *Ibid.*

52. Bill James, "Phoenix," *The Bill James Guide To Baseball Managers*, pp. 242–243. This move, along with the concurrent shift of Terry Forster to the rotation, choked off the 24-year-old Pete Vuckovich's chances at a starting berth. After winning the 1982 Cy Young Award, Vuckovich would remember Richards as "the guy who made a reliever out of me and a starter out of Goose Gossage."

OK Pete, you did end up with an impressive trophy for your rec room and Gossage didn't do particularly well as a starter (9–17 with a 3.94 ERA) after an excellent 1975 season in relief, but before we consign Richards to pathetic old-fogey hell, consider that:

1. Gossage had been a fine starter in his minor league days. At Appleton in the Midwest League in 1971, the Goose had worked over seven innings a start en route to an 18–2 record with a 1.83 ERA and 149 Ks in 187 innings pitched. (*Who's Who In Baseball* [1980 Edition], pp. 137–138.)

2. Vuckovich, a guy whose success was driven by eccentric mechanics as much as sheer power, was coming off a season in which he'd gone 11–4... but with a 4.34 ERA. Sure, he'd recorded those numbers in Denver, but the Bears' staff ERA that year was 4.23; Vuckovich was

dragging the team down in that area. The Bears' 1975 ace was Steve Dunning, a 26-year-old right-hander who had absorbed 380-plus innings of punishment as an Indians starter in the early 1970s. Dunning went 15–9 that year with a 3.49 ERA and virtually identical stats to those of Vuckovich except that he was significantly less homer-prone. (1975 American Association Pitching Statistics, *1976 Official Baseball Guide*, pp. 367–369.)

Dunning, like Vuckovich, would get a shot at the Show in 1976 ... and post a 2–6 record with a 4.35 ERA in 97 innings worked primarily for the Montreal Expos. (Bucek [ed.], *The Baseball Encyclopedia* [Tenth Edition], p. 1955.) *Now* we know that such moves rarely work, but back then the situation was much more fluid with a Skip Lockwood or Ron Reed seemingly coming out of nowhere every season to have a big year in relief. An ace closer is of minimal use to a team if they can't pass a lead to him; Richards was desperate for starters in the aftermath of Kaat's trade, Gossage appeared to be one of the four or five best possibilities he had at his disposal, and Vuckovich didn't. That's all there is to it, Pete.

53. Jerome Holtzman, "Wood Injury Caps Sox' Tale of Woe," *The Sporting News*, May 29, 1976 p. 20. The Tigers' Ron LeFlore hit the drive.

When Wood returned from Detroit, Veeck went out to meet him at Chicago's O'Hare Airport. Showing that he hadn't lost his sense of humor, the White Sox owner quipped upon seeing the wheelchair-bound knuckleballer, "If it was the other one, I could have given you one of my wooden legs."

54. Veeck with Linn, *Veeck as in Wreck*, p. 386.

From the "what might have been" files, a little lefty named Ron Guidry who was having a terrible spring (Billy Martin supposedly said to him at one point, "If there's anybody you can get out, tell me and I'll let you pitch to him") was originally slated to be the pitcher in the deal. Gabe Paul, however, talked Steinbrenner out of moving Guidry at the last moment (Lyle and Golenbock, *The Bronx Zoo*, p. 39).

55. In August 1975, Soderholm broke a

couple of ribs when he fell into a 12-foot-deep storm sewer. While in the hospital, he decided to have surgery done on a knee that had been locking up on him from time to time. The surgery didn't go well; after two additional operations, Eric was told that his chances of playing again were less than 50-50. (Eric Solderholm as told to George Vass, "The Game I'll Never Forget," *Baseball Digest*, May, 1981, p. 86.)

Once out of the hospital, though, Solderholm decided to "give it everything I had to attempt to rehabilitate the knee." Eric and his family lived in a Florida trailer while the third baseman took part in a strenuous Nautilus program to strengthen the joint — so strenuous, in fact, that he actually lived at the weight training center for an extended period of time.

Unimpressed, the Twins released Soderholm at the end of the 1976 season. (George Vass, "These Are Baseball's Biggest Player Bargains!" *Baseball Digest*, July, 1977, pp. 23–24.)

56. Jerome Holtzman, "Gamble, Zisk Fueled Rejuvenated Chisox," *1978 Official Baseball Guide*, p. 59.

57. Holtzman, "Gamble, Zisk Fueled Rejuvenated Chisox," p. 59.

58. Veeck and Linn, *Veeck as in Wreck*, p. 393.

59. *Ibid.*, p. 387. The practice had reportedly spread to Kansas City and Texas by the end of the season (Holtzman, "Gamble, Zisk Fueled Rejuvenated Chisox," p. 59).

60. Veeck and Linn, *Veeck as in Wreck*, p. 387.

61. Caray and Verdi, *Holy Cow!* pp. 210–211. Harry had sung "Take Me Out to the Ballgame" along with the organist for years, but none save the people in the press box and those fans seated close by had heard him before Veeck snuck a PA microphone into the booth one day early in the 1976 season.

"Harry," Veeck said after the game, "I've been looking for a guy to do that for thirty years, but I could never find the right guy before. Well ... you're the right guy."

The reason that Caray was right for the part, however, was something less than 100 percent flattering. "Harry," Veeck continued, "anybody in the ballpark hearing you sing 'Take Me Out to the Ballgame' knows that he can sing as well as you can. Probably *better* than you can. So he or she sings along. Hell,

if you had a good singing voice you'd intimidate them, and *nobody* would join in."

62. Jerome Holtzman, "Players, Lawyers Gained; Attendance Up," *1978 Official Baseball Guide*, p. 329.

63. Zander Hollander, *The Complete Book of Baseball* (1975 Edition), p. 119. Gamble's hair (which reportedly added four inches to his height) almost kept him from playing with the Yankees in 1976. Oscar finally agreed to have his hair cut if the Yankees would pay for the job ... and as a result an anonymous Fort Lauderdale barber ended up $33 richer (Phil Elderkin, "The Power Hitter the Yankees Dealt Away, *Baseball Digest*, December, 1977, p. 96).

64. Veeck and Linn, *Veeck as in Wreck*, pp. 389–390.

65. Forman, *Baseball-Reference.com*.

66. John A. Grunnell (ed.), *Standard Catalog of American Cars 1946–1975*, p. 311.

67. David Halberstam, *The Reckoning*, p. 529.

CHAPTER 30

1. 1968 American Association statistics, *1969 Official Baseball Guide*, pp. 361–371.

2. 1969 American Association statistics, *1970 Official Baseball Guide*, pp. 393–400.

3. Anderson had won pennants in each of his final four seasons as a minor league skipper (Jack Zanger, *Major League Baseball 1970*, p. 29) but had only one year of managerial experience above the A level at the time of his anointment by the Reds.

4. Hal McCoy, Untitled, *Baseball Digest*, September, 1975, p. 28. Pittsburgh broadcaster Bob Prince took to calling Bourbon "Dracula" after the incident.

5. Pietrusza, et al. (ed.), *Baseball: The Biographical Encyclopedia*, p. 324.

6. Nixon may have crossed paths with Anderson when both men were in the Boston organization — Russ as the team's number two catcher and Sparky as a member and then manager of their AAA Toronto squad. Nixon's FSL teams generally finished just over .500, a "good enough to keep but not good enough to promote" record which probably explains why he spent five seasons at the A level. His only divisional crown came in 1974, when all the good teams were

in the other bracket (*1975 Official Baseball Guide*, p. 476).

7. Spink, *1977 Official Baseball Guide*, p. 341 (Minor League Manager of the Year List), pp. 372–381 (1976 American Association statistics).

8. In "The Lost Decade ... Cards Went From '68 Pennant To '70s Sleepwalkers" (Mike Eisenbath, St. Louis *Post-Dispatch*, August 23, 1992, p. 1F), Bob Forsch remembered the complacency that marked the Cardinals' collective attitude in those days. "I remember one year Mr. Busch, who very rarely came around the ballpark in those days, came into the clubhouse," Forsch recalled. "We were fighting with the Mets for last place, and he told us, 'Whatever you do, finish in front of the Mets.'

"That's when reality slapped us in the face. You know you're going bad when your owner has to ask you not to finish last."

9. Mike Eisenbath, "The Lost Decade ... Cards Went From '68 Pennant To '70s Sleepwalkers," St. Louis *Post-Dispatch*, August 23, 1992, p. 1F. Ted Simmons put it succinctly—"We had a number of characters. We didn't have enough ballplayers."

10. James, *The Bill James Guide to Baseball Managers*, p. 252.

11. *Ibid.*

12. *Ibid.*, p. 251.

13. Neal Russo, "Mad Hungarian Excites Fans and Chills Hitters," *The Sporting News*, August 16, 1975, p. 3. Hrabosky's psych routine had its origins in his minor league days, but Al's act didn't really blossom until the after the 1974 All-Star break. "After struggling so much in the first half [15 hits and nine runs allowed in his first eight innings worked], I thought of psyching myself by walking around the mound and talking to myself. Every athlete or businessman uses something to boost himself. My method was just wide open."

14. Jeff Meyers, "The Cardinals' 'Mad Hungarian'," *Baseball Digest*, January, 1975, p. 54.

15. Pietrusza, et al. (eds.), *Baseball: The Biographical Encyclopedia*, p. 526.

16. "It's gotten to the point where [the batters] are psyching themselves out," Hrabosky once said to St. Louis *Post-Dispatch* reporter Jeff Meyers (Meyers, "The Cardinals' 'Mad Hungarian'," p. 55). "But they're doing it. What I do out there is strictly for my own benefit."

17. Neal Russo, "Clean-Shaven Cards Earn Rapp Okay," *The Sporting News*, March 12, 1977, p. 36.

18. James, *The Bill James Guide to Baseball Managers*, p. 252.

19. Forman, *Baseball-Reference.com*.

20. Bill James, *The Bill James Guide to Baseball Managers*, p. 252.

21. Unattributed, "The Sounds of 1978: Some Memorable Lines from a Forgettable Season," St. Louis *Post-Dispatch*, July 20, 1988, p. 3D.

22. Forman, *Baseball-Reference.com*.

23. Bucek (ed.), *The Baseball Encyclopedia* (Tenth Edition), p. 739.

24. James, *The Bill James Guide to Baseball Managers*, p. 252.

25. Spink, *1978 Official Baseball Guide*, p. 181. Five of the eight losses were credited to either Hrabosky or setup man Rawly Eastwick.

26. James, *The Bill James Guide to Baseball Managers*, p. 252.

27. *Ibid.*, p. 253.

28. *Ibid.*

29. *Ibid.*, p. 252.

30. *Ibid.*, p. 253.

31. *Ibid.*

32. Keith Hernandez and Mike Bryan, *If At First ...* p. 159.

33. Neal Russo, "Flashy Forsch Laboring in Cardinals' Shadows," *The Sporting News*, August 23, 1975, p. 16.

34. Dave Leucking, "'78 Cards: A Lost Cause," St. Louis *Post-Dispatch*, July 20, 1988, p. 1D.

35. Unattributed, "The Sounds of 1978: Some Memorable Lines from a Forgettable Season," 3D.

36. Luecking, "'78 Cards: A Lost Cause," p. 1D.

37. *Ibid.*

38. Unattributed, "The Sounds of 1978: Some Memorable Lines from a Forgettable Season," p. 3D.

39. Luecking, "'78 Cards: A Lost Cause," p. 1D.

40. Unattributed, "The Sounds of 1978: Some Memorable Lines from a Forgettable Season," p. 3D.

41. *Ibid.* Obviously referring to Buck, Rapp would comment after his firing, "I feel sorry for individuals who felt they had to get me because they really don't know what

it is to be a class person. If it was his intent to get me fired, I feel very sorry for him."

42. Bucek (ed.), *The Baseball Encyclopedia* (Tenth Edition), p. 579.

43. A good example of this genre is Dave Nightengale's "Did Orioles Lose Because of Weaver?" (*Baseball Digest*, January, 1972, pp. 27–28), which states in its opening paragraph that "Manager Earl Weaver cost Baltimore the championship by his refusal to substitute Paul Blair for Boog Powell in the final five games of the [1971] World Series." The premise was that Powell's wrist was still tender after being fractured in August and was thus responsible for his poor Series performance (three singles in 27 tries), while Blair's defense might have saved Game 7 for the Os.

Well, Dave ... first of all, Boog's wrist injury was originally suffered while sliding during a June 21 game with the Senators; the mammoth first baseman was back in the lineup on a regular basis by July 27 (Phil Jackman, "Baltimore Foes Get Bad News: Boog's Back and Bat Is Booming," *The Sporting News*, August 21, 1971, p. 7). Secondly, while the wrist problem did limit Boog's availability down the stretch (he played in 47 of the Orioles' final 57 games), he certainly carried his share of the load while in there. Powell hit .303 in the final two months of 1971 with eight homers and 37 RBIs, then followed that up with a couple of monstrous dingers in the ALCS to help the Os sweep the A's. As for Blair, he hit a very respectable .292 over the same period but with only three homers and 12 RBIs.

Sure, both played well, but with a team on which Frank Robinson was the only other big-time power source, one would have to imagine that 99 out of 100 managers would have gone with Boog if at all possible. Weaver, however, was roasted by Nightengale for it because Powell had a poor Series, and writers in general didn't like Earl, and thus put every decision of his under a microscope until he was anointed as a certified genius in the latter half of the decade.

44. In a highly publicized 1973 incident, Weaver was handcuffed and taken to jail after verbally abusing a Maryland state trooper and causing $75 worth of damage to his squad car after being stopped on suspicion of driving while under the influence of alcohol. "It all boils down to a personality conflict," Earl said at the time, a reasonable statement given that the Baltimore manager had called the arresting officer "crater face" (he suffered from acne) and a "pig _____" during the confrontation. "Yet I understand that the man was only doing his duty ... When the policeman pulled me over, I should have closed my mouth and accepted it." (Lou Hatter, "Earl the Weaver Gets in a Few Rips," *The Sporting News*, May 5, 1973, p. 8.)

45. James, *The Bill James Guide to Baseball Managers*, p. 254.

CHAPTER 31

1. Steve Garvey with Skip Rozin, *Garvey*, p. 19.

2. *Ibid.*, pp. 30–31. Garvey's mania for sartorial conservatism extended to those around him. When his father once came to watch him play in khakis, the younger Garvey noticed ... and commented on it once they got home.

3. *Ibid.* Garvey remembers that at age 12 he hit .750 with 20 homers while throwing three no-hitters. OK, perhaps he's rounding off those numbers — but Steve recalls later on (p. 34) that he hit .472 and .465 in his final two years at Chamberlain High.

4. *Ibid.*, p. 18. According to Garvey, he crouched down at the plate to the point that his strike zone was approximately six inches high, thus walking many times and scoring a number of runs despite the lack of hits. It is interesting to note that Garvey was unable to retain this sense of plate discipline in his professional years.

5. *Ibid.*, pp. 38–39.

6. "I admire him for some of the same reasons I admired [Gil] Hodges," Garvey explained in a 1975 interview. "Guys like this create good publicity for baseball. Pete's tremendous energy and hustle on the field are great assets for the game. And he does everything well. He plays cleanly and fairly, and takes the game seriously. You have to admire a guy like that." (Larry Bortstein, "Six Stars Name Their Baseball Idols," *Baseball Digest*, July, 1975, p. 59.)

Pete Rose mentioned in the same breath with Gil Hodges?

7. Garvey and Rozin, *Garvey*, pp. 127–

130.

8. "I know that in order to get my 200 hits a year, I must hit safely in 75 to 78 percent of the games," Garvey noted in a 1980 interview. "I'm aware, for instance, that I must average 17 RBIs a month to get my 100. I must average 33 hits a month to get my 200. And always in my mind is my slogan — .300-200-100. That means a .300 average, 200 hits, 100 RBIs."

As for fielding, "I allow myself one error a month. Anything more than that is counterproductive to winning, which should be the chief goal of all of us." (Melvin Durslag, "Steve Garvey: The Majors' Newest 'Iron Man'," *Baseball Digest*, p. 30.)

9. Forman, *Baseball-Reference.com*, Steve Garvey career statistics.

10. John Kuenster, "How Major League Players Are Rated in Special Talent Categories," *Baseball Digest*, April, 1979, p. 17. Garvey was also named in the poll as the NL's smartest player.

11. Gordon Verrell, "Good-Guy Garvey Cast in Dodger Villain Role," *The Sporting News*, July 19,1975, p. 15.

12. Garvey with Rozin, *Garvey*, p. 115.

13. Sid Bordman, "Steve Garvey, the Making of a Dodger Legend," *Baseball Digest*, June, 1979, p. 21.

14. Anthony Perry, "Developer Make Pitch for Garvey as Candidate," Los Angeles *Times* (San Diego County Edition), October 12, 1988, p. 1.

15. Forman, *Baseball-Reference.com*, *The Great American Stat Book* (1986 Edition), p. 233.

16. Dave Distel, "Garvey Ends Career in Baseball, Turns Eye Towards Politics," *The Los Angeles Times* (San Diego County Edition), January 14, 1988.

17. Pietrusza, et al. (eds.), *Baseball: The Biographical Encyclopedia*, pp. 765–6.

18. *Bill Mazeroski's Baseball '86*, p. 49.

CHAPTER 32

1. Forman, *Baseball-Reference.com*.

2. Larry Whiteside, "163rd Game — No Special Badge for Red Sox," *1979 Official Baseball Guide*, p. 27.

3. Forman, *Baseball-Reference.com*.

4. George Vass, "Here's How the Major League Pennant Races Shape Up," *Baseball Digest*, April, 1978, p. 23. "He's the guy we need to solidify our infield defense and give us speed at the top of our batting order," manager Don Zimmer said. "We don't have much speed and we need all we can get."

Remy also apparently arrived in Boston with the right attitude. "The first time we played the Yankees," Bill Lee commented, "he said, 'I hate every one of those pinstriped sons of bitches'." (Bill Lee with Dick Lally, *The Wrong Stuff*, p. 177.)

5. Weaver with Stainback, *It's What You Learn After You Know It All That Counts*, p. 223.

6. Bucek (ed.), *The Baseball Encyclopedia* (Tenth Edition), p. 2564.

7. Forman, *Baseball-Reference.com*.

8. Lee with Lally, *The Wrong Stuff*, pp. 171–172. Eckersley didn't go to a bar to drink, he went there to "get oiled" (Dennis's oil preference in those days, by the way, was what he called "eighty weight," which meant Jack Daniels). The Eck was good at nicknames, too: Lee was Sherwin Williams for his ability to paint the corners of the plate ("Why don't you call me Picasso or Renoir?" the Spaceman asked), while he himself was the Cheese Master.

9. Larry Whiteside, "163rd Game — No Special Badge for Red Sox," *1979 Official Baseball Guide*, pp. 29–30.

10. Lyle and Golenbock, *The Bronx Zoo*, p. 113.

11. Steinbrenner had paid the Atlanta Braves $100,000 for the final year of Messersmith's three-year, $1 million contract, which doesn't seem extraordinary until one considers that Andy had missed much of the previous season after undergoing reconstructive elbow surgery. Messersmith came back from the separated shoulder in June, pitched a couple of games, and was observed by Sparky Lyle after a July 1 start attempting to dress one-handed, his right arm rigidly at his side (Lyle and Golenbock, *The Bronx Zoo*, p. 149). Outside of a brief comeback attempt with the 1979 Dodgers, that episode would mark the end of Andy Messersmith's career.

In one sense it was probably just as well that things worked out as they did. Messersmith was a sensitive individual at heart, and he took the random screaming fits (manager Billy Martin once chewed him out for not wearing his cap), posturing, and pressure incumbent with the Yankee experience too much to heart. "He's amazed we can still play ball at all," Lyle remarked on June 10 (*Ibid.*, p. 114).

12. Gullett, a heavily muscled onetime farm boy who'd grown up hoisting 100-pound hay bales, began experiencing arm problems during the lockout-shortened 1976 spring training camp. Not having thrown a ball all winter prior to reporting to camp, Gullett starting airing out his arm too soon, which when combined with his natural crossfire delivery limited him to 23 1976 starts.

Though an examination by Dr. Frank Jobe showed "nothing of a serious nature" wrong with Don's arm at the time, the Kentucky-born lefty would never work as many as 160 innings in a season again, and his shoulder would be beyond repair by his 27th birthday (Earl Lawson, "Anatomy of an Arm Problem," *Baseball Digest*, December, 1976, pp. 40–42).

13. Lyle and Golenbock, *The Bronx Zoo*, p. 91. According to Lyle, by late June Hunter could barely shave with his right hand.

14. On the downside of his career, the midwestern native would only agree to be traded to either Chicago or Milwaukee. Holtzman's wish was granted on June 10, when he was sent to the Cubs for what Sparky Lyle termed "a minor league pitcher with a 7.00 ERA" (Lyle and Golenbock, *The Bronx Zoo*, p. 115). That pitcher, however, was Ron Davis, who as the result of a Bob Lemon experiment would become the first modern "setup" man (*1979 Official Baseball Guide*, p. 387).

15. Lyle and Golenbock, *The Bronx Zoo*, p. 222.

16. James, *The New Bill James Historical Baseball Abstract*, p. 376.

17. Martin and Peter Golenbock, *Number 1*, p. 217. Rivers's money problems led to a highly publicized altercation between Martin and Thurman Munson on a flight to Chicago in mid-May. While Martin characterizes the incident as teasing gone slightly amok, Lyle (*The Bronx Zoo*, pp. 89–90) tells of a nearly berserk Billy being restrained by his coaches from attacking the catcher while Munson stood at the ready laughing and shaking his head. "I never saw anything like that flare-up," Lyle recalled, "and really it

never should have happened. If Billy had something to say to Mickey, he should have said it."

"When he [Rivers] was upset about money he'd become moody, and he wouldn't run out ground balls and wouldn't play well in the field," Martin observed in *Number 1* (p. 89). "Sometimes I'd have to lend him some money just so he'd feel better about things."

18. Jackson with Lupica, *Reggie*, p. 156. There were actually two "straw that stirs the drink" quotes in the *Sport* article, and it would be the second one that would cause the biggest headaches for Reggie. In regards to Thurman Munson's role as team captain, Ward quoted Jackson as saying, "Munson thinks he can be the straw that stirs the drink, but he can only stir it bad."

Though the tremendously insecure catcher would eventually get over the slight, Reggie would find himself essentially alienated from his Yankee teammates for the remainder of his New York career. Carlos May and Mickey Rivers moved their lockers away from Jackson's immediately after the article came out, while the clubhouse began to fall silent when Reggie made his entrance each afternoon. "Every day I'd walk in," Jackson remembered (*Ibid.*, p. 189), "and it would be like there were these imaginary arrows showing me the way to my locker…. If I could connect the dots, there wouldn't be any trouble. Walk to the middle of the room, stop before I got to the buffet table, take a sharp military left turn, sit down, start getting dressed. Talk to Fran Healy if he was around. If not, keep the mouth shut. Don't go near Nettles. Don't want to mess with Nettles; it would be like betting against the house. Don't go near Lyle. Don't go near Munson. Just get the T-shirts out, get the sweatshirt, get the wristbands, get the batting gloves, get the bats, get the spikes. Get dressed. Get ready to go out and try to take it all out on a pitcher.

"As they say in show business, it was a tough room to work."

19. "He can tell a writer that you're the biggest moron and the worst ballplayer who ever lived," Sparky Lyle noted in *The Bronx Zoo* (p. 32), "and the next day Reggie will come over and smile at you and say 'Hey, how're you doing, buddy?' as if to say, 'I wasn't serious about the stuff I said. I was just doing my thing for the writers.'

"And the thing is, not many guys rip Reggie as hard as he should be ripped because they don't want to be like he is.... Instead of confronting him and telling him, 'You asshole' and putting an end to that crap, they figure 'Screw it. I don't want to be like him'."

20. "If I live to be 100, I could never repay Fran Healy for his friendship and kindness," Reggie stated in *Reggie* (pp. 204–205). "To this day, I am overwhelmed by the reservoirs of compassion he showed for me, almost from the first day. It was not a brilliant political posture around the Yankees to be Reggie Jackson's friend."

21. The desire to be a two-way player was one that Reggie shared with many of uncertain fielding prowess, but being a cleanup hitter appears to have been a core feature of Jackson's personality at the time. Reggie mentions his position in the lineup on several occasions (*Ibid.*, pp. 162, 196–7, 199, 222, 233) and even devotes a portion of a chapter title ("On Stayin' Alive in the Clubhouse, Batting Cleanup, and Winning the Division: Not Altogether Unrelated Events," *Ibid.*, p. 187) to the concept. Consider Reggie's comments regarding the early weeks of the 1977 season on page 162:

"Arm's sore. Can't hit. Booed wherever we went including Yankee Stadium. Hitting third, fifth, sixth, everywhere but where I should have—fourth."

Ah, Reggie ... has it ever occurred to you that a player on the same team as men like Craig Nettles, Chris Chambliss, and reigning MVP Thurman Munson probably shouldn't be in the number four slot when he isn't hitting? That perhaps one of those other guys could step in and keep the team going while you get your swing back in gear?

22. This viewpoint is admittedly based upon the opinions of Jackson (*Ibid.*, p. 167), Lyle (*The Bronx Zoo*, p. 177) and others rather than those expressed by the man himself in *Number 1*. In reading that book, one gets the impression that Martin's problems with Reggie were as much a matter of Steinbrenner's meddling as it was anything that Reggie himself did (see *Number 1*, pp. 105, 119–20, 234, 237–8, 305, 326 for examples). The Yankee manager even goes so far as to characterize himself and Jackson as becoming friendly upon Billy's return to the team in 1979 (pp. 326–327), a comment that stands in contrast to Reggie's statement (*Reggie*, p. 273) that "Billy and I *had* gotten

along well through the end of the [1979] season, mostly because we stayed out of each other's way.... In the back of my mind, though, I felt that things were never really going to change for us."

That's basically the way *Number 1* reads in general: outside of George Steinbrenner, Twins traveling secretary Howard Fox and perhaps George Weiss, everybody comes off as a good guy in Martin's estimate—a little misguided at times perhaps, but A-OK just the same. Martin remembers himself as being like a father to Minnesota pitcher Dave Boswell, yet that pseudo-relationship apparently wasn't strong enough to keep him from beating Boswell to a pulp in a Detroit bar (pp. 272–274). Similarly, though Thurman Munson is characterized as "a fun-loving, good-natured kid who loved to agitate me" (*Ibid.*, p. 218) Billy was still able to denigrate Munson's influence on the team at top volume on a commercial airline flight (Lyle, *The Bronx Zoo*, p. 89).

23. "Once again, he [Martin] and I had no relationship at all," Jackson recalls (Jackson and Lupica, *Reggie*, p. 218), "unless we happened to be in the same newspaper story. The only time Billy and I spoke was if we happened to be walking through the clubhouse door at the same time.... As far as Billy and Reggie were concerned, it was the same old nightmare."

Martin, however, remembered it differently, stating that "Reggie was super" about being moved down in the order and occasionally to the bench as the result of a midseason slump. "I don't know what he told the writers, but I felt he and I had a great rapport. He'd come into my office, we'd talk, and he'd lay a little poem on my desk for me to read. He was just super, didn't give me any trouble." (Martin and Golenbock, *Number 1*, p. 233.)

24. Jackson and Lupica, *Reggie*, pp. 222–223.

25. On May 16 in Chicago, Martin almost passed out on the bench by both his recollection (*Number 1*, pp. 220–221) and Lyle's (*The Bronx Zoo*, p. 91). A doctor summoned to the dugout thought Martin might have a heart problem and should go to a hospital immediately; when Martin refused, the doctor said, "Well, I'm not responsible if anything happens." (Martin and Golenbock, *Number 1*, p. 221.)

"Billy's pale and looks terrible," Lyle

stated in his journal (*The Bronx Zoo*, pp. 91–92). "Everyone's been telling him to take it easy, but he takes losing so hard, and with this other stuff popping up, it's killing him... Billy's deathly afraid he's losing control of the ball club, and I think that if he continues the way he has been, he just might."

26. Jackson and Lupica, *Reggie*, pp. 227–228. "He wanted to be Mr. Fixit," Jackson said of the Yankee owner. "It's another one of George's favorite roles. I sometimes think that when George shaves in the morning, he looks in the mirror and sees six or seven faces staring back at him. George the patriarch. George the sportsman. George the tycoon. Tough George. Fair George. And you can take it from me, there *are* a lot of Georges.

"I just hope you get a nice one."

27. Holtzman, "More than 40 Million Caught 'Baseball Fever'," p. 322. Practically every independent observer characterizes Martin as having increasingly taken solace in the bottle in the days leading up to this climatic quote. (See Lyle, *The Bronx Zoo*, pp. 93–94, 105, Jackson and Lupica, *Reggie*, pp. 216, 217–8; Holtzman, "More than 40 Million Caught 'Baseball Fever'," p. 322.) Martin himself, however, never mentions alcohol in his recounting of the crises leading up to his dismissal.

28. Consider this August 22 entry: "We really don't think we can do it. We're seven and a half back with 39 games to play, and even if we beat Boston all seven games we have remaining with them, if we lost a couple of games and they won, it would be church.... Boston's not about to fold with the club that they have." (Lyle, *The Bronx Zoo*, p. 201.)

29. Larry Whiteside, "Lee Punches Out a Six-Week Vacation," *The Sporting News*, June 5, 1976, p. 6.

Lee tore ligaments in his left shoulder as a direct result of his close encounter with the Yankee third baseman, then hyperextended his elbow as a result of favoring the shoulder while rehabbing. According to the Spaceman, the injury robbed him of the ability to back batters off the plate with hard stuff, forcing him thereafter to concentrate more on changing speeds and throwing to spots. (Lee with Lally, *The Wrong Stuff*, pp. 157–158.)

30. "He didn't have a clue on how to run a pitching staff," Lee stated (*Ibid.*, p. 165). "At one point [this was during the 1977 season] he had eight guys moving in and out as starters.... None of us could establish a good working rhythm pitching under those conditions. Laboring in the bullpen for him wasn't a treat either."

Zimmer was apparently also a big proponent of the brushback pitch, which caused an unnamed Red Sox hurler to ask "How bright can this guy be? Here he is walking about with a plate in his head, the souvenir of a serious beaning, and he's talking about knocking guys down." (*Ibid.*, p. 162.)

31. *1979 Official Baseball Guide*, pp. 102, 417.

32. Lee with Lally, *The Wrong Stuff*, p. 166. The Order's name was derived from a moniker hung on the Boston manager by Ferguson Jenkins, who believed buffalo to be the stupidest creatures on Earth.

33. Whiteside, "163rd Game — No Special Badge for Red Sox," p. 27.

34. Forman, *Baseball-Reference.com*.

35. *Ibid.*

36. Pietrusza, *Baseball: The Biographical Encyclopedia*, p. 46.

37. Boggs, just 20 at the time, hit .311 in 354 at-bats while contributing an additional 53 walks, which led to 63 runs scored in 109 games. However, Wade was no power hitter (just one homer and 16 other extra-base hits on the season) and didn't have a defensive position (he played second, short, third, and the outfield that year) , so despite finishing third in the Eastern League batting race he was destined to stay at Bristol for the 1979 season. (*1979 Official Baseball Guide*, pp. 449–453.)

38. According to Reggie Jackson (Jackson and Lupica, *Reggie*, p. 232), Lemon set a minimalist tone during his first team meeting. "You guys won last year," the one-time Cleveland right-hander reminded his new charges, "which means you must have been doing something right. So what do you say you go out and play just like you did last year, and I'll try to stay out of the way."

39. Actually, Dalton didn't require a lot of persuading. After the Halos lost $600,000 in 1977 despite setting a single-season franchise attendance record (just over 1.4 million), owner Gene Autry coerced longtime Dodgers/Padres GM Buzzie Bavasi out of retirement to handle the team's purse strings.

Looking a $400,000 player development budget cut in the face, Dalton was thus receptive when Selig came calling in November with a six-year deal in hand (Newhan, *The California Angels: The Complete History*, pp. 158–161).

40. Lou Chapman, "More Changes Were Foreseen for Brewers," *1978 Official Baseball Guide*, pp. 43–44. Hegan was released shortly after making his comment.

41. Bucek (ed.), *The Baseball Encyclopedia* (Tenth Edition), p. 2657. Rich Folkers, a 31-year-old lefty with 195 big-league appearances under his belt but none in front of him, went with Slaton to the Tigers.

42. *Who's Who In Baseball* (1980 Edition), p. 68. You couldn't blame the Brewers, though; an All-American shortstop at the University of Minnesota, Molitor had hit .346 with eight homers and 50 RBI, in his 64 games at Class A Burlington (Iowa). A last-place team at the time of Molitor's arrival, Burlington won the Midwest League's Southern Division title for the second half of the season by seven games, then defeated Waterloo in the playoffs to cop the league title (*1978 Official Baseball Guide*, p. 534).

43. Mike Gonring, "Bamberger Brewed Up Winning Concoction," *1979 Official Baseball Guide*, p. 31.

44. *Ibid.*, p. 30.

45. As is so often the case, it was another player's misfortune — in this case a crippling shoulder injury that essentially ended Larry Hisle's career — that gave the free-swinging Oglivie his break (Okrent, *Nine Innings*, p. 16).

46. Terence Moore, "Mike Caldwell: Heart of the Brewers' Success in '78," *Baseball Digest*, December, 1978, p. 39.

47. Bucek (ed.), *The Baseball Encyclopedia* (Tenth Edition), p. 548.

48. The Brewers' closer platoon that season consisted of Bob McClure and Bill Castro, nicknamed Ethyl and Premium by a press box sage for their erratic performance. (Okrent, *Nine Innings*, p. 7.) McClure, despite a 1981 rotator cuff tear that would place his career in jeopardy, would parlay his left-handedness and the developing trend towards situational relievers into a 19-year career. Castro, on the other hand, as an undersized right-hander who lacked Grade A heat and had trouble staying healthy, would disappear from the majors before his 30th

birthday. (Forman, *Baseball-Reference.com*.)

49. Tom Weir, "A's Three-Month Miracle Short of Paradise," *1979 Official Baseball Guide*, pp. 71–72.

50. Larry Whiteside, "Red Sox Battled Yanks to Wire," *1978 Official Baseball Guide*, pp. 33–4, and Whiteside, "163rd Game — No Special Badge for Red Sox," p. 29.

51. Lyle, *The Bronx Zoo*, pp. 215–216.

52. *Ibid.*, p. 216.

53. *Ibid.*, pp. 217–218.

54. *1979 Official Baseball Guide*, p. 417. By fingering Sprowl, the Red Sox passed up a 24-year-old lefty swingman who had posted a 7–4 record with a 3.09 ERA in 105 innings. His name was John Tudor.

55. Lyle, *The Bronx Zoo*, p. 218.

56. *1979 Official Baseball Guide*, p. 49.

57. *Ibid.*, p. 30.

58. Lyle, *The Bronx Zoo*, pp. 241–242.

59. *1979 Official Baseball Guide*, p. 30.

60. Phil Pepe, "Well-Traveled Stanley Settles Down as Yank," *The Sporting News*, June 28, 1975, p. 9.

61. Jackson and Lupica, *Reggie*, p. 241.

62. Larry Wigge, "Dent's HR Shocked Red Sox for A.L. East Title," *1979 Official Baseball Guide*, p. 240.

63. Jackson and Lupica, *Reggie*, p. 241.

64. Lyle, *The Bronx Zoo*, p. 244.

65. Wigge, "Dent's HR Shocked Red Sox for A.L. East Title," p. 240.

66. Lyle, *The Bronx Zoo*, p. 243.

67. Forman, *Baseball-Reference.com*.

68. Pietrusza, et al. (eds.), *Baseball: The Biographical Encyclopedia*, p. 1140.

69. Jackson and Lupica, *Reggie*, p. 242. According to Jackson, Dent had been using Rivers's bats in recent days.

70. Wigge, "Dent's HR Shocked Red Sox for A.L. East Title," p. 240.

71. Jackson and Lupica, *Reggie*, p. 243.

72. *Ibid.*, p. 244.

73. *Ibid.*

CHAPTER 33

1. MacPhail, *My Nine Innings*, p. 116. From the Insensitivity Hall of Fame: A film on relief pitching unveiled at the Shea Stadium Diamond Club on October 21, 1970 featured a vignette from a June 24 Cleveland–New York games in which Indians first

baseman Tony Horton literally crawls back to his dugout after being embarrassed by a couple of Hamilton's "folly floaters" (Jack Lang, "Rescue Artists Are Heroes in New Film," *The Sporting News*, November 7, 1970, p. 48). By the time the film was released, everybody in baseball knew that Horton's antics were anything but a put-on: Tony had been institutionalized with a nervous breakdown a few months after his unsuccessful duel with the Yankee hurler and would never play baseball again. Yet the clip still found its way into the finalized film.

2. Forman, *Baseball-Reference. com.*

3. *Ibid.*

4. Harry Shattuck, "Jose Cruz of the Astros: Under-Rated No Longer!" *Baseball Digest*, February, 1981, p. 55. Cruz's introductions became something of a fan participation event over time, though Jose once said, "Sometimes I don't know if they are booing me instead."

5. Bucek (ed.), *The Baseball Encyclopedia* (Tenth Edition), pp. 417–419, 496–499.

6. The Bull also had a standing agreement with Larry Bowa that the rangy shortstop would take every popup/fly ball that he could get to (Calabria, "Greg Luzinski: The Maturing of a Major League Slugger," p. 48).

Stan Hochman ("Greg Luzinski: 'I've Got To Make Good'," *Baseball Digest*, February, 1973, p. 37) said that "if you put a bell around Luzinski's neck, he'd look like a neighborhood ice cream truck. Which is the way he plays left field for the Phillies, like a truck with a student driver."

7. Forman, *Baseball-Reference. com.*

8. *Ibid.*

9. Pietrusza, et al., *Baseball: The Biographical Encyclopedia*, p. 129.

10. Neal Russo, "Fans Enchanted by Theft Artist Brock," *The Sporting News*, August 23, 1974, p. 3.

11. *1975 Official Baseball Guide*, p. 73, 187.

12. *Ibid.*, p. 187.

13. Bucek (ed.), *The Baseball Encyclopedia* (Tenth Edition), p. 38.

14. Though Washington was the first (and thus far only) man to make his living entirely via his feet, Finley had experimented before with guys whose primary purpose was to pinch run. The most famous of these men was Allen "The Panamanian

Express" Lewis, a switch-hitting outfielder with zip power and little idea of how to use his speed either on the basepaths or in the field. Like Washington, Lewis's teammates did little to make his life as a half-player any easier; according to Wells Twombly ("Washington's Curious Legacy: 31 SBs, No ABs," *The Sporting News*, May 24, 1975, p. 13), one Oakland player dubbed Lewis "The Panamanian Local" because of his penchant for advancing one base at a time.

15. Ron Bergman, "Finley's Speed-to-Burn Plan Gives Athletics Sudden Chill," *The Sporting News*, April 6, 1974; p. 18.

16. *Ibid.*

17. *Ibid.*

After watching Washington ply his unusual trade for a couple of months, one A's player was inspired to quip, "He'd better win 13 between now and the end of the season because he's already minus four" (Kuenster, "The Mad, Mad World of the Oakland A's," p. 8).

18. Ron Bergman, "Loss of Catfish Hastened Herbie's Farewell," *The Sporting News*, May 24, 1975, p. 13. Despite being a pleasant, intelligent man, Washington was roundly disliked by most of his Oakland teammates, who felt that Herb's presence on the roster denied a *real* player his shot at the Show. Graciousness was in short supply even with Washington's demise; team captain Sal Bando remarked that "I'd feel sorry for him if he were a player. He got a bonus and a salary and a full World Series share, didn't he?."

19. Spink, *1978 Official Baseball Guide*, pp. 419–457.

20. Bill James wrote a highly descriptive and entertaining piece about Smith's defensive misadventures in the *Bill James Guide to Baseball Managers* (pp. 263–264). James pointed out that Lonnie's problems weren't as damaging as they looked "because, since Smith fell down chasing the ball all the time, he knew that you couldn't just lie there and look embarrassed, you had to hop right back up and start chasing that ball again."

21. Bucek (ed.), *The Baseball Encyclopedia* (Tenth Edition), pp. 522–561.

22. Forman, *Baseball-Reference.com.*

23. *Ibid.*

In the late 1970s, Indian farm system chieftain Bob Quinn began rating high school and college athletes on their quickness in what he called the Speed Book. According to Quinn, in the amateur draft's later rounds the Tribe would often select players based upon their Speed Book ratings alone. "You used to hear it said that speed is no help if he can't get to first base," Quinn remarked. "But we have seen enough of them now who learned to make contact well enough so that they could use their speed by the time they got to the major leagues." (Bob August, "Why There's A Surge In Base Stealing," *Baseball Digest*, August, 1977, p. 61.)

24. *Ibid.*

25. Bucek (ed.), *The Baseball Encyclopedia* (Tenth Edition), p. 2683. Lest we forget, Larry Bowa accompanied Sandberg in the famous/infamous January 27, 1982 deal.

26. Forman, *Baseball-Reference.com.*

27. *Ibid.*

28. *Ibid.*

29. *Ibid.*

CHAPTER 34

1. Bill James, *The Bill James Baseball Abstract 1984*, p. 131.

2. Pietrusza, et al. (eds.), *Baseball: The Biographical Encyclopedia*, pp. 760–761.

3. Jack Lang, "Sky King Writing Tape-Measure Tale," *The Sporting News*, May 8, 1976, p. 3.

4. Hal McCoy, "Dave Kingman: The Emergence of a New Home Run Star," *Baseball Digest*, August, 1976, p. 34.

5. *Ibid.*, p. 35.

6. *Ibid.*

7. John Kuenster, "Pitchers Hate Tape-Measure Home Runs," *Baseball Digest*, September, 1971, p. 4.

8. Forman, *Baseball-Reference. com.*

9. *Ibid.* Thomas as the AL's home run champ finished seventh in the 1979 MVP balloting, then managed an eighth-place finish in 1982 when he repeated as dinger king. Oddly enough, though, that eighth-place finish pegged him as just the third most valuable Brewer in the voters' minds that season — Robin Yount took the 1982 MVP home with him, while first baseman Cecil Cooper finished fifth.

10. Dick Young, "Dave Kingman: Home Runs Turn Him On," *Baseball Digest*, June, 1977, p. 67.

11. Pietrusza, et al. (eds.), *Baseball: The Biographical Encyclopedia*, p. 610.

12. Bill James, *The Bill James Baseball Abstract*, p. 214.

13. "It's just that I prefer a private life of my own," Kingman noted in a 1976 interview (Lang, "Sky King Writing Tape-Measure Tale," p. 3). "I like to live quietly."

While playing for the Mets, the then-single Kingman chose a large house in Cos Cob, New Jersey over the bright lights and fast-paced lifestyle of the Big Apple. "I enjoy playing in New York," Dave explained, "but I don't enjoy living in the city. I like peace and quiet. I like to get away from it all. I enjoy woodworking. I enjoy making things. I'll have my own shop in this place."

CHAPTER 35

1. Merrill with Dent, *You're Out and You're Ugly, Too!* p. 28.

2. *Ibid.*, p. 41.

3. *Ibid.*, pp. 40–41. After a Sunday afternoon brouhaha in which a number of players and coaches from both sides were thrown out of the game when Durwood's partner lost a fly ball in the sun, the two neophyte umpires were locked in the Bakersfield (CA) umpire's room until 6 a.m. the following morning. Once released, Merrill's partner dropped him off at the hotel, said "Durwood, I'm not putting up with this," and drove away, never to return.

4. *Ibid.*, p. 48.

Dave Pallone earned $600 a month flat for his early 1970s work in the New York-Pennsylvania League, which after taxes and expenses associated with the job came to about $10 a day. He and his partner "could only afford a room with one bed, so we switched off each night: one of us on the bed and one on the floor. We went to the market and bought a loaf of bread, a pound of bologna, some mustard and tomatoes, and that's what we ate every day." (Dave Pallone with Alan Steinberg, *Behind The Mask: My Double Life In Baseball*, pp. 51–52.)

5. Ron Luciano and David Fisher, *The Umpire Strikes Back*, p. 41.

6. This was Al Salerno's pay rate in his final season as an arbiter. (Jack Craig, "Stanky Goes to Bat for Ousted Umpires,"

The Sporting News, August 1, 1970, p. 10.)

7. Holtzman, "Players, Umpires, Books, Law Suits...," *1971 Official Baseball Guide,* p. 287.

8. Thomas Boswell, "The Umpire: He's Baseball's Indispensable Man," *Baseball Digest,* April, 1979, p. 78.

9. Jerome Holtzman, "Expansion, Canadian Club, Feature 1968," *1969 Official Baseball Guide,* p. 196.

10. *Ibid.*

11. *Ibid.,* pp. 197–198.

12. Jerome Holtzman, "Players, Umpires, Books, Law Suits...," *1971 Official Baseball Guide,* p. 286.

13. Holtzman, "Two Divisions, Rules, Player Demands, Etc.," p. 307.

14. Holtzman, "Players, Umpires, Books, Law Suits...," pp. 286–287. The American League made four attempts to settle with Salerno and Valentine — the final one 24 hours before the scheduled opening of the initial NLRB hearing on July 7, 1970. One of the agreements would have called for the two umpires to have started the 1970 season in the minors, be promoted after two months, and receive retroactive pay and benefits for the missed 1969 season.

Salerno apparently had financial difficulties (he reportedly told his attorneys that he owed $40,000) and didn't really want to return to baseball anyway, which made him especially susceptible to his attorney's assurances that a NLRB ruling would yield $250,000 or more. Since the AL was demanding that both umpires drop their suits as a condition of any agreement, this left Valentine — who consistently agreed to every proposal baseball offered — out in the cold.

15. Jerome Holtzman, "'71 Saw Gate Up, Short Move, Alex Angry," *1972 Official Baseball Guide,* p. 311.

16. *Ibid.,* pp. 287–290.

17. Stan Isle, "Umps' New Pension Plan Sets $17,076 Tops," *The Sporting News,* April 19, 1975, p. 20.

18. "Average Hours and Earnings of Production Workers, 1966–94," *The World Almanac* (1996 Edition), p. 153.

19. Jerome Holtzman, "More Than 40 Million Caught Baseball Fever," *1979 Official Baseball Guide,* p. 313.

20. Merrill with Dent, *You're Out and You're Ugly Too,* p. 80. Merrill missed his daughter's wedding, high school gradua-

tion, and was even denied a furlough when in 1977 she developed a health issue that required immediate surgery. Instead of being at her side, Durwood was the home plate umpire at Cleveland's Municipal Stadium that night. After the game, he found out that his daughter was going to be fine ... then went back to his hotel room and cried.

21. Luciano and Fisher, *The Umpire Strikes Back,* p. 232.

22. Phillips played a cameo role in the 1981 players' strike, suing to deny the clubs the $50 million in strike insurance payments available under the policy they had taken out with Lloyds of London (Kuhn, *Hardball,* p. 352). He also appears to have been utilized as a middleman by George Steinbrenner in an attempt to settle the strike's key issue via the establishment of a compensation pool to reimburse teams that lost free agents (Miller, *A Whole Different Ball Game,* pp. 379–382).

Interestingly, neither baseball's commissioner nor the MLBPA leader mentions the 1979 umpires' strike in their memoirs.

23. Clifford Katchline, "Ump Walkout, Yanks' Troubles Dominate," *1980 Official Baseball Guide,* p. 300.

24. Holtzman, "More Than 40 Million Caught Baseball Fever," pp. 313–314.

25. Katchline, "Ump Walkout, Yanks' Troubles Dominate," p. 300.

26. *Ibid.* As a side note, while the agreement between baseball and the umpires allowed for salaries to exceed the contract minimums based upon performance, none of the 51 arbiters who submitted their contracts to Phillips were offered more than $3,000 above the base rate for their years of experience.

27. *Ibid.*

28. *Ibid.,* p. 301.

29. *Ibid.*

30. *Ibid.*

31. *Ibid.,* pp. 300–303. Hendry was an 11-year minor leaguer who had been recently elevated to replace future Hall of Fame arbiter Nestor Chylak, who became an assistant supervisor of umpires for the American League. Pryor, on the other hand, was an 18-year veteran who "for personal reasons" (i.e. he needed the money) signed a two-year contract in early March. Pryor was roasted by his fellow umpires for breaking ranks while Hendry wasn't, but both would

ultimately resign their positions and join their brother arbiters on the picket line.

32. *Ibid.*, p. 301.

33. Solomon, *The Baseball Timeline*, p. 821.

34. *Ibid.*, p. 822.

35. Forman, *Baseball-Reference.com.*

36. Katchline, "Ump Walkout, Yanks' Troubles Dominate," p. 300.

37. Feeney's and Luciano's remarks were actually pirated from ex-Cubs manager Herman Franks, of whom umpire Ken Kaiser once said (Boswell, "The Umpire: He's Baseball's Indispensable Man," p. 80) "I hope he goes 0 and 162 some year."

So much for burying the hatchet....

38. "Work Stoppages (Strikes and Lockouts) in the U.S., 1960–99, *The World Almanac* (2001 edition), p. 169.

39. Katchline, "Ump Walkout, Yanks' Troubles Dominate," p. 304. A 200-man picket line established on Easter Sunday reduced turnout for a game with divisional rival St. Louis to 3,012 hardy souls.

40. *Ibid.*

41. *Ibid.* The local organizations that honored the umpires' picket lines were in Cleveland and San Diego.

42. *Ibid.*, p. 306.

43. *Ibid.*, p. 307.

44. Pallone with Steinberg, *Behind The Mask: My Double Life In Baseball*, pp. 128–142.

45. In the days when he was a "swing" umpire, filling in for arbiters who were on vacation, Dave Pallone once arrived in San Francisco to find:

   a) The word "scab" emblazoned in red across the top of his equipment trunk.

   b) His shin guards slashed.

   c) His hat shredded.

   d) A padlock fastened across the bar of his face mask.

"*Now* it seems funny," Pallone remarked, "but when it happened I went through the roof" (Pallone with Steinberg, *Behind The Mask: My Double Life In Baseball*, p. 131).

46. Katchline, "Ump Walkout, Yanks' Troubles Dominate," p. 306.

47. *Ibid.*, p. 307.

48. *The World Almanac* (2001 Edition), p. 171.

Chapter 36

1. Luciano and Fisher, *The Umpire Strikes Back*, p. 36.

2. Dave Kaye, "Ron Luciano: Flashiest Ump in the Game," *Baseball Digest*, October, 1977, p. 26.

3. *Ibid.*, pp. 70–72. Luciano did apologize to Patek later on.

4. *Ibid.*, pp. 61–62. Stanley, the guy who became a first-time shortstop during the 1968 World Series when Tiger manager Mayo Smith decided that he couldn't put up with Ray Oyler's bat (or lack thereof), was hearing Ron LeFlore's footsteps behind him. Luciano's mission failed: Stanley announced his retirement almost immediately after the season ended.

5. *Ibid.*, p. 65.

6. *Ibid.*, pp. 32–33. In 1965, Luciano ejected 26 players, coaches, and managers in 140 Eastern League games, including Elmira manager Earl Weaver in four consecutive contests, thus setting the stage for their future travails.

7. Trying to stem the tide of Luciano's words, Frank Robinson upon becoming manager of the Cleveland Indians instigated a $200 fine for anyone who talked to the Roman Umpire. See *Ibid.*, pp. 54–55.

Carl Yastremzski was normally good for a friendly hello at a minimum, but once when he was going through an 0-for-20 slump, Yaz greeted Luciano with "Listen, you [expletive deleted]. My wife is OK, my kids are OK, I'm OK, I don't know any good eating places in town and keep your mouth shut." (Kaye, "Ron Luciano: Flashiest Ump in the Game," p. 27.)

8. Luciano and Fisher, *The Umpire Strikes Back*, pp. 34–35.

9. *Ibid.*, p. 166. Ellie Hendricks, Ed Herrmann, and Johnny Roseboro were the designated umpire/catchers.

10. John Lindblom, "An Ex-Ump Calls Them as He Saw Them," *Baseball Digest*, December, 1980, p. 43.

11. *Ibid.*

12. Bill Lyon, "Please Don't Kill the Umpires!" *Baseball Digest*, February, 1980, p. 49.

13. *Ibid.*

14. Weaver and Stainback, *It's What You Learn After You Know It All That Counts*, p. 51. "I think his antics were definitely good

for the game ... until he began putting more effort into them than he did into his work. It suffered along with those of us who were engaged in our profession that particular day. Luciano just got caught with his thumb up his butt too many times."

According to Durwood Merrill (Merrill with Dent, *You're Out and You're Ugly Too!*" p. 235), "Ronnie's biggest problem was that he spent too much time with his eyes in the stands and his head in the clouds, and even though he was funny at times, enough was enough."

15. Ken Nigro, "Weaver, Ump Luciano Resume Trading Insults," *The Sporting News*, March 10, 1979, p. 39.

16. A good example was Weaver's public (and successful) agitation to have umpire Bill Haller removed from any games involving the Tigers and Orioles during the tight 1972 pennant race due to the fact that Haller's brother Tom played for Detroit (Lou Hatter, "'Weaver Wrong!' Ump Haller Fires Rebuttal," *The Sporting News*, August 12, 1972, p. 19). "When brothers are in the same league," Earl commented at the time, "especially when one of them catches for a contender, I don't think the brother umpire should be umpiring games involving the Orioles.... Rather than have something build up inside of me or anybody else, Haller should exclude himself, or the league should act, so that we do not see him umpiring any games involving contenders any more this year."

In abstract Weaver's request was not unreasonable ... until one realizes that Tom Haller was a 35-year-old third-string catcher at the time, and he recorded a big ten at-bats after August 31.

The umpire had the last laugh, however; the Orioles fell five games short of the Bengals and Haller was named as one of that season's World Series officials (Robert L. Burnes, "Season's High, Low Spots," *Baseball Digest*, January, 1973, p. 77).

17. Nigro, "Weaver, Ump Luciano Resume Trading Insults," p. 39.

18. Tom Fitzpatrick, "Ron Luciano: The Ump Who Tells It Like It Is," *Baseball Digest*, September, 1976, p. 23.

19. Luciano and Fisher, *The Umpire Strikes Back*, p. 30. Whenever Luciano's umpiring crew crossed paths with the Orioles, the Baltimore players would set up a pool each night to bet on how long Weaver would last that particular day. "I might dump him in the fifth inning," Ron commented in his book, "and look into the Oriole dugout and Mark Belanger or Jim Palmer or Don Buford would be jumping up and down and cheering 'Fifth inning, that's me!'."

20. Lindblom, "An Ex-Ump Calls Them As He Saw Them," p. 40.

21. Merrill with Dent, *You're Out and You're Ugly Too!* pp. 234–235. "I really don't believe that Ronnie had fun his last couple of years," Merrill continued. "The bosses were on his case, and even some of his fellow umpires wanted him to tone it down."

22. Ron Luciano & David Fisher, *Strike Two*, pp. 1–2. "Actually," Luciano commented, "I was surprised I hadn't done better. There are many things I'm not good at. I'm not good at video games. I'm not good at yachting. I'm a terrible typist. But talking? With all the practice I've had?"

23. Associated Press, "Luciano's Death Is Classified as a Suicide," Los Angeles *Times*, January 20, 1995, p. 10.

CHAPTER 37

1. Charley Feeney, "Willie Stargell: A Super Star at Last?" *All-Star Sports*, September, 1971, p. 10.

2. Charley Feeney, "Graveyard Strolls Keep Slugger Stargell Slim," *The Sporting News*, May 22, 1971, p. 3. Stargell was 5'10" and 152 pounds when he broke in with the Sophomore League's Roswell team in 1959.

3. Pietrusza, et al. (eds.), *Baseball: The Biographical Encyclopedia*, p. 1074.

4. When asked in a 1970 interview why he seethed at small indignities like being asked by little old ladies to carry their bags in hotels, Gibson replied, "It's not small. It's a big thing. It happens every day of your life. It's one of the underlying reasons why you are not accepted and respected the same as everyone else."

On whether an African American could go through an entire day without being slighted: "He would probably have to stay home and not turn on the radio or TV set. The kids would have to stay in the house and not go to school.... It would be very difficult to go a day without being reminded you're not what you're supposed to be." (George Kiseda, "Dash of Bitters Sours Gibby Success Saga," *The Sporting News*, October 10, 1970, p. 17.)

By the early 1970s, Gibson's wife was no less reticent than her husband about expressing her dissatisfaction with the plight of blacks in American society. "If Bob and I are treated better than most blacks," Mrs. Gibson commented in early 1973, "it's only because he's a celebrity. It's a mark of our society that a man earns equality by throwing a baseball harder than someone else." (Bob Hertzel, "Racial Prejudice a Definite Stranger to Reds," *The Sporting News*, April 28, 1973, p. 7.)

5. Wills and Celizic, *On the Run*, pp. 153–154. Wills was given the sobriquet by Dodgers coach Charlie Dressen, who disliked Maury's quiet way of coming back to the dugout after making an out. Wills, to his credit, did try it Dressen's way one time though, cursing and kicking as he returned to the bench after being retired, culminating in a grand finale in which Maury flung his bat down the bench past first baseman Gil Hodges.

The legendarily strong Hodges called the 170-pound Wills over and said quietly, "You gotta be careful throwing those bats. Because if you hit somebody — especially me — you might get your butt kicked."

Thus ended Maury's career as a bat thrower.

6. Charles Feeney, "Willie Stargell Puts It All Together," *Baseball Digest*, September, 1971, p. 19. Stargell suffered from double vision for the remainder of the 1968 season, contributing mightily to his .237 average that year with 24 homers.

Willie felt that he erred early in his career by taking minor injuries too lightly. "I used to think a muscle pull would go away if I forgot about it," Stargell commented in 1971. "I'd play two, three weeks with a bad leg instead of sitting out a game or two and allowing it to heal. Then, when the leg would get so bad, I'd have to sit down for two or three weeks."

7. Feeney, "Willie Stargell: A Super Star at Last?" p. 13.

8. Most of the cartilage had been removed from Stargell's knees by 1973 (Charley Feeney, "HRs Are Mere Frosting on Stargell Swat Cake," *The Sporting News*, June 9, 1973, p. 16).

9. Phil Musek, "The Roberto Clemente I Know," *Baseball 1972 Yearbook: A Popular Library Publication*, pp. 7–8 gives a good (if slightly fawning) overview of a typical Clemente interview. Roberto was a shouter who emphasized his points in the Latin tradition by gesturing, which made him seem more dramatic and bombastic than would otherwise have been the case. Furthermore, he wasn't a man to forget a slight; a routine 1969 interview with the right fielder apparently devolved into a discussion of why Roberto had finished a poor eighth in the 1960 MVP balloting ("I do not remember 1960," Clemente said coldly) as well as a 1967 incident in a furniture store and early-career warnings from the front office to stay away from white girls.

10. *Ibid.*, p. 7.

11. Clemente utilized a Puerto Rican chiropractor by the name of Arturo Garcia to take care of his myriad aches and pains. Among his various ministrations, Dr. Garcia, according to one observer, "rubs on a potent orange ointment called Atomic Balm, 'cauterizes' tendons with a black plastic cylinder that emits crackling blue sparks, and heats aching muscles with a small infrared lamp." (Quoted in Pietrusza, et al. [eds.], *Baseball: The Biographical Encyclopedia*, p. 210.)

Roberto was commonly considered to be a hypochondriac by Pittsburgh sportswriters and Pirates management during his lifetime (and, indeed, it was a rare Clemente interview that didn't include a description of some physical malady that was plaguing him at the moment). Having said that, it should be noted that as the 2002 season began, Clemente ranked 57th all-time in number of games played and might well have made the top 20 if fate hadn't intervened.

12. Oscar Palacios, "The Man in Right Field: Roberto Clemente," *Ballpark Sourcebook: Diamond Diagrams*, p. 148.

13. Larry Eldridge, "Willie Stargell: Pirate Treasure," *Baseball Digest*, December, 1974, p. 55.

14. Cord Communications Corporation, *Major League Baseball 1974*, p. 95.

15. Bill James, *The Bill James Historical Baseball Abstract*, p. 587.

16. Les Biederman, "Former Baseball Heroes Remember Their Failures Too!" *Baseball Digest*, December, 1979.

EPILOGUE: AUGUST 9, 1979

1. Pietrusza, et al. (eds.), *Baseball: The Biographical Encyclopedia*, p. 849.

2. O'Malley also demanded that the Halos become his tenants once Dodger Stadium was completed (Veeck with Linn, *Veeck as in Wreck*, p. 365).

3. Golenbock, *Bums*, p. 438.

4. Bavasi and Savage, *Off the Record*, p. 145.

5. Gordon Verrell, "Rehired Walt Starts Search for Sock," *The Sporting News*, October 4, 1975, p. 8.

6. Porter Bibb, *It Ain't As Easy As It Looks*, p. 80. This figure was triple the amount that NBC affiliate WSB, the perennial number one in the Atlanta market, had been paying the Braves previously. Turner wasn't being philanthropic, however; the contract he signed with the parent LaSalle-Atlanta Corporation allowed him to broadcast 60 games per season as opposed to the 20 that WSB had aired.

7. *Ibid.*, p. 85.

8. *Ibid.*, p. 136.

9. *Ibid.*, pp. 139–40.

10. *Ibid.* As part of his testimony in front of a House communications subcommittee, Turner observed that "While voicing support for retransmission consent, these monopolistic sports interests know full well that they have absolutely no intention of granting consent. This new law, if passed, will result in the smaller cities and towns across America being deprived of the same variety and high quality of sports broadcasts available in major cities like New York, Chicago, and Los Angeles. The open and competitive market we see today will become totally non-competitive if restrictive retransmission consent becomes law. And I don't think any of you gentlemen here today would stand up and say you are in favor of a monopoly."

11. Kuhn, *Hardball*, pp. 366–403. As early as December 1981, nine owners had issued a letter calling for Bowie's resignation. Since a 75 percent plurality of each league's owners was required to elect a commissioner, the five National League signees (New York's Nelson Doubleday, Houston's John McMullen, St Louis's Gussie Busch, San Diego's Ballard Smith, and Bill Williams

of Cincinnati) represented an effective block to any attempts to reelect Kuhn. Despite two years of politicking by Bowie and others (including Peter O'Malley, who threatened to toss Budweiser out of Dodger Stadium) nothing much changed over time except for Smith being replaced by Ted Turner in the opposing camp.

12. Katchline, "Ump Walkout, Yanks' Troubles Dominate," p. 318.

13. Forman, *Baseball-Reference.com*.

14. Katchline, "Ump Walkout, Yanks' Troubles Dominate," p. 317.

15. *Who's Who In Baseball* (1980 Edition), p. 176.

16. Phil Elderkin, "Steve Howe: Another Great Arm for the Dodgers!" *Baseball Digest*, April, 1981, p. 55.

17. Miller, *A Whole Different Ball Game*, pp. 296, 298.

18. Kuhn, *Hardball*, pp. 332–333. Milwaukee GM Harry Dalton, a member of the owner/player committee studying compensation issues, was dinged $50,000 in May 1980 for saying "I hope that we are not about to witness another macho test of wills. From what I hear, the Players' Association is genuinely looking for a compromise if we'll just give them something that they can accept without losing too much face." (Miller, *A Whole Different Ball Game*, p. 291.)

19. Kuhn, *Hardball*, p. 333. Miller (*A Whole Different Ball Game*, p. 295) states the fund was $15 million in size; Katchline ("Ump Walkout, Yanks' Troubles Dominate," p. 314) pegs it at $3.5 million.

20. Katchline, "Ump Walkout, Yanks' Troubles Dominate," p. 314.

21. Miller, *A Whole Different Ball Game*, p. 319.

22. Kuhn, *Hardball*, p. 169.

23. In Bouton, *Ball Four*, p. 212, Don Mincher estimates that more than half of all major league ballplayers take greenies. "Just about the whole Baltimore team takes them," Mincher told Bouton at dinner one night. "Most of the Tigers. Most of the guys on this club. And that's just what I know for sure."

24. Kuhn, *Hardball*, pp. 303–304.

25. Katchline, "Big Salaries, Labor Strife Topped '80 News," p. 329.

26. *Ibid.*

27. Burt Solomon, *The Baseball Timeline*, pp. 831–832. Pitcher Randy Lerch was the

only Phillie to admit anything in the trial, testifying that he purchased 75 Preludins (a psychomotor stimulant considered to have a high potential for abuse) from Dr. Patrick Mazza from $15 while implicating several of his teammates. All charges against Dr. Mazza were dropped in February, 1981 (*ibid.*, p. 843): Lerch was traded less than a month later.

28. Katchline, "Big Salaries, Labor Strife Topped '80 News," p. 328.

29. Kuhn, *Hardball*, p. 308.

30. *Ibid.*, p. 309.

31. *Ibid.*, p. 311. Sullivant in his decision acknowledged that a professional athlete's life "is not all roses.... But all the Court can do is take the totality of circumstances as found in the record in this case and the limitations imposed by the statute and impose a sentence which the Court feels will meet the objectives in this particular case and that is rehabilitation and deterrence to others similarly situated as well as to others that hold you out as a model, a role model, in their lives, particularly the younger individuals."

32. *Ibid.*, p. 306. An insight into Kuhn's vision of baseball is contained in his characterization of arbitrator Raymond Goetz's decision as a "grave disservice, not only to those of us in sports administration, but to concerned parents and citizens everywhere. Athletes have a tremendous influence on our youth an on society in general.... I believe vast segments of society are outraged that some athletes do not show a greater sense of responsibility to a public that idolizes and imitates them, particularly the youngsters who make heroes of athletes."

Jenkins ultimately agreed to contribute $10,000 to a drug education program and make some public service announcements for Major League Baseball.

33. *Ibid.*, p. 309. Kuhn found out about the under-the-counter payments some two years after the fact from MLBPA executive director Donald Fehr. As one of his last acts as commissioner, Bowie fined the Padres $50,000 for this transgression.

34. *Ibid.*, p. 310.

35. *Ibid.*, p. 314.

36. Katchline, "Ump Walkout, Yanks' Troubles Dominate," p. 329.

37. "Major League Attendance for 1979," *1980 Official Baseball Guide*, p. 394.

38. "Best Major League Attendance Marks," *1980 Official Baseball Guide*, p. 394.

39. Jerry Green, "Membership in the 3,000 Hit Club Bloomed in the '70s," *Baseball Digest*, December, 1979, p. 36. Another exhibit in the NL-AL talent gap is the fact that seven of the nine most recent men to top 3,000 hits were senior circuit lifers.

40. Chuck Pickard, "These Were The Best Big-League Marks of the 1970s," *Baseball Digest*, February, 1980, p. 60.

41. Katchline, "Ump Walkout, Yanks' Troubles Dominate," pp. 312–313. After his second dismissal from the Yankees, Billy was anything but contrite. He released a statement on October 30 stating that "I do not want or need any more of George Steinbrenner's so-called help" and characterized The Boss during a December 11 Q&A session at the University of Rhode Island as "sick."

None of which, of course, kept Martin from returning to the Yankee manager's office a couple of years later.

42. Bavasi and Savage, *Off the Record*, p. 170. Bavasi's book was written in 1987, by which time it was pretty clear that Ryan was going into Cooperstown. However, Buzzie stands by his statement in the book because "he [Ryan] was never much more than a .500 pitcher." Exactly how good the Angel teams that had supported him were was left uncommented upon.

43. Pietrusza, et al. (eds.), *Baseball: The Biographical Encyclopedia*, p. 1130. The vision in Thon's left eye never came all the way back; he would have problems against right-handers with good breaking stuff for the rest of his career, and would even quit the Astros in mid-1987 out of frustration (*Bill Mazeroski's Baseball '88*, p. 51).

44. After posting a 21-8 record with a 1.93 ERA for the 1985 St. Louis Cardinals, Tudor went through a four-year span of ailments that one wouldn't wish on their worst enemy. John:

1. Came down with shoulder problems in 1986 ... and still worked 219 innings while posting a 2.92 ERA (Jayson Stark, *Bill Mazeroski's Baseball '87*, p. 24).

2. Lost three and a half months of the 1987 season to a busted kneecap suffered when Mets catcher Barry Lyons charged into the Cardinals'

dugout after a foul pop and landed on the seated left-hander. Though Tudor would go 8–1 down the stretch and twirl a postseason shutout, the knee was never quite right and would require off-season arthoscopic surgery (Jayson Stark, *Bill Mazeroski's Baseball '88*, p. 30).

3. Underwent Tommy John surgery after walking off the mound in pain during the second inning of Game 3 of the 1988 World Series (Randy Youngman, *Bill Mazeroski's Baseball '89*, p. 42).

4. Ached in each of those surgically repaired joints throughout the 1990 season (*Bill Mazeroski's Baseball '91*, p. 42).

But during that four-year time span, Tudor posted a 45–21 record with a 2.77 ERA.

The pitcher with the most similar career record to Tudor's, according to Sean Forman's *Baseball-Reference.com*, is Gary Nolan; others in the top ten include Preacher Roe, Mort Cooper, Don Gullett, and Mel Parnell.

45. According to Bill James (James, *The New Bill James Historical Abstract*, p. 892), in his days as part of the Royals' broadcasting team Quisenberry would play a game with lead announcer Denny Mathews in which each would select an off-beat word like "xenophobic" or "divericate" for the other to use during the game without the audience suspecting that something was up.

"He was, in fact, a gentle man," said James, who participated in a call-in radio program with Quisenberry, "but he had an edge to him too. Like a lot of bright people,

he was very aware that he was living in a world inhabited by more than a few morons. A lot of times, when he said all the funny things that are collected in all of the quote books, he was actually directing attention away from something he didn't want to talk about.

"I never knew anyone who would give an unexpected answer to a question more often than Quiz, unexpectedly honest, unexpectedly profound, or just off-the-wall. 'I never asked "Why me?"' he said about the brain tumor. '"Why not me?"'

46. Okrent, *Nine Innings*, p. 46. According to Luis Tiant, Thomas was so ugly that he "could be anything in the jungle [he] wanted to be, but not the hunter."

47. Richard had complained of numbness in his shoulder throughout the first half of the 1980 season (the team's doctors and some sportswriters thought it was all in his mind) and had been diagnosed with a circulatory problem that restricted the flow of blood to his arm just four days earlier. The restriction turned out to be caused by a blood clot behind J.R.'s right collarbone; the resulting stroke resulted in partial paralysis on the left side of his body that lasted for several months (Cliff Katchline, "Labor Strife, Big Salaries Top '80 News," *1981 Official Baseball Guide*, pp. 325–326).

48. Dan Berger, "Padres Shortstop Ozzie Smith: A Future Star," *Baseball Digest*, September, 1978, p. 78. An addendum was printed shortly after the season opener adding Ozzie to the roster.

Bibliography

Books

Aaron, Hank, with Lonnie Wheeler. *I Had a Hammer: The Hank Aaron Story*. New York: HarperCollins, 1991.

Allen, Dick, and Tim Whitaker. *Crash*. New York: Ticknor & Fields, 1989.

Bak, Richard. *Cobb Would Have Caught It: The Golden Age of Baseball in Detroit*. Detroit: Wayne State University Press, 1991.

Bavasi, Buzzie, with John Strege. *Off the Record*. Chicago: Contemporary Books, 1987.

Baylor, Don, with Claire Smith. *Nothing but the Truth: A Baseball Life*. New York: St. Martin's Press, 1989.

Bibb, Porter. *It Ain't as Easy as It Looks*. New York: Crown Publishers, 1993.

Bouton, Jim. *Ball Four*. Cleveland: The World Publishing Company, 1970.

_____. *I'm Glad You Didn't Take It Personally* (ed. by Leonard Shecter). New York: William Morrow, 1971.

Bucek, Jeanine (ed. dir.). *The Baseball Encyclopedia* (10th ed.). New York: Macmillan, 1996.

Caray, Harry, with Bob Verdi. *Holy Cow!* New York: Villiard Books, 1989.

Cosell, Howard. *Cosell* (Mickey Herskowitz, ed.). Chicago: Playboy Press, 1973.

Dewan, John (ed.). *The Scouting Notebook 2001*. Morton Grove, IL: STATS, 2001.

Doctor X. *Intern*, New York: Harper & Row, 1965.

Down, Fred (Cord Communications Corp). *Major League Baseball 1975*. New York: Pocket Books, 1975.

Durocher, Leo, with Ed Linn. *Nice Guys Finish Last*. New York: Simon and Schuster, 1975.

Elias Sports Bureau. *Who's Who in Baseball*. New York: Harris Press, 1973.

Flood, Curt, with Richard Carter. *The Way It Is*. New York: Trident Press, 1971.

Garvey, Steve, with Skip Rozin. *Garvey*. New York: Times Books, 1986.

Golenbock, Peter. *Bums*. G.P. New York: Putnam's Sons, 1984.

Grunnell, John A. (ed.). *Standard Catalog of American Cars 1946–1975*. Iola, WI: Krause Publications, 1987.

Halberstam, David. *The Reckoning*. New York: William Morrow, 1986.

Hernandez, Keith, and Mike Bryan. *If at First....* New York: Viking Penguin, 1986, 1987.

Hollander, Zander (ed.). *The Complete Handbook of Baseball* (1975 edition). Bergenfield, NJ: New American Library, 1975.

Jackson, Reggie and Mike Lupica. *Reggie*, New York: Villiard Books, 1984.

James, Bill. *The Baseball Book*. New York: Villiard Books, 1990, 1992.

_____. *The Bill James Baseball Abstract*. New York: Ballantine Books, 1985, 1986.

_____. *The Bill James Guide to Baseball Managers*. New York: Scribner, 1997.

_____. *The Bill James Historical Baseball Abstract*. New York: Villiard Books, 1986.

_____. *The New Bill James Historical Baseball Abstract*. New York: The Free Press, 2001.

_____. *The Politics of Glory*, New York: Macmillan, 1994.

_____, John Dewan, and Project Scoresheet. *The Great American Stat Book*, New York: Ballantine Books, 1987.

_____, John Zminda, and Project Scoresheet. *The Great American Stat Book*, New York: Villiard Books, 1988.

John, Tommy, with Dan Valenti. *T.J.: My 26 Years in Baseball*. New York: Bantam Books, 1991.

Kuhn, Bowie. *Hardball: The Education of a Baseball Commissioner*. New York: McGraw-Hill, 1988.

Lee, Bill, with Dick Lally. *The Wrong Stuff*. New York: Viking Penguin, 1984.

Luciano, Ron, and Dave Fisher. *Strike Two*. New York: Bantam Books, 1984.

_____. *The Umpire Strikes Back*. New York: Bantam Books, 1982.

Lyle, Sparky, and Peter Golenbock. *The Bronx Zoo*. New York: Crown Publishers, 1979.

MacPhail, Lee. *My Nine Innings*. Westport, CT: Meckler Books, 1989.

Martin, Billy, and Peter Golenbock. *Number 1*. New York: Dell, 1981.

McGeveran, William, Jr. (ed. dir.). *The World Almanac*. Mahwah, NJ: World Almanac Books, 1996, 2001.

Merrill, Durwood, with Jim Dent. *You're Out — and You're Ugly, Too!* New York: St. Martin's Press, 1998.

Miller, Marvin. *A Whole Different Ball Game*. New York: Fireside Books, 1991.

Morrison, Samuel Eliot. *The Oxford History of the American People*. New York: Oxford University Press, 1965.

Newhan, Ross. *The California Angels: The Complete History*. New York: Simon and Schuster, 1982.

Okrent, Daniel. *Nine Innings*. New York: Ticknor & Fields, 1985.

Palacios, Oscar and Eric Robin. *Ballpark Sourcebook: Diamond Diagrams*. Skokie, IL: STATS, 1998.

Pallone, Dave, with Allen Steinberg. *Behind the Mask: My Double Life in Baseball*. New York: Viking Penguin, 1990.

Palmer, Jim, and Jim Dale. *Palmer and Weaver. Together We Were Eleven Foot Nine*. Kansas City: Andrews and McMeel, 1996.

Pietrusza, David, Matthew Silverman, and Michael Gershman. *Baseball: The Biographical Encyclopedia*. Kingston, NY: Total Sports Publishing, 2000.

Reidenbaugh, Lowell. *Take Me Out to the Ball Park*. St. Louis: The Sporting News Publishing Company, 1983.

Roth, Allen (ed.). *Who's Who in Baseball*, New York: Harris Press, 1968, 1970, 1971, 1972.

Rowe, Chris, and Dick Kaegel (eds.). *Baseball Dope Book* (1968, 1970, 1972 eds.). St. Louis: The Sporting News Publishing Company.

Rowe, Chris, Joe Marcin, and Larry Wigge (eds.). *Baseball Dope Book* (1973, 1976 eds.). St Louis: The Sporting News Publishing Company.

Solomon, Burt. *The Baseball Timeline*. New York: Avon Books, 1997.

Spink, C.C. Johnson (publisher). *Official Baseball Guide* (1969–1981 eds.). St. Louis: The Sporting News Publishing Company.

Swioff, Seymour (ed) *Who's Who in Baseball*. New York: Harris Press, 1974, 1980.

Veeck, Bill, with Ed Linn. *Thirty Tons a Day*. New York: The Viking Press, 1972.

_____. *Veeck as in Wreck*. Chicago: The University of Chicago Press, 2001.

Ward, Geoffrey, and Ken Burns. *Baseball: An Illustrated History*. New York: Alfred A. Knopf, 1994.

Weaver, Earl, and Berry Stainback. *It's What You Learn After You Know It All That Counts*. Garden City, NY: Doubleday & Company, 1982.

Wills, Maury, and Mike Celizic. *On the Run*. New York: Carroll & Graf Publishers, 1991.

Woodward, Bob, and Scott Armstrong. *The Brethren*. New York: Simon and Schuster, 1979.

Zanger, Brenda, and Dick Kaplan. *Major League Baseball 1971*. New York: Pocket Books, 1971.

_____. *Major League Baseball 1972*. New York: Pocket Books, 1972.

Zanger, Jack. *Major League Baseball 1970*. New York: Pocket Books, 1970.

Zminda, Don (ed.). *Diamond Chronicles*. Morton Grove, IL: STATS, 1999, 2000.

YEARBOOKS

California Angels, 1967.
Cincinnati Reds, 1971, 1973.
Los Angeles Dodgers, 1967.
Oakland A's, 1973, 1974.
Philadelphia Phillies, 1972.
Detroit Tigers, 1971, 1976, 1990.
Chicago White Sox, 1970.

WEBSITES

Forman, Sean. Baseball-Reference.com.
Doyle, Pat. Old-Time Data. WebBall.com.
National Baseball Hall of Fame.
BaseballLibrary.com.
CBSSportsline.com.

PERIODICAL ARTICLES

"A Tried and True Showcase." *The Sporting News*, July 29, 1972.
Allen, Maury. Untitled, *Baseball Digest*, January 1972.
_____. Untitled, *Baseball Digest*, January 1977.
_____. Untitled, *Baseball Digest*, September 1972.
Associated Press. "Luciano's Death Is Classified as a Suicide." *The Los Angeles Times*, January 20, 1995.
Atkin, Ross. "Bobby Bonds Takes a Giant Step Forward." *Baseball Digest*, October 1973.
Atkinson, Lewis F. "How Mexican Raids Threatened to Ruin Majors 25 Years Ago." *Baseball Digest*, July 1971.
August, Bob. "Why There's a Surge in Base Stealing." *Baseball Digest*, August 1977.
"Beer Bust or Ball Game?" *The Sporting News*, June 22, 1974.
Berger, Dan. "How Richie Allen Finally Became a Complete Baseball Player." *All-Star Sports*, September 1971.
_____. "Padres Shortstop Ozzie Smith: A Future Star." *Baseball Digest*, September 1978.
"Bergman Bounced by Finley." *The Sporting News*, September 23, 1972.
Bergman, Ron. "A's Charge Double Standards in North Case." *The Sporting News*, June 9, 1973.
_____. "A's Discover Mr. Kleen in SuperWash." *The Sporting News*, August 9, 1975.
_____. "A's Sit Quietly, Awaiting Bando Bat Boom." *The Sporting News*, September 23, 1972.
_____. "Athletics Avoid Deep Water When Horacio Is on Bridge." *The Sporting News*, May 19, 1973.
_____. "Athletics' Sizeup of Rudi: Greatness Without Glamour." *The Sporting News*, June 8, 1974.
_____. "Bando Bat Mark Plummets, Worst Season for A's Star." *The Sporting News*, September 6, 1975.
_____. "Bando's Outburst Just the Tonic A's Needed." *The Sporting News*, July 13, 1974.
_____. "'Call Me Dumb, Not Cheap,' Fumes Finley in Ring Furor." *The Sporting News*, March 23, 1974.
_____. "Diary of Defeat — A's Were Losers Even in Bus League." *The Sporting News*, June 12, 1976.
_____. "Fan Appreciation Day Revived." *The Sporting News*, October 2, 1971.
_____. "Fingers Points Way for Athletics." *The Sporting News*, August 19, 1972.
_____. "Finley Blisters A's After Jackson-North Bout." *The Sporting News*, June 22, 1974.
_____. "Finley's Speed-to-Burn Plan Gives Athletics Sudden Chill." *The Sporting News*, April 6, 1974.

_____. "Girls Swoon, Batters Fade When A's Put Rollie on Hill." *The Sporting News*, September 8, 1973.

_____. "Green Right at Home as A's Moving Man." *The Sporting News*, November 25, 1972.

_____. "Heavy Frost Killing Good Will in Finleyland." *The Sporting News*, May 4, 1974.

_____. "Hunter Dropped His Hands to Raise Win Total to 20." *The Sporting News*, October 2, 1971.

_____. "Injury to Rudi's Thumb Darkens A's Prospects." *The Sporting News*, August 30, 1975.

_____. "Loss of Catfish Hastened Herbie's Farewell." *The Sporting News*, May 24, 1975.

_____. "Mincher Weary of Bench Duty, Retires as 200-Homer Belter." *The Sporting News*, January 13, 1973.

_____. "Moody Jackson: A Fascinating Riddle." *The Sporting News*, April 13, 1974.

_____. "Peace Reigns Briefly, Then A's Blow Stacks." *The Sporting News*, April 27, 1974.

_____. "Reggie and Charlie Kiss and Make Up, or Do They?" *The Sporting News*, September 26, 1970.

_____. "Rollie's Follies Real Oakland Thigh-Slapper." *The Sporting News*, March 3, 1973.

_____. "Series Still the Big Thing to 20-Win Holtzman." *The Sporting News*, September 22, 1973.

_____. "Sharp Bullpen Halts A's Skid — Offsets Anemic Bat Production." *The Sporting News*, September 16, 1972.

_____. "A Strutting Finley Hogs the Spotlight — As Usual." *The Sporting News*, August 2, 1975.

_____. "Tenace Size-Up of Blue — 'Mentally Still Not Ready.'" *The Sporting News*, July 7, 1973.

_____. "What Happened to the Mustache Gang?" *Baseball Digest*, September 1973.

Biederman, Les. "Former Baseball Heroes Remember Their Failures Too!" *Baseball Digest*, December 1979.

Bisher, Furman. "Hank Aaron Tells a Secret." *Baseball Digest*, November 1971.

Blackman, Ted. "Mike Marshall: The Pitcher Nobody Wanted." *Baseball Digest*, December 1973.

Bordman, Sid. "'I Hope I'm Never Satisfied'— Busby." *The Sporting News*, August 3, 1974.

_____. "Steve Garvey: The Making of a Dodger Legend." *Baseball Digest*, June 1979.

Bortstein, Larry. "How 14 Leading Hitters Rate Best Pitchers." *Baseball Digest*, January 1975.

_____. "Six Stars Name Their Baseball Idols." *Baseball Digest*, July 1975.

Boswell, Thomas. "Certain Ballparks Have Their Own Special Charm." *Baseball Digest*, August 1979.

_____. "The Umpire: He's Baseball's Indispensable Man." *Baseball Digest*, April 1979.

Brauchner, Bill. "Fred Norman's Long Search for Big League Stardom." *Baseball Digest*, June 1975.

Broeg, Bob. "Three Rivers Stadium — Ball Park With Perfect Name." *The Sporting News*, July 27, 1974.

Brown, Doug. "Orioles' Tommy D. Looks Back in Anger." *The Sporting News*, August 11, 1973.

_____. "Earls of Baltimore Having Their Problems." *The Sporting News*, June 29, 1974.

Burdick, Si. "Hal McRae: A Premier Designated Hitter." *Baseball Digest*, July 1977.

_____. Untitled, *Baseball Digest*, October 1971.

Burnes, Robert L. "Season's High Spots ... and Some Low Ones." *Baseball Digest*, January 1973.

Calabria, Pat. "Greg Luzinski: The Maturing of a Major League Slugger." *Baseball Digest*, November 1975.

Chass, Murray. "Curt Flood: Baseball's Forgotten Pioneer." *Baseball Digest*, January 1977.

Claflin, Larry. "Kasko Finds 2-Year Contract in Midst of Bosox' Flag Ruins." *The Sporting News*, October 21, 1972.

Collier, Phil. "IRS Could Nip Padre Plans to Move." *The Sporting News*, August 25, 1973.

_____. "Zimmer's Goal: To Vacate Dungeon." *The Sporting News*, October 7, 1972.

Condon, Dave. "Charlie O.: Amazing Sports Maverick." *The Sporting News*, January 6, 1973.

Conlin, Bill. "Lefty Says Goodbye." *Philadelphia Daily News*, June 26, 1986.

Craig, Jack. "Stanky Goes to Bat for Ousted Umpires." *The Sporting News*, August 1, 1970.

Didinger, Ray. Untitled, *Baseball Digest*, September 1969.

Distel, David. "Garvey Ends Career in Baseball, Turns Eye Towards Politics." Los Angeles *Times* (San Diego County edition), January 14, 1988.

Donley, Paul. "The New Challenge Facing Pete Rose." *Sport World*, April 1969.

Dunn, Bob. "McNally Declares His Decision to Retire Is Firm." *The Sporting News*, June 28, 1975.

Durslag, Melvin. "Carew admits stealing home is one feat that turns him on." *Baseball Digest*, July 1979.

_____. "A Duster Artist." *The Sporting News*, August 25, 1973.

_____. "Steve Garvey: The Majors' Newest 'Iron Man.'" *Baseball Digest*, July 1980.

Eisenbath, Mike. "The Lost Decade ... Cards Went from '68 Pennant to '70s Sleepwalkers." *St Louis Post-Dispatch*, August 23, 1992.

Elderkin, Phil. "Bobby Bonds Pays Off with Speed and Power.'" *Baseball Digest*, December 1977.

_____. "David Clyde: The Fireball Who Survived a Flameout." *Baseball Digest*, November 1978.

_____. "Master of the Game's Best Split-Fingered Fastball." *Baseball Digest*, December 1979.

_____. "The Power Hitter The Yankees Dealt Away." *Baseball Digest*, December 1977.

_____. "Rod Carew: 'Home Runs Don't Interest Me.'" *Baseball Digest*, August 1973.

_____. "Steve Howe: Another Great Arm for the Dodgers!" *Baseball Digest*, April 1981.

Eldridge, Larry. "Mark (The Bird) Fidrych: A New Folk Hero Arrives." *Baseball Digest*, October 1976.

_____. "Willie Stargell: Pirate Treasure." *Baseball Digest*, December 1974.

Falls, Joe. "Now It's Time for a Few Laughs." *The Sporting News*, May 17, 1975.

Feeney, Charles. "Graveyard Strolls Keep Slugger Stargell Slim." *The Sporting News*, May 22, 1971.

_____. "HRs Are Mere Frosting on Stargell Swat Cake." *The Sporting News*, June 9, 1973.

_____. "Robertson's Home-Run Barrage Just a Mirage?" *The Sporting News*, June 22, 1974.

_____. "Rooker Feels Cheated: Low ERA, Few Victories." *The Sporting News*, June 8, 1974.

_____. "Willie Stargell: A Super Star at Last?" *All-Star Sports*, September 1971.

_____. "Willie Stargell Puts It All Together." *Baseball Digest*, September 1971.

Fetzer, John. "Fetzer Fires a Rebuttal at Critics of Gen. Eckert." *The Sporting News*, May 29, 1971.

Fink, David. "The Other Side of Alex Johnson." *Baseball Digest*, June 1974.

Fitzpatrick, Tom. "Ron Luciano: The Ump Who Tells It Like It Is." Chicago *Sun-Times*, September 1976.

"Flood's Loss Is Baseball's Gain." *The Sporting News*. July 8, 1972.

Flynn, John. "Steve Carlton: At Last, a Winner for the Phils." Philadelphia *Inquirer*, November 1972.

Fowler, Bob. "Bert Blyleven — The Touch of a Dutch Master." *The Sporting News*, August 4, 1973.

_____. "Critics Take New Look, Salute Clouting Carew." *The Sporting News*, July 7, 1973.

Frizzell, Pat. "Bonds Rates as Giants' No, 1 Candidate for Laurels as MVP." *The Sporting News*, October 2, 1971.

_____. "Ex-Whiz Clyde Facing Fight to Regain Ranger Job." *The Sporting News*, September 27, 1975.

_____. "Gilt-Edged Bonds Supporting Giants' Flag Bid." *The Sporting News*, June 26, 1971.

_____. "Hunt Sets N.L. Plunk Mark." *The Sporting News*, August 1, 1970.

Galloway, Randy. "Bibby on Hill, Anything Can Happen." *The Sporting News*, August 10, 1974.

_____. "Ranger Clyde Sweeps in Like Texas Tornado." *The Sporting News*, July 21, 1973.

_____. "Rangers Flash Slowdown Sign to Eager Young Clyde." *The Sporting News*, March 30, 1974.

_____. "Superstitions are Still Part of the Major League Scene." *Baseball Digest*, October 1979.
_____. "Teen-Ager Clyde Taming Hitters with Wise Pitches." *The Sporting News*, June 1, 1974.
_____. "Who's Jim Bibby? The Rangers' New Mound Whiz." *The Sporting News*, August 4, 1973.
Gammons, Peter. "Jim Kern: Best Reliever in the American League." *Baseball Digest*, September 1979.
_____. "Spear-Carrier Guerrero? He's Bosox Beaut at Short." *The Sporting News*, May 4, 1974.
Goldstein, Alan. "Frank Robinson's Dream: Can He Ever Reach It?" *All-Star Sports*, April 1969.
Green, Jerry. "Membership in 3,000-Hit Club Bloomed in the '70s." *Baseball Digest*, December 1979.
_____. "Will Mark Fidrych Defy the 'Sophmore Jinx.'" *Baseball Digest*, April 1977.
Gross, Milton. Untitled, *Baseball Digest*. September 1971.
Hagan, Paul. "Rangers' Bullpen Takes a Zany Road for Relief." *Baseball Digest*, June 1980.
Hatter, Lou. "Blair Regains Star Route with Aid of Hypnotist." *The Sporting News*, July 14, 1973.
_____. "Cuellar Authority on Whammies and Hoodoos." *The Sporting News*, August 5, 1972.
_____. "'Earl the Weaver Gets in a Few Rips.'" *The Sporting News*, May 5, 1973.
_____. "Giant Pleasure Dome in Baltimore Future." *The Sporting News*, June 23, 1973.
_____. "Study Indicates Face-Lifting Could Save Oriole Park." *The Sporting News*, January 20, 1973.
_____. "'Weaver Wrong!' Ump Haller Fires Rebuttal." *The Sporting News*, August 12, 1972.
Hawkins, Jim. "Alex Johnson: A Defiant Champion." *Baseball Digest*, July 1971.
_____. "The Bird Amuses Tigers, Befuddles Enemy Swingers." *The Sporting News*, June 5, 1976.
_____. "John Hiller: Tigers' One-Man Bullpen." *The Sporting News*, June 1, 1974.
_____. "Rod Carew: He's in a Class by Himself." *Baseball Digest*, December 1975.
_____. "Tigers Purr Happily Under Houk's Easy Leash." *The Sporting News*, April 6, 1974.
Heiling, Joe. "Cedeno's Life Periled by Pittsburgh Caller." *The Sporting News*, August 3, 1974.
Heisler, Mark. "Why Rod Carew Is the Best Hitter in the Majors." *Baseball Digest*, July 1979.
Hersch, Phil. "Chet Lemon: The Struggle for a 'Spot in the Sun.'" *Baseball Digest*, June 1981.
Hertzel, Bob. "How About Some Recognition for Lee May?" *Baseball Digest*, August 1979.
_____. "Racial Prejudice a Definite Stranger to Reds." *The Sporting News*, April 28, 1973.
Heryford, Merle. "Short Sells Rangers to Texas Group." *The Sporting News*, April 20, 1974.
_____. "To Find Rangers, You Have to Visit Infirmary." *The Sporting News*, August 11, 1973.
Hinton, Ed. "Why Hitters Call Atlanta Stadium the 'Launching Pad.'" *Baseball Digest*, July 1981.
Hochman, Stan. "Greg Luzinski: 'I've Got to Make Good.'" *Baseball Digest*, February 1973.
Holtzman, Jerome. "Behind the Scenes." *The Sporting News*, August 12, 1972.
_____. "Bill Melton ... from Agony to Ecstasy." *The Sporting News*, September 4, 1971.
_____. "Doc Veeck to Try His New Theories on an Old Patient." *The Sporting News*, October 18, 1975.
_____. "Charlie-Jerry vs. Establishment." *The Sporting News*, August 2, 1975.
_____. "Chisox' Allen Swings Hot, Heavy Bat." *The Sporting News*, June 29, 1974.
_____. "Chisox Quaff Champagne — Toast Homer Champion Melton." *The Sporting News*, October 26, 1971.
_____. "Gura Geared for Spring Assault on Spot as Cub Mound Regular." *The Sporting News*, December 23, 1972.
_____. "Holcomb Quits Chisox, Hemond Replaces Him." *The Sporting News*, August 11, 1973.

_____. "'Santo's Our Guy!' Cubs' Fans Chorus." *The Sporting News*, June 23, 1973.

_____. "Wood Injury Caps Sox' Tale of Woe." *The Sporting News*, May 29, 1976.

Hudspeth, Ron. "Rico Carty: He's No Longer the 'Beeg Boy.'" *Baseball Digest*, February 1973.

Hunter, Bob. "Dodgers' Ailing Hurlers Look Sharp in Action." *The Sporting News*, July 3, 1971.

_____. "Swap to L.A. Gives Andy 'Good Feeling.'" *The Sporting News*, January 6, 1973.

Isle, Stan. "Kuhn Hails Supreme Court Decision." *The Sporting News*, July 1, 1972.

_____. "Umps' New Pension Plan Sets $17,076 Tops." *The Sporting News*, April 19, 1975.

Jackman, Phil. "Baltimore Foes Get Bad News: Boog's Back and Bat Is Booming." *The Sporting News*, August 21, 1971.

Jacobs, Hal. "Lester! The Strange but True Tale of Georgia's Unlikeliest Governor." *Creative Loafing*, March 20, 1999.

Joyce, Dick. "They Can Cram the Money!" *All-Star Sports*, June 1979.

"Judge Points the Way." *The Sporting News*, August 29, 1970.

Justice, Richard. "Al Oliver's Inside Tips on Hitting." *Baseball Digest*, July 1979.

Kaese, Harold. "It Won't Be Baseball — It'll Be Dumbball." *Baseball Digest*, April 1973.

Kaye, Dave. "Ron Luciano: Flashiest Ump in the Game." *Baseball Digest*, October 1977.

Kelly, Ray. "Quakers Miffed by Scarcity of Mac's Headlines." *The Sporting News*, June 8, 1974.

Kiseda, George. "Dash of Bitters Sours Gibby's Success Saga." *The Sporting News*, October 10, 1970.

Klein, Moss. "When Billy Martin 'Went to Bat' for Rod Carew." *Baseball Digest*, March 1978.

Kuenster, John. "A's at Their Best When Fighting." *Baseball Digest*, January 1974.

_____. "Added Pitching Bolsters Dodgers and Astros for Coming Pennant Scramble." *Baseball Digest*, February 1980.

_____. "Brock and Grich: Top Candidates to Win 'Comeback Player' Awards." *Baseball Digest*, September 1979.

_____. "Double Play Kings of the Majors." *Baseball Digest*, March 1974.

_____. "How Major League Players Are Rated in Special Talent Categories." *Baseball Digest*, April 1979.

_____. "It's Been a Wild and Cra-a-zy Sort of Season in the Majors!" *Baseball Digest*, October 1978.

_____. "The Mad, Mad World of the Oakland A's." *Baseball Digest*, November 1974.

_____. "Pitchers Hate Tape-Measure Home Runs." *Baseball Digest*, September 1971.

_____. "Prediction: Mark Fidrych and Dave Kingman Will Make Big News in '78." *Baseball Digest*, April 1978.

Lang, Jack. "Fabled Yanks Sold for Cut-Rate $10 Million." *The Sporting News*, January 20, 1973.

_____. "Majors Draft Record Low of 785 Prospects." *The Sporting News*, June 23, 1973.

_____. "Rescue Artists Are Heroes in New Film." *The Sporting News*, November 7, 1970.

_____. "Sky King Writing Tape Measure Tale." *The Sporting News*, May 8, 1976.

Lawson, Earl. "Anatomy of an Arm Problem." *Baseball Digest*, December 1976.

_____. "Hustler Pete Rose: Baseball's Best Ad." *The Sporting News*, July 18, 1970.

_____. "Reds Offer Thanks to Padres After Early Norman Conquests." *The Sporting News*, July 14, 1973.

_____. "The Reds' Pitching Staff Went That-A-Way!" *Baseball Digest*, April 1979.

_____. "Reds' Rose Still Has Rifle Arm, Foes Discover." *The Sporting News*, April 28, 1973.

_____. "Today's Reds— Greatest in Rhineland History?" *All-Star Sports*, November 1970.

_____. "Tolan Barks Once Too Often, Winds Up in Red Doghouse." *The Sporting News*, September 15, 1973.

Leucking, Dave. "'78 Cards: A Lost Cause." St. Louis *Post-Dispatch*, July 20, 1988.

Lewis, Allen. "Connie Mack Stadium Destroyed by Blaze." *The Sporting News*, September 11, 1971.

Lindblom, John. "An Ex-Ump Calls Them as He Saw Them." *Baseball Digest*, December 1980.

Littwin, Mark. "Pitching Arms Should Get Special Care." *Baseball Digest*, September 1977.

Lockwood, Wayne. "The Funny Side of Baseball Brawls." *Baseball Digest*, August 1973.

Lyon, Bill. "Please Don't Kill the Umpires!" *Baseball Digest*, February 1980.

MacDonald, Ian. "Expos' Hunt Handles Bat Like Baton." *The Sporting News*, August 5, 1972.

_____. "Hunt Makes 'Hit' as Expos' MVP." *The Sporting News*, October 16, 1971.

_____. "Hunt, Pitchers' Favorite Target, Says Hurlers Are Much Too Wild." *The Sporting News*, September 4, 1971.

"Major Changes in Baseball Playing Rules." *Baseball Digest,* April 1973.

Markus, Robert. "Don Sutton: Will He Be the Best Dodger Pitcher Ever?" *Baseball Digest*, May 1977.

McCormick, George. "Denny McLain & His Feuds with the Tigers." *All-Star Sports*, September 1970.

McCoy, Hal. "Dave Kingman: The Emergence of a New Home Run Star." *Baseball Digest*, August 1976.

_____. Untitled, *Baseball Digest*, September 1975.

McGuff, Joe. "Royals' Fans Expect Tallis to Swing a Big Deal." *The Sporting News,* November 25, 1972.

_____. "Royals Find Bullpen Help in the 'Hall-Way.'" *The Sporting News*, June 5, 1976.

_____. "Royals Flush a Quartet of First-Rate Starters." *The Sporting News*, September 6, 1969.

_____. "Slowdown at Gate Could Speed Lemon's Exit from Kansas City." *The Sporting News*, October 14, 1972.

Meyers, Jeff. "The Cardinals' 'Mad Hungarian.'" *Baseball Digest*, January 1975.

"Mileti Out and Bonda In." *The Sporting News.* September 22, 1973.

Miller, Dick. "Alex Johnson's Dogging It Leads to Angels' Doghouse." *The Sporting News*, June 5, 1971.

_____. "Angels Hailing Zing in Singer's Fast Ball." *The Sporting News*, June 30, 1973.

_____. "Angels Perform Like Demons with Sulking Alex on Bench." *The Sporting News*, June 26, 1971.

_____. "Hard-Luck King? Angels' May Qualifies Easily." *The Sporting News*, July 10, 1971.

_____. "Singer Undergoes Surgery." *The Sporting News*, June 29, 1974.

Minshew, Wayne. "Evans' Batting Feats Lost in Aaron's Shadow." *The Sporting News*, August 18, 1973.

_____. Untitled, *Baseball Digest*, July 1977.

Moore, Terrence. "Mike Caldwell: Heart of the Brewers' Success in '78." Baseball Digest, December 1978.

"More Power to the Rabbits." *Baseball 1976.*

Munzel, Edgar. "Allyn Backs Holcomb Against Non-Signers." *The Sporting News,* August 4, 1973.

_____. "Chisox to Make Stretch Bid Minus Melton." *The Sporting News*, August 12, 1972.

_____. "Hard Nosed Ron Santo: Modern Gashouser." *The Sporting News*, September 6, 1969.

_____. "Initial Allen Proves Super, So White Sox Go for Two." *The Sporting News*, April 21, 1973.

_____. "Wood's Knuckler a Mystery to A.L. Batters." *The Sporting News*, June 2, 1973.

Murphy, Jack. Untitled, *Baseball Digest*, June 1972.

Murray, Jim. "Murray's Best: Rose Is Red-Hot Item." *The Sporting News*, September 5, 1970.

Musick, Phil. "The Roberto Clemente I Know." *Baseball 1972 Yearbook: A Popular Library Publication.*

Newhan, Ross. "Do Dodgers' Hurlers Cheat? A Silly Question!" *The Sporting News*, May 25, 1974.

_____. "Iron Mike — What's Behind Brilliant Record?" *The Sporting News*, July 27, 1974.

Nightingale, Dave. "Did Orioles Lose Because of Weaver?", *Baseball Digest,* January 1972.

_____. "The Human Side of Richie Allen." *Baseball Digest*, July 1972.

Nigro, Ken. "Weaver, Ump Luciano Resume Trading Insults." *The Sporting News*, March 10, 1979.

"The 1968 Who's Who in the Majors." *Sport World,* October, 1968.

O'Boynick, Paul. "Rooker Curbs Wildness, Saves Job." *The Sporting News*, August 23, 1969.

O'Brien, Andy. "Ron Hunt: No. 1 on the Majors' Hit Parade." *Baseball Digest*, August 1972.

Ogle, Jim. "Yanks' Rebuilding Job Is Ahead of Schedule." *The Sporting News*, June 27, 1970.

Pepe, Phil. "Bonds Promises Gilt-Edged Payoff Next Year." *The Sporting News*, October 4, 1975.

_____. "Gabe Defends Hefty Outlay of Talent to Get Chambliss." *The Sporting News*, May 18, 1974.

_____. "Well Traveled Stanley Settles Down as Yank." *The Sporting News*, June 28, 1975.

Perry, Anthony. "Developer Make Pitch for Garvey as Candidate." Los Angeles *Times* (San Diego County edition), October 12, 1988.

Pickard, Chuck. "These Were the Best Major League Marks of the 1970s." *Baseball Digest*, February 1980.

Piellisch, Richard. "Do Artificial Surfaces Help or Hinder the Game?" *Baseball Digest*, June 1980.

Rapoport, Ron. "Should the Spitball Be Legalized?" *Baseball Digest*, December 1972.

Reich, Kenneth. "Hank Aaron in Countdown on Ruth Mark." *Baseball Digest*, January 1972.

Riger, Robert. "The Pitch That Changed the Game." *Baseball Digest*, February 1972.

"Robertson Has Doubts." *The Sporting News*, September 15, 1973.

Roewe, Chris. "Pitching Averages—Including Games of August 23." *The Sporting News*, September 8, 1973.

Ronberg, Gary. "From the Archives: A New 'Interview' with Steve Carlton." Philadelphia *Inquirer*, September 26, 1983.

_____. "Steve Carlton: Pitcher with the Classic Style." *Baseball Digest*, December 1977.

Rosen, Byron. "Rebellion by Indians Socks it to Boss Paul." Washington *Post*, July 4, 1979.

Rubin, Bob. "Trick Pitches Spell Success in the Major Leagues." *Baseball Digest*, November 1978.

Russo, Neal. "Cardinals Finally Sign Simmons." *The Sporting News*, August 12, 1972.

_____. "Clean-Shaven Cards Earn Rapp Okay." *The Sporting News*, March 12, 1977.

_____. "Fans Enchanted by Theft Artist Brock." *The Sporting News*, August 24, 1974.

_____. "Flashy Forsch Laboring in Cardinals' Shadows." *The Sporting News*, August 23, 1975.

_____. "Mad Hungarian Excites Fans and Chills Hitters." *The Sporting News*, August 16, 1975.

_____. "Steve Ditches 'Made in Japan' Slider." *The Sporting News*, May 8, 1971.

Ryan, Bob. "An Analysis of the Fine Art of Pitching." *Baseball Digest*, November 1977.

Sanders, Cooper. "Inside Pete Rose." *All-Star Sports*, August 1970.

Schlossberg, Dan. "How the Players Rate Their All-Stars." *Baseball Digest*, July 1972.

Schneider, Russell. "Alex an Early Arrival in Tribe's Overhaul." *The Sporting News*, October 23, 1971.

_____. "Incident or Riot? That Depends on Who's Talking." *The Sporting News*, June 22, 1974.

_____. "Nettles Fires Departing Salvo at Pilot Aspro." *The Sporting News*, December 30, 1972.

Scott, Jim. "Alex Johnson vs. Ron Johnson—A Study in Moods." *Super Sports*, June 1971.

_____. "Is There a New Reggie Jackson?" *All-Star Sports*, July 1971.

Seltzer, Robert. "Unheard, Unseen Dorchester Neighbors Knew Little of Carlton." Philadelphia *Inquirer*, June 27, 1986.

Shattuck, Harry. "Jose Cruz of the Astros: Under-Rated No Longer!" *Baseball Digest*, February 1981.

_____. "Soaring Debts Pick Hofheinz Off Astro Perch." *The Sporting News*, July 12, 1975.

Siegel, Eric. "Ken Singleton: He Tries to Get on Base Any Way He Can!" *Baseball Digest*, February 1979.

Snyder, Brodie. "Ross Grimsley: Master of the Changeup." *Baseball Digest*, September 1978.

Solderholm, Eric (as told to George Vass). "The Game I'll Never Forget." *Baseball Digest*, May 1981.

"The Sounds of 1978: Some Memorable Lines from a Forgettable Season." St. Louis *Post-Dispatch*, July 20, 1988.

Spander, Art. "Giants Discover Landlord Camped on Their Doorstep." *The Sporting News*, July 12, 1975.

_____. "Rumors Fly, Fans Flee as Giants End Season." *The Sporting News*, October 11, 1975.

Spink, C.C. Johnson. "We Believe...." *The Sporting News*, August 24, 1974.

Spoelstra, Watson. "Timmerman a Blue-Chip Reliever." *The Sporting News*, October 3, 1970.

Stark, Jayson. "The Door Remains Shut as Carlton Toasts 300." Philadelphia *Inquirer*, September 25, 1983.

_____. "St. Louis Cardinals Team Review." *Bill Mazeroski's Baseball '87.*

_____. "St. Louis Cardinals Team Review." *Bill Mazeroski's Baseball '88.*

Stolze, Craig. "A Pitcher with a Heart — That's John Hiller." *Baseball Digest*, March 1974.

Strauss, Joe. "Palmer, Weaver Burn Roast." Baltimore *Sun*, November 4, 2000.

Sudyk, Bob. "The Travels and Travails of Pat Dobson." *Baseball Digest*, January 1977.

Twombly, Wells. "Cause for Concern — A's Seem Too Peaceful." *The Sporting News*, April 26, 1975.

_____. "Washington's Curious Legacy: 31 SBs, No ABs." *The Sporting News*, May 24, 1975.

_____. "Crosley Field Dimensions." *Baseball Digest*, October 1975.

Vass, George. "Are Major League Batting Championships Overrated?" *Baseball Digest*, June 1975.

_____. "Fergie Jenkins Wants to Go Out a Winner." *Baseball Digest*, August 1979.

_____. "Five Biggest Surprises, Disappointments of 1980." *Baseball Digest*, December 1980.

_____. "Here Are the Six Biggest Free Agent Flops!" *Baseball Digest*, May 1979.

_____. "Here's How the Major League Pennant Races Shape Up." *Baseball Digest*, April 1978.

_____. "Spite Trades Can Ruin Flag Hopes." *Baseball Digest*, July 1972.

_____. "These Are Baseball's Biggest Player Bargains!" *Baseball Digest*, July 1977.

Verrell, Gordon. "Good-Guy Garvey Cast in Dodger Villain Role." *The Sporting News*, July 19, 1975.

_____. "Messersmith Heads an Elite Corps of Dodger Hill Artists." *The Sporting News*, October 18, 1975.

_____. "Rehired Walt Starts Search for Sock." *The Sporting News*, October 4, 1975.

Whiteside, Larry. "Lee Punches Out a Six-Week Vacation." *The Sporting News*, June 5, 1976.

Whittlesey, Merrill. "Did High Court Err? Everybody Has Opinion." *The Sporting News*, July 8, 1972.

_____. "Problem-Plagued Flood Seeks Haven in Europe." *The Sporting News*, May 15, 1971.

Wiebusch, John. "'I Lead Two Lives' ... by Alex Johnson." *The Sporting News*, June 27, 1970.

Young, Dick. "The Comeback of Luis Tiant." *Baseball Digest*, December 1972.

_____. "Dave Kingman: Home Runs Turn Him On." *Baseball Digest*, June 1977.

_____. "Young Ideas: Braves' Fans Snub Aaron." *The Sporting News*, July 5, 1975.

_____. "Young Ideas: Fights Routine with A's." *The Sporting News*, June 22, 1974.

_____. "Young Ideas: Rose Does His Thing." *The Sporting News*, August 1, 1970.

Youngman, Randy. "Los Angeles Dodgers Team Review." *Bill Mazeroski's Baseball '89.*

FILMS

Twentieth Century–Fox Film Corporation. *Wall Street*, 1997.

Madacy Entertainment Group Inc. *Wild World of Sports Bloopers: The Best of Baseball*, 1996.

Index